Human Aging

Human Aging

Paul W. Foos

University of North Carolina at Charlotte

M. Cherie Clark

Queens University of Charlotte

Boston ■ New York ■ San Francisco ■ Mexico City
Montreal ■ Toronto ■ London ■ Madrid ■ Munich ■ Paris
Hong Kong ■ Singapore ■ Tokyo ■ Cape Town ■ Sydney

Senior Acquisitions Editor: Stephen Frail
Executive Marketing Manager: Karen Natale
Production Supervisor: Liz Napolitano
Editorial Production Service: Marty Tenney, Modern Graphics, Inc.
Composition Buyer: Linda Cox
Manufacturing Buyer: JoAnne Sweeney
Electronic Composition: Modern Graphics, Inc.
Photo Researcher: Naomi Rudov
Cover Designer: Joel Gendron

For related titles and support materials, visit our online catalog at www.ablongman.com.

Between the time website information is gathered and then published, it is not unusual for some sites to have closed. Also, the transcription of URLs can result in typographical errors. The publisher would appreciate notification where these errors occur so that they may be corrected in subsequent editions.

ISBN 13: 978-0-205-54401-1
ISBN 10: 0-205-54401-0

Library of Congress Cataloging-in-Publication Data

Foos, Paul W.
 Human aging / Paul W. Foos, M. Cherie Clark. -- 2nd ed.
    p. cm.
 Includes bibliographical references and index.
 ISBN-13: 978-0-205-54401-1 (alk. paper)
 ISBN-10: 0-205-54401-0 (alk. paper)
 1. Aging—Textbooks. I. Clark, M. Cherie. II. Title.

 QP86.F67 2008
 612.6'7—dc22

                                                                                    2007046013

Printed in the United States of America

10   9   8   7   6   5   4   3   2   RRD–VA   11   10   09

Credits appear on page 489, which constitutes an extension of the copyright page.

CONTENTS

PART FOUR   Aging and Our Survival   275

12 Psychopathology   277

13 Healthy/Helpful Environments: Places and People   317

PREFACE

We began this book after searching for a textbook for our own undergraduate classes in adult development and aging that better fit our model of gerontology education. We searched for a book that balanced science and application; was complex enough to challenge students to think critically about issues; was interesting, friendly, and readable without being demeaning, shallow, or all too often, unfortunately, boring; and one that reflected the diversity and multidisciplinary nature of gerontology. Unable to find a textbook that fulfilled all our needs, we set out to produce one that would. We hope we have succeeded in all our aims.

Organization

Human Aging is organized like many other adult development and aging books in that it begins with an overview of gerontology and research methods. **Chapter 1** introduces gerontology and will give you an idea of why the study of aging is more important now than ever before. **Chapter 2** presents the basics of the research methods used in aging and introduces the guiding principles and major issues addressed by the research and theory described in the remaining chapters. The next thirteen chapters are divided into five major sections.

- **Aging and Our Bodies**(Chapters 3, 4, and 5) looks closely at physical changes, proposed explanations for why those changes occur with advanced age, and what can be done to prolong health and longevity. We believe it is important to cover these physical changes first since much of what comes later depends on these changes.
- **Aging and Our Minds** (Chapters 6, 7, and 8) progresses from changes in our senses, how these affect perceptions, and the slowing that occurs with advanced age. These changes underlie many of the changes in memory and higher cognitive processes, which are covered in the latter two chapters. Later sections depend on students knowing the mental and physical changes that can occur in adulthood.
- **Aging and Our Selves** (Chapters 9, 10, and 11). The focus in this section is on our social selves. We examine personality, social support, and social relationships, and end with work and retirement. You will find our chapters on personality and social relationships quite different from those in other texts.
- **Aging and Our Survival** (Chapters 12, 13, and 14) looks at those conditions that threaten or facilitate our survival. From the psychopathologies of Chapter 12, through the environmental design and caregiving of Chapter 13, to death and bereavement in Chapter 14, we try to clarify complex issues and tie them back to the material presented earlier.

- **Aging and You** (Chapter 15) reviews some of the most important information you have learned in relation to the principles raised in Chapter 2, discusses the overall well-being of older adults today, and projects the likely state of affairs for your bodes, minds, selves, and survival over the next 30 to 50 years.

Features

Our approach has several main features. First, we try to make it clear that to understand aging and older adults it is necessary to integrate research and theory from a number of different disciplines; gerontology is inter- and multidisciplinary. We, thus, include work from biology, medicine, psychology, sociology, and even economics in our presentation. Second we try to focus the reader on the science of aging. The questions in aging are difficult to answer and we want to make it clear (1) why they are difficult, (2) how social scientists attempt to handle such difficulties, and (3) the successes (and failures) they have had so far. Real age differences and age/cohort differences are explained first and then highlighted throughout the discussion of research findings in various content areas. We present both sides of all issues as fairly as we can and the evidence as it exists currently.

Third, we tried to write the text to be friendly, active, and fun. It contains projects that you can try out (at home), a fair amount of humor, and is, hopefully, relatively easy to read. We attempt to relate the research findings to real life experiences and to use familiar examples. We have tried to clarify rather than simplify. We believe that learning should be an enjoyable and active experience; therefore, we attempt to engage the reader with thought-provoking questions.

Fourth, the text has applied foci throughout. We try to show how current research findings are now being applied in the real world and/or how they might be applied in the near (or not so near) future. Some applications are general and some are specific. Some applications are ones that you can use to help yourself and/or aging relatives and/or friends. We strongly advocate this application.

Fifth, the text is realistic and positive. Using the results of research, we present things as they are. Too often texts in aging become either negative or overly jolly. Our approach is positive because we believe there are many more genuine pluses to aging than there are minuses. We are conscious, however, of the "glossing" of aging that often occurs in some publications and we try to avoid excesses in this direction.

Sixth, we have tried to weave the evolution of the field throughout our presentation. The study of older adults is continually changing and, as cohorts also change, some findings may be only temporary. What we know now may be very different than what we know by the time our readers are old—just as what we thought we knew in decades past may no longer be true today.

Seventh, we have tried to include crosscultural comparisons and ethnic group comparisons whenever possible. Diversity is an important part of the study of aging and where available we have discussed group and cultural differences both for the aging population in the United States and across the world.

Learning Aids

Each chapter also contains a number of specific learning aids to assist the reader. Each chapter opens with a quote from some well-known person that sets the tone and expresses the main theme of the chapter. We want to focus the reader on the important point(s) right at the start.

Each chapter also presents a **Senior View**. Senior Views are interviews that were conducted with a number of different adults and include a photograph of each senior that helps introduce the main topics in each chapter. We believe that information should be presented in a number of different ways if it is to be assimilated successfully—these interviews are one way of presenting important information. When the theory, research, and a real older adult all agree on some finding, that finding is likely to be remembered. When they disagree, that disagreement is also likely to be remembered. We were very impressed with the knowledge displayed by these older adults. Senior Views make the presentation more varied and show the operation of chapter content in real life with real people. Many students miss the opportunity to discuss class material with an older adult; this is an attempt to give you that source of information. *This is a unique aspect of our text.*

Each chapter includes a **Project** that you can do. The emphasis is on attempting to address some question raised in the text and providing a project that can either be done relatively simply or turned into a more elaborate project for possible independent study at a later date. Active learning is important; this is an attempt to provide such opportunities. Our projects have been tested successfully in the classroom and have been found to be helpful and enjoyable.

Each chapter contains a number of **Boxes** that add information to the text presentation. Generally the information added is outside the main focus but clearly of related interest. Some of these are in-depth looks at particular pieces of research, others are vignettes that describe real people experiencing the situations covered in the text, some are applications of the research that has been discussed, and some just provide interesting information. New to this edition are a number of **Social Policy Application** boxes that highlight important issues that are currently or soon will be topics of pubic debate. We try to be neither conservative nor liberal in our presentation and hope our readers will draw their own conclusions. More importantly, we hope that readers will see areas in which they can actively participate in advocating for older adults.

Each chapter contains numerous **tables and figures** to present relevant procedures, methods, and results. We have received permission to reproduce some of these from other authors whereas we have created others ourselves. This graphic presentation helps students assimilate written text.

Each chapter ends with a section containing **Chapter Highlights** and **Study Questions** which summarize the main points and allow readers to test themselves on knowledge gained and on where to study more.

We have provided **Recommended Readings** and **Internet Resources** for the topics presented in each chapter. We know that most students (most people) use the Internet today and we hope that our listed sites will encourage an active search for additional and related information.

Supplementary Materials

An *Instructor's Manual and Test Bank* is available. The manual portion contains suggestions for lecture presentations and classroom discussions. We have included extra information for the instructor on various topics discussed in the text. Many of these suggestions will assist the instructor who wants a lively class discussion; others are simply extra background material for the instructor's use. The test bank contains a range of easy to difficult multiple-choice questions for every chapter plus a number of essay questions.

Allyn and Bacon has also provided a website where interested readers can learn more and listen to interviews conducted with older adults on many of the topics discussed in the text.

Acknowledgments

We want to thank a great number of people who helped us in preparing this new edition. From Allyn and Bacon we tip our hats to Stephen Frail and Mary K. Tucker for their continual involvement with the book. We owe much to Marty Tenney of Modern Graphics for her advice and assistance.

We wish to thank our colleagues, friends, and family who said encouraging words, smiled, and always gave us thumbs up. We thank the University of North Carolina and Queens University of Charlotte for their continued support.

We wish to thank the reviewers, hired by Allyn and Bacon, who gave us much encouragement along with constructive criticism and helpful suggestions.

John Coggins, Purdue North Central
Joanne Gonsalves, Salem State College
Lesea Lorenzen Huber, Indiana University
David Layman, New York University
Cheeryl Shirley, Drury University

We thank all the older adults who gave of their time and knowledge for each chapter's Senior View: Joyce Shealy (1), Arthur and Ruth Kingberg (2), Clifford and Lucia Pauling and Lori Fincher (3), Martha Russell (4), Walter Donham (5), Mabel Davis (6), Edward and Isabelle Peltz (7), Mae Taylor and Jack Palis (8), Jane Hege and Tolly Kleckley (9), Pauline and Lister Hopkins, Tom and Eleanor McNair, Edwin Schmidt, and Carol Milheim (10), Frank Ochoa and Pat Shelley (11), Edna Carpenter and Wanda Washburn (12), May Lee (13), and Tat Kleckley (14).

We thank our students who assisted in gathering data for many parts of the book including the Senior Views in each chapter. We especially thank Arlo Clark-Foos who is currently a graduate student in psychology at the University of Georgia and has taught us how to appreciate our field through new eyes. He has been quick (perhaps too quick) to offer suggestions on how to appeal to college students in writing, pictures, graphs, and other aspects of the text. As parents we know that we learn much from our children. We have high hopes that the next generation of our family, starting with Aleigha, will carry on the tradition of honoring our elders. A final thanks goes to our parents, Clarence, Joan, Norma, John, and Madge and Grandma and Grandpa Clark, Collignon, Halm, and Foos who instilled in us the spark that became our love for aging.

Paul W. Foos
M. Cherie Clark

Human Aging

CHAPTER

1

An Introduction to Human Aging

Old age is like everything else. To make a success of it you have to start young.

—*Fred Astaire*

You have to start young. Regardless of how young, or old, you now are, you are continually becoming older. To make your aging successful, you need to start young and our text and this course will help you do just that. You will learn about things that typically change as we grow older and things that typically do not. You will learn that some change is beneficial while other change is not. We will examine the mind and body, our inner and outer selves, the society we live in, and the interactions among these different components of human aging. To give you an up close and personal view, each chapter will begin with the views of an older adult about the topics covered in that chapter. In our first Senior View, Dr. Joyce Shealy tells about her early introduction to the importance of learning, her relentless pursuit of education—sometimes in the face of obstacles—and her continuing quest to know more. She shows how the search for knowledge can be a habit, one that serves well into old age and one that brings lifelong fun. Let us begin the joy of learning about aging, about ourselves.

Why Study Human Aging?

Why study human aging? Why study older people? One might also ask why study children, history, poetry, or why study at all? A simple answer is that we study things so that we can know more about them. We want to know more about them because we as humans value knowledge and because knowledge can help improve our lives. One reason for studying human aging is that we value knowledge and want to learn more.

We also study aging because it is something that we all are doing every day, and hope to continue doing for many more decades. The alternative could be quite unpleasant. The study of human aging has direct relevance to the way we live. Every day that you live, you are aging, as are your family and friends. The things you learn from this book—and any other reading that you do—can influence the choices you make for yourself and your loved ones for the rest of your life. Another major reason for studying human aging is because you are human and you are aging. The things you learn may help you to age successfully.

1

Senior View

We talked with Dr. Joyce Shealy, professor emeritus of psychology at Queens University of Charlotte, North Carolina, about the importance of education and learning. Joyce was 80 years old when we spoke with her and recently retired from a career of over 40 years of teaching.

Joyce was born in Bucyrus, Ohio, and moved with her family to Chicago, then New Jersey, and finally to the South Carolina pecan farm where her family originated. We asked her to share the educational influences and experiences she had across her life. She said her father influenced her love of learning that has pervaded her life. She repeated his words of advice: *Don't get married right away; learn who you are first; never stop learning.* Here is what she told us.

I spent 2 years at Winthrop University, where my mother went to school. Despite my mother's urging to stay there, I needed to branch out. I wanted to go someplace else; my dream was New York. My parents let me transfer to the University of South Carolina in Columbia because that's where my brother was and they believed he would watch over me. I earned my BA and MA in political sci-

ence. Even then I had an interest in psychology as my thesis examined the personality characteristics of South Carolina legislators. I compared them to a control group of similar men who were members of a club my father belonged to. This was a fun study but my advisor published my thesis and put me in a footnote.

I had a hard time finding a job I really liked. I taught modern dance for a year and then taught history, political science, psychology, and sociology at Lees McRae College for another year. I served as faculty sponsor for a number of student organizations but still had the itch to see and do more. I moved back to Columbia and worked as a research assistant for the Bureau of Public Administration.

I was interested in personnel issues and my father thought a psychology degree was the best a person could get so I went to Ohio State to get another graduate degree, this time in industrial/organizational psychology. When I completed my MA, my professor told me that as a woman, I could not continue there for my doctorate in I/O psychology and should consider a counseling degree. That's not what I wanted so I took the next semester off and moved to UNC Chapel Hill to work on my PhD.

My specialization there was in psychometrics and I was fortunate to have worked with Dr. Thurstone. When I finished, I got a research assistant position working in special education at the University of Delaware. However, I was not happy there as my heart was in the south, so I returned to North Carolina where I became a professor of psychology at Queens College (now Queens University) of Charlotte. I loved teaching and miss it now that I've retired. I still get together, once a year, with some former students who are now psychologists and judges. I also love learning and have not retired from that. I take classes at Wake Forest University and take advantage of other opportunities as they arise. I am now a docent at the Reynolda Museum and a volunteer at the humane society. I won't stop learning and you shouldn't either.

My advice is to continue your education.

Finally, we study human aging because that area of study is becoming more important with each passing year. A major reason for the importance of this area of study, and the increasing interest in aging, is because changes are occurring in the world population, particularly in countries such as the United States. The number and proportion of older adults in the U.S. population is likely to increase for quite some time. The growing number of older adults will impact everything in our lives. Here are just a few examples. Transportation will change as older drivers demand better public transportation. Older people vote in greater numbers than other age groups so policies and legislation will reflect their interests. More leisure and recreation opportunities will be developed in response to this large age cohort. Family dynamics may change as more grandparents and great-grandparents are available to give advice and help to younger people. Finally, this growing segment of the population will create job and career opportunities in fields that serve older consumers. The population is changing and the more we learn about it, the better equipped we will be to succeed.

Changes in Population

The number and proportion of older adults among the world population will continue to increase for the foreseeable future. In 1900, about 4 percent of the U.S. population was 65 and older (about 3 million people). In 1996, about 13 percent were 65 and older (about 35 million) (U.S. Bureau of the Census, 2000). It is not just that there are a greater number of older people; the population has grown and there are more people of every age. The important point is that the proportion of older people continues to increase. In 1900, 1 out of every 25 people was 65 and older. In 1990, it was 1 out of every 10. By 2030, it is expected that 1 out of every 4 or 5 will be 65 or older. That's 85 million older Americans. This change is taking place in technologically advanced and industrialized countries all over the globe. Can you imagine how different things might be with such a large proportion of older adults? How old will you and your loved ones be in 2030?

There are a number of factors that are responsible for the drastic change in population including the unprecedented number of people in the baby boom generation, lower birth rate, and changes in life expectancy.

Soon there will be many more older adults.

Baby Boom Generation.   The baby boom generation refers to those individuals born between 1946 and 1964. Following the end of World War II, there was a huge increase in the number of births as soldiers returned home to their families or married and began a family. There were feelings of victory, security, and prosperity and couples felt good about bringing children into these happy times. They were very successful at having babies and averaged close to three births per fertile woman (U.S. Bureau of the Census, 1989). This was the highest birth rate since right after the Civil War (1865–1900). The impact of the baby boom generation on society can be seen throughout history by looking at the growth of products and programs to serve the needs of the "boomers" and their families. The first wave of the baby boom generation will reach age 65 in the year 2011. The proportion of older adults in the population will continue to increase from 2011 until at least 2030.

Birth Rate.   Following the great increase after World War II, birth rate has declined. The average number of births per fertile woman is now less than two and some experts expect the number to go as low as 1.7. The total proportion, as well as number, of older adults will be greater over the next several decades than it has ever been. This is where developing countries differ from developed nations. In developing countries, populations of older persons are not yet on the rise. While their birth rates are still quite high, their life expectancy remains low.

Lifespan and Life Expectancy.   Lifespan refers to the maximum number of years that an organism in a species can live. Clearly, the lifespan for different species is very different and not many species live longer than humans do. Table 1-1 provides some examples

TABLE 1-1   Estimated Lifespans for Some Friends and Acquaintances

Queen honey bee	6 years
Rabbit	13 years
Cat	28 years
Cow	30 years
Dog	34 years
Tape worm	35 years
Gorilla	39 years
Alligator	56 years
Horse	60 years
Eagle	65 years
Elephant	70 years
Blue whale	80 years
Human	122 years
Tortoise	170 years
Italian cypress	2000 years
Bristle cone pine	5000 years

Source: Most of these estimated lifespans were taken from Comfort (1964) and Kimmel (1990).

of lifespans for several different common, and not so common, species. Cover the right column of the table and see if you can guess the lifespan for these different forms of life. These numbers come from reports from naturalists, scientists, zookeepers, and everyday people about the lives of animals that they have observed. They are not absolute values because it is possible that a member of that species might break the current record and live a little longer. At the same time, the numbers can be considered pretty good "ballpark" figures because these current records have, in many instances, stood for quite some time.

The estimated lifespan for humans was 120 years but since Jeanne Calment (see photo) had her 122nd birthday on February 21, 1997, and died in August 1997, 122 years is the current lifespan. Who is the oldest person alive today, and how old is he or she? While that may seem like a simple question, it is not. How do you determine a person's age? What documentation do you use? A registered birth certificate is the most accepted record of age. However, many people born in the late 1800s either never had a birth certificate or no longer have that documentation, especially in countries where record keeping is not advanced. Regardless of how you answer that question, many older adults seem to be rapidly closing in on the record. Earlier this year Maria Esther de Capovilla of Ecuador celebrated her 116th birthday before passing away. What do you think should be required as proof?

Many scientists would argue that lifespan, once we figure out what it is, cannot be changed. (See Chapter 5 on longevity.) Life expectancy can, however, be changed and has changed since humans began recording such statistics. Life expectancy refers to the age at which half of a given birth group is expected to be living and half is expected to have died. Thus, we expect that for people born in 1993, half will live to be 75.4 years of age and half will die before reaching that age. This number is life expectancy at birth (LEAB) and, thus, takes into account all the deaths for that 1993 group that will likely occur during the first few years of life, adolescence, and young adulthood. An important factor underlying the

Jeanne Calment, the current record holder for oldest person, age 122.

improvement in LEAB over the past century is the significant improvement in sanitation and health care for infants and children. Since 1900, we have seen a dramatic drop in the number of young people dying from what were once common and terminal childhood diseases. Because LEAB counts all these early deaths in calculating life expectancy, one might expect that individuals who make it past those early challenges will live longer than the average 75.4 years. After all, their average will not include those early deaths that go into calculation of LEAB. Today, LEAB is estimated to be 77.9 for newborn Americans.

Life expectancy at a specified age (LEASA) estimates the age at which people are expected to die, given that they have made it to a certain age. In this case we can estimate how many more years people who are a certain age can, on average, expect to live. The number refers to the number of years past which half of the group should still be living and half will have died. LEASA is longer than LEAB because it does not include any of those early deaths in its calculation. Therefore another major reason for the increases in proportion and number of older adults is that LEAB and LEASA have both increased. Birth groups can expect to live longer than they could at the turn of the century as we continue to improve our ability to live through early life illness and disease; adults who make it to an older age can expect many more years ahead of them than could adults who made it to that same specified age several decades ago. Figure 1-1 shows differences in life expectancy at birth for people who lived in the distant past, not so distant past, and today. Some very well-known individuals did not live very long although some others lived well past the life expectancy for people living in their times. Generally, people can expect to live much longer today than they could in the past.

Clearly, there will be many more older people over the next several decades and those older people can also expect to live longer. Table 1-2 shows life expectancy at the specified age of 65 for people making it to that age at the beginning and end of the twentieth century. Older people can expect to live longer than older people could just a few decades ago. In fact, the biggest increases over the next several decades will be for the oldest-old, people 80 years of age and over.

TABLE 1-2   Twentieth Century Changes in Life Expectancy at the Specified Age of 65

If you reached age 65 in this year	You could expect to live this many more years	For a grand total of this many years
1900	11.65	76.65
1920	12.30	77.30
1940	12.65	77.65
1960	14.40	79.40
1980	16.20	81.20
2000	18.01	83.01

Source: Adapted from Hooyman & Kiyak (1996); Kimmel (1990); U.S. Bureau of the Census (1993); and the authors' own estimations.

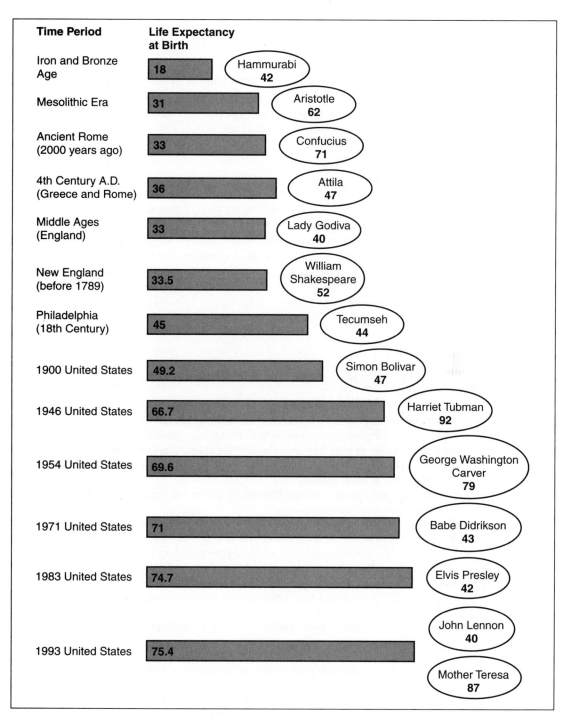

Time Period	Life Expectancy at Birth	
Iron and Bronze Age	18	Hammurabi 42
Mesolithic Era	31	Aristotle 62
Ancient Rome (2000 years ago)	33	Confucius 71
4th Century A.D. (Greece and Rome)	36	Attila 47
Middle Ages (England)	33	Lady Godiva 40
New England (before 1789)	33.5	William Shakespeare 52
Philadelphia (18th Century)	45	Tecumseh 44
1900 United States	49.2	Simon Bolivar 47
1946 United States	66.7	Harriet Tubman 92
1954 United States	69.6	George Washington Carver 79
1971 United States	71	Babe Didrikson 43
1983 United States	74.7	Elvis Presley 42
1993 United States	75.4	John Lennon 40 / Mother Teresa 87

FIGURE 1-1   Historical Changes in Life Expectancy.

Sources: Adapted from Katchadourian (1987); Laslett (1985); and Worldwatch Institute (1994).

In short, there will be a greater number, and a greater proportion, of older adults over the next several decades as a result of the great number of births which followed World War II (baby boom), the lower birth rate in more recent decades, and the continued increases in life expectancy. These numbers carry important implications for careers and employment opportunities in the twenty-first century.

Career Implications

It is important that we know as much as we can about aging so that we can be prepared for these millions of people. This might mean the creation of new direct service jobs in fields such as elder law, geriatric health care, gerontological social work, or advocacy for elders. The U.S. Labor Department predicts a 36 percent increase in gerontology-related jobs by 2012. Box 1-1 contains a list compiled by the Association for Gerontology in Higher Education (AGHE) of jobs in the field of gerontology. While this is an impressive list, knowl-

---

BOX 1-1

Careers in Gerontology

Gerontological specialists work in a variety of different settings that can be listed in the following broad categories:

- Direct Service Provision—Provide care for elders in homes, hospitals, clinics, or through adult service programs; these can include health care provision, counseling, advising elders, and developing programs and activities for elders in a wide variety of settings.
- Program Planning and Evaluation—Design, implement, and evaluate programs designed to meet the needs of older persons.
- Management and Administration—Oversee operation, staffing, and evaluation of organizations and institutions serving elders.
- Marketing and Product Development—Many corporations, institutions, and organizations want employees to help develop and market new products and services for older persons.
- Advocacy—Work with or on behalf of older persons before legislative bodies, politicians, or institutions; often advocating for specific programs, services, or policies.
- Education and Training—Educate and train older people and their families, health care and other service providers, and future gerontological professionals in a variety of educational settings.
- Research—Design and conduct a wide variety of research projects dealing with aging issues.

Newer jobs for gerontological professionals are emerging including:

- Entrepreneurs—Self-employment, often as consultants on a variety of aging issues to businesses, individuals, organizations, and corporations.
- Geriatric Care Managers—Assist with planning services for elders, often acting as a liaison with service providers; care managers are often hired by family members to help arrange care for an elderly relative.

edge of aging and older people can serve you well in any career you choose simply because there will be more older customers/clients, supervisors, and employees as you travel through your work life. In all cases, jobs that are geared toward serving the public will need to take into consideration the growing number of older consumers. A major portion of the consuming public will be over age 65 and you can be sure that corporations will want to sell to them. After all, there will be many more of them in the not-too-distant future and many of them have substantial discretionary income. New jobs, such as elder law, will emerge to serve the older population. Entrepreneurs in this area can make a substantial impact.

The Study of Aging

The study of aging and older adults is known as **gerontology**. This word comes from "ology" meaning "the study of," and the Greek word "gero" referring to elders. A related term is **geriatrics**, which refers to the specialty within such health care fields as medicine, social work, nursing, and dentistry; it is concerned with health, disease, care, and treatment of older adults. Gerontology is multidisciplinary, which means it includes the perspectives of many traditional disciplines like anthropology, biology, business administration, economics, nursing, psychology, and sociology; it assumes multiple influences on development. In this book we examine gerontology primarily from the perspective of the sciences (anthropology, biology, psychology, sociology, social work) but, by definition, there will be topics that will be discussed that draw on or emanate from many of these other disciplines. Working individually or together, these researchers advance an understanding of aging.

All sciences use similar methods to study aging and older adults. We will examine these basic common methods in the next chapter. An understanding of methods and some of the problems confronted by researchers will help you to understand the findings, theories, and conclusions drawn throughout the rest of the book.

What Is Aging/Who Is Old?

Aging refers to an individual passing through time and all that occurs during the passing of time. We age from birth onward. Changes that occur during aging can be quick or slow, positive or negative. For example, we may hear a proud parent of a 7-year-old say, "He's such a big boy now; he acts so much older." Clearly, the notion of aging and getting older in this situation is a positive experience. You may also have heard people say about a grandparent, "He seems so much older than when we saw him last." Here the connotation is somewhat negative, suggesting that some major decline connected to getting older has occurred. As the lifespan developmental perspective suggests, development at every age is made up of both gains and losses. You can think of things that you are better at now than you were 10 years ago and also things you do not do as well anymore.

Undoubtedly you know many older adults. Your parents are certainly older than you are, although we might still count them as middle-aged. Your grandparents are older adults and, if all are still living, you probably know them fairly well. Many of your teachers are older adults; at least the ones that you had years ago in elementary school. Look to the front of the room in all of your classes; are any of your current teachers older adults? You may have neighbors and friends who are older adults. You certainly see senior citizens whenever you go out. Of course, looking at these people may have alerted you to the fact that you may not be sure what counts as old. Where is that line between middle and old age? Or between middle and young age? Is there such a line at all?

One of the most commonly used markers to identify the boundary between old and middle-age is chronological, the age of 65. The U.S. Bureau of the Census (1993) provides three subcategories of the older population: (1) the young-old (65 to 74 years); (2) the middle-old (75 to 84 years); and (3) the old-old (85 and over). Although some research, particularly marketing studies, has tried to provide support for differences among these three groups, other research has failed to find significant differences. Centenarians, people who are 100 and older, are often regarded as another separate group, and, as you will see, a number of research studies have examined this oldest of the old groups separately from those youngsters only in their 80s. Regardless of how many groups are used or how the elderly population is divided, it is important to remember that much of this division is done for convenience and to identify gross differences that might apply to many, but certainly not all, members of a group. You can probably think of someone who is quite old but who looks and acts much younger. You have probably also seen someone who is fairly young but who looks and acts quite old. Gerontologists agree that the elderly, as a group, are more heterogeneous or different from one another than any other age group. Individual differences only get stronger as you get older, as your biology and the environment continue to interact to make you unique.

Despite what researchers say, many lay people have similar ideas about when they think old age begins. The American Association of Retired Persons (AARP) compiled information from three different surveys with thousands of respondents and found that the majority of respondents said old age started between 60 to 69. Researchers found that the older the person answering the question was, the older the age they assigned to being old. What age would you say begins old age? You might try the exercise in Box 1-2 and learn how your answers compare to others older and younger than you are.

What can we conclude about when old age starts? Only that a commonly perceived marker is between the ages of 60 and 70 and that old age is divisible into subcategories. Keep this in mind as we discuss the scientific literature on aging. Gerontology literature attempts to provide accurate and reliable information about aging regardless of when old age begins and hopes that such information can counteract the stereotypes about aging that are prevalent in society.

Stereotypes

Many sources provide us with stereotypes of older adults and the aging experience. We see older adults portrayed on television, in movies, and in advertisements. We meet older characters in books, hear about them in jokes, and read how aging is depicted in most birthday cards. Much of what the average person knows, or thinks they know about aging comes from these sources, and these sources are never entirely right.

B O X **1-2**

Who Is Old?

The authors (1994) did a follow-up study on what people think about aging and older people. We collected information from a regional sample in order to compare it to the national sample reported by AARP, which is discussed in the text. Answer each of the following questions before reading the results described later, in order to compare your answers to the answers found:

1. At what age do you consider someone to be old?
2. Describe your image of a typical old person.
3. How do you feel about your own aging?

These questions were asked of 301 men and women ranging in age from 14 to 97 (mean age of 35). There was strong agreement that the age at which someone is considered to be old is about 70. Remember that the national survey found 60 to 69 as the average age of an old person. How close was your answer to this number?

For Question 2, the most frequent characteristics listed by the adults surveyed were the following: retired, grandparent, wise, slow, handicapped/weak, wrinkled, gray hair, cheerful/happy, inactive, isolated, fearful, and confused. Some of these images seem positive and some negative. Although all of them are true of certain individuals, none are true of all individuals. There is enormous diversity among older adults and we will explore this diversity throughout this book. Although some of these characteristics fit the typical stereotype of an older adult, you will soon learn that stereotypes are not very accurate and that they can be quite damaging.

For Question 3, the vast majority of people (67 percent) said that they looked forward to aging. Another 21 percent said that they were scared and 12 percent said that they couldn't imagine growing old. Which group do you find yourself in? Why?

Stereotypes often lead naive people to believe that exaggerations and half-truths (in many cases outright falsehoods) are not only true but are also true for every member of that group. Some anthropologists say that stereotypes influence people to believe that older adults are typically confused, disoriented, maladjusted, and incoherent. These believers then seem surprised when meeting an older adult who does not show such characteristics and may believe that the individual is simply having an unusually good day. Evidence that older adults are not confused, disoriented, maladjusted, and incoherent is often considered suspect because everyone knows they are (Hazan, 1996).

Maggie Kuhn, who founded the Gray Panthers, has been very active in trying to change stereotypes about older adults, and aging, in general. In an interview in 1989, she said, "The first myth is that old age is a disease, a terrible disease that you never admit that you've got, so you lie about your age. Well, it's not a disease. It's a triumph, because you've survived. Failure, disappointment, sickness, loss, you're still here."

Such positive views of aging are all too rare in the television shows, movies, advertisements, books, jokes, and birthday cards that continue to portray aging in a negative light. In what follows we describe some of these stereotypes and their presentation in the

Not your stereotypic older adult.

media. Generally, researchers have looked at the portrayal of older adults in two ways, quantitatively and qualitatively. A quantitative analysis is done to assess whether the proportion of older adults in a media presentation is equivalent to the proportion of older adults in the general population. If older adults comprise about 20 percent of the total population but older characters comprise only 2 percent of the population in a novel, then older adults are underrepresented in the novel. Of course, in some novels such an underrepresentation might be expected. A novel about an adolescent youth camp will, of course, underrepresent older and probably middle-age adults. A qualitative analysis is done to assess whether the older adults who are presented are portrayed in positive, neutral, or negative terms. If older adults are portrayed as wise, then that would be considered positive; if they are portrayed as confused, then that might be considered negative. We will examine portrayals in electronic and print media separately.

Electronic Media

Electronic media refers to television, movies, radio, and Internet portrayals of older adults, although only television has received extensive assessment. In a quantitative analysis of 22,315 television characters, most studies found an underrepresentation of older adults. This underrepresentation was particularly low during prime-time shows. Females were underrepresented to a greater extent than males. On the other hand, television commercials and daytime soap operas represented older adults at about the same proportion as in the population (Vasil & Wass, 1993). A study (Robinson & Skill, 1995) compared roles held by older persons in 1995 to those reported in previous studies from the 1970s. Older people were actually more underrepresented than in the 1970s. So, despite the fact that the number of older people in the population has grown, and that public opinion about the elderly seems to have improved (Ferraro, 1992), their portrayals in prime-time shows have not improved. Swayne and Greco (1986) found the same underrepresentation of older people in television commercials. Women, again, were even more underrepresented.

Qualitative analyses show that older adults are more often portrayed negatively than positively and that this is especially true of older females. Older adults are most frequently portrayed as foolish and eccentric (Bishop & Krause, 1984). Older women are often shown as silly, lacking common sense, and unsuccessful (Gerbner et al., 1980) while older men are sometimes portrayed as problem solvers (Dail, 1988). Thus, even though all older adults suffer from negative portrayals on television, older females seem to suffer more. As in the quantitative analyses, the least negative portrayals are found in daytime soap operas.

Print Media

Print media refers to newspaper, magazine, book, and greeting card portrayals of older adults. As with electronic media, older adults are underrepresented in print and this is particularly true for older women (Vasil & Wass, 1993). Qualitative analyses of print media, like electronic media, shows that older adults are more likely to be portrayed in a negative way than are other age groups and the most frequent negative themes are of extreme conservatism and sexual dysfunction (Smith, 1979).

One might expect that advertisements would provide positive portrayals of aging and older adults since such advertisers are often attempting to attract older consumers. In fact, this does seem to be the case. One major study of 30 years of advertisements in *Modern Maturity* magazine (published by AARP) found that persons 50 and older were shown as healthy, important, capable, and socially active (Roberts & Zhou, 1997). They also found that 96.4 percent of the older persons in these advertisements were white. What about mainstream magazines? Miller et al., (1999) examined advertisements in several popular U.S. magazines (e.g., *Better Homes and Gardens, Popular Mechanics*) for evidence of elderly stereotypes. They were particularly interested in examining change over time so they analyzed magazines from 1956 to 1996. Similar to the findings with electronic media, the elderly were greatly underrepresented in these ads with the percentage decreasing over the years. Overall they found little stereotyping of elders but for those few stereotypes, there was an increase in negative stereotyping and a decrease in positive stereotyping.

Birthday cards and jokes provide other examples of negative stereotyping of older adults and aging. Of course, these jokes and cards are meant to be humorous and many are quite funny. Nevertheless, one must distinguish between a good joke and a damaging stereotype. See Box 1-3 for an example of a good and positive joke. An analysis of

BOX **1-3**

Positive Humor

Most jokes about older adults carry negative connotations and portray old adults as confused, incapable, disoriented, incoherent, and even maladjusted. Once in a while, however, a joke can carry positive connotations as the following illustrates.

> A wise old gentleman retired and purchased a modest home near a junior high school. He spent the first few weeks of his retirement in peace and contentment. Then a new school year began. The very next afternoon three young boys, full of youthful, after school enthusiasm, came down his street, beating merrily on every trash can they encountered. The crashing percussion continued day after day, until finally the wise old man decided it was time to take some action. The next afternoon, he walked out to meet the young percussionists as they banged their way down the street. Stopping them, he said, "You kids are a lot of fun. I like to see you express your exuberance like that. Used to do the same thing when I was your age. Will you do me a favor? I'll give you each a dollar if you'll promise to come around every day and do your thing." The kids were elated and continued to do a bang-up job on the trash cans. After a few days, the old-timer greeted the kids again, but this time he had a sad smile on his face. "This recession's really putting a big dent in my income," he told them. "From now on, I'll only be able to pay you 50 cents to beat on the cans." The noisemakers were obviously displeased, but they did accept his offer and continued their afternoon ruckus. A few days later, the wily retiree approached them again as they drummed their way down the street. "Look," he said, "I haven't received my Social Security check yet, so I'm not going to be able to give you more than 25 cents. Will that be okay?" "A lousy quarter?" the drum leader exclaimed. "If you think we're going to waste our time, beating these cans around for a quarter, you're nuts! No way, mister. We quit!" And the old man enjoyed peace and serenity for the rest of his days.

> *Source:* Contributed by Tim Rehahn.

---

birthday cards found that 88 percent portrayed aging in a negative way (Demos & Jache, 1981). Look at birthday cards the next time you are in a card store and you will probably see that very few portray aging in a positive way. If you want to try this in a slightly more systematic way, you might try Project 1.

Stereotyping can be found in a content analysis of jokes. We have all heard jokes about a number of different groups and they are generally not very flattering for the groups portrayed in the joke. An analysis of jokes about old people shows that 59 percent portray old age and old adults negatively while only 23 percent portray them positively (the remaining 18 percent were considered neutral). The most negative portrayals were in jokes about death, age concealment, mental and physical ability, and appearance (Palmore, 1986). The next time you hear a joke about an older person, substitute a minority for the older person and see if it still sounds funny. We no longer consider racist and sexist jokes funny but we often don't think twice about laughing at or telling an ageist joke. Would your grandmother think that joke you are hearing or reading is funny? If you agree that these negative portrayals should be curtailed, look in Box 1-3 for information on one way to do something positive.

A major problem with stereotypes is that they often lead to prejudice and discrimination against older people. Age discrimination against older adults is different than

---

PROJECT 1

Although the text claims that most portrayals of older adults and aging are quite negative, perhaps you are wondering if this is true. To some extent, the amount of negativity depends on the source of the stereotype. Birthday cards about aging are almost always negative, whereas advertisements are far more positive.

Go to a major source of birthday cards, such as a large department store, card store, or drug store, and read 20 cards for children, 20 for older adults, and 20 for people of unspecified age. Rate each card as being positive, neutral, or negative about that birthday age. What did you find?

The 20 cards for children are likely to be positive; the 20 for older adults are likely to be negative. You may notice, however, a sudden shift in cards designed for the very old. These cards turn sweet and gentle. Why do you think this is? How positive or negative were cards for individuals of unspecified age?

What stereotypes about aging are portrayed in these cards? Was Maggie Kuhn right?

---

other forms of discrimination since, as time passes, the persons doing the discrimination are likely to be among those discriminated against (Garstka et al., 2004). **Ageism**, a term coined and first described in detail by Butler (1969), is very prevalent in society. If you think older people are forgetful, then you may not trust directions or instructions given to you by an older relative. If you think older people are confused, then you may interpret a pause at the snack counter in a theater as a reason to start offering alternatives or to skip over that person. You may not hire an older person if you think that they will have physical or mental problems on the job. Ageism is supported by, and to some extent grows out of, negative stereotypes and can result in negative attitudes toward aging and older adults.

BOX 1-4

Be Fair

As persons interested in the welfare of older adults, we should all work to eliminate ageism in all of its forms. Ageism is any form of discrimination against an individual because of his/her age. If you see a product or service that is itself or in its advertisement offensive to older persons, let the manufacturer or service provider know. Gently reminding people that jokes about older persons are demeaning can go a long way toward raising the consciousness of others. Negative portrayals in the media also should be protested. Contact media outlets (and their advertisers!) and let them know what the objectionable material is and how they can change. The organization Fairness and Accuracy in Reporting (FAIR) has developed a media contact list that can serve as an excellent first step to advocacy for fair treatment of older persons in the media. Go to www.fair.org and click on "Activisim" to obtain the media contact list and other activisim tools. Tell your friends to help the cause. Pretty soon it will be a movement!

Attitudes Toward Aging

Negative portrayals of older people often result in negative attitudes toward aging. What do most people think about old people? Most Americans tend to see older persons with many more serious problems than they really have, especially regarding health, loneliness, and financial worries (AARP, 1995). Even children, as young as 8, tend to have negative views of older adults (Aday et al., 1991) and individuals with some intellectual disability have more negative attitudes than those experiencing normal development (Lifshitz, 2002).

There are also age, gender, and racial group differences in attitudes toward aging and older adults. Older adults are generally more positive about aging than are younger adults (AARP, 1995; Kalavar, 2001). Work on gender differences has provided mixed results. Adolescent women and female graduate students generally are more positive than their male counterparts (Haught et al., 1999; Gellis et al., 2003). Other work shows, however, that young women report more anxiety about aging than do young men (Barbee, 1989; Cummings et al., 2000) and older women are more likely than older men to conceal their age (Harris, 1994). A more recent study by DePaola et al. (2003) found no gender differences in attitudes among older adults. Gender differences are not consistent and appear to depend on other factors.

Very few studies have been focused on racial and ethnic group differences in attitudes toward aging (e.g., DePaola et al., 2003). Some work has found that young African and Hispanic Americans reported more anxiety about their own aging than young Caucasian Americans (Cummings et al., 2000). Research that has examined the attitudes of old as well as young African and Caucasian Americans found far less-positive attitudes about aging for African Americans, perhaps because of the double difficulty of being both black and old, their lower financial status, and their higher risk of disability and disease (Foos et al., 2006). It is difficult to draw many conclusions regarding Native Americans since there is great variety among the 307 officially recorded political entities (tribes, clans, nations). There is a range of attitudes toward older adults from that of respected elder to worthless burden who should be abandoned by the young. Across all groups, however, for those Native Americans who hold to traditional culture, respect for family leads to positive attitudes toward older adults. Mexican Americans have a very strong filial (family) obligation and thus tend to view their older family members positively. Old age in Mexican American families comes with increased status. Finally, Holmes and Holmes (1995) suggest that Asian Americans hold tightly to traditional respect for family and hold their elders in high esteem. What is your family background? Can you identify traditions in your family that give guidance to the treatment of elder members?

Are older adults viewed differently in other cultures around the world? Sokolovsky (1997) summarizes the results of several anthropological crosscultural studies by saying that attitudes toward elderly persons vary tremendously both within and across cultures. This fact makes it very difficult to draw generalizations or discuss the variety in a short space. Furthermore, as fast as a culture is studied, changes in the society and around the world make the data somewhat obsolete. Given those caveats, what can we say about images of aging in other places? In many cultures, aging carries high status and prestige and is associated with great respect. This seems to be the case in Japan, China, and many eastern countries as well as in Africa as seen in the ¡Kung of Botswana and Hausa of Nigeria.

On the other hand, young adults in Nigeria often describe older adults as sickly, conservative, suspicious, secretive, and acting like children although they also say that these older adults impose few demands on their children (Okoye & Obikeze, 2005).

In Turkey, only about 6 percent of the population is 65 or older and people consider themselves old by the time they reach their late 40s. Turkish residents, especially men, have high concerns about aging and many fear growing old, perhaps due to the economic and social turmoil in Turkey (McConatha et al., 2004). German young people are more negative about growing old than are American young people while, at the same time, they view old age as starting in the mid 60s while young Americans see it as starting in the early 50s (McConatha et al., 2003). In Samoa, according to Holmes and Holmes (1995) old age is a prerequisite for family and political leadership; in other words, one must be old to be the boss. Elders in other countries do not fare as well. For example, elderly in Hong Kong experience very low status (Keith et al., 1994), and frail elders in Polynesia are considered decrepit and ghost-like and therefore neglected and left to die (Barker, 1997). Sokolovsky reports that very low favor characterizes the view of elderly in the Siriono people in East Bolivia and also the Chippewyan Indians in Northern Canada.

As you can see, the attitudes toward older adults worldwide are mixed, at best. Although there seem to be groups in which increased status, respect, and prestige is the norm for older members, there are still others for which aging has a negative connotation, much as seen here in the United States. Can we hope for better days ahead in the view of old persons? Even today, not all views are negative. We know that older adults have positive stereotypes too. They are often considered wise, helpful, caring, and generous. Work that has presented positive stereotypes for young (e.g., energetic) and old (e.g., experienced) along with negative stereotypes for both age groups (reckless for young and forgetful for old) has found much quicker responses to positive than to negative stereotypes suggesting that they are stronger (Chasteen et al., 2002). It is encouraging to find that, although there are many negative stereotypes, positive views may be the stronger views.

Findings with children and persons with disabilities suggest that persons with less knowledge about aging have more negative attitudes and that appears to be the case. As you might then expect, increased education about aging improves attitudes (Funderbunk et al, 2006; O'Hanlon & Brookover, 2002). Research also has shown that positive attitudes can be fostered by providing opportunities for contact between young and old. Contact with unrelated older adults improves attitude particularly when the contact is positive (Funderbunk et al., 2006; Meshel & McGlynn, 2004; Schwartz & Simmons, 2001). There is empirical evidence that both education and contact are important. Think about your contact with older persons and how that might have influenced your current views of aging; think about your own education with respect to aging. The questions in Box 1-2 can help you think through this issue.

As the population ages and more persons enroll in classes like the one you are now taking, more accurate knowledge of aging should translate into better images of aging in general and more positive anticipation of our own aging. That more accurate knowledge comes from research in gerontology.

SOCIAL POLICY APPLICATIONS

Any major change in population is bound to influence a society's policies. For example, we have seen policies proposed to handle increases in the number of immigrants. If children were rare (as in *Children of Men*), policies would be created to increase their numbers, perhaps by providing support and protection for those capable of giving birth and for the few existing children. The U.S. population is changing in the other direction as the number and proportion of older adults increases and continues to increase over the next several decades. Should we create new policies to provide support and protection for them? Because older adults are increasing rather than decreasing in number, perhaps they are already too supported and protected. Do you think this is the case? Will an increased proportion of older adults exert undue influence on future policy decisions? Members of the baby boom generation, followed by their children, will be a major political force not just because of their numbers but also because older adults typically vote at a higher rate than younger adults. In addition, life expectancy is increasing so these voters will be around and voting for quite some time. Social policies are more and more likely to focus on the needs of these older adults; the United States already has had several policies changed and others proposed in response to the growing needs of the growing older population in the areas of Medicare, Medicaid, social security, estate issues, employment, and others. Policy and aging will no doubt be intricately tied to one another in the next few decades. Remain knowledgeable about aging and policy and weigh in with your state and federal policy makers to be sure that votes do not begin to favor one age group over another—and of course, vote.

CHAPTER HIGHLIGHTS

- There are three reasons to study human aging:
  1. We value knowledge and want to learn more.
  2. The things you learn may help you to age successfully.
  3. The area of aging is becoming more important with each passing year.
- The number and proportion of older adults in the population is and will continue to increase in the future. By 2030, there will be approximately 85 million older adults, or one out of every four people will be over the age of 65. This has been called the graying of the population.
- A number of factors underlie the growth in the older population including: the graying of the baby boom generation, lower birth rates, and increases in life expectancy.
- Lifespan is the maximum number of years that an organism in a species can live. There are great differences in lifespan among species. Lifespan has changed very little over time. The lifespan of humans currently is believed to be 122 years of age.
- Life expectancy at birth (LEAB) is how long an individual is expected to live, on the average. It is calculated as the point at which 50 percent of the people born in any given year are dead. Life expectancy has increased dramatically over the years of human existence and continues to increase. Currently, life expectancy is about 75.4 years of age for someone born in 1993.
- Life expectancy at a specific age (LEASA) is how much longer a person is expected to live once they have reached a certain age. It is calculated like LEAB except that only those who have made it to the specific age are included.
- Increases in LEAB and LEASA contribute to more people reaching old age than ever before, and to more people reaching advanced old age; people age 85 years and over make up the fastest growing segment of the population.
- The study of aging is called gerontology; the health care field focusing on older people is called geriatrics.

- Aging refers to an individual passing through time and all that occurs during that passing of time; old age is considered by most scientists to begin at 60 or 65, however, this is just a convenient reference point; there is no one point at which old age starts.
- Researchers often divide the older segment of the population into subcategories: 65 to 74 years are the young-old, 75 to 84 years are the middle-old, 85 and over have been considered the old-old, and, recently, 95 years and over are the very-old. Centenarian are those 100 and older.
- Society holds many stereotypical views of older persons, some positive, some neutral, and many negative.
- Quantitative analyses of electronic and print media have found that elderly people, especially older women, are greatly underrepresented relative to their numbers in the population.
- Qualitative analyses have found that older adults are often portrayed negatively, for example, foolish, eccentric, and mentally impaired.
- Negative stereotypes can lead to ageism, prejudice, and discrimination against older people.
- Negative portrayals of the elderly often results in negative attitudes toward aging and the aged; research supports the existence of significant negative attitudes.
- Not all cultures, within the United States or across the world, hold negative views of aging; in some cultures, increased age is a sign of status and prestige, in other cultures, negative views abound.
- Research suggests that improving portrayals of older people, increasing positive experiences younger people have with older people, and education about aging can all reduce negative attitudes toward aging and the elderly.

STUDY QUESTIONS

1. What change(s) in population can we expect over the next several decades?
2. What three reasons were given for the population changes that are occurring now and will continue to occur for the next several decades?
3. Name several areas of society that have been impacted by the baby boom generation. Name several areas that will be impacted by an aging baby boom generation.
4. To what do the terms lifespan and life expectancy refer?
5. What is the difference between life expectancy at birth and life expectancy at a specified age? Which is longer? Why?
6. What are some common stereotypes about the elderly? How do print and electronic media contribute to stereotypes about aging?
7. Explain the cultural differences in attitudes toward aging.
8. What are the roles of education and contact?

RECOMMENDED READINGS

Cole, T. R., & Winkler, M. G. (1994). *The Oxford Book of Aging: Reflections on the Journey of Life*. Oxford: Oxford University Press. This book offers 250 short essays, poems, and reflections on growing and being older. Reflections come from ancient times to present day (or at least the early 1990s).

King, S. (1994). *Insomnia*. New York: Viking Press. In this book, the hero and heroine are a pair of older adults. This is a positive view of older adults who are the heroes in this major work of fiction.

Martz, S. (1987). *When I Am an Old Woman I Shall Wear Purple*. Watsonville, CA: Papier–Mache Press. This book and two other books edited by the same author, *If I Had My Life to Live Over I Would Pick More Daisies* (1992) and *Grow Old Along With Me the Best Is Yet to Be* (1996) are compilations of wonderful short stories and poems written by and about older adults.

Palmore, E. B. (1999). *Ageism: Negative and Positive* (2nd ed.). New York: Springer Publishing. An excellent resource on the topic of ageism and attitudes toward aging. The book includes a review of findings in this area and addresses ways that people have attempted to reduce ageism. The book includes facts on aging quizzes, examples of ageist humor, and an annotated bibliography on ageism.

INTERNET RESOURCES

www.iog.wayne.edu/APADIV20. A number of sections on aging are available through individual professional organizations such as the American Sociological Society and the American Anthropological Society. Division 20 of the American Psychological Association deals with adult development and aging and also maintains a web site with useful information and links to other sites.

www.msstate.edu/org/gerontology/index.html. Facts on Aging Quizzes (1999). See how much you know about aging.

http://news.aarp.org/UM/T/asp?A910.52851.2518.5.5080. An excellent site with links to over 900 of the best sites that provide information about aging resources. This site will give up-to-date information about people currently closing in on Jean Calment's record lifespan.

www.iog.wayne.edu/APADIV20. Information from the American Psychological Association's Divison 20 (this is the division for adult development and aging).

www.geron.org. The Gerontological Society of America. This site has information on the study of aging, the society, news releases about aging, fact sheets, interest groups in gerontology, and links to other sites.

CHAPTER

2 Research Methods and Issues

Art is I; science is we.

—Claude Bernard

Science is the work of a community and brings forth knowledge for all to share. In this chapter, we will examine the methods that scientists use to gain knowledge about aging and older adults. Gerontological scientists, part of the "we" in the opening quote, come from anthropology, biology, medicine, psychology, sociology, and several other disciplines as well. Their findings are for all of us (another part of the "we" in the quote).

In this chapter, we will examine some of the guiding principles that influence research in gerontology and some of the important issues to which much research is directed; then we will look at theory that is meant to explain the phenomena that occur with increasing age. Finally, we will examine the methods that researchers use to test these theories and their hypotheses about aging and older adults. Some basic understanding of these principles, issues, theories, and methods are necessary if you are to understand the information presented in the rest of this text and this course. As always, let's begin with a Senior View.

Guiding Principles and Issues

Over the course of any research enterprise, guiding principles become evident and are shared by most involved in the field. Important issues or questions also evolve over time to be shared in the search for knowledge.

Table 2-1 on page 23 shows the set of principles that many researchers have adapted from the **lifespan perspective** (Baltes, 1987). This perspective says that we cannot look at any aspect of development in isolation; development is complex with myriad interrelated parts. *Development is a lifelong process.* It doesn't stop when someone reaches old age and it doesn't start only when adulthood begins. What happens early in life affects later life. *Development is multidisciplinary.* As noted earlier, anthropology, biology, medicine, psychology, sociology, and many other disciplines take part in the exploration of aging. One perspective is not sufficient if we are to truly understand human aging. *Development is composed of both gains and losses.* It is false to think that all of early life is gain and all

Senior View

We spoke with Arthur and Ruth Kingberg about the importance of research for answering questions about aging. Both were 83 and two of the healthiest older adults we'd ever met. They told us about leaving Germany—when they were still children—in the late 1930s to escape the Nazi persecution. Ruth escaped to England and then to the United States on a ship, dodging torpedoes, while Art escaped to Switzerland and then to the Philippines until after World War II. Both came without their parents. They met in New York (on the subway) and now have been married for 56 years.

When we asked what the important research questions were, Ruth told us, *Alzheimer's needs to be researched.* Art quickly added, *you have to limit medications if you can; the side effects of drugs are a real problem. Each person should do their own careful experimentation. Have semiannual checkups to gather data to see what works and what doesn't. Don't just do what someone tells you. You know your body best, so you can tell best what level of drug to take. Do your own research.*

An important topic in this chapter concerns distinguishing between age differences and cohort or generation differences. Do older people behave differently because they're older or because they grew up in different times? Ruth told us, *it's upbringing and not aging that usually is most important. It's how you were raised.*

Art told us, *you must take lifestyle factors into account; even people who were brought up conservatively can end up spoiling their kids.*

Ruth added, *the research is not yet strong enough; more needs to be done. Even what you eat is important and needs to be examined more closely.*

Would they be willing to participate in research? Art said *there should be an age limit in research participation; maybe at 50.* Ruth said *no, don't stop at any age.*

Art conceded saying that *it depends on the type of research.* For medical research, they both said no but for social research, they both said yes. For memory research, they were less certain. Ruth said, *memory is difficult and each brain may not be able to carry it through.* Art added, *memory is individual and with aging, the time line changes. Old memories come back faster than new.* Ruth quipped, *not necessarily* and they both laughed.

In parting they gave a list of tips for aging gracefully: *Stay in love and respect each other, eat the right food (use unbleached flour), never fry, leave the dinner table not fully satisfied, watch your weight, maintain general good health, have annual checkups, exercise, socialize, plan ahead, own and operate a computer for the wealth of information, practice religion, have a hobby and travel, be financially secure, maintain your own home, prevent bone loss, and do not smoke.* You will see throughout this book that their tips are well supported by research. No wonder they look so young!

TABLE 2-1   Important Features of the Lifespan Development Perspective

Feature	Description	Example: Math Ability in Old Age
Development as a lifelong process	Development takes place over the entire lifespan and all age periods are equally important to development and so must considered in research.	The development and maintenance of math ability at all previous ages should be considered important to present ability.
Development as multi-disciplinary	Development in any area is intricately tied with development in other areas (e.g., social relies on cognitive) and so research must consider all disciplines to understand the totality of development.	How can the fields of biology, anthropology, sociology, computer science, etc., contribute to the research question regarding the development of math ability?
Development as gains and losses	At all ages, development consists of both gains and losses and so research must examine both types of change.	Consider the gains in math ability in old-age along with the losses: for example, does wisdom result in more efficient ways to complete math tasks?
Development shows plasticity	Any individual's development shows considerable modifiability: at any point a person's experiences could changes the course of development and so developmental research must identify the degree of plasticity and its constraints.	How has math ability been affected by education or other experiences? Can current math ability be modified with training?
Development as embedded in history	Development occurs with a given historical-cultural context so research must examine development as it occurs within specific sociocultural conditions and how these change over time.	What historical and cultural factors have influenced math ability: for example, did growing up in the Great Depression result in poor nutrition and less formal schooling, which in turn affected math ability?
Development occurs within a context	Individual development is influenced by an interaction among many influences: some of which are biologic and some enviornmental, some experienced uniquely by an individual, and some experienced similarly by many individuals, and so research must consider the multitude of influences on development.	How was math ability learned and how was it maintained? Did parents or teachers provide basic instruction? How much practice, formal and informal, with math tasks was maintained in young and middle adulthood?

Source: Adapted from Baltes (1987).

of late life is loss, although, as you have already learned, many stereotypes of aging adopt this view. Children lose their innocence as they gain experience. Older adults gain perspective as they lose the speed with which they work. *Development shows plasticity.* The ways in which we develop always can be modified and much of this, although by no means all, is in our own hands. We decide to exercise or not; we decide to take risks or not; our decisions influence our development. *Development is embedded in history.* Human aging is strongly influenced by the times and places in which humans live. Throughout much of this text, we will examine these influences as we examine crosscultural factors and their effects on older adults and aging in general. *Development occurs within a context.* The context for a developing individual is comprised of their genes and all the environmental factors that influence their progression through life. Your parents, your home, your town, your job, your friends, your socioeconomic status (SES), and so on have all influenced who you are now.

These principles guide much of the research that is done to investigate aging and much of the thinking about older adults. Life is complex and the way we think about development should be equally complex. These principles are not always on center stage as we examine aging and older adults but they always are there even if sometimes behind the scenes. Take a minute and think about how these principles help explain your own development.

Researchers in gerontology are concerned with some general issues as well as the very specific problems they address. For example, a researcher might work to investigate changes in memory with advanced age but also know that any answers they find will contribute some knowledge about one or more of these general issues. We will only briefly describe some of these issues so that you can better understand the origins of much of the research discussed in this text. If you would like to learn more, a good source is provided by Lerner (1986).

The first issue, **nature–nurture**, refers to the relative contributions of genetics, and the environment to human aging. For example, does the occurrence of high cholesterol levels in some people over the age of 65 result from a genetic predisposition (dad, mom) or environmental influences (all those butter and bacon sandwiches)? We know that the answer is that both contribute. The more frequently asked questions emanating from this issue are concerned with the relative contributions of nature and nurture and how they interact to produce a given outcome.

A second issue is whether aging is **mechanistic–organismic**. The mechanistic view proposes a rather passive role for the individual as genetic and environmental forces shape development. The organismic view proposes that each of us play a very active role in our own development. What happens to us is largely up to us. Think of an older man who is socially isolated and experiencing loneliness. Has this happened because his genetic endowment did not make him very sociable and the friends he once had have all passed away? Or is it the case that he himself has discouraged others from coming too close and has not sought to make new friends? As with the prior issue, we expect that it is a little bit of both. We cannot control all of the things that happen to us but we can make choices and play an active part in our own development.

Continuity–discontinuity is the third issue and asks whether the changes we experience with age (the gains and losses) are smooth and gradual or sudden and abrupt.

Older twins.

Do we change in a nearly steady quantitative way gaining and losing a little with each step forward or do we remain stable for a time and then show a large qualitative shift up or down? Think of how the speed of responding might change with age. Do we grow a little slower with each passing year, perhaps as a result of a continual loss of neurons and muscle fibers? Or does the slowing occur in big and discontinuous steps because we do not feel the loss of nerves and fibers until they reach some critical level? We expect some of the changes that accompany aging to be continuous while others will be discontinuous.

The last issue is **stability and change**. We want to know what aspects of aging remain the same over time and what aspects change as we grow older. We will see that there are many aspects that do not seem to change or to change very much with age while other things show considerable change. For those that change, we will want to know when during development that the change occurs. For a long time, development was viewed as a series of big and small changes. If you didn't see change, it was because you weren't looking hard enough. Now we have clearly defined aspects of development that do not change, at least for a long period of time. Accepting that development is characterized by both stability and change at all ages is a relatively new way of looking at development in old age.

It is important to remember that not many researchers take a side on these issues. Most work is being done in the middle ground area. These issues guide research in various ways. It could be the way a topic is investigated, what is investigated, or even how results are interpreted. Studying aging is a gigantic job and we are thankful that much has already been achieved. A large part of that achievement is embodied in current theories about human aging.

Theory

Theories are built from the accumulation of knowledge. We investigate some phenomenon like whether longevity is affected by diet and exercise or why older adults are more likely than younger adults to show wisdom. Research reveals a number of facts about the phenomenon. Not all older adults seem to develop wisdom. Furthermore, some young adults are wise. We propose explanations for our findings in the form of theories. It is not age per se that leads to the development of wisdom; it is having enough of the right kinds of experiences that is most important (see Chapter 8).

Besides offering possible explanations for research findings, theories also function to guide research. They often make clear what the next step in a line of investigation should be. Researchers conduct research to test the explanations offered by theory. Theory helps organize a wealth of accumulated findings and may suggest connections where none were previously apparent.

In this text, we will examine a number of theories that attempt to explain why older adults often experience physical and mental decline: why older adults slow down, why some older adults live longer than others, why some aspects of personality and ability to cope with stress change and some do not, why the social relationships of older adults sometimes differ from those of young adults, why dementia occurs in some but not in others, why older adults are more likely to develop wisdom, and so on. Theories will not, however, be the main focus. We are researchers and are interested in the facts. We will present theory but be assured that we are not married to any of them. We, like you, will try to keep an open mind as we examine human aging.

Research Methods

We have guiding principles, important issues, and theory to guide the investigations of aging and older adults. We use research methods to gather data to learn whether hypotheses can be supported. We first divide these methods into those that are designed to answer questions about the relationships between variables and those that are designed to tell whether age groups differ with respect to some variable. Although this division is somewhat artificial, it should help organize your thinking about the methods used most frequently. We then will examine a few less-powerful methods that are nonetheless capable of revealing important clues as to where relationships and/or differences might lie.

Relationship Methods

There are many variables that a researcher might believe to be related to a person's age. Is age related to the number of friends that a person has, to their likelihood of being involved in a traffic accident, to their overall world knowledge, to their overall productivity at work, or to their flexibility when confronted with a new situation? Relationship questions usually are addressed by conducting correlation research. A **correlation** is a statistic that tells whether variables are related and, if they are, the direction of that relationship.

Using this method, a researcher would measure the variable of interest on a large group of people and then compute a correlation, symbolized by the letter r. Let's suppose we're interested in whether a person's age is related to their overall interest in politics. We might ask people outside a shopping mall (with, of course, permission of the mall) to tell us their age, their level of education, and to rate their overall interest in politics on some rating scale (e.g., from 1 = very uninterested to 5 = very interested). We gather data from a large group of adults ranging in age from 18 to 84 and obtain the correlation, $r = .37$. The statistical program tells us that this is significant (it's probably not just due to chance). This is a positive correlation and that means that people with high values on one variable (age) tend to have high values on the other variable (interest in politics). If the correlation were negative, that would mean that younger adults showed more interest in politics than older adults. In fact, adult age and interest in politics are positively correlated. It seems to be consistent with other findings such as more older, than younger, adults vote on election days.

Does being old cause one to become more interested in politics? Does an increased interest in politics cause one to become older? With a correlation, we cannot draw any conclusions about cause and effect. The two variables are related but we do not know how or why. Think for a moment about a strong correlation ($r = .86$) between the number of older adults living in a community and the number of violent crimes in that community. Clearly these variables are strongly related but is one the cause of the other? If we could get those older adults to move out of town, would the crime rate go down? No. The size of the community's population is the important variable. Bigger communities have a greater number of older adults and also more violent crime while smaller communities have fewer of each. Correlations do not reveal causes of relationships; they only reveal the strength and direction of relationships.

Difference Methods

Difference methods are designed to tell whether age groups differ on some important variable: Are older adults unable to remember as much as younger adults, are they more or less likely to help in an emergency, are they more spiritually oriented, more generous, less sociable, and so on. These methods generally are referred to as **quasi-experimental** methods. They are not true experiments in which the researcher can decide who receives different levels of some variable like different amounts of time to study some information for a memory test or different numbers of people to wait with in a scary room. In a quasi-experiment, the variable of interest, age, cannot be assigned to people; they already have an age of their own. For instance, compare different aged people on their ability to remember, willingness to help, or their spirituality, generosity, or sociability.

If we find that older adults are different than younger adults on some measure, can we say that age is the cause of this difference? Again the answer is no. The cause must lie in some process, some physical or mental change, and some factor that accompanies aging. The investigation has just begun. There are three general ways that such investigations are carried out and all have both advantages and disadvantages. We must first, however, step back and look at the variables that are always present in any investigation of age differences and can act to disguise or confound the research findings.

These three variables, all of them having to do with time, are age, cohort, and time of measurement. **Age** of the participants is usually the variable of primary interest. Researchers in gerontology want to know if age differences are real. When we ask if 70-, 60-, and 50-year-olds have different attitudes toward retirement, we want to know if age is an important factor worth further exploration. Do 70-year-olds differ from 60-year-olds and do 60-year-olds differ from 50-year-olds? We want to know if older adults, regardless of when they were born and when they were tested, have different attitudes than younger adults.

However, people in different age groups were, of course, born in different times; they are of different generations. This is the second variable, a participant's **cohort**. A cohort is a group of people who have been born at or around the same time (those born in 1950 or those born in the 1950s) and/or those who lived through the same historical period (the Vietnam generation). Maybe people in an older cohort, with different life experiences, have very different views about retirement than people born more recently. Furthermore, they might have these different views regardless of how old or young they are. These differences would be due to their experiences, not their age.

The third variable is **time of measurement**. Perhaps if we measured attitudes toward retirement at a time when the unemployment rate was very low, we might get more positive attitudes than we would during times when unemployment is very high and these attitudes might exist for people of different ages and/or different cohorts. Furthermore, if we measured people at two different times and, thus, two different ages, any obtained differences could be due to time or age or both.

These three variables—age, cohort, and time of measurement—are the ones of concern as we attempt to conduct research to investigate age differences. Figure 2-1 shows the relationship among these variables; we will refer to this figure as we examine the first two methods of conducting this type of research. On the left are three cohorts, representing people born in 1940, 1950, and 1960. At the bottom are three times of measurement, 2000, 2010, and 2020. The numbers in the boxes are the ages of individuals. For example, if we tested people born in 1950 during the 2000 measurement year, they would have been 50 years old when measured (they are in the middle box in the left column). If we test people born in 1960 during our 2010 measurement year, they will be 50 years old (see middle box on bottom row).

If we test our three age groups—70-, 60-, and 50-year-olds—at the same time of measurement (the year 2010), we have conducted cross-sectional research. **Cross-sectional research** is when the different age groups tested are composed of different people. The cross-sectional research is represented by the middle column in the figure. Cross-sectional research is the most frequently used method for determining differences between age groups. The data collection is relatively quick (all in 2010) and costs usually are minimal. There is, however, a problem and that is that the different age groups come

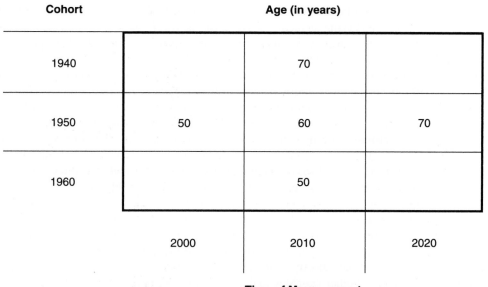

FIGURE 2-1   **The Relationship Among Age, Cohort, and Time of Measurement.**

from different cohorts (1940, 1950, and 1960). Maybe the differences obtained have to do with when these people were born and what they lived through rather than how old they are. Of course, it could be the case that both age groups and cohort groups differ in their attitudes toward retirement. One cross-sectional study does not allow us to determine which factor is the important one (perhaps they both are).

If we choose instead to test the same people, at different ages, over time, we are using a **longitudinal** method. We'll test them when they're 50 years old and come back and test them when they're 60 and come back and test them again when they're 70. This is represented by the middle row in the figure. Longitudinal research can permit us to reach conclusions about individual change with age; we measure the same people and see if their attitudes change as they grow older. There are, of course, some problems. You will have noticed right away from the figure that all of the people tested this way are from the same 1950 cohort. If we find differences, we must be cautious when generalizing to other co-horts. Longitudinal research also is far more costly and clearly takes more time (in this case from 2000 to 2020) to conduct than a cross-sectional study. Finally, we always have attrition and time of measurement problems with longitudinal research and these can be very damaging.

Attrition refers to the loss of participants over time. Suppose we start with 300 people aged 50 and test them all in the year 2000. In 2010, we come back and try to retest the same

300 people who are now 60. Some will have died, some will have left no forwarding address or any way to contact them, and some will no longer be willing to have their attitude toward retirement measured. We end up testing only 240 of the original 300. Another 10 years go by and in 2020 we end up testing only 170 of the original 300. Attrition always occurs but the crucial question is whether this attrition has been selective. **Selective attrition** occurs when those who no longer participate are different in one or more important ways from those who continue to participate. For example, suppose we notice that the people who remain in our sample (the 170) are all of higher SES (socioeconomic status) than those who dropped out (the 130). If SES is related to attitudes toward retirement, then we have a biased sample and any age differences obtained may only be true for those with higher SES. Work examining health and mortality as a function of aging can be particularly difficult since those who do not make it to the final point of measurement have probably declined more rapidly and may even have died. This is clearly selective attrition and the rate of decline for the survivors is not then a good model of general decline with age (Feng et al., 2006).

Although it may be relatively easy to monitor the mortality of participants, how would a researcher know the SES levels of these groups? Researchers are well aware of the dangers of selective attrition and typically measure a very large number of demographic and other variables so that they can determine whether their final sample might be biased in some way(s).

The third method for conducting research into group differences is referred to as sequential design and grew out of the work of K. Warner Schaie (1965; 1977; 1990). **Sequential designs** combine aspects of cross-sectional and longitudinal research. Of the three types of sequential designs, only the cohort sequential will be discussed here since it is the one used most frequently. A **cohort sequential design** separates the effects that are true age differences from those that are cohort differences. This design is illustrated in Figure 2-2. In our cohort sequential example, we began in 1990 and tested a group of 50-year-olds (all born in 1940). In the year 2000, we retested as many of these people as we could; they were 60 then, and we added another group of 50-year-olds (all born in 1950). In 2010, we again tested the original 50-year-olds (who are now 70), the 50-year-olds tested in 2000 (who are now 60), and we added another group of 50-year-olds. In 2020, you can probably figure out who is tested and who will be added.

At this point, we can examine age differences and control cohort. We'll compare the attitudes toward retirement of people aged 50, 60, and 70 and if we use the right groups (boxes), we can control for any potential cohort differences. The responses given by those age 50 come from three different cohorts (1940, 1950, and 1960) but the 60- and 70-year-olds come only (so far) from the 1940 and 1950 cohorts. We then will compare 50-, 60-, and 70-year-olds from the two common cohorts, 1940 and 1950, and be pretty confident that any differences obtained are age differences because the three age groups are all from the same two cohorts. In terms of the figure, the comparison would be between all the responses made when people from the 1940 and 1950 cohorts were in their 50s to responses from when they were in their 60s to responses made when they were in their 70s.

We also can make cohort comparisons and keep the ages the same. We will compare the attitudes of those born in 1940 to those born in 1950 and the age of these two cohorts are the same; that is, each cohort has responses from 50-, 60-, and 70-year-olds. From the figure, we would be comparing the top and middle rows on overall attitude.

Cohort   **Age (in years)**

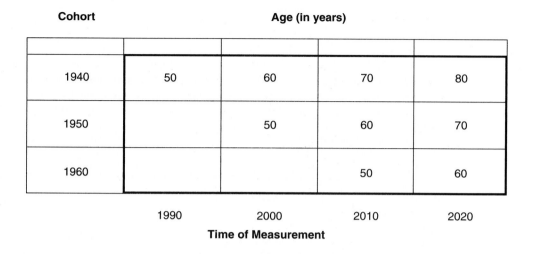

Cohort	Age (in years)			
1940	50	60	70	80
1950		50	60	70
1960			50	60
	1990	2000	2010	2020

Time of Measurement

FIGURE 2-2   **An Example of a Sequential Design.**

Cohort sequential designs have the enormous advantage of allowing researchers to separate genuine age and cohort differences. You may have noticed, however, that, in this example, the 50-year-olds were tested in 1990 and 2000 while the 60-year-olds (yes, they're the same people) were tested in 2000 and 2010. The 70-year-olds were tested in 2010 and 2020. Time of measurement is not the same for all age or cohort comparison groups. This is clearly a disadvantage when time of measurement differences are likely. Although this is not often the case, a good researcher always will attend to possible time effects. The other disadvantage is that, like longitudinal methods, sequential designs take a great deal of time and a great deal of money. Sequential designs are very large and expensive studies to conduct and, as a result, there are not many of them underway and those that are, go on for long periods of time.

Descriptive Methods

Not all gerontology research involves correlation or quasi-experimental methods. Here we will examine observational research, case studies, and focus groups.

Observational research involves observing, and often recording, people's behavior in a natural setting; for intance, are there age or gender differences in where people go to first when they enter a mall? The researcher might station herself near a door close to the food court and see if younger adults go more often for the food while older adults go more often to a store. Simple observations like these do not allow us to conclude very much about the differences obtained. If we found that younger adults went first to the food court while older adults went to a store, we then might attempt to learn why by conducting further research using a more sophisticated technique such as a survey asking people where they first go and why.

PROJECT **2**

As you can imagine, it can be quite difficult convincing people to participate in ongoing research. While a fair number of people are willing to give some of their time to participate when they need only do it once, longitudinal and sequential research designs expect continued participation over years, and sometimes decades. How likely is it that you would volunteer to participate in such long research enterprises?

To gauge how difficult it can be to recruit participants we want you to ask three young adults, three middle-aged adults, and three older adults to use the following rating scale to express their agreement or disagreement with the numbered statements that follow.

Strongly Disagree	Disagree	Neither Disagree nor Agree	Agree	Strongly Agree
1	2	3	4	5

1. I would be willing to give an hour of my time to participate in research.
2. I would be willing to give an hour of my time each month for a year to participate in research.
3. I would be willing to give an hour of my time each year over the next five years to participate in research.
4. I do not want to participate in research.

Did you find that people more often agreed with the first statement than with the second and third ones? Did they agree more often with the second (where 12 hours of participation are needed but only over one year's time) or with the third (where only 5 hours are needed but over a 5-year span)? Did you obtain any age difference on the last statement?

Researchers frequently have to provide incentives to convince people to give their time to research. What types of incentives do you think are most powerful? Do you think this would vary by age of participant? How and why?

One special kind of observation involves the presence of a **participant observer**. This is when the researcher takes part in the situation being observed. For example, one way to gather data on how well older adults enjoy participating in annual senior games would be to participate in the games and observe the other participants. Participants may reveal their true feelings to another participant more often than they would to some objective observer. Personal experiences with the other players would be a major part of the data. This technique can give valuable information that can be explored with other methods.

Case studies refer to the extended collection of information on some individual or, less often, some group of individuals. When doing a case study, researchers often tend to accept any and all information obtained, striving to have a complete picture of the case. That, in fact, is the main advantage of case studies; they provide so much information. On the down side, however, the information is, of course, limited to what is observed. The researcher cannot know why some behaviors occurred while others did not; they cannot be sure what factors are related to other factors. However, case studies make for interesting reading and often suggest the next step in a line of research.

SOCIAL POLICY APPLICATIONS

If we are to gain an understanding of the factors that underlie changes due to age or cohort, then we must conduct research. Research is, however, expensive. As you know, sequential and longitudinal studies especially are expensive and even cross-sectional studies are not free. Costs include paying participants for their time and effort and buying the equipment and/or materials needed to gather data. The salaries of researchers and assistants are another major cost. The costs also vary as a function of what it is that's being examined. It's less expensive to do a study on age differences in memory than it is to do a study on age differences in the effectiveness of some new medical treatment.

These costs can be paid for by federal and private grants. Much research in gerontology is funded by the National Institute on Aging, the National Science Foundation, and other federal granting programs but with a limited budget, not all research can be funded. We must consider social policy to increase the funding of research.

Focus groups are yet another way of collecting data. A focus group is a collection of a small number of people (usually 6–10) brought together to discuss and give their opinions on some topic. The group is run by a facilitator who tries to make sure that everyone gets a chance to talk and that the group stays on topic. These groups can be fairly costly and are used most frequently when a company is considering a new product or the legislature is considering a new program like the Medicaid prescription benefits program.

Data Sources

In our discussion of methods, we have acted as if the actual collection of data was obvious. When we want to assess age differences in attitudes toward retirement, we simply. . . .

Staying Informed.

If we want to know whether old adults remember stories better than young we just . . . just what? The answer is that we need a measure of the variable that we think is related to age or that we think age groups will differ on. For every variable, there are multiple ways of measuring it. For the memory-for-stories example, it seems pretty clear to present some stories and then test memory by having old and young people attempt to retell the stories. Variables like memory, speed of responding, and perception can be measured in a rather straightforward way. Other variables are more abstract and require some effort to measure. For attitudes toward retirement, we could simply ask people "what is your attitude toward retirement?" and record the answers received. For some of those types of answers it may be hard to interpret the data. Box 2-1 illustrates these difficulties. It is possible to devise a rating scale and have people select a number that describes how positive or negative their attitude is toward a subject (1 = very negative, 2 = negative, 3 = neither negative nor pos-

BOX **2-1**

What Do You Mean?

When we ask open-ended questions, we might have considerable difficulty in deciding exactly what the answers mean. Let's suppose we are interested in age differences in attitudes toward retirement and we ask people, "How do you feel about retirement?" Here are the responses given by the first four people we talk with.

Person 1. I feel fine about it; you gotta have some money though; otherwise you gotta work; unless you got a rich spouse; course then you're probably already retired; heh heh heh.

Person 2. I'm not ready yet; it could be OK if you can do it.

Person 3. Retirement could be very good; you don't have to get up and go to work but you have to have your health; I guess if you didn't have your health, you'd have to retire so maybe it works both ways.

Person 4. Sounds OK.

Would we want to say that these four people all have the same attitude? Probably not since numbers 1 and 3 seem more positive than 2 and 4. Are 2 and 4 the same? Is "OK" the same as "could be OK"? For persons 1 and 3 are the answers "I feel fine about it" and "could be very good" the same? What if someone else says "pretty good"; is that the same as "feel fine" or "could be very good"? What about "certainly good," "not bad at all," and "it rocks"? Is "very good" the same as or not as good as "excellent"? It can become very difficult to know where the lines are between different answers.

Person 1 talked about finances as being important while Person 3 talked about health but did not make a very clear statement. Instead it sounds like you should retire when you have good health but have to when you have bad health.

Problems in interpreting what people give as answers to open-ended questions involves a careful analysis of content and at least two independent readers/raters so that the reliability (see text) of the ratings can be assessed.

itive, 4 = positive, and 5 = very positive). We could ask people to rank the good things and the bad things in life and have retirement on the list of things to be ranked. There are a number of ways of doing this. Two important criteria that allow us to choose the best measure available follow.

Measures need to be **reliable** or consistent. If we ask people to rate retirement one day and ask them to do it again a month later, we expect to get essentially the same ratings from the same people. They may not be identical because the measure is not perfect but if they are not reliable or if there is very little agreement between what people said the first and second times, then the measure is not worth using. If you measure your weight 3 days 1 week and get numbers like 98 lbs, 178 lbs, and 230 lbs, you will conclude that the scale you're using is unreliable and you then may purchase a better one. If, on the other hand, the three measures are 157 lbs, 158 lbs, and 156 lbs, you will probably conclude that the scale is reliable but your weight fluctuates a little. We want measures that are as reliable as can be.

Our measures also must be **valid**; that is, they must really be measuring the thing they claim to measure. If your reliable scale gave you readings of 10, 10.5, and 10.75, it would clearly be doing something reliably but it's probably not measuring your weight unless you are a baby. A measure without reliability cannot be valid but reliability does not guarantee validity.

In short, some measures are fairly straightforward because the variable we are dealing with is concrete while other measures are less direct because the variable being measured is more abstract. In all cases, we want the measures to be reliable and valid. Let's end this discussion by briefly examining two fairly common sources of data: archives and surveys.

Archival research refers to the use of public records. These are data that have been collected by others. Much archival research is conducted on data collected by the U.S. Census Bureau although there are many other sources as well. For instance, if we are interested in the relationship between age of driver and motor vehicle accidents, these archives contain the relevant information. Sometimes, however, archives are in a different form than the researcher would like them to be and so some transformation of the data may be needed. If, for example, one county counts motor vehicle accidents as being any reported incident while another counts only those in which some property damage has occurred, then the researcher may have to dig through the former record excluding all without property damage to achieve the same data base. Archival data usually are used in relationship rather than quasi-experimental research.

Surveys also are frequently used for relationship research. Researchers may ask younger and older adults to fill out a survey on their attitudes toward retirement and learn that age and attitude are strongly correlated. Of course we could take these survey data and look for age differences as in a quasi-experiment. Either is possible depending on the researcher's main interests. Surveys generally ask for other information in addition to the variable(s) of main interest. In the survey on age and attitudes toward retirement, we probably would want to know the gender of each respondent, their education level, the type of job they have or are working, their salary, their health, and their financial status. What other information do you think we should ask for? Both open-ended questions and rating scales frequently are used in surveys.

Ethics

Whenever we collect data from others to help us explore aging and to examine differences between age groups, we must do so ethically. In fact, all research conducted with human or animal participants must follow ethical guidelines such as those designated by the American Psychological Association (2003). All of these guidelines are important but the ones of greatest concern are informed consent, protection from harm, confidentiality of information, and debriefing.

Informed consent means that the person participating in the research has been given all information that could influence their willingness to participate, that they understand this information, that they are competent to make the decision to participate, and that they participate voluntarily. This means that potential participants must be provided with understandable and relevant information before beginning testing. Participants are frequently asked to sign an informed consent form before participating.

Not all participants are old enough or competent enough to sign for themselves. If we compare adults to children and adolescents under the age of 18, then we must gain informed consent from the parents or guardians of these children and adolescents. If we are studying older adults who have been diagnosed with dementia, we need to gain the informed consent of a spouse, caregiver, or someone with the power to make such decisions for that person. People with dementia eventually become incapable of making such informed decisions about participating in research.

Research also must **protect participants from harm** while they participate in a study. We do not want to frighten participants or put them in a stressful situation or cause any physical damage. If there is to be some stress involved, then participants must know before they agree to participate.

Sometimes medical research may cause some physical damage. If we have found laser surgery to restore vision then, as with any surgery, there is the potential for physical damage. Again, people undergoing this surgery must know ahead of time what the risks are; they must be fully informed. Testing new medicines which are designed to treat some disorder always carries the risk of unwanted and unexpected side effects. A lot of work in certain areas of gerontology carries with it the risk of some harm. *A good guiding principle is that participants should leave the research better off or at least the same as when they started.*

All information gathered in a research study must remain **confidential**. Participants' responses must not be able to be connected to individual participants. No one should know which 70-year-old rated retirement as "very positive." You might wonder how this works in a longitudinal or sequential design study. In those cases, researchers must be able to go back to the original participants and gather additional information from them. To know if individuals change as they grow older, researchers must be able to follow the responses made by individuals. There are a couple of answers to this question. Researchers must know who the individual participants are if they are to contact them for more information. The responses can, however, be coded so that all examinations of data tell only that the responses of Person MO87 have not changed since the last time he or she was tested. When researchers know the identity of individual respondents, they are ethically obligated to keep that information confidential.

Finally, it is always important to **debrief** the people who have participated in the research. We must be willing to take the time to tell them what we are investigating, what we expect to find, why it's important, and how they have helped. We should thank them and be sure that they are no worse off. We always should offer to share the results with them once the results are known. You will find that a lot of people are very interested and will ask intelligent questions during a debriefing while some others have far less interest. Whether they are interested or not, we must debrief as best we can.

How are these guidelines checked? How do we know that researchers are following ethical practices? The answer is that institutions that conduct research and receive federal funding must have an **institutional review board (IRB)** composed of members of the institution and at least one outside member who review all proposed research to be certain that these guidelines are followed. One is not permitted to begin data collection until the work has been approved by an IRB. Ultimately, however, ethics are the responsibility of each researcher.

CHAPTER HIGHLIGHTS

- Research on aging and older adults is guided by several well-adopted principles that are:
  Development is a lifelong process.
  Development is multidisciplinary.
  Development is composed of both gains and losses.
  Development shows plasticity.
  Development is embedded in history.
  Development occurs within a context.
- Research on aging and older adults is guided by several important issues and attempts to answer important questions about human aging. These issues are nature-nurture, mechanistic-organismic, continuity-discontinuity, and stability-change.
- Research also is guided by theories that pull together collections of facts and attempt to explain them.
- Theories suggest hypotheses and the steps to take next in a line of investigation.
- Research methods are ways of collecting data to test hypotheses and are of two general types: relationship and difference methods.
- Correlations are the major relationship method and are used to test whether variables are related to one another. They do not tell about cause and effect.
- Quasi-experiments are the major difference methods and are used to test whether age groups differ from one another.
- The variables of age, cohort, and time of measurement all are involved when conducting research in gerontology.
- Cross-sectional research involves testing age groups composed of different people. Obtained differences could be due to age or cohort or both.
- Longitudinal research involves testing the same people over time. Researchers can examine individual changes but it takes a long time, the cost is high, and selective attrition is a possibility.
- Cohort sequential research designs separate true age differences from cohort differences but are also time consuming and expensive.
- Observation, case studies, and focus groups are descriptive methods used to gather information about aging.
- All measures must be reliable and valid.
- Data, in addition to direct measurement, frequently comes from archives or surveys.

■ All researchers must follow ethical guidelines including informed consent, protection from harm, confidentiality, and debriefing.

STUDY QUESTIONS

1. Define/describe the guiding principles used in research on aging.

2. Define/describe the major issues for gerontology researchers. Think of examples of each issue and how it might be approached in research.

3. What are the advantages and disadvantages of cross-sectional and longitudinal research methods in revealing age differences?

4. Explain the advantages and disadvantages of cohort sequential design. Give an example of a question that might be addressed with this design and why this might be better than using a cross-sectional or longitudinal design.

5. Describe observation, case study, and focus group methods.

6. What is meant by reliability and why is it important? What is meant by validity and why is it important? How are these criteria related to one another?

7. How are archives and surveys used in gerontological research? What are the advantages and disadvantages of these methods?

8. Describe the main ethical guidelines used by researchers. What are special ethical considerations for gerontological researchers?

9. How is ethics ensured for research participants?

RECOMMENDED READING

Schaie, K. W. (1990). Developmental designs revisited. In H. W. Reese & S. H. Cohen (Eds.), *Life-Span Developmental Psychology: Methodological Issues*. Hillsdale, NJ: Erlbaum. This chapter presents an overview of sequential and other designs.

INTERNET RESOURCES

www.webster.edu/woolflm/methods/devresearchmethods.html. Contains a good general discussion of many of the research methods discussed in this chapter.

http://sageke.sciencemag.org; www.seniornet.org; www.apa.org/pi/aging. For a view of some current research.

Aging and Our Bodies

PART ONE

Aging and Our Bodies

CHAPTER

3 Physical Aspects of Aging: Changes in Our Bodies

Life is like riding a bicycle. You don't fall off unless you stop pedaling.
—*Senator Claude Pepper*

As we grow older, our bodies change—but how we see those changes undergoes a transformation during adulthood. As children, we are proud to be older and can't wait to be older yet. Tell an 8-year-old that you think they're 12 and they're delighted. Tell a 40-year-old that you think she's 60 and you will not get delight. We say that some people "look young for their age" and act like this is a compliment but when we say he's "old before his time," we convey a sadness. The passage of time is neither good nor bad; it is what we do with our time that is important. We have to keep pedaling and as we move forward, as we age, marks will be left on our bodies. Those marks, those bodily changes, are what we examine in this chapter.

Individual Differences

Some people who are past the age of 65 look as if they're still in their 40s or 50s while many others look much older. Part of this difference is due to our inability to judge a person's age by how they look. We are simply not very good at making such judgments. Take a look at the photographs shown on page 44 and see if you can judge the age of each person. Who do you think is the oldest? Who is the youngest? To find out how accurate you were, look for the answers at the end of this chapter.

One reason why it can be difficult to judge another's age is because the storms that people weather over the course of their lives can be quite different. An individual who has had a relatively easy, stress-free life with very little hard physical labor, the best doctors, excellent nutrition, and good exercise is bound to look different than an individual who has had trying times, worked hard in the fields most of their lives, experienced lots of stress and danger, has poor health, and poor nutrition. It is not the passing of time per se that causes these changes, it is the events and experiences that occur over time and how they are dealt with, that are responsible. Furthermore, the influence of some of these environmental factors can depend on when they occur and whether they occur with other factors or by themselves. If you work on a farm, your muscles and bones may grow stronger than those of a person who works in an office. If you work in an office, you are protected from the harsh elements of weather. If you are born with cerebral palsy, your hips may deteriorate faster due to an uneven gait wearing down the joints. If you live in the desert, you may be ravaged by the sun and sand. If you live in a monsoon area you may fall prey to bacterial infections.

People look different in part because of the things that they have been through, when those things occurred, and their constitutional ability to deal with their experiences. The results of life's storms depend to some extent on the psychology of the individual who experiences them and the social support that assists them.

Another reason why it is difficult to judge age is because the very same individual can show a lot of change in some ways and hardly any in other ways. One's heart and lungs may be as strong as those of a much younger person while one's digestive system has declined to a very low level and can handle only very bland foods. One's muscles may be weak and one's bones fragile while one's mind is sharp and quick. Different organs, tissues, systems, and bodily functions seem to age at very different rates. Many researchers

Senior View

We spoke with Clifford and Lucia Pauling about some of the physical changes that have occurred in their own bodies over the years. Clifford was 75 and a retired custodian and Lucia was 69 and retired from a nursing center when we spoke with them. When Clifford retired, he was awarded a plaque from the school board for outstanding service. They have been married for 35 years and have seven children.

My kidneys gave out when I was only in my 40s, Lucia told us. *It was tough at first, I've been on dialysis for more than 20 years; wish I could get a new kidney.*

She didn't even tell me when it happened; I got told by her mother. Lucia is the type of person

who won't ever complain. They taught me how to do her dialysis right here at home, said Clifford.

I can still travel but sometimes have to set up a dialysis appointment somewhere where we're going, said Lucia. *I like to travel and I wouldn't want to give that up.*

Lucia told us about other physical changes as well. *I've got high blood pressure and had a thyroid removed; the only other time I was in the hospital was to have my children . . . since then I've gained a little weight,* she said smiling. *Things change slow, even physical things.*

Clifford told us, *I had no physical problems till I turned 70 and then they told me that I had a touch of colon cancer but it wasn't bad. I have to go now for regular checkups.*

We also spoke briefly with Lori Finch about physical changes. She is a retired nurse who is widowed and was 76 when we talked.

My health is just fine except for three little problems. I've got asthma, kidney disease, and osteoporosis. Kidney problems, as you will learn, occur more frequently for older adults and seem to be related to bone loss.

I've also lost 4 inches and that's the important one; it's a lot harder to reach stuff that's high up. For my kidneys, I have to be careful not to overexert myself, watch my diet, and not lift heavy objects. I frequently forget how old I am and get a little carried away in my activities. I've not noticed any new changes over the last 5 years.

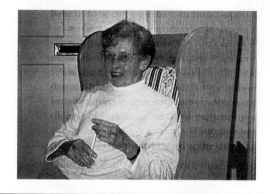

When we asked Lori if she would like to tell younger adults anything about the changes that occur with age, she told us, *physical changes make you determined to maintain your independence; physical changes are a threat to your independence and once you lose your independence, you feel old. I'm just going to keep going until I can't go anymore and I don't want someone overtreating me or overmedicating me.*

We like the spirit of Clifford, Lucia, and Lori. Physical changes depend a great deal on mental attitude and we will spend some time talking about the influence of positive attitude later in this chapter. The mental attitude of these three seniors is one major factor in their success at dealing with the physical changes they have experienced.

refer to these differences by using the term **biological age(ing)**. Biological aging refers to the physical, chemical, and biological changes that occur in vital organ systems, tissues, and physical appearance over time. Systems that are biologically old have changed quite a lot as the person has gotten older. Systems that are young are those that have changed very little. Biological aging may increase the vulnerability of those bodily systems making them more prone to accidents, disease, and longer recovery times. The decline in bodily systems and the resulting increased vulnerability is referred to as **senescence**.

It is very important to keep in mind that different physical components of our bodies change at different rates. Although one's chronological age is the same for all bodily organs because they were all formed at the same time, one's biological age may be different for different physical components. Some components show more change than others and are, as a result, biologically older. These biologically older components are likely to show more senescence, or vulnerability, than components that are biologically younger. An individual also is unlikely to show the same vulnerability for all biological components. On the other hand, an individual is quite likely to show varying amounts of senescence for different biological components. All components have grown older and are, thus, subject to biological aging and the influence of numerous external factors (Miller, 1999). It is important to remember as you read about these changes that individual differences are paramount. Some people experience far less change than others.

Changes in Physical Appearance

Skin

As one ages, wrinkles appear in the skin. In fact, wrinkles appear fairly early in life and by age 30, most adults show lines in the forehead. Between 30 to 50 years of age, additional lines on the face appear. For example, "crow's feet" may appear around the eyes and

Who is oldest? Who is youngest?

the lines linking the nostrils to the side of the mouth may become more prominent. One may develop a furrowed brow as wrinkles on the forehead become more pronounced. Beyond age 50, wrinkling continues and becomes more extensive with each passing decade.

Mark Twain said, "Wrinkles should merely indicate where smiles have been." This is a nice thought but in fact, wrinkling occurs because of stiffening and a decrease in the underlying connective tissue whether you smile or frown. The connective tissues, composed of a protein called collagen, underlie the skin, surround all bodily organs, and cover the walls of blood vessels. Connective tissue and elastin fibers, which maintain normal tension in the skin, become less flexible, more rigid, and also decrease in amount after age 30. The sweat glands also are likely to show diminished function leading to less moisture in and under the skin. Wrinkles in the skin are less likely to disappear when the skin is less flexible because of the more rigid underlying elastin fibers and less moisture. Thus, wrinkles increase with advanced age (DiGiovanna, 1994).

Skin also shows the effects of a lifetime of exposure to the sun as one grows older. Skin exposed to the sun becomes stiffer and loses elasticity like leather. Skin cancers increase in frequency with age and much of this is due to extended exposure to the sun. Individuals who experience severe sunburns when they are young are far more likely to experience skin cancer as they grow older. Take this seriously and protect your skin. The outside layer of the skin, the epidermis, becomes flattened and new cells are less organized than old cells. One can see this loss of organization in the changes in geometric furrows visible on the skin's surface. Compare your skin with that of your parents and grandparents and see if you can notice the differences in epidermal organization. Subcutaneous fat, which provides the smooth padding and curves of youth, decreases on limbs in old age and collects in deposits at the waist and hips (Whitbourne, 1996).

The production of sweat glands and of skin oil, called sebum, declines after menopause for women, and females are strongly encouraged to use lotions and protective creams at that point in their lives. For males, the production of sebum remains relatively stable although moisturizing lotions are still recommended.

The coloring of light-skinned people alters due to changes in melanocyte, the pigment containing cells in epidermis. The total number of such cells declines and the ones remaining contain fewer pigment granules. Irregular dark spots, called age or liver spots, appear on the skin as do dark moles and angiomas. Angiomas are small blood vessels elevated to the surface of the skin. Capillaries and small arteries often dilate and look like small, irregular colored lines on the skin. In other cases, capillaries may be lost causing individuals to look pale.

The result of all these varied changes in the skin may be a negative effect on protective functions. With advanced age there may be a limit in temperature adaptation with less perspiration in the heat and less conservation of heat in the cold. The recovery from surface wounds may be impaired and cuts and burns may take longer to heal (Whitbourne, 1996). Biological aging of the skin can result in senescence.

Hair

As one grows older, hair turns gray due to the loss of pigment. Most adults experience the beginning of graying in their early 40s. The loss of pigment appears to have a strong genetic component, and men and women whose parents or grandparents turned gray are likely to do the same (DiGiovanna, 1994).

Pattern baldness or hair loss also is very likely. For men, baldness typically begins at the temples and proceeds to a circle in the top and back of the head. Hair loss then proceeds until the entire top of the head is bald. Baldness is largely hereditary (Rexbye et al., 2005) and, like graying, can be predicted with a reasonably high level of accuracy by looking at the father, uncles, and grandfathers of a given individual. Baldness also affects about 75 percent of women but to a much lesser extent. In women, hair tends to thin all over the scalp rather than proceeding from one starting point (Kligman et al., 1985). The drug finasteride can be used to prevent hair loss. Finasteride is not recommended for women of childbearing age because it can cause birth defects.

For men, hair loss on the top of the head is only half the picture. Men are very likely to find hair growing in and around their ears, out of their nostrils, and all over their backs. Also, the eyebrows become courser and longer. Some women, particularly those of Mediterranean or Middle Eastern origin, may grow long, dark, and thick hair over their lips and on their chins. Some also develop hair around the nipples and in the middle of the chest or abdomen (Lorber & Lagana, 1997).

Height and Weight

Height and weight also change with age, although there is some debate about the latter. Of course, there are enormous individual differences in height and weight as you can tell simply by looking around. Nevertheless, older adults typically lose height and weight, occurring at a greater rate after the 50s, and this is truer for women than for men.

On average, men lose about 1.25 inches in height between the ages of 30 and 70 while females lose about 2 inches. The greater loss for women is, in part, due to greater incidence of bone loss. Functional height, which measures how high one can reach, also decreases with advanced age. You can estimate your own functional height by standing and reaching high on the wall with a marker. Make a mark at your reach level and then measure the difference between that level and your height. That difference is your functional height. The lower the number, the lower your functional height. For older adults, functional height can be as low as 7 inches due to changes in muscles and bones.

The typical pattern of weight change is one of gain followed by loss. From young adulthood to middle age, weight typically increases due to changes in metabolic rate and lifestyle. Basal metabolism slows down 3 percent every 10 years. At the same time, middle-age adults may continue to eat the same amount of food that they did when they were younger. With the slow down in metabolism, less food is converted to energy and is, instead, accumulated resulting in weight gain. Also, many middle-age adults are not as physically active as when they were younger. Together these factors typically result in weight gain for middle-age adults. For most individuals, weight levels off and then declines from middle-adulthood to old age. Senescence in tissues and muscles results in weight loss as heavier muscle tissue is replaced by less heavy fat (DeGiovanna, 1994). Older adults also typically eat less than middle-aged adults in part because of declines in the ability to smell and taste as discussed in Chapter 6.

Although this weight gain/loss pattern is thought to be typical, most evidence comes from cross-sectional comparisons and any differences could be cohort differences rather than real age differences. High fat and high carbohydrate diets used to be much more the norm than they are now, so older cohorts may have eaten very differently than more recent cohorts. Recent cohorts have developed different, healthier, eating habits. At the same time, there are more overweight Americans now than at any other time. At present it is not clear whether the obtained patterns of weight change are due to age or cohort or both effects (Whitbourne, 1996). Do you think changes in weight are due to cohort or age (or both)? What differences in your cohort would you expect if it were one or the other?

Voice

Voice lowers in pitch with age and can decrease by two or three notes on the musical scale. This lowering is far greater for those who smoke (Verdonck-de Leeuw & Mahieu, 2004). Loss of muscle control over the vocal cords also may produce a quaver in the voice.

Facial Appearance

Changes in facial appearance are the easiest to see. After all, the face is the most exposed area of skin. There are exceptions in certain cultures. Muslim women, for example, cover much of the face. Facial muscles are always being used for eating, talking, and facial expressions. Skin on the face is, thus, more likely to show biological aging than skin on any other body part.

The accumulation of cartilage also shows on the face and head. This accumulation makes the nose grow $\frac{1}{2}$-inch wider and $\frac{1}{2}$-inch longer, on average, by age 70. Earlobes become fatter and the ears grow $\frac{1}{4}$-inch longer.

The head increases in circumference and has been increasing since birth. The circumference of the skull increases by $\frac{1}{4}$ inch every 10 years as the skull thickens. At 20 years old, the skull is about $\frac{1}{2}$ inch bigger in circumference than it was at birth. By 80, it will be about $1\frac{1}{2}$ inches bigger than it is now or 2 inches bigger than it was at birth.

Changes in skin, hair, and cartilage can be easy to hide and many adults attempt to do just that by using make-up, hair color, and even plastic surgery. Are older adults less satisfied with their physical appearance than are younger adults? Survey research has found that physical appearance is regarded as important especially by women. When old and young adults were asked about how satisfied they were with the way they looked, men were fairly satisfied at all ages. For women, however, age made a big difference. The oldest women were the most satisfied with their bodies (Öberg & Tornstam, 1999). Garson Kanin said, "Youth is a gift of nature; age is a work of art." Changes in physical appearance can create some beautiful works of art. Sopia Loren, Paul Newman, Jessica Tandy, Robert Redford, and perhaps your own grandparents are prime examples of older art.

Internal Changes

Muscles

Muscles decline in strength, tone, and flexibility as one grows older. Muscle fiber is often replaced by connective tissue, which tends to become stiff. As a result, injured muscles are slower to heal for older adults.

Overall muscle strength begins to decline between the ages of 40 and 50 and can decline by as much as 10 to 20 percent by age 70. More severe loss occurs as one grows older. Muscle decline is most pronounced in the lower extremities (McArdle et al., 1991). Grip strength and muscle flexibility also decline (Kozma et al., 1991). Figure 3-1 shows the average changes for grip strength across different adult ages. The muscle groups used for grip are referred to as "fast twitch" muscle fibers and are associated with rapidly accelerating, powerful contractions. These fibers atrophy and are first replaced by connective tissue and later by fat. Although nothing at present can be done to stop the loss of muscle fiber, the remaining fibers can be strengthened and made more efficient for individuals at any age through techniques such as resistance training. Recent work suggests that it is not just the loss of muscle mass that reduces strength but the loss of muscle quality with advanced age (Goodpaster et al., 2007). Although it is not yet clear what, if anything, can be done to reduce the loss of quality, this is still a situation where the decline in strength depends to some extent on the physical activities of the individual.

Eccentric strength, involving the muscles used in lowering arm weights, slowing down while walking, or going down a flight of stairs remains stable until age 70 to 80 (Hortobágyi et al., 1995). These muscle groups are referred to as "slow twitch" muscle fibers and are associated with maintaining posture and muscle contractions over long periods of time. These fibers remain relatively constant with age.

Does the loss of muscle strength influence losses in other systems? All systems influence one another and the overall health. Muscle strength is an important component of stamina; muscle strength may also be associated with cognition. One recent study of over

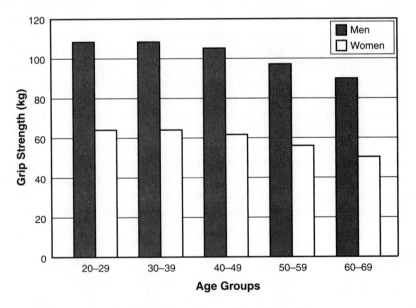

FIGURE 3-1   Average Grip Strength as a Function of Age.

Source: Adapting from Kozma et al. (1991).

2000 Mexican Americans found that over a 7-year period, those with the lowest strength experienced the most cognitive decline (Alfaro-Acha et al., 2006). What factors do you think might account for this relationship?

A study examined the relationship between grip strength, weight, and mortality in a sample of 6000 healthy men over a 30-year period. Men with the lowest grip strength in middle age had the highest probability of dying earlier, independent of how much they weighed, while those with the highest grip strength had the lowest probability of dying. The researchers strongly recommend increasing muscle strength by exercising because such increased strength "may provide greater physiologic and functional reserve that protects against mortality" (Rantanen et al., 2000, p. M168). Do you exercise?

Skeletal System

The skeletal system is composed of the bones and cartilage of the body. As you learned previously, cartilage continues to increase with age and, as a result, the nose and ears grow with each passing year. The circumference of the skull also increases but the rest of the bones in the body tend to show the opposite effect.

Bone represents the deposit of calcium phosphate and calcium carbonate by cells called **osteoblasts** (think of builders, osteoblasts are bone builders). These cells take calcium from the nutrients in the blood and build bone. Thus, strong bones depend on a diet with sufficient calcium. To keep bone growth and replacement in balance, another set of cells, called **osteoclasts**, resorb bone. Resorption refers to the process of dissolving and assimilating bone tissue. When we are young and growing, the action of osteoblasts is greater and bones get bigger. During adulthood, osteoblasts and osteoclasts work in balance to maintain a strong, healthy skeletal system. As we grow older, however, the action of osteoclasts is greater; as a result, the resorption of bone increases and we lose bone. Bone density decreases. This is one reason for the loss of height that we discussed earlier. Old bones become weaker and withstand pressure less well. Since more bone is being resorbed by osteoclasts than is built up by osteoblasts, older adults are frequently advised to increase their intake of calcium to 1200 to 1500 mg from the recommended daily allowance of 800 mg (Hermann, 1998).

The loss of bone has been attributed to three main factors: genetic, hormonal, and lifestyle. Together, genetic and hormonal factors account for close to 40 percent of the variability in bone loss. Individuals whose parents experienced significant bone loss are likely to have the same experience when they grow old. The hormonal changes that occur following menopause result in significant bone loss in many women. The third factor, lifestyle, accounts for the remaining 60 percent. Lifestyle refers to a number of variables such as one's diet, physical activity, the amount of alcohol consumed, and whether one smokes. Consuming large amounts of alcohol and/or smoking blocks the body's ability to use calcium to build bone.

In terms of diet, one must not only consume sufficient calcium but must also get vitamin D to enable osteoblasts to use that calcium. The best source of vitamin D is sunlight. The consumption of meat in greater abundance than vegetable proteins contributes to bone loss and the consumption of more vegetable products may help protect bone density as we grow older (Frasetto et al., 2000). In one large study, researchers in Boston and the Netherlands measured levels of an amino acid called homocysteine in several hundred older adults and then monitored them for 5 to 8 years paying particular attention to bone fractures. Homocysteine is high in individuals who do not eat certain nutrients such as vitamins B_6 and B_{12} and folic acid. Over the years that they were monitored, individuals with high levels of this amino acid had nearly double the risk of fractures (van Meurs et al., 2004). Researchers strongly recommend that older adults take a multivitamin and eat plenty of green leafy vegetables and fortified grains to help maintain bone density.

A lack of physical activity results in loss of bone density. Bones and muscles need to be pushed to remain strong so lifting weights or using elastic bands to stretch helps maintain that strength; people who don't exercise experience a loss of bone density. This also occurs for people who are on bed rest for some illness. This even can occur for astronauts who spend time in weightless outer space. A loss of bone density increases the risk of fractures and, among old adults, hip fractures are an all too common occurrence. Each year, over a quarter of a million people are hospitalized with hip fractures and close to 40 percent of these individuals are over 65. Hip fractures are a major cause of long-term disability and can lead to death within a year of the fracture. Regular resistance training exercise can increase bone density and help protect against fractures. In one study, women spent time jumping while wearing weighted vests. They did this three times a week for 32 weeks a year for 5 years and significantly increased their bone density compared to non-jumping women (Snow et al., 2000). What are you doing right and what are you doing wrong for your bone density?

Some recent work has found that the loss of bone density is related to declining function in other parts of the body. Researchers examined the relationship between kidney dysfunction and loss of bone density in the hips. Kidney dysfunction was assessed by measuring cystatin-C and bone density was measured over a 4-year period for 1500 adults age 65 and older. Kidney dysfunction was strongly related to bone density loss especially for men perhaps because of lower levels of vitamin D and decreased physical activity that often accompany kidney dysfunction (Fried et al., 2006).

In extreme cases, the resorption of bone by osteoclasts is so great that bones become brittle and fragile, resulting in a disorder known as **osteoporosis**. Osteoporosis is particularly prevalent in postmenopausal white and Asian American women. About 90 percent of older adults with osteoporosis are women and most of them are white or Asian (Gambrell, 1987). The difference between men and women is largely due to the relatively rapid lowering of estrogen levels in postmenopausal women (DiGiovanna, 1994). The older treatments for osteoporosis involved injections of calcium in the form of calcinate or hormone replacement therapy (HRT). Injections, however, are not easy to administer and HRT has been associated with increased rates of uterine, ovarian, and breast cancers. Newer treatments work by inhibiting the action of osteoclasts to slow down the resorption of bone and to give osteoblasts a chance to "catch up." Estriol (a form of estrogen) and alendronate (sold under brand names) seem fairly effective. In one study, women using estriol and all over the age of 75 showed a 3.5 percent increase in bone density after only 30 weeks of treatment (Hayashi et al., 2000). In two large studies, researchers found an increase of over 8 percent for women using alendronate over a longer, 3-year period (*Laboratory Medicine*, 1996). One might expect that the relationship of an older couple would suffer when she has osteoporosis and may no longer be able to function as well. The husband will have to do more and may worry about his ailing wife but recent research shows that husbands and wives report no decline in the quality of their marriage as a result of the wife's osteoporosis (Roberto et al., 2004). Long marriages are strong marriages.

Cardiovascular System

The cardiovascular system can be broken down into a number of different components, some of which show senescence and some of which do not. Because heart disease is the number one cause of death in the United States, we will examine the system in detail.

Blood Pressure. Blood pressure signifies the structural health and functioning of the entire cardiovascular system. Blood pressure is signified by two numbers called systolic and diastolic pressure. Thus, a blood pressure of 120 over 80 means that the systolic pressure is 120 and the diastolic is 80. Systolic pressure occurs when the heart contracts pushing blood into the arteries and diastolic pressure is when the ventricle refills with blood from the veins. Elevations in blood pressure are clear warning signals and should be dealt with by a physician.

As one ages, systolic pressure typically shows moderate increases while diastolic pressure tends to remain stable. Many researchers, however, find no change in systolic pressure with age when physiological status and fitness are controlled (Gardner & Poehlman, 1995). Perhaps obtained differences are due to an inclusion of individuals with hypertension and/or cardiovascular disorder in larger numbers in older samples. At present, it is not clear why systolic differences are frequently found but it is possible that these too are cohort differences. Older cohorts may have ingested more fatty foods than more recent cohorts.

The Heart. The heart, like other muscles, shows some deterioration with advanced age and pumps less blood. One reason less blood is being pumped is the change that can occur in veins and arteries. As one grows older, the heart gets bigger, literally. Some think that this is a built-in compensation for the muscle loss that occurs with aging but the increase in size is mostly in the left ventricle due to a thickening of the walls.

Blood Vessels. Blood vessels can show a lot of senescence. Both veins and arteries are prone to calcification and the accumulation of fatty materials and cholesterol. These changes result in slower and less efficient contraction of the heart and reduced and delayed filling. Less blood is sent to the body. Calcification is particularly common at the aortic valve leading from the heart, and the diameter of the aorta increases with advanced age becoming less flexible and less able to push blood into the arteries. Cardiac output decreases linearly throughout adulthood dropping to 30 to 40 percent by age 65.

The clogging of blood vessels with fat and cholesterol, a condition called **atherosclerosis**, means the heart must work harder to pump the same amount of blood. Atherosclerosis is a type of arteriosclerosis, which is the name for a thickening and hardening of arterial walls. In atherosclerosis, this thickening is the result of accumulated fat and cholesterol. Oxygen consumption at rest and during exercise is diminished when the vessels are clogged and this clogging begins as early as age 20. With the recent increases in numbers of obese children, atherosclerosis is beginning to appear much earlier in life.

Blood.   Blood is composed of plasma, red and white blood cells, and platelets. Plasma is the fluid that carries cells and platelets. Red blood cells or hemoglobin carry oxygen from the lungs to all the tissues in the body. The amount of hemoglobin does not decline with age for nonsmokers. White blood cells, which are part of the immune system, show no change in number with aging. Platelets are the clotting agents in blood and, like the cells, show no change with age. Blood clotting times are not influenced by an individual's age. Blood remains healthy while the path it travels may deteriorate and become blocked.

Exercise is the primary means of enhancing the cardiovascular system. Aerobic exercise increases heart muscle strength, lowers average heart rate, and helps to counteract the negative effects of cholesterol. We discuss exercise in Chapter 5.

Respiratory System

Several changes that affect the intake of oxygen through the lungs take place with aging. The muscles that operate the lungs, like other muscles in the body, weaken and some muscle tissue may be replaced by stiffening connective tissue. The connective tissue that surrounds the lungs also stiffens, reducing the ability of the lungs to fully expand. Maximum lung capacity is typically reached between the ages of 20 and 25 and then shows progressive decline. Table 3-1 shows average maximum intake of quarts of air for different age groups. Beginning at age 40, the average decrease in input is close to 1 percent per year (Lakatta, 1990).

Within the lungs, other changes occur. At birth, the lungs contain about 24 million alveoli or air sacs. This number increases to about 300 million by age 8 and then remains constant throughout young adulthood. By age 40, however, the ducts that carry oxygen from the sacs to the blood vessels, and that also have been increasing since birth, begin to crowd out the air sacs that they serve. These changes decrease the surface area in the lungs that is available for the exchange of gases. At age 50, the air sacs, like connective tissue, lose elasticity and become more rigid and flatter. Gravitational pull on the lower, larger part of the lungs, where more blood flows, also results in less oxygenated blood. The air

TABLE 3-1   Approximate Average Intake of Air for Adults of Different Ages

Age (in years)	Quarts of Air Inhaled
20	
30	
40	
50	
60	
70	
80	

brought in is not sufficient to fill the lungs and, thus, the lower blood-rich lungs receive less air. Respiration becomes progressively more difficult beginning at about the age of 40 (DiGiovanna, 1994).

The changes that are typical in the muscles, cardiovascular, skeletal, and respiratory systems frequently produce a shortage of **stamina** in the older adult. It may take longer to catch one's breath and for a racing heart to slow down after some strenuous physical activity, or even after climbing a flight of stairs. The muscles are stiffer, the lungs cannot take in as much oxygen, bones may be fragile, and the heart may have to work extra hard to push blood through partially clogged arteries. Much of this, of course, depends on how frequently an individual exercises. Remember, however, that not all changes happen to all people at the same time. For some real-life examples of older adults with very little loss of stamina read about Dorothy Cheney, Jim Eriotes, Norman Vaughan, Carol Johnston, George Ezzard, and Don Robitaille in Box 3-1. Clearly, one can maintain very healthy muscular, cardiovascular, skeletal, and respiratory systems; one can maintain stamina.

Digestive System

Like the cardiovascular system, the digestive and elimination systems are composed of several components each of which may show senescence to a different degree. Overall, the capacity to digest and absorb food does not diminish with age.

The surface epithelium, or membrane of the **mouth**, shows some atrophy with advanced age and the underlying connective tissue may degenerate. The loss of bone, may result in the loss of teeth because the roots are no longer held in place. Teeth may become loose and move easily creating pockets for bacterial infection in the gums. Many older adults lose teeth and use dentures. Because of this, many low-income older adults who cannot afford dentures or dental care eat far less than is healthy and may suffer pain.

As one grows older, the lining of the **stomach** may atrophy. Although this has very little effect on the overall digestion of most food, two important nutrients, which are absorbed in the stomach, may be affected. Vitamin B_{12} and iron are absorbed in the stomach and, if the stomach lining has deteriorated, less of these two important nutrients are obtained. Vitamin B_{12} is very important for normal cognitive functioning and a symptom of vitamin B_{12} deficiency can resemble dementia. Older adults with deterioration of the stomach lining often are advised to increase their intake of these nutrients because, even if they are taking the minimum daily requirement, they may not be absorbing that minimum.

The intestines, particularly the **colon**, have decreased motor function and muscle tone, as do other muscles in the body. Peristalsis or contractive movement slows down. Changes in the intestine also result in increased loss of water from the intestine. The loss of muscle tone and water results in frequent constipation for older adults. Most constipation, however, results from lack of fiber, recent stress, or sedentary periods. The natural frequency for defecation ranges from three times per day to once every 3 days. Someone who experiences a bowel movement once every third day is within the normal range and overuse of laxatives is a major cause of constipation (Minaker & Rowe, 1982).

The **liver**, which is responsible for the metabolism of drugs, hormones, and alcohol in the body, is not functionally impaired in older adults who are free from alcohol-related disease. There is a lot of redundancy in the liver so that even with major structural change

BOX 3-1

Short on Stamina? I Don't Think So.

At age 80 Dorothy Cheney has won 279 National Tennis Championships and in 1997 won the Southern California Tennis Association Lifetime Achievement Award. She began playing when she was a child. Her mother, May Sutton Bundy, was her primary teacher. May won Wimbledon in 1905 and 1907, and Dorothy won the Australian Championship in 1938 and ranked among the top U.S. tennis players for 10 years. She plays in the senior national championships four times a year. Opponents say she will win if they make the slightest misstep. Dorothy remembers female tennis champion Billy Jean King and played her when Billy Jean was 10 or 11. "After the match I gave her a little advice," she said. Billy Jean won many major tennis tournaments and the advice she got from Dorothy played some role in her success. Dorothy Cheney said she is not finished winning yet and expects to continue playing for a long time. Dorothy Cheney has a lot of stamina.

Jim Eriotes, at age 74, is the champion of the batting cages in Elmhurst, Illinois. In his younger years, Jim was a minor league outfielder. He decided in the late 1980s to begin batting again. In spite of glaucoma and being nearsighted, Jim hits balls thrown at Nolan Ryan speeds and once hit 20 of 30 pitches thrown at 110 mph. Running 100 yard sprints and weight-lifting keep him in shape. Also, he swings at 140 to 300 pitches a day. It doesn't matter whether the pitch is a fast ball, curve, slider, or change-up; he hits all of them. Jim said he told his wife that, "I plan to be hitting baseballs when I'm 80 or 90." Jim Eriotes has a lot of stamina.

Norman Vaughan was the chief dog sledder for Admiral Byrd's expedition to the Antarctic in 1928. He was the first American to drive a dog team in Antarctica. Byrd named a peak in the Queen Maud mountains for him and Vaughan has wanted to return and climb 10,302-foot Mount Vaughan ever since. In 1995 he reached the summit on December 16, 1995, just 3 days shy of his 89th birthday. Norman, with a fused ankle and a reconstructed knee, hauled 75 pounds of equipment, including a portable computer, up that slope. "I couldn't believe it was happening," he said. Norman Vaughan has a lot of stamina.

Carol Johnston of Walnut, California, is a champion pole vaulter. Carol is 85 years old, still vaulting, and the holder of the world record for his age group. That vault was 7 feet 6 inches. Carol Johnston has a lot of stamina.

George Ezzard of Salisbury, North Carolina, was named Mega Man of the Year by General Nutrition Centers. George swims 16 laps underwater every day, plays ping pong, pool, and basketball. He hit 99 out of 100 free throws to celebrate his 84th birthday in 1997. George is interested in trying a few new sports. "I've got to find out something about golf," he said. George Ezzard has a lot of stamina.

Don Robitaille is 70 years old and loves to ride his, also old, Trek bike. In the last 9 years, he's put over 85,000 miles on that bike and recently, for a bit of an outing, biked the 5000 miles from Bar Harbor, Maine, to the Pacific Coast in Washington. Don Robitaille has a lot of stamina.

Source: Modern Maturity magazine, Front Lines (1997); Charlotte Observer (1995); AARP Magazine (2006).

function remains unaffected. The liver also has good regenerative capacity. Up to 80 percent of the liver can be removed without significantly affecting function (Schmucker, 1998).

Gallbladder problems are more prevalent in older adults and are probably a result of lifelong dietary patterns of fat intake rather than structural changes with age.

The **kidneys** decrease in weight and volume by 20 to 30 percent, mainly, in outer filtration units by the early 70s. The filtration rate declines by about 1 percent every year past the age of 40. The kidneys of older persons are, however, still able to meet the body's needs as long as they are not placed under extreme physiological stress. There are three conditions with which we should be concerned. First, renal blood flow is reduced during aerobic exercise as the blood is diverted to the skeletal muscles. Second, under conditions of intense heat, as well as during exercise, sodium and water can become depleted. Older adults must be careful when exercising and/or under conditions of hot temperatures. It is especially important for older adults who have not exercised, and who now are beginning to do so, to seek the guidance of a physician. Finally, the kidneys of an older adult are less efficient at transporting chemicals. When an older adult takes the same dosage of medicine as a younger adult, more of the drug remains behind in the bloodstream. Harmful levels can, thus, build up over time with repeated dosages. Drug dosage must be carefully monitored by and for older adults (Whitbourne, 1996).

The **bladder** loses 50 percent of its capacity by age 65 and, like many other tissues in the body, becomes stiffer and less flexible. As a result of these changes, the bladder can no longer hold the volume of urine that it could in the past and can no longer completely empty itself. There is a higher volume of residual urine following each urination. As a result, older adults tend to urinate more often but less each time (DiGiovanna, 1994).

Reproductive System

Male and female differences in biological aging are most evident in the reproductive system because women experience a major change during **menopause**. Menopause refers to the cessation of menstruation and the accompanying changes in hormone levels. Throughout the 40s, there is a gradual decline in female reproductive ability ending with menopause, which is when menstruation ceases completely, around age 50 to 55. The process usually takes 2 to 3 years with irregular menses until complete cessation. Most women report little discomfort although some experience "hot flashes," characterized by feeling overheated, sweaty, and flushed. Estrogen levels drop dramatically and this relatively sudden drop is a factor in the development of osteoporosis. The physical changes that accompany menopause include a loss of skin elasticity, replacement of mammary tissue with fat leading to sagging breasts, and the appearance of facial hair. None of the changes directly affect sexual function but can affect the way a woman feels about her appearance. Some women may experience serious adjustment problems as a result of these changes (see Chapter 10).

Males do not experience any such dramatic change in such a short period of time. Sperm-producing tubules decline in function over a much longer period of time and the number of sperm gradually decline. For most older men, sexual functioning is not affected and they gradually adapt to and often enjoy the slower pace that accompanies these changes. Many older men do, of course, experience some sexual dysfunction but it is not due to declining levels of testosterone.

Many men experience a very noticeable change in the size and weight of the prostate gland as they grow older. The weight of the prostate can double by the time a man reaches his late 70s. Many men also contract prostate cancer as they age. Regular checkups after 50 are recommended.

Immune System

The body's defense against harmful invaders in the form of bacteria, germs, viruses, and toxins is called the immune system and consists of three major components. These components, when functioning correctly, recognize cells of the host body and do not attack them, are usually specific in attacking only one type of invader, and can develop memory cells in case an invader attacks again at a later date. These defensive cells are produced in bone marrow and then converted to specific types of defenders.

The first defense consists of **T cells** which are converted in the thymus gland residing above the heart and behind the sternum. Each type of T cell is built to recognize the host body and one type of invader. It is estimated that there are as many as 100 million different types of T cells; one for each type of danger from cancer, bacteria, germs, and viruses. T cells are thought to be the primary defense against virus infection and cancer. The efficiency of T cells is influenced by a chemical called thyroxin produced by the thyroid glands on either side of the throat. The second defense consists of **B cells** which are converted at an unknown site. B cells manufacture and secrete antibodies and those antibodies attack the invader. B cells can attack at a distance because the antibodies they produce are carried through the blood stream. The action of B cells is influenced by T cells. B cells are thought to be the primary defense against bacterial infection and poisons. The third type of defense cells are called **natural killer cells**. Unlike T and B cells, they are not specific to certain forms of intrusion but are stimulated by T cells. These cells function as hunters when danger is present.

Several changes in the immune system accompany aging. The thymus begins to shrink soon after puberty until close to age 50. At that point, it may be only 5 percent of its original size. The hormones produced by the thymus cease by age 60. The production of new T cells does, however, continue and the migration of those new T cells to the body is proportional to the relative size (e.g., 5 percent) of the still functioning thymus (Rodewald, 1998). Research also suggests that the changes that occur in T cells are due to the increases in chronic disorders and inflammations that so often accompany aging rather than to some innate aging process (Boucher et al., 1998). Thyroxin, produced by the thyroid glands, also declines with advanced age. As a result of the changes in the thymus and the production of thyroxin, T cell production and efficiency typically decline with advanced age and about 75 percent of older adults show moderate or severe declines in T cell response to invasion. Because T cells are a primary defense against viral infection and cancer, these problems increase with advanced age. Cancer, in particular, is far more common in older than in younger adults.

B cells are influenced by T cells, so some changes in B cells occur. For older adults, antibody production is slower, ends sooner, and the level reached declines faster. Older adults who encounter an invader that they encountered when young are usually very successful at fighting off the invasion. It is the production of new antibodies for new invaders that functions less efficiently. One implication of these findings is that vaccinations are more effective when given to young adults, and are maintained by booster shots, than are vaccinations given for the first time to older adults. Why then do you think individuals, especially older individuals, are encouraged to get a flu vaccine every autumn?

There are a number of things that are thought to boost the functioning of the immune system. You have probably heard that vitamin C, echinacea, and zinc accomplish this task but the evidence is not actually very convincing, particularly for echinacea. Some other work suggests that certain exercises may boost the immune system. In one study, adults over the age of 60 who had a virus responsible for one form of herpes were randomly assigned to a group that performed tai chi chih exercises for 15 weeks or to a control group that did not. Tai chi chih is a modified form of the Chinese exercise and involves simple careful movements that emphasize balance and postural changes. The adults performing tai chi chih showed a significant increase in immune system reaction to the virus at the end of the study (Irwin et al., 2003). The bodily systems do not operate in isolation but rather influence one another.

Nervous System

Studies have found changes in the nervous system with advanced age. Most of the changes are in the number of nerve cells or **neurons**. Sensory neurons decline in number with age so it may become more difficult to detect a touch on the skin, a scent in the air, or the taste of salt in food. Changes in senses influence changes in perception and cognition (see also Chapter 6).

Motor neurons also decline in number reducing the number of cells that can be stimulated in a muscle. Muscle cells that are no longer stimulated degenerate and may be replaced by stiffening connective tissue (DiGiovanna, 1994). Loss of muscle fiber is usually the result of loss of motor neurons. Loss of motor neurons is typically the result of clogged blood vessels, which can no longer nourish the neurons. Clogged blood vessels are one of the most harmful physical changes that occur with aging.

The **brain** decreases in size and weight with advanced age by nearly 5 percent. Weight loss seems to accelerate after age 60 (Cunningham & Brookbank, 1988) but is not equally distributed across the entire brain. Some areas of the brain lose many neurons while others seem to show little or no loss. Loss typically occurs in visual, hearing, smell, and voluntary movement areas of the brain. Individual neurons also show structural change with advanced age. Figure 3-2 on page 58 shows a neuron from a young person and one from an old person. The number of connective spikes, called dendrites, is far fewer on the old neuron. This loss of density, as well as loss of whole cells, accounts for the observed changes in size and weight with advanced age.

There is some debate as to whether the loss of dendrites and whole cells influence behavior. Much of the brain is redundant and it may be that some back-up systems have been lost but that no real effect on performance can be detected under normal conditions. At the same time, differences in performance are found on a number of tasks and, perhaps, some of those differences are due to the loss of dendrites and cells in the brain.

Nerve cells communicate with one another and with sensory and muscles cells by way of chemicals called **neurotransmitters**. The nervous system has a number of different neurotransmitters, and several pathologies of the brain are particular to a single class of neurotransmitters (see also Chapter 12). In general, the function of major brain pathways is unaffected by normal healthy aging.

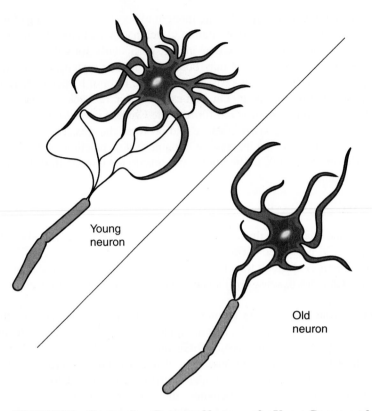

Young
neuron

Old
neuron

FIGURE 3-2   Comparison Between Neurons of a Young Person and an Older Person.

Chronic Conditions

With the physical changes and senescence that can occur in so much of the older body, the number of chronic conditions experienced by older adults is, as you might expect, fairly high. **Chronic conditions** refer to physical ailments characterized by slow onset and a long duration. Most do not cause death and the 10 most frequent for older adults are shown in Table 3-2. We will examine the hearing and visual conditions in Chapter 6.

    Arthritis comes in two forms both of which are more frequent in women and involve a breakdown of bone and cartilage at the joints: **Osteoarthritis** is the more frequent form while **rheumatoid arthritis** is a type of autoimmune disease. An **autoimmune disease** is when the immune system attacks some part, in this case the joints, of the host organism. Many older adults suffer from both forms. There is no cure for these conditions and sufferers must rely on pain medication, exercise, and even joint replacement for relief.

    Hypertension refers to abnormally high blood pressure. It is the second most frequent chronic condition and affects 38.1 percent of adults age 65 and older. Hypertension is more frequent in older men than in older women. In hypertension, systolic pressure is 140 or higher and diastolic pressure is 90 or higher. High blood pressure is a clear warning signal of blockage in the arteries and an increased risk of blood clots. Blood clots can produce stroke and major loss of nerve cells in the brain. Blood clots can produce fatal

PROJECT 3

One of the major points in this chapter is that physical change, biological aging, is highly variable both between and within individuals. It has been said that when you look at the physical changes within an individual it's a little like walking into a clock shop where all the clocks tell a different time. Some are fast, some are slow, and some show the true time. For the first part of this project, record the physical changes that you notice while observing older people in a public place, such as a mall. What changes are easiest to notice? What changes are not noticeable at all?

For the second part of this project, look at the following list of possible physical changes:

Your hair turns gray and you lose half of it.

Your bone density declines and you are in danger of developing osteoporosis; this loss of bone has loosened most of the teeth in your mouth.

Your blood pressure is now 145 over 95 and you have atherosclerosis.

Colon cancer is a danger for people in your family and your doctor wants to perform an examination every 2 years.

Your immune system is functioning at a very low level. You are prone to getting infections and diseases whenever you are exposed to them.

You have lost almost all feeling in your feet and hands.

Based on this list of physical changes, create an older adult by randomly selecting any three changes. Now create three more older adults by selecting randomly (with replacement) any three of these changes. Describe the adults you have created. Who is the healthiest and why? Who is least healthy and why?

Is this the way that real aging operates? Do you think that physical changes are randomly selected for older adults or do you think that some changes tend to occur together and that they depend on the choices made when we are young?

TABLE 3-2   The 10 Most Frequent Chronic Conditions for People Age 65 and Over (in percent)

Arthritis	48.3
Hypertension	38.1
Hearing impairment	28.6
Heart disease	27.9
Cataracts	15.7
Orthopedic deformity	15.5
Chronic sinusitis	15.3
Diabetes	8.8
Visual impairment	8.2
Varicose veins	7.8

Source: National Center for Health Statistics (1990).

heart attacks. It is important to monitor blood pressure and seek immediate consultation with a physician for any signs of elevation (Kannel, 1996).

Heart disease is the number one killer of Americans and affects 27.9 percent of people 65 and older. A major cause of heart disease is blockage of blood vessels caused by the accumulation of fat and cholesterol. Studies show that women are 14 percent more likely than men to die after a heart attack, and that the likelihood of death after a heart attack also is greater for older individuals (Malacrida et al., 1998).

Chronic sinusitis refers to inflammation of the sinus cavities. Such inflammation can be quite painful producing sinus headaches and burning sensation.

Diabetes refers to a reduction in or cessation of the production of insulin by the pancreas. Without insulin, the body cannot process sugars and, as a result, sugar accumulates in the blood, causing damage to some organs and tissues, while other organs and tissues in need of sugar starve without it. Adult onset diabetes occurs more frequently in older adults but it can usually be controlled by careful diet and medication.

Varicose veins refers to veins that have a larger than normal diameter due to the accumulation of blood in the vein. The vein may become permanently stretched. Stretched veins are more common in the legs and abdomen. This disorder is thought to be caused by the reduction of circulation due to congestive heart failure, wearing very tight clothing, or standing still or sitting for long periods of time with little movement. Besides being unattractive, varicose veins can be painful, result in clots and blockage of blood flow, and can result in tissue damage and even death. It is important to keep moving or elevate your legs if you find yourself standing still for long periods of time.

One common complaint that may be heard from older adults is that they have **insomnia** and never get a good night's rest. Insomnia is not regarded as a common chronic condition. Box 3-2 will provide some of the more recent information on this chronic complaint and Box 3-3 tells a little about the dreams of those who do make it to sleep.

Interactions

We have tried to point out in this chapter instances of interactions among the different body systems. We saw that kidney dysfunction predicts bone loss and that exercise influences immune function. The body systems also are influenced by interactions with the environment and our attitude. It probably will not surprise you to learn that SES is strongly related to health as those with higher SES have greater access to the best doctors, physicians, and insurance. Other research shows that our parents influence our physical health, decades after we are no longer children. One recent study measured grip strength and balance in a sample of several thousand adults in their 50s. They found that the occupation of their fathers predicted low functioning while their mother's education level predicted high functioning; that is, adults whose fathers had low-paying, low-status jobs did not function well, while adults whose mothers were well educated functioned very well (Guralnik et al., 2006). Our early years influence our later years. How do you think these influences operate?

We have known for a long time that negative attitudes can result in low functioning and poorer health and some of this work will be discussed in Chapter 5. Over the last several years, however, psychologists have become more interested in the influence of posi-

BOX **3-2**

Sleeping and Aging

Dorothea Kent tells the story that, "a man 90 years old was asked to what he attributed his longevity. I reckon, he said, with a twinkle in his eye, it's because most nights I went to bed and slept when I should have sat up and worried." Getting adequate sleep is very important for healthy aging and yet many older adults express complaints about their sleep. One survey of over 9000 older adults found that more than half said they had difficulty falling asleep, trouble staying asleep, or early morning awakenings (Foley et al., 1995). Women going through menopause often experience these same sleep problems. Difficulty falling asleep and/or maintaining sleep are referred to as **insomnia**. Some of these problems can be attributed to the environment in which one sleeps, some to normal physical changes that can occur with aging, and some may be due to a serious sleep disorder.

Environment

If the bedroom is too hot or too warm, sleep will be affected. If it's noisy or there's too much light in the room, we may all have difficulty falling asleep. Drinking caffeine or eating or exercising before going to bed also make falling asleep harder than it should be. All of these problems are solved rather simply and, if you have an older relative who complains about insomnia, these are the first things to check.

Normal Changes

Monitoring of adult sleep suggest that insomnia may result from a decline in quantity or quality of sleep. Several factors play a role. You already know how the bladder can disrupt normal sleep for older adults. Older adults also generally get far **less deep sleep** than do younger adults (Dement et al., 1985). Deep sleep is when the brain shows a very low level of activity. Older adults get mostly light sleep and REM (rapid eye movement) or dream sleep; the loss of deep sleep results in a less-satisfying rest. Considerable research shows that deep sleep can be restored by sleep deprivation (Carskadon, 1982). In one study, older adults who went to sleep a half hour later than they normally would have, but who still got up at their usual time, recovered deep sleep, had fewer awakenings at night, and reported high levels of well-being in the morning (Hoch et al., 2001).

Another factor is the change in **circadian rhythm** that frequently occurs with advanced age. These rhythms govern body temperature and hormone secretions. For most of the day, we are in the warm segment of this rhythm and wide awake, while at night, we are cool and generally sleeping. As we age, the hypothalamus, which regulates this rhythm, can deteriorate and produce an advance in the rhythm such that these people are warm very early in the morning and cool during the last half of the day. They then try to stay up to their usual bedtime even though they're cool and should be sleeping and wake up earlier than they want because their body is warm early. The treatment is quite simple. The warm segment of the rhythm responds to bright light so one can simply make sure to be in bright light during the afternoon and early evening. After a short period of time, those daytime hours will become once again part of the warm rhythm and the night and early morning will be cool. One caution is to avoid bright light in the morning hours (wear sunglasses if you go out) or you may shift the rhythm back to its previous sleep disrupting state (Fetveit et al., 2003).

(continued)

BOX **3-2** Continued

Sleep Disorders

Sleep apnea, which is a cessation of breathing while asleep, is fairly common among older adults. Estimates suggest that close to 35 percent experience apnea (Stone, 1993). Apnea is increased by sleeping pills but decreases as a result of sleep deprivation (Davies et al., 1986; Carskadon, 1982).

　　Periodic limb movement disorder (also called nocturnal myoclonus) is characterized by rhythmic movements of the legs and sometimes arms and also is fairly common among older adults (Youngstedt et al., 1998). The movements typically occur every 20 to 40 seconds for much of the night and disrupt sleep for the sleeper and, sometimes, for anyone sharing their bed. This is distinct from **restless leg syndrome** which is a strong urge to move due to extended discomfort. The latter can be successfully treated by regular exercise and soaking the legs in warm water (Hornyak & Trenkwalder, 2004) but the former usually requires some medication.

Good Sleepers

So are good sleepers those who are getting 8 or more hours every night while all those with less are poor insomniacs who pay the price with lower mental acuity, more irritability, and lower energy levels all day every day? We're happy to say that the answer is no. It is sleep disturbances, such as those just described, that produce difficulties and not the total amount of time slept (Blackwell et al., 2006). In fact, the amount of sleep that individuals need is highly variable. Some need 8 hours or more while others can get by on much less. Good sleepers are those who get the sleep they need; poor sleepers, among them insomniacs, get far less than they need. One study looked at sleep for a large number of adults between the ages of 55 and 87. All regarded themselves as good sleepers so the researchers divided them into two groups by the hours they slept. About 30 percent of the sample got 8 or more hours each night while 20 percent got fewer than 6 hours. These "long" and "short" sleepers then were compared on 48 different measures including daytime pleasantness, anxiety, depression, neuroticism, cognition, and life satisfaction. The main differences found were that "long" sleepers got up later, spent more time in bed, fell asleep sooner, and had breakfast later. "Short" sleepers weren't suffering at all (Fichten et al., 2004).

---

tive attitude and this area of research has been referred to as **positive psychology**. This work shows that people with a consistent positive attitude are subject to less-frequent injury (Koivumaa-Honkanen et al., 2000), lower rates of stroke (Ostir et al., 2001), and fewer readmissions to the hospital following cardiovascular problems (Middleton & Byrd, 1996). One study measured mood over a week by asking participants to rate, every day, how well positive adjectives (like *happy*, *lively*, and *cheerful*) and negative adjectives (like *sad*, *nervous*, and *hostile*) described the way they felt. They then were exposed to viruses that cause the common cold and monitored for symptoms. Those with positive attitudes were less than half as likely to develop a cold when compared to those with negative attitudes; those in the middle in attitude were also in the middle on catching colds (Cohen & Pressman, 2006). Such work offers some support for the organismic theory of development rather than the mechanistic view.

　　Findings such as these should make it clear that some of the physical changes that can occur with advanced age are largely beyond our ability to alter but most allow us some degree of control. Not all physical changes happen to all people and not all changes occur at the same time. Diet, exercise, and even attitudes play an important role.

BOX **3-3**
Dreaming and Aging

It is difficult for most people to remember their dreams so any analyses of dream content are based only on the relatively small proportion of dreams that are remembered. Perhaps because of this, not a lot of systematic research has examined the differences in dreams between young and old adults. Some work has, however, found that older adults report far less visual imagery in their dreams (Fein et al., 1985) and fewer themes (Soper et al., 1992). Young adults report more emotions in their dreams (Zanasi et al., 2005) and the emotions most frequently reported by young and old dreamers differ. Younger adults report more anger and fear in their dreams while older adults report more enjoyment and joy (Blick & Howe, 1984). Related to this, older adults report fewer nightmares than college-age dreamers (Salvio et al., 1992). Levels of apprehension seem to be lowest in the dreams reported by middle-aged adults while younger and older adults are more apprehensive, at least in their dreams (Clark et al., 2001). Perhaps these differences reflect the uncertainties of young and old age compared to middle age. Some work has used a survey named the BEM sex role inventory, named after the researcher who first created this measure of masculinity, femininity, and androgyny (Bem, 1974). High masculinity scores were associated with more aggressive dream content for young and old (Clark et al., 2006). Finally, with respect to erotic dreams, the number reported seems to vary with age (Funkhouser et al., 1999). One study of older women found that dreams about sex were reported by 67 percent of women between the ages of 50 and 59, 68 percent between 60 and 69, 74 percent between 70 and 79, but by only 33 percent of those over the age of 80 (von Sydow, 1992). Do you think these differences are genuine age differences or could they be a cohort difference in reporting erotic dreams?

SOCIAL POLICY APPLICATIONS

You now know that there are many physical aspects that change and many that don't change in old age. For those that change, we see both increase as well as decline. Two areas of change that have had a significant impact on a great many people regarding health and morbidity in old age are cardiovascular disease (CVD) and osteoporosis. Both of these conditions produce significant disability and health problems for a great many older persons. Bone deformities in general and heart disease are major chronic conditions and together account for a significant number of deaths of older persons. These two conditions often can be prevented. As researchers, we continue to call for more research into the etiology and treatment of these diseases but we also call for more advocacy in prevention. Insurance companies, among others, need to step up to the plate, and several have, to pay for prevention. Education programs to inform individuals at all ages about how to attain and maintain bone and heart health are critical. Public health programs must also be more proactive in identifying and treating early signs of osteoporosis and CVD. The trend of restaurants and even cities to eliminate trans fats from menus is an excellent first start. We need to go farther to promote more heart and bone healthy items at all restaurants including fast food places along with explanations of why these foods are important. We need to make walking a priority by creating better environments conducive to walking. We need programs like "take a walk with your neighbor" or "walk with grandma" to encourage young folks to get active early and support mobility in older residents. Service learning programs could be designed to help older community and facility residents eat better and exercise more, simply by spending quality time interacting during these activities. Try it yourself, you'll like it!

CHAPTER HIGHLIGHTS

■ There is great variability in the physical changes that occur across the older adult population and within each individual.

■ Skin shows changes in color, accumulation of dark spots, wrinkling, and decreased moisture. Changes in the skin can have a negative effect on protective functions.

■ Hair usually turns gray and is lost in varying amounts; these changes seem to be largely genetic.

■ Older adults lose height. Weight change, which may be a cohort effect, increases during middle age and decreases during old age.

■ Voice lowers in pitch.

■ The skull, ears, and nose grow as we age.

■ Fast twitch muscle fibers are lost between age 40 and 70 while slow twitch fibers remain intact until 70.

■ The increased action of osteoclasts lessens bone density in older adults, particularly white and Asian American women. This loss is due to genetics, hormones, and lifestyle factors and can become osteoporosis, which is severe loss of bone.

■ The cardiovascular system shows higher systolic pressure for older adults but intact heart and blood. Blood vessels, however, clog as one ages and can result in atherosclerosis. Be careful what you eat and exercise regularly.

■ The lungs take in less air as we grow older due to changes in muscles, increases in ducts, and the effects of gravity.

■ In spite of changes in muscles, cardiovasular system, and respiration, many older adults are able to maintain a high level of stamina.

■ The overall functioning of the digestive system shows very little decline although the lining of the mouth and stomach may deteriorate, the colon loses moisture and muscle, the kidneys slow down under stress, and the bladder becomes smaller and more rigid. Kidney dysfunction is related to bone loss.

■ Women experience a relatively sudden change in their reproductive system and levels of the hormone estrogen when they go through menopause. This change in estrogen plays a role in bone loss. Men experience no such sudden change but often experience an enlargement of the prostate gland.

■ T cell production and efficiency decline with age due to a shrinking of the thymus gland and increases in chronic disease and inflammation. The efficiency of B cells and natural killer cells is influenced by the decline in T cells, and a vulnerability to a number of disorders, especially cancers and viral infections, increases with age.

■ Nerve cells in the periphery and in the brain decline with age in part because of clogged blood vessels. Cell loss in the brain tends to occur in specific areas.

■ Older adults frequently experience a number of chronic conditions such as arthritis, hypertension, cardiovascular disease, osteoporosis, chronic sinusitis, diabetes, and varicose veins.

■ Complaints about insomnia are frequent among older adults and research suggests several reasons for lower quality sleep among older adults: loss of deep sleep, apnea, myoclonus, and smaller bladder. Education about healthy sleep and sleep deprivation are reasonably effective treatments.

■ The bodily systems do not operate in isolation but influence one another. Physical changes also can be influenced by behaviors (what we eat, how we exercise) and attitude. Positive attitudes produce positive results in health and well-being.

STUDY QUESTIONS

1. Distinguish among chronological age, biological age, and senescence. Give an example of biological aging without significant senescence.

2. What major systems are involved in maintaining stamina and how can senescence in these systems affect one's stamina?

3. What are the major changes in physical appearance? How do these affect function?

4. What changes typically occur in the cardiovascular system? The digestive system? The nervous system? The immune system?

5. What aspects of the nervous system change and which do not? Is behavior affected by these changes? Why or why not?

6. Describe the influence of clogged blood vessels on muscles, nerves, and chronic conditions.

7. What advice would you give to an older friend who claims to be having difficulty sleeping or complains about poor quality sleep?

8. Describe at least three instances of interactions between bodily systems that influence senescence. How are physical changes influenced by diet, exercise, and attitude? Give specific examples of each.

9. Consider the issue of individual differences in senescence. Think about and describe the differences between people you know who are the same age.

RECOMMENDED READINGS

DiGiovanna, A. G. (1994). *Human Aging: Biological Perspectives*. New York: McGraw Hill. A good, readable description of the major biological changes that accompany aging.
Seuss, Dr. (1986). *You're Only Old Once*. New York: Random House. A humorous view of an old man's encounter with the medical establishment.
Whalley, L. (2001). *The Aging Brain*. New York: Columbia University Press. A good and readable overview of the changes that can occur in the aging brain.

INTERNET RESOURCES

www.nof.org/. For information on osteoporosis.
www.americanheart.org/. For information on heart disease.
www.arthritis.org/. For information about arthritis.
www.ppc.sas.upenn.edu/. For information about positive psychology.
www.sleepfoundation.org/. For information about sleep and sleep disorders.

Look at the photos shown at the beginning of this chapter. The order from oldest to youngest is bottom left, middle, bottom right, top left, and top right. Look at your own grandparents. Are they not beautiful? Older adults are among the finest art ever produced.

4 Theories of Senescence and Aging

Age is not all decay; it is the ripening, the swelling of the fresh life within, that withers and bursts the husk.

—*George MacDonald*

In Chapter 3 we talked about the marks left on aging bodies, "the husk withered and burst by the swelling within." In this chapter, we will examine some of the explanations given for this "withering." We will examine theories that attempt to explain how and why senescence occurs. If we understand what causes those increased vulnerabilities, we will be better informed and may be able to minimize senescence so that old age can be a healthy, active time, a time for the "swelling of the fresh life within." In this chapter's Senior View, Martha Russell gives us her views on some of these theories.

An Overview

Virtually all organisms show senescence if they live long enough. Most animals in the wild do not show senescence because they fall to predators at the first signs of weakness. Animals held in captivity or pets show senescence because they are protected from predation. Humans show senescence because they grow old with a fair amount of protection from predators too. There are, however, instances of wild animals that seem to live for long periods of time but do not show significant senescence.

Turtles, and their large relatives tortoises, live for long periods of time and show little senescence. Careful examination of turtle tissues shows that older tissues are not much different from younger tissues. Turtles and tortoises do not seem to die because of the increased vulnerability to injury and disease that is characteristic of senescence. They die because of predators, usually humans. Some fish (sturgeons), amphibians (alligators), and sponges (regardless of their life in Bikini Bottom) also seem to avoid senescence as they age.

An animal's size is related to its longevity and when senescence begins. Generally, smaller animals live shorter lives than larger animals and, consequently, show senescence at a much earlier chronological age. Turtles are an exception to the general rule, because they are relatively small animals but live a long time.

Animals who live a long time with no apparent senescence, the relationship between size and longevity, and the fact that different species have very different life expectancies suggests a strong role for genetics. Different species live in the same environments but have different genes. Genes must be one major reason why a horse lives longer than a dog. Furthermore, members of the same species (e.g., humans, cats, antelopes) have about the same life expectancy regardless of where they live. A cat living in Japan has about the same life expectancy as a cat living in Canada. Genetics clearly plays an important role in longevity. On the other hand, the environments for these different species are not identical. Different species, eat different things (e.g., horses and dogs) and the life expectancy of some species, notably humans, has changed dramatically over time. Human life expectancy at the beginning of the twentieth century was about 49 and now it's over 75. This difference clearly is environmental. The environment has changed over the last 100 years but human genes have not. Both genes and environment play a role in longevity.

Theories of senescence must deal with the findings that the members of some species live longer than members of other species, that some species seem to show no senescence, that environments are rarely identical, and that the life expectancy of a species

Senior View

Martha Russell, a widow living alone, was 78 when we spoke with her. She and her husband used to own a rug company. We asked Martha her opinions of the theories presented in this chapter. Here's what she had to say.

My health is just fine so any theory that says you get sick when you get old has to be wrong. Martha would not be a fan of the programmed theories you will learn about in this chapter.

That evolution theory says that you live only to reproduce and then you have to go ahead and die. That can't be right because I had my child many, many years ago and I feel fine today. We're not programmed to die; we're programmed to live.

It is quite possibly true that our own garbage kills us. There's so much pollution in everything and a lot of cancers come from that. I guess it could hurt our DNA and we just couldn't get it all fixed. I know I already have too much to do. Martha smiled as she said this last statement.

The things we eat and vitamins might give us some protection. Pollutants are in a lot of things and are very bad for you.

We're supposed to get old and that's what happens but you shouldn't try and hurry it up. We agree.

A turtle.

can change as the environment changes. Such theories often are complex and always difficult to test. When there is evidence for or against one of these theories, it is usually indirect. In the following discussion, the theories are divided into programmed and nonprogrammed categories: **Programmed theories** claim senescence follows a predetermined plan and **unprogrammed theories** mean ones where no such plan exists. As you will see, it is difficult to place some theories into either of these categories.

Programmed Theories

Biological Clock

Biological clock theory is the leading programmed theory. Our genes were considered to be a ticking clock that would stop at a given point and, at that point, we would fall apart and die. The theory has evolved quite a lot since that simple version and now many think that the ticking clock itself has been found.

Cells are not immortal. They divide and reproduce a limited number of times and then die. That number is known as the **Hayflick number**, named for its discoverer Leonard Hayflick (1965; 1996). Cells from different species have different limits on cell division. The Hayflick number for human cells is about 50. The Hayflick number for a giant tortoise, which can live to 175 years, is about 110. A species' longevity is related to the upper limit on cell division, the Hayflick number. To produce a human adult from a fertilized egg takes about 40 divisions. When cells can no longer divide, they deteriorate and die, although such cells living in a culture may survive for quite some time. The limit on cell division seems very much like a biological clock.

The limit on cell division resides on the DNA-carrying chromosomes that carry the cell's genetic code. During cell division, the DNA molecules on chromosomes split and rebuild themselves as each adenine base acquires a new thymine partner (and vice versa), and as each cytosine base acquires a new guanine partner (and vice versa) from the nutrients in the cell. The two new cells are identical to the old cell from which they came. At the ends of DNA chromosomes are a series of repeating units called **telomeres**. Telomeres carry no genetic information and are shortened with each succeeding cell division. Figure 4-1 shows what this might look like. Cell division stops when the telomere sequence has been sufficiently shortened. This might occur because further cell division would damage genetic material, and so the telomere protects the genetic information while division occurs. When the telomere strand is too short to protect genetic information during cell division, the cell stops dividing. At that point, the cell is assumed to grow old and experience senescence (Hayflick, 1996). Telomere length is influenced by several factors examined later. The length you start with is inherited (Nawrot et al., 2004). Not all humans inherit sufficient length to experience 50+ cell divisions; some have more and some have less. Some believe that we should measure physical fitness by measuring average telomere length (Aviv, 2006). Perhaps long-lived parents pass long teleomeres to long-living children.

This theory has strong appeal because it seems very logical and relatively simple but there is some evidence that is problematic. Research has found deteriorating cells that still have long telomere sequences (Ferenac et al., 2005). Perhaps the deterioration in such cells is not due to senescence but some other cause. Other research with cloned mice has found evidence for no loss and perhaps an increase in telomeres (Wakayama et al., 2000). If the

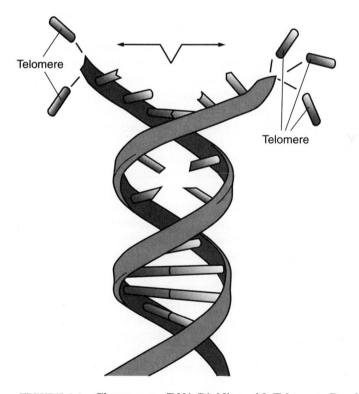

FIGURE 4-1   Chromosome/DNA Dividing with Telomeres Breaking Away.

shortening telomere length with each cell division produces senescence, then one might wonder why the brain can become senescent because nerve cells in the brain do not typically divide (Cohen, 2000). These findings are not easily explained if telomeres are programmed to shorten and lead to senescence.

One line of indirect but interesting evidence for a telomere clock comes from the study of cancer cells. Cancer cells seem to be immortal. They do not ordinarily stop dividing; they have no known upper limit. Cancer cells also have telomere sequences at the ends of their chromosomes and those telomeres are lost during cell division just as in normal cells. Cancer cells, however, have an enzyme called **telomerase** that rebuilds the telomere sequence following each cell division. In this way, one can think of cancer cells as being able to reset their biological clock so that it never runs down (Landman et al., 1997). Stem cells also have telomerase and can rebuild their telomere sequences. That is one reason why stem cells are considered by some as a promising potential cure for many disorders.

Evolution

Another set of theories argues that senescence is programmed to occur as a result of our genes much like the original biological clock theories. Our genes, according to this view, are meant to ensure the survival of the species rather than the survival of the individual. The survival of the species depends on reproduction and raising and protecting the young until they also can reproduce. Natural selection should eliminate those young, who would pass on faulty genes, before they are able to reproduce. One expectation of this view is that death rates for individuals in their childbearing and rearing years should be lower than death rates for the very young (because some of them carry faulty genes) and the old (because they are past their reproductive years). When researchers have examined these death rates and excluded deaths that might be considered unnatural, such as homicides and accidents, they have found lower death rates for those in their reproductive years (Olshansky et al., 1998). Death rates also have been examined for dogs and mice and they too have lower death rates during their reproductive years (Carnes et al., 1996).

Evolution would want organisms to spend their resources on reproducing. When they are spent on reproducing, fewer resources are available for the repair of physical problems that might occur (e.g., illness or injury). Those who reproduce while young should, thus, experience high levels of senescence as they age while those who put off reproducing should experience healthier aging. Some work supports this general notion. In a comparison of opossums living in two different environments, those on an island on which there were no predators reproduced later and showed less senescence with age while those living near predators reproduced earlier and declined much sooner (Austad, 1997).

Some theorists believe that this difference is controlled by one's genes and refer to it as **antagonistic pleiotropy** which means that genes that increase the probability of good reproductive years decrease the probability of long life. In humans, there seems to be at least one such gene (called p53). It instructs cells that are damaged to stop dividing or to die and is thought to help prevent cancer in young adults. Once adults reproduce and become older, this gene lessens the ability to replace damaged tissues in various physical systems (Williams, 1997).

Evolution theories make some sense and there are findings consistent with their predictions but there are also other possible explanations for those findings and some seeming inconsistencies. Could it be, for example, that a reason for the faster decline of mainland opossums is the presence of predators? Other work shows that men and women who have more children live longer, although for women age of the last birth is the more critical factor. A later last birth is associated with longer life (McArdle et al., 2006).

Hormones

Hormones are chemical messengers that provide instructions to different types of cells throughout the body. They are produced by endocrine glands such as the thyroid, the parathyroid, the adrenal cortex, the pancreas, and the ovaries and testes, all of which are controlled by the "master" gland, the pituitary at the base of the brain. The pituitary is, in turn, largely controlled by the hypothalamus, a brain structure responsible for body functions such as eating, temperature regulation, and sexual desire. Because hormones control the actions of cells in many different systems, it seems possible that they might also control the aging of cells in those different systems. Glands follow a schedule and decrease the production of certain hormones as we grow older. Those lowered levels of hormones may produce increased vulnerability (senescence) in other parts of the body.

Table 4-1 lists glands of the endocrine system, some of the major hormones, and some implications for human aging and senescence. As you know from the last chapter, the immune system functions less efficiently as one ages because of the decline in T cell efficiency. As suggested in Table 4-1, this immune system decline may be the result of changes in the thyroid and thymus glands. You also know that bones weaken with

TABLE 4-1 Endocrine Glands, Hormones, and Implications for Aging

Gland	Hormones and Function	Implications for Aging
Pituitary	Human growth hormone that promotes tissue development and carbohydrate metabolism.	Growth hormone and tissue development decline with age.
Pineal	Melatonin hormone regulates biological rhythms.	Some claim that melatonin reverses aging; it does not.
Adrenal	DHEA that is converted to estrogen and testosterone and may serve other functions as well.	Research has found positive and negative effects for DHEA intake in older humans.
Thyroid	Thyroxin that affects T cell efficiency and with triodothyronine increases oxygen consumption and regulates growth and maturation of tissues.	T cell efficiency and, thus, the immune system decline with age.
	Calctitonin that lowers calcium in blood by inhibiting bone resorption.	Bone resorption increases with age.
Parathyroid	Parathormone that increases calcium in blood by increasing bone resorption.	Bone resorption increases with age.
Thymus	Responsible for development of immune system.	Is replaced by fat in adults; immune system declines.
Ovaries	Estrogen that is necessary for development of sex organs and secondary characteristics.	Menopause results in loss of estrogen.
Testes	Testosterone that aids development of secondary sexual characteristics and helps blood clot.	Testosterone levels decline as one grows older; blood clots may increase.

advanced age due to increased resorption of bone by osteoclasts. As shown in Table 4-1, bone resorption is to some extent controlled by the parathyroid gland and the loss of estrogen following menopause. There is, however, no direct evidence that declining hormones are responsible for senescence so researchers have tried to determine whether increases in these declining hormones would reverse aging.

In an early 1990s' study, medical researchers injected 12 volunteers, older men age 61 to 81, with doses of **human growth hormone**, three times a week. Human growth hormone is produced in the pituitary gland and is known to decline with age. It was hypothesized that the decline of human growth hormone might be partly responsible for observed senescence so restoring higher levels through injections might reverse any decline. These dozen men showed significant change: decreased fat, increased muscle mass, and increases in skin thickness. They appeared to look younger. Very soon, however, some men developed diabetes-like symptoms, carpal tunnel syndrome, and the growth of breasts. When they stopped taking the hormones, their bodies returned to their prior states. Work by other researchers found some of the same positive effects but also some negative effects such as swollen ankles, stiffened joints, and stiff hands. Generally, the results have been very disappointing (Cohn et al., 1993; Dinsmoor, 1996; Rudman et al., 1990; Weiss & Kasmauski, 1997).

Melatonin is a hormone produced in the pineal gland located near the center of the brain. Melatonin regulates biological rhythms and has been used to help people sleep better (Garfinkel & Zisapel, 1998; Sack et al., 1997). Melatonin has been referred to as an antiaging drug and a protection against cancer. Although there is some evidence of such benefits with animals, it is possible that the obtained results may be due to lower caloric intake (Hayflick, 1996). Work with humans suggests no antiaging effects or protection against cancer (Dickey, 1996; Panzer et al., 1998).

The hormone **DHEA** (dehydroepiandrosterone), which also declines with advanced age, is being investigated. In humans, this hormone is produced in the adrenal glands and its production declines about 2 percent every year following puberty. Preliminary work with rats has found that DHEA inhibits lung, breast, and skin cancers (Hayflick, 1996; Ogin et al., 1990; Porter & Svec, 1996). Work with aging humans also seems to indicate benefits in terms of increased muscle strength, leaner body mass, and activation of immune functions (Yen et al., 1996). Some work has found that older men with the lowest levels of DHEA are much more likely to die, particularly from cardiovascular disease, than are men with higher levels (Triveldi & Khaw, 2001). Older women with some disability, those with very low or very high levels of DHEA were more likely to die over the 5-year span of a recent study (Cappola et al., 2006). In the short term, large doses of DHEA have resulted in hair loss, acne, and deepening of the voice in female users and may increase the risk of ovarian cancer (Helzlsouer, 1995; Mack, 1997). At present it appears that DHEA supplements could benefit some people while seriously hurting others. The long-term effects of DHEA supplements are not yet known.

In sum, hormone theories of aging have appeal because of the great influence of hormones on all bodily systems and organs. Such theories do not, however, have any evidence to support their claims that hormones are responsible for senescence or are able to reverse biological aging.

While biological clock, evolution, and hormone theories are programmed theories, there are theories that are not as easy to categorize. The following theory is placed in a middle category.

A Middle Category

Immune System

Like hormones from the endocrine system, the immune system exerts influence in all other systems as it functions to protect the body. A decline in the immune system is hypothesized to produce senescence in two different ways that we refer to as the leaky defense and the autoimmune hypotheses.

   The leaky defense hypothesis claims that senescence is a result of invasion by environmental toxins and organisms that damage cells, tissues, and organs throughout the body. This damage is a direct result of the less-efficient functioning of the immune system as we age. The defense is leaky and allows more invasion and, thus, damage. Some have suggested that the thymus gland, which produces T cells and slowly disappears as we grow older (see Table 4-1), may function as a biological clock; when it is gone, we die (Walford, 1969). The leaky defense theory usually is considered a programmed version of immune system theory. The immune system is programmed to deteriorate according to a predetermined schedule and that deterioration results in greater amounts of less-efficient functioning.

   The autoimmune hypothesis says that senescence and damage increase with age because the immune system begins attacking portions of the body it is meant to protect. Body tissues and organs show senescence because the body's own immune system is destroying parts of itself. It may be that the immune system is correct in attacking these body parts because they have been radically altered over time due to interactions with the environment. The alterations have made these body parts appear to be invaders. This is an unprogrammed version of immune system theory. Attacks depend on nonscheduled and damaging interactions with the environment in which one lives.

   Immune theories of senescence have some problems. We already know that the immune system declines with age. Can the immune system be causing its own senescence and then go on to damage the rest of the body or is there another cause that results in senescence in all systems? A problem for immune theories is one of determining what causes senescence in the immune system in the first place. Another problem is that the immune system may be responding correctly when it attacks its own body. The attack may be on molecular tissue that has been altered by mutation, free radicals, error, or unrepaired damage. In such a case, it would be those errors, rather than the immune system itself, that led to any observed senescence.

Unprogrammed Theories

Wear and Tear

The wear-and-tear theory claims that senescence is a result of using the body too much and of exposing it to damaging situations. In other word, the body just plain wears out. Some early views of wear and tear were based on concepts borrowed from physics. For example, the Second Law of Thermodynamics says that energy dissipates over time; this is known as **entropy**. Perhaps it is this entropy that leads to the senescence found in aging living tissue. Tissues lose energy as they are used again and again and, as a result, they become more vulnerable.

Wear-and-tear theories have no real support and several problems. First, senescence seems to be too regular to be the result of random wear and tear. Certain organs and systems are most likely to show senescence before others and the pattern of decline in many systems is not random. Second, one might think about the wear and tear that could be produced by certain behaviors such as eating fiber and roughage. It seems like these should produce considerable wear and tear on the body. They should tear the lining of the stomach and intestines and leave them more vulnerable, but such foods contribute to health rather than senescence. Third, think about the wear and tear on the muscles, lungs, and heart as we exercise, particularly if we exercise strenuously and on a regular basis. Wear-and-tear theories seem to suggest that we would be better off sitting comfortably on the couch, eating pudding. Wear and tear is a popular notion with lay people but not with most researchers (DiGiovanna, 1994).

Free Radicals

Free radical theory states that senescence is the result of damage produced by free radicals. Free radicals are atoms or molecules with an odd number of electrons and, as a result, they are very reactive and unstable. Free radicals attempt to take on an electron or contribute an electron to other molecular structures in the body and react with almost anything nearby, such as the nucleic acids of DNA and RNA, the lipids that make up the cell's membrane, or proteins that govern the functions of cells. Molecules that interact with free radicals then may cease to function or may function incorrectly (Balin, 1982; Hayflick, 1996).

Free radicals are produced during normal metabolism. The metabolic furnace that roars in the body to provide the energy needed to function also may damage the body with the waste products that result. Free radicals are one such waste product. Free radicals also result from actions of the immune system on invaders, and from exposure to sunlight and radiation. After a lifetime of metabolism, immune responses, and sunlight, the damage from free radicals may eventually result in observable senescence. The effects may accumulate the longer we live (Sohal & Allen, 1985; Weiss & Kasmauski, 1997). This theory is an unprogrammed theory, because there is no plan for senescence; it occurs as more free radicals are produced and interact with cell tissues and chemicals and result in damage. Damage is more probable as one experiences more interactions with free radicals, but damage is not certain.

The body has some defense against the action of free radicals in an enzyme known as sodium oxide dismutase (SOD). SOD sweeps up free radicals and neutralizes their action. Also, there is a relationship between the longevity of a species and the level of SOD; higher levels of SOD are generally found in long-lived species (Cunningham & Brookbank, 1988). Free radical theorists argue that the presence of SOD in the body is evidence for the harm that free radicals can produce. It would be senseless to provide a protection against some agent that could cause no harm. Some work has, however, shown that an abundance of SOD does not increase length of life for mice (Huang et al., 2000).

PROJECT **4**

This project is designed to illustrate how random events such as DNA damage and/or free radical damage and/or damage from accumulated garbage could result in fairly regular patterns of senescence. This project is best done with a group of individuals.

Prepare the materials. Write the names of 10 errors on 10 different pieces of paper. Five of them are meaningless errors, and you should just write something like "oops." These are errors resulting from a metabolic mistake, free radicals interacting with some body protein, or a "bump" from accumulated garbage but one from which no damage occurs. On the other five pieces of paper, write the following errors that result in senescence: senescence to the arteries, senescence to the lungs, senescence to the skin, senescence to the bones, and senescence to the muscles. Put all 10 pieces of paper in a box, hat, or bag so that they can't be seen.

Have several individuals draw papers from the hat, write down the errors as their own, and return them to the hat before the next person draws. Each draw can count as a 2-year period. People are 60 years old when they start, and after five draws are 70. Thus, everyone will draw five papers to get from 60 to 70 years of age. This random assignment of errors will result in some individuals who have very little senescence, others with quite a lot, and most with a moderate amount. Although the draws from the hat are random, the obtained patterns of senescence are quite regular. Why? How did you fare?

A variation of this game is played by allowing individuals to draw the same error more than once or by making them draw a different piece of paper if they already drew one in a previous draw. Allowing them to draw the same senescence result more than once can be described as "three strikes and you are out." If they draw "senescence to the arteries" once, then they are said to have experienced a heart attack and must take it easy. If twice, then they have had major heart surgery. If three times, then they are no longer with us. The same rule applies to the other senescence events for lungs, skin, bones, and muscles.

Free radicals are neutralized by antioxidants, which are chemicals that inhibit oxygen from combining with susceptible molecules to produce free radicals. A normal, healthy diet contains a number of antioxidants, such as beta-carotene and vitamins C and E. Studies of animals given higher levels of antioxidants in their diet have found that the animals live longer than control animals not given the extra antioxidants. Mice, for example, can live 30 percent longer. Such studies are difficult to evaluate because the higher levels of antioxidants often suppress appetite, and many of the animals eat less. It may be less eating, rather than or in addition to the higher level of antioxidants, that is responsible for longer life (Yu, 1995). Some work with humans has examined the relationship between certain antioxidants in the blood of older individuals and their level of independence; individuals with higher levels of the antioxidant lycopene seem to be more independent than those with lower levels (Snowdon et al., 1996).

Although the evidence for free radicals as the cause of senescence is indirect, the theory has been well accepted in and out of the scientific community. Clearly free radicals can cause damage, bodies do have a built-in protection, and some work even has found higher free radical levels in older animals (Balin, 1982). Of course, it is possible that those higher levels are the result of senescence rather than the cause.

Garbage Accumulation

Garbage accumulation theories suggest that over time, garbage from the environment accumulates in the cells and tissues and eventually results in senescence. It is not that the materials accumulated are necessarily toxic but that their mere presence interferes with normal cellular processes. At some point, after decades of such accumulation, cells and tissues break down under the load of accumulated garbage. If the theory is correct, then we ought to be able to find much higher levels of waste in older cells, tissues, and organs. In some cases we do.

We know that **lipofuscin** accumulates. Lipofuscin is composed of a number of metabolic waste products and accumulates in various cells throughout the body. Cells cannot eliminate it and lipofuscin appears as a dark pigment in older cells on the skin, the heart, and the brain. Such spots on the skin are referred to as liver spots. Although it is true that this particular garbage accumulates with age, it is not clear whether it results in any damage. At present, the answer seems to be that it does not.

Amyloid protein is a byproduct of normal metabolism and is found throughout the body. It accumulates between the cells in the brain, heart, and other organs. One type, beta amyloid, plays a major role in Alzheimer's disease discussed in Chapter 12—however, we must be cautious because senescence is not a disease like Alzheimer's. It is increased vulnerability. Furthermore, ordinary amyloid seems to produce no ill effects.

In short, garbage accumulation theories point to a number of substances that accumulate with age and suggest that such accumulation is the cause of senescence. Strong

SOCIAL POLICY APPLICATIONS

In this chapter, you have seen what is known so far about how and why people age. Clearly more research is needed to give a clearer picture of senescence. Despite this, research has spawned many products with dubious claims to reverse or prevent aging. When you combine the negative attitudes toward aging that exist (see Chapter 1) with the easy availability of various antiaging products, including supplements, lotions, and even beverages, people in today's youth-oriented society can fall prey to these claims. They want products that are antiaging even though there is no accepted definition of antiaging or other such claims. Furthermore, the term "antiaging" carries very negative connotations. Aging must be something very awful if so much are against it. Some say we need to eliminate the term antiaging completely and rely solely on research terms, for example, antioxidant. There is some merit in this approach because it is more factually based and less prejudicial. Many say that if we are to fight prejudice, we need to start with the words we use. We think, however, that some of the negative connotation might vanish if we had an agreed upon definition of antiaging. To this end, we need to be proactive with companies that are currently selling, or who wish to sell in the future, antiaging products and urge them to endorse a unified definition of the term antiaging based on research. If companies, large and small, would support basic research, going beyond testing their own products, society could move much faster with breakthroughs in the aging field and people might understand that antiaging is really an attempt to prolong health. Advocate for uniform definitions and ask corporations to help sponsor basic research in senescence.

supporting evidence for these interesting theories has not been found. There does not seem to be enough garbage accumulation to produce the senescence that occurs and the garbage accumulation that does occur doesn't seem greater in tissues showing senescence than in those not showing it.

DNA Damage and Repair

DNA damage and repair theories come in several different forms. We will describe one of the simpler versions. As you probably know, all of the information to generate a complete organism is carried on that organism's DNA. Cloning (and *Jurassic Park*, Crichton, 1990) depends on this. Cells do not, however, need the complete DNA molecule to function. There is no need for a liver cell to know how to build and function like cells in the kidneys, heart, skin, lungs, or brain. Only a small portion of DNA is actually used by the cells of various tissues while the remaining, close to 95 percent, can be ignored. One form of DNA repair theory says that cells receive the wrong instructions from their small portion of the DNA strand and that this results in the production of aberrant cells, incorrect structures, and the wrong chemicals and, finally, senescence. Why do cells receive the wrong instructions? Perhaps they do this because the DNA no longer carries the correct information. It has been damaged over time by exposure to radiation from the sun, the actions of free radicals, exposure to toxins and pollutants, and other damaging environmental conditions. In some cases, the damage is unimportant because it is on a part of the DNA strand that is ignored by those particular cells but in other cases the damage is on the crucial part. Thankfully cells have DNA repair units to mend damaged DNA and prevent errors in producing new cells and chemicals.

Much of the work on this theory has focused on these DNA repair units to see if they decline with age. If so, then that decline might be a reason for senescence. DNA repair units are measured by damaging cells, usually with ultraviolet radiation, and then monitoring repair. Some early work showed that long-lived species have more repair units than short-lived species (Hart & Setlow, 1982) but, while that is interesting, it is not the important question for the theory. Researchers want to know if there are fewer repair units for older members of a single species. Work with dogs and with mice suggests that the answer is yes (Modak et al., 1986; Cabelof et al., 2006, respectively). There also is some work with human cells that examined postmortem tissue from the frontal cortex in 30 deceased individuals between the ages of 26 and 106. The research found little DNA damage among the brains of the young (those less than 40), great damage among the brains of the old (older than 70) but considerable diversity among the brains of the middle-aged individuals. It is possible that DNA repair begins to decline rapidly in some middle-aged people and that if researchers could detect this early decline, they might be able to delay senescence (Lu et al., 2004).

All (Many) of the Above

Clearly, no theory, at present, has much support. It is probably unwise to assume that senescence in all different cells, tissues, and organs has a single cause. Some instances of senescence may result from multiple causes, or causes may be linked to one another. Researchers are beginning to look at the interactions among several of these different theories (Torre et al., 1997).

We have thought about the connections among these different theories. In Figure 4-2, seven of the theories are included (we have not included wear and tear) and arrows connecting them suggest possible causal links. The theories at the top are all programmed theories and some think they may share a connecting link through the evolution theory. If one believes that humans are programmed to live long enough to produce offspring and that when those years are over, they are set to deteriorate and die, then connections between evolution theory and biological clock, hormone, and immune system theories all seem possible. These other theories may specify the deterioration predicted by evolution theory.

At the middle and bottom are unprogrammed theories. Others think a connecting link could be provided by free radical theory. Damage from free radicals may build up over a long life and lead to damaged DNA, the accumulation of certain types of garbage, a breakdown in immune system protection, and a decline in the production of certain hormones. Free radical damage can be hypothesized to underlie all sorts of senescence in the body.

As you consider these theories and the possible connections among them, keep in mind that the research evidence is conflicting. More needs to be done.

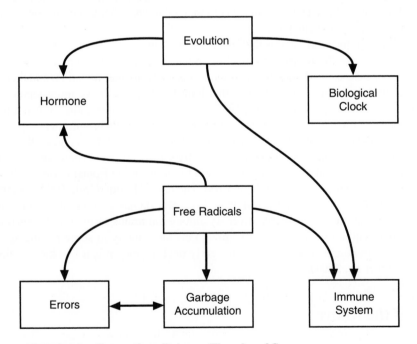

FIGURE 4-2   Connections Between Theories of Senescence.

CHAPTER HIGHLIGHTS

- There are a number of theories that attempt to explain senescence but none have strong supporting evidence.
- All theories must deal with great variability in length of life and degree of senescence among different species, some of which seem to show very little senescence (e.g., turtles); variability within a species, and variability across different environments.
- Programmed theories suggest that senescence is predetermined by a plan and occurs on a relatively fixed schedule. The following three theories are programmed theories.
- Biological clock theory says that senescence is determined in the genes. The latest version of this theory says that senescence begins when cells stop dividing which occurs when telomere sequences at the end of DNA strands become sufficiently shortened.
- Evolution theory says that humans are programmed to deteriorate and die after they reproduce and raise their offspring. Certain genes that result in productivity may also lead to lower levels of protection against senescence, causing environmental factors.
- Hormone theories say that glands are programmed to end production of certain hormones and that the lower levels of these hormones produce senescence.
- Immune system theories claim that decline in the immune system produces senescence.
- Unprogrammed theories say that there is no plan for senescence, and that it occurs as a result of interactions with the environment and/or between environmental and genetic factors. The following four theories are unprogrammed.
- The wear-and-tear theory claims that the body wears out from a lifetime of use.
- The free radical theory says that reactive molecules produced during metabolism, exposure to radiation, and actions of the immune systems produce senescence by damaging the molecules that make up important chemicals, tissues, cells, and proteins in the body.
- Garbage accumulation theories say that waste products accumulate over time, damage tissues, and interfere with the normal functioning of the body resulting in senescence.
- The DNA damage and repair theory says that as people age we have fewer repair units to fix the damage caused by environmental agents. The cells then follow incorrect instructions from this damaged DNA and the result is senescence.
- It is most probable that no individual theory explains all of senescence and, it is more likely that some combination of them, perhaps with theories not yet known, will be the best description of the causes of senescence.

STUDY QUESTIONS

1. Do the lives of turtles offer strong support for a biological/genetic theory of senescence? Why or why not?

2. Describe the theory (theories) that claims that senescence is entirely genetic. Entirely environmental?

3. What evidence is there for the notion that senescence is due to both genetic and environmental factors?

4. Is the length of a young organism's dependence on parental care related to the life expectancy of that species?

5. How can random errors in DNA replication, or free radical damage result in regular patterns of senescence?

6. Distinguish between programmed and unprogrammed theories of senescence. Describe several theories of each type explaining why they are regarded as programmed or unprogrammed theories. What support exists for these theories?

7. Is evolution theory a programmed or unprogrammed theory? Why?

8. Can you find and describe connecting links among all seven theories?

RECOMMENDED READINGS

Hayflick, L. (1996). *How and Why We Age*. New York: Ballantine Books. Hayflick provides a very readable view of the factors that may produce senescence and a broader discussion of the points made in this chapter.

Ferrini, A. F., & Ferrini, R. L. (1993). *Health in the Later Years* (2nd ed.). Madison, WI: Brown & Benchmark. The Ferrinis present a condensed version of many of the theories described in this chapter.

Kirkwood, T. (1999). *Time of Our Lives*. New York: Oxford University Press. Tom Kirkwood presents a stimulating discussion of aging and attempts to combine many of the theories presented in this chapter. We think some such combination is inevitable.

INTERNET RESOURCES

www.experiencefestival.com/a/Aging. Once you arrive at this site you will have to search for theories of aging. The site discusses a number of theories including many discussed here.

If you simply use a search engine such as Google for the phrase "senescence theory," you will find thousands of sites, most of which discuss a single theory.

5 Health and Longevity

I don't want to achieve immortality through my work. . . .
I want to achieve it through not dying.

—*Woody Allen*

Immortality is not something that any of us will achieve by not dying no matter how hard we try. We might, however, delay that dying by being blessed with the right genes and making the right choices. In this chapter we explore the factors that influence health and longevity; that influence not dying.

Longevity depends on remaining healthy. Many of the factors discussed are beyond the control of individuals. Genetic inheritance and gender are two such factors. Other factors such as diet, exercise, and smoking are yours to manipulate to your advantage, although not many people do so. Finally, some factors beyond our control are associated with factors that are potentially within our control. Factors like race and socioeconomic status (SES) may influence health and longevity because of differences in behavior, nutrition, and access to health services. There is no magic formula for living a long, healthy life but there are a number of things that you can do to increase the odds in your favor. People have looked for ways to lengthen their life as long as there have been people and some of the stranger ways to do this are discussed in Box 5-1. We will look at more realistic methods and at the end of the chapter we will briefly examine the quality of life for very old adults to see if living long is worth the effort.

Overview

The desire to live a long and healthy life is an old one. A myth from ancient Greece relates that there was a place in the world where people, favored by the gods, lived long healthy lives. Although there is no spot on earth where people do not age, there are huge differences in longevity around the globe. Japan is the world leader in terms of life expectancy. The life expectancy for men in Japan is 76.6 and for women 83. The longevity of residents of Japan also is evident when one examines the large number of centenarians. **Centenarians** are people who are 100 years and older and Japan has over 28,000, of whom about 85 percent are women. Out of every 100,000 residents, 22 are 100 or older, while

B O X   **5-1**

Increasing Longevity in WEIRD Ways

One of the very first attempts to increase length of life (or at least one of the first to be written down, in the *Ebers papyrus*, 1600 BC) was the ancient Egyptian practice of *eating the internal organs of young animals*. Although no evidence was obtained to show that this worked, the idea hung around. In the late nineteenth century, an older (he was 72) French physician named Brown-Séquard told other prominent people how he *injected the crushed testicles of puppies* into his arms and legs. He claimed it had restored his youth and that he was now able to pay a visit to his young wife. Although there was an initial rush to find crushed puppy testicles, the fad did not last and the professor lost his reputation, young wife, and died of a stroke shortly thereafter.

Some ancient Chinese (those with sufficient funds) believed that *drinking tiny pieces of gold* mixed in a medicine could result in long life. The gold, however, could not be gold from your vault or mine but must instead be gold that was made from mercury! A person transformed mercury into gold, put that gold in a medicine, drank it, and then, and only then, would live for a long, long time. Many of these practitioners are believed to have died from mercury poisoning.

George van Tassel was a test pilot for Howard Hughes who quit his job and moved to Landers, California, near Giant Rock. Giant Rock is a huge (7 stories high) boulder that was once considered sacred by Native Americans. He changed his life, got into meditation, and was visited by aliens from Venus. These aliens told him the secret of regenerating cells and living a long life so he spent the next 18 years building *the Integratron*. The Integratron is a 50-foot diameter, 38-foot-high wooden dome made from Douglas firs with no metal fittings. Inside the dome, a turbine generated electricity and walking around the device would regenerate one's cells. Van Tassel said "the purpose of the Integratron is to recharge energy into living cell structure, to bring about longer life with youthful energy." Sadly he died in 1978 before completing the dome and some say that is why it does not work.

Source: Cohen (2000).

only 10 of every 100,000 U.S. residents live that long. In Okinawa, 54 of every 100,000 make it that far; Okinawa has the longest lived residents on the planet.

The life expectancies for men and women in the United States are 71.8 and 78.8, respectively. Within the United States, residents of Hawaii live the longest while residents of Washington, D.C., have the shortest average lives. The life expectancy for men and women in D.C. are 62 and 74.2, respectively (Kranczer, 1998). Of course, life expectancy estimates change for each new cohort. Today life expectancy in the United States is estimated to be 77.9.

Clearly people in different places have different life expectancies and this suggests a strong environmental influence that may be within one's control. At the same time, women usually live longer than men and this suggests a genetic factor beyond personal control. As we examine these and other factors, we will see that it is not quite that simple. For example, the long lives of those living in Okinawa seems to be due in large part to genetics while the short lives of men seems to be due in part to the behaviors they engage in (Willcox et al., 2006).

Factors Beyond One's Control

If you were born with a congenital heart condition would that affect your longevity? Probably yes. You would probably die sooner than a person born without such a condition, but that condition could be due to genetics or to your prenatal environment or both. It is not always easy to determine whether nature or nurture are more important.

Genes influence life expectancy indirectly and it is likely that many genes are involved (Carnes et al., 1999). Genes influence susceptibility to a number of diseases, influence behavioral and biochemical responses to stress, and may influence personality characteristics, such as risk-taking behavior, for example. It is estimated that about 25 to 35 percent of the variability in human longevity is directly attributable to genetic factors (Vaupel et al., 1998; Finch & Tanzi, 1997).

A typical method for assessing the relative influence of genetic factors has been to examine the longevity of a large sample of individuals and then correlate the lengths of those lives with the lives of their parents and grandparents. For example, almost one quarter of the immediate ancestors of Jeanne Calment, lived more than 80 years. In a comparison group of shorter-lived individuals, only 2 percent of immediate ancestors lived that long (Robine & Allard, 1998). Long-lived people tend to have long-lived ancestors. An investigation examined the longevity of 8409 men and 3741 women of European royal and noble families (because such families kept extensive records). Results showed that 18 to 34 percent of male longevity and 20 to 58 percent of female longevity was accounted for

Four generations of a Cakchiquel Mayan family in Guatemala.

by the longevity of their fathers. The influence of genetic factors was highest when fathers lived past the age of 70 (Gavrilova et al., 1998).

Other work suggests that the maternal influence on longevity is greatest when deaths from cardiovascular diseases are examined, and that the longevity of grandmothers on both sides of the family is predictive of the longevity of grandchildren (Brand et al., 1992; Vandenbroucke, 1998). The influence of the mother and grandmother on the longevity of offspring had been assumed for a long time (Pearls, 1931), but the genetic influence on longevity comes from both sides of the family and may be slightly higher for the paternal side (Gavrilov et al., 1998). Regardless of which side of the family exerts the most influence, longevity clearly runs in families.

Other researchers have compared DNA samples from centenarians to younger adults of the same gender, health, and sometimes geographic origin. Comparisons were made between DNA samples. This work has produced mixed results. The genes that are most strongly related to heart disease do not differ between centenarians and younger comparison groups (Bladbjerg et al., 1999). On the other hand, one type of protein found in the blood has been found to be more frequent in centenarians than in a comparison group (Thillet et al., 1998). Another group of researchers compared 212 centenarians with 275 younger adults and found differences in mitochondrial DNA (de Benedictis et al., 1999). Mitochondria are microscopic bodies found in the cells of living organisms that convert food to usable energy. Animal studies of mitochondria suggest that they are more likely than other structures to be damaged by free radicals. Perhaps some forms of inherited mitochondria are less susceptible to such damage (Schäcter, 1998). Other work has identified a gene (YTHDF2) that is more similar in centenarians and more variable in younger adults. This gene may be involved in glucose metabolism and, thus, influence longevity through metabolism (Cardelli et al., 2006). Those who inherit the right form live longer. Finally, some work has examined the presence of different forms of the apolipoprotein E (Apo-E) in different aged adults. The Apo-E protein functions to transport cholesterol in the body and comes in three different types: Apo-E 2, Apo-E 3, and Apo-E 4. A person inherits one type from the mother and one from the father so that person could be a 2-2, 2-3, 2-4, 3-3, 3-4, or 4-4 combination. The presence of Apo-E 2 is much greater in older men, including centenarians, than in men under the age of 60 (Seripa et al., 2006). Whether this type somehow promotes longevity or whether another type (we will look at Apo-E 4 in Chapter 12) increases the risk of cardiovascular disease is not clear but the type inherited clearly plays some role in longevity (Johnson et al., 2003).

Besides genetics, other factors such as gender and race are also beyond our control but their influence on longevity may be potentially controllable.

Factors Within One's Control

If you were born in Japan and moved to India, would your life expectancy change? Would it depend on how old you were when you moved? If you answered yes to these questions then you must believe that the environment in which we live contributes to longevity—and it does. Many researchers argue that genes play an important role but place no firm limit on how long a person might live (Finch, 1998). Given a perfect environment (whatever that might be) humans might live for a very long time.

The relative impact of genes and environment can be assessed by studying twins as well as by looking at the longevity of immediate ancestors. A major study of identical twins reared together or apart and fraternal twins reared together or apart looked at mortality rates. The influence of genes on longevity is assessed by comparing individuals with the same genetic inheritance (identical twins) to individuals without identical genetic inheritance (fraternal twins) to see whether the twins died closely together. If those with the same genes died closely together while those with different genes did not, then that would support a genetic influence. The influence of environment is assessed by comparing those reared together and, thus, having similar although not identical environments to those reared apart. If those from the same environment died close together while those from different environments did not, then that would support an environmental influence. The findings suggest that longevity is largely determined by environmental factors with a minimum of 66 percent of the variance in longevity due to environmental, rather than genetic, influences (Ljungquist et al., 1998). This estimate is virtually the same as that provided earlier and taken from the studies of ancestors. It is clear that environmental factors strongly influence longevity. This is good news for all wanting to live longer. We examine the influence of a few of the more well-known environmental factors: diet, exercise, supplements, tobacco, alcohol, and stress.

Diet

The relationship between diet and longevity has been examined in animals more than in humans. Animal studies usually compare animals who have experienced restricted diets to those who have had no restrictions while human studies usually correlate longevity with **body mass index (BMI)**. BMI is used rather than weight because it takes height and weight into account. For a description of how to calculate your own body mass index, see Box 5-2.

The research on the health and longevity of animals raised under different levels of calorie-restricted diets has produced positive results for over 70 years. Although most of these studies have examined mice and rats, the benefits of caloric restriction also have been found for fruit flies, spiders, water fleas, guppies, protozoa, monkeys, and many more species (Masoro, 2002; Sell et al., 1996; Weindruch, 1996). With caloric restriction, a wide range of ordinary age changes are slowed down, age-related diseases are often postponed or slowed down, and restricted rats outperform well-fed rats on measures of learning and coordination (Ingram et al., 1987). These benefits are stronger for rats that are not well exercised, showing that exercise also increases longevity (Holloszy, 1998). Some recent work suggests that the benefits derived from caloric restriction occur because such restriction results in lower levels of oxidative damage (Faulks et al., 2006). This is similar to the kind of damage produced by free radicals.

It is unethical to conduct such calorie-restriction research with humans. Can you imagine signing up to participate in a study in which your current caloric intake would be cut by 30 to 60 percent for the rest of your life? Yet, many of us do try to cut our intake and with good reason. It's estimated that over 67 percent of Americans are overweight and about 25 percent are obese (Ravussin, 2005) and these numbers have increased since 1995. About 25 percent of men and 40 percent of women are actively trying to lose excess weight and quite a lot of research suggests that is the right thing to do (Serdula et al., 1994).

Senior View

Dr. Walter Donham was in very good health and 70 years old when we spoke with him about longevity. Dr. Donham received his doctorate in chemical engineering from the Ohio State University and then worked for Ethel Corporation in Baton Rouge, Louisiana, for 37 years. Walter and his wife are now retired. When we arrived at his home for the interview, he was repairing his roof.

When asked about genetic influences on longevity, Walter said that, *most of my older relatives have lived quite long. My maternal grandfather lived to be 98 and both of my paternal grandparents lived to their late 80s. My own mother died at 93 but my father died at 54 from a heart attack. I know several people who are 94 or 95 and I hope to make it to 100.*

Exercise also is important. Walter said, *my wife and I walk one mile a day, 4 or 5 days a*

week. On two other days, I work for Habitat for Humanity doing general carpentry. I don't do much lifting though because my shoulder has been a little sore lately. My doctor told me to start lifting 3 to 5 pound weights, 30–40 times each day but I haven't been very diligent about following his advice.

Diet is yet another important factor: *Most afternoons I eat an apple for a snack. I don't really believe in all those so-called benefits from various herbs but I have begun taking a multivitamin every day.*

Alcohol also influences longevity. *The wife and I don't drink very much. I have a bottle of wine in there and it's likely to last a year. Drinking is just not one of our habits but I see no harm in having a glass of wine each day. Most people who get in trouble with alcohol, start early in life. In small amounts, it has some benefits. It apparently thins the blood slightly. That helps prevent clotting, heart attacks, and strokes.*

Doesn't aspirin do the same thing? *I won't use aspirin because it thins my blood too much. If I take aspirin very often and scratch myself, I bleed very easily so I don't take aspirin on a regular basis.*

The most important things for maintaining good health and living to 100 are exercise, diet, and having good genes; that's really what it gets down to. Also important is mental stimulation. It is very important for maintaining good health. Being physically and mentally active is a necessity to a long life. As you will see many researchers would agree with Dr. Donham.

As we were leaving, Walter was climbing back on his roof to finish his repairs.

Both low and high BMIs are dangerous. A BMI of less than 20 has been associated with increased risk of death, particularly death from respiratory causes (Adams et al., 2006; Jee et al., 2006). Obesity, defined as a BMI of 30 or more, is strongly associated with early death, particularly from diabetes, cancer, and cardiovascular disease (Adams et al., 2006; Jee et al., 2006; Manson et al., 1995). Obese individuals increase their risk of death by two to three times. Recent work shows that even being overweight rather than obese (BMI of 25 to 29.9) results in a 40 percent increase in the risk of early death (Adams et al., 2006). In an examination of longevity, 2000 Japanese American men were followed for

36 years. Those with below-average caloric intake had the lowest death rate over this time period; their average BMI was 23.9 (Willcox et al., 2004). Men and women of all ethnic groups with high BMIs die sooner and women are more likely than men to be obese or underweight (Wray et al., 2005).

Why do very high or very low BMIs shorten life? There are several possible answers to that question. In an examination of white blood cells in over a thousand women, obesity was strongly associated with shorter telomeres (Valdes et al., 2005). If telomere length functions like a biological clock, then any shortening might result in earlier death (see Chapter 4). A high BMI also might be viewed as only one part of an overall lifestyle that includes little exercise or any physical activity (Simoes et al., 1995). Such individuals are likely to lose bone density and muscle fibers at a much higher rate. A very low BMI may indicate poor nutrition and be indicative of an eating disorder such as anorexia or bulimia. Each person should strive to reach a normal BMI of 18.5 to 24.9. What is your BMI?

Of course, it is not always easy to bring your BMI down (or up if very low) even though there are dozens of diet plans to follow, pills to pop, surgical procedures to undergo, and exercise regimens to undertake. Some argue that the problem is largely genetic and, thus, very difficult to manage. For example, some comparisons of people with high and with normal BMIs show that normal weighted individuals have nonexercise activity thermogenesis (NEAT). **NEAT** refers to unplanned physical activities like fidgeting, walking, gesturing, standing, and other daily activities (Ravussin, 2005). In one study, 10 thin and 10 obese persons were monitored for body posture and movements over a 10-day period. On average, the obese individuals were sitting 2 hours longer every day than the thin individuals. The researchers estimate that, if the obese individuals moved as much as the thin persons, they would burn an additional 350 calories each day. In another study, obese persons were put on a diet for 2 months while thinner persons were overfed for those 2 months. The obese lost weight and the thin gained weight but both groups maintained their original NEAT suggesting that these activities are built in rather than a result of some environmental factors (Levine et al., 2005). We might all lose weight if we just moved and fidgeted a little more but it would still be important to watch what we eat.

Some research suggests that dietary restriction can help protect older adults from the effects of degenerative diseases (like cancer) but may increase the risk of mortality in younger adults by making them more vulnerable to infectious diseases (like the flu) (Pletcher et al., 2000). Dieting is not to be taken lightly. Everyone, old or young, must be very careful to get the right nutrition in their diet. The wrong diet can produce frailty in older adults. **Frailty** is defined as the combination of feelings of exhaustion, low physical activity, poor muscle strength, and very slow walking speed. An examination of diet and frailty in over a thousand older adults found that low intake of protein and of vitamins C, D, and E was strongly associated with increased frailty (Bartali et al., 2006). Related work has found that vitamin E reduces senescence in the nervous system (Martin et al., 2000) but does not reduce the risk of cardiovascular disease and cancer (Lee et al., 2005). Other work has suggested vitamin E as the source for far less mental decline in those who consume more than two servings of vegetables, especially leafy greens like spinach, per day (Morris et al., 2006). Another nutrient, omega-3, found in fish and also in flax seed, appears to reduce the risk of cardiovascular disease. Fish highest in omega-3 are salmon, sardines, and herring. However, one must be careful of mercury levels, which are generally higher in larger predatory fish such as sharks and swordfish, but researchers believe that the benefits outweigh the risks (Mozaffarian & Rimm, 2006). Table 5-1 gives some of the specifics on where to find essential nutrients and the benefits that seem to occur with their intake.

In sum, we want to maintain a BMI somewhere in the normal range while making sure that we get all of the essential nutrients. The U.S. Department of Health and Human Services recommends a diet rich in grains and sparse in fats, oils, and sweets; these recommendations are shown in the traditional food pyramid of Figure 5-1 and readers are advised to examine the newer versions at www.mypyramid.gov. Some research, however, suggests that certain sweets may not be so harmful as long as you don't overdo it (see Box 5-3). The diet recommendations for older adults are essentially the same as for younger adults although increased intake of calcium, fiber, and protein and decreased vitamin A often are recommended for older adults. One caution, however, watching what we eat, following these recommendations, and trying to lower the BMI can be stressful. Recent work with postmenopausal women has found elevated levels of stress in women worried about their weight and trying to restrict their diet (Rideout et al., 2006). As soon noted, stress is not beneficial for longevity.

TABLE 5-1   The Benefits of Vitamins

Vitamin	Where Found	Possible Benefits
A	Dairy products and eggs	Eye health and helps skin retain moisture
B_1 (Thiamine)	Beans, fish, oatmeal, nuts, raisins	Nerve function
B_2 (Riboflavin)	Dairy, eggs, grains, some vegetables	Reduces homocysteine (see Chapter 3)
B_3 (Niacin)	Beans, dairy, eggs, fish, nuts	Lowers bad cholesterol
B_6	Bananas, brown rice, cabbage, carrots	Heart and nerve function
B_{12}	Dairy, fish, meat	Reduce risk of cancer and heart disease
C	Green peppers, broccoli, citrus, leafy greens	Strong blood vessels; reduce cancer risk
D	Sunlight, egg yolk	Absorption of calcium
E	Almonds, rice, oatmeal	Reduce risk of nerve senescence and some visual disorders (see Chapter 6)
Folic acid	Citrus, leafy greens, peas	Reduce risk of some cancers and birth defects
Lycopene	Tomatoes, watermelon	Reduce risk of some cancers
Omega-3	Fish, flax	Reduce risk of cardiovascular disease

Source: Norton (2002).

BOX 5-2

Determining Your Body Mass Index

Body mass index (BMI) is found by dividing your weight in kilograms by your height in meters squared. A relatively quick and easy way to compute BMI without converting to metric measures is to take your weight in pounds and divide by your height in inches squared. Multiply that answer by 703 and you have your BMI.

$$\text{BMI} = \frac{\text{Weight in pounds}}{(\text{height in inches})^2} \times 703$$

For example, if you are 5 feet 3 inches, then your height in inches would be 63 (i.e., 5 feet × 12 inches per foot = 60 + 3 inches = 63). Your height squared would be 63 × 63 = 3969. If you weighed 120 pounds, then your BMI would be 120/3969 × 703 or 21.25.

A BMI between 18.5 and 24.9 is considered normal and healthy. Anything less than that is dangerous. An overweight BMI is 25 to 29.9 and obese is 30 and over.

If this math is intimidating, go to the website of the National Heart, Lung, and Blood Institute and your BMI will be calculated for you: *www.nhlbisupport.com/bmi/bmicalc.htm.*

Exercise

Exercise, usually is divided into two types: aerobic and resistance. **Aerobic exercise** consists of activities that increase heart rate like jogging, biking, dancing, and swimming. **Resistance exercise** is muscle training involving pushing or pulling against a force as in weight lifting. Many exercise routines are composed of both types. Aerobic exercise promotes blood flow and resistance exercise strengthens bones and muscles. Together they promote flexible joints and a healthy heart while reducing hypertension and the risks of adult-onset diabetes, cancer, and osteoporosis. Regular exercise may reduce anxiety and depression (see Chapter 12) and increase cognition (Colcombe & Kramer, 2003). Exercise even increases feelings of self-efficacy and well-being (Netz et al., 2005). Those who exercise feel more competent and in control. Exercise is a major factor in increasing health and longevity (Cress et al., 1999; Lee & Paffenbarger, 1992).

Some researchers go so far as to claim that much of the senescence that appears to come with advanced age really is due to a failure to continue using the body in effective ways (Peeke, 2005). This is particularly true for muscles and bones (see Chapter 3) and this loss of muscle strength and bone density is referred to as **hypokinesia**; it is thought to be a major contributor to functional decline. People become sedentary and, as a result, become frail. The effects of not exercising increase past the age of 50 so it is even more important for middle-aged and older adults to exercise on a regular basis although it is, of course, important for everyone.

A number of studies have examined the effects of exercise programs on older adults. In one study, several thousand older adults in Dallas were followed for 8 years and at the end of that time, the death rate in the least-fit group was more than double that in the most-fit group. The differences were primarily in deaths from heart disease and cancer (Blair et

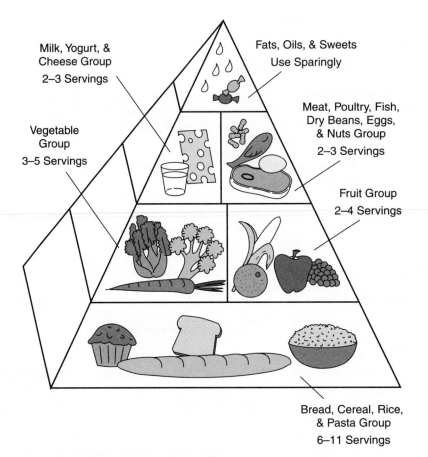

Milk, Yogurt, &
Cheese Group
2–3 Servings

Fats, Oils, & Sweets
Use Sparingly

Vegetable
Group
3–5 Servings

Meat, Poultry, Fish,
Dry Beans, Eggs,
& Nuts Group
2–3 Servings

Fruit Group
2–4 Servings

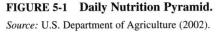

Bread, Cereal, Rice,
& Pasta Group
6–11 Servings

FIGURE 5-1   Daily Nutrition Pyramid.

Source: U.S. Department of Agriculture (2002).

al., 1989). Other work with older adults has found increases in oxygen consumption, muscle strength, flexibility, endurance, and coordination for those who exercised at least three times a week for only 4 to 6 months (Cress et al., 1999; Lazowski et al., 1999). More recent work has found that aerobic and resistance exercises improved the metabolism of glucose in older men who were overweight or obese. Improved glucose metabolism reduces the risk of diabetes and cardiovascular disease (Ferrara et al., 2006).

Exercise also has been used to reduce frailty. Frail adults usually do not exercise. A study of frail residents of nursing homes found that fewer than 20 percent were physically active and those who were active had a much lower mortality rate (Landi et al., 2004). In another study, frail residents of nursing homes randomly were assigned to one of three resistance exercise groups: high-intensity, low-moderate intensity, or no exercise. Exercise

BOX **5-3**

Sweets for the Sweet

Most dieticians and nutritionists recommend avoiding too much sugar. A common assumption is that chocolates, candy, and other sweets are never good, always harmful, and should be avoided. Dentists say candy causes tooth decay, and they are undoubtedly right that candy does contribute to the growth of cavity-producing bacteria. Many people believe that sugar makes kids hyperactive, but they are wrong. Research evidence indicates no relationship between hyperactivity and sugar consumption. Perhaps these findings mean that candy in some instances may not be a bad thing. But is it ever a good thing?

One study suggests that might be true. Candy consumption was examined in 7841 men who had no heart disease or cancer when the study was initiated. Participants were between the ages of 60 and 72 and were asked about their consumption of candy, cigarettes, red meat, alcohol, vegetables, and vitamins over a year's time. Death rates were followed from 1988 to 1993 and 7.5 percent of those who did not consume candy died while only 5.9 percent of candy consumers died. Candy consumers were less likely to smoke, drank less alcohol, ate more red meat and vegetables, and were less likely to take vitamins. Both groups had the same levels of physical activity. On average, candy consumers lived almost a year longer than those who did not consume candy (Lee & Paffenbarger, 1998).

Chocolate, particularly dark chocolate, may also be beneficial (Kirschbaum, 1998). Dark chocolate contains flavonoids that stimulate antioxidant and blood clot inhibiting effects in the blood; platelets do not stick to one another as well after a small amount of dark chocolate (Becker et al., 2006; Rein et al., 2000). The possible benefits of candy are not easy for many professionals to swallow but the majority of folks probably welcome this news.

---

intensity was determined by first measuring the maximum weight in an ankle cuff that could be lifted one time when the person was seated. High-intensity exercisers were trained at 80 percent of their maximum weight while low-moderate exercisers were trained at 40 percent. All exercisers performed three sets of eight lifts, three times a week for 10 weeks. At the end, both exercise groups improved in the distance they could walk in a short period of time, their stair-climbing ability, the time they took to rise from a chair, and overall strength and endurance; improvement was greatest for the high-intensity group (Seynnes et al., 2004).

Clearly exercise is beneficial, yet estimates suggest that only about 10 to 15 percent of older adults engage in regular aerobic and/or resistance exercises. Exercise takes motivation and self-discipline. In one examination of the leisure activities that very old adults (85 and older) are most interested in and do on a regular basis, exercise was ranked very low. Older adults generally were not motivated to exercise and did not see any benefits for people their age (Nilsson et al., 2006). Researchers know, however, that the benefits of exercise do not depend on how old you are and work such as this reveals a need for educational interventions for older adults. Other work has looked at the influence of recommendations to exercise given by physicians to sedentary middle-aged and older adults. Over a 6-week period following their physician's recommendation, adults increased their walking and other physical activity more than a group who received no such recommendation (Calfas et al., 1996). Education about exercise and a recommendation from a respected authority like a physician might go far in promoting exercise for older adults.

The barriers to exercise that are named by older adults are large in number. Even older adults who are aware of the benefits of exercise say they feel self-conscious about exercising, lack the self-discipline to stick with it, don't find it to be an interesting activity, have no one to exercise with, do not enjoy it, cannot find the time, and do not know how to exercise properly (Dergance et al., 2003). The easiest way for most people to begin is to start walking or to increase the walking already done. Walking is regarded as good aerobic exercise as long as one walks briskly. Once exercise is begun, however, exercising with others appears to be beneficial for keeping the person involved. In the words of one woman: "I don't make time unless I have a specific class to go to" (Caserta & Gillett, 1998, p. 607). Exercise groups provide social as well as physical reasons for going and continuing to go.

What can researchers conclude? Exercise is very beneficial but is not practiced by a great number of people. The number of people who exercise might be increased by effective education about the benefits and how to do it, by recommendations from respected authorities, and by involving people in a group-exercise setting.

Supplements

People who want to live longer lives have often sought quick and easy remedies for aging. Claims for lotions, pills, herbs, beverages, and other products that will reverse aging and prolong life will exist as long as people are willing to buy them. Manufacturers are not hesitant about offering new products containing the latest herbal remedy for some aspect of aging (Feig, 1998). Figure 5-2, provides a fictional example of these types of products.

In Chapter 2 we looked at the claims often made for the hormones DHEA, melatonin, and human growth hormone and saw that none of these supplements reversed aging or lengthened life although moderate levels of DHEA may offer some protection against cardiovascular disease. One must exert caution when taking supplements, especially those with extravagant claims, because their use can be quite dangerous (Schulz & Salthouse, 1999). Pantothenic acid found in royal jelly makes queen bees live far longer than worker bees but seems to have no effect on humans. Gerovital may make you feel better because it contains novacain but it does not affect aging. Ginseng can produce anxiety, insomnia, gastrointestinal disorders, and elevated blood pressure. Selenium can be toxic in large doses but may retard cancer growth in mice.

Other supplements may, however, have some benefits. Applications of **Retin A,** over a period of several months, reduced lipofuscins (dark spots; see Chapter 3) and some wrinkling of the skin in close to 75 percent of test participants. However, almost as many adults experienced reddening, swelling, and irritation of the skin. Most often these unwanted side effects disappear after several months of use. **Alphahydroxy acids (AHAs),** which often include citric acid, may decrease the thinning and wrinkling of the skin that occurs with aging. AHA treatments do not appear to produce the skin irritations that frequently accompany the use of Retin A, but also do not reduce lipofuscins on the skin (Rowe & Kahn,

Older adults participating in the Senior Games.

1998). Little is known about the long-term effects of using these products. However, to keep wrinkles and/or lipofuscins at bay, one must continue using the supplement.

Aspirin is another effective agent for reducing the risk of stroke, myocardial infarction, and in some cases heart attack. One dose of 325-mg aspirin daily can reduce the risk of heart attack by 50 percent in men with high levels of C-reactive protein. C-reactive protein is an indicator of inflammation and accumulation of blockage of blood vessels in the heart and brain (Mahoney & Restak, 1998). Aspirin can, however, also increase the risk of brain hemorrhage and can be very damaging to the lining of the digestive system and should be taken in a buffered or coated form. **Folic acid** is associated with reduced risk of heart disease and cancer in the colon and rectum.

Drinking green tea, but not black tea, seems to reduce mortality. In an examination of over 40,000 older Japanese, researchers found that the death rate from all causes was lower for those who consumed at least one cup of green tea every day and the death rate from cardiovascular diseases, especially stroke, was lowest of all. Green tea, however, had no association with deaths from cancer (Kuriyama et al., 2006). Other work, so far only with animals, has shown that a chemical found in red wine, resveratrol, appears to turn on a gene that produces an enzyme that repairs DNA damage. DNA damage was discussed in

FIGURE 5-2   "Fountain of Youth" Supplements.

Chapter 4. Mice given resveratrol live up to 70 percent longer (Baur et al., 2006; Valenzano at al., 2006). Some researchers believe that this DNA-repairing gene also is turned on when cells are starving and that may be the reason for the benefits of low-calorie-diets. It would be far easier to drink red wine than to cut back on calories but to get enough resveratrol from red wine would mean drinking much more than a moderate amount.

In summary, some supplements are helpful, some may turn out to be helpful, and some should be kept at a distance.

Tobacco

Tobacco, in the form of cigarettes, is responsible for over 3 million deaths each year, worldwide (American Cancer Society, 1994). Cigars, pipes, chewing tobacco, and snuff account for additional cancers and deaths, as does secondhand smoke. Smoking is strongly associated with cancer of the lungs, esophagus, bladder, mouth, larynx, kidneys, pancreas, and cervix; it is also strongly associated with heart disease, emphysema, and bronchitis (Katchadourian, 1987; Menotti et al., 1998; U.S. Department of Health & Human Services, 1987). Tobacco smoke contains a number of harmful substances that contribute to

---

PROJECT **5**
Searching for the Fountain of Youth

Take a trip to a local health store or try a large pharmacy or department store instead. Go to the sections that have dietary supplements and cosmetics and look for antiaging products. You may be surprised at how many you find. Americans spend millions of dollars every year trying to reverse, or stop, aging. Many vitaminc, herbs, minerals, ointments, and other more mysterious substances are advertised for their antiaging properties. For each product you find:

■ Record the name, the company that makes it, and the specific claim(s) made.
■ Which ingredient is the one that is supposed to produce the antiaging effect?
■ If the active ingredient is one of the ones discussed in this chapter (e.g., ginseng, pantothenic acid, selenium, Retin A) or in Chapter 4 (melatonin, SOD, DHEA, growth hormone, beta-carotene), then you know how valid the claims made for antiaging benefits are. Were any of the claims based on current evidence?
■ If the active ingredient is not one discussed (e.g., lamb fetus, crocodile tears), how valid do you think the claims are? Why?

It is sad that so many people search for youth while it slips through their fingers. All of us grow older and each day should be appreciated rather than spent yearning for days already past. Old age is a time to be welcomed and celebrated. The real fountain of youth is in your mind. You are only as old as you think you are or as the great Satchel Paige asked, "How old would you be if you didn't know how old you was?"

---

these disorders. Nicotine is an addictive alkaloid (like caffeine, morphine, and strychnine) that causes small blood vessels to constrict while increasing the heart rate. This results in an increase in blood pressure. Smoke particles and tar produce respiratory problems. Tar is carcinogenic. Toxins such as carbon monoxide and cyanide combine with red blood cells and block the transportation of oxygen to body tissues and the brain. Smokers get a constriction of small blood vessels, a racing heart, a jump in blood pressure, a blockage of oxygen, and the ingestion of cancer-causing substances with every smoke inhalation. Some recent work even shows that cigarette smoking is strongly associated with an 18 percent reduction in average telomere length (Valdes et al., 2005). Earlier (Chapter 3) we saw that strength declines with loss of fiber and quality of muscles with age. Some work suggests that, at least for women, loss of muscle quality may be related to smoking (Rapuri et al., 2007).

For men, the effects of smoking may be quite important long before the end of life. The incidence of erectile dysfuncion is far higher in smokers than in nonsmokers (Sofikitis et al., 1995). For couples hoping to conceive, researchers also have found that the sperm of smokers shows lower quality than the sperm of nonsmokers (Zavos et al., 1998).

Clearly smoking is very harmful. In the United States, about 28 percent of men and 24 percent of women smoke. The highest proportion of women smokers are in Denmark (41%) and men smokers are in Japan (61%) (Starfield, 2000). Most smoking individuals began in adolescence or young adulthood (Giovino et al., 1995). Some quit but many continue. Even second hand smoke is dangerous and people who live with a smoker or work in a smoke filled environment place their health at risk.

When one quits smoking, the improvements in blood circulation begin immediately. Within the first year, the risks of heart attack and stroke decline dramatically. Even the likelihood of cancer returns to normal levels after 10 or more years following quitting (National Institute on Aging, 1993). If you are currently a smoker, the greatest influence you can have on your own longevity and on those who breathe your smoke is to quit. If you are not a smoker, the greatest influence you can have on your own longevity is to never begin and avoid exposure to the smoke of others.

Alcohol

It is common knowledge that the effects of alcohol can be devastating. Excess consumption of alcohol is associated with early death particularly from liver damage and disease (cirrhosis), accidents, and suicide. Excess use is associated with depression and even memory loss and functional impairments (Perreira, 2002). Moderate consumption, however, appears to be beneficial. Those who drink moderately are generally healthier and live longer than both those who abstain and those who drink excessively. Study after study has found moderate consumption to be associated with longevity (Williams, 1988), with improving cholesterol levels in blood (Doll & Peto, 1994; Langer et al., 1992), and with reduced cardiovascular disease (Doll, 1997; Moore & Pearson, 1986). One recent study of alcohol use in women who were 70 or older found that moderate use compared to no use was associated with less cognitive decline over a 2-year period (Stampfer et al., 2005).

How much is a moderate amount? Three or four drinks may be moderate for someone who is very large but way too much for someone smaller. Moderate consumption for women is about 70 percent of what is considered moderate consumption for men because of size and other biological (hormonal) differences. In most research, moderate drinking is regarded as one to three drinks per day; a single drink is one bottle of beer or 5 ounces of wine or 1.5 ounces of liquor. Clearly moderation also depends on experience. Even moderate drinkers are advised not to drive or to handle any potentially dangerous equipment.

Stress

Stress refers to life events that produce mental and/or emotional disruption. Life is full of such events and the amount of disruption produced depends on the amount of change that accompanies the event and the individual's own coping skills. Positive events such as moving to a new home, getting a better paying job, getting married, or having a baby produce considerable amounts of disruption just as negative events do—such as the death of a parent, a divorce, being fired at work, or developing a serious illness. Ratings of the stressfulness of different events place death of a spouse and divorce very high while having a baby or moving to a new home are much lower. The relationships among level of stress, coping skills, health, and mortality have been investigated, and the general finding is that people under a lot of stress, particularly those with poor coping skills, experience a decrease in health and a shorter life (Karlamangla et al., 2002; Yong-Xing et al., 1998).

How do stressors produce such effects? There are both biological and behavioral answers to that question. Biologically, the adrenal cortex increases the secretion of cortisol when we experience stress. We are prepared for fight or flight; the heart rate increases and blood pressure rises. If the secretion continues as a result of continued stress, heart rate returns to normal and we are able to adapt. During this adaptation, many of the body's resources are depleted. If the stress continues, the high levels of cortisol suppress the immune system, leading to increased susceptibility to infections, colds, and cancers; the individual may become dysfunctional and suffer a heart attack or stroke and some believe that inflammation is the link between the continuing stress and heart disease (Miller & Blackwell, 2006). Prolonged stress is very damaging (Seeman et al., 1997; Tennant, 2000; Yusef et al., 2004). Older adults are particularly vulnerable to stress because they are likely to secrete higher levels of cortisol and for a longer time than are younger adults (Lakatta, 1990). Negative health symptoms as a result of stress are high for both men and women (Weekes et al., 2005). Some recent work shows that telomere length is associated with cortisol; more stress leads to more cortisol which appears to lead to a shortening of telomere length (Epel et al., 2006). Continued stress (6 months or longer) depletes the body's defenses and increases the likelihood of serious health problems.

Behaviorally, people under stress increase their intake of fatty foods, exercise far less (if at all), and smoke more (Ng & Jeffrey, 2003). People may eat more snacks and fast food and drink more caffeine while stressed (Epel et al., 2000; Pak et al., 2000). Some may drink alcohol to excess (Heslop et al., 2001). Women tend to eat more candy and sweets (Steptoe et al., 1998); while men eat more red meat (Spillman, 1990). People do not take care of themselves when they are stressed which also increases the likelihood of serious health problems.

Clearly stress, particularly prolonged stress, is damaging. Before we reach that point, we need to find effective ways to handle and reduce our stress. One of the hypothesized reasons for the long life of Hawaiians is that they have learned to relax when minor frustrations occur. One indicator of this relaxed attitude is the absence of horn blowing, even during rush hour, on the streets and expressways of Hawaii (Glatzer, 1999). Different strategies work well for different people but the usual recommendations are to increase exercise, try to sleep more, learn to meditate, learn to relax, do things you enjoy, and try to laugh (by renting a Mel Brook's film).

Other Factors

In this section, we examine factors that are not clearly in or out of our control. One cannot change one's gender or race/ethnic group but many of the factors that contribute to gender and race/ethnic group differences in longevity can be changed. The behaviors we engage in are one such factor. Our SES also influences these differences and can undergo change as we develop.

Gender

Females live longer than males and this difference in longevity is referred to as the **gender gap**. From conception onward males have higher death rates than females (Smith, 1993).

This difference in favor of females occurs in species other than humans and, in humans, it occurs worldwide. Over the last 100 years, the size of the gender gap has fluctuated and grown. Figure 5-3 shows female and male life expectancies in the United States over the last 100 years.

The gender differences in death rates are particularly high for certain forms of death. It is estimated that about 40 percent of the gender gap is due to gender differences in heart disease and stroke due to atherosclerosis. Another 33 percent of the gender gap is thought to be due to social and behavioral differences. Men have much higher rates of suicide, cirrhosis of the liver, lung cancer, and emphysema. Men tend to smoke, drink, and use guns more than women do. It is expected that the gender gap will decrease, somewhat, as individuals begin eating better, exercising more, and paying more attention to their health; the gap might never, however, disappear (Kranczer, 1999).

Genetic/Biological Explanations.   There are several different genetic and biological explanations for the gender gap. One hypothesis is that the differences in longevity between females and males are due in part to inherited sex chromosomes. Females receive an XX sex chromosome while males receive an XY sex chromosome. This difference is known to play a role in disorders such as color blindness and hemophilia. When a gene is carried on the X chromosome, females receive two while males receive one. If the gene is recessive and codes for a negative trait, then females who receive that gene on one X chromosome still have a chance to inherit the healthy dominant gene on the other X chromosome. Males do not because they receive only the one gene on their one X chromo-

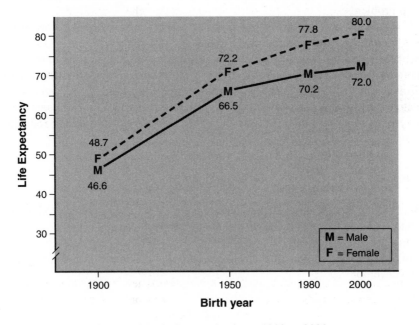

FIGURE 5-3   Gender Gap in Longevity from 1900 to 2000.

some. Perhaps some negative factor(s) associated with longevity are carried on the X chromosome. For example, the X chromosome appears to carry the gene or genes that determine initial telomere length and we know that women, on average, have longer telomeres (Nawrot et al., 2004). Deaths from infectious diseases are far more likely for individuals with shorter telomeres (Samani et al., 2001).

A second genetic/biological hypothesis is that the gender gap is due to hormonal differences. Men and women have many of the same hormones but the relative amounts differ. Men have more testosterone while women have more estrogen (DiGiovanna, 1994). Testosterone is known to increase blood clotting while estrogen reduces clotting. Testosterone then may account for some of the higher levels of atherosclerosis in males. Females might have some protection against atherosclerosis because of the positive effects of estrogen (U.S. Department of Health & Human Services, 1992). One way to investigate the effects of these hormones is to eliminate them. Researchers have eliminated testosterone in male rats by castrating them when they are young. Generally these rats live longer than usual but often not as long as well-exercised intact rats. In humans, castration was not an uncommon treatment for some forms of psychosis, certain cancers, and mental impairment during the last decades of the nineteenth century and the early decades of the twentieth century. Many years ago, researchers interested in the relationship between testosterone and longevity examined several hundred institutionalized persons with mental impairment. Some of them had been castrated. On average, the females outlived the males by just over 6 years while the castrated males outlived those females by about the same amount (Hamilton, 1948). Of course, there are some problems with such comparisons. Perhaps, the castrated males were treated better than other persons in the institutions because their lack of testosterone made them more docile than the other males and females. People who work in institutions often favor docile residents. Although we cannot be sure what factors resulted in the obtained differences in length of life, the results are very interesting and do correspond with the results from many animal studies.

Environmental Explanations. One environmental difference that may contribute to the gender gap is the difference in proportions of female and male tobacco users. As noted earlier, a greater proportion of men than women smoke. Because tobacco use is a major factor in the production of cancer and heart disease, the gender differences in smoking must be responsible for some of the gender difference in longevity.

A second environmental explanation is that men are more likely to engage in risky behaviors (beyond smoking) than are women. More men than women drink alcohol excessively and die from cirrhosis of the liver. Men are more likely to isolate themselves socially while women are more likely to use social supports to assist them in times of trouble (see Chapter 10). Social supports are known to help buffer individuals against certain diseases and to assist individuals in getting well (Eckert & Rubinstein, 1999). Men are more likely to commit suicide than are women. Men are more likely to drive fast, jump from airplanes, wrestle alligators, and shoot guns than are women. These differences are largely cultural and some expect that the gender gap may narrow as women begin doing the same sorts of things in greater numbers than they have in the past.

An older person sky diving.

Race/Culture/SES

There are large life expectancy differences between various racial, cultural, and ethnic groups. In the United States, Asian Americans live longest, followed by whites and Hispanics, then Africans, then Native Americans (National Center for Health Statistics, 2003; Smith, 1993; Williams, 2005). Among older adults, however, African, Hispanic, and Native Americans have lower death rates than white Americans (Zopf, 1992). These differences are due to a number of different factors.

Asian Americans have much lower rates of heart disease and stroke than the other groups and a part of this is undoubtedly due to much lower rates of smoking and alcohol abuse (Yee & Weaver, 1994). The rate of cancer also is lower except for stomach cancer which is much higher than other groups (Weisburger, 1991). Which foods do you think contribute to this effect? Asian Americans also have high rates of tuberculosis, anemia, and hepatitis. Most of the research has been done only on Japanese Americans so generalizations are difficult to make.

For **African Americans**, the death rates from cancer, heart disease, stroke, cirrhosis, pneumonia, and influenza are very high (Otten et al., 1990). They are also six times more likely than white Americans to be murdered. A greater proportion of African American men smoke than white American men but a smaller proportion of African American women smoke than white women (Smith, 1993).

Hispanic Americans die from homicide nine times more frequently than white Americans. Heart disease, cancer, diabetes, and stroke are the most frequent causes of death and the incidence of AIDS also is high. Most of the research has been done only on Mexican Americans so generalizations are difficult to make and the overall death rate for Hispanic Americans is surprisingly low. Some say this is paradoxical because Hispanic Americans have low SES levels as do African and Native Americans. Recent work suggests that the death rate may be low due to a strong tendency for less-healthy Mexican Americans, especially men, to return to Mexico and not, therefore, be counted among those dying in the United States (Markides & Eschbach, 2005).

For **Native Americans**, diabetes occurs at 10 times the rate of white Americans and is, thus, a major cause of death along with heart disease, cancer, stroke, pneumonia, and influenza (American Association of Retired Persons, 1993). Alcohol abuse also is more frequent for this group than for any other. As with Asian and Hispanic Americans, one must be cautious in generalizing because there are many different groups of Native Americans. For example, the incidence of lung cancer among those living in the southwest is very low while the incidence among those living in the northwest is much higher (American Cancer Society, 1991).

White Americans also have high rates of death from cancer, heart disease, and stroke and higher rates from chronic obstructive pulmonary disease. The suicide rate for white Americans, particularly older men, is extraordinarily high (see Chapter 12).

To determine what factors might be responsible for these group differences, some research has examined the risky behaviors, such as smoking, excess drinking, obesity, and physical activity, that different groups engage in (Crimmins et al., 2003). One examination of these factors in several thousand adults found that African Americans were more likely than white Americans to be obese. Men and unmarried adults were more likely to smoke cigarettes than women and married couples. African and Hispanic Americans, especially women, were more likely to abstain from alcohol. Hispanic Americans, especially older adults, were less likely to be physically active (Wray et al., 2005). These differences must account for some of the differences in longevity; can you think of other possible reasons for longevity differences?

One strong hypothesis to account for group differences in longevity is that they are largely due to differences in SES. In the United States, white Americans, on average, have higher SES than other groups while African, Hispanic, and Native Americans are often at the lowest SES level. People who make less money may have more hazardous jobs, poorer nutrition, less access to doctors and hospitals, less ability to pay for prescriptions, and be less likely to have health insurance. For example, white Americans are more likely than all other groups to have major surgery performed at hospitals of higher volume (one measure of quality) than all other groups (Liu et al., 2006). African Americans are less likely to be admitted to a hospital and when admitted tend to stay longer with a higher probability of dying (Ferraro et al., 2006). When African and white Americans have been enrolled in the same health plan and compared on their control of blood pressure, diabetes, or cholesterol levels, white Americans have done much better. Researchers believe these differences may be due, in part, to white Americans having higher SES to afford the better hospitals and any needed medications (Trivedi et al., 2006). People at low SES levels also are more likely to smoke and drink excessively. As a result, they are not as healthy and do not live as long (Escobedo & Peddicord, 1996). Group SES differences are greatest among older adults (Crystal & Shea, 1990). In addition to higher income to pay for better care, recent work suggests that stress also may be a factor. People with low income experience far more financial strain in trying to pay bills, feed families, and care for themselves (Kahn & Fazio, 2005). We know how harmful prolonged stress is on the body's defenses.

Some work suggests that another part of the problem for some groups is that they may have low levels of health literacy. They are not able to understand the directions given by doctors or the instructions given for prescription drug use. They remain uninformed about health problems and solutions. This problem is greater for old adults than for young adults and greater for those with lower education levels, lower SES levels, those who have more severe sensory problems (seeing and hearing), and those who are relatively recent immigrants and have not yet learned English well (Gazmararian et al., 1999; Morrow et al., 2006; Parker et al., 2003). These individuals need assistance in understanding the health alternatives available to them and the directions given but seem to be less willing to ask for this assistance. They may be embarrassed by their inability to understand and are more likely to be socially isolated (Lee et al., 2006b). Health illiteracy is yet another factor contributing to group differences in longevity.

Social Support

One of the most well-known longitudinal investigations of longevity began in 1965 near San Francisco. Participants were followed for 17 years. As you might expect, results showed strong influences for many of the factors already discussed. For example, smoking, not exercising, having a high BMI, and abusing alcohol were strongly associated with shorter life expectancy. Results also showed a large difference in life expectancy between those who were socially active and had a lot of social support from family and friends and those who were socially isolated. Those with social support had less than half the mortality rate of those who were socially isolated (Berkman & Breslow, 1983). People with strong social support groups live longer.

Social support can come from a number of sources. In a successful marriage, husband and wife can rely on each other in times of stress or ill health and support each other in healthy habits and outlook. Married people live longer than divorced, widowed, or single people of the same age (Eriksson et al., 1999). Maintaining close ties and interactions with family and friends and/or being socially active in religious or cultural groups or other social organizations also offer social support (Berkman, 1986; Cohen et al., 1985). Another form of social support can come from serving as a volunteer. Volunteers typically meet new people and develop new social relationships and research suggests that a moderate amount of volunteering is associated with longer life (Musick et al., 1999). It is important to emphasize that it is the quality of the social relationships rather than the number of relationships that is most important. Furthermore how we perceive the support given to us by others is important. If we think that people are helping because they are obligated to help, it is their duty, then we may not benefit as much. Support might mean doing more things for a person such as driving them to appointments, helping them with everyday tasks that they can no longer do, and providing advice and information on financial or health matters but such things are easily seen as obligations. One recent study found that these assistive supports had no influence on the mortality of older men or women. Higher quality includes emotional closeness, reassuring the person of their worth, making them feel that they belong in addition to assisting with everyday tasks. This type of support had no influence on the mortality of older men but was strongly related to a lower death rate for women (Lyyra & Heikkinen, 2006).

How does social support contribute to longevity? A favorite hypothesis is that support serves as a buffer against stress. As noted earlier, high levels of stress are strongly associated with poor health and shorter life. Family, close friends, and other social groups can offer help in times of stress and so relieve some of the negative effects. An examination of police officers on traffic duty in New York City found, to no one's surprise, that the level of stress on this job is very high. These officers are cursed more often than most other groups. Those with good social support in the form of encouragement from other officers and supervisors had much lower blood pressure levels than those without much support (Karlin et al., 2003). Other work has found better cardiovascular health and immune system functioning in those with good levels of social support (Uchino et al., 1996). Those who support us socially watch out for us; they make us feel better; they help relieve our stress.

Other work has examined the characteristics of those who have higher levels of social support and found that these individuals are more open to others, more trusting, and more optimistic. People with higher levels of trust tend to live longer (Barefoot et al., 1998). Those who have a more positive attitude about their own aging tend to function better (Levy et al., 2002) and those who are dissatisfied with aging die sooner (Maier & Smith, 1999). Generally those with higher levels of optimism and/or religiosity live longer (Antonucci et al., 1997; Danner et al., 2001; Oxman et al., 1995). It's not yet clear, however, whether high levels of social support lead to more positive attitudes and trust or whether more positive attitudes and trust lead to more social support. What do you think? More about social support is given in Chapter 10.

Quality of Life

Quality of life is, of course, a subjective judgment by the individual. You may be quite healthy but report a low quality of life if you are without friends and lonely. You may be relatively unhealthy but report a high quality of life because of the support of family and friends who love you dearly. Nevertheless, physical and mental health are important components of quality of life and those with high levels of health are more likely to have high quality of life (Kaplan et al., 2004). When older adults have been asked about their health, many more white Americans (70%) than African (52%) or Hispanic (50%) Americans rate their health as good or excellent. People who perceive their health to be good live longer

SOCIAL POLICY APPLICATIONS

Clearly the population is growing and we are living into very old age. We have seen how genetic and environmental factors contribute to these population trends. A number of organizations have studied these trends and contributing factors with an eye toward making predictions for future programs and services. The Population Council has brought together a number of these international government and nongovernmental organizations to gather and analyze data in order to achieve a sustainable balance between what people need and what the world can provide. Like many of the studies discussed in the chapter, one factor that they found strongly related to health in old age is education. Beyond all other environmental factors, having more education predicts a healthy old age, and a healthy very old age both over short time periods and over the lifespan. They suggest that education may operate to improve health through a number of different channels such as producing better memory and reasoning skills, changing brain biology, or producing better health self-management behaviors. Although these routes should be investigated further (and thus we should advocate for more money for longitudinal research), we can impact the future health of the growing older population by improving the education system today. We should be sure that quality education is truly available to every child and we should make secondary and higher education better and more available (more affordable) for everyone as well. If better education leads to better health, the money the government spends early on education will be saved many times over in old age.

than people who perceive their health to be poor (Kaplan et al., 1988). If we consider only perceptions of health, we would expect to find group differences in quality of life and those differences would correspond to SES levels.

It's a mistake to think that disability is a natural part of aging. Estimates suggest that at least 40 percent of those 85 and older have no major disability. Less than 6 percent of older Americans live in nursing homes. Even among centenarians, 20 percent are able to care for themselves and 17 percent live by themselves (Rowe & Kahn, 1998). People who make it to that 100-year mark often are categorized as being of three types. Survivors are those who developed an age-related disorder, like osteoporosis or heart disease or stroke, and kept going; about 38 percent of centenarians are this type. Delayers are those who developed a disorder but later than the life expectancy for their cohort; about 43 percent are this type. Escapers are those who made it to 100 without a diagnosis of any age-related disorder; about 19 percent are this type (Evert et al., 2003). Clearly one can succeed by avoiding, postponing, or battling the disorders of old age. In an investigation of their quality of life, centenarians were compared to younger adults aged 86 to 99, and even younger adults aged 75 to 85. Centenarians reported more lost functions, such as the ability to shop, maintain their finances, and use the telephone, than those in the two younger groups. The youngest group, however, complained the most of discomfort and had the greatest number of painful symptoms. Centenarians showed good mental functioning and reported higher levels of life satisfaction and more satisfaction with their social lives than the two younger groups. People who live to be very old adapt well to change, generally have a positive outlook, and maintain good social relationships (Buono et al., 1998).

Positive attitude and an optimistic outlook are part of positive psychology discussed earlier. Older adults who are satisfied with their lives tend to live longer (Lyyra et al., 2006) and people who believe they have some control over possible physical and/or mental decline generally are more optimistic. They are more likely to engage in health promoting behaviors and to adopt successful strategies (Lachman, 2006). Their quality of life can be quite high.

From what you have read, you know there are no simple formulas for living longer and remaining healthy and a great many factors that play a role. Complete the exercise in Box 5-4 and estimate your own life expectancy. Would you really want to live that long? Your answer should depend to some extent on the quality of life for those who are already living that long.

One good example of a person with these characteristics is Jeanne Calment (see Chapter 1). She exercised on her bicycle until she was 100 years old. Until she was 110, she lived independently and maintained her own home. She ate chocolate, drank red wine, and didn't quit smoking until she was 117. She is said to have had an excellent sense of humor and an extremely positive outlook on life. Bernadine Healy (1997) relates the story of a visitor leaving Jeanne Calment's presence and saying on the way out, "until next year, perhaps." Jeanne Calment answered, "I don't see why not! You don't look so bad to me."

BOX 5-4
Estimating Your Own Life Expectancy

This test is designed to estimate the life expectancy of people with different genetic endowments and different life experiences. The numbers that result are only estimates. To begin, you will need to determine your life expectancy at your specified age. Take that number from the following (choose the age that is closest to your own).

Age	Men				Women			
	Asian	Black	Hispanic	White	Asian	Black	Hispanic	White
20	74	68	67	73	81	75	73	80
30	75	69	68	74	82	76	74	81
40	76	70	69	75	83	77	75	82

Use your beginning life expectancy to add or subtract as you answer the following questions.

1. If you are now over age 50, **add 10**.
2. If your mother or father lived beyond 80, **add 3**.
3. If any grandparent lived beyond 80, **add 1** for each grandparent who did. For those who made it to 70, **add .5**.
4. If any close relative (defined as parent, grandparent, or sibling) died of a heart attack or stroke before age 50, **subtract 4** for each death.
5. If any close relative died before 60 of diabetes, **subtract 3** for each death; of stomach cancer, **subtract 2** for each death; of any cause (except accident or homicide), **subtract 1** for each death.

(continued)

B O X **5-4** Continued

6. **Women only**—if a close relative died of breast cancer before 60, **subtract 2** for each death. If you will not have children or if you're now 40 or older and have not had children, **subtract .5**.
7. If your mother was over 35 or under 18 when you were born, **subtract 1**.
8. If you are the first born or an only child, **add 1**.
9. If you believe you are more intelligent than almost everyone you know, **add 2**.
10. What is your BMI? If it's below normal (<18.5), **subtract 5**; if it's between 25 and 25.9, **subtract 8**, if it's 30 or higher, **subtract 12**.
11. If you eat a lot of vegetables and fruits rather than fats and sugars, **add 1**.
12. If you smoke a pack of cigarettes or more a day, **subtract 15**; if you smoke less than a pack, **subtract 6**.
13. If you do aerobic exercise at least three times a week, **add 3**.
14. If you sleep excessively (10 or more hours a night) or very little (5 or fewer hours), **subtract 2**.
15. If you are frequently ill or have a chronic health condition such as diabetes, cancer, high blood pressure, or ulcer, **subtract 5**.
16. If you are married and living with your spouse, **add 1**. If you are past the age of 25 and have never married, **subtract 1.5** for each decade past 25. If you are a divorced, separated, or widowed man, **subtract 6**. If you are a woman in those same circumstances, **subtract 3.5**.
17. If you take risks (drive without a seatbelt, speed, take dares), **subtract 2**. If you always use your seatbelt, **add 1**.
18. If you've spent most of your life in an urban area **subtract 1**; if you've spent most of your life in a rural area, **add 1**.
19. If you have completed at least 2 years of college, **add 3**; if you are a freshman or sophomore, **add 1.5**.
20. If you enjoy regular sexual activity at least one or two times per week, **add 2**.
21. If you are an alcoholic, **subtract 8**. If you drink a moderate amount (half a liter of wine or three to four glasses of beer or two whiskeys) most days, **add 3**. If you drink some, but less than a moderate amount, **add 1.5**.
22. If you are always changing things in your life (jobs, where you live, friends, spouses, your appearance), **subtract 2**.
23. If you generally like people and have at least two good friends in whom you can confide, **add 1**.
24. If you are rigid, dogmatic, and set in your ways, **subtract 2**.
25. If you are a calm, reasonable person who is easy going and adaptable, **add 2**. If you are aggressive, under time pressure, and sometimes hostile, **subtract 3.5**.
26. If you are basically happy and content and have a lot of fun in your life, **add 2**.

Source: Adapted from Perls et al. (1999) and Foos (2001).

CHAPTER HIGHLIGHTS

- A number of factors are thought to influence the probability of living a long and healthy life.
- Differences in longevity are found worldwide; people in Japan live longer than people elsewhere do and, within the United States, residents of Hawaii live the longest and Washington, D.C., the shortest.
- Genetic influences are estimated to account for 25 to 35 percent of the variability in human longevity.
- Genes from both parents influence longevity by producing life-threatening disorders (e.g., through the apolipoproteins [APOE]-producing genes), influencing body chemistry (e.g., through free radical production and mitochondria damage), and generating the stability of telomere sequences or the entire genetic code.
- Genetic influences are not yet clearly understood and may be considered to be out of our control, at least for now.
- Environmental influences on longevity are within our control.
- Healthy, low-fat diets are related to longevity; a high or low BMI is associated with a higher risk of death, perhaps, because of other factors such as lack of exercise or eating the wrong foods.
- Exercise is another important factor and seems to produce benefits relative to the amount of exercise; cancer and heart disease may be especially reduced by regular vigorous exercise.
- Not many older adults exercise regularly. Education and recommendations from authority figures, and having people to exercise with are major factors for encouraging exercise.
- A number of supplements claim to have aging-reversal effects but, in fact, do not.
- Green tea may reduce the risk of cardiovascular diseases, especially stroke.
- Tobacco use shortens life and is dangerous for those around the smoke of others.
- Alcohol is thought to be beneficial in moderate amounts because it may reduce the risk of heart disease; the general finding of a benefit of moderate consumption over no consumption at all is, however, still questioned.
- Reactions to stress can be very unhealthy and can increase blood pressure and release immune suppressing hormones.
- Stress increases less-healthy behaviors like smoking and drinking; stress depletes the body's resources.
- Gender differences in longevity appear to be due to biological factors such as telomere length and behavioral factors such as smoking and risky behaviors.
- There are a number of differences in most frequent causes of death and life expectancy among African, Asian, Hispanic, Native, and white Americans. These differences seem to be due to social factors.
- Race, culture, and ethnic group differences in longevity exist for a number of reasons. Different groups engage in harmful behaviors to varying degrees. SES differences influence longevity by providing better doctors and care for those at high levels and more stress for those at low levels. Health literacy differences exist for different groups and influence health through knowledge.
- People with good social support live longer; social support may buffer individuals against stress and it may be that certain characteristics (e.g., optimism) and behaviors (e.g., volunteering) of sociable individuals are what influence length of life.
- Very-old adults who retain their health live longer and seem to be satisfied with life; they report having good quality of life.

STUDY QUESTIONS

1. Describe how researchers attempt to determine whether longevity is due to genetic or environmental factors. What have researchers concluded?

2. Why does a very low or very high BMI seem to shorten life? What factors are involved?

3. Describe four types of exercise that are aerobic and beneficial. How does exercise help lengthen life?

4. How might we get older adults to begin exercising? What is a good beginning exercise?

5. What do the benefits of diet and exercise say about the mechanistic-organismic issue?

6. Name and describe five supplements intended to reverse aging. Is there any evidence to support the claims?

7. Why is tobacco harmful? What ingredients produce the harm?

8. Why might nondrinkers die sooner than people who drink a moderate amount of alcohol?

9. Why does stress often produce poorer health and shorten life? How can one learn to handle stress. Describe specific techniques.

10. Describe four factors that might account for the gender gap in longevity.

11. Describe some of the race/ethnic group differences in longevity and possible reasons for these differences.

12. Explain how SES affects longevity.

13. Explain how social support affects longevity.

14. What do you think is the "perfect" environment for increasing longevity?

15. How high is the quality of life for people who live long lives? What factors make a difference and why?

RECOMMENDED READINGS

Allard, M., Lebre, V., & Robine, J. M. (1994). *Jeanne Calment: From Van Gogh's Time to Ours*. New York: W.H. Freeman. This is a delightful little book written by Jeanne Calment's physician and two gerontologists. We get a look into the life of the world's oldest person. Filled with Calment's humorous quips and sayings, this book makes living to 122 a wonder and a joy.

Rowe, J. W., & Kahn, R. L. (1998). *Successful Aging*. New York: Pantheon. This is an easy-to-read description of factors that influence health and longevity.

Weil, A. (2005). *Healthy Aging: A Lifelong Guide to Your Physical and Spiritual Well-Being*. New York: Knopf. This book presents an overview of aging and offers specific suggestions for how to improve your own aging.

INTERNET RESOURCES

www.attitudefactor.com. Offers useful information about aging but may be overly optimistic about some of the factors that influence longevity.

www.northwesternmutual.com/games/longevity. Gives life expectancy estimates.

www.deathclock.com. See how life is slipping away.

http://news.aarp.org/UM/T.asp?A910.52851.2518.4.5090. For information about health and aging.

PART TWO

Aging and Our Minds

6 Sensation, Perception, and Slowing with Age

The same space of time seems shorter as we grow older.

—*William James*

William James and others claim that our perception of time seems to change as we age. When we are very young, a year seems to take forever but as we grow older, the years seem to fly by. We will examine changes in our sensations and perceptions as we age. Perhaps the perception that time moves faster is related to our own slowing down, or because we value time more because each passing year means one less in the future.

Sensation and Perception

Many bodily organs and tissues change with age and senescence. Sense organs are likely to change and show senescence although not all changes occur in all people and not all changes occur at the same time. **Sensation** refers to the stimulation of sensory cells in the body's sense organs. That stimulation then is passed on to centers in the brain. **Perception** refers to the interpretation of sensory stimulation and takes place in the brain. Perception gives meaning to sensory stimulation and may signal the organism as to which stimulation should receive the greatest amount of attention. Changes in sense organs frequently influence perception. If you cannot taste the sugar in coffee, you may add more sugar until you are finally able to detect the sweetness. At the same time, sensory changes can take place over relatively long periods of time and, thus, enable individuals to compensate. Such compensation can result in little, or no, significant change in perception. Some changes in senses may influence perception while others may not. Some changes may be compensated for while others may not.

Vision

A diagram of the human eye can be seen in Figure 6-1. The outer membrane covering the eye is called the **cornea**. Light rays enter the eye through the **iris** which expands or contracts depending on the level of illumination. When the light is dim, the iris opens wide to

111

let in more light; when the light is bright, the iris closes to reduce the amount entering the eye. Light is focused by the **lens** onto the **retina**. The **ciliary muscles** function to change the shape of the lens to focus the image, which might be near or far from the viewer. The inside of the eye is filled with a fluid called the **vitreous humor**. The retina converts the light rays into electric impulses for the nerve cells and those impulses are carried to the visual cortex at the back of the head. Cells in the retina are called cones and rods. **Cones** number close to six million and respond to color and high levels of illumination; they are for daytime/light vision. **Rods** are cells distributed throughout the retina but concentrated in the periphery. They respond to low levels of illumination as in night/dark vision.

Senior View

We visited Mabel Carson Davis to ask about changes in sensation, perception, and slowing. Mabel was born in 1912 and worked as a registered nurse until she retired in 1982. We first asked about her vision.

I don't see things the same way now that I'm older. Colors were especially difficult until I had my cataracts removed. Before that I was arguing with everyone in the country about what color I was seeing. Having the operation was like a yellow sheet was removed. (We'll talk about that yellowing in this chapter.)

We asked about her hearing. *Three years ago I had a bad cold and sore throat with a lot of drainage. When I was blowing my nose, I went deaf in both ears! My doctors could not figure out what happened and for about 6 weeks I couldn't hear anything at all. It finally got better but after a year I needed a hearing aid. The hearing aid is an advantage because when people see it, they speak more directly to me.*

I've not noticed any change in my sense of smell or my taste and I still have a very high threshold for pain. My breakfast this morning did not taste very good so I'm sure I can taste quite well.

We asked Mabel about slowing down. *I'm not sure whether I've slowed down or not. I can't do as much yard work as I used to be able to do but that might be because I get tired sooner. I still drive but not as fast as I used to. That's because I have an old car, not because I'm old. I don't go 85 any-*

more. Sometimes I have to reread things to get it right.

Finally we asked whether she thought time moved faster now. *When I was young I used to think Christmas and my birthday* (December 27) *would never get here and now on Monday it's Friday before I know it. I'd like to say "stop" to the world.*

Mabel left us with this thought. *Each part of life is interesting and can be exciting if you look for the excitement. Youth is wonderful but old age is not bad at all.* We agree.

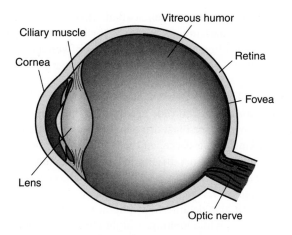

FIGURE 6-1   **Diagram of the Normal Eye.**

Physical Changes.   After age 40, the cornea begins to increase in curvature and thickness and loses luster. Over the years, many individual's eyes appear to stick out more and appear duller as a result of these changes in the cornea and surrounding skin and bone.

A number of changes occur in the lens. First, the lens of the eye becomes flatter and the ciliary muscles, like other muscles in the body, become stiffer. Between the ages of 40 and 50, the result of these changes moves the point of clearest vision farther from the eye. This is called **presbyopia**. Older individuals often hold a book or newspaper at arm's length to read it and many purchase magnifying glasses for reading or change their glasses to bifocals. Another result of these lens and ciliary muscle changes is a decreased ability to shift back and forth between near- and far vision. This ability to shift back and forth is called **distance accommodation** and is important in many tasks, particularly driving. Some middle-age and older drivers have difficulty shifting focus from the roadway to the dashboard and back as a result of declines in distance accommodation.

The lens of the eye also turns more yellow as it accumulates insoluble proteins. The change to yellow, however, is so gradual that it does not affect perception in all cases. Your lenses are already turning yellow even if you are only in your early 20s but you probably won't notice this gradual change until you are in your 90s. For older adults with yellow lenses, everything does not appear yellow but the ability to distinguish certain colors, particularly in the green-blue-violet end of the spectrum, can be greatly reduced (Whitbourne, 1996). Please don't reset the color on your grandparents' television unless they ask you to. It may look "off" to you but looks just fine through yellow lenses.

The lens of the eye also grows thicker as we age. This thickening, along with yellowing, allows less light to reach the retina. As a result, older adults are less able to perceive clearly when the lights are low and generally need higher levels of illumination for good visual perception. It is very important that there be adequate lighting, particularly in unfamiliar environments and on stairways, to prevent falling accidents.

As we grow older, particles of insoluble protein, called "floaters," accumulate in the vitreous humor. When we are young, the vitreous humor is thicker like gelatin but as we age, it becomes more liquid. Floaters often are remaining pieces of gelatin floating in liquid humor. They are normal, harmless, and ordinarily do not affect perception.

Changes in Visual Perception.   The **adaptation from light to dark** is slower and less efficient for older eyes. Shifting from cones to rods takes longer because there are fewer cells. Driving at night, particularly when one must drive in and out of lighted areas, can be dangerous for older drivers. Walking into a darkened theater should be done much more slowly when one is older. Even in the daytime, driving in and out of a tunnel can be more difficult for older drivers. Having a picture taken with a bright flash has a more pronounced effect on older adults; it takes longer to recover normal vision.

With aging, **peripheral vision** also declines. Peripheral vision is measured by testing vision for objects seen at the sides while looking straight ahead. For young adults, the typical peripheral vision range is about 170 degrees. By age 50 peripheral vision range is only 140 degrees and continues to decrease as one ages (Kline & Schieber, 1985). The replacement of muscle fiber with stiffer tissue in the ciliary muscles contributes to this decline. To see things in the periphery, we must turn our heads more as we grow older.

Visual acuity refers to the ability to identify objects in space and is the ability to resolve images and then to identify them. This is what most people think of when they think of vision. The ability to detect where one object ends and another begins underlies the ability to perceive those objects. There are two forms of acuity. **Static acuity** is the identification of stationary objects and is measured using an eye chart. This form of visual acuity and the eye charts used to measure it were first created by a Dutch physician named Hermann Snellen (Sekuller & Blake, 1994). **Dynamic acuity** is the identification of objects when they are moving or you are moving or both.

Both types of acuity decline with age especially under low light levels but the decline in dynamic acuity is greater. The decline in dynamic acuity is partly dependent on the speed of moving objects with older adults, particularly women, having more difficulty at higher speeds (Atchley & Andersen, 1998). Research suggests that older adults show virtually no deficit in static acuity, compared to younger adults, when levels of illumination are sufficiently high (Long & Crambert, 1990). Higher levels of illumination help the sensitivity to contrast or detection of the edges of objects. Researchers have compared the static acuity of younger and older adults with 20/20 vision under conditions of high contrast and low contrast. In the high-contrast condition, letters were printed in black ink on a white board while in the low-contrast condition letters were printed in gray ink. The acuity of the young and old were the same in the high-contrast condition but in the low-contrast condition, older adults performed much worse (Adams et al., 1988). When you renew your driver's license, static acuity is tested by having you identify letters or road signs in a viewer under high-contrast conditions. While driving, you are more likely to need dynamic acuity; signs must be identified while you are moving. Furthermore, contrast is frequently not very high. Changes in dynamic acuity, dark-light adaptation, distance accommodation, and peripheral vision also affect driving as examined in Box 6-1.

Older adults are more likely than younger adults to experience certain eye problems and Table 6-1 presents some of these. You may recall from Chapter 3 that cataracts and

BOX **6-1**
Older Drivers

Several normal changes that occur in the eyes of older adults and in their vision have implications for safe driving. Do you recall what those changes are? Older adults are likely to process important information more slowly and this also has implications for safe driving. Do these changes mean that older adults are less safe behind the wheel?

For every 1000 drivers aged 75 to 84, there are 30 driving accidents but for drivers 16 to 24 there are 120 (AARP, 2003a; Barnhill, 1998). The most dangerous drivers are young drivers. Nevertheless, the rate for older drivers is higher than for other age groups. Older drivers who are depressed or on medications that cause drowsiness are the ones most likely to be involved in an accident (Sims et al., 2000). In terms of traffic accidents for older adults, however, the most frequent accident does not occur while they are driving. It is when they are on foot and get hit by a moving vehicle (Aiken, 1995). Changes in vision, including peripheral vision, and in hearing are thought to be major reasons for this as older adults step into the way of oncoming traffic, exit their own car without looking, or enter a busy intersection without seeing the traffic light or "don't walk" sign. When driving in an area where there are likely to be older pedestrians, drivers of all ages need to be very alert.

Some adults with sensory decline are not always aware of their loss and may continue to drive as before (Holland & Rabbitt, 1992). Adults who are aware—or who are made aware—change their behavior. They drive less at night, avoid unfamiliar areas, use greater caution at dangerous intersections, and drive slower (Mancil & Owsley, 1988; Morgan, 1988).

Because older drivers have the second highest rate of traffic accidents, many states have insisted on more frequent and/or more stringent testing of older adults when they renew their license. Illinois and New Hampshire require a road test for older adults. Eighteen other states and the District of Columbia have more stringent license renewal requirements for older adults (AARP, 2003a). Others would argue that the focus on older drivers is misplaced. Not all older drivers have problems; not all younger drivers have problems; not all drivers have problems. The focus, they say, should be on problems. All drivers, regardless of age, should have the quality of their driving assessed when they renew their license or none should. What do you think?

other visual problems rank fifth and ninth among chronic conditions. Cataracts can be very successfully treated with laser surgery but other problems, like macular degeneration, are not so easily fixed and individuals may lose much of their sight and have to compensate for this loss. One may no longer be able to read but compensate by using audio books. Some recent work has found that compensatory devices that do not make up for the loss of vision but instead provide an alternative means (like audio books to compensate for visual reading) do not reduce depression or restore function nearly as well as optical devices that do restore, at least partially, the ability to see (Horowitz et al., 2006).

Hearing

Physical Changes.   Figure 6-2 shows a diagram of the ear. Changes in the muscles and bones, and the degeneration of sensory cells in the base of the cochlea are physical changes

TABLE 6-1 Disorders of Vision and Hearing that Increase with Age

Disorder	Description	Treatment
Vision		
Cataracts	Cloudy, opaque areas on lens, blurred vision common	Can be surgically removed
Glaucoma	Excessive fluid pressure in eye, can cause retinal damage, not noticeable by individual	Can be medicated with drops and/or marijuana if detected early
Macular degeneration	Central part of retina does not function effectively, blurred vision when reading, dark spots, distortions when viewing vertical lines	Amenable to laser treatments in some cases; vitamins C and E may help
Retinal detachment	Inner and outer layers of retina separate	Can be surgically reattached
Retinopathy	Small blood vessels that nourish retina do not function properly as a result of diabetes	Amenable to laser treatments
Hearing		
Central auditory impairment	Difficulty in understanding language but external sounds are heard; nerve centers in brain are damaged	None at present but advances in technology look promising
Conductive loss	Sound does not travel through outer or middle ear due to blockage from wax, fluid, or abnormal bone growth; sounds seem muffled while one's own voice may sound louder	Treated by flushing ear, medication, or surgery
Presbycusis	Progressive loss of hearing for high-frequency tones due to deterioration in inner ear	Hearing aid

that contribute to hearing loss in older adults (Schneider, 1997). The most typical loss is a deficit in hearing for high-pitched tones. This deficit is called **presbycusis**. Hearing impairments are one of the most frequent chronic conditions of older adults and are reported in 28.6 percent of individuals aged 65 and older. Hearing loss is more frequent for men than women (Fozard, 1990). One might expect that such hearing loss would result in greater difficulty in speech perception for older adults.

Although debate continues over whether environment or heredity is primarily responsible for hearing loss, clearly both contribute. In an examination of women, aged 63 to 76, who were identical or fraternal twins, over 60 percent of the variance in hearing loss was attributed to genetic factors (Viljanen et al., 2007). In another study, several hundred adults age 70 and older had their hearing and their belief in age stereotypes measured. When their hearing was measured again, 3 years later, those with the most negative views showed the greatest loss of hearing. Authors suggest that this may happen as those who be-

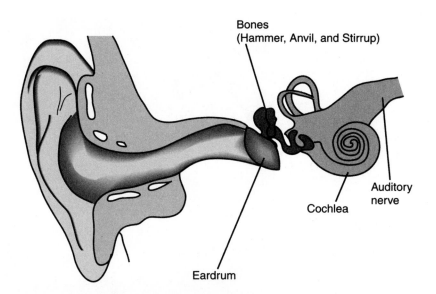

FIGURE 6-2 Diagram of the Normal Ear.

lieve negative stereotypes may not try to offset declines and may experience significant stress from those stereotypes. Perhaps the chemical components of stress (see Chapter 5) contribute to hearing loss (Levy et al., 2006).

Research has examined age differences in **speech perception** under a variety of conditions and found age differences under noisy conditions (Fozard, 1990). These studies used a cross-sectional approach and compared adults of different ages on their ability to perceive speech when presented by itself, or in the presence of other competing voices in the background, or in the presence of other noises such as electronic static. Results show little decline in speech perception from age 20 to 89 when speech is presented by itself but show progressively more decline in the presence of other voices and especially static noise (Bergman et al., 1976; Heller & Wilber, 1990). Studies like this are often criticized for failing to consider the possibility that any obtained differences could be cohort differences.

Longitudinal studies allow one to examine this question by following the same group or groups of adults over longer periods of time and measuring the same individuals at several points. In one such study, adults ranging in age from their 20s to their 80s were tested two to six times with an average interval of 3 years between tests. Results showed a steady rate of hearing loss for high frequencies even in the young and an increased loss for older adults in the perception of sound frequencies at the level of speech (Brant & Fozard, 1990). Note that such longitudinal work may tell that changes in hearing occur with age and are not simply cohort differences but do not tell whether those changes are due to exposure to noise over one's life.

The most common device to assist people who are losing their ability to hear well is the hearing aid. There are many different types of hearing aids but generally they amplify sound and can be viewed as beneficial, in part, because they restore hearing rather than

Driving means freedom at any age.

compensate for its loss. Because the two ears are not equal in terms of speech perception (Sininger & Cone-Wesson, 2006), one is advised to place the aid in the right ear which is better at detecting speech.

There are a number of important points to consider when talking to an older person with a hearing impairment (Cheesman, 1997). As with vision impairments, hearing impairments are more likely in older adults (see Table 6-1). Raymond Hull (1980) says that when conversing with a person with a hearing impairment, one should talk a little louder (do not shout) than one ordinarily would and should not speak too rapidly. Face the person when speaking to them so that they can see your lips move. Do not try to make the person hear you when there is a lot of other noise around. If the individual does not understand you, do not repeat what you have said. Try saying it a different way. Do not shout into a person's ear; that is insulting and takes away any use of visual cues that might help the person understand what is being said. Treat older adults who have a hearing impairment with respect; treat them as you would wish to be treated.

Smell, Taste, Touch, and Balance

The olfactory bulb in the brain is the center for **smell** and shows cell loss with advanced age. Tests of 1955 people ranging in age from 5 to 99 were conducted to see if simulated aromas such as cinnamon, cherry, pizza, mint, and lemon could be detected and named (Doty et al., 1984). Best performance was by people between the ages of 20 and 40. After age 50 decrements appeared and after age 70 there was rapid decline. One-half of the adults over the age of 80 seemed to have lost all ability to detect aromas. As with vision and hearing, some researchers believe that this loss of smell is not the result of aging. Instead, loss of smell may be the result of a lifetime of exposure to airborne toxic substances such as car exhaust fumes, pesticides, factory waste, cigarette smoke, and other pollutants. People living in a pollution-free environment may show little or no decline with age while those living in a very polluted environment may show great loss at a relatively young age. Clearly, the total loss of sense of smell influences perception. As you might imagine, this could be a very dangerous loss in situations where one might be unable to detect a gas leak or the smell of spoiled food. One's enjoyment of foods also may decline due to a loss of sense of smell.

Humans have four types of **taste** buds on the tongue resulting in four basic taste sensations: bitter, sour, salty, and sweet. Taste buds are short-lived but are continually replaced. The total number of taste buds declines with age starting at about age 40 because the rate of replacement declines. Some individuals show a loss of nearly two-thirds of total taste buds by age 70 and the buds most frequently lost are those for sweet sensation (Aiken, 1995). Many older adults compensate for this loss by adding extra sweetener to coffee, desserts, lemonade, and other items. Have you ever had a grandparent offer you a glass of lemonade that was too sweet for your taste? It may not have tasted that sweet at all to the person who made it. At high concentrations, older adults are as able as younger adults to differentiate all tastes (Bartoshuk et al., 1986). You might notice that older adults often put more salt, pepper, or other condiments on their food. They need what appears to be an excess amount so that they can taste it. The amount of salivation also decreases with age and saliva may become thicker. As a result, older adults often drink more fluids with a meal than younger adults do and are often less tolerant of dry foods such as potato or corn chips (Cunningham & Brookbank, 1988).

Sensitivity to **touch** also declines with age. As discussed in Chapter 3, fewer nerve cells are present to detect contact on the skin as one grows older and the skin itself has changed. Older adults may not be as sensitive to changes in temperature as a result of this loss or may not easily detect a light pressure stimulus such as a mosquito on the skin. In very cold climates, the danger of frostbite can be much greater for older adults because their skin is less sensitive to temperature. Burns also are more frequent for older adults because they may not feel the heat of a stove, match, or fire and may not pull away until the skin is burnt.

Sensory cells in the vestibular system located in the ears also decline with advanced age and can produce more difficulty in maintaining **balance**. Older adults with such decline are more likely to experience vertigo or dizziness. Research has shown that reductions in lower body strength, poor vision, and cigarette smoking all contribute to loss of balance and that women over 85 have the most difficulties (Satariano et al., 1996). The loss of sensory cells in the vestibular system can be compensated for by relying more on other sensory information to help maintain balance. Adults in their 80s have been trained to improve their balance and strength by performing leaning exercises on balance boards and lifting sandbags with their legs. Following training, gains have been maintained by teaching adults to practice low-intensity tai chi (Wolfson et al., 1996). **Tai chi** is a Chinese system of physical exercises that involves slow, rhythmic movements. Six months after learning tai chi, adults showed higher levels of balance and strength than untrained control participants (Wolf et al., 1996). Other work has found that vibrations in the feet can help

Tai chi may help one's balance.

adults control their balance. In one study, younger and older adults had their balance measured while they stood on vibrating gel-based insoles or simply stood. In both young and old, balance was better on the vibrating insoles but especially for older adults (Priplata et al., 2004). The vibration may restore the brain's attention to sensory messages about posture and balance from the feet.

Changes in senses can affect perception but often do not because they usually occur over an extended period of time, allowing individuals to adapt. In addition, devices and/or treatments often are available to restore sensation. When that cannot occur, compensation can. The ability to perceive information and act on it also is influenced by the slowing that occurs with age.

Slowing

Measurements of response time have been made since psychologists began systematic investigations of human behavior. In 1884 at the International Health Exhibition held in London, England, Sir Francis Galton measured the response times of 9337 men and women ranging in age from 5 to 80, who paid three pence each for this privilege. Individuals responded as quickly as they could when a tone was sounded and when a light was flashed. People responded quicker to the tone than the light and the fastest people responding were between the ages of 18 and 20. Older adults were consistently slower (Boring, 1950). This finding has been replicated many times over the last century and is one of the most certain findings in gerontology. Without a doubt, people slow down as they age.

Reaction time measures are usually divided into three different types. The kind of response or reaction time measured by Galton is referred to as **simple reaction time**. One stimulus is presented and when it occurs, the person makes one response. For example, a clock might start when a light comes on and, when the light is seen, a person presses a button as quickly as they can; the button stops the clock and, over a series of trials, average simple reaction time is recorded. **Choice reaction time** refers to the situation in which two different stimuli are presented and a different response for each one is required. When there are more than two stimuli and two responses, the situation is referred to as **complex reaction time**.

Think for a moment about what sorts of internal processing must go on for a person to react in one of these situations. Table 6-2 illustrates the steps involved. *First*, you must sense the stimulus when it is presented; failure to sense that the light has come on would result in no response at all. Once the sense has registered, it must be correctly perceived as being the relevant stimulus. Then, you must decide to respond, and you must initiate the response. These components of perception, decision, and initiation are central and take place in the brain. They make up the *second* step. Third, nerve signals must be sent to the correct muscles and those muscles must move and press the button. Motor action is the *third* step.

In simple, choice, and complex reaction time situations, all three steps must occur but in choice and complex situations, the second step requires more processing. In Table 6-2, the steps shown above the line always occur whether the situation is simple, choice,

TABLE 6-2   Three Components of Response Time: Sensory, Central Processing, and Muscle

Step 1 (Sensory)	Step 2 (Central processing in the brain)	Step 3 (Muscle response)
The stimulus must be sensed by the appropriate sense organ.	Stimulus must be perceived as the one requiring a response. One must decide whether to respond. One must initiate the response.	When the nerve impulse reaches the muscle, the response occurs.
	One must determine which of two (choice) or several (complex) stimuli was sensed. One must determine the correct response for the stimulus that was perceived.	

or complex. In choice and complex situations, however, the additional central processing shown below the line also takes place. You must perceive which of the relevant stimuli has occurred and which response is appropriate for that stimulus. For example, you must decide whether the red or the green light has come on and to press the button on the right if the red light came on or the button on the left if the green light came on. Choice and complex situations involve more central processing at the level of the brain but the work of the sense organs and muscles, steps one and three, are largely the same in simple, choice, and complex situations.

If older adults respond more slowly because of a slow down of central processing in the brain, then we would expect them to be much slower as the task becomes more complex and that is exactly what happens. Age differences in simple reaction time are much smaller than age differences in choice and complex situations (Birren et al., 1980; Fozard et al., 1994; Salthouse, 1985). The decrease in response speed, between age 20 and 60, is about 20 percent for simple situations and about 50 percent for complex situations (Welford, 1984). Although there is some slowing in sensation and motor movement as we grow older, the major slowing is in central processing in the brain.

To investigate this slowing in the brain, researchers now are examining different components of the mental processing that takes place. The range in response times is much wider for older than for younger adults suggesting that some particular aspects of central processing have changed and may be the main reasons for the slowing (Ratcliff et al., 2000). When a particular aspect is affected, that individual will slow down a great deal while slowing is minimal for those with no change in this particular aspect. The range of response times for such a group is greater than for a group with no change in that aspect of processing. In some of this work, younger and older adults responded to asterisks or dots presented on a screen and judged whether there were many or few or whether they were close together or far apart. Results showed that much of the slowing in these tasks for older adults was due to their setting a very conservative response strategy; that is, they tended to delay their response until they were certain they were correct. This more conservative response strategy is one aspect of central processing that contributes to age differences in reaction times (Ratcliff et al., 2001).

The slowdown in the brain also may be due, in part, to physical factors (Schaie & Willis, 1991). We know that some areas of the brain lose more nerve cells and connections than other areas. Areas with the greatest loss may operate at a much slower rate than they once did. The finding that slowing with advanced age occurs for some aspects of various tasks but not for others fits well with this hypothesis (Sliwinski, 1997). Blood flow also declines as we grow older so the brain receives less oxygen and glucose than it once did (Hagstadius & Risberg, 1989). Increasing blood flow with aerobic exercise can significantly increase speed of responding (Dustman et al., 1984; Spirduso & McRae, 1990) and older adults who are athletic have faster reaction times than younger adults who are not (Spirduso & Clifford, 1978).

In most of the laboratory work on response time and aging, the differences found between older and younger responders are less than a second (Salthouse, 1985). Such response differences are barely visible to the casual observer and require careful measurement to be noticed. One might think, therefore, that these small slowdowns are relatively meaningless, and in many situations they are. If one seals envelopes or squeezes toothpaste a little slower, it is unlikely to make much of a difference. Think for a moment, however, of all the central processing that goes on in a situation such as driving down an unfamiliar street when something suddenly appears ahead in the road. Your visual sense detects the object and now you must try to perceive what it might be. Is it a child in the road? A dog? A newspaper? A shadow? If it is a dog, is it standing still or moving? Is it in your way? Will its movement put it in your way when you arrive at that location? What, if any, response should you make? Should you blow your horn? Should you swerve to avoid a collision? Should you apply the brakes? A little bit of slowing may not be a problem but the cumulative effect of a little bit of slowing in each of these steps could make the difference between a close call and a disaster. Slowing with advanced age can, in all too many situations, make a major difference in the outcome.

In summary, the slowing that accompanies old age varies from individual to individual. Adults who have worked in jobs demanding mental processing as opposed to physical labor tend to respond faster (Simonen et al., 1998). Any slowdown in central processing can be quite serious in some situations but not in others. We will see how it can affect performance in certain jobs when we examine work in Chapter 11. Some recent research shows that the slowdown in muscle movement also should be considered as serious. An examination of men participating in the Baltimore Longitudinal Study examined the relationship between the speed with which they tapped with a pencil, their reaction time, and their mortality over more than 20 years. The risk of death was significantly higher for those who showed muscle slowing, but not central slowing. The control of muscles is related to mortality although the reasons for this connection are not yet clear (Metter et al., 2005). Other work has found that central slowing also is related to mortality. Several hundred older adults were followed from their early 50s to their 70s and results showed higher mortality rates for those with the slowest initial simple and choice reaction times (Deary & Der, 2005). It appears that some inefficiency in processes that takes place in the brain and muscles predicts mortality. When mental processes slow down, they may not function as efficiently. Older persons may not be able to take in as much information in a short period of time as they did in the past. They may, however, be able to take in the same information if given sufficient time. They may have more difficulty remembering information previously presented because the search of memory operates much slower than previously. At the same time, they may be able to remember just as well if given sufficient time to remember. Slowing has implications for the ways in which we evaluate the memory, cognition, and intelligence of older adults both in the laboratory and in everyday settings. We will see in the next two chapters that one must be careful about drawing conclusions regarding changes in mental processes above and beyond the slowing that occurs in those processes.

Falls

Older adults who have deficits in one or more senses and who respond slower are more likely to be involved in an accident. Driving, traffic accidents, and license renewal are discussed in Box 6-1. Fires and burns also are fairly frequent. The loss of smell contributes to the former because smoke from a fire may go undetected (please check the batteries in your grandparents' smoke alarms) while the loss of sensitivity to touch contributes to the latter (Aiken 1995; Sterns et al., 1985). The most frequent accident for older adults is, however, falling. Falls are the leading cause of accidental death in adults 65 and older (Morse et al., 1985). Each year, it is estimated that about a third of older, healthy adults living in the community fall at least once (Tinetti et al., 2006). Falls are even more frequent among frail, nursing home residents.

Falls occur more often for women than for men; about 80 percent of those who fall are women. Falls occur more often for white Americans than for other ethnic groups; about 90 percent of those who report a fall are white. Every year, more than 200,000 not only fall but fracture a hip during the fall. In many of these cases, it is believed that the hip fractured first, because of osteoporosis, and then the person fell. About 20 percent of older adults who fracture a hip never recover and die of pneumonia within 6 months; within the first year half die this way (Peterson & Rosenblatt, 1986; Tinetti, 1989). The risk of mortality during that first year is greater for men than for women and men typically have more other health problems, such as chronic obstructive pulmonary disease and stroke, before the fall occurred (Hawkes et al., 2006). A hip fracture can be very frightening and many individuals are unwilling to risk getting up and moving about for fear of fracturing the other hip. They spend their time in bed as fluid builds up in their lungs and bones become weaker; they catch pneumonia and die. Exercise is very important following a hip (or knee) replacement. Staying in bed is a serious mistake.

When a fall does not result in a serious fracture, it still has consequences. In one recent study, Chinese adults 65 and older were assessed before and after falling. Over a year's time, those who fell had reduced walking speed, balance, and more difficulties with activities of daily living (ADLs) (Chu et al., 2006). People who have fallen are more cautious and often change the way they walk; they are not as steady on their feet but a change in walking often increases, rather than decreases, the likelihood of falling again (Campbell et al., 1981).

Why do falls occur? Certainly osteoporosis and a change in gait following a prior fall increase the risk. Diseases like diabetes increase the risk of falls because the person may lose sensitivity in their lower extremities (Blaum et al., 2003). People who have had a stroke, who take many prescription medications, or who have lower levels of physical functioning, are more likely to fall (Quandt et al., 2006). Alcohol consumption, at a moderate to high rate (14 or more drinks per week) increases the risk of falling (Mukamal et al., 2004). Declines in vision increase the risk of falling. When moving from a room with a light-colored flooring to one with a dark-colored flooring, a visually impaired person may see the change in coloring as a change in elevation. They may raise their foot expecting to step up and lose their balance when no such elevation occurs. If that person also responds slower, then the sudden loss of balance may not be corrected before they fall. A fall that might not injure a younger person can be quite serious for an older person.

Because falls are very frequent among older adults and can be serious and even fatal, many older adults are quite fearful about falling. Ask an older adult if they know anyone who has fallen recently and you will find that most do; ask them if they know of anyone who fractured a hip and then died and very many will answer yes. Ask them if they're afraid of falling. Studies have shown that a high fear of falling is yet another factor that increases the risk of falling (Cummings et al., 2000). Having already fallen, being 80 or older, having a visual impairment, a sedentary lifestyle, and no emotional support all increase the fear of falling (Murphy et al., 2003). Social support from family, although not from friends, decreases fear (Faulkner et al., 2003). Family members may provide assistance when it is needed, be ready to come when needed, and may warn the person of hazards and environmental conditions that could result in a fall.

It is important to prevent falls and to reduce fear of falling. As you learned earlier, tai chi has been shown to help older adults maintain balance. In one study, physically inactive older adults, between the ages of 70 and 92, were randomly assigned to 6 weeks of tai chi training or 6 weeks of stretching exercises. Their balance, number of falls, and fear of falling were measured before the training, immediately after, and 6 months after the end of training. Those in the tai chi group maintained better balance, had fewer falls, and had a much lower fear of falling than those in the stretching exercise group (Fuzhong et al., 2005). We also can work to make the environment safer for older adults who may fear falling. One of the most dangerous places to fall is on a stairway. Stairs should be well lit and light switches should be located at both the top and bottom of the stairway. Stairs could be painted different colors or the rise and run could be different colors to aid vision. Nothing should be placed on stairs or floors that might be accidentally stepped on. The next time you visit the home of an older adult, look for these dangers and fix them if you can.

Time

At the beginning of this chapter we quoted the famous psychologist William James who expressed the belief that time is perceived as passing more rapidly when we grow old. Mabel Davis, in this chapter's Senior View, says that time passes far too quickly for her ("on Monday, it's Friday before I know it"). It is, in fact, a common belief that time passes more rapidly as we age (Fraisse, 1984; Ross, 1991). Research shows that students perceive

SOCIAL POLICY APPLICATIONS

Policies govern who should be permitted to have a driver's license and who should not. You must be a certain age and be able to pass the tests. Clearly we want those with licenses to be capable of driving safely and all states test adults of all ages when it is time to renew their licenses. You will learn in Chapter 14 that motor vehicle accidents are a major cause of death. Does this suggest that we need more stringent tests for license renewal? Won't more stringent tests be more expensive? Will you have to wait in line even longer? Are there too many unsafe drivers on the road? Should only older adults have to take more stringent tests and more often than middle-aged and younger adults since, as you now know, they may have sensory deficits and respond more slowly? Should we incorporate more tests of dynamic acuity as indicated in this chapter? Will we provide transportation to older adults who end up unable to renew their licenses? How will they access groceries, or doctors, or attend religious services or community events? Would we doom them to a life of homebound isolation? Policies with regard to who should have a driver's license are difficult to design and implement. The implications and consequences for society are great.

PROJECT **6**

This project is based on work conducted by Michael Flaherty and Michelle Meer (1994). You will need a group of volunteers to participate. Each person is asked to estimate the passage of time using the following scale:

1 = Very slowly

2 = Slowly

3 = Normally

4 = Quickly

5 = Very quickly

Select a few different time periods for them to estimate. For example, Flaherty and Meer used yesterday, last month, and last year. You might try the same time periods or others.

Flaherty and Meer also used young (mean age of 19.8), middle-age (mean age of 38.4), and older (mean age of 71.2) adults. You might use the same age groups or different groups. Children, for example, might provide different estimates than adults.

Each person is told to think about the things they did and experienced during a time period, such as last month, and to estimate how they remember time as passing using the scale, ranging from very slowly (1) to very quickly (5). They then are asked to think about another time period and estimate time for that period. You should be careful to present the time periods that you are using in different orders for different people.

When you finish, calculate scale means for each time period for each group. Flaherty and Meer found means of 3.79, 4.03, and 3.80 for young, middle-age, and older adults, respectively. Time was reported as fastest for the middle-age participants. They also found means of 3.46, 3.95, and 4.22 for estimates of time passing yesterday, last month, and last year, respectively. More recent time seemed slower than more distant time. How do your means compare?

The researchers found that all three age groups rated time as passing more quickly last year than last month and more quickly last month than yesterday. They assume that this difference is largely due to memory. People remember a lot that happened yesterday but not as much for last month and even less for last year. The less that is remembered, the quicker time is perceived as having gone by. What do you think of this explanation? Can you think of any other possible reasons for the obtained difference?

They also found that time moved quicker for their middle-age group than for younger and older adults. The middle-age group was involved in the most routine of activities while the younger and older adults were experiencing new things. Did you also find age differences? If so, do they seem to be due to the routine of life?

---

time as having passed slower when they were younger (8- to 10-years-old) and fully expect it to pass more rapidly as they grow older (Joubert, 1990). Adults are often heard to remark how fast the week, month, or year has gone.

It has been suggested that this difference in perception is a result of memory and novel activity (Flaherty & Meer, 1994; Pedri & Hesketh, 1993). If we do not remember much happening over the last few years, then that time may seem short compared to time in the distant past when many new things were happening. If you do the same thing over and over, year after year, time, in retrospect, seems to have passed quickly. If you move slowly and take a long time to finish a task, then later it will seem as if time flew by since you accomplished so little. Older adults may have fewer new experiences and this lack of novelty may make time seem to move faster for them (Fraisse, 1984).

Other research has found that time perception is influenced by memory for past events and that ratings of how quickly time went by are faster for events of 1 year ago than of 1 month ago, and of 1 month ago then of yesterday for adults of all ages. When events are well remembered, time seems slower than when events are not so well remembered (Flaherty & Meer, 1994). Try a version of this study by completing Project 6.

Time may seem to move more rapidly as we grow older but it is obviously perception and not time that has changed. The changes in perception and the slowing that occur with age have strong influences on our cognition and it is to cognition that we now turn in Chapter 7.

CHAPTER HIGHLIGHTS

- Some changes in senses affect perception while others do not.
- Physical changes in the eye include an increase in curvature/thickness of the cornea, and the lens become flatter, yellow, and thicker. These changes result in presbyopia (when point of clearest vision moves farther from the eye), altered perception of some colors, less light entering the eye, and reduced distance accommodation. Floaters also increase, some rod and cone cells are lost, and ciliary muscle fibers are lost.
- Adaptation from light to dark is slower and less efficient for older eyes.
- Periperal vision declines with age.
- Visual acuity declines (especially dyamic acuity). These declines make reading more difficult and driving less safe.
- Physical changes in the inner ear and/or exposure to noisy environments may produce hearing loss. The most common loss in older adults, especially men, is presbycusis (a deficit in hearing for high-pitched sounds).
- Older adults have no difficulty perceiving speech unless other talking or noise occurs at the same time.
- Loss of cells in the olfactory bulb often results in loss of smell for older adults. Such loss can be dangerous.
- The rate at which taste buds are replaced slows as one grows older and many older adults need higher concentrations of a flavor to perceive the taste.
- Sensitivity to touch declines as nerve cells under the skin are lost.
- Loss of cells in the vestibular system often occurs in older adults and can result in loss of balance. Tai chi is effective in helping adults improve and maintain balance.
- The finding that older adults respond more slowly is one of the most certain findings in gerontology.
- Age differences in response time increase as situations change from simple to complex. These results support the hypothesis that the slowing that occurs with advanced age is in the central processing that takes place in the brain.
- The slowing of central processing in the brain may be due to the loss of nerve cell connections or decreased blood flow.
- The slowing of muscle response is related to increased mortality.
- Small amounts of slowing in a number of central processes can result in serious problems in some complex real-life situations.
- Falls are the most frequent and most deadly accident for older adults. A hip fracture especially is dangerous and many older adults do not recover.
- The likelihood of a fall is higher for those with osteoporosis, increased fear of falling, reduced vision, diabetes, stroke, a large number of prescription medications, higher alcohol consumption, and lower levels of physical activity.

- Fear of falling is higher for those who have already fallen, are 80 or older, have a visual impairment, are sedentary, and have little emotional support.
- Fear of falling is reduced by social support from family, exercise (such as tai chi), and maintaining a safe environment.
- Time perception seems to change with age. Older adults frequently perceive time as passing quickly. This perception could be due to memory for events, absence of novel activities, and/or the speed with which tasks are performed.
- Sensory changes, perceptual changes, and the slowing of central processing influence many types of cognition.

STUDY QUESTIONS

1. Which of the changes in the eye that are typical of advanced age, begin when we are very young and which do not begin until we are older?

2. Explain why perception is not always affected by changes in sense organs.

3. Name some ways in which the risk of falls can be prevented. Why do older adults fall so often?

4. Why do you think your grandmother puts so much sugar in her tea? Is it because she likes sweet tea or because of changes in her sense of taste? Explain.

5. Could changes in senses be due to exposure to the environment? What things in the environment could produce sensory decline? Can anything be done to lessen the effects of these environmental factors?

6. Older adults respond slower than younger adults but only by a fraction of a second. Explain how such a small difference could make a big difference in some real-life settings.

7. Why do we conclude that most of the slowing with advanced age is in the brain rather than in the sense organs or muscles? Explain the steps involved in responding and the research findings.

8. What factors influence the perception of time?

9. What findings in the present chapter can you relate to the issues of mechanistic-organismic development and continuity-discontinuity?

10. What sensory changes are influenced by both genetics and environment? Give examples.

11. What factors increase the likelihood of a fall? What factors decrease this likelihood?

RECOMMENDED READING

Draaisma, D. (2006). *Why Life Speeds Up as You Get Older: How Memory Shapes Our Past*. New York: Cambridge University Press. This book presents an entertaining and informative presentation of several interesting phenomena (*deja vu*, near death experiences) including the perceived speeding up of time with age.

INTERNET RESOURCES

www.eurekalert.org/releases/better-smeller.html. For information on loss of smell due to breathing in pollutants.

nidcd.nih.gov/. National Institute on Deafness and other communication disorders website supporting human communication research.

www.hear-it.org/?gclid=CJre7cSJpogCFSdpNAodkD-y7Q. Site on hearing and hearing loss.

www.99main.com/~charlief/blindness.html. Site on vision loss.

www.stopfalls.org. Site on fall prevention.

www.aarp.org. Scroll down and go to the Driver Safety Online Course. For information on safe driving for older adults.

CHAPTER

7   Memory and Cognition

The true way to render age vigorous is to prolong the youth of the mind.
—Mortimer Collins

It is commonly believed that memory declines as we age. Older adults are said to forget things, even things that just happened. They are said to remember the "good old days" but fail to remember appointments, names of people they just met, items they were supposed to pick up at the store, and so on. Such beliefs are as common among older adults as among younger adults (Hertzog et al., 1990).

This chapter examines the changes that seem to occur with advanced age. Also, we try to dispel some of the false beliefs, and suggest ways to improve memory. First, take a brief look at how memory is thought to operate.

An Overview of Memory Processing

While different views of the details of memory and processing exist, most have a common configuration. It is this common configuration, or skeleton of memory, that we use for this discussion.

This common view suggests that there are three basic components of memory processing (Figure 7-1) and that incoming information must be processed in order to be remembered. Memory does not operate like a video camera or a tape recorder; it does not simply record events. The information that gets put into memory is information that we have thought about, reacted to, or mentally processed in some way. Memories are a result of processes that we apply to information. For example, we select items to remember or ignore, we abstract information, we condense or expand it, we associate it with other things we know, we concentrate or hardly pay attention, and the final product is as much a result of processing (probably more) as of any actual experience. We know that three people witnessing the same event may remember it in three different ways. Each person's memory of the same event is a result of each person's processing of that event.

It is also the case that processing depends on many factors, each of which influences our memory for an event. For example, the amount of time available to process informa-

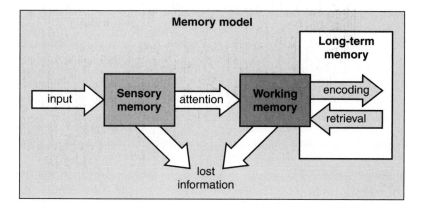

FIGURE 7-1   Illustration of the Memory System.

tion will influence how well it is processed. A familiarity with the information, the complexity of the situation, physical and mental health, a knowledge of processing techniques/tricks, and so on, influence one's memory for information by influencing the processing of that information. In short, memories depend on processing and processing depends upon a number of other factors. Finally, these factors may be influenced in the same or different ways for different people.

Sensory Memory

The first part of memory is called **sensory memory** and consists of a different and brief memory for each sense. For example, visual memory stores information received by the eyes and auditory memory stores information received by the ears. The amount of information received by the eyes and ears is too much to process and so most of it is discarded immediately (Neisser, 1967). Box 7-1 gives an example of how sensory memories are bombarded with information, most of which is lost. Information in sensory memory is there for only a very brief period of time as new information is continually received by the senses. Although vision and hearing frequently decline with advanced age and older adults may have a harder time seeing or hearing information (see Chapter 6), once it is seen or heard, evidence suggests that those sensory memories decline minimally (Craik & Jennings, 1992; Poon, 1985).

Working Memory

Working memory is assumed to be centrally located in the brain and, as the name implies, this part of memory does the real work of paying attention to information in the sensory memories (or ignoring that information), encoding, abstracting, selecting, retrieving, and other mental processing. One simple way to think about working memory is to equate it with consciousness. If you are consciously aware of something, then that something must be in working memory.

Senior View

We spoke with Edward and Isabelle Peltz about changes in their memories as they have grown older. Ed was 72 and Isabelle was 69 when we spoke with them. Before his retirement, Ed was a teacher, then a principal, then the superintendent of schools. Isabelle worked as a medical assistant and then a registered nurse until their children were born. Have their memories changed?

Isabelle told us, *My memory is still quite good but I have a lot of difficulty recalling names; sometimes it's right on the tip of my tongue.*

Ed, on the other hand, said, *My memory is nowhere near as good as it used to be.*

Isabelle went on to say, *I have no trouble at all recalling events that happened whether they happened in the past or were very recent. My hus-*

band claims that I don't remember certain things but that is under dispute at all times.

Ed chuckled and asked, *What was the question again?*

We asked them what kinds of things they did to keep their memories sharp.

We read a lot, said Isabelle.

Ed told us, *We also belong to a number of organizations and that gives us opportunities to meet and interact with a very wide variety of people. It forces you to stay mentally active. I try to remember the names of new people by associating each name with some familiar object that I can see in my mind.*

Isabelle said, *I have to write down new names and other things I want to remember. Just the act of writing it down and then looking at it later helps me remember pretty well.*

Following a set routine is helpful for remembering to do certain things. Doing them becomes automatic, said Ed.

So how much information is stored in your memory and does it help or hurt? we asked. Isabelle told us, *The amount of information can be a help; if you have more information, it makes your memory better. Your organization may improve.*

Ed said, *Everything you experience goes into your memory and stays there but you still don't run out of room. Memory's not always accurate though. Different people tend to remember the same thing in different ways.*

Isabelle finished this thought by saying, *The way you perceive it at the time is the way it is stored in the memory, not necessarily the actual facts.* It would be hard to find a cognitive psychologist who did not agree with her.

Working memory can be considered as a pool of processing resources that can be allocated to different processing tasks by a central executive (Baddeley & Logie, 1999). It is very limited in the amount of processing that can be done at one time because the pool or pools of available resources are quite small. The central executive cannot allocate to all tasks demanding processing when the demands of such tasks exceed the available resources. In such cases, choices must be made. We are aware of the difficulties encountered

BOX **7-1**

A Walk Through the Library

To get a feel for the three components of memory, imagine you are entering the library to check out a certain book. As you enter, your senses are bombarded. The walls may be covered with shelves that are filled with books of different sizes and colors. There may be paintings on the walls and tables and chairs in the room. There are people everywhere and all are different. They are wearing a wide variety of clothing of assorted colors. The lights may be bright, dim, white, or yellow. Even though this is a library, there are sounds everywhere: people whispering, copy machines running, people walking, and doors, elevators, and heaters/air conditioners quietly humming. You can feel the floor under your shoes and the temperature of the room. You can feel your backpack on your back and pen in your hand. You might detect the cologne of other students or the musty scent of books. All of this information impinges on your sensory memories but almost all of it is immediately discarded. Most information gets no further than sensory memory.

Working memory has allocated resources to finding a particular item. As you examine a row of books looking for that item you come upon a book laying on the floor. You bend to pick it up and see that it is *The Life and Times of S. V. Shereshevskii*. This information has made it past your sensory memory and into your working memory; you have noticed it but because it means nothing, you discard the information from working memory and place the book on a shelf. You do not process it further. Most information is lost at the sensory memory level and some which makes it past that level to working memory also is lost.

Suppose, however, that you know that Shereshevskii is the famous memory magician described by Luria (1968). You then might open the book and examine it; you might consider borrowing it and reading about this famous mnemonist. You are processing information about the book and encoding that information into permanent episodic memory. Even if you discard the book, you are more likely to remember having seen it if you ever see it again or the next time someone talks about memory.

Try to examine all the information that is discarded at the level of working memory and the even greater amount lost at the sensory memory level the next time you enter the library or grocery store, or the next time you go to a concert, dinner, or movie. It is a good thing about memory that most information is discarded. We could stand there forever, in a daze, if everything were processed for storage in permanent memory.

---

when we are asked to do too many things at the same time. We cannot do them all at once. Some information will be lost but what is processed in working memory is stored in long-term memory, the last component.

Long-Term Memory

The third component is **long-term memory** and is assumed to reside in the cerebral cortex as a vast interconnected network of stored memories. In fact, it is often assumed that two or three different networks of long-term memories exist and are interconnected. For our purposes, assume that there are three major parts of long-term memory: procedural, episodic, and semantic memories (Tulving, 1985), although there are other ways to categorize these different aspects of permanent memory (Schacter, 1992).

Procedural memory refers to memory of how to do something. Permanent memories of how to tie your shoes, wash your hands, make a bed, and open a door are examples of procedural memories.

Episodic memory refers to memory for the episodes/events of your life. Permanent memories of where you grew up, your first date, where you parked your car, and what you did last night would be episodic memories.

Semantic memory refers to memory for knowledge and meaning. Permanent memories of the meanings of words, the location of Mexico, the difference between a liquid and solid, and which way is up would be semantic memories.

Most of the research conducted on memory has measured episodic memory rather than procedural or semantic memory. Research participants typically are presented with some items (e.g., a list of words, a story, face–name pairs) and then, after some period of time, tested for the items presented. They might be asked to recall or recognize the presented items. Because the presentation of the items was an event in their life, it is memory for that event that is being tested.

Long-term memory is assumed to have no upper limit to its storage capacity. Think of it as a structure being built with Legos. The bigger the structure gets, the more places there are to add on more pieces.

Memory System

It is important to think of the various components of memory as working together but the heart of the system is working memory. Working memory can be viewed as a pool of processing resources. It is a very limited pool. We can carry on only so many processing tasks at the same time. For example, you cannot sing the National Anthem while reading a book and jumping rope. You do not have enough processing resources to do all these things at the same time although you undoubtedly have sufficient resources to do any one of them, or a combination if you are resourceful.

These resources can be allocated to paying attention to new information; that is, working memory may select some of the information impinging on sensory memory and pay attention to it. It is, thus, being processed in working memory.

In working memory, the information can be encoded (e.g., rehearsed or pictured) in an attempt to lay down a permanent representation. You might try associating it with other information that you already know. In this case, you are clearly using some resources to retrieve information from permanent memory to relate to the new information. In this case, you can allocate some resources to retain the new information while you allocate others to retrieving information from permanent memory.

The interactions between working memory and permanent memory can be thought of as going in two different directions. When resources are being used to place information into long-term storage, they are referred to as **encoding** processes. Thus, rehearsing information or trying to form a mental image or associating information with prior information are considered forms of encoding processes. The more distinctive these encoding operations are, the better the *copy* in permanent memory (Schmidt, 1991). The better the copy, the easier it will be to find at another time. When resources are devoted to finding something in long-term memory and bringing it to conscious attention in working memory, they are referred to as **retrieval** processes. Thus, trying to recall the name of someone you met or recognizing the correct item on a multiple-choice test are considered forms of retrieval.

Memory and Aging

Although many adults believe that memory declines with advanced age, the evidence is not convincing. Clearly, some parts of memory change while others seem to stay the same or even improve (Cerella et al., 1993). Remember when discussing sensory memory, there seems to be little or no decline with age.

Working Memory and Aging

Working memory does seem to change with advanced age. Research suggests that typical changes in working memory for older adults are due to a decline in available resources and a slowing in the rate at which information is processed. Thus, older adults may have more difficulty paying attention to more than one thing at a time and, typically, have to devote more effort to learning something new (Fogler & Stern, 1994).

The decline in working memory resources with advanced age has been documented a number of times (McCabe & Hartman, 2003). With fewer resources available, older adults often must decide which of several pieces of information or ongoing tasks should receive their attention and processing effort (Brébion, 2003; Foos, 1995). This means that older adults have far more difficulty when more than a single task must be completed in a given period of time and their performance on at least one task suffers (Barrouillet et al., 2004; Verhaeghen & Cerella, 2002). The need to make such a decision can occur quite frequently in real life because, as noted earlier, sensory memories are continually awash in information. When, on the other hand, older adults can process information a piece at a time in a distraction-free environment, they generally do quite well. When they do not, we must have some concern about their health (see Chapter 12). Some work shows that even the normal loss of resources in working memory contributes to the difficulties that older adults can have with understanding new medical information given to them by their physician or written on a prescription bottle. Health providers need to be aware of this loss of processing resources and be willing to provide continuous access to information (on the Internet or by answering questions on the phone) (Brown & Park, 2003).

Processing speed is also an essential element in the observed decline in working memory (Salthouse, 1990; Salthouse & Babcock, 1991). For example, Fisk and Warr (1996) tested older and younger adults on several measures of working memory and perceptual speed. Perceptual speed refers to how quickly an individual can make a decision about presented materials. For example, participants were shown two strings of letters on a computer screen and had to answer as quickly as possible whether they were the same or different. They also had to answer questions about sentences that they had just read and later recall the last words of several sentences. These and other tasks showed that differences in perceptual speed accounted for many of the obtained age differences in working memory. Older adults may not only process less but they process less at a slower rate. It seems likely, as suggested by Babcock and Salthouse (1990), that resource space and speed each contribute, perhaps equally, to the deficits in working memory that are observed in older adults (Brébion, 2003).

Long-Term Memory and Aging

The changes that occur in long-term memory with advanced age depend to some extent on which component of long-term memory is under investigation: procedural, episodic, or semantic (Cherry & Smith, 1998).

Procedural Memories. Procedural memories appear to remain relatively intact for healthy older adults. One does not forget how to drive a car, boil an egg, swim, or brush one's teeth as one ages unless something is seriously wrong. Even tasks that are not performed on a regular schedule seem to remain strong in procedural memory.

Episodic Memories. Encoding of information into episodic memory is influenced by the lower level of resources and the slower processing speed that characterize older working memory. As a result, older adults seem to encode items less distinctively and less distinctive encoding results in more difficulty in retrieving items (Isingrini et al., 1995; Zacks et al., 1987).

Retrieval of information from episodic memory is a frequent difficulty for older adults. Sometimes the information cannot be found at all and the individual gives up, while at other times it simply takes far longer to find the wanted information (Fogler & Stern, 1994). You may have heard older adults say things like "now why did I come in here? It's slipped my mind." In a situation like that, it often helps to go out and come in again. The classic and personal study of this retrieval difficulty was conducted over several decades by Smith (1935; 1951; 1963). At age 10, she learned the 107 questions and answers of the Westminister catechism. When she was 43-, 63-, and 73-years-old, she tested her memory for the catechism with the help of a friend. At each test she remembered all of the items but, as she grew older, she needed more prompting to aid her retrieval. For instance, when she was 43, only 9 items required extensive prompting; when she was 63, 15 items needed this extra help; and when she turned 73, 34 items were very difficult to retrieve. All the information was still there in long-term memory but was far more difficult to retrieve as she became older.

This retrieval difficulty seems to be due to several factors. For one, the amount of information that is stored in episodic memory increases with every conscious moment and so older adults have far more information to search through to find the correct item. We regard this factor as quite positive. The difficulty in retrieval with advanced age is, in part, due to the wealth of knowledge and experiences stored over a long, rich life. In support of this, some work has found slower decline for those with higher education (Alley et al., 2007). A second factor, as just mentioned, resides in working memory. Older adults, perhaps because of fewer resources, seem to devote less-conscious processing to retrieval and, as a result, may retrieve the wrong or incorrect information (Jacoby & Rhodes, 2006). These conscious control processes involved in coordinating information, planning, and the functioning of activities in working memory can be greatly enhanced by regular aerobic exercise (Colcombe & Kramer, 2003). This suggests that a lack of physical activity may be another factor and some work shows that regular exercise can improve even the retrieval of ordinarily difficult (verbal) items (Woo & Sharps, 2003). Mental activity also is important and one longitudinal study that followed older adults for 6 years found very little decline for adults who were regularly engaged in intellectually challenging activities such as learning a new language or playing bridge (Hultsch et al., 1999). Do you remember what challenging mental activities Ed and Isabelle Peltz engage in to preserve their memories?

Age differences in retrieval are dependent on the type of memory being tested and the aspects of that memory being tested. For example, compared to younger adults, older adults have more difficulty recognizing faces they have seen but not in recognizing other complex objects such as houses and chairs (Boutet & Faubert, 2006).

Aspects of memories that are less likely to be remembered are the source of the information and the context in which the information was presented. Although most people have more difficulty remembering the source of information and the context in which it was presented than in remembering the information itself, the forgetting of source and/or context is greater in older adults (Erngrund et al., 1996; Siedlecki et al., 2005; Spencer & Raz, 1995). The relevance of the source or context also plays a role and we are more likely to remember more relevant contexts than less-relevant ones. If you read in the paper that a good friend of yours is wanted by the FBI, you probably would remember the content but may not later remember whether you read it in the paper, saw it on TV, or heard about it on the radio. If, however, the FBI came to see you and ask where your friend is, you are very likely to remember the source as well as the content of the message. Perhaps our limited resources, as we age, are allocated to the content of the message rather than the source because the content usually is more important.

Age differences also are dependent on the way in which memory is tested. Older adults perform better at retrieving episodic memories when the instructions given do not mention that memory is being tested. For example, an instruction like "you will be tested on this information later" results in better performance by older adults than one like "you will be tested on your memory for this information later" (Rahhal et al., 2001).

Another aspect of episodic memory that has received some attention in aging is whether the memory is prospective or retrospective. **Prospective memory** refers to remembering to do some future behavior such as remembering an appointment or remembering to take medication. **Retrospective memory** is for information that has already occurred and you now try to remember it such as remembering what you did last weekend. The work discussed so far has all been retrospective and most of the research done on memory and aging has examined various aspects of retrospective memory. In laboratory studies of prospective memory, individuals might be told to remember to press a certain key several seconds after they complete some other task; in these studies, younger adults perform better than older adults (Einstein et al., 2000). In more natural studies of prospective memory, individuals might be told to phone an experimenter at a certain future time or following completion of some everyday task; in these studies, older adults perform better (Henry et al., 2004). Generally, older adults remember appointments and to take medication quite well (Cohen, 1993). It is believed that part of the advantage for older adults in a naturalistic setting is that they can plan effective strategies to assist their performance perhaps as a result of their greater experience and knowledge about their own memory. We will discuss knowledge about personal memory when we talk about metamemory.

Clearly retrieval from episodic memory declines as we grow older. Some even believe that this retrieval difficulty is greatest for the newest memories and that old memories are remembered very well by older adults. They can tell you what happened in 1930 but can't remember what they did last weekend. Take a look at Box 7-2 to find out more about this common myth.

Semantic Memories.   Semantic memories, like other types of long-term memory, also accumulate with age. We have much greater knowledge of more things as we grow older and this great store of knowledge is considered to be one kind of intelligence (crystallized) which we will discuss in the next chapter. Think about how much more general knowledge

BOX 7-2

Remembering Old Memories Better than New Memories

A common myth about older adults' memories is that older adults remember things that happened a long time ago but not things that happened recently. My grandfather remembered a lot of stories about the Great Depression but could not always remember what happened a few days, hours, or minutes ago. There are, of course, enormous difficulties with these comparisons. We know that everyone remembers more meaningful material better than less meaningful material, and the Great Depression was clearly more meaningful than yesterday's lunch. We know that everyone remembers well-rehearsed stories better than stories that have never been told. Finally, we do not have a way to estimate the total amount of stored information from which these items are being retrieved. If grandfather remembers one of the four items we had for lunch, then he is remembering 25 percent. If he remembers one of 10 Great Depression stories, then he is only remembering 10 percent. We do not know how many total stories there are and so we cannot estimate the amount remembered. In spite of such difficulties, two lines of research offer some evidence on remembering old memories.

Hulicka (1982) interviewed several older adults in a congregate living facility who told her that they frequently spoke about old memories around young listeners in an attempt to increase the listener's interest. Memories of a 70-year-old might be quite unique for a 20-year-old whereas memories of recent events would be of less interest to the young listener. Hulicka recorded the conversations of one 93-year-old man to learn what memories were discussed in conversations among older adults. The tapes showed that recent (last 20 years), old (those of 60+ years ago), and in-between memories were equally likely to be brought up in conversations. Perhaps older adults discuss old memories with young listeners but discuss any memory (new or old) with their peers.

Other work has shown that when adults are asked to recall events in their lives they tend to recall recent events and then fewer older memories except for an unusually high recall of adolescent memories. This is referred to as the reminiscence bump (Fitzgerald & Lawrence, 1984; Robinson, 1976). To examine this phenomenon, Jansari and Parkin (1996) had adults in their late 30s, 40s, and 50s recall under instructions to avoid recent memories. This instruction resulted in a reminiscence bump, not just for the oldest participants, but for the younger ones as well. They then had other participants recall and rate the memories on several dimensions (e.g, vividness, pleasantness, importance, etc.). Although these dimensions did not differentiate new from old memories, old memories were more often first-time or unique experiences. The authors state that "firsts are more abundant in early-life and are also easy to retrieve" (p. 89). It may not be that older

BOX **7-2** **Continued**

adults remember old memories better; it may be that everyone remembers their first-time better (better than their eighth time or forty-second time, and so on).

Test yourself and see if you can remember your:

- first car
- first date (how about your eighth date?)
- the house you grew up in
- first job

Finally, some recent work shows that you obtain the typical reminiscence bump when you present older adults with words and pictures as cues (does the word "tar" bring back a memory?; How about "anise" or "cinnamon?") but when you present an odor, the most frequent memories retrieved are from childhood rather than adolescence (Willander & Larsson, 2006). Why do you think this occurs?

---

you have now than you had when you were 10. How much more might your grandparents have? One might expect older adults with such a vast store of knowledge to have retrieval difficulties just as they do with episodic memory but the story with semantic memory is a bit different.

Most of the work that has examined semantic memory for older adults has found no evidence of a deficit and, in some cases, evidence for improved semantic memory (Mayr & Kliegl, 2000; Nyberg et al., 1996; 2003). In one study of semantic memory, younger and older adults were asked to retrieve general knowledge pertaining to history (name the U.S. presidents), geography (name countries in South America), geopolitics (name the 50 U.S. states), biology (name animals native to Africa), and several other knowledge domains. On all tests given, older adults performed significantly better. Table 7-1 shows these semantic memory results for presidents and states. In a second study looking at episodic memory, younger and older adults were presented the names of 20 presidents and 25 states and later asked to recall or recognize them. On these tests, younger adults performed sig-

TABLE 7-1 Mean Proportions Correct for Semantic and Episodic Tests of Presidents and States

	Age Group	
	Old	Young
Semantic Memory for		
Presidents	.73	.65
States	.83	.74
Episodic Memory for		
Presidents	.58	.77
States	.69	.90

nificantly better. Table 7-1 also shows these episodic memory results. It is not the type of information that makes the task easy or difficult but the type of memory. Older adults generally are very capable of retrieving information from semantic memory but, as you already know, have considerable difficulty in retrieving information from episodic memory (Foos & Sarno, 1998).

Other work related to semantic memory shows that older adults have more of one common retrieval difficulty than young adults do. That difficulty is the tip-of-the-tongue or TOT experience. A **TOT** is when you have difficulty finding the right word or name but you know that you know the answer; it's right there on the tip of your tongue. TOTs are quite common when you try to remember the name of someone whose face you recognize. People having this experience frequently can remember what sound or letter the name begins with and how many syllables it is but not the item itself until working at it for a period of time or asking another for the answer. Older adults experience more TOTs than younger adults and, while in a TOT state, recall less information about the target name or word (Fraas et al., 2002; James & Burke, 2000). Nevertheless, they are as able as young adults to finally retrieve the correct item.

Older adults perform as well as younger adults on most tests of semantic memory and probably have more general knowledge than younger adults. At the same time, older adults more frequently have difficulties accessing that knowledge. Information can be harder for older adults to retrieve especially when it is information that is not used very often. Given sufficient time, older adults are very able to access a wealth of information. Semantic memory, as a component of long-term store, remains stable through the adult years and some would argue that this network of associations is even improved with age (Laver & Burke, 1993).

Metamemory

Metamemory refers to knowledge about one's own memory. If you know how well your memory works, if you know what strategies are likely to be effective in different situations, if you can successfully predict your own performance, if you know how much you know, you probably have a very good metamemory. For example, as a student, you may know how well you perform on essay versus multiple-choice tests or in English versus math. Such knowledge, if accurate, will allow you to allocate your study time efficiently and to select more effective test-taking strategies. If your metamemory is not very good, then you may end up prioritizing tasks inefficiently and using your time and strategies ineffectively. Researchers typically measure metamemory by using a questionnaire such as the Metamemory in Adulthood (MIA) (Dixon & Hultsch, 1983), Memory Self-Efficacy (Berry et al., 1989), or Memory Functioning (Gilewski et al., 1990). Table 7-2 provides examples of the types of questions asked on these questionnaires.

Older adults generally believe that their memories have declined and so they rate their memory fairly low on metamemory questionnaires although the answers you get from older adults depend to some extent on the way the questions are asked (Cavanaugh, 1996; Hertzog et al., 1990). Although young adults say their memory is now better than when they were younger, older adults say their memory now is worse than when they were younger (Reese & Cherry, 2006). When one then tests their memory, it frequently is found,

Project 7

The text says that older adults often underestimate their own memory because they believe the stereotype that says memory declines with age. You now know that some components of memory do show a decline (the capacity of working memory, retrieval from episodic memory), while others remain stable or even improve (sensory memory, procedural memory, semantic memory). Younger adults also tend to believe this negative stereotype about older adults' memory. This project gives an opportunity to see how older and younger adults rate their own memory compared to people in other, younger and older, age groups. Duplicate the brief survey given here and ask some younger and some older adults to fill it out.

For each statement, use this scale

1 = MUCH BETTER
2 = BETTER
3 = ABOUT THE SAME
4 = WORSE
5 = MUCH WORSE

Put the number that best describes your current belief on the line at the end of each statement.

A. Compared to people much younger than myself, my memory is _____.
B. Compared to people younger than myself, my memory is _____.
C. Compared to people the same age as me, my memory is _____.
D. Compared to people older than myself, my memory is _____.
E. Compared to people much older than myself, my memory is _____.

What did you find? Did younger adults tend to say their memory was better than those older than themselves? Did older adults tend to say their memory was worse than those younger than themselves?

How did people of different ages rate their own memories compared to those older than themselves? Did everyone think that they had better memories than older people?

What factors do you think explain these results?

---

however, that those who believe their memory has declined a lot tend to perform fairly well while those who complain very little of memory decline often perform fairly poorly (Kaszniak, 1990; McDonald-Miszczak et al., 1995; Smith et al., 1996). Metamemory in older adults is based, to some extent, on their belief that memory declines with age and, therefore, their memory must be worse now than it was in the past (Blatt-Eisengart & Lachman, 2004; Lane & Zelinsky, 2003). On the other hand, if your memory really has declined, you may defensively assert that it functions just fine.

Do older adults just not know whether their memories are good or bad and rely on stereotypes for their information? One longitudinal study conducted on very-old adults (mean age at first testing was over 86) found that low self-evaluations of memory at the

TABLE 7-2 Sample Metamemory Questionnaire Items

For each of the items listed here, (1) rate how often remembering that item presents a problem for you (i.e., always, sometimes, never), and (2) for each problem item rate how serious you consider the problem to be (i.e., very serious, somewhat serious, not serious):

Names	Faces	Appointments
Where you put things	Phone numbers	Directions
Your shoe size	Words	Things people tell you
Day of the week	Date	Taking a test

Is your memory the same, worse, or better than it was . . .

One year ago?
Five years ago?
Ten years ago?

How often (always, sometimes, never) do you use the following techniques to help you remember things?

Appointment book	Reminder notes
Mental repetition	Making a list

How would you rate your memory in terms of the kinds of problems you have?

Major problems			Some minor problems			No problems
1	2	3	4	5	6	7

Source: Adapted from Gilewski et al. (1990).

first testing were predictive of decline and, in some instances, a diagnosis of dementia, 2 to 4 years later (Johansson et al., 1997). This may mean that older adults know their memories better than memory researchers do. They may be able to detect changes that cannot be detected by traditional tests of memory until the change is quite severe. Low self-evaluations may turn out to be useful for identifying individuals who are at risk for dementia and, as noted in Chapter 12, even mild cognitive impairment can be a warning sign.

What factors might affect metamemory? One hypothesis that has received attention recently contends that because beliefs about memory and age vary from culture to culture perhaps the memory performance of older adults also varies. Some cultures, particularly Asian and African, have greater respect for older adults. While older adults in American culture are believed to have declined quite a bit, older adults in some of these other cultures are believed to remain quite capable and wise. An initial test of this hypothesis provided promising results (Levy & Langer, 1994) but more recent work found no differences. A comparison of younger and older Anglophone Canadians to younger and older Chinese Canadians found older adults of both cultural groups performing poorer than younger adults on a number of memory tests (Yoon et al., 2000).

"I don't remember."

Another factor may be education. Older (and younger) adults with greater ability and/or higher levels of education have more positive views of their own memory and generally perform better when memory is tested (Reese & Cherry, 2006). Their self-efficacy is higher and they tend to perform better (Ryan & See, 1993). Such older adults may believe their memory is largely within their own control and that if they work hard or learn some memory improvement techniques, they will improve their ability to remember information. Others believe that abilities decline with age and that there's very little that they can do about it (Bieman-Copland & Ryan, 1998). People who believe they have control seem to try harder and perform better while those who believe they are powerless to prevent or stop decline generally perform worse on tests of memory and may not learn or use effective strategies even when such strategies are provided to them (Lachman et al., 2006; Riggs et al., 1997). Perhaps if older adults understood the changes that occur in memory with advanced age, confidence in their own memory ability might increase and such an increase might lead them to adopt effective strategies and perform much better (Cavanaugh, 1996; Welch & West, 1995). Take some time to reassure and educate an older loved one about their memories.

Memory Improvement

Everyone can improve their memory but as you just learned, those who believe that memory decline is inevitable are less likely to attempt to do so. It is important to teach older adults about memory and the changes that are typical with advanced age as well as specific improvement techniques.

Most of the work on improving memory has focused on the use of internal, mental techniques. For example, you may already use acronyms to remember the colors of the spectrum (ROY G BIV) or the names of the Great Lakes (HOMES). Most of the books on memory improvement are filled with these and other mental tricks like imagery, peg words, digit/sounds, and other memory aids (Brown, 1989; Lapp, 1992) and several studies have demonstrated their usefulness (Glass & Holyoak, 1986). Interestingly, however, when people are surveyed about the memory aids they use, most report using external techniques such as making written lists, using appointment calendars, and setting timers (Park et al., 1990). People know they often need help but are not often familiar with the internal techniques that can provide that help. Table 7-3 provides examples of some memory problems and internal and external techniques designed to solve those problems.

To improve the memory of older adults, a number of studies have shown that internal techniques improve memory for the types of items used in the training but do not reduce anxiety about declining memory (Neely & Bäckman, 1995; Scogin et al., 1985). At the same time, efforts to improve self-efficacy and reduce anxiety have been successful at that but do not improve performance (Dittman-Kohli et al., 1991). Both are needed. Furthermore, older adults may be more likely to continue using a technique if it is one they

TABLE 7-3 Some Memory Improvement Tricks

Problem	Technique
I forget to do something when I get home.	Call home and leave yourself a message on your answering machine.
I leave the car lights on after driving in the rain.	Keep a clip in your car and attach it to the keys when you turn on the lights. You will feel that reminder when you turn the engine off.
I forget to get something when I'm out.	Create an acronym. To remember to get *m*ilk, *a*spirin, *g*reen pepper, *i*ce cream, and *c*andy at the store, remember the word *magic*.
I forget where I parked my car.	When you exit the parked car, pay careful attention to where it is. Look back at the car before entering the building.
I can't remember numbers.	Convert the numbers to words by replacing each digit with a word that has that many letters. The number *549* could be remembered as *learn* (5) *this* (4) *technique* (9).
I forget new names right away.	When you learn a new name, say it out loud ("I'm pleased to meet you _____").
	Look at the person's face several times over the next several minutes and practice mentally retrieving the name each time you look at or later picture the face in your mind.

Source: Techniques and examples taken from Foos (1997).

have chosen (Best et al., 1992). In one study, older adults were taught a variety of techniques and chose which ones to practice and use and which ones to ignore. In an attempt to reduce their anxiety, they also were taught about the changes that normally occur with age. Immediately after their 4 weeks of training and a month later, they had greatly reduced anxiety about their memories and performed very well on remembering a variety of types of information different from the original training materials (Foos, 1997).

Aside from internal and external techniques, some believe that memory can be improved pharmacologically; if you take the right supplements, your memory could get much better. Studies with animals suggests that the neurotransmitter acetylcholine can improve memory and that for humans, it plays a major role in the consolidation of new memories during sleep (McGaugh, 2000; Power, 2004). Other work shows, however, that simply taking acetylcholine to improve memory does not work (Lombardi & Weingartner, 1995). It is important for memory but is part of a larger neural processing system. Although most supplements that have been tested have turned out to be ineffective in improving memory, gingko biloba has shown some promise. Gingko is an extract from the fan-shaped leaves of the maidenhair tree that was once considered a sacred plant in China and Japan. Some research has found significantly better memory with large doses of gingko extract over an extended period of time but only for those with serious impairment (Deberdt, 1994; Hofferberth, 1994). It has not yet been shown to help ordinary people with ordinary memories.

Some components of memory change with age and some do not. Some change can be considered as gain and some as loss. Some loss can be offset by reducing the amount of information that must be dealt with at a single time and learning specific improvement techniques. Although many younger and older adults believe the negative stereotype of memory loss with advanced age, it just isn't that simple.

SOCIAL POLICY APPLICATIONS

One thing you learned about in this chapter is memory improvement techniques. As you noticed, the best techniques are rooted in the basics of how memory and cognition operate. You also may have noticed that you can benefit from these techniques as much as older persons. Everyone at any age can use memory and cognitive training. In fact, recent research suggests that the more cognitively active you are when you are young, the more active you will remain in middle and then old age. It is true: the more you use, the less you lose, so you need to begin training better memory and cognition early. Education curricula need to include specific program components on how memory and cognition work and what things can be done to keep cognitively "fit." We need to have cognitive "bees," not just spelling bees. Children need to learn how and why to keep cognitively active. This curriculum needs to be incorporated at all levels of education, including college and university levels. Moreover, this training needs to be extended to lifelong learning—but who will pick up the task of training after formal education ends? Perhaps the media could be held responsible for incorporating cognitive education and training into their public service programs. Perhaps they could be required to include a certain number of quality programs, announcements, or articles that encourage cognitive fitness. What about sponsoring an adult cognitive bee or race, an American Memory Idol? If we all take up the task of remaining cognitively active, we certainly will be rewarded in later years. We can age well if we work at it!

Good memory is important, if you want to win the game.

CHAPTER HIGHLIGHTS

- All memories are the result of processing that takes place using resources held in working memory. Memory is assumed to have three major components: sensory memory, working memory, and long-term memory. Long-term memory is also divided into three components: procedural, episodic, and semantic.
- Older adults show no decline in sensory memory.
- Older adults show declines in working memory that appears to be due to a loss of resources and a slowing in processing.
- Older adults show no decline in procedural memory but very little research has been done.
- Older adults show a decline in encoding and retrieval from episodic memory. These declines seem to be due to the changes that have taken place in working memory and to the accumulation of information in long-term memory.
- Among the factors that influence retrieval from episodic memory are physical and mental activity, the type of memory being tested (faces versus other picture; prospective versus retrospective), the instructions given, and aspects being tested (content, context, and source).
- Semantic memory seems stable or improved in older adults although retrieval can sometimes take longer (TOTs).
- Tests of metamemory in older adults show mixed results and the answers one gets often depend on how the questions are asked. Older adults believe their memories have declined but such beliefs do not generally correspond to beliefs about specific items or actual performance. This may be due to the common belief that memory declines with age or to the inability of our current tests to detect changes that can be detected much earlier by the individual experiencing them.
- Memory improvement techniques can work well for older adults but it is important to teach them how memory works and to reduce their anxiety about what many believe to be an inevitable decline.

■ While most of the pharmacological agents tested have not been shown to improve memory, recent work on ginkgo biloba seems promising.

STUDY QUESTIONS

1. Describe the three components of memory and explain how they work together.

2. Give an example of memory and aging findings that illustrate stability rather than change. When change occurs, is it always negative? What is gained and what is lost? Give examples.

3. Are the changes that occur with memory over the adult years more likely to be continuous or discontinuous?

4. Why does Grandpa remember stories about the Great Depression and his adolescence when he cannot remember what he had for lunch an hour ago?

5. Explain how the decline in encoding with advanced age might be due, in part, to changes in working memory resources and speed. Could these changes in working memory also be responsible for the decline in retrieval? Why? Are there other factors that influence the decline in retrieval?

6. Older adults frequently have difficulty coming up with the right word or name. What positive thing might you tell an older adult with this difficulty?

7. When older adults complain about their memories, it could be due to two factors. What are those factors?

8. What is a TOT and what does it tell us about semantic memory for older adults?

9. What findings suggest that semantic memory for older adults is as good as it is for younger adults (and maybe better)?

10. Why don't some older adults use memory improvement techniques? Give at least two reasons. What can be done to encourage older adults to learn and use such techniques?

RECOMMENDED READINGS

Lapp, D. C. (1992). *Maximizing Your Memory Power*. New York: Barron's Educational Series. This book on memory improvement gives a number of techniques to use.

Park, D. C., & Hedden, T. (2001). Working Memory and Aging. In M. Naveh-Benjamin, M. Moscovitch, & H. L. Roediger III (Eds.), *Perspectives on Human Memory and Cognitive Aging* (pp. 148–160). New York: Taylor & Francis. This chapter presents one common view of the changes that occur in working memory as we grow older.

INTERNET RESOURCES

www.psywww.com/mtsite/memory.html. For information on memory techniques and mnemonics.

www.memorydoc.org/aging.php; www.familydoctor.org/124.xml. These two sites provide information about memory and aging.

8 Intelligence, Wisdom, and Creativity

Wisdom doesn't necessarily come with age.
Sometimes age just shows up all by itself.

—Tom Wilson

Wilson makes it clear that not all older adults are wise. In this chapter we will see that—just as this is true—so also is it true that not all older adults lose intelligence or their creative abilities. In Senior View, May Taylor tells us that she has slowed down and has difficulty paying attention to more than one thing at a time but that her intelligence and wisdom have increased and that she is more creative now than in the past. Jack Palis, on the other hand, says that he is much wiser than he used to be but that his intelligence and creativity are not called into play as much anymore because he no longer has to confront problems. These different perceptions of what has happened to intelligence, wisdom, and creativity are much like the research. In some cases there appear to be increases in all three while in other cases the opposite seems true. The answers to if and how intelligence, wisdom, and creativity change with age may be less clear than in any other area.

Intelligence, wisdom, and creativity are related. They all rely on similar mental processes, such as attention, encoding, and retrieval. Intelligence might be thought of as the ability to remember information and to use it effectively when necessary. One might become very intelligent in some specific area with continued experience and practice; we would say that such a person has developed expertise in that area. Wisdom might be considered an overall perspective on knowledge and the ability to use it in practical situations; wisdom can be viewed as expertise for matters of real life. Creativity might be thought of as going beyond what is known in an attempt to create something new. Robert Sternberg (1990) says:

> If we view existing knowledge as setting constraints much like a prison, we might view the wise person as seeking to understand this prison and just what its boundaries are, the intelligent person as seeking to make the best of life in prison, and the creative person as seeking to escape from the prison. (p. 153)

Intelligence

Age differences in intelligence and the relationship between age and intelligence have received more research attention than almost any topic in gerontology. Among lay people, there is a general belief that "you can't teach an old dog new tricks," but most researchers

Senior View

We spoke with May Taylor and Jack Palis about intelligence, wisdom, and creativity. Mae was 85 and Jack was 82. May is a widow now and lives with her dog while Jack is still married and living with his wife in an apartment in the city.

I'm in very good health and just as smart now as I ever was [pause] but I've slowed down. Everything takes a little longer and I'm not as sharp as I used to be after playing bridge for 4 hours, May said with a smile.

I've grown more intelligent since my husband passed away. I've had to learn how to handle financial matters. I believe that intelligence is the ability to handle any crisis—or anything that comes up—well. One good measure of intelligence is the way people drive. I've seen some really stupid driving.

Regarding wisdom May told us, *I'm wiser now than I used to be because of the experiences I've had over my long life.* You will see later that many theorists would agree with May about the importance of experience.

I'm still creative now that I'm older but in

different ways than when I was young. I have new interests. I took some painting classes and now I love to paint.

Jack said this about intelligence: *I believe that intelligence is the ability, when confronted with a situation, to be able to cope with it. I'm much wiser now than when I was young but I was better at coping with situations when I was young.*

My wisdom has increased because of all my experiences. I think a lot of people become more experienced with age but they do not necessarily become wiser. Some people will never learn and they act on impulse all their lives.

I don't get many opportunities to be creative anymore and so I'm less creative. When I was young, I constantly had problems to solve and that's what makes you creative. People need problems to solve if they're going to be creative. Here's my advice for young people: Before you act on impulse, think of the possible outcomes; if the possible negative outcomes outweigh the gratification you may get now, then do not act on that impulse. That seems like pretty wise advice.

know better. Older animals, including humans, may seem to lose some ability to learn and remember; they may seem to lose intelligence but some aspects of memory and cognition change with age while others do not. Those that change can increase as well as decrease in efficiency. There are gains and losses at all stages of development and this is certainly the case when intelligence is measured.

What Is Intelligence?

Although there are many ways to measure intelligence and probably many different kinds of intelligence, most researchers would agree on the major aspects and might, thus, define intelligence as some overall ability. **Intelligence** is a general proficiency at cognitive tasks (Glaser, 1986). An intelligent person can be expected to perform well on most, but not all, types of tasks that demand some form of thinking and remembering. Most people are better at some tasks than others. Most people are intelligent in some ways but not all ways. This is one of the problems in defining and measuring intelligence; it seems to be more than one thing. A number of researchers have even proposed very specific and different kinds of intelligences and sought ways to measure them individually (e.g., Gardner, 1993; Sternberg, 1985).

One way to conceptualize these different views is to say that there is a general and universal factor, the **g factor** (general proficiency), which underlies intelligent performance on most tasks and, at the same time, some very specific factors that underlie intelligent performance on different tasks. Thus, the g factor might contribute to performance in learning new information rapidly, remembering verbal information, remembering spatial information (where did I park that car?) while other specific factors contribute to only one or the other of these forms of intelligence (Neisser et al., 1996).

TABLE 8-1   Primary Mental Abilities Test of Intelligence

Thurstone's Primary Mental Abilities Test has several subtests to measure different aspects of intelligence. The five most frequently used in investigations of age differences in intelligence are briefly described here.

Subtest	Sample Item/Description
Verbal Meaning	What does fossil mean? or What is a silo?
Numerical Ability	How many carrots can you buy if they are 6 cents each and you have 42 cents?
Word Fluency	Name as many words as you can that contain the letter G in a two minute period (also used to measure Divergent Thinking which we will discuss later in this chapter).
Inductive Reasoning	What would be the next letter in the following series? A, E, F, H, I, K, _____, *
Spatial Orientation	Which of the following is the same as ▲ but is rotated? ●, ■, ◆, ▶, ▬

*This one may be more difficult than the others so we have provided the answer later in the chapter.
Source: Adapted from Thurstone, L. L., & Thurstone, T. G. (1941). *Factorial Studies of Intelligence*. Chicago, IL: University of Chicago Press.

Intelligence first was measured by Alfred Binet (1903) and his test was intended to determine whether French children were of average intelligence for their age or whether they were above or below average. Lewis Terman of Stanford University imported the test to this country and created the Stanford-Binet IQ test. Other tests were created later including the Army Alpha for recruits in World War I, the Wechsler Adult Intelligence Scales (WAIS), and the Thurstone test of primary mental abilities. These last two tests consist of several subscales designed to measure different aspects or kinds of intelligence (or g and specific factors). The Thurstone test is described in Table 8-1 because it is the test that most often has been used in research in early investigations of intelligence and aging.

Age Differences in Intelligence

Evidence for Declining Intelligence. When the U.S. Army recruited soldiers to fight in World War I, those recruits took the Army Alpha (or Beta) intelligence test. Test scores were obtained for tens of thousands of men ranging in age from 18 to 60 and the scores for officers were examined, after the war, by Yerkes (1921). Yerkes found that past the age of 25, intelligence, as measured by the Alpha test, declined. The older the recruit, the worse he did on the test. These data were recalculated years later and the original result was confirmed (Jones, 1959). These average scores for different age groups are shown in Figure 8-1. The belief that intelligence declined with age was so strong that older test takers had a constant added to their score to make up for their "constant decline."

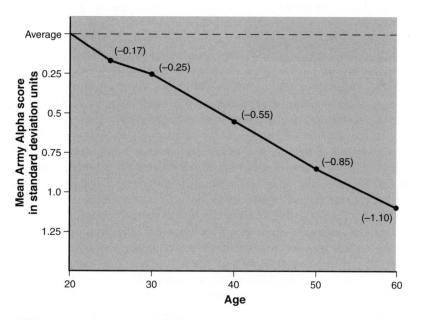

FIGURE 8-1   Graph of Age Differences in Intelligence Based on Army Alpha Data.
Source: Yerkes (1921).

Not every researcher, however, obtained evidence for this decline. When Terman imported Binet's test and created the Standford-Binet test, he administered the test to a large number of people and recruited over 1500 gifted boys and girls whom he and others followed over the course of their lives. This large gifted sample named themselves the "Termites" and a little over half now are dead. Work examining their longevity found many of the same factors discussed earlier (Chapter 5) to have played a role in their life expectancy (Friedman et al., 1995). Tests of their intelligence over a 12-year-time period showed that, rather than declining, they improved (Bayley & Oden, 1955). If you think about the work conducted on this gifted sample and the type of research design used with army recruits, you will notice that the type of person tested, gifted versus average, is not the only difference between these studies. Think critically for a moment and apply what you know about the differences between longitudinal and cross-sectional research.

Evidence for Cohort and Other Effects.   K. W. Schaie and his associates understood that the decline in intelligence found with the army recruits, and in other cross-sectional comparisons, could be due to cohort rather than age differences. Individuals who entered the army in 1917 at the age of 50 had been born in 1867, right after the Civil War, and belonged to a much older cohort than the 20-year-olds who also joined the army in 1917. Perhaps the differences that were found on the tests were due to differences in the experiences and environments of these different cohorts.

Schaie and his associates have been conducting the Seattle Longitudinal Study of Adult Intelligence for several decades (Schaie, 1979; 1983; 1990; 1994; 2005). The study began in 1957 with a sample of 500 people selected from the roster of a prepaid medical plan. Fifty people, 25 males and 25 females, at each 5-year age group from 20 to 65 participated. Every few years those who are willing are tested again and, thus, provide longitudinal information on any intellectual changes. At each test, new samples are added providing data for cross-sectional comparisons. What kind of design do we call a study like this?

Using Thurstone's Primary Mental Abilities Test of Intelligence, Schaie tested these individuals looking for differences that could be attributed to age, or cohort. Schaie showed that most of the obtained results on intellectual decline can be attributed to cohort, rather than age, differences. Older cohorts scored lower especially on tests of verbal meaning, inductive reasoning, and spatial orientation. Older and more recent cohorts scored about the same on tests of number and word fluency while middle cohorts, born in the 1920s and 1930s, scored higher on number but lower on word fluency. These cohort differences accounted for most of the previously assumed decline with age.

Cohort effects could be due to a number of environmental differences between generations. Today, younger cohorts may have more years of schooling; more exposure to information from television, movies, and the Internet; more work experience requiring thought rather than physical labor; and, probably, have taken tests recently. Undoubtedly all of these, and many other differences, play some role in the obtained cohort differences in intelligence. With no control over the environmental circumstances in which different cohorts developed, it is impossible to know for certain which factors are most important in producing the obtained cohort effects. It is, however, certain that effects due to cohort, rather than age, underlie most of the obtained differences in overall intelligence.

With respect to actual age differences, primary mental abilities seem to increase until people reach their early 40s. They then tend to remain stable until the early 60s when some decline begins (Schaie, 1989; 2005). By age 80, most older adults show some significant decline but only on one or two of the five tested abilities. Less than 10 percent show decline on four or five. Some types of intelligence also are more likely than others to change with age just as some are more likely than others to show cohort effects. At the same time, the relative contributions of g and specific factors to performance on these different tests, seems to remain constant at least from age 8 up to age 54 and probably doesn't change for older adults as well (Juan-Espinosa, 2006).

One way of categorizing different forms of intelligence that has been fairly influential in gerontology has been the division into **crystallized** and **fluid** intelligence (Horn, 1982). Crystallized intelligence refers to accumulated knowledge gathered over a lifetime of experiences and is very similar to semantic memory discussed in the last chapter. Intelligent people will have gathered and remembered more information than less-intelligent people. Fluid intelligence refers to the ability to deal quickly and efficiently with new situations and unfamiliar circumstances. This is similar to the definitions given by May Taylor and Jack Palis in this chapter's Senior View. Intelligent people are able to learn new things quickly.

If you look at the subtests of the Thurstone test described in Table 8-1, you might suspect that some of these tend to measure crystallized intelligence (e.g., verbal meaning) while others tend to measure fluid (e.g., inductive reasoning) and still others have components of each (e.g., word fluency). The same can be said for the WAIS test which is frequently used in research conducted on intelligence and aging. As a general rule, older adults perform poorly on tests of fluid intelligence but better on tests of crystallized intelligence (Ackerman & Rolfhus, 1999). Poorer performance on tests of fluid intelligence is thought to be due, in part, to the brain status changes examined earlier and to the slowing that occurs with advanced age (see Chapter 6; Zimprich & Martin, 2002). Averaged across all these different subtests, researchers may find very little difference in overall intelligence until very old age. This is illustrated in Figure 8-2.

These age differences in intelligence could be due to a number of factors. Age differences obtained in cross-sectional studies could reflect gender differences as well as cohort differences. Because women live longer than men, older age groups have many more women than men. Some work has found that men perform better on some measures involving visual and spatial processing while women perform better on some episodic memory tasks (Maitland et al., 2004). In one longitudinal study, older women outperformed older men on several tests including vocabulary which is much like the verbal meaning subtest of the Thurstone (Gerstorf et al., 2006). This gender difference is less of a problem when one examines intelligence longitudinally because both men and women show some decline, although not always the same decline. Women show more decline in fluid intelligence while men show more in crystallized (Dixon & Hultsch, 1999).

Health is a factor that exerts some influence on age differences in intelligence. Older adults are more likely than younger adults to be in poor health and, as you know from Chapters 3 and 6, are more likely to have serious chronic conditions. Those with health problems generally score lower on measures of intelligence and research suggests that this relationship is not simply due to difficulties in seeing and hearing while taking a test but

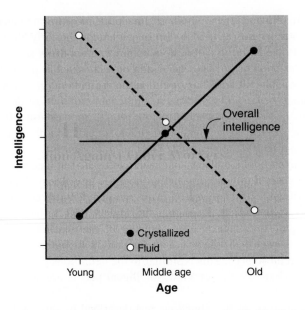

FIGURE 8-2   Graph of Age Differences in Fluid, Crystallized, and Overall Intelligence.

to more central changes in the brain (Lindenberger et al., 2001; Rosnick et al., 2004). When older adults score lower on tests of intelligence, some of that deficit can be attributed to declines in health.

As you remember, nature–nurture is one of the developmental issues addressed by researchers in gerontology and plays a role here because intelligence is made up of both genetic and environmental factors. Older adults do not have different genes but frequently have different environments than younger adults. Does this contribute to age differences in intelligence? The answer appears to be yes because longitudinal research conducted with twins has shown that genetic factors largely are responsible for individual differences in intelligence but environmental factors largely influence the rate of decline as we grow older (McGue & Christensen, 2002; Reynolds et al., 2002). Less-rapid decline occurs for those with more education, better social support, good nutrition, physical activity, and mental stimulation. Many older adults do not eat well, exercise, or engage in mentally challenging activities and so score lower on tests of intelligence.

Another factor that has received some attention is the phenomenon known as terminal drop. **Terminal drop** refers to a relatively sudden decline in some cognitive abilities shortly before death. Although this might occur for any individual close to death, it is undoubtedly the case that many more older than younger adults are close to death and, therefore, more likely to show this decline. Box 8-1 describes some of the research examining this factor.

If older adults perform well on some tests but not on others, maybe they have learned different ways to deal with problems that arise in real life. Perhaps they compensate for any deficiencies but are unable to use such strategies when taking intelligence tests. Using standard tests of intelligence then might not tell about adult intelligence in real-life situations or when real-world problems arise.

BOX **8-1**
Terminal Drop

Terminal drop refers to a relatively sudden decline in cognitive abilities shortly before death. If terminal drop really occurs in a high proportion of individuals near death, then it may be that obtained deficits in memory, cognition, and intelligence may reflect terminal drop and not be genuine aging differences. In other words, these deficits are only an artifact of the methods used (Jarvik & Cohen, 1973). Imagine that we conduct a longitudinal study and follow a group of 100 adults from age 20 and we measure their abilities every 10 years. Imagine that we also could measure how many people at each testing were experiencing terminal drop. These imaginary figures are shown here (Baltes & Labouvie, 1973):

Age	Average IQ	Number with Terminal Drop
20	115	0
30	114	1
40	113	2
50	113	2
60	105	10
70	95	20
80	85	30

Each person with terminal drop declines enough in measured intellect to reduce the group average by 1 point. Because the person with terminal drop dies before the next test is given, the average is assumed to be at the highest level, 115, before the effects of terminal drop are subtracted. Terminal drop could, thus, produce large differences in IQ measured in the same individuals over a long period of time. If we looked at only the healthy 80-year-olds (those without terminal drop), their average IQ could be the same 115 of the 20-year-olds.

How would near death produce such changes in cognition? It may reflect the high rate of deaths from heart disease and other cardiovascular problems, the brain receives less oxygen as the disease worsens. Without adequate oxygen, the brain functions less efficiently.

Is there evidence for terminal drop? The first study was conducted over 40 years ago and examined older men four times over a 12-year period. The results showed a more rapid decline for those who died compared to those who lived (Kleemeier, 1962). Work conducted in Sweden tested men and women aged 80 and older. Participants were tested three times over a 6-year period and much lower scores were found for those who died before the last test (Johannson & Zarit, 1997; Johansson et al., 1992). A study conducted on 1000 older adults living in Florida found a decline but only on vocabulary skills and only in adults who were younger than 70 (White & Cunningham, 1988). Other work also has shown declines on usually stable verbal skills shortly before death (Small & Bäckman, 1997). Because fluid abilities may decline with age, perhaps terminal drop only is evident, or most evident, on tests of crystallized intelligence. Another study found declines, shortly before death, on verbal meaning, word fluency, number, and spatial orientation subtests but not on inductive reasoning (Cooney et al., 1988). Finally, one study followed 2000 older adults who had been assessed for mental competence. After 4 years, 85 percent of those who showed no cognitive impairment were still alive while only 51 percent of those with severe impairment were still living (Kelman et al., 1994). Even though a greater proportion of cognitively

(continued)

B O X   **8-1**   Continued

impaired adults died, many impaired adults still were living at the end of the 4 years. Furthermore, not all older adults tested who later died showed terminal drop; many died with no cognitive impairment. In some cases, the proportion showing a sudden decline is less than 20 percent (Siegler, 1983).

Is terminal drop responsible for the obtained age differences in IQ? At this point in time the answer seems to be no. Not all adults show terminal drop and when it does appear, it is not always on the same measures. Terminal drop may, however, account for some proportion of the obtained differences. There are still too many unanswered questions regarding terminal drop to allow researchers to reach any firm conclusions (Small & Bäckman, 1999). Remember the earlier example was just that: an example. Nevertheless, terminal drop clearly does occur in some people. An older adult who exhibits a relatively sudden and major loss of cognitive abilities is an older adult who needs to be examined.

Real-World Adult Intelligence

Does your score on an intelligence test relate to your ability to act intelligently in the real world? Many would argue not. Real-world adult intelligence may involve many components of dealing with real-world situations, using effective strategies to compensate for physical or mental deficiencies, getting along with diverse groups of people, being able to plan ahead, knowing when to argue and when to keep quiet, and seeing things from a broader perspective. If the heat goes out in your cold apartment, are you able to persuade the owner to fix it right away? If so, society might regard that as one component of real-world adult intelligence that is probably not measured by standard IQ tests. The work that has examined this issue is mixed and it appears that IQ tests measure some components of real-life intelligence while not measuring others.

In one study, researchers administered tests of fluid and crystallized intelligence to adults aged 66 and older. Participants also were given a measure referred to as observed tasks of daily living (OTDL) that examines performance on nine food preparation, nine phone, and 13 medication-type tasks, all designed to be different from the way such tasks might ordinarily be performed. For example, instead of simply making a cake, they were asked to make a cake for someone on a low-cholesterol diet. The correct response in this case was to replace eggs with some form of egg substitute. The results showed strong correlations between performance on the modified everyday tasks and the measures of intelligence, particularly fluid intelligence (Diehl et al., 1995). Other work also has found a positive relationship between measures of intelligence and many everyday tasks (Allarire & Marsiske, 2002; Marsiske & Willis, 1998). This is to be expected if the g factor truly underlies performance on tasks that require some level of intelligence.

On the other hand, some studies have found no relationship between standard measures of intelligence and performance on real-world tasks. In a comparison of young and old bank managers, older managers scored lower on an intelligence test but much higher on tacit, on-the-job knowledge (Colonia-Willner, 1998). Tacit knowledge refers to knowledge gained implicitly by working on a task. An examination of intelligence and ability to pick the winners at the horse track showed no relationship between the two tasks. The top man at the track picked the winning horse in 10 straight races and the top three in five of those races; his tested intelligence was well below average (Ceci & Liker, 1986). Still other work found older adults performing better than younger adults when the measure of intelligence involves going beyond the presented material and using other knowledge and a broader perspective. Older adults have scored higher when classifying short stories into categories and themes, when asked to provide endings for partially completed stories, and even when asked to complete Piagetian tasks of cognitive development (Kramer & Woodruff, 1986; Labouvie-Vief, 1985).

Figure 8-3 shows an example of Piaget's conservation task for space (1972; Flavell, 1985). In this task, the individual views two same size properties with exactly the same layout of buildings. All the empty spaces are green and represent yard to be mowed. The person first would see two properties both arranged like the layout on the left in the figure. The individual is asked whether the same amount of time would be spent mowing the two yards and the answer is clearly yes. The buildings on one of the properties are then moved as in the layout on the right and the person again is asked whether the same amount of time would be spent mowing. How would you answer this question? The expected answer again is yes because the number of green grass spaces is exactly the same and this is often taken as the most intelligent response because it indicates conservation of space. Older adults, however, have a tendency to say the one on the right would take longer. Perhaps they cannot count the number of green spaces to see that they are identical in the two arrangements? When asked to explain their seemingly unintelligent answer, older adults point out that the mowing on the right would be more difficult and time consuming *because* there are fewer long straight paths, many corners to turn, and far more weed whacking in tight places, even though the total amount of grass is the same (Newman-Hornblum et al., 1980). When one goes beyond the materials presented at test, one is likely to score lower on standard measures of intelligence.

Going beyond presented test materials can be seen as a component of real-world adult intelligence. In the real world, one is intelligent to consider as many factors as possible when confronted with a problem. Older adults also are more likely to consider their own feelings and the feelings of others when thinking about problems; we regard this as a second component. Older adults are more willing to accept ambiguity. Adolescents and

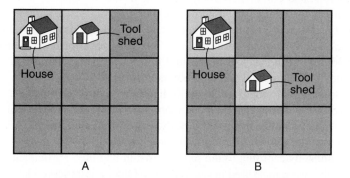

A   B

FIGURE 8-3   Conservation Task Used to Measure Adult Intelligence with House and Shed Arranged Two Different Ways in the Yard.

younger adults may seek a single correct answer while older adults may believe that there is no single correct answer for real-world problems. A fourth component is a tendency to seek new problems and new perspectives as opposed to attempting to avoid any new problems or perspectives. Older adults have a greater tendency to seek new ways of looking at the world and their place in it. Questions may be as important as answers (Belsky, 1999; Labouvie-Vief, 1992; Sinnot, 1991; Stevens-Long, 1990). These four components of adult intelligence are quite different than the primary mental abilities tested by intelligence tests and, of course, both these components and primary mental abilities are important.

In summary, measured intelligence is different for different cohorts and different ages of adults. Some types of intelligence, such as crystallized intelligence, generally improve while other types, such as fluid intelligence, generally decline. Measured intelligence is associated with performance on some everyday tasks and clearly plays a role in real-world intelligence. At the same time, other aspects of real-world intelligence seem unrelated to standard measures. Everyone is more intelligent in some ways and less in others.

Problem Solving

You might expect that because measures of intelligence are related to some everyday tasks but not others, then measured intelligence might be important for solving some kinds of problems but not others. To see if this is so, divide problems into different types. One division is between problems that are abstract and those that are practical. **Abstract problems** are ones encountered in a testing situation and do not deal with concrete objects or real-life situations. For example, you might be asked to determine which letter is next in this sequence A, K, M, N, _____ (this answer is at the end of the chapter). Older adults generally have a bit more difficulty in solving abstract problems like this and performance is correlated with standard measures of fluid intelligence in large part because the test items and abstract problems very often are similar and often timed (Denney & Palmer, 1981; Heidrich & Denney, 1994).

Practical problems are those encountered in real life and can be divided into social and instrumental. Some practical problems have high emotional content while others do not. For example, if two of your friends are very angry and arguing with one another and you want to intervene and end this conflict, then that would be regarded as a social problem with high emotional content. If you come home and find water all over the kitchen floor around the base of your refrigerator, that would be regarded as an instrumental problem and, in this case, with low emotional content. The category, instrumental problems, includes (among others) those that revolve around financial issues. Should you spend your hard-earned money to fix your old car or to pay next semester's tuition?

Research on practical problems generally has found better performance at least up to middle age and stable or even improved performance into old age (Cornelius & Caspi, 1987; Denney & Pearce, 1989). In one such study, younger adults aged 19 to 37 and older adults aged 60 to 80 read or viewed brief problems like the one shown in Box 8-2 and their solutions were evaluated according to the scale shown in that box. Participants' neuropsychogical abilities also were measured in several ways. Older adults scored lower on almost all of these measures except problem solving. The problem solutions provided by older adults were fewer in number for each presented problem but of much higher quality

---

BOX **8-2**

Problem Solving

In one study, older and younger adults read problems like the following (Crawford & Channon, 2002, pp. 13–14):

Anne is in her office when Tony comes in. She asks how he is, and he says he is alright, but tired. She agrees that he looks tired, and asks what is the matter. He has new neighbors who moved into the flat above his a couple of weeks ago. They are nice people, but they own dogs and keep them in their kitchen at night, which is directly above Tony's bedroom. All night, and every night since they moved in, the dogs jump around and bark. He finds it impossible to get to sleep. He says he has had a word with the neighbors, and although they were very reasonable, they said they had nowhere else to put the dogs because it is a block of flats.

Participants were asked to describe each problem to ascertain whether they understood and to generate possible solutions. Solutions were scored as adequate or poor. For this problem, adequate solutions include answers like *going to the landlord or police, buying earplugs*, or *moving*; poor solutions included answers like *killing the dogs*.

Younger adults generated more total solutions than older adults but the solutions generated by older adults were of higher quality.

(Crawford & Channon, 2002). This suggests that ordinary assessments of cognition do not relate very strongly to practical problem solving.

Older adults might be as good or better at solving practical problems simply because they have had far more life experience than younger adults. They have witnessed many more disagreements among friends and wet kitchen floors than younger adults have. This increased knowledge facilitates problem solving and, as you then might expect, practical problem solving is correlated with crystallized intelligence and domain specific knowledge (Allaire & Marsiske, 1999; Heidrich & Denney, 1994). As a result of this greater experience and knowledge, older adults have and employ a wider range of strategies when confronted with problems. When dealing with instrumental problems, such as a puddle around the refrigerator, they more often choose action strategies like putting towels on the floor and turning off the water connection to the ice maker. When dealing with social problems, such as an argument among friends, they more often choose an emotion-managing strategy such as first sitting everyone down and serving warm tea (Blanchard-Fields et al., 2004). Older adults often consider fewer facts when solving problems and making decisions than do younger adults, but, at the same time, provide solutions of high quality, particularly for familiar situations (Chen & Sun, 2003). In many ways, older adults might be considered experts at problem solving.

Selective Optimization with Compensation

One practical problem that can confront an older adult is how to deal with physical and/or mental decline. Increased difficulty hearing or seeing usually can be dealt with by using assistive devices like better glasses or a hearing aid but in some other cases, the older adult must find a more sophisticated and even life-altering strategy. One such strategy is referred to as selective optimization with compensation (Baltes, 1993; Marsiske et al., 1995). This three-part strategy is meant to assist adults of all ages in learning to deal with changes but is usually described for older adults because they are more likely to show some decline. Being **selective** refers to choosing those activities—mental or physical—that you still can perform while discarding others. **Optimization** refers to increasing knowledge and performance in the activities you have chosen. **Compensation** refers to adapting to change by finding new ways, techniques, or assistance to maintain a high level of performance. Box 8-3 provides some examples of selective optimization with compensation.

Selective optimization with compensation is a wise strategy to use when one is confronted with some deficit that was not previously present. Research has found this strategy being used by younger as well as older adults in both work and social settings (Abraham & Hansson, 1995; Baltes & Graf, 1996). Employment of this strategy can help older adults maintain their independence and that is an important goal.

Expertise

People may select physical or mental activities, optimize performance in those areas, and use compensation when necessary to achieve or maintain a high level of performance.

B O X **8-3**

Examples of Selective Optimization with Compensation

Tom and Sarah have always loved camping and hiking in the woods. In their younger days they would often spend several weeks camping and hiking miles of trails in the mountains. They would set up camp by a lake or stream and do a little fishing too. Now they find hiking in the mountains to be difficult even though they both walk regularly. Steep rocky paths make it difficult for Tom to maintain his balance and he is afraid of falling and fracturing a hip. As a result, they have now **selected** fishing as their primary activity during a camping trip. To **optimize** this activity, they have been reading about different types of mountain trout and the best ways to catch them. They have talked with experienced people who fish about the best locations and the best way to cook trout. To **compensate**, they invested in new fishing gear, wading boots, and are thinking about purchasing a small boat.

Jean has been on the police force for 40 years and spent most of those years as a plain-clothes detective investigating violent crimes. She has always been in charge at the crime scene making sure that everything was dusted for prints, photos were taken, all evidence was bagged, and witnesses were interviewed and had their names and addresses taken. Now, at 60, she finds it more difficult and less rewarding to be in charge and to organize all this activity. She has **selected** witness interviewing as her primary task and has given up the rest. To **optimize** her interviewing skills, she has read several reports and attended a training session where she got to meet Dr. Ronald Fisher, one of the creators of the Cognitive Interview Technique for interviewing eyewitnesses. She uses her knowledge to help guide her questioning of witnesses. To **compensate**, Jean takes her time and tape records witness interviews.

SOCIAL POLICY APPLICATIONS

The governments of the world expect to spend a greater and greater proportion of their budgets on caring for an increasing numbers of older adults. We know that as we age we are more likely to become dependent on others for assistance with everyday tasks, transportation, practical problems, and our own care. We need to find ways to keep older adults as independent as possible for as long as possible and, of course, loss of independence can be due to physical and/or mental decline. One may have increasing difficulties with cooking, shopping, cleaning, using the phone, caring for oneself, and other activities because of physical factors, such as severe arthritis, or mental factors, such as poor planning and memory (Rowe & Kahn, 1998).

To help older adults maintain their independence, several lines of research have focused their efforts toward improving or at least maintaining higher cognitive abilities in older adults (see Chapter 7 for examples of memory improvement work). Because fluid abilities decline and influence performance on other measures (e.g., wisdom), much of the work in two major undertakings (ADEPT and ACTIVE) has attempted to train older adults to use effective strategies and study techniques. This work has shown stable performance for those trained in many cases and even improved performance in some (Ball et al., 2002; Dunlosky et al., 2003; Willis, 1990). Fluid abilities in general and problem solving in particular can significantly improve with training. It is hoped that this work might lead to intervention programs for older adults in the form of educational and training programs to improve performance and help maintain independence.

They may become experts in performing the activities they have chosen. **Expertise** refers to very high performance in some activity and typically results from both genetic and environmental factors. Practice seems to be the most important environmental factor. Generally, middle-aged and older adults have higher levels of expertise than younger adults because of the amount of time and experience that it takes to develop expertise. For many activities, older adults have had much more practice (Ericsson & Charness, 1994).

We know that older adults have diminished working memory capacity, process information more slowly, and perform lower on measures of fluid intelligence. One might expect that older adult experts would lose some of their expertise and advantage over nonexperts. Nothing, however, could be further from the truth. Researchers have compared younger and older experts and nonexperts in a number of different areas. Older typists who are experts are as quick and error-free as younger experts. Experts, young or old, are quicker and more accurate than nonexperts (Salthouse, 1984). Older expert pilots perform at higher levels than younger pilots or nonexperts (Morrow et al., 1994). Older expert baseball players maintain high levels of performance for longer periods of time and decline more slowly in baseball skills than less-expert younger or older players (Schulz et al., 1994). Older and younger medical laboratory experts are equally proficient at identifying clinically significant information presented on a previously seen slide even while performing another task at the same time. Experts were much better than nonexpert, younger and older lab technicians (Clancy & Hoyer, 1988). Older chess experts have been found to perform as well as younger chess experts at selecting the best move from among presented alternatives (Charness, 1981). Age does not seem to diminish expertise even though some of the mental operations involved in such expert performance may have declined. One study

*Expertise comes with
practice.*

of expert and nonexpert *GO* game players found that experts had developed expertise at deductive reasoning and working memory involved in playing *GO*. Researchers suggest that these expertise abilities are forms of adult intelligence not measured by standard IQ tests (Masunaga & Horn, 2001). It is clear that age does not ordinarily diminish expertise.

Wisdom

Wisdom often is regarded as the highest level of cognitive development that a person can attain and can be viewed as expertise but in matters of real life rather than in some specific task (Dittman-Kohli & Baltes, 1990). Wise people are experts at life and wisdom is viewed as "expert-level knowledge in the fundamental pragmatics of life" (Baltes & Smith, 1990, p. 95). To have such expertise, a person must balance their own interests with those of others and of society as a whole. A wise person values the common good (Sternberg, 2004). To be an expert in real life, one must have lived a long time; expertise, after all, takes practice. It is, thus, quite common to believe that wisdom is a special characteristic of older adults, or at least of some older adults (Clayton & Birren, 1980). The phrase "wise beyond their years" carries the implication that age brings wisdom. When individuals have been asked to define wisdom or to describe a wise person, they generally name such characteristics as extensive experience, being able to control emotions, considering all points of view, concentration, and going beyond the limitations of persons or situations; when asked to name wise individuals, generally older adults are named (Birren, 1985; Simonton, 1990). Besides age, two other factors also are thought to be important for the development of wisdom (Baltes & Staudinger, 1993).

Personality traits are thought to be important for the development of wisdom. People with some personality types are more likely to learn from extensive experience and be more open to the relativism and uncertainties of life. A person who is very rigid or set in their ways is unlikely to learn much from experience; a person who shuns new experiences is not likely to develop wisdom.

A third factor important for the development of wisdom has to do with having the right kinds of life experiences. Someone who has had experience with personal, ethical problems and planning under difficult, complex situations is more likely to develop wisdom than someone without such life experiences. Thus, being older, having the right personality characteristics, and having experiences dealing with life should contribute to the development of expertise in life or wisdom (Baltes & Staudinger, 1993; Smith & Baltes, 1990).

Paul Baltes and his colleagues attempted to find ways to measure wisdom and test hypotheses about its development (Baltes & Staudinger, 1993; 2000). According to their view, wisdom consists of five characteristics shown in Figure 8-4. First, wisdom depends on **factual knowledge** about life. Second, **knowledge about strategies and procedures** is necessary for wisdom. Without factual knowledge or knowledge of strategies and procedures one cannot be wise. A third characteristic is referred to as **lifespan contextualism**,

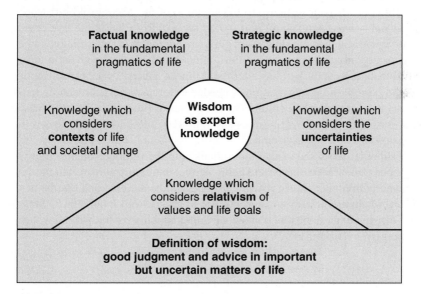

FIGURE 8-4   Five Components of Wisdom.

Source: From Baltes, P. B., & Staudinger, U. M. (1993). The search for a psychology of wisdom. *Current Directions in Psychological Science 2,* 75–80. Copyright © 1993 Blackwell Publishing. Reprinted with permission.

which means that someone with wisdom considers multiple contexts for problems and dilemmas. Different cultures may do things differently. The wise person is aware of differences due to context. The fourth characteristic is **relativism**, or the realization that life's goals and values are relative. What is important for one person may be less important for another. The last characteristic is **uncertainty**. The wise person has the ability to recognize and manage life's uncertainties.

To test this model of wisdom, researchers asked individuals to respond to imaginary life situations. Their responses are recorded and then observed by raters who attempt to determine how an individual rates on factual knowledge, procedural knowledge, contextualism, relativism, and uncertainty. For example, individuals might be asked to respond to the following situation: A 15-year-old girl wants to get married right away. What should she do and consider (Baltes & Staudinger, 1993, p. 77)? Think for a moment about how you might respond to this situation.

Generally, researchers have found no overall age differences when the responses of younger and older adults are compared. Age, by itself, does not generate wisdom. Using adults with different life experiences does, however, result in differences. Comparisons between clinical psychologists, who are assumed to have had extensive experience with life's problems, and accountants, who have had extensive experience with business problems, show that clinical psychologists score higher on the five characteristics of wisdom. Persons nominated as wise by others also score as high as clinical psychologists and nominated individuals were all older adults. The highest score on the characteristics of wisdom ratings are obtained by older persons who have been nominated as wise and older clinical psychologists (Baltes et al., 1995; Smith et al., 1994; Baltes & Staudinger, 2000). It appears that older people and/or people with the right kinds of experiences generally score well on this test of wisdom.

Think about your response to the situation of the 15-year-old girl who wants to get married right away. A response that would score fairly low on the five characteristics of wisdom might say that she should not get married; that it is unacceptable to get married so young. A response that would score fairly high might say that special circumstances might be involved; perhaps the girl has a terminal illness; perhaps she is from another culture or historical period; more information is needed before any decision can be made. The wise response takes into account culture (which is part of lifespan contextualism), sees that the situation is relative to different times and religions, and knows that there is no single correct response. There is uncertainty.

Still other work shows that individuals with the right personality traits score higher. Being open to new experiences and being neither extremely extroverted nor introverted are associated with higher levels of wisdom. These traits are examined in the next chapter. In addition, wisdom is related to fluid but not to crystallized intelligence (Staudinger et al., 1998). Finally, older adults who show wisdom generally report a high level of satisfaction with their lives (Ardelt, 1997).

Creativity

Another aspect of cognition is creativity. Creativity is different from general intelligence and wisdom and seems to be a distinct cognitive ability (Guilford; 1956; 1967; McCrae et al., 1987). **Creativity** is defined by its newness and difference from the ordinary. Creative responses are unusual, original, and unique. They may be relevant to some problem but are out of the ordinary (Botwinick, 1984). Creativity has been one of the most difficult concepts to define clearly and often is thought to be of two different types. **Exceptional creativity** refers to the creativity of well-known persons who may be artists, authors, scientists, or other professionals and whose work is recognized as creative by experts in and out of that particular discipline. **Ordinary creativity** refers to the creativity of persons whose work is not recognized by experts although often recognized by others. Finding a new way to keep the squirrels off the bird feeder or changing the old recipe for meat loaf, if done successfully, would be examples of ordinary creativity (Weisberg, 1986). Researchers interested in the relationship between aging and creativity have used three general approaches.

One way to examine creativity, particularly ordinary creativity, has been to administer a standardized test. Just as there are standardized tests of intelligence, there are also standardized tests to measure aspects of creativity. These tests are referred to as tests of **divergent thinking** (Guilford, 1967). Divergent thinking involves coming up with multiple solutions to a problem. Problems such as what would happen if people no longer needed air to breathe, how can garden pests be eliminated, or how many uses can you think of for a hammer, have many possible answers and the number and uniqueness of such answers is regarded as one aspect of creativity. In fact, some have argued that divergent thinking is a necessary condition for creativity. If one cannot think divergently, then one cannot think creatively although the ability to think divergently may not, by itself, be enough to produce creativity (Rebok, 1987). The creative individual not only may need to come up with a wealth of divergent ideas but also be able to separate good ideas from bad ideas (Csikszentmihalyi, 1996). Table 8-2 gives examples of tests of divergent thinking.

Cross-sectional comparisons of older and younger adults on tests of divergent thinking have generally resulted in lower scores for older adults particularly on timed tests (Ruth & Birren, 1985; Schaie & Hertzog, 1983). In longitudinal comparisons, adult men scored lower as they grew older on the five timed tests shown in Table 8-2 (McCrae et al., 1987). Other work shows, however, that when these tests are given with no time limit, older adults score just as high as younger adults (Foos et al., 2003). It appears that this aspect of creativity has not diminished with age but, as with many cognitive processes, has very much slowed down.

A second approach to measuring changes in creativity with age looks at productivity. In some comparisons, the quantity produced at different ages is regarded as the important measure because it is assumed that to come up with a truly creative accomplishment one must accomplish a great deal (Dennis, 1966). Others make some effort to look at the quality of accomplishment at different ages. The classic example of this work was begun by Lehman over 50 years ago (1953). Lehman examined the references listed in key texts in a number of different disciplines. Those who were cited in such texts were believed to have made a significant creative contribution to the discipline. One could easily determine then how old each contributor was when they made each of their creative contributions. Figure 8-5 illustrates the finding typical for many disciplines. The peak occurred in the late 30s to early 40s. Poets, however, showed their peak about 10 years earlier and authors of best sellers about 10 years later than this common peak. Musicians showed two peaks: the usual one in their late 30s and a second in their early 70s.

TABLE 8-2   Tests of Divergent Thinking

The following tests are from a set of tests used to measure different aspects of divergent thinking.

Test	Example
Associational fluency	This test has two parts. Each part contains two words and you try to write as many other words that have similar meaning in the two minutes allowed. Try it. In 2 minutes (time yourself), write as many words as you can that are similar in meaning to the word LARGE and to the word DRY.
Consequences	This test has five parts. In each part you try to write as many consequences as you can for a new and unusual situation. You are allowed 2 minutes for each part. Try it. In 2 minutes (time yourself), write as many consequences as you can for the situation that EVERYONE ON THE PLANET NOW IS BLIND.
Expressional fluency	This test has four parts. In each part you try to write sentences made up of four words with each word beginning with the letter given. You are allowed 2 minutes for each part. Try it. In 2 minutes (time yourself), write as many sentences as you can in which the four words begin with the following letters in the following order R__A__T__B__.
Ideational fluency	This test has four parts. In each part you try to name as many things as you can that belong to a certain category. You are allowed 3 minutes for each part. Try it. In 3 minutes (time yourself), write down as many things as you can that are TREES THAT GROW FRUIT.
Word fluency	This test has two parts. In each part you try to name as many words as you can that contain a certain letter. You are allowed 2 minutes for each part. Try it. In 2 minutes (time yourself), write down as many words as you can that contain the letter *D*.

For associational fluency, a score of 7–10 is about average. For consequences, a score of 4–7 is about average. For expressional fluency, a score of 6–8 is about average. For ideational fluency, a score of 12–14 is about average. For word fluency, a score of about 23–25 is about average.

If you scored about, or higher or lower, than average, please remember that you were not taking the tests under normal, standard testing conditions and took only one part of each test. Your scores are fun scores rather than reliable, valid measures of your divergent thinking.

Source: Christensen & Guilford (1957a, 1957b, 1958a, 1958b); Christensen, Merrifield, & Guilford (1958).

Using a variation of this method, researchers divided the adult years (from age 20 to 79) into six decades. If one makes the simple assumption that productivity has nothing to do with age, then about 17 percent of a person's creative productivity should occur in each of these decades. If Lehman is correct and productivity declines with age, then far less than 17 percent should occur in the last several decades while far more should occur in the second (the 30s) and third (the 40s) decades. The results suggest that age is a factor but not simply one that is related to decline. For the disciplines of history, literature, and philosophy, more than 20 percent is produced in each of the last two decades. Well-known inventors produced 53 percent of their work in their 60s and 70s. This is far more than the expected 34 percent (2 × 17 percent). On the other hand, artists produced only 14 percent

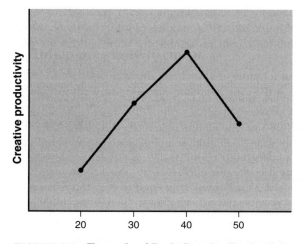

FIGURE 8.5   Example of Peak Creative Productivity.

Source: Based on data from Lehman (1953).

in their 60s and only 6 percent in their 70s (Dennis, 1968). The relationship between creative productivity and age varies for different disciplines, which clearly indicates that there is no validity to the simple belief that creative productivity declines with age.

Some work has argued that career age rather than chronological age is the more important factor (Simonton, 1991; 1998). According to this view, creativity is a function of the creative potential that a person has, their ability to come up with creative ideas (divergent thinking?), and their ability to turn those ideas into products. In a career, individuals with the right potential have ideas and products over their early decades but as they spend more time in that career, they no longer have as many remaining ideas or are less willing to pursue them. These possibilities have not always been easy to test. Some people switch careers at midlife or start their first career somewhat later, but their productivity has not been carefully monitored by researchers. One frequently cited example is Grandma Moses who did not begin painting until she was in her 70s and continued painting past the age of 100.

Another way to examine the relationship between creativity and aging is to look at the lives of creative individuals or groups to see whether change occurs (Sasser-Coen, 1993). Some of this work shows that the best predictor of a person's creative productivity is their past productivity rather than their chronological or career age (Horner et al., 1986). Many adults, however, spend very little time on creative activities during their younger and middle years because there is so much else that needs to be done. Caring for children and/or aging parents, maintaining a household, and working to advance a career or to get a better position leaves little time for painting. When one retires and the children are on their own career paths, older adults frequently take up creative activities. Several lines of research show that these creative activities increase social engagement with others, give the person a sense of control, and may even grow new connections in the higher centers of the brain (Cohen, 2006). These are strong factors for maintaining health and life satisfaction as we grow older. Creative activities should be strongly encouraged for older adults whether they have been creative in their earlier years.

Studies that have followed composers of classical music found that their later compositions were shorter, simpler, and more restrained but equally creative to their early compositions (Simonton, 1989). A similar phenomenon has been found for artists, authors, and religious leaders whose later works often eliminate details but focus on the underlying meaning of the product (Hall, 1992; Lindauer, 1998). Such findings are sometimes referred to as a "swan song" phenomenon. Legend has it that the swan sings but once in its life and that is just before its death. It appears instead that creative older adults produce much more that just a single song and have been producing most of their lives. Look at some of the older creative adults listed in Table 8-3 and see if you can think of still more for Project 8.

TABLE 8-3   Examples of Older Creative Individuals

Person	Creative Accomplishment and Age
Maya Angelou	Continues as a best-selling novelist and poet in her 70s.
Helen Hooven Santmyer	Wrote the 1985 bestseller *And the Ladies of the Club* longhand on paper while she was a resident of a nursing home in Ohio at age 86.
Sophocles	Greek poet wrote *Oedipus Rex* when he was 75 and *Oedipus Coloneus* when he was 89.
Mary Ann Smith	Developed the Granny Smith apple when she was in her 60s.
Claude Monet	Impressionist/artist began his water lily series at age 73.
Eudora Welty	Wrote numerous novels and short stories and won a Pullitzer Prize when she was 65.
Helen Keller	Published her book, *Teacher*, the story of Anne Sullivan, at age 75.
Frank Lloyd Wright	Architect who completed the Guggenheim Museum at age 91.
Franciso de Goya	Painted many great works such as *The Milkmaid of Bordeaux* (at age 81) in his later years.
George Abbot	Directed a broadway musical at age 100.
Mary Baker Eddy	Founded the *Christian Science Monitor* at age 87.
Mahatma Gandhi	Began the Indian Independence Movement at age 72 and completed negotiations for India's independence at age 77.
Benjamin Franklin	Invented the bifocal lens at age 78.
Mary B. H. Cartland	Wrote 26 books in 1 year (1983) when she was 82.
Dr. Seuss (Theodore Geisel)	Published his adult bestseller *You're Only Old Once* at age 82.
Susumu Mikami	Started his own business producing artificial caviar that he created from seaweed, squid ink, and seafood; he was 66.
Jesse J. Aaron	Descendant of Seminole Indians and slaves; became an awarded wood carver at age 88.
Charles G. Abbot	Invented a device that converted solar energy into electric power just before his 100th birthday.
Antonio Stradivari	Created two famous violins, the *Muntz* and the *Habeneck* in his early 90s.
I. M. Pei	Designed the Rock and Roll Hall of Fame in Cleveland at age 78.

Project 8

In this chapter you learned that many older people are very creative although general trends suggest a decline in creative productivity with aging. Research also shows that the peak age of creative productivity is very different for different disciplines. For this project find someone in your major who was creative after age 65. If you have not declared a major, then choose an area in which you might be interested.

Please note that you are not looking for someone who was very creative when they were younger and who has now passed the age of 65. Find someone who did something creative *after* 65. Try to answer the following questions:

Who is this creative person? How old are they now? How old were they when they made this creative contribution? Are they still making creative contributions?

Was this person always creative or did their creativity begin late in life? If this person is someone who has always been creative, have their creative "products" changed?

Why do you consider their contribution to be creative?

Do you think that there are a lot of people in the area you have chosen who have made creative contributions during old age? Why or why not?

Most students find this project to be relatively easy to complete. Maybe that means that there are a lot of older creative persons in a number of different disciplines.

What Can We Conclude?

Does higher cognition change with age? The answer is yes—and no. Changes in intelligence do occur with age but mostly in fluid abilities. Crystallized intelligence increases for many older adults. These measures are related to performance on some everyday tasks but not on others and the ability to solve practical problems seems to increase as we age. Expertise does not seem to fade with age and many older adults find sophisticated strategies to continue performing at a high level. Wisdom occurs more frequently with advanced age and creativity seems to remain stable.

CHAPTER HIGHLIGHTS

- Intelligence, defined as performance on IQ tests or subtests, initially was thought to decline with age but longitudinal and sequential design research shows that age changes are relatively modest compared to large cohort differences. When age deficits are obtained, they are typically on measures of fluid intelligence, the ability to respond quickly to a novel situation. Older adults frequently perform quite well on measures of crystallized intelligence, the accumulated knowledge of a lifetime of experience, and vocabulary increases are seen well into old age.
- Gender, health, education, diet, social support, and even terminal drop seem to play some role in lower intelligence test scores for older adults.
- The intelligence measured by standardized tests correlate well with some real-life activities but poorly with others.

- Older adults generally solve practical problems very well perhaps because of their greater knowledge or expertise.
- Expertise depends on extensive practice at some task and does not seem to decline with age.
- Wisdom may be thought of as expertise in matters of life and, thus, develops as one gains life experiences which is more likely as one grows older. To develop wisdom, one must not only have experiences, they must be of the right kind and one must have a personality to learn from such experiences.
- Baltes and his associates define wisdom as being composed of factual knowledge, strategic knowledge, contextualism, relativism, and uncertainty. Research has found higher levels of these components in older individuals nominated by others as being wise and in persons with appropriate life experiences and personality characteristics.
- Other measures of wisdom, such as an ability to solve everyday problems, have shown better performance by older, than younger, adults. Old age does not guarantee wisdom but it may make it more probable.
- Creativity involves unusual, original solutions to problems and has been measured in three ways.
- Measures of divergent thinking generally have found lower scores for older adults until the time limits are removed. Older adults then perform as well as younger adults.
- Measures of lifespan productivity generally have found peak performance at some age followed by a gradual decline. The peak age is quite different for different disciplines and, in some cases, the peak is during advanced age.
- Measures of individual creative people suggest that the nature of creativity may change as one grows older and that a great many older adults have made major creative contributions.
- Creativity does not decline with age.

S T U D Y   Q U E S T I O N S

1. Why did early researchers believe that intelligence declined with age? What research changed their minds and why?

2. What is the g factor and how does it influence performance on various tests of intelligence? Does its influence change with age?

3. Compare and contrast fluid and crystallized intelligence. Give an example of a subtest that measures each and a subtest that has both fluid and crystallized components.

4. Describe how factors like gender, health, education, training, the type of test, and terminal drop influence intelligence.

5. Are intelligence test scores related to real-world intelligence? Practical problem solving? Expertise? Wisdom? Creativity?

6. Why might one older adult exhibit a high level of wisdom while another might not?

7. Describe the five characteristics of wisdom. Write down examples for each.

8. Describe the three ways in which creativity and aging have been examined in research and tell what these results have shown.

RECOMMENDED READINGS

Csikszentmihalyi, M. (1996). *Creativity: Flow and the Psychology of Discovery and Invention*. New York: HarperCollins. This book examines the creativity of 90 older adults.

Cohen, G. D. (2000). *The Creative Age*. New York: Quill, HarperCollins. This book is a refreshing and very positive view of creativity during the second half of life.

Simonton, D. K. (1990). Creativity and Wisdom in Aging. In J. E. Birren & K. W. Schaie (Eds.), *Handbook of Psychology and Aging* (3rd ed., pp. 320–329). New York: Academic Press. This chapter presents an overview and summary of a lot of the earlier work on creativity, wisdom, and aging.

Sternberg, R. J., & Lubart, T. I. (2001). Wisdom and Creativity. In J. E. Birren & K. W. Schaie (Eds.), *Handbook of the Psychology of Aging* (5th ed., pp. 500–522). San Diego, CA: Academic Press. This chapter is a good review of the latest research on wisdom, creativity, and aging.

INTERNET RESOURCES

www.newchurch.org/sermons/individualsermons/oldage.html. A more personal view and an interesting sermon on old age and wisdom.

www.healthandage.com/html/min/afar/content/other6_1.htm. A brief discussion of fluid and crystallized intelligence and aging.

www.brucereed.com/Humor. Scroll down and click on the Aging Intelligence label for a humorous view of aging intelligence.

The answer to the inductive reasoning question in Table 8-1 is "L." The letters are those made with straight lines and no curved lines. The answer to the next letter sequence in the text (A, K, M, N, _____) is R. Only letters that have a diagonal line are used in this sequence.

PART THREE

Aging and Our Selves

9   Personality

*The man who views the world at 50 the same as he did at 20
has wasted 30 years of his life.*

—Muhammad Ali

Muhammad Ali says we must see the world differently, we must change and grow, if we are truly to have productive lives. At the same time, we must remain true to ourselves or we will lose so much of what we have gained. In this chapter, we examine what is meant by personality and the ways in which we change and stay the same. Do we see things differently as we age? To many, some aspects of personality change as we age while others remain stable through life.

An Overview of Personality

You often hear people referring to someone who has a "good" or "bad" or even "no" personality. Usually what they mean is that the person has good or bad or no reactions to other people or events around them; this you can sometimes change. Although social or emotional reactions are part of what we know about personality, psychologists define it far more broadly. In fact, **personality** is one of the broadest terms in psychology. In general it refers to those traits, behaviors, ways of thinking, motives, and emotions that make us who we are. These are all aspects of personality. To know someone's personality is to know them. We would know a person's traits such as how outgoing, how friendly, how aggressive, and how anxious they are. We would know how they act in different situations and at different times. We would know their motivation for doing the things they do and why they avoid doing other things. We would know their emotional reactions to various people and situations and how intense such reactions tend to be for them. To know someone's personality is to know a lot about them. Personality is so all encompassing that it can be difficult to even know ourselves, let alone someone else. As difficult as it is to define and understand, personality is equally difficult to measure.

Senior View

We spoke with Jane Hege and Tolly Kleckley about personality and whether they think it changes as one grows older. Jane was 69 and still employed as a receptionist and switchboard operator when we spoke with her. She has been happily married for over 50 years and has three grown children.

Personality is one of the most important factors in your home life, your church life, and in every aspect of your life. You should hold onto the personality you had when you were young because you can't change it very much anyway. Be happy with who you are. She gave us a big smile.

A good personality and outlook will help you be healthy and overcome obstacles in life. It's especially important in old age because older adults often depend on others for assistance. Somebody who complains all the time, somebody with a poor personality and never has a kind word to say, somebody who is always downing everyone is likely to have difficulty finding help when they most need it.

When asked about midlife crises, Jane said, *men are more prone to midlife crises than women because men are less mature. Crises tend to occur when one partner is not attentive to the needs of the other, so one goes astray. Most men need a lot of attention.*

Tolly was 77 when we spoke with him. He also is happily married and is retired from the furniture retail business.

Your personality is how other people see you; it's the image you project and how you feel about yourself.

My personality has pretty well stayed the same. I believe most people keep the same personality all their lives. It's not totally the same; some aspects of personality vary but not by a lot. Most people don't change much. They have a way of being themselves and they are just that way whether they want to be or not.

When you get older, the best personality to have is one that doesn't worry about the past but instead thinks about what you're gonna do in the future.

When we asked Tolly about a midlife crisis he said, *I'm not even sure what a midlife crisis is but people sometimes worry about what they used to do or do things that they never did before. It's not good to worry but trying new things can be good.*

Measures of Personality

Because there are so many different aspects of personality, there are a number of ways to measure these aspects. No single measure can encompass them all. The measures of personality used most frequently fall into two large groups: objective and projective measures.

Objective Measures of Personality. Objective measures of personality are those that measure characteristics or aspects of personality by directly asking a person to list, sort, or rate typical features or behaviors. A number of objective measures of personality are paper-and-pencil tests. Individuals are asked to respond, true or false (or agree/disagree), to a number of statements such as those shown in Table 9-1. Responses to these items then are compared to the responses made by people in a standardization sample who took the test when it was first developed. If the individual being tested responded the same as highly aggressive people in the standardization sample, then the individual would be assumed to be highly aggressive. Another type of objective test is the Q-sort. In this type of test, the person is given a stack of cards each with a different description of some characteristic of personality. For example, cards might say things like "I really enjoy the company of others" or "I feel lonely most of the time." The person sorts the cards into piles depending on how well each statement matches their personality. In all cases, the individual decides how true a statement is, how much they agree with it, or how well it describes them. Sometimes the measures are made by interviewing an individual and evaluating their answers to standard questions about different aspects of their personality.

Objective personality tests generally have a number of scales that examine different characteristics, such as outgoingness and typical ways of dealing with certain situations.

TABLE 9-1 Sample Items from an Objective Measure of Personality*

For each of the following statements answer True (T) or False (F):

1. I prefer to be by myself. _____
2. I am a flexible person. _____
3. Most people like me. _____
4. I tend to avoid new places. _____
5. Birds frighten me. _____
6. I like to wear mittens. _____
7. I like to meet new people. _____
8. I control my own destiny. _____
9. My life is full of adventure. _____
10. I am often bored. _____
11. I like to party. _____
12. I read a lot of books. _____
13. When I am angry, I try to deal with the situation immediately. _____
14. My family thinks I'm crazy. _____
15. I often feel sad. _____

*These are exemplar items and are not taken from any standard test of personality.

The most frequently used objective measures of personality include the California Psychological Inventory (CPI), the Minnesota Multiphasic Personality Inventory (MMPI), the Myers-Briggs Type Indicator (MBTI), the Revised NEO Personality Inventory (NEO-PI-R or the NEOFFI), and the Inventory of Psychosocial Development (IPD), as well as several others.

Projective Measures of Personality.   Some researchers and theorists believe that objective measures of personality are incomplete. Although they may measure certain traits and habitual ways of behaving quite well, they may miss other and/or unconscious aspects of an individual's personality. Projective tests are designed to tap into these aspects by presenting some ambiguous figure to the individual and allowing the person to reflect on the figure and, thus, project their personality onto that ambiguous figure. As the person does this, they may reveal aspects of their personality that would not be evident by directly asking using an objective test or interview. Generally, the reliability and validity of projective tests are lower than for objective tests.

The Rorschach Inkblot Test and the Thematic Apperception Test (TAT) are two examples of these projective tests. In the former, individuals are shown a series of 10 inkblots, one at a time, and are asked to describe what they see in each one. In the TAT, the individual is shown a series of black-and-white pictures of one or more people in an ambiguous situation. The person is asked to describe the situation. An example of a picture like those found in the TAT is shown in Figure 9-1.

FIGURE 9-1   An Example of a Picture that Would be Part of a Thematic Appreciation Test (TAT).

If we were to use one or more objective tests, a projective test or two, an interview to measure an individual's personality, and if we also asked that person's family to rate them on a number of dimensions, we might expect to have a fairly complete picture of that person's personality. We would have information about several different aspects of their personality but to get a complete picture, we would have to obtain much more information at several different levels. One way to combine all the information or aspects of personality is to think of a description of personality as operating on different levels.

Levels of Personality

Dan P. McAdams proposed that a person's personality be considered as being composed of three levels of description (1994a; 1994b; 1994c; 1995). The three levels are assumed to be distinct and nonoverlapping. Knowing one level of an individual's personality may tell nothing about that person's position on the other two levels. In this chapter, we will use McAdams's proposal to organize the different aspects of personality. The first level of personality description is the level of traits, the second level is that of personal concerns, and the third level is identity. After we have examined the change or stability found for these levels, we will discuss the relationships found between personality, health, and satisfaction with life.

Traits

A **trait** is a distinguishing feature of a person's character and is assumed to remain stable over the course of adult development. Traits may be largely genetically determined. A person who is very aggressive is likely to be that way in a number of different situations and to remain aggressive throughout life. Gordon Allport was among the first to describe personality in terms of traits or enduring characteristics (1937). An individual's personality could be described by specifying where they placed on each of these traits on a continuum ranging from an extremely low score to an extremely high score. The extremes of each trait are labelled with terms indicating their opposition, such as dominant/submissive. An individual would reflect behavior indicative of traits such as dominance-submission, extraversion-introversion, friendly-unfriendly, nervous-calm, and so on. Allport believed that there were close to 5000 different traits. Other researchers have identified smaller numbers of traits as representing personality. Today, the major trait theory of personality that has been tested for age differences is the Big Five Theory.

Five-Factor Theory of Personality

Paul Costa and Robert McCrae (1994; McCrae & Costa, 1990) have argued that all important traits can be grouped into five dimensions of personality. Each dimension is composed of several different but related traits. The five dimensions are: neuroticism, extraversion, openness to experience, agreeableness, and conscientiousness. A persons' place on these dimensions is measured by an objective test of personality.

Neuroticism refers to level of anxiety or emotionality. Neurotic people are anxious, hostile, irritable, overly sensitive to criticism, and often sad and lonely. People low in this trait are emotionally stable, secure, and fairly relaxed even under stressful conditions.

Extraversion refers to how outgoing an individual is and is the opposite of introversion. Extraverted people are very sociable, enjoy being the center of attention, and seek excitement. Introverts are more serious and prefer to be by themselves.

Openness to experience refers to a willingness to try new ways of doing things. People high in this trait are imaginative, and always ready to go somewhere new or try something different. People low in openness are more traditional and set in their ways. They may be more rigid.

Agreeableness refers to being warm hearted with a strong tendency to cooperate. Agreeable people are trusting, submissive, and may be easily persuaded by others. People low in agreeableness are skeptical of others, stubborn, proud, and often, very competitive.

Conscientiousness refers to a tendency to accomplish things. Conscientious people are well organized, competent, and have a high level of self-discipline. People low in this trait tend to be easygoing, disorganized, and may even be careless or lazy.

Although you can score high, low, or in the middle on any or all of these dimensions, most people reside somewhere in the middle. We generally are calm but sometimes experience feelings of anger or sadness. We enjoy being with other people but enjoy our privacy as well. We try to balance old and new ways of doing things. We usually are agreeable but can be stubborn too. We are fairly well organized but do not work all the time.

Costa and McCrae and others argue that traits are biologically based, genetic in origin, and only slightly modified by environment. To understand a biological base, think of how you feel when you are in front of a classroom making a presentation. Everyone is a little nervous at first. Some people calm down fairly quickly while others get more nervous and experience stage fright. They can hear their heart racing. That "gut feeling," whether you calm down or get more nervous, indicates your biological system's involvement in this reaction. Costa and McCrae claim that your personality is tied to your biological system. Although we do not know the exact genetic origins of personality traits, many believe we inherit these traits. To examine genetic influences, researchers have compared identical twins who have the same genetic endowment with fraternal twins who do not. They found that identical twins were much closer to each other on each of the five dimensions, but not the same as were fraternal twins (Plomin et al., 1997). Such work suggests both genetic and environmental influence on traits.

Age Differences in Traits

Cross-sectional, longitudinal, and sequential research strategies (see Chapter 2) have been used to investigate age differences in personality traits. Cross-sectional research on personality and aging also has been used to assess the influence of genetic and environmental factors. If traits depend to some extent on the cultural environment in which people live, then people in different cultures may show different traits or some traits may be more common in some cultures than in others. In one study, researchers measured the five factors on young and middle-aged adults in Croatia, Germany, Italy, Korea, and Portugal and compared their findings to those obtained in the United States. In all six cultures, they found lower levels of neuroticism, extraversion, and openness and higher levels of conscientiousness and agreeableness in middle-aged adults. Because the same differences were obtained in different cultures, these findings support a genetic, rather than a cultural/environmental influence on traits. If it were environmental, then different cultures should have shown different results (McCrae et al., 1999). Another study compared traits for adults living in the United States and in China. Older adults living in both cultures scored lower on extraversion and flexibility but higher on self-control and orientation toward accepted norms. The younger Chinese participants, however, scored more like residents of the United States than did older Chinese, suggesting cultural/environmental influences. Recent moves toward modernization and westernization in China seem to have influenced younger Chinese adults who are now closer to their U.S. counterparts on many measures (Labouvie-Vief et al., 2000).

Other cross-sectional studies also have obtained age and/or cohort differences on a number, but not always the same, traits. Higher levels of neuroticism and extraversion for young adults and higher levels of agreeableness for older adults have been found (Zonderman et al., 1993). Using different measures, others have found older adults to be more cautious, less energetic, and more conforming to society's rules. This work did not, however, find any age differences on extraversion (Stoner & Panek, 1985). Still other work shows that traits are far more stable in older adults than in younger adults. While younger adults show variability in how neurotic or extraverted they are, older adults show far more stability; they seem to have settled into a more consistent pattern of behavior (Lee & Hotopf, 2005). With only a few exceptions (Stoner & Spencer, 1986) cross-sectional studies have found age differences in a number of traits. If these differences are truly age, rather than cohort, then we would expect to find the same results when we use a longitudinal or sequential design.

The results, however, from longitudinal and sequential studies, have been somewhat less supportive of age differences than cross-sectional studies, although some changes have been found. In an initial examination of participants in the Baltimore Longitudinal Study, researchers found stability for neuroticism, extraversion, and openness over periods of time as long as 45 years (Costa & McCrae, 1988; Costa et al., 1986). In an examination of over 3000 adults over a 7-year period, other researchers also found cohort but not age differences (Schaie & Willis, 1991). More recently, however, researchers have shown, that in spite of great stability, small but consistent changes in traits often occur as age increases. These changes tend to be similar to those found in many cross-sectional studies. In an examination of data from 92 different longitudinal studies and over 50,000 participants, it was found that conscientiousness and social dominance (an aspect of extraversion) tended to increase between the ages of 20 and 40 while neuroticism decreased. Openness and social vitality, which is another aspect of extraversion, tended to decrease in old age (Roberts et al., 2006). Additional work from the Baltimore Longitudinal Study found that from middle to old age, conscientiousness and agreeableness tended to increase while openness decreased (Terracciano et al., 2005). Generally, however, people tend to believe that they have changed far more than they actually have (Fleeson & Heckhausen, 1997; Troll & Skaff, 1997).

When change was observed, it tended to be during young adulthood. Researchers believe that young and old age changes in traits may be due to environmental factors. The demands on younger adults to do well in college, begin a career or work path, get married, start a family, and establish oneself and during older age to prepare for and enter retirement, lose some physical abilities, and become more dependent on others may result in the obtained age differences in traits. Think for a minute about the value of conscientiousness for your work in classes like this one or the value of agreeableness for getting others to lend a hand when you're older. Because these demands and changes occur in most cultures, it is not surprising that most cultures show nearly the same trait differences when young and old are compared.

It appears then that traits, as predicted, tend to remain relatively stable over the adult years, although there are some changes that occur. Some argue that this stability can be a handicap when one begins to draw closer to old age; Box 9-1 describes some of this work.

Personal Concerns

Your biggest concerns today are probably very different from those that you had 10 years ago. Your biggest concerns after you finish college and have begun a career and, perhaps, a family are likely to be different than the ones you have now. Personal concerns are likely to change. This second level of personality description, personal concerns, encompasses what individuals want and the techniques, strategies, and plans that people use to achieve those wants (McAdams, 1995). What people want can, of course, vary as a funtion of age, time of life, and social role. At the level of personal concerns, we expect to see some changes as people grow older. Project 9 offers the opportunity to compare the personal concerns of different aged adults and to relate those concerns to some of the theories

BOX **9-1**

Traits and Fears of Aging

In Chapter 1, we talked about different attitudes toward aging and older adults and how negative attitudes can lead to ageism. Fear of aging is another aspect of these negative attitudes and can take four different forms. Fear of old people refers to a discomfort when around older adults and an unwillingness to be with them; psychological concerns refer to a belief that when you're old, you'll be bored and unable to find pleasure; physical appearance refers to worry about how you will look when you're older; and fear of losses refers to concerns about loss of independence, friends, and abilities with advanced age. Some research has found that those who have little contact with older adults have higher fear of physical appearance and of losses while those with low-quality contact have higher levels of psychological concerns (Lasher & Faulkender, 1993). Perhaps such fears are related to personality traits.

To examine this question, Lori Harris and Stephanie Dollinger (2002) measured the four types of aging fears in young people aged 17 to 25 and also measured the five factors of personality. They found that those high in neuroticism showed higher levels of fear of losses, physical appearance, and psychological concerns. Those high in extraversion had less fear of losses and psychological concern. Those high in agreeableness were lower on all four types of fears. Those high in conscientiousness had lower levels of fear of older people, psychological concerns, and physical appearance. Openness was not related to any of the measured fears.

If you're high on neuroticism but low on agreeableness, extraversion, and conscientiousness, you may have a fairly high fear of aging and if traits remain relatively stable as we grow older, your adjustment to your own old age may be quite difficult. What trait changes with aging may help in this adjustment?

PROJECT 9

Age/Cohort Differences in Personal Concerns

In this project we want you to examine the personal concerns for different age individuals. Remember, these different age individuals are members of different cohorts.

Using the rating scale shown, rate the items on the "concerns list" for how concerned you are about them at this point in your life.

Make copies of the scale and list and ask family members and friends to rate the same items using the same rating scale. Make an effort to test people of different ages. What items do you expect them to rate almost the same as you did and what items do you expect them to rate differently? Why?

Are your expectations based on age, cohort, or specific environmental circumstances (e.g., dad's car just broke down so I know he wants a new one).

Compare the different ratings and see which items were rated differently and which were rated the same. Are the differences and similarities the ones that you might expect on the basis of things that you have learned about adult development and aging? Are the differences that Erikson might expect (in intimacy? in generativity?) present in the ratings you obtained?

We hope you also will take the time to talk about the similarities and differences with your parents, grandparents, and/or the people who completed the ratings for you. We expect that you will learn much from your discussions with these older adults.

Use the following Rating Scale to rate how important each item on the concerns list is to you at the present time.

- Not important at all   1
- Not very important   2
- A little important   3
- Fairly important   4
- Very important   5

Being with my family   _____

Making money

Being with my friends   _____

Traveling to new places

Making new friends   _____

Nurturing my family

Protecting my family   _____

Teaching younger people

Maintaining my health   _____

Improving my health

Changing my life   _____

Finding true love

Starting a family   _____

Getting a new car

Staying out of trouble   _____

Losing weight

Being happy   _____

Avoiding rating scales

discussed in this section. One way to view the level of personal concerns is to view those concerns as being a function of stage of life. At different life stages people tend to have different social roles and tend to focus on different concerns. We will examine one major theory of life stages and then look at changes in another type of personal concern, the ways that people cope with stress and problems as they grow older.

Erikson's Stages of Lifespan Development

The Theory.   Erik Erikson studied with Sigmund Freud but, unlike Freud, did not believe that personality development ended in early childhood (1963, 1968, 1982; Erikson et al., 1986). He proposed that we continue to experience life stages that may alter aspects of personality development. In fact, he was the first to propose a detailed lifespan theory of development in any area. Erikson's eight stages are shown in Table 9-2. Developmental stages represent qualitative changes in behavior and thought, occur in fixed order, and cannot be skipped. They represent discontinuous change although the transition from stage to stage is thought to be gradual. It is not that one becomes less concerned with trust as one grows older; it is that trust is a major concern very early in life and the level of trust we take up depends very much upon early experiences. We view Erikson's stages as representing major personal concerns or tasks that must be dealt with (Havighurst, 1972), rather than true developmental stages. We will examine the three concerns that Erikson refers to as the adult stages of development but remember that dealing with these concerns is affected by how we dealt with earlier concerns.

The first of these concerns is that of **intimacy versus isolation** and occurs during young adulthood. Although young adults are, of course, concerned about many things; a primary, and perhaps universal, concern is to merge with another human being in an intimate relationship. It is thought that we experience both social and biological pressures to achieve this and if we fail, we experience feelings of isolation. Intimate relationships typically involve courtship, marriage, and often the beginning of a family. Relationships may be heterosexual, gay, lesbian, or even very close friendships. In Erikson's view, you gain

TABLE 9-2   Erikson's Stages of Personality Development or Personal Concerns

Age	Personal Concern
First year of life	Trust vs. mistrust
Second year	Autonomy vs. shame and doubt
Age 3 to 5	Initiative vs. guilt
Age 6 until puberty	Industry vs. inferiority
Adolescence	Identity vs. role confusion
Young adulthood	Intimacy vs. isolation
Middle age	Generativity vs. stagnation
Old age	Ego integrity vs. despair

ego strength when you resolve this concern by successfully forming an intimate relationship with another person. This successful resolution is dependent to some degree on your success at forming a self-identity during adolescence (and your level of trust and successful resolution of other concerns). Your success at forming an intimate relationship enables you to better handle the concerns of later years.

The second concern takes place in middle age and is that of **generativity versus stagnation**. Erikson believed that during middle age, people become concerned about their own and future generations of people. They may strive to create something that would contribute to the welfare of humanity and that could be passed on to younger generations. Generativity might be achieved by rearing strong, smart, and healthy children and/or by working hard to be a success or role model in one's career or place of employment. Those who stagnate during their middle years may be those who experience a **midlife crisis** (Levinson, 1996). They don't want to generate something for the younger generation; they want to be a member of that generation. They attempt to hang on to their youth and often attempt to rid themselves of the vestiges of middle age and approaching old age. Divorce, sports car sales, plastic surgery, and hair dye may be higher for this group. The proportion of people experiencing a midlife crisis is quite low, however, and men are more likely than women to have this experience (Chiriboga, 1989). Perhaps most middle-aged adults become generative rather than stagnant.

It is important to point out that one cannot determine another's generativity simply by knowing the kind of work that a person does or the size of their family. It is the feeling they have about the work they do or the family they care for that determines generativity or stagnation. An artist may appear to be generative because she creates works of great beauty that attract praise from others in her own generation and that will undoubtedly be appreciated by many future generations. She may, however, feel that her work is repetitive and only done to fund her lifestyle; she may be stagnant. An auto mechanic may appear to be stagnant doing the same jobs over and over again but she may feel very generative as she works to make the repairs that keep others and their children safe on the highways and as she teaches future mechanics her trade and skills.

The last adult concern is **ego integrity versus despair**. During old age, Erikson believed that a person looks back over life and attempts to determine whether that life has been coherent, whole, and fulfilling. If so, one experiences feelings of integrity and can face decline and accept mortality without regrets. If, instead, one looks back and wishes they had made other choices in their youth and middle years, then they are likely to experience despair because it is too late to make those changes.

Other theorists have argued that Erikson stopped short and that older adults can better be described as having three major concerns, rather than just one (Peck, 1968). During young-old age, adults are concerned with a **redefinition of self versus a preoccupation with work**. As people approach retirement, they must decide whether to continue in their jobs or to make a major change in their lives by retiring. With retirement comes a new view of oneself. A second concern is **body transcendence versus body preoccupation**. As you know our bodies undergo significant changes as we grow older (see Chapter 3). If one becomes focused on graying hair, wrinkles, declining physical abilities, slowing, and other signs of biological aging, then one may lose sight of the important components of life. If one can cope with these physical changes, if one can transcend them, then one can attend

A generative act.

to social relationships, health, finances, and overall well-being and have a higher quality of life. Finally, older adults become concerned with **ego transcendence versus ego preoccupation**, which is much like Erikson's original ego integrity versus despair. People must understand that death is inevitable and see that their contributions in the form of children, grandchildren, work, and perhaps civic activities will be there when they are gone.

Testing the Theory.   Most of the work that has been done to test Erikson's theory has been cross-sectional and focused on generativity, a proposed major concern of middle-aged but not young adults. Older adults also may have generative concerns but their concerns should lessen with age and as they turn to retirement, physical changes, and life review. Defining what is meant by generativity and measuring it have not, however, been easy tasks. Some researchers suggest that obtained age differences in generativity will depend on the type of generativity being measured. For example, the *desire* to be generative might be high in young adults, the *capacity* for generativity might be high in middle age, and the *feeling* of generative accomplishment might rise through adulthood and be highest in old age (Stewart & Vandewater, 1998).

Researchers have attended to these different ways of measuring generativity. In a comparison of 51 young adults (ages 22 to 27), 53 middle-age adults (ages 37 to 42), and 48 older adults (ages 67 to 72), researchers used four different measures of generativity and a measure of life satisfaction and retested 70 percent of the sample 6 months later. The measures of generativity assessed how much each person was concerned with future generations, how committed they were to doing something to help, what actions they were taking presently that were generative (e.g., actions like donating blood or teaching somebody a new skill were classified as generative while actions such as buying a new car or going bowling were not), and how much their recall of important life events included generative themes. The results generally were supportive of Erikson's theory. On all four measures, young adults were less generative than middle age and older adults and on measures of generative commitment and generative themes older adults also were less generative than middle-age adults. Overall, middle-age adults showed consistently high levels of generativity. Generativity was not related to an individual's marital situation or the presence of children (McAdams & de St. Aubin, 1992; McAdams et al., 1993). Perhaps a reason for higher levels of generativity in middle age compared to young age is that one becomes more generative as one spends more time in a career or in raising children. After a certain amount of experience one may be expected to share the knowledge they have gained and to teach members of the next generation. Other work has obtained similar results with middle-aged adults showing more generativity than younger adults but older adults being nearly as generative as those in middle age (Zucker et al., 2002). It is, of course, possible that older adults are generative but it may be the case that those older adults tested were not yet old enough to turn to the concerns of ego integrity.

Some longitudinal work also has examined generativity. In one study, women from Smith College, Mills College, and the University of Michigan were tested for generativity, identity certainty (discussed later in this chapter), confidence, and concerns about aging. All of these were higher for women in their 40s and 50s than earlier in their lives (Stewart et al., 2001). Another longitudinal study began testing 20-year-olds in 1966. They were tested again in 1977 when they were 31 and again in 1988 when they were 42. New samples of 20-year-olds also were added in each of those years. Higher levels of intimacy concerns were found for those in their 20s but because the oldest age tested thus far was only 42, no conclusions regarding generativity are yet possible (Whitbourne et al., 1992). These studies and others generally support Erikson's predictions that different age adults have different personal concerns and that those age-related concerns occur quite often.

The generative years, middle age, once were thought to be a time of crisis (midlife crisis) but now are generally viewed as a time of great relief from the strivings of young adulthood. The concerns of old age are far in the future; men and women have raised their children, established their careers, and have money to spend on themselves (Gallagher, 1993). Middle age could be the best time of life. Some research supports this positive view. In one such study, a sample of women who had graduated from Smith College 30 years earlier were asked how they felt about turning 50. Nearly half, 48 percent, had very positive feelings while only 18 percent were very negative (21% were neutral and 13% were mildly negative) (Steward & Ostrove, 1998). Other work on middle-age personal concerns has focused on differences between men and women in terms of their changing gender roles and is described in Box 9-2.

Overall, some changes in personal concerns seem to occur as one grows older, and research supports Erikson's prediction of increased generativity during middle age. If a number of different changes in personal concerns occur during middle and old age, then it seems likely that a number of different changes in strategies for dealing with life's events and attempting to resolve personal concerns also might occur. As you recall, part of the

---

BOX **9-2**

Age and Androgyny

Although both men and women show many of the same personality traits, they tend to differ in terms of the way they perceive themselves and react to others and events in their lives. These different ways are referred to as gender roles. Those who attempt to be in charge, be dominant, and change the world rather than change themselves are said to be high in **masculinity**. Those who tend to be more submissive and to change themselves in order to meet the needs of others are said to be high in **femininity**. Some people are high in both masculinity and femininity and are said to be **androgynous**. They can be in charge or follow orders; they can be dominant or submissive; they can change the world and themselves. Some people are, of course, low in both masculine and feminine characteristics and are said to be **undifferentiated**. David Guttman (1987) proposed that during young adulthood, men and women tend to be gender stereotypical, very masculine or very feminine, because they are raising children. A division of labor and nurturing leads them to become more masculine or feminine than they already were. During middle age, when the children begin to leave or have left the home, men and women can show their other sides. Men become more feminine without abandoning their masculinity and women become more masculine without abandoning their femininity; men and women become androgynous.

The work testing Guttman's predictions has shown some of these changes and others as well. Middle-aged men often are more nurturant and feminine than young men and middle-aged women are more assertive and masculine than young women (Huyck, 1990). A longitudinal examination of women found that they increased in femininity between the ages of 21 and 27 and increased in masculinity between the ages of 27 and 52. The changes, however, were unrelated to the presence or absence of children (Helson & Wink, 1992). In another study, men and women between the ages of 13 and 81 were measured over a 10-year period. Both men and women increased in femininity; that is, men became more androgynous but women simply became more feminine (Hyde et al., 1991). Changes in gender roles frequently occur but the changes are not always the same and may depend on cohort, age, and a host of other factors rather than the demands of parenthood.

---

definition of this second level of personality description includes the strategies and plans that people use to achieve the things they want (McAdams, 1995). It is, therefore, expected that those strategies and plans often will change over the course of a person's life. People with different experiences may cope differently and because experiences and personal concerns change with age, coping too should change.

Age Differences in Coping

An important part of personality is the way individuals cope with everyday situations and with high-stress situations. Research has shown that coping strategies change with age. In examining these changes, consider two different views of why such changes occur: research that examines responses to stressful situations and research that examines different types of control over the events of life.

Two Views

Strategic Knowledge.   One view of why coping strategies might change with age is simply that older adults know more strategies. The phrase "been there, done that" more readily applies to older than to younger people. Because older adults have lived longer and, thus, had more experiences, they are bound to have developed many more coping strategies than younger adults. They are able to select from a wider variety of strategies. This view expects that older and younger adults will choose the same type of coping strategies in many situations but that older adults are more able to change strategies when the situation changes while younger adults may not yet be aware of other strategies that might be more effective in certain situations. Older adults also may value outcomes differently than they once did. They may alter strategies because they now focus more on the emotional and social aspects of problems while younger adults may nearly always focus on finding a problem solution (Carstensen & Freund, 1994).

Compensating for Loss.   The second view is that older adults may *have* to change strategies. As you know, all development is comprised of gains and losses but some believe that losses outweigh gains as we grow older. You know about the physical changes that occur as we age and that many of those are senescent. You know that we slow down and some aspects of our cognition decline while others improve. This view says that older adults change coping strategies to compensate for these losses and, in some instances, because they are no longer able to use a preferred coping strategy. They may know a number of strategies but, because of losses, can no longer use very many of them. They have no choice but to change if they are to successfully solve the problem.

Whether older adults use different coping strategies because they have to or because they have a wider variety of strategies to choose from, some recent work suggests that either the availability and/or the choices made have strong genetic, as well as environmental, learning components (Busjahn et al., 2002). A recent examination of middle-aged and older, identical and fraternal twins, reared apart or reared together, showed that genes played a larger role than environment in the coping strategies used by these adults. Furthermore, problem-solving coping strategies were strongly related to high levels of extraversion and openness while emotion-managing strategies were related to neuroticism (Kato & Pedersen, 2005). The same genes that influence personality traits also may influence the ways in which a person copes with life's problems.

Responding to Problems

Much of the research on age differences in strategies used to solve life problems has involved presenting vignettes and asking people to discuss their solutions. They are asked to tell what they would do if they were in such a situation or what advice they would give to someone in such a situation. Typically vignettes are designed to vary the emotional content of the situation (Blanchard-Fields, 1986). If older adults are aware of more strategies and/or attend more to the social/emotional content, then they should use different strategies when the emotional content of the vignette is high. Coping strategies are classified in a number of ways but for our purposes, we will describe four different types: (1) problem solving—two kinds of emotion-managing strategies; (2) passive emotion regulation; (3) proactive emotion regulation; and (4) avoidance (Blanchard-Fields et al., 2004). Read the following vignette and think of how you might handle this situation:

> A young couple plan to get married next summer so that his parents will be able to attend. His parents live in France and can only get away during July. They have made it very clear that this is the most important event in their lives because he is their only child. They would be very upset, angry, and perhaps disown him if they were unable to attend. Her mother, however, has been diagnosed with a terminal illness and her doctors say she will be lucky to live as long as March. Her last hope is to see her daughter happily married. The young man wants to please his parents while she wishes to please hers and they have begun to disagree and argue. What should the young couple do?

If your answer is a **problem-solving** solution, then you would try to find an answer without considering emotional content. You might suggest that they have two ceremonies, one now and one in July. If you chose a **passive emotion regulation** strategy, then you would not deal directly with the problem but instead try and remain calm. You might say that it is important for the couple to stay calm and not fight while the two sets of parents should work together to solve this situation. If you chose a **proactive emotion regulation** strategy, then you would confront the emotions and consider accepting responsibility. You might try to make it clear to his parents the seriousness of her mother's illness, that the couple is in love and will get married no matter what, and ask them to find another way to celebrate the wedding. If you chose an **avoidance** strategy, then you would act as if there was no problem. You just might assume that things will work out and no action at present is needed. What strategy did you use?

When the emotional content of vignettes is fairly low, such as whether a person should accept a lower paying job close to home or a higher paying job farther away, age differences usually are not found. Adults from adolescence to old age resort to problem-solving strategies such as taking the job of greater interest or with better probability of advancement. When, however, the emotional content is high, age differences appear. Adolescents often fail to solve these problems and seem to have few available strategies. Younger and older adults still offer problem-solving strategies most often but older adults use far more emotion managing strategies in these situations (Blanchard-Fields, 1986; Blanchard-Fields et al., 1995; Folkman et al., 1987). Generally such work supports the view of greater strategic knowledge for older adults.

This work is sometimes criticized for being artificial. People may say they would solve the problem in a certain way but would they if they really were in that situation? To solve this problem researchers have asked people about real-life situations that they have encountered and how they handled their own situations. In one such study, men were asked to describe real situations that had happened in their lives and the strategy that they used to solve the problem. Older men were less likely than middle-age men to use avoidance strategies in situations that occurred in their lives when the situation involved confronting an authority or making an important decision. The research also showed that both middle-age and older men had and used a wide variety of strategies. Older men, who did not have to worry about the same repercussions in the workplace that middle-age men did, tended not to avoid confrontation as often as middle-age men (Feifel & Strack, 1989). Older adults, including middle-age adults, appear to have a wide variety of coping strategies and select an appropriate strategy based on a number of relevant factors.

In another study, Fredda Blanchard-Fields and her colleagues (2004) asked young, middle-aged, and older men and women to talk about family problems of their own that had occurred during the past year. They were told that one problem should be "highly emotional for you" while the other should be "not real emotional for you" (p. 262). They also described how they handled the situation and its emotional aspects. All age groups showed more use of strategies in their own situations which were high in emotional content and women used more emotion-managing strategies than men did. Over all situations, problem-solving strategies were, however, the most frequently used. Looking at types of emotion-managing strategies, middle-aged adults more frequently used proactive emotion regulation while older adults more frequently used passive emotion regulation (Blanchard-Fields et al., 2004). Middle-aged and older adults seem to have more available strategies than younger adults but their coping strategy use is different. Do you think these effects could be cohort differences? The researchers note this as a possibility and suggest that their middle-aged adults (baby boom generation people) generally may be more proactive in confronting life's problems. Why do you think this might be?

Of course, not all of life's problems are social and emotional. Age differences in coping may occur because older adults typically face different problems than do younger adults (Neugarten & Neugarten, 1987). Severe arthritis may lead to a loss of mobility; macular degeneration may result in the loss of a driver's license and some independence; presbycusis may lead to a loss of willingness or ability to participate in social conversations. How older adults cope with such losses also has been investigated. One model of the strategies used to cope with such losses says that there are three general strategies.

1. **Assimilation** strategies are those in which the individual modifies her or his behavior to meet a goal or maintain performance. For example, you wish to live a long healthy life so you quit smoking.
2. **Accommodation** strategies are those in which the individual modifies the goal that is being sought, substitutes a different goal, or lowers one's acceptable standards for performance. For example, your arthritis will no longer allow you to be a member of the softball team so you take up coaching.
3. **Immunization** strategies are those in which some evidence of loss is reinterpreted in a more positive way or is regarded as irrelevant. For example, you frequently forget appointments but claim it's because you had more important things on your mind.

The use of these strategies is thought to change as we grow older. Younger adults rely more on assimilation strategies while middle-aged, and especially older, adults rely more on accommodation and immunization strategies (Brandstädter & Greve, 1994).

In cross-sectional studies designed to test the predictions made by this model, nearly 4000 men and women ranging in age from the early 20s to the late 70s responded to measures of assimilation and accommodation strategy use. Results from this and other studies showed a consistent decline in scores on the assimilative measure and an increase on the accommodative measure as the age of the respondents increased (Brandstädter, 1992; Coleman et al., 1999). A more recent longitudinal study looked at the coping strategies used by over 700 adults ranging in age from 58 to 81 who showed some functional impairment. Their sense of control over their performance, compensatory efforts, perceived losses, personal standards of performance, and overall contentment were measured over a 4-year time span. Results showed, as you might expect, that perceived losses increased with age while perceived control decreased. Compensatory effort, a form of assimilative strategy, increased up to age 70 and then declined. Older adults lowered their performance standards which is one type of accommodation strategy. Over all ages, contentment with performance was maintained, suggesting that both assimilation and accommodation strategies are effective for dealing with loss (Rothermund & Brandstädter, 2003).

Control

The study just discussed found a decreased sense of control over functional impairment for the oldest adults with such impairment. Considerable research has examined age difference in the concept of control over life events and specific aspects such as impairment. **Locus of control**, which was originally considered a personality trait, refers to one's beliefs about the positive and negative things that happen (Rotter, 1966). Control has two extremes which are referred to as internal and external. A person high in **internal control** believes that their successes and failures depend primarily on their own actions. A person high in **external control** believes that their successes and failures depend on forces over which they have no control. Control may be in the hands of powerful others or simply chance (Levenson, 1974). Control typically is measured by asking persons to express their degree of agreement or disagreement with general statements about their lives. For example, one might agree or disagree that "as long as I exercise my mind I will always be on top of things" or "I can understand instructions only after someone explains them to me" or "to a great extent my life is controlled by accidental happenings." Strong agreement with the first statement would be a sign of internal control while strong agreement with the second or third statements would be signs of external powerful others or external chance, respectively.

When researchers have examined age differences in sense of control over general life events, the results have been mixed. Both cross-sectional and longitudinal studies have obtained higher and lower levels of internal control for older adults (Lachman, 1983; 1985; Ryckman & Malikioski, 1975; Siegler & Gatz, 1985; Wolf & Kurtz, 1975). Some have argued that older cohorts, and perhaps older adults, have been more willing to accept responsibility and that acceptance, rather than locus of control, is the factor responsible for seemingly high levels of internal control in the older respondents.

When, however, control in some specific domain is measured (as with impairment), the results are more consistent. Marge E. Lachman (1986) tested younger and older adults on their general sense of control and on control in the areas of intellect and health. People expressed agreement or disagreement with internal statements such as "it's up to me to keep my mental faculties from deteriorating" for the intellect domain and "if I take care of myself I can avoid illness" for the health domain. Powerful other statements for intellectual and health domains included "I wouldn't be able to figure out the postal rates on a package without a postal worker's help" and "regarding my health, I can only do what my doctor tells me." External chance statements for these domains included "I have little control over my mental state" and "no matter what I do, if I'm going to get sick, I will get sick." Tests of several hundred adults showed no age differences on the general scale of control but in the specific domains of intellect and health, older adults showed more external control. The loss of some abilities with advanced age may produce increased effort to maintain performance until resources begin to deplete. With fewer remaining resources, older adults may begin to believe that their successes and failures are no longer their own to control.

Control can be thought about in terms other than internal and external. Another way to think about coping and control is to think in terms of primary and secondary control (Schulz & Heckhausen, 1996). **Primary control** refers to exerting influence on the external world. If the environmental situation is not acceptable, a person using primary control changes that environment. **Secondary control** refers to change within the individual. If the environmental situation is not acceptable, a person using secondary control changes him- or herself. Figure 9-2 illustrates the expected availability and use of these two types of control over the course of a person's life. During childhood, adolescence, and young adulthood, we learn both strategies but we mainly use primary control as we explore and shape our environments. All through our lives we strive for primary control. In middle adulthood, we use both strategies but in different situations. In late adulthood, our ability to change the environment and exert primary control declines and we rely much more heavily on secondary control strategies. At the same time, we become much more selective in our choice of goals and use primary control strategies whenever possible. In very old age, we may have to rely entirely on secondary control. Some research shows that very old adults strive

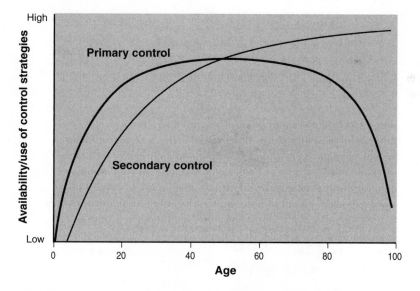

FIGURE 9-2   Primary and Secondary Control Across the Lifespan.

Source: Reprinted with permission from Schulz, R. & Heckhausen, J. (1996).

to avoid problems whenever possible and to accept what they cannot change (Aldwin et al., 1996). Older adults often rely more heavily on religion which is seen as a form of secondary control (McFadden, 1999). In one examination of the coping strategies reportedly used by older adults, religion was named more frequently than any other strategy (Koenig et al., 1988).

In one test of this model of coping, younger, middle-age, and older adults answered questions about their life goals and took standardized measures of tenacity and flexibility. Researchers found that older adults were less optimistic about attaining their goals and believed that they had less control over that attainment. Older adults were more concerned with health, leisure, and community goals than were the other groups but less concerned with family, financial, and work goals. Older adults strove for primary control but were more flexible in their approach and more willing and likely to use secondary control strategies (Heckhausen, 1997). Other studies also found that older adults use secondary control in many situations and more often than younger adults (Wrosch & Heckhausen, 1999).

In 2000, 1013 younger adults, 1650 middle-age adults, and 827 older adults participated in a half-hour phone survey and provided, by mail, ratings for their well-being, control strategies, and their current level of stress in health and financial matters. Control strategies were evaluated by having people rate three types of control statements on a scale ranging from "not at all" (a 1 on the scale) to "a lot" (a 4 on the scale). An example of a primary control statement is "Even when I have too much to do, I find a way to get it all

Coping strategies change with age.

done." Secondary control was measured in two forms: positive reappraisal and lowering aspirations. The former is described as seeing the good side of a bad situation. A statement characteristic of this strategy is "I find I usually learn something meaningful from a difficult situation." The latter type of secondary control refers to changing goals or giving up. A statement characteristic of this strategy is "When I can't get what I want, I assume my goals must be unrealistic." Researchers found that primary control was positively related to well-being for younger adults while the positive reappraisal form of secondary control was positively related to well-being for middle-age and older adults. Lowering aspirations was negatively related to well-being for adults of all ages. These findings were particularly strong for individuals who had relatively high levels of health or financial stress. Older adults also showed a higher level of reliance on primary control strategies than did younger adults suggesting that older adults rely more on all control strategies than do younger adults (Wrosch et al., 2000).

It appears that personal concerns tend to change as we grow older. We tend to become more concerned with generative issues in middle age. In old age, our concerns may shift to issues of health, leisure, and community. The strategies used to cope with various situations also seem to broaden and change and beliefs in how much control we have and how much we are able to exert also seem to shift with advanced age for certain domains. We may become more focused on social and emotional ties and worry less about the future. At this point in our exploration of personality, it appears that traits tend to remain relatively stable and personal concerns tend to change.

Identity

The third level of personality description is one of identity. **Identity** refers to a continuing and coherent sense of self over time. Even though concerns and strategies for coping with various situations may change, we still see ourselves as being basically the same person that we have always been. One factor that helps us to maintain a coherent and lasting sense of identity is the relative stability of the traits discussed earlier. Our continuing neuroticism, extraversion, openness, agreeableness, and conscientiousness help make us feel like we are the same person but, as these traits change, adjustments to our self-identity also may occur. The culture in which we live and the things we experience play a role in our identity. Our culture can influence the identity we construct for ourselves and events in our lives may force us to reevaluate who we are and alter our identity. Another contributor to the maintenance of self-identity is our life story. Many people, but not all, have fashioned a story of their lives in which they are the central character. Life stories will be examined later in this section.

One way of examining identity is to ask individuals to respond to specific questions about their sense of identity. In longitudinal work with students who graduated from Mills College (Helson, 1993), Radcliffe (Stewart & Vandewater, 1993), Smith College, and the University of Michigan (Tangri & Jenkins, 1993; Cole & Stewart, 1996), researchers asked individuals to respond to scales that measured identity certainty, which is the "sense of having a strong and clear identity" (Stewart & Ostrove, 1998, p. 1189). This work and others have found an increasing awareness of self-identity, and an increasing certainty of self, as individuals aged through their 40s and up to their 60s (Miner-Rubino et al., 2004; Stewart et al., 2001; Whitbourne & Waterman, 1979). Adults become more sure of who they are as they grow older and gain more experience.

Typically one grows older and gains experience within some cultural context and some work has looked at the influence that culture has on self-identity. One such study examined identity in Dutch and Spanish adults over the age of 60. Identity was measured by having each respondent complete a number of sentences with truthful statements about themselves. Sentence stems included "I am best at _____"; "Others think I am _____"; "My life's goal"; and so on. Although all the responders were similar in most ways, an important difference was found in the proportion of responses that related to family and to personal activities. Spanish older adults responded more frequently with reference to members of their family ("Others think I am a very good father who cares for his children") while Dutch older adults responded more frequently with reference to their own free time activities ("Others think I am one of the best fishermen in our town"). It is believed that differences such as this result from the more collectivist Spanish culture and the more individualistic Dutch culture (Katzko et al., 1998).

Another cross-cultural study looked at attitudes toward older adults and views of one's self-identity in China, Japan, and the United States. Older adults are not viewed very positively in any of these cultures although they are treated more favorably and with greater respect in China and Japan. Japanese culture maintains a strong distinction between the outer and inner self that the other two cultures do not. The outer self in Japan is the identity that interacts with the world while the inner self is free from influences of the material and social world. Other studies have shown that success or failure in social situations seems not to affect the self-esteem of the Japanese because the inner self is not affected by such external events (Kitayama et al., 1997). In this study of attitudes, older adults in these three cultures were asked what the first five words or phrases were that came to mind when they thought about themselves and when they thought about an older person. The results showed that in China and the United States, views of self and of an older person were mostly the same and fairly negative. The negative stereotypes of older people in these cultures is related to the negative views that older adults have of themselves. In Japan, however, older adults also viewed an older person negatively but viewed themselves very positively. The cultural emphasis on an inner and an outer self seems to protect the identity of older adults in Japan from any damaging influences of attitudes toward older persons (Levy, 1999).

For most people, such cultural influences operate throughout their lives as most people are born into and remain in one primary culture. The influence must, therefore, start fairly young. Erikson put self-identity as the personal concern of adolescents but the beginning of its formation may be much earlier. We try several different possibilities (the brain, the clown, the model, the lover, the athlete) until we find ourselves. According to Erikson, failure to find ourselves during adolescence results in role confusion; we don't know who we really are and will have trouble establishing intimate relations with others as we reach young adulthood. Some work supports the formation of identity during adolescence (Habermas & Bluck, 2000) although its formation may start much earlier (Cohler, 1982). The roots of identity are seen in the development of self-concept that is affected by parents, culture, and society. As children, then adolescents, then adults, people encounter more feedback about themselves from others and are able to put all the information about themselves together. With higher level thinking, self-concept and identity broaden and change (Harter, 1990).

The processes involved in the maintenance and altering of identity in old age have been described by Susan Whitbourne (1985; 1989; 2001). When we attempt to fit life events into a preconceived view of who we are and to downplay events that don't fit, that process is called **identity assimilation**. At other times, events happen that do not fit our view and we alter our identity; that process is called **identity accommodation**. (In other words, if I see myself as a generous person, then I may tend to think of my purchase of lottery tickets as just being one way of contributing money to the funding of public education. I assimilate the event into my preconceived view of myself.) One example of such assimilation was found with older psychiatric patients. These individuals greatly downplayed, and in some cases even denied, that they had spent major parts of their lives in the hospital. Spending time in a psychiatric hospital did not fit well with their self views (Whitbourne & Sherry, 1991). Sometimes, however, events that do not easily fit cannot be easily ignored. If a person believes that they will never marry and then find themselves taking those vows, some accommodation clearly is necessary. In the course of identity maintenance and change, both processes play a role and healthy development occurs when a balance between the two processes is present.

One means that some people use to maintain their identity is the personal **life story**. Simply saying, "this is my life story" seems to indicate a strong sense of identity and these stories have been collected and analyzed by a number of researchers examining identity. It is important to keep in mind that identity itself is not the life story. The story is a way for the individual to maintain a coherent identity and, when written down, for the researcher to examine that identity and to investigate why some people construct life stories while others do not.

Virtually everyone can tell you about the major events that occurred to them during their life. Such a telling is not, however, regarded as being a life story. To be a life story, the information provided by an individual must have four important characteristics (Coleman, 1999). The first is **coherence** which refers to a linking thread that makes the story whole and not just a sequence of events. Linking threads are commonly family and/or career but can also be psychological constructs. Stories must show **assimilation** (yes, still another type of assimilation) which refers to the interpretation of the events that are presented rather than just their presentation. The third characteristic is **structure** which means that life stories have some beginning, middle, and anticipated end. Finally, stories must be the **truth**. They are more like works of history than works of fiction. They should tell the truth from the viewpoint of the person who has constructed the story. Box 9-3 provides an example of a sequence of events and those same events told as a life story. Can you distinguish the two?

Using some of these characteristics, Coleman and his colleagues have begun to examine life stories. In one study, 18 men and 25 women ranging in age from 80 to 98 were interviewed about the course of their lives. Of these 43 people, 28 saw their life course as a story and many (27) thought it worth telling or writing about. Story coherence was most typically maintained by long-term relations with family and friends who provided the links between past and present. For others, work provided this important link. Ten of the

BOX 9-3

A Life Story

The following are excerpts from two imaginary older adults asked to tell us about their lives. One is told as a sequence of events and the other as a life story. Can you detect any of Coleman's criteria as you distinguish the two?

Jake

. . . and then, let's see, I guess it must have been my tenth birthday, I got this really cool bike and I used to ride it everywhere. It was stolen a year later. It made me mad but we never found it. Some people just take whatever they want. I never stole anything. When I was 14, we moved to Boise. My mom got a transfer and we had to move. I didn't make any friends for a while but finally I got used to it and made some really good friends. I took a girl to a movie when I was 15 and kissed her. I don't remember the name of the movie. Some of the other kids who had already been dating made fun of us. Kids will be kids. . . .

Bart

. . . I got a really cool bike for my tenth birthday. Riding it made me feel free because I could go anywhere I wanted. A year later it was stolen and I felt really mad for a while but never got it back. I never forgot that feeling of freedom and have strived to feel like that all my life. At 14, we moved to Springfield. I enjoyed exploring my new territory and felt excited and free in this new place. It took a while to make new friends but I did. One of them, Gary, is still a good friend and we still get together once a year to catch up on things. When I was 15, I exercised my freedom and took a girl to a movie and kissed her. Some other kids made fun of us. I think that experience made me a little shy around women but my wife, Bu, says she likes me that way. . . .

You should be able to find evidence for coherence and assimilation in Bart's excerpts but not in Jake's. The criteria of structure cannot be determined from such a short piece of life telling because we've eliminated the beginning and end. How might you determine the truth of these excerpts?

individuals interviewed saw their life course as disconnected or as a series of events rather than as a story. Eight of these 10 individuals without coherent life stories were women. Three years later, 10 men and 17 women of the first sample were interviewed again. The majority of these individuals still reported life stories with family relationships as the main theme for both men and women (Coleman et al., 1998). In a continued investigation involving these same people, five individuals were selected for a more intensive case analysis. These individuals maintained their life stories even in very old age and used these stories "not only in making sense of the past but interpreting the present as well" (p. 843). The results from these case studies suggest that perceived control is an important factor in whether one constructs a life story. As you might expect from the earlier discussion of control, people who believe they have little or no control are more likely to perceive their lives as disconnected events (Coleman et al., 1999). Perhaps women of that older cohort (these people were born between 1895 and 1913) grew up and lived in times when women perceived little control over their lives. Would women in the present cohort be more likely to construct life stories?

Clearly the same life events are presented very differently by people listing sequences of events and by those telling a life story. Even two different story tellers may describe the very same events quite differently (McAdams, 1998). Telling a life story involves looking at the past and some research shows that older adults are more likely to do this than younger adults (Runyan, 1980; Vaillant & McArthur, 1972). Older adults may be more likely to have greater coherence and structure in their life stories than middle-aged and younger adults. Of all the criteria, it may be coherence that is most likely to be changed by a major life event such as a serious illness or the onset of disability. Story assimilation, structure, and truth may remain while the thread of coherence might be frayed by such cataclysmic events (Warren, 1998). Loss of job or loss of family can radically alter the coherence of one's life story.

Finally, some research has attempted to compare the stories told by people with different traits or different personal concerns. In one study, researchers examined the life stories told by highly generative and less generative adults who ranged from 25 to 72 years of age. Generativity was measured by scores on a test of generative concern, a test of daily generative acts, and the individual's professional and/or volunteer activities. Interviews were conducted to gather the life stories of 40 adults who were highly generative and of 30 adults who scored low on generativity. Stories were scored by independent raters. The life stories told by highly generative adults showed a sensitivity to the feelings of others early in life, a stable morality, a tendency to obtain good outcomes even from bad situations, and the setting of future goals that were intended to benefit the greater society rather than the self (McAdams et al., 1997). The life stories of generative adults were quite different from the life stories told by less generative adults.

The work on life stories is still relatively new and many additional studies will be needed before researchers can be sure how often such stories are used to maintain identity. Even people without a life story have, of course, a self-identity and some recent work suggests how important that identity can be for adults who have begun to lose their connections with their memories and their families. In this study, adults diagnosed with dementia randomly were assigned to a treatment or to a control group. The treatment consisted of determining an important component of self-identity for each individual person and then providing activities related to that identity for 30 minutes a day for 5 days. For example, a person whose family and social role were important for her identity might spend the treatment days working on creating a family tree using photographs. One whose role as an aviation engineer was an important component of his identity might help construct a model plane. At the end of this short treatment period, those provided with identity-related activities had fewer instances of agitation, greater orientation, and more interest, involvement, and pleasure in their activities (Cohen-Mansfield et al., 2006). Maintaining one's self-identity is an important part of overall well-being.

Personality, Health, and Well-Being

The examination of personality and aging has shown that traits remain relatively stable although there are some common changes that do occur. Younger adults tend to become a little more conscientious and extraverted and less neurotic while older adults tend to become a bit more agreeable and less open to new experiences. We also have seen how some personal concerns, control, and coping styles change through the adult years. Finally we have found that identity tends to remain stable and more certain as one grows older, although major life events can result in changes even here. What does all this mean for a person's health and well-being, for a person's success at aging? Does it matter which traits or which style of control you have when it comes to your health and longevity? The answer is yes.

As you might expect, people high in *neuroticism* tend to experience higher than normal levels of anxiety and depression (Bagby et al., 1995; Costa et al., 1998; Shea et al., 1996). This work strongly suggests that it is the neuroticism that leads to depression rather than the other way around. For example, a recent longitudinal study examined neuroticism, self-esteem, health, and several other factors over a 6-year period for 1500 adults 55 and older and found that the strongest predictor of depression was a high level of neuroticism (Steunenberg et al., 2006).

People high in *neuroticism* also perceive their own physical health to be poor. They say they get sick easily and expect their health to get even worse (Chapman et al., 2006). Another recent longitudinal study followed adult centenarians and younger adults in their 60s and 80s for 18 months to 5 years. Those with higher than average levels of *anxiety*, an important part of neuroticism, became less physically active, reported higher stress levels, had poor nutrition, and, perhaps as a result of these factors, lower energy levels and more functional limitations (Martin et al., 2006). They were worn out, perhaps by their continual worry. You already know that higher levels of stress, lower levels of physical activity, and poor nutrition reduce longevity. One study of clergy over a 5-year period found the highest levels of mortality for those highest in neuroticism. This same study found relatively low mortality rates for those highest in *conscientiousness* (Wilson et al., 2004). Finally, one recent study found particularly high mortality for men who showed an increase in neuroticism over a 12-year span. While neuroticism is predictive of mortality, increases in neuroticism are the stronger predictors (Mroczek & Spiro, 2007).

Conscientiousness, even measured as early as childhood, is associated with longer life (Friedman et al., 1995) and a higher survival rate for those with chronic illness (Christensen et al., 2002). An examination of traits with U.S. Navy and Marine corps personnel found that high *conscientiousness* and *agreeableness* were associated with higher levels of self-care behaviors while high levels of *extraversion* and *openness* were associated with a tendency toward risk taking with alcohol (Booth-Kewley & Vickers, 1994). Women high in *extraversion* and *conscientiousness* have been found to be far more likely to adhere to a regimen of regular breast cancer screening while those with high levels of *neuroticism* and low levels of extraversion are far less likely (Siegler & Costa, 1994). These traits are even related to oral hygiene. In a longitudinal study of several hundred dental patients, researchers found that high levels of *extraversion* were strongly associated with flossing, use of gum stimulators, and using mouthwash while those high in *neuroticism* tended to brush their teeth less often than others (Kressin et al., 1999).

Clearly one's traits relate to a number of different health factors with high neuroticism being the most negative factor and high conscientiousness being the most positive. One can imagine—and the research suggests—how these relationships work. For example, the anxiety that often accompanies neuroticism and the depression that follows may lead to feelings of constant stress and stress is a very unhealthy state (see Chapter 5). Those high in conscientiousness are well organized, make plans, strive for goals, and seem far more likely to follow any regimen necessary to maintain their health or to recover from illness (Smith, 2006).

Locus of control also has been linked to health. Those with external locus, whether powerful others or chance, are far more likely to experience anxiety, which is strongly related to factors that contribute to ill health. These individuals also can become almost fanatically concerned about health issues; they may become **hypochondriacs** (Frazier & Waid, 1999). A sense of control also is related to health behaviors. One study of over 7000 adults over the age of 70 found that those with an internal locus were more than twice as likely to engage in physical activity and walked a mile or more several days per week (Friis et al., 2003). Exercise is very important for maintaining good health.

With relative stability in traits that may or may not be favorable to health and well-being, with changes in personal concerns and an increasing sense of external control in many of life's domains, with declines in physical and changes in cognitive abilities, with retirement and loss of status and income, one might expect to find many older adults having problems and difficulties adjusting to old age. We saw earlier how a positive attitude can be beneficial to one's health and well-being and talked about this as a component of positive psychology. Some work shows that those who maintain a positive outlook, who tend to be optimistic even in the face of problems, live longer than those with a more neutral or, worse yet, pessimistic view of life (Giltay et al., 2006). Clearly then, some do maintain a positive view but are more older adults saddened by loss and fraught with problems? Here the answer seems to be no. Older adults are generally as satisfied, or even more satisfied, with their lives as are younger and middle-aged adults (Diener & Suh, 1998; Lawton et al., 1992).

SOCIAL POLICY APPLICATIONS

We talked about several personality components including identity through life story, generativity, and coping. In all of these, people who have developed life stories, who are more generative, and who use more positive coping styles have a pretty happy and successful old age. Can we facilitate this in any way? Although at first glance these components of personality seem to be somewhat automatic and pretty individual, and while they clearly are, one can always learn from others. Reviewing others' life stories may reveal what is good and what is not so good and provide models for generativity and coping. Research has shown that people benefit by reading about how others have coped (Cook & Oltjenbruns, 1998). How might this be done? With cooperative sponsorship, perhaps including government granting agencies like the National Institute on Aging and the National Endowment for the Arts, corporations, local universities and organizations, and individual artists, a repository of video and or audio life stories from older Americans could be collected. Local aging organizations and facilities could encourage and assist older folks to read/listen to/see these interviews and perhaps even post their own. National Public Radio's StoryCorps and this text's website present brief versions of parts of life stories. These could serve as a springboard for the life story collection project. Maybe you could start by collecting life stories now and encouraging others to join you. While you are at it, encourage your instructor to look into organizing a life story collection effort in your area.

Perhaps older adults simply are reluctant to express their dissatisfaction. Members of older cohorts may have learned to "grin and bear it." Perhaps they need to be asked several times or in different ways before they are willing to talk about their troubles. In an attempt to determine whether this is the case, one group of researchers pushed, pulled, and coaxed adults to respond to questions about their troubles and problems. Over a thousand men first received a standard stress-and-coping interview and many denied having any problems. Interviewers then asked them to "identify the most serious problem or concern they had had in the past week and to describe it briefly" (Aldwin et al., 1996, p. P181). If an individual still did not respond with a problem, the interviewer told them that the problem did not have to be major but could be anything that bothered them during the past week. For those who still did not report a problem, the interviewer asked about any problems at work or at home, with their family, their health, or even their automobile. This intense interview and repeated questioning resulted in higher levels of reported problems for all age groups. The overall proportion reporting one or more problems grew from the typical 75 percent (Aldwin & Revenson, 1987) to 90 percent. It was still the case, however, that older adults reported fewer problems. While only 3 percent of middle-aged men reported no problems, more than 17 percent of the oldest men reported no problems at all (Aldwin et al., 1996).

Older adults are mostly satisfied and don't seem to have as many problems as younger and middle-aged adults but are they really happy? Younger adults generally believe that older adults cannot be very happy with all the losses they experience and death just around the corner. Of course, one's happiness may depend more on the experience and skill one has for dealing with life's problems rather than the problems themselves. Older adults clearly are more experienced and as noted have a wider array of coping strategies and often

*I'm quite happy with my life,
thank you for asking.*

become wise (Chapter 8). A recent online survey investigated the happiness of different aged adults. Each participant rated their own happiness on a 10-point scale and also rated the happiness of an average person the same age as themselves. They rated how happy they would be (or were) at age 30 and at age 70 and how happy average 30- and 70-years-olds were. Results showed that nearly everyone thought the average 30-year-old would be happier than the average 70-year-old but self ratings for the 70-year-olds were higher that self ratings for younger adults (Lacey et al., 2006). There are certainly happy and unhappy people in all age groups but, on average, older adults are happier.

CHAPTER HIGHLIGHTS

- We examined personality, one of the broadest terms in all of psychology. Because of this breadth, it is difficult to measure and researchers have had to use techniques that measure only some aspects of personality. These measures are typically divided into objective and projective assessments.
- To examine personality we, like McAdams (1995), divided the aspects into three levels. The first level, traits, are characteristics assumed to have a genetic component, although environmental factors also play a role.
- We examined the five dimensions of traits proposed by Costa and McCrae (1994): neuroticism, extraversion, openness, agreeableness, and conscientiousness. Although there is great stability in these traits over the course of adult development, there are also some common changes.
- The second level, personal concerns, is assumed to show change as we grow older or our circumstances change.
- Erikson proposed three major concerns during the adult years: intimacy/isolation during young adulthood, generativity/stagnation during middle age, and ego integrity/despair during old age. Peck has proposed three additional concerns for older adults.
- In general, changes in personal concerns are well supported.
- Changes in coping strategies with advanced age could be due to the greater strategic knowledge of older adults and/or a need to compensate for lost abilities. There is evidence to support both of these views.
- Although older adults have a good sense of internal locus of control for general matters, they often show external control in specific domains such as cognition or health.
- Research on the third level of personality description, the level of identity, shows that identity certainty increases with age and that one's identity is influenced by one's culture.
- Identity may be maintained by a balance between assimilation and accommodation. Many people, especially those with a sense of internal control, use a life story to help maintain their identity.
- Traits and locus of control are associated with health and longevity. A high level of neuroticism and/or a low level of conscientiousness appear to be especially harmful.
- Older adults are far less likely to have, or at least to report, serious problems than are other aged adults and older adults are as satisfied and seem to be more happy than other aged adults.

STUDY QUESTIONS

1. Name some characteristics of a person that do not fit under the broad heading of personality.
2. Compare and contrast objective and projective measures of personality.
3. Define each of the following traits: neuroticism, extraversion, openness, agreeableness, and conscientiousness.

4. Do traits change with age? With cohort? What factors account for these differences?

5. Describe Erikson's three stages of adult development. Are these stages supported by research?

6. What might a mid-life crisis be? How often do these crises occur?

7. Describe Peck's additions to Erikson's theory.

8. Describe the strategic knowledge and the compensating for loss views of changes in coping strategies and some evidence for each.

9. How does the emotional level of a situation change the coping strategies used? Who are influenced most by emotional levels when selecting a coping strategy? Why?

10. Describe age differences in locus of control overall, and for specific domains. Why do such differences occur?

11. Explain the differences in primary and secondary control. Which is used most often? Under what circumstances might the other strategy be used?

12. Explain what is meant by the three kinds of assimilation described in this chapter.

13. Do older adults present more problems when they are asked several times in several different ways? Do they present more problems than other age adults?

14. Describe some of the cultural differences that have been found with respect to adult identity.

RECOMMENDED READINGS

Ryff, C. D., Kwan, C. M. L., & Singer, B. H. (2001). Personality and Aging: Flourishing Agendas and Future Challenges. In J. E. Birren & K. W. Schaie (Eds.), *Handbook of the Psychology of Aging* (5th edition, pp. 477–499). San Diego, CA: Academic Press. This chapter is the latest review of theory and research in the personality of aging.
Willis, S. L., & Reid, J. D. (1999). *Life in the Middle: Psychological and Social Development in Middle Age*. San Diego, CA: Academic Press. This book presents a series of readings on different topics in middle age.

INTERNET RESOURCES

www.issid.org/issid.files/research.html. Links to personality research.
www.personalitypage.com and *www.queendom.com/tests/personality/index.html*. These sites will let you take personality tests and give information about your traits.

CHAPTER

10 Relationships

You can't help someone get up a hill without getting closer to the top yourself.

—*Norman Schwarzkopf*

Schwarzkopf tells us that we are helping ourselves when we help another—and in this chapter we will examine the help, the social support, we give and receive from those closest to us. We will examine the importance of social relationships with family members and friends and the effects of this social support on our ability to carry on and reach the top. This chapter's Senior View gives several different perspectives on several different social relationships that we will examine in this chapter but first let's look generally at the importance of social relationships and support.

Social Support

Think about the relationships you have had with people in your life. You've had relationships with parents and/or guardians; perhaps with siblings; perhaps with grandparents and other relatives; with teachers and other students; with supervisors and coworkers; with friends. What are some common factors across these relationships? How are they different? Did they all offer social support when you were in need and did you offer such support to them as well? These are the types of questions that researchers have asked and we will examine their answers as we progress through this chapter. As we do this, we will follow the lead of Mary Levitt (2000) and use social support as our unifying theme.

Social support refers to assistance received from other persons who are close to us; it is assistance received from or given to those in our social network. Our **social network** is that group of friends and family who are close to us. Social support and social networks are, thus, fundamentally connected. Human beings are social creatures and it appears that an important part of being social is the support we give and receive from others.

Senior View

There are many different kinds of social relationships that we enter into over the course of our lives. In this Senior View, we tried to talk with a number of older adults about different relationships discussed in this chapter.

Marriage

Pauline Hopkins was 70 and Lester was 74 when we spoke with them about marriage. Pauline told us, *Bat* [Lester's nickname] *came over to her parents' farm to help in the wheat field, met me, and didn't leave until he got me.* Lester said he served in the army and when he returned he told her, *we'll get married if you want to.* They eloped but told no one. Each lived with their parents for 5 months before revealing their secret. *We saved and made a down payment on our own house. He put the ring on my finger and looked at momma and said "she's mine now."*

They've lived together in that house for 46 years and raised two children. *The best years of our marriage were when we raised our children; we were surrounded with family. We talk less now because we know each other so well.*

Siblings

We spoke with Eleanor McNair (70) about sibling relationships. *I have two little brothers and one little sister. My youngest brother is proactive like me; we like to get a lot done. He's a salesman, talks loud, and has a loving heart. My older brother is slower than molasses in January. My sister is a worrier.*

We asked if these very different people got along with each other. *We never had any sibling rivalry. The worst time was when my sister and I had to share a bed when we were little. Now that we're all grown up, we're all friends. Last year our dad died and we became even closer. The comfort and support we gave each other was a big help during that hard time.* Time of loss often serves to bring siblings closer together although sometimes it can work the other way.

Children and Grandchildren

We spoke with Reverend Edwin R. Schmidt, age 69, about his four children and his six grandchil-

dren. *It was very challenging to raise four children. You can't treat them like possessions. The hardest part was knowing when to discipline, and come down hard, not abusively, but hard, and knowing when to let them loose and let them make their own mistakes. We always told them we loved them. You only owe your children two things: roots and wings. They need a solid base and the ability to find their own way. I think we succeeded.* Today he happily sees his children and grandchildren about once a year; his children live all over with one each in Illinois, Minnesota, North Carolina, and Oregon.

With grandchildren you don't feel quite as responsible; you can spoil them and not feel bad. You try and teach some values but you don't impose. What you do teaches them more than what you say.

The worst thing about having grandchildren is that they are not always here. I don't expect them to be so close to me when they're adolescents but to be very close again once they're young adults. When they get older they realize how much you know.

Friends

Carol Milheim was 68 when we asked her about friends. *I have several friends but two very close friends who I can trust with anything. We've been close over the last 20 years and have shared caring for sick parents, divorce, and death of a husband. One of my friends is like the sister that I never had. I have no siblings and neither does she; this has been an important part of our relationship.*

I've moved many times in my life and had to leave friends behind. Making new friends is often difficult; you have to work at it. I've been pretty successful at finding friends who have different religions, belong to different ethnic groups, and have different backgrounds. Diversity is rewarding and educational.

It fills a tremendous need to have a close personal friend. We shop together, eat together, discuss grandchildren, generally socialize, and, most important, confide in each other. Friends are people I would trust with anything I said to them.

About her closest friend, Carol said, *if I needed her tomorrow, she would be here without question and vice versa. I value and need my friends.*

Support typically is divided into two general types: instrumental and emotional. **Instrumental support** usually is help with specific tasks, such as shopping, transportation, repairs, or housework. **Emotional support** is help that is intended to lift our spirits, relieve our sadness, or comfort us in time of need. Some researchers also discuss informational support, which is knowledge provided to us by people in our network. When support is needed, friends are more likely to give emotional forms of assistance while family members are more likely to give instrumental forms of assistance (Antonucci, 1990). Spouses tend to provide both types of assistance.

To measure social support and the social network providing this support in adulthood, researchers have used a number of different techniques including the Interpersonal Support Evaluation List (Cohen et al., 1985), the Lubben Social Network Scale (Lubben, 1988), and the hierarchical mapping technique using the concentric circle diagram shown in Figure 10-1 (Kahn & Antonucci, 1980). As you can see, the center circle in this diagram is labeled *you* and it is surrounded by three other circles in which the respondent places people they know. In the inner circle, closest to you, are those who you could not live without and with whom you share confidential information. In the next circle are those who are also very close to you but not quite as close as the person or persons in the inner circle. In the last circle are people you like and are friendly with but who are not as close to you as those in the two inner circles. Each circle can be full or empty or anywhere in between. Researchers use this, and the other techniques, to compare the social networks of men and women, young and old, people of different cultures, and so on to see if the networks differ and to determine the support provided by these networks. Try measuring your own network and social support with Project 10.

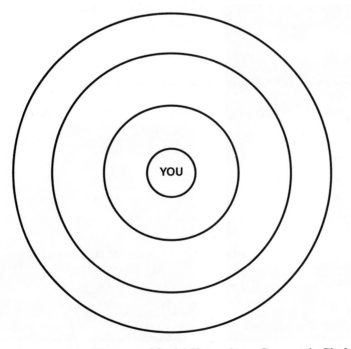

FIGURE 10-1   Diagram of Social Networks as Concentric Circles.

PROJECT **10**
Social Networks

This project will allow you to get an idea about your own social support system using a modified version of the scale developed by Kahn and Antonucci (1980). Keep in mind the characteristics of social support and what friends versus family do for one another when you consider your own convoy of social support. One other thing that you might find interesting is to identify the different types of support provided by various network members. Kahn and Antonucci's convoy model suggests that social support has three different components: aid, affect, and affirmation. Aid is the physical help given and received, affect is the emotional support shared, and affirmation are the things people do to make you feel good about yourself; make you feel worthwhile. Start thinking about the people in your life and see how they all fall into place in the convoy model.

Look at the concentric circle diagram in Figure 10-1 and recreate it on a piece of paper. Put yourself in the very center. Now beginning with the first circle out from you (considered your inner circle), write the names of all of those people in your life who you feel so close to that you cannot imagine life without them. People who you do not feel quite *that* close to but who are still very close go in the second circle. People to whom you feel less close, but are still important to you go in the third circle. Circles can be full, empty, or anywhere in between.

Now answer the following questions about the people in your network. Write the names of the people who fit the description in each question.

Are there people who reassure you when you are feeling uncertain about something?

Are there people who make you feel respected?

Are there people who would make sure that you were cared for if you were ill?

Are there people you talk to when you are upset, nervous, or depressed?

Are there people who you talk to about your health?

Are there people who you talk to about your family?

Are there people you confide in about things that are important to you?

Now compare your answers to these questions to your answers on the next set of questions:

Are there people who you reassure when they are feeling uncertain about something?

Are there people who you make feel respected?

Are there people who you would make sure were cared for if they were ill?

Are there people who talk to you when they are upset, nervous, or depressed?

Are there people who talk to you about their health?

Are there people who talk to you about their family?

Are there people who confide in you about things that are important to them?

One last set of questions to consider.

Would you want to have more people, fewer people, or do you think you have the right number of people in your network?

(continued)

P R O J E C T **10** **Continued**

Would you want to have more people in your network that you could depend on?

Now you have a clearer understanding of how the concentric circle diagram is used in measuring social networks and social support. What did you learn about your own network and support that you did not realize before doing this project?

Using these measures, researchers have found that most people place close to 20 people in their network with half or more of these being in the outermost circle. Those placed in the inner circles tend to remain there when examined longitudinally although over time, older adults do lose some of their network members, especially those in the outer circle (Antonucci, 2001). This consistency in social networks over time has been taken as support for the **convoy model** of social support that says that a network is dynamic and its members move together through life, watching out for and supporting each other (Kahn & Antonucci, 1980). Think for a minute about who is in your network, who has been there for more than a few years, and who is relatively new. You will probably find that those in the inner circle have been there for a while whereas some in the outer circle are new.

When the networks of men and women are compared, women typically have larger networks with more family members than men do (Antonucci & Akiyama, 1991). This difference is largely due to the fact that women place more people in their inner circle while men and women are close to the same in their outer circle. Both men and women tend to place their spouse in their inner circle but women also tend to place others there like a sister and/or a best friend. Men more likely place siblings in the second rather than inner circle (Antonucci & Akiyama, 1997). Women are more likely to maintain close, confiding relationships with people other than their spouses while men are more likely to confide only in their spouses. We will see later that this difference can be very important when one loses a spouse (Chapter 14). These gender differences tend to disappear for older men and women (Reinhardt et al., 2003).

The support networks of gay and lesbian couples tend to be about the same as the convoys of heterosexual couples with the exception that their convoys contain more gay or lesbian people or people with an awareness of the individual's orientation. Awareness of the individual's gay or lesbian orientation is regarded as the single most important factor in the individual's overall satisfaction with the support received (Grossman et al., 2000).

Race and ethnicity have been examined in relation to social support revealing considerable commonality across groups. Differences stem more from customs that affect relationships than from group membership, per se. Those holding to traditional customs tend to have similar social support networks that differ slightly from others. The role of family, friends, and church as support providers is very important in the African American elderly community. More relatives are in African American networks than networks of whites, but being married predicts this more than race. Race emerges as a difference because fewer African American elders are married. Hispanic American elders tend to have a lot of people in their networks including nuclear and extended family members. Older Chinese

Americans rely primarily on their children for support, especially their daughters (Antonucci, 2001).

Some work has examined social networks as a function of age, gender, education, and SES level and found that those with higher levels of education tend to have larger overall networks but not larger inner circles. Women with higher SES have a higher proportion of friends in their networks than do those with lower SES while men with higher SES have networks that are more likely to contain people at some geographic distance. Inner circles were, however, unaffected by age, education, or SES level (Ajrouch et al., 2005).

Researchers also have examined the social networks for people living in different cultures. In a comparison of U.S. networks with those of people living in Liverpool (in the United Kingdom) and in Beijing (China), it was found that, in all three places, the primary source of social support was the spouse, followed by children especially daughters, followed by friends (Wenger & Jingming, 2000). The inner circles of social networks and social support are largely the same for older men and women with different education and SES levels and from different ethnic groups and different cultures.

While these factors do not produce major differences in the inner circles of social networks, there are large individual differences. Some people have bigger networks with more close family and friends that they can rely on during times of need while others have much smaller networks and much less social support. As discussed in Chapter 5, those who have strong ties to family and friends generally live longer than those without such ties. Over 80 studies have examined the relationship between social support and health and found that relationship to be strong and positive. Those with strong support have healthier cardiovascular, endocrine, and immune systems. Strong social support seems to slow down some aspects of biological aging (Urchino et al., 1996). Those who express high levels of satisfaction with their networks also have high levels of psychological well-being (Antonucci et al., 1997; Newsom & Schulz, 1996).

As we grow older, our need for social support is likely to increase. Older adults are more likely than younger adults to experience some disability due to chronic conditions like arthritis or advanced stages of illnesses like cancer. Researchers have examined social support for older adults with such clear needs. In one study, older adults who had experienced a loss of vision and who were entering rehabilitation services were interviewed three times over an 18-month interval about their networks of family and friends and the support they received. Participation in rehabilitation was associated with a larger network of friends perhaps because participants made new friends while at rehabilitation. Those with increased disability had strong support from family networks. Family members help those in need. Results also showed a decrease in the size of both family and friendship networks over this time period but it is not clear whether these decreases might be due to the individual striving to maintain independence, an increased difficulty in maintaining ties to less-close network members, or from network members not wanting to deal with an impaired friend or family member (Reinhardt et al., 2003). What do you think?

It is important to remember (Chapter 5) that help must be perceived as social support in order to have an effect on one's health and well-being. If we observe family members helping an impaired relative, then that relative clearly is receiving support. The individual may, however, not see the help as support at all; it may be perceived as something done out of obligation: "They're only helping me because they have to; I'm their father." In such a case, the benefits of support are far less than in a situation where one believes the support comes from the heart. An examination of the relationship between disability and depression makes this point very clearly. In this study, over 1000 adults 65 and older were measured for disability, depression, and support received and perceived beginning in 1986 and again in 1990, 1993, and 1996. Results showed a clear and strong relationship between disability and depression. Increasing and greater disability led to greater depression. This relationship was not mediated by received support but perceived support eliminated the growth of depression as impairment increased. Those who became more disabled over the 10 years of the study and who perceived themselves as receiving strong support from family and friends did not become more depressed while those without such a perception, even when receiving support, became more and more depressed (Taylor & Lynch, 2004).

Perceived social support also is related to cognition and an examination of cognition, emotional support, and the frequency of contact with network members found that, over a 12-year period, those who perceived the most emotional support and had the most frequent contact with network members showed the least decline in cognitive function (Holtzman et al., 2004). A related study found good maintenance of cognitive function over a 7-year period for those with the strongest family ties and who perceived themselves as being valued members of their families (Béland et al., 2005). Clearly, perceived social support plays a very important role in the functioning and health of adults and several views of how this support operates have been advanced.

Some believe that the benefits of support are due to three sets of factors (Cohen, 1988). **Social factors** include the buffering of stress provided by family and friends. Stress is easier to handle when you have an ally who can share and mitigate your stress. Someone who can tell us how they solved a similar problem or perhaps just empathize with us can reduce the stress we feel. We saw earlier (Chapter 5) how damaging stress can be and so social factors operating through stress reduction can produce great benefits.

Psychological factors refer to the positive emotions and sense of control that friends and family can engender. Contact with those in a social network is most often in the context of good times as family members visit on holidays or friends accompany us to concerts. They make us feel good and discourage negative emotions (Cohen & Herbert, 1996). We saw earlier how a positive outlook can play a major role in health and longevity. When people support you, you also may get the message that you are a worthwhile and competent person; you may perceive yourself as having more control over your life and we know that a good sense of control can result in more effort to maintain health and well-being (Antonucci, 2001; Krause, 2001).

Behavioral factors refer to healthy and unhealthy behaviors and habits that are influenced by social support. Smoking, driving recklessly, and drinking to excess (or doing all three at the same time) clearly are unhealthy behaviors while exercising and watching your nutrition are healthy. Friends and family may nag us to quit the unhealthy behaviors and start or maintain the healthy ones. Of course, it is possible for a particular social network to do quite the opposite. Perhaps because of that, work has found good support for social and psychological factors but less for behavioral factors (Urchino et al., 1996).

In sum, humans need strong social relations with others. Social relations provide social support and are related strongly to physical and psychological health and longevity. Spouses, children, parents, grandparents, siblings, and friends are our most valuable asset.

Members of the Red Hat Society.

Think about how each of these types of people has provided you or your loved ones with social support across the lifespan. We will now examine these different supportive social relations in greater detail.

Family Relationships

Family relationships have received more attention from researchers than any other type of relationship. This makes sense because most of the relationship types that we experience in our lives are those with various family members and such relationships usually are quite long lasting. We have a set of caregivers, most typically one or two parents; we may have one or more siblings; we have extended families in our grandparents, aunts, uncles, cousins, and in-laws; we usually marry and have one or more children; and, most of us eventually become grandparents. In this section we examine the major types of family relationships including marriage, divorce, sexual relations, elder abuse, siblings, and grandparenting.

Marriage, Gay/Lesbian Unions, Divorce, and Remarriage

Marriage.   **Marriage** is a legal union and has been defined by many courts as that of a man and woman as husband and wife. Of all relationships, marriage has been studied the most. Most people get married at least once. In fact, about 95 percent of U.S. residents have been married at least once.

Although many marriages last, almost 50 percent end in divorce. Divorce is the legal dissolution of a marriage. The divorce rate was at its highest in 1980 but has gone down since then. In 1980, close to 60 percent of marriages ended in divorce while in present times about 45 percent are expected to end in divorce (Whitbourne, 2001). Usually, divorce happens within the first 3 years of the marriage; men are usually in their early 30s and women in their late 20s at the time of this first divorce (Clarke, 1995).

These statistics have prompted researchers to investigate the factors that are responsible for long-lasting marriages and those responsible for divorce. Why do some marriages last while others do not? One factor is marital satisfaction. Marital satisfaction is usually measured by asking individuals to rate their overall satisfaction with a number of different aspects of their marriage. Figure 10-2 illustrates what has become known as the curvilinear pattern of marital satisfaction for couples who have remained married. The early years of the marriage, during young adulthood, generally are quite high in marital satisfaction; this seems reasonable. If satisfaction were not high the marriage might never have taken place or could end in divorce soon after the marriage. Marital satisfaction often declines with the birth of the first child. This also seems reasonable. That very high level of satisfaction during those early years could only change in one direction. Typically satisfaction is lower for couples who have settled into a routine and who are raising a family. These couples, particularly those with children, often face increased financial obligations and fewer interactions with each other. Marital satisfaction is usually high again when the last child has left home and husband and wife have more time together. This frequent pattern

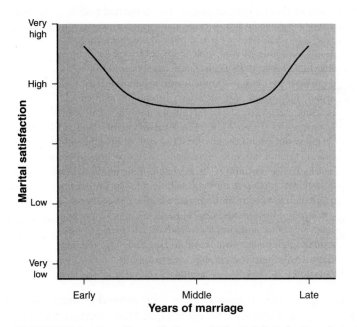

FIGURE 10-2   Curvilinear Pattern of Marital Satisfaction Over the Course of a Long-Term Marriage.

has been found in a large number of studies (Miller et al., 1997). The next most frequent pattern is one of relatively high marital satisfaction at all ages, with no decline in middle age (Anderson et al., 1983; Atchley, 2000). In a survey of over 3000 married adults over the age of 50, 85 percent reported being satisfied and happy with their marriage (Brecher, 1984).

Another way to examine the factors that underlie long-lasting marriages is to compare couples who have been married for different numbers of years. The differences between middle-age and older married couples and between satisfied and dissatisfied married couples have been examined by Carstensen and her colleagues (1995). In these studies, married couples often are videotaped while discussing topics such as money, children, communication, recreation, sex, and in-laws. Independent raters code the tapes and several findings are common. Older couples, who have been married for a longer period of time than middle-aged couples, show higher levels of affection and lower levels of disagreement even when discussing topics on which they disagree. For older couples, children and grandchildren are a major source of pleasure while for middle-aged couples, children are often a problem area. Older couples seemed to approach their problems with more humor and affection for one another and negative emotions were rare in these discussions (Carstensen et al., 1995; Levenson et al., 1993). Although these comparisons are cross-sectional, they suggest that older couples may have learned more effective ways of dealing with life's problems as discussed in Chapter 9. Couples also seem to become more like one another in their beliefs, attitudes, and behaviors as their years together increase (Davey & Szinovacz, 2004).

Researchers also have interviewed middle-aged couples who have been married for at least 15 years and older couples who have been married for at least 45 years (Lauer & Lauer, 1985; Lauer et al., 1990). When asked what factors contribute to their long-lasting relationship, husbands and wives and middle-aged and older couples generally agreed. The most frequently named reason was "my spouse is my best friend," followed by "I like my spouse as a person," "marriage is sacred," "we agree on aims and goals," and "my spouse has grown more interesting." Do you think that spouses seem more interesting because they now are more alike? Older couples also added humor as an important contributor to their long-lasting marriages. Couples said they laughed together every day, kissed each other daily, and confided in one another.

Although ratings of marital quality typically remain high for couples who remain married, they do show some decline over time and are generally lower for women than for men (Van Laningham et al., 2001). One study examined marital strain for 1000 husbands and wives over an 8-year period. Over this time period, strain increased but was nearly the same for men and women under 30 but greater for women than men after age 40. Although middle-aged men showed increases in strain over time, no increase was observed for men over 60 (Umberson & Williams, 2005). At all older ages, women reported more strain than men. Some of this increased strain is due to the change in roles that can occur when one person becomes disabled or ill and the other becomes their caregiver. Wives are more likely than husbands to become caregivers (more about these situations in Chapter 12). We also know that marital quality is associated with physical and psychological health. In comparisons of satisfied and dissatisfied couples, researchers have found that satisfied couples have much higher levels of physical and psychological health. Marital dissatisfaction leads to lower levels of health rather than low levels of health leading to dissatisfaction and this is particularly true for women (Robles & Kiecolt-Glaser, 2003). A recent study examined self-reported health and marital strain for husbands and wives and found that health decreased as strain increased, particularly for older adults (Umberson et al., 2006). It is believed that marital strain produces stress which, if continued over a long period of time, results in ill health (see Chapter 5). If women show more strain, then they are likely to have more stress-related health problems.

Sometimes marital strain is too much for some and results in abuse, although for older adults abuse is often at the hands of children rather than spouses. Box 10-1 gives some information about this sad state of affairs. Marital strain, although often greater for older than for younger couples, is not the typical state of affairs for long-married couples. As noted before, marital satisfaction generally is quite high for long-time married couples even when some strain is present.

Gay and Lesbian Unions.   Although marriage between gay and lesbian partners is not often legally sanctioned, there are many long-term relationships of homosexual couples (Peplau, 1991). It has not, however, been easy for researchers to investigate these relationships because many, until recently, have been difficult to find. It is important to remember that older cohorts of gays and lesbians grew up in a time of strong hostility against homosexuals. In the early 1970s, the American Psychiatric Association classified homosexuality as a mental illness and did not remove it from the *Diagnostic and Statistical Manual of Mental Disorders* until 1986. Most of these couples kept their relationships secret to avoid discrimination from employers, society, friends, and even family. Such couples report the highest levels of social support from those family and friends who are aware of their sexual orientation (Grossman et al., 2000). Of course not all gay and lesbian older couples have remained in hiding and those who have been open have had to develop strong coping strategies. This strength seems to have been useful not just for dealing with discrimination against homosexuals but also for meeting late-life challenges (Quam & Whitford, 1992). It is possible that older homosexual couples are, in many ways, stronger than older heterosexual couples.

Not having legal status has presented these couples with many obstacles and these difficulties are fairly widespread (O'Brian & Goldberg, 1999). For gay men, the likelihood of a steady relationship with one partner increases with age and is highest when they are between the ages of 46 and 55 (Yoakam, 1999). These are ages when, as you know, chronic disorders such as arthritis or severe illnesses such as cardiovascular disease are more likely to begin. Increased contact with physicians and hospitalization can result in obstacles not faced by heterosexual couples. When, for example, one partner is hospitalized, the other partner often is denied access to areas restricted to "next of kin" (Cahill et al., 2000). Without a power of attorney, hospital personnel and physicians do not recognize the authority of a partner to make health care decisions. Even with a will, many older gay men and lesbian survivors find that family members can successfully contest their right to inheritance (Wojciechowski, 1998).

Although there is not yet a wealth of research on older gay and lesbian couples, the work that has been done suggests that these relationships show many of the same characteristics as those of heterosexual couples. Communication is an important factor

BOX 10-1
Elder Abuse

Elder abuse is a pervasive and growing problem. Elder abuse occurs in all settings; it occurs in homes (domestic), assisted living centers, and nursing homes (institutional). Domestic elder abuse is the hardest to detect and prevent. Currently six types of abuse are generally agreed upon. **Physical abuse** includes inflicting pain or injury or depriving a basic need. **Sexual abuse** includes nonconsensual sexual contact of any kind. **Emotional** or **psychological abuse** is the infliction of emotional anguish or distress. **Financial** or **material exploitation** involves funds, property, and assets. **Neglect** is the loss of food, shelter, health care, or protection and is the most common type in domestic settings. Self-neglect is any act by the elder him- or herself that threatens health or safety. Finally **abandonment** is the desertion of an elder by anyone who has assumed responsibility for care.

In the United States, 1 to 2 million adults over the age of 65 have experienced some type of abuse in institutional and/or domestic settings (Wolf, 1998). It is believed that only a portion of elder abuse cases is ever reported. Vulnerable elders are even less able or willing, and thus less likely than are victims of other domestic abuse, to report abuse or neglect. Current estimates suggest that only one out of every five cases in all settings is reported; only 1 in every 14 cases in domestic. Elder abuse is, of course, not just a U.S. phenomenon and is found all over the world. Recent reports have documented elder abuse in Japan (Arai, 2006), Germany (König & Leembruggen-Kallberg, 2006), Israel (Rabi, 2006), and Brazil (Bezerra-Flanders & Clark, 2006). In considering these data, it should be remembered that both the population of elders and vulnerable elders is increasing.

Research has examined both who is most likely to be abused or neglected and who is more likely to perpetrate these crimes. The median age of abuse victims in 1996 was 77.9. In 2004, more than two in five of the cases reported involved older adults age 80 or over. In 1996, 66.4 percent of the victims of domestic elder abuse were white, while 18.7 percent were black; Hispanic elders accounted for 10 percent of the domestic elder abuse cases. Minority elders may be even less likely than majority elders to report abuse, because doing so would bring shame on the family. Men and women equally are likely to be abused; men may be more likely to be victims of self-neglect. Elder abuse is more likely in situations where the husband has a lower level of education (wife's education does not seem to play a role), when family income is low, when depression is present, and when abuse occurred earlier in the household (Bonomi et al., 2007; Harris, 1996).

Perpetrators of abuse and neglect are most often children of the victim (32.6%) followed by other family members (21.5%) and then spouses and intimate partners (11.3%). Early data indicated that men were more likely to be abusers but more recent research suggests that both men and women equally are likely to perpetrate elder abuse and neglect crimes. Research has yet to clarify the profile of perpetrators based on type of abuse.

Finally, in regard to prevention, several experts in the field have implicated the widespread ageism present in society that allows elder abuse and neglect to flourish. Studies have shown that the same services available for victims of child or domestic abuse (e.g., foster homes, women's shelters) are not available for elders. Funds devoted to prevention and treatment of elder abuse are significantly less than that devoted to other types of crimes. The paucity of law on the federal level and the inconsistency of state laws (although all 50 states and most territories do have laws regarding elder abuse; Lachs & Pillemer, 1995) are indicative of the poor view of elders. There is substan-

(continued)

B O X **10-1** **Continued**

tial literature on the negative view of elders in society and the potential for maltreatment as a result of these stereotypes. In a study of perceptions of abuse, six different scenarios were presented to college students who rated whether abuse was present in the scenario, whether the caregiver or the older adult was the abuser, and how justified the abuse was. Scenarios included a daughter throwing a frying pan at her mother, a daughter threatening to poison her mother's food, a daughter withholding money belonging to her mother, and a daughter refusing to take her mother to a doctor's appointment. Students also answered questions about their relationships with their grandparents. Results showed that students found caregiver abuse to be more justifiable when the older adult was portrayed as being agitated or senile but less so when the older adult was helpless. Students who reported closer contact with their own grandparents found more instances of abuse to be unjustifiable than those students who did not maintain close ties with grandparents (Mills et al., 1998).

It is clear that much more research is needed in all areas of elder abuse in order to best serve today's vulnerable elders. Be watchful and willing to report any instances of elder or other abuse to the proper authorities.

---

contributing to long-term relationships, partners tend to be best friends, conflicts often center on finances and relations with family members, and strain increases with age undoubtedly due, in part, to the difficulties of dealing with health care (Berger, 1990). In

Still together after all these years.

comparisons of gay men and lesbian couples, it has been found that lesbian couples place more emphasis on equality between the two partners than do gay or heterosexual couples (Kurdek, 1995a; 1995b). Overall, gay men and lesbian couples seem to cope as effectively as heterosexual couples in dealing with the strain of long-term relationships and perceived inequities and are generally successful at maintaining a positive outlook in the face of often considerable stress (Patterson, 2000).

Cohabitation.   Because marriage rarely is legal for gay and lesbian couples, they are nearly always cohabiting. As a result, one cannot examine differences between marriage and cohabitation for these groups and because of this, the research on and this discussion of cohabitation is restricted to heterosexual couples. Cohabitation among heterosexual couples has increased from about a half a million couples in the early 1970s to 5.5 million in the year 2000 (U.S. Census Bureau, 2001). Of these, 1 million are 51 years of age or older. More than 70 percent of these older cohabiters have been divorced or separated (18 percent widowed and 11 percent never married) and the biggest proportion are aging baby boomers between the ages of 51 and 59. Cohabiters are more likely to be African than white Americans, report lower levels of involvement in organized religion, are more likely to consume excess alcohol, and appear to have smaller and, perhaps less supportive, social networks when compared to those who have remarried (Brown et al., 2006). Parents and married children report much closer relationships than parents and cohabiting children (Aquilino, 1997; Nock, 1995). Perhaps many older cohabiters, like older homosexual couples, attempt to conceal their relationship from family and friends. About half of cohabiting relationships end within the first year as the couple marries or separates; marriage is more probable than separation (Bumpass & Lu, 2000; Centers for Disease Control, 2002).

One study compared younger and older adults who were cohabiting to see if cohabitation was different for different age/cohort groups. Nearly 1000 adults were surveyed. Older cohabiting adults reported higher quality relationships. They spent more time with their partners, argued less frequently, believed they were treated fairly, and were far less likely to report that the relationship would end. Younger couples were more concerned about compatibility and tended to view their cohabitation as a step toward marriage while older couples tended to view it as an alternative to marriage (King & Scott, 2005). It is expected that as baby boomers grow older, the number and proportion of cohabiting older adults will continue to increase but the age differences may remain. What do you think?

Divorce.   Not all relationships succeed. Between 40 and 50 percent of marriages end in divorce and, although that is high, the divorce rate has gone down since the early 1980s when it was close to 60 percent. Divorce is 30 percent more likely for low-income couples, 24 percent more likely for those who marry young, 14 percent more likely for those who are less religious, 13 percent more likely for those with a lower level of education, and 9 percent more likely for those who cohabit before marrying (Centers for Disease Control, 2002). This latter finding often surprises people but research suggests that those who cohabit are different in important ways from those who do not. Cohabiters tend to have more liberal attitudes toward the roles of men and women, have more negative attitudes about marriage, and to be more accepting of divorce (Seltzer, 2000). It is not cohabiting that produces divorce; it is that cohabiters tend to be people more accepting of divorce.

The reasons for divorce have been examined in two primary ways and both involve surveying or interviewing. One way to do this is to interview people who are already divorced to learn what factors produced the divorce. This approach has been used a number of times and generally has found good agreement between men and women as to what the major factors were. Poor communication, basic unhappiness, and incompatibility are named most frequently. Children rarely are mentioned as a problem. There are also some gender differences because men are more likely to blame their own abuse of alcohol or drugs while women are more likely to blame emotional and/or physical abuse or their husband's infidelity (Cleek & Pearson, 1985; South & Lloyd, 1995). Of course a problem with this approach is that people may not clearly remember exactly which factors led to the divorce and which may have been revealed during or after the divorce. Lack of communication may have led to a person's divorce but later they found out about their spouse's infidelity. Now they name them both as causes.

To solve this problem, many researchers use the second approach which is to survey married people and follow them until a divorce happens. In one example of this, 2000 married people were surveyed and followed for 12 years. At the end of this time, those who divorced and those who remained married were compared. Divorced women named themselves as often as they named their husbands as the source of the problem. Divorced men blamed themselves more than they blamed their wives. The factors that were the strongest predictors of divorce were infidelity, jealousy, irritating habits, foolish spending, and the use of drugs or alcohol (Amato & Rogers, 1997). Other similar work has found that when husbands report low levels of affection for their wives, when both husband and wife express disappointment in their marriage, and when they act as individuals rather than as a couple, divorce is far more likely (Buehlman et al., 1992).

Clearly some of the factors found using these two different approaches are the same. Infidelity and alcohol/drug abuse are commonly given as reasons for divorce. Other factors differ (e.g., irritating habits, incompatibility) and it is not at present clear whether these differences are due to the use of different samples of people or whether they are due to the method of data collection.

The consequences of divorce can be quite severe for some people. Women are more likely to suffer economic hardship following a divorce than are men. Some of this difference is due to the fact that many divorced men avoid paying alimony and/or child support. It is typical for a man's standard of living to increase after a divorce while a woman's is most likely to decrease. Men are more likely to lose custody of their children than are women. In 72 percent of divorce cases where children are involved, the woman is granted custody while only 9 percent of such cases result in the man receiving custody. Divorced individuals show higher rates of emotional and physical disturbances than single, married, or remarried persons. They are more likely to die from cancer, heart disease, cirrhosis of the liver, or in an accident (Clarke, 1995).

Remarriage. "Well I'm glad that's over. Whew, what a relief to be away from that *%$#*#. I'll never make that mistake again. The next time I marry I'm going to make the right choice." Many people who divorce remarry with exactly this belief: "I'll do it right the next time." The probability of a divorce is, however, actually higher for a remarriage than for a first marriage (Martin & Bumpass, 1989). Furthermore, second marriages, on average, last about 1 year less than first marriages and third marriages are shorter, on average, than second marriages (Clarke, 1995). Instead of getting better, do things get worse with each subsequent marriage? People who have been divorced may find it easier to choose divorce when marital satisfaction declines and may even turn to divorce for fewer reasons than they did the first (or second) time. Things may not really be worse in a second, or subsequent marriage, but remarried people may be less willing to take as many bumps as they did the first time.

Many more men remarry than women and one reason for this is that, as you know, for middle-aged and older adults there are many more women than men. For women, the probability of remarriage is highest for white Americans (58% remarry within 5 years), than for Hispanic (44%) or African-American women (32%) (Centers for Disease Control, 2002). Young divorcees also are more likely to remarry than are older divorcees (U.S. Bureau of the Census, 1997). As you know, older divorcees frequently turn to cohabitation as an alternative to remarriage. A second reason for men being more likely to remarry is that men seem to experience greater loneliness and a greater need for companionship following a divorce than do women (Chipperfield & Havens, 2001). Recall the differences in the social networks of men and women. In one major study, over 3000 married, divorced, remarried, cohabiting, widowed, and never-married men and women were compared on measures of loneliness. Those who were married or cohabiting showed the lowest levels of loneliness. People in their first marriage were less lonely than those who were remarried. Men without a partner were more lonely than women without a partner. Those who never married were less lonely than those who once had a partner but no longer did (Peters & Liefbroer, 1997). A more recent study looked at life strain for divorced, widowed, and never-married older adults and found greater strain for those who had been married at one time (divorced and widowed) than for those who never married (Pudrovska et al., 2006). Tennyson said that it is "better to have loved and lost, than never to have loved at all" but these results suggest that, with respect to loneliness, Tennyson was wrong. It is better to love but losing can be very hard.

Sexual Relations

Sexual relations are not mentioned frequently as a factor in long-lasting marriages or as a problem that led to divorce. Nevertheless, sex is an important part of life for most younger people but not for very many older people. Did you believe that last statement? Although it is a common belief that once you are old you are no longer sexually active, it simply is not true. Do you think of your parents or grandparents (or great-grandparents) as being sexually active? Most likely they are.

Sexual Activity.   Sexual activities almost always are examined by use of a survey and ordinarily quite a large number of people respond. At the same time, responders are more likely to answer some questions than others. Questions about frequency of activity, intercourse, and satisfaction are more likely to be answered than are questions about masturbation or oral sex, particularly by older cohorts. Sexual activity is usually an important part of marriage and cohabitation and many would say an important part of life.

Most surveys indicate that sexual activity declines through the adult years but not to the extent that many believe. For example, in one survey, the average frequency of sexual intercourse for younger adults (18 to 30 years old) over a 1-year period was 78 times, for middle-aged adults (40 to 49 years) 67 times, for slightly older adults (50 to 59 years) 46 times, and for old, but not very old, adults (60 to 69 years) 23 times (Seidman & Rieder, 1994). Generally, men report higher levels of activity than do women and marital status makes a difference for women but not for men. Women who are married report higher levels of activity than those who are not (Matthias et al., 1997). How do you think cohort effects contribute to these reports? For men and women, the level of sexual activity is generally higher for those who are healthy, married, confident, educated, and who have good social support networks (Buono et al., 1998).

Other surveys have obtained similar results and when one asks about sexual activity rather than just intercourse, the numbers are, of course, higher. The majority up to age 70 report being active at least once a month (Ade-Ridder, 1990; Marsiglio & Donnelly, 1991). In another survey of adults between the ages of 60 and 91 years, 80 percent reported that they were sexually active. Some work has found no decrease in activity between the ages of 80 and 102 with 83 percent of the men and 64 percent of the women reporting regular sexual activity (Bretschneider & McCoy, 1988). When older adults are asked about their satisfaction with their recent sexual activity, the majority report being satisfied or very satisfied (Matthias et al., 1997). In one study, 36 percent said it was better now than when they were young (Starr & Weiner, 1981).

Research on gay and lesbian couples has found similar results. Older adults report less activity but still find that activity satisfying. Older lesbians are more likely to discontinue sex altogether just as older heterosexual women are less likely than men to engage in sexual activities. Older gay men and lesbians report a preference for partners who are as old as they are (Adelman, 1990; Pope, 1997; Van-de-Ven et al., 1997).

Are these cross-sectional findings due to older cohorts being less active than younger cohorts? It's a little hard to imagine that our parents and grandparents were any less active than we are when they were our age although they may be less active now that they are older. The decline in activity is primarily age, rather than cohort, related as shown by the few longitudinal studies that have been conducted. In one such study men in their 40s, 50s, and 60s were followed for 9 years and results showed a decline in activity for all three groups but a smaller decline for those in their 40s and a greater decline for those in their 60s (Araujo et al., 2004). A similar study followed women between the ages of 45 and 55, the period of menopause, and found that over the 8 years of the study, sexual activity decreased (Dennerstein et al., 2002). We will examine menopause later as we look at the factors responsible for these decreases in sexual activity for men and women.

Explanation for Declining Sexual Activity.   The most frequently cited reasons for the decrease in sexual activity with age are hormonal, physical changes, poor health, unavailability of a partner, and the social unacceptability of sex between older adults.

As you learned in Chapter 3, men and women experience changes in the relative quantities of sex **hormones** as they grow older. For women these changes are far more abrupt than they are for men and this period of change is referred to as **menopause**. Although the average age of menopause is 52, it can start as early as 40 or as late as 58. Estrogen production is greatly reduced in menopause and lower levels of estrogen are associated with lower levels of sexual activity (Dennerstein et al., 2002). Some research has found that it is not just sexual activity that declines for women as they go thorough menopause but sexual desire as well (Sheehy, 1992). More recently a number of publications have begun discussing the relatively slow changes in hormone levels for men and referring to these changes as male menopause. These changes also are associated with lower levels of sexual activity for men. It appears, however, that, rather than being a direct cause of declines in sexual activity, hormone changes are more of an indirect cause. The changes in hormone levels do not affect an individual's ability to engage in sexual activity although they do have some influence on sexual desire (Burleson et al., 1995; Wallen & Lovejoy, 1993). Many women report that menopause means that a person is now an old woman and not expected to have sexual desires (Nobre & Pinto-Gouveia, 2006; Wilk & Kirk, 1995). Research on attitudes toward older adults has found that older woman are viewed more negatively than older men and the portrayals of older women in the media also are more negative (Arber & Ginn, 1991; Hurd, 1999). A women past menopause can easily view herself in these same negative ways and believe that she is no longer a desirable or suitable partner.

Physical changes also contribute to reduced activity. The loss of peripheral nerve cells reduces sensitivity in the genital areas and can make it more difficult for older adults to become aroused (Berger et al., 1994). Reduced blood flow to the penis is another factor for older men. This makes it difficult to obtain and maintain an erection (Rieske & Holstege, 1996); this problem is far more likely for smokers. Most of the pharmaceuticals that are designed to increase performance for older men work by increasing blood flow. Older men with erectile dysfunction do not, however, report a lowering of their self-esteem or any feelings of being sexually deprived (Schiavi, 1999). For women, the thinning of the vaginal wall that frequently occurs after menopause and a reduction in lubrication with advanced age can lead to pain during intercourse and lower sexual activity.

Sexual activity also is influenced by **health** and the **medications** used to treat health problems. One study of over 1000 men between the ages of 40 and 70 found that men with diabetes, heart disease, and/or hypertension had the greatest difficulties and that the prescribed medication was often at fault (Goldstein & Hatzichristou, 1994). Women with multiple sclerosis have great difficulty in achieving orgasms in part due to medication. Even some of the medications used to treat less life-threatening disorders like arthritis, insomnia, and sinusitis can influence sexual responsiveness and lead to lowered levels of activity. Psychiatric medications also have been implicated as a contributor to sexual dysfunction in both men and women (Segraves & Segraves, 1995).

For women, but not men, the **decreased availability of a partner** in older age is another factor in decreased sexual activity. Women tend to marry older men, live longer, become widowed, and outnumber older men, their most likely partners, by more than two to one. Even when male partners are present, they may be unable to perform for reasons such as those just given (Roughan et al., 1993).

The **social unacceptability** of sex among older adults is the final factor influencing sexual activity. Most people do not realize that older adults are still active and many find the thought of such activity to be repugnant or amusing. A large proportion of the jokes about aging have always been jokes about the loss of ability to function sexually (Palmore, 1971). These false beliefs and negative attitudes influence a large number of older adults and lead them to give up sex prematurely (Teitelman, 1990). No one wants to be thought of as repugnant or a joke. Those who maintain their activity generally do so surreptitiously. In a nursing home, however, such concealed sexuality is not possible and staff often may have very narrow views about such activity among residents and actively inhibit such activity even though, by law, older adults have the same rights as all Americans to privacy (Glass et al.,

Your kiss is still so sweet.

1986). Typically for safety reasons, older residents are not permitted to be behind locked doors and staff may "forget" to knock when interrupting the sexual activities of older adults. Older adults, interrupted in such a rude manner, become less likely to continue their embrace. Researchers who have compared the responses of staff and older residents on questions regarding sexual activities have obtained some interesting findings. Older residents were more likely than staff to agree that sex improved quality of life, that relationships among residents should be encouraged, and that sexuality promotes well-being. The majority of both residents and staff agreed that both gay men and lesbians should be allowed to live at the facility in which they lived or worked. When asked whether members of the staff should help obtain erotic videos or magazines for the residents, only 10 percent of the staff but 43 percent of the residents said yes (Walker et al., 1998). Many staff, like members of the general population, find sex among older adults to be unacceptable. How sad for older adults.

Siblings

Siblings are usually the longest social relationship that individuals have. Your older siblings have known you since you were born and your younger siblings have known you since their birth (or shortly thereafter). Siblings, like parents, are not a social relationship that we choose. Having siblings is beyond our control. Like them or not, they are still our siblings.

Most people have at least one sibling and close to 80 percent of older adults have at least one living brother or sister. When asked how close they felt to the sibling(s) that they see most often, most older adults report being close or very close while a small minority, only 5 percent, report not being close at all (Atchley, 2000; Bedford, 1996). Close relationships can be of several different kinds and researchers have attempted to characterize these different kinds of close and not-so-close sibling relationships.

Deborah T. Gold and her colleagues (1989; 1990; Gold et al., 1990) have provided the most commonly used typology of sibling relationships. Five types of sibling relationships were revealed and are summarized in Table 10-1. Intimate siblings are very close and are friends that one can confide in at any time. Congenial siblings also are close and friendly but not as close as spouse or adult child. Loyal siblings are close because they belong to the same family; they may or may not like one another. Apathetic siblings do not like or dislike one another; they are indifferent. Hostile siblings avoid one another and are resentful and/or angry with each other. In a later analysis of these relationship types, four rather than the original five, types of relationships were identified. Later analysis showed that the apathetic and hostile relationship types were very much the same on several measures, such as amount of contact between siblings.

Your relationship with your sibling(s) and how often you contact one another are undoubtedly influenced by a number of factors, and this is true for all adults. Research has revealed several life events and situations that generally improve but can worsen these relationships under some circumstances. In one study, extensive interviews were conducted with 120 adults ages 20 to over 80 who had at least one living sibling. Results showed that marriage and having children usually had little effect on the sibling relationship while divorce, widowhood, illness, or death of a close family member usually strengthened the relationship (Connidis, 1992). Other work suggests that these same events can, in some circumstances, result in renewed antagonism between siblings. The death of a parent may eliminate any perceived obligation to remain quiet about perceived injustice and siblings

TABLE 10-1 Types of Sibling Relationships

Type	Characteristics
Intimate	Strong feelings of love and trust; may regard each other as best friends; have frequent contact (through visits, letters, e-mail, phone); provide support and whenever it is needed without being asked.
Congenial	Feelings of love and trust; may regard each other as good friends; contact is less frequent; feel closer to their spouse or children; provide support if asked; get along well with one another.
Loyal	Relationship based on beliefs about family ties and responsibilities that siblings have to be a good brother or sister; may not have much contact except at traditional family gatherings.
Apathetic	Rarely contact or even think about each other; no strong positive or negative emotions about each other; it is as if they have no sibling(s)
Hostile	Feelings of resentment, anger, and occasionally envy toward each other; no intentional contact and effort to avoid each other; usually a result of some specific event (battle over an inheritance, feeling less loved by a parent, and so on).

Source: Gold (1989).

may confront or avoid one another following the funeral. Generally, however, sibling relationships grow stronger as siblings grow older and in cases where there were earlier disagreements and negative feelings, they tend to lessen (Schulman, 1999).

Frequency of contact also is influenced by several factors. Siblings are more likely to remain in contact with one another when they are emotionally close to one another, feel responsibilities to the family, and live in close proximity. Women, particulary sister-sister pairs, are more likely than men to maintain contact and people without children tend to feel more obliged to maintain contact than those with children. People with children feel more obligation toward their children than toward their siblings (Lee et al., 1990).

When help is needed, those without a spouse or children are more likely to turn to a sibling for help than are those with a spouse or children (Connides, 1994). Most older adults are confident that they could call on a sibling for help if needed but that spouse and children, if present, would be called on first (Cicirelli, 1985). Siblings may be the next line of support following an individual's own nuclear family but fewer than 5 percent of older adults are cared for by siblings (Coward et al., 1992). We saw earlier that social support is important at all ages. Given the length of the sibling relationship, you might think that these individuals would provide an important lifespan source of social support. In fact, many people report just that. But siblings may be more likely to play a role in lifelong psychological support, which is not often reported in the research. More research on the role of siblings and lifelong social support is needed.

Intergenerational Relationships

Intergenerational relationships are relationships between parents and adult children, grandparents and grandchildren and, of course, children, parents, and grandparents.

Parents and Children.   Relationships between parents and young children or adolescents are covered in child or adolescent development or lifespan development. Our discussion will, thus, be limited to parents and their adult children.

Over the last 20 years, more adult children have continued to live with their parents or returned to their parents' home after residing elsewhere for some brief period of time. For example, an adult might return to a parents' home following a divorce. One national survey found that 30 percent of parents had an adult child between the ages of 22 and 24 living with them, 19 percent had a child between the ages of 25 and 29, and 10 percent had a child 30 years of age or older (Hamner & Turner, 1996). Two-parent homes are more likely to have an adult child living with them than are homes with only one parent or homes in which a remarriage has taken place. The adult child who is most likely to live with parents is one attending a school that is within commuting distance from the parents' home.

The opposite situation, a parent moving in with an adult child, usually occurs because of a crisis involving a parent's health and the need for care. These relationships typically are handled quite well but sometimes deteriorate because the child did not fully understand the demands of caregiving, conflicts between caregiving and employment, or a need for professional caregiving that arises as the health of the parent grows worse (Brackbill & Kitch, 1991). You will learn more about these situations in Chapters 11 and 12. Most parents and adult children do not live together.

The amount of contact between parents and adult children who do not live together varies as a function of number of adult children, proximity, and affection. Parents with only one adult child do not have contact as frequently as parents with more than one adult child but still 75 percent have contact at least once a week with their one child (Uhlenberg & Cooney, 1990). Parents and children who feel strong affection for each other maintain contact even at great distance and most parents and children report strong positive feelings. Parents remain concerned about their child's welfare regardless of that child's age. Having a child with serious problems is a major cause of parent depression (Pillemer & Suitor, 1991).

The quality of the parent-adult child relationship is influenced by a number of events. An examination of some of these events was conducted by surveying several thousand adult children in 1988 and again in 1994. These surveys were part of the National Survey of Families and Households (NSFH). Close to 60 percent of the relationships did not change over that time period while 20 percent improved and another 20 percent got worse. Relationships tended to improve when a parent's health improved, when the child got married, when a son's work hours increased, or when a son (but not a daughter) had an additional (not a first) child. Relationships tended to worsen when parents divorced, when a daughter got divorced (but not when a son did), or when a daughter's work hours increased. Having a first child or remaining single had no consistent effect on the quality of the relationship. Women who remained single were among those reporting either improved or worsened relationships with their mothers (Kaufman & Uhlenberg, 1998). One can imagine both of these cases because some parents support their single child while others show great impatience. Although there are many reasons for remaining single, one may be competence in managing a romantic relationship. Some work suggests that the success of romantic relationships for adult children is strongly influenced by the nurturance they received from their parents when they were much younger. Those who had very nurturant parents were seen to be supportive and warm toward romantic partners and to show far less hostility than those from less nurturant parents (Conger et al., 2000). This nurturance is more likely to continue in advanced age.

Grandparents and Grandchildren. Everyone has or has had a grandparent and most adults will become grandparents. Using data from the NSFH, it is estimated that 67 percent of adults who have children of childbearing age are grandparents and by the time their children are 40, close to 95 percent will be grandparents. Most grandparents have more than one grandchild and the average number is between five and six (Kivnick & Sinclair, 1996; Szinovacz, 1998). Eons ago, when life expectancy was very short, you might guess that grandparents were rare because not many people lived long enough to become grandparents. Some anthropological evidence shows that, about 30,000 years ago, there was a great increase in the number of older adults probably due to a change in culture and, perhaps, domestication. The value of grandparents was recognized and it is believed that these older adults took care of, fed, and taught their grandchildren, allowing parents to have more children, colonize new territories, and devote childrearing time to the development of new forms of hunting, farming, and civilizing the world (Caspari & Lee, 2006; O'Connell et al., 1999). Grandparents may have been a major force in the development of human civilization and still are highly valued family members today.

Grandparents play a number of important roles in today's families depending on the family itself and the particular situations that arise. Typical roles include providing children and grandchildren with information about family history, keeping track of family members, serving as mediators when conflicts arise between parents and children or siblings, and even filling in as custodial parents for their grandchildren when parents are unable to fill that role themselves (Atchley, 2000). This latter role can be quite difficult for grandparents and some recent work has found much higher levels of family strain and lower health scores for custodial grandmothers. These grandmothers perceived far lower levels of family functioning than did noncustodial grandmothers and usually for good reason (Musil et al., 2006). Box 10-2 takes a closer look at the issues and problems for grandparents and grandchildren in these custodial situations.

Grandparents generally are older adults and older adults, especially older women, are often portrayed negatively in the media (see Chapter 1). Children typically have a very negative view of older adults (Haught et al., 1999; Lichtenstein et al., 2003). When, however, young children are asked about their own grandparents, they view them very positively, especially when contact is frequent (Creasey & Kaliher, 1994). A description of grandparents written by a 9-year-old girl illustrates this positive view (McElreath, 1996):

> A grandmother is a lady who has no children of her own, so she likes other people's little ones. A grandfather is a man grandmother . . . they drive us to the market where the pretend horse is and have lots of dimes ready. Or, if they take us for walks, they should slow down past things like pretty leaves and caterpillars. When they read to us, they don't skip or mind if it's the same story again. Everybody should try to have one, especially if you don't have a television, because grandmas are the only grown-ups who have got time.

Contact between grandparents and young grandchildren is not in the hands of the grandchildren and is largely dependent on the relationship between parents and grandparents. In these cases, African American grandparents are more likely than white American grandparents to be involved with their grandchildren and to spend more time with them (Strom et al., 1996). Even very old (85 and older) African American grandparents spend considerable time with their grandchildren and great-grandchildren and report significant emotional benefits and pride in their role as grandparents (Barer, 2001).

When grandchildren are grown, contact depends on them more than on anyone else. College students report contact once a month or less on average. This is not surprising because most college students live some distance from their parents and grandparents. Young adults usually report that such contact is very important to them and that their closest grandparent has had great influence on their life (Boon & Brussoni, 1996). When asked about activities that they shared with their grandparents during a visit, they most frequently named being together at family events, just "messing around," eating out, spending the night at a grandparent's house, watching TV together, discussing recent events in each other's lives, playing games, and going shopping (Kennedy, 1992). Young adults report more of these shared activities and a stronger relationship with grandmothers than with grandfathers (Roberto & Stroes, 1992). For African American grandmothers, some work shows that their children and grandchildren perceive their teaching as their greatest strength (Strom et al., 2005).

Grandparents have been asked many of the same questions and their answers are essentially the same as those received from grandchildren. Most grandparents say they have

BOX **10-2**

Custodial Grandparents

Custodial grandparents refer to those grandparents who are raising their grandchildren for short (a couple of weeks) to long (until the children are grown) periods of time because the children's parents are unable or unwilling to do so. Parents may have died, been involved in substance abuse, been imprisoned, been disabled, been ill, have severe psychological or financial difficulties, or neglected the child (Sands & Goldberg-Glen, 2000). It is estimated that there are about 1.5 million custodial grandparents at any one time (Simmons & Dye, 2003). About 12 percent of African American grandparents and about 4 percent of white American grandparents have had this experience (Thomas et al., 2000). Grandmothers who are younger and who never completed high school are the most frequent custodial grandparents (Minkler & Fuller-Thomson, 2000). A number of studies have looked at the effects this situation has on grandparents and grandchildren.

One study found lower health and more strain for custodial grandmothers (Musil et al., 2006). Other studies also have found more health problems, higher levels of depression, and greater stress (perhaps a cause for those health problems) for custodial grandparents (Goodman, 2003; Minkler et al., 1997; Musil & Ahmad, 2002). These difficulties are even greater for the many older adults experiencing a chronic disorder or serious health problem of their own. In one study, custodial grandparents suffering from arthritis perceived themselves as having greater difficulty raising grandchildren and, as a result, felt high levels of anger, frustration, guilt, and depression (Barlow et al., 1999). Grandparents also often have difficulty in managing the behavior of grandchildren, particularly adolescents, and the problems seem to be worldwide. A recent study conducted in Kenya found the same types of problems for custodial grandparents there as in the United States (Ice et al., 2006).

These difficulties are not always the same for grandmothers compared to grandfathers. One interesting study found that grandmothers showed more depression when the grandchildren first moved into the home while grandfathers showed more when they moved out. It is thought that grandfathers may be less involved with the actual custodial care (feeding, clothing, disciplining) but benefit from the companionship they receive and being viewed as a wise elder. When the grandchildren leave, they lose these benefits (Szinovacz et al., 1999).

Grandchildren in these situations are more likely to have some behavioral, emotional, school-related, or neurological problems than those living with their parents (Hayslip et al., 1998). Such problems may have been present before moving in with grandparents. They seem, however, to be at the same overall level of health and school performance as children living with their parents rather than grandparents (Solomon & Marx, 1995).

---

seen a grandchild within the last month, talked on the phone, and/or sent a card. The activities that they report sharing with a grandchild include eating a meal together, watching TV, and having the grandchild spend the night (AARP, 1999). Grandparents of college students report great pride in the accomplishments of their grandchild (or -children), feel especially loved when the grandchild visits or calls unexpectedly, and enjoy being asked for and providing advice (Harwood & Lin, 2000).

Grandparenting usually is very rewarding for those older adults who experience it. Although custodial grandparents (see Box 10-2) have more difficulties than other grandparents, they still derive benefits. One survey of over 800 grandparents, in various circumstances, asked them to rate their relationship with their closest grandchild on a scale of

1–10 with 10 reflecting a very strong and very enjoyable relationship. The average rating was 8.7 (AARP, 1999). Other work has shown that grandparents under the age of 50 and over the age of 80, rate grandparenting as less enjoyable than those between 51 and 79. Younger grandparents still were engaged in jobs or careers and had little time to enjoy grandchildren while older grandparents were sometimes too frail to enjoy interacting with grandchildren. Those who found grandparenting enjoyable gave four main reasons: They could spoil the grandchildren; they enjoyed being respected as a wise older person; they felt a sense of immortality looking at their grandchildren, and, in many instances, great-grandchildren; and they were reminded of their experiences with their own grandparents (Kivnick, 1982). Some work shows that those who have a strong identity as a grandparent (or parent) tend to have higher self-esteem and much lower depression than those who do not (Reitzes & Mutran, 2004). Being a grandparent is, for the most part and for most people, a very positive experience.

Friends

How many friends do you have? In answering this question you probably responded as most people do and counted individuals who are and are not all that close to you. If asked how many good friends you have, you would undoubtedly give a smaller number. Recall where you placed your friends in your social network (Project 10).

Friendships are defined by a number of characteristics and close friendships have more of those characteristics than less-close friendships. Friendships are **voluntary**. Unlike sibling, parent, or grandparent relationships into which you are born or adopted, one

Grandparents may experience a form of immortality when they are close to their grandchildren.

selects friends. Friendships are **reciprocal**. Each person gives as well as receives. When a friend needs help, a friend is ready to help. **Self-disclosure** is a characteristic of friendships. Friends share secrets that they would not share with other people; they know each other's likes and dislikes, they confide in one another. It is the mutual nature of this self-disclosure that is most important. We are not close friends if you know everything about me and I know nothing about you. Women are more likely than men to have more than one close friend in whom they confide; men are more likely to confide only in their best friend, their spouse. **Equality** is another characteristic. One person is not always the leader while the other follows. They may alternate these roles or never engage in them at all. Friendships have **emotional attachment**; friends care about each other. Friends have **overlapping interests**. They enjoy many of the same things and like to do things together (Atchley, 2000; Schulz & Salthouse, 1999). Men friends are more likely than women friends to do things together (Cavanaugh, 1998). Thinking about some of the people you regard as friends, you might try the scale in Table 10-2 that measures these characteristics. Did you notice that the scale includes a few other common characteristics, such as physical appearance and intelligence? Close friends tend to be close to each other in these characteristics too.

Friends, of all types, are important in a number of ways. Long-term close friends tend to be placed in the inner circle of older people's social support network. They are a major source of social support as are family members. Older adults in need are sometimes more willing to ask a friend for support than a child because the help of a child may produce a loss of independence or, at least, the perception of such loss (Lee, 1985). Friends are less likely to take away your feelings of independence. People with friends, regardless of their age, have more social support and, as a result, seem to enjoy better health and lower mortality rates (Berkman, 1995; Penninx et al., 1997). Friends help each other cope with stress (Cavanaugh, 1998). Friends play a more important role in older adult's well-being and life satisfaction than income and marital status (Siebert et al., 1999). In addition, older friends serve as important caretakers of our memories. They share a large part of our lifetime and bring back happy memories, cushion sad memories, and reminisce as no others are able (Stowe et al., 1997).

By now you have witnessed the shattering of so many common myths about older adults that it will not surprise you to learn that older adults do not have fewer friends than other aged adults. The number of close friends that most people have remains relatively stable over the course of their adult years (Antonucci, 1990). People who have a large number of close friends when they are young tend to have a large number of close friends when they are old, while those with fewer close friends when young tend also to have fewer close friends when old. Of course, the chances of losing a friend are higher for older adults than for younger adults, but older adults are usually quite successful at forming new friendships when older ones are lost (Johnson & Troll, 1994). Older adults most often lose close friends as a result of relocation, retirement, or death. On average, adults of all ages have five to six persons that they name as close friends (Stowe et al., 1997).

There are, however, age differences in the number of acquaintances and casual friends in the outer circle of older and younger adults; older adults have fewer of these types of friends (Antonucci, 2001; Carstensen & Charles, 1998). These findings and others have led Laura Carstensen (1992; 1995) and colleagues to develop a theory of why older people have fewer casual friends and fewer people in the outer circle of their social

TABLE 10-2   Are Your Friends Really Friends?

Think about and answer the following questions about your relationship with a person who you regard as being a close friend. Add up your score and see if your friendship also would be regarded as a friendship by those who conduct research on friendships.

1. If you truly regard this person as a close friend, **start off with a score of 1**; after all, you're probably right.
2. Do you and this person get together even when you don't have to? If you only see this person in class or in church or at gatherings held by family or some social organization, that does not count. If you can answer "yes" to this question, **add 2**.
3. When is the last time you did something to help this person? How important was the thing you did? If you did something to help within the last 6 months and the thing you did was important, **add 1.**
4. When is the last time this person did something to help you? How important was the thing he or she did? If this person helped you within the last 6 months and the help was important, **add 1**.
5. Think of your three biggest secrets. How many of these have you told this person? **Add 1 for each secret you revealed**. If you have not yet revealed any of these secrets to this other person but you plan to tell sometime soon, **add 1**. If you think that you will never reveal any of these secrets to this other person, **subtract 2**.
6. Has this other person told you any of their secrets? If "yes," **add 1**; if "no," **subtract 1**.
7. Are you or the other person the boss in your relationship? If either of you is the boss, **subtract 3**.
8. How strong are your feelings for this other person? If you rate them as very strong and positive, **add 2**.
9. How strong are this other person's feelings for you? If you rate them as very strong and positive, **add 2**.
10. Think of your five most favorite things to do. How many of these are favorites for this other person? **Add 1 for each thing that is a favorite for both of you**. If none of the five things you thought of are favorites for this other person, **subtract 3**.
11. Do you and this other person like the same music? The same movies? The same books? The same sports? If you answered "yes" to at least two of these categories, **add 1**. If you did not answer "yes" to any of the categories, **subtract 1**.
12. Is this other person as physically attractive as you are or are they better or worse? If you think that they are about the same as you, **add 1**.
13. Is this other person as smart as you are or are they smarter or not as smart? If you think this other person is as smart as you or smarter than you, **add 1**.
14. Do you have other close friends in addition to this person? If "yes," **add 1**; if "no," **subtract 1**.

If your total score is 12 or higher, most researchers would agree with you that the person you thought of is a close friend. Try the scale again thinking of a different person.

support network. This **socioemotional selectivity theory** holds that older people develop an increased attention to emotional factors in their relationships due to an awareness that their time may be limited. Carstensen suggests that older people reduce the total number of people in their lives who do not provide emotional closeness and focus more on those

My friends know who I am.

who do. Their increased attention to emotional factors may be part of the reason that older married couples show less negative and more positive emotions when discussing a disagreeable topic or why older adults more often turn to emotion management coping strategies when dealing with an emotional situation (see Chapter 9). In one study, young, middle-aged, and older adults were asked who they would rather be with if they had a half hour open and could spend it with the person they chose or if they were moving across the country with no accompanying family or friends. They were allowed to choose from a member of their immediate family or a person they recently met and who appeared to have a lot in common with them or an author of a book they had read. All aged adults selected a family member in the situation where they were moving across country but, as expected by socioemotional theory, only older adults selected a family member when they had a half hour to spare (Fredrickson & Carstensen, 1990).

In addition to age differences in the number of casual friends, there are occasional age differences in the characteristics that define friendship. Both young and old friendships tend to be voluntary and to have strong emotional attachment. Some work has found, however, less self-disclosure as older adults often express an unwillingness to bother others with their troubles because others, who also are old, have enough troubles of their own (Johnson & Troll, 1994). Other work has found that, for older adults, satisfaction with friends was not related to reciprocity or equality in the friendship (Jones & Vaughn, 1990). Older women have sometimes downplayed the importance of overlapping interests (Roberto, 1997). Although these characteristics are important for close friendships, they may often be less important for older adults. Think of an older adult who cannot share equally or reciprocate with a good friend because of some disability; who does not want to disclose any pain or suffering; and who is no longer able to participate in interests that were once shared. Is such a person incapable of having a good friend? We think we would all agree that the answer is no.

Because older adults lose friends more often than younger adults, some work has examined the coping and making of new friends for these individuals. In one longitudinal study, older adults were interviewed in 1979 and again in 1995 when the youngest person still in the study was 81. Over that 16-year interval, many lost close friends. Most (70 percent), however, still had good friends and were quite satisfied. Ten percent had good friends and wanted still more. One interesting finding was that the new friends selected by these older adults were as likely to be different gender as same gender. Young adult friendships are usually among men or among women but older adult friendships are frequently mixed gender. Another 15 percent had no good friends and did not wish for any. Only 5 percent had no good friends but wished they did. Older adults like this or those who have good friends but wish they had more can benefit from programs that teach specific skills, practice those skills in role-playing sessions, and emphasize pragmatic factors. Such programs have been shown to be quite effective in reducing loneliness and increasing the friendships of older women (Stevens et al., 2006).

Religion

All of the social relationships so far have been with individual people. We are close to and receive social support from a significant other, a sibling, parents or children, grandparents or grandchildren, and friends. Social support also can come from groups to which we belong such as clubs, professional organizations, and religious congregations. In this section we will look at **religion**, which for our purposes refers to a community of individuals who share common beliefs and participate together in faith-based common activities or rituals. All religions provide social links, and frequently social support, to their members that would otherwise not be available. Religion is the public and social side of theological belief systems and is different from spirituality. **Spirituality** is the private, emotional, and/or intellectual connection that one makes to an accepted higher power. People who are members of a religion may or may not be spiritual and people with spirituality may or may not be members of a religion. Most of the research conducted in this area is relatively new and has focused more on religion than on spirituality.

A common belief is that older adults are more religious and more spiritual than younger adults. In support of this, a number of cross-sectional surveys have found higher attendance at religious gatherings for older adults (Krause, 1997). When people have been asked whether they believe in a higher power, about two-thirds of those between 15 and 34 answered yes while 87 percent of those 55 and older answered yes (Jacobs & Worcester, 1990). These differences could, however, be associated with cohort rather than age. Older adults grew up in times when religion was a more central part of life. One longitudinal study followed a large group of adults for 20 years and found that attendance at services was higher for older adults between the ages of 60 and 75 but declined past the age of 75. One might guess that this decline could be due, in part, to increased illness or disability for those older adults but, in fact, many who became ill or disabled increased their attendance while others with no apparent disability attended less often than they had in the past (Atchley, 1999). It is not clear whether this decrease in attendance was accompanied by a decrease or perhaps an increase in spirituality. Religion and spirituality, as with intelligence and personality traits, may be other cases where we find both age and cohort differences.

SOCIAL POLICY APPLICATIONS

Clearly it is important for human beings to perceive that they have social support from family and/or friends. Such support contributes to health and longevity. Well-supported people are of benefit to society as they, in turn, support others. Social support has not, however, been the business of government but maybe it should be. Many believe that state, county, or city governments should provide opportunities for adults of all ages to interact and get together. One of the best mechanisms is to provide accessible recreation and entertainment and better transportation to prevent isolation and loneliness. For the first, many think that this is the role of local government in partnership with arts organizations and private organizations and donors. Providing more low cost or subsidized arts events (music, plays, art shows, etc.) and in more locales (rural and suburban shopping centers, churches, community centers, etc.) would increase access for individuals who normally do not or are not able to attend arts events. The 2005 White House Mini Conference on Aging and Creativity stressed the role of the arts in promoting community and social engagement in older persons.

The second recommendation involves transportation. Think about what happens when your car is in the shop or you can't get anyone to give you a ride when you need one. It is very frustrating. For older persons, it is isolating and can promote depression and loneliness. On a given day, about 3.6 million Americans over 65 stay home because they lack transportation. This means they make fewer trips to the doctor, fewer shopping and eating out trips, fewer trips to entertainment opportunities, and fewer trips for social, family, and religious activities. Trips outside a neighborhood involve asking someone else for a ride in the majority of cases because public transportation is not available to many older adults. When it is, they use it. Therefore, local governments (state and county/municipal/city) must increase public transportation options for older Americans. In addition, studies indicate that when there are good walking and bicycle paths, older adults use them on a regular basis. Clearly, these options also need to be expanded. Given what we know about the benefits of exercise and socialization, it would be a crime to not make these improvements for our older citizens. How can you help?

Religion and spirituality have been associated with a number of benefits for adults of all ages. In a review of over 200 prior studies and three national surveys, Jeffrey Levin found that religion was strongly and positively related to health and that a large number of health problems were less frequent among adults who reported more religious involvement (1994; 1998). In one longitudinal study, those who attended religious services during the early years of the study had far fewer and less serious disabilities 12 years later (Idler & Kasl, 1997a; 1997b). Psychological well-being and life satisfaction also have been associated with religion (Johnson, 1995). In this case, however, the association is U shaped. Those with higher involvement in religion and those with no involvement in religion tend to have higher levels of psychological well-being than those with moderate levels (Krause, 1995). Finally, religion also is related to mortality. In one study, 2023 California residents, ages 55 and older, were asked about their attendance at religious services. As in other studies, attendance was higher for women than men and lowest for the youngest (middle age) and oldest (old-old) adults in the sample. Over the next 5 years, mortality data were collected by continual reading of obituary notices in newspapers and attempts to contact participants for later interviews. The death rates were highest for those who had earlier reported no attendance at religious services and lowest for those who had reported weekly attendance (Oman & Reed, 1998). In a direct comparison of the benefits associated with religion and with spirituality, one longitudinal study interviewed adults when they were in their 30s, 40s, 50s, and late 60s. Higher levels of religion were strongly associated with more positive relationships with other people, well-being derived from such positive relationships, and generativity. As you recall, generativity refers to the feelings associated with providing something of value to the next generation(s). Higher levels of spirituality were strongly associated with personal growth, being involved in creative or learning tasks, and wisdom. Perhaps very spiritual people develop more insight into human life and become experts. You will remember that wisdom can be thought of as expertise at life (Wink & Dillon, 2003). Factors underlying the relationships between religion and spirituality on the one hand and health, well-being, generativity, wisdom, and mortality on the other have been the focus of much research.

One factor is the set of rules or **demands** made by some organized religions on their members. One religion may prohibit behaviors such as drinking alcohol, using drugs, smoking, extramarital sex, and other behaviors that may be dangerous. The demands of Buddhist, Hindu, Muslim, Mormon, Seventh Day Adventists, and several other religions are such that many unhealthy behaviors are unacceptable. A reason for better health for religious people may be that they are less likely to engage in unhealthy behaviors.

A second factor may be relaxation from a form of **meditation**, particularly in the face of stress. Meditation is known to reduce blood pressure and decrease heart rate (Holmes, 1987). The meditation practiced by highly spiritual people may involve reading religious writing, listening to religious programs, and reciting prayers as one might recite a mantra. In one study of 1300 older adults, more than half reported reading the Bible, one-third listened to or watched religious programs, and 60 percent reported praying every day (Koenig, 1995). Highly spiritual people may have a very effective technique for ameliorating stress.

A third factor is the **social support** coming from a religious community beyond that provided by family and friends. Members of religious communities may offer instrumental and/or emotional support to one another at times of need whereas such support might come only from family and friends for those who are not part of a religious community. As you know, more support is better than less. In one survey of African Americans, researchers found that 60 percent reported receiving support from members of their religion; 80 percent also received support from a good friend and 50 percent from family (Taylor & Chatters, 1986). It has been suggested that the support actually received from a religious community is very much like the support received from family and friends but may be more likely perceived as social support because most religions advocate concern and care for others (Krause, 2001). Recall the earlier discussion of how it is the perception of social support that is important.

Another form of social support occurs as religions offer opportunities to form new friendships and to, thus, expand social networks. Box 10-3 describes Shepherd's Centers that provide activities and learning opportunities for older adults at a number of religious organizations across the country. Gatherings for religious services, for festivals, and for other sponsored events also offer opportunities for **network expansion**.

Social support from a religion also can be more abstract than instrumental or emotional. A sick member of the community might be provided with meals and with people to talk to but also be prayed for. **Prayer** may be a kind of social support that only religions

BOX 10-3

Shepherd's Centers

Religious groups in your community may sponsor a number of activities managed by **Shepherd's Center**. Shepherd's Center was founded in 1972 by Dr. Elbert Cole as a way for older adults to provide services for other older adults. The national headquarters in Kansas City offers assistance to those interested in beginning a local center. There are now over 100 local centers in more than half the states and over 100,000 members (Atchley, 2000). Space for activities usually is provided by a religious group that has ample space available and funding is donated by a number of local religious groups and participants. Shepherd's Center activities are open to older adults regardless of religion. Centers provide classes on a number of different topics, companion aide service, transportation for grocery shopping or doctor's appointments, handyperson services, hot meal deliveries, and other activities.

Available activities at our local Sheperd's Center includes information on income tax assistance and travel; transportation and aides; and classes on bridge instruction and play, creative writing, current events, line dancing, memory improvement, music appreciation, origami, portrait drawing, romantic poetry, water exercise, and wood carving. Classes usually are taught by older adults or by volunteers from the community who have some expertise in the topic. A different variety of classes is offered each fall and spring and usually meet once a week for 6 to 7 weeks. Participants pay a minimum fee to participate in one morning and one afternoon class.

---

provide and so researchers have examined the effectiveness of this support. In one examination of the effects of prayer and of music/imagery/touch therapy on cardiac patients, no benefits were found (Krucoff et al., 2005). More recently, researchers compared cardiac patients who were randomly assigned to receive standard treatment or standard treatment combined with prayer. For those assigned to receive prayer, half were randomly assigned to a group who were told that they would be receiving prayer. Other groups did not know whether prayers would be said for them. Three groups prayed daily for 2 weeks for all patients assigned to the two prayer groups. Results showed that those who knew they were being prayed for had more complications following the surgery than did the other two groups (Benson et al., 2006). Being prayed for had no benefit over not being prayed for but being prayed for and knowing it resulted in more difficulties. Researchers suggest that being told that people are praying for you might lead you to expect the worst and increase your anxiety level which then might increase complications following surgery. As a form of social support from religious groups, prayer has not been found to be a health benefit but may, of course, be beneficial in other, as yet untested, ways.

Finally, some have suggested that religion or spirituality may be beneficial because they provide hope and a more **positive outlook** for those in the religious community and/or those who believe in a higher power. These individuals may be able to place their problems in a broader context of human suffering and salvation and be more happy with their lives. Some work has found a strong positive relationship between religiosity and happiness while other work has not (Lewis & Cruise, 2006). Perhaps many religious people have a more positive outlook and a number of studies in positive psychology have found benefits associated for those who have such an outlook.

Religion and spirituality are associated with a number of benefits and appear to operate through several different factors but even in studies where many of these factors have been controlled for (size of social support network, healthy behaviors, drinking, smoking), researchers have still obtained lower mortality rates for religious people especially women (Koenig et al., 1999; Strawbridge et al., 1997). Perhaps meditation/relaxation and positive outlooks account for the association or perhaps there are other factors that have not yet been systematically investigated. What do you think these other factors might be?

Isolation and Loneliness

Although a common misperception of older adults is that they are isolated and lonely you now know better. The social networks of older adults are quite strong and more focused on those who are emotionally closest and in their inner circles. Older adults, like all other adults, derive social support from their relationships and often from religious communities as well. In an early examination of loneliness, researchers looked at 15 different studies that had investigated levels of loneliness for older adults. These studies showed that about 10 percent reported being very or often lonely, 20 percent lonely sometimes, and 70 percent rarely or never lonely. For each hour spent alone, younger adults reported more loneliness than older adults (Malatesta & Kalnok, 1984; Wenger et al., 1996). Do not fear being alone in old age; it is highly unlikely.

Five generations.

CHAPTER HIGHLIGHTS

- Social support from family and friends seems to remain stable across the adult years and to be a major factor in physical health, psychological well-being, and longevity.
- Most people have about 20 people in their social networks but older adults tend to lose those in the outer circle and focus more on those closest to them.
- For social support to have a beneficial effect, it must be perceived as well as received.
- Family relationships begin at birth for most people and relationships with parents and siblings are typically the longest relationships in an individual's life.
- Most people marry at least once in their lives but close to half of these marriages end in divorce.
- Generally, marital satisfaction is relatively high in the early years of a marriage, declines somewhat during the years in which children are present, and rises again following the departure of the last child from home.
- Long-lasting marriages tend to be those in which the couple agrees on many important topics, where marriage is regarded as a major commitment, where humor and affection reside, and where spouses are regarded as best friends.
- Marital strain increases over the years of marriage especially for women.
- Despite encountering more obstacles, gay and lesbian couples report many of the same levels of satisfaction and strain as do heterosexual couples.
- Divorce tends to occur when there is lack of or minimal communication between partners and/or infidelity.
- Many more men than women remarry and such second, third, and so on marriages are less likely to succeed than first marriages.
- Many older adults are turning to cohabitation as an alternative to marriage following the loss of a spouse.
- Sexual relations continue into very old age but at a reduced rate. A number of reasons are thought to underlie this lower activity level.
- Most parents become grandparents before reaching age 50.
- Grandparents generally enjoy being grandparents for a number of reasons including the chance to spoil the grandchildren.
- Custodial grandparents have higher levels of strain and depression than other grandparents.
- Friendships are characterized as being voluntary relationships in which each person gives and receives. Friends typically confide in one another and are equals in the relationship. Friends have close emotional attachments and share common interests.
- The number of friends does not seem to change with age. For older adults, friendships are more often cross-gender, less confiding, and less reciprocal.
- Religion plays an important role in social relationships and is related to health, well-being, and mortality. Several factors are known to underlie this relationship while others are, as yet, unclear.
- Most older adults report being rarely or never lonely.

STUDY QUESTIONS

1. Describe the convoy model of social networks and social support. Are there age and gender differences in social networks and support?

2. How does social support exert an influence on physical health, psychological well-being, and mortality?

3. What factors play a role in long-lasting marriages? In divorce?

4. What are the types of elder abuse? How frequent is such abuse?

5. Is it better to have loved and lost than to have never loved at all? Explain the reasons for your answer.

6. Describe/discuss changes in sexual activity with age and the reasons for these changes. Are the reasons the same for men and women?

7. Describe sibling relationships. Do sibling relationships change with age? With the loss of parents? With changes in health?

8. What factors influence the relationships between parents and adult children?

9. What are the similarities and differences in the relationships between grandparents and young versus adult grandchildren? What factors play a role?

10. Do grandparents enjoy being grandparents? What factors play a role? Do grandparents enjoy acting as parents again? What factors play a role? Do grandchildren benefit or suffer when they are parented by their grandparents instead of their real parents? Do grandparents benefit or suffer?

11. What criteria do researchers use when defining a friendship? In your opinion, which of these criteria are most/least important?

12. Are the friendships of older adults different than those of younger adults? Of men than those of women?

13. What is the difference between religion and spirituality?

14. What accounts for the relationship found between religion/spirituality and health/mortality?

15. How do you think that social support might bring all of the aspects of social relations together in a comprehensive view of lifespan social development?

RECOMMENDED READINGS

Hanson, W. (1999). *Older Love*. Minneapolis, MN: Waldman House Press. This very short book or very long poem (36 pages) is a description of the love that resides in a long-lasting marriage.

Krause, N. (1999). *The Healing Power of Faith: Science Explores Medicine's Last Great Frontier*. New York: Simon & Schuster.

Lee, J. A. (Ed.). (1991). *Gay Midlife and Maturity*. Binghamton, NY: Harrington Park Press. If you are interested in learning more about older gay persons and their adjustment to aging, this older book is a good place to start.

Werking, K. (1997). *We're Just Good Friends: Women and Men in Nonromantic Relationships*. New York: Guilford. This book examines cross-gender friendships and their survival in U.S. culture.

INTERNET RESOURCES

www.census.gov. Find some of the latest statistics on marriage, divorce, and other relationships.

www.shepherdcenters.org. Learn more about Shepherd's Centers of America and the activities offered, how to start a local center, and other information.

www.elderabusecenter.org. Information about Laws Related to Elder Abuse.

www.elderabusecenter.org. Offers a fact sheet on elder abuse prevalence and incidence.

www.aoa.gov. Learn about elders rights and resources.

CHAPTER

11

Work and Retirement

We've put more effort into helping folks reach old age than into helping them enjoy it.

—Frank A. Clark

Frank Clark is right. You have read the work on increasing longevity and remaining healthy in old age. The time to enjoy this longevity and health is, for most, the time of retirement. In this chapter we will examine how good that time is and what factors influence an enjoyable retirement. Many retired adults report it as the busiest time of life; our retired friend Grace Holden says, "you'll wonder how you ever had time to go to work." Unfortunately, as Frank Clark suggests, many find retirement to be a letdown or a great expense with little enjoyment and, as just suggested, there is little effort to help such individuals. On the other hand, many continue working well into old age so that is where we will begin.

Work

The average age of the American worker has increased over the last several years and will undoubtedly continue to increase as older, still working baby boomers, age. In 1996, the average worker was 38 years old and in 2006 that average was close to 41. As you might expect, younger workers are employed in a wider variety of jobs than are middle-aged and older workers. Middle-aged and older workers are relatively settled into a job while younger workers often are still searching for the right position to match their skills and interests. Younger adults also are more likely to take temporary, hazardous, and physically difficult jobs than are older adults. Men are employed in a wider variety of jobs than are women, although this is far less true for young men and women. Older cohorts of women were not employed in many jobs that were regarded as the domain of men. A glance at Table 11-1 gives an idea of what some of these restricted jobs were and where women of this older cohort were most likely to be employed (Czaja, 2001).

The frequent and persistent negative view of aging and older adults and negative stereotypes about older adults discussed earlier have influenced the evaluation of older workers by management, supervisors, coworkers, and even older workers themselves. It is thought that older workers are more likely to be hurt on the job, get sick and be absent, perform at a lower level, be more forgetful and unable to learn new procedures, and cost far more than they are worth to the employer (Wegman, 1999). Many believe older minds and bodies simply do not work as well anymore. They are burned out and no longer

TABLE 11-1   Percentage of Middle-Age and Older Men and Women in Different Job Types (in percent)

Men Age 45–64		Women Age 45–64	
Crafts	21	Clerical	40
Management	19	Service	21
Professional/Technical	17	Professional/Technical	19
Total	57	Total	80
Men Age 65+		**Woman Age 65+**	
Management	18	Clerical	25
Professional/Technical	15	Service	21
Service	13		
Total	46	Total	46

Source: Adapted from Czaja (2001).

interested in or satisfied with their jobs. None of these beliefs are, however, supported by the evidence and some are refuted.

Injury and Absence

In terms of injuries and absences from work, older adults have fewer of each (Laflamme & Menckel, 1995). Experienced workers are, of course, less likely to have an accident in the workplace and become injured regardless of age and the highest accident rate is for inexperienced, young workers under the age of 25. The accident rate for workers 25 and older does not vary as a function of age (Cleveland & Shore, 1996). Other work shows that today's older workers are healthier and more able to work than older workers 20 years ago (Crimmins et al., 1999). It is, however, the case that when an older worker is injured on the job, more time typically is lost to recovery than for a younger worker. A large part of this seems to be due to the fact that management insists and/or encourages an older worker to take more time because an older worker is expected to need more time to heal (Wegman, 1999). This is often the case but it is not clear whether it is better to have three younger workers gone for 1 day each or one older worker gone for 3 days. It probably depends on what the job is. Another interesting thought is whether it is better to cut back on recovery time for older workers or extend time for younger workers. What is the right amount of time? Is it age that is the important consideration or something else?

Some types of injuries are more frequent in older workers but are due to the amount of time on the job or tasks of the job rather than to the age of the worker. Cumulative trauma disorders and repetitive strain injuries result from performing a job while standing in an awkward posture, repeating the same motions, and/or having to exert excessive force. The longer you do this sort of work, the more likely you are to suffer, and some of these strains, such as carpal tunnel syndrome, can be quite severe. Generally, the incidence of such disorders are about the same for younger and older workers but the prevalence rates are higher for older workers. For example, problems of pain in the lower back are as likely to first occur (incidence) among younger workers as among older workers, but more older workers have such pain (prevalence) because they have had it for a long time (de Zwart et al., 1997). The effects of continual standing at work and repetitive motions decrease work ability especially for older workers who are more likely to have decreased muscle strength and who have been at the job for a longer period of time (Tuomi et al., 1997).

Senior View

Frank Ochoa was 75 when we spoke with him about his work and his farm. Frank's parents were migrant workers from Mexico and he recalls those days. *We would travel 2 or 3 days to get to a location then either there was a job or there wasn't. The most we ever stayed at a place was a month; then we would pick up and go. All of your belongings had to fit in the car. Finally when I was 8 (in 1939), we came to Washington and there was a lot of work there. In 1941, my dad rented some land*

and started farming on his own; we worked from daylight to dark raising cattle and produce. I learned young, 11 or 12, about mortgages and interest because I had to interpret for my dad and so I was beyond my years in knowledge.

I went to school only 3 days a week because of working but I graduated high school and then took a college correspondence course. I couldn't finish because of work and because my parents didn't speak English so I had no one to help me with the lessons. It taught me that there are better things in life than just to work day in and day out. I found out that you have to have goals and you have to set them early in life to obtain them. I worked on the railroad, in a bean processing plant, a potato plant, and on the police force but went back to farming when I was 28.

We asked if he had experienced any discrimination. *Some people do discriminate but you can work hard and earn respect. When I started my farm, I had to go to three banks to find one that would give me a loan. They trusted me and I didn't let them down. I have 500 acres now and farm another 1400. Some farmers here, when they need a job done, will hire Hispanics and they are nice to them till the job is done and then they can't get rid of them fast enough. I see there is a lot of hidden prejudice and racism that people have to rise above and prove themselves. I have no animosity against people who were prejudiced against me. My best recollection, probably my best teacher was this Swedish guy who took me under his wing. I learned from observing the way he handled himself in different situations. Observance is very important. You know you learn more by listening than by talking.*

We asked Frank to what he attributed his success. *I learned that one way to be successful is*

(continued)

Senior View *Continued*

to learn to say no. I had friends my age and they would come and say "let's go hunting or let's go here or there" and I would say "no, I can't." I worked. A person has to work hard in order to obtain success. Also, I was always positive. I always stood up for myself. I married and had eight children and now many grandchildren. My children all went to college.

We asked Frank if he would ever retire. *I don't think I will retire. I want to raise cherries. I got 5 acres already and it's a trial basis and if that works well, then I'm going to put in another 20 acres. Twenty-five acres of cherries is an awful lot; it's different from regular farming. I think that staying active is what kept me going for so long.*

We think he's right and you will learn in this chapter about the importance of remaining active in both work and retirement. To talk about retirement we scheduled an appointment with Pat Shelley, a former schoolteacher. She stays busy with her volunteer work taking care of "old folks" during the week. Pat has a set routine of visiting shut-ins in the community and driving folks to the store and doctor's appointments. We also had to schedule our meeting around the Atlanta Braves because Pat is an avid fan. We caught up with her after a game (the Braves won) one afternoon to get her views on work and retirement.

I've been happily retired for about 12 years

after an enjoyable 39 years of teaching third and fourth grade children. One of the best parts is that I still get notes, letters, and messages from some of those kids. I love to hear from them and especially love them to visit. Some even remind me when I had to spank them so many years ago. In those days that was the expected punishment for misbehaving.

We asked why she had decided to become a teacher. *I always knew I wanted to be a teacher. In those early days of the 20th century, career decisions were easy for women. If you wanted a career you had to be a teacher or a nurse. My parents encouraged me to be a teacher and I had older sisters who also went into teaching. When you pick your career you have to go with your personality. I've always been a very happy, energetic person and loved children. I had the right personality for teaching.*

With respect to retirement, Pat told us, *my husband, who was a barber, and I always tried to save for the future and for our retirement. We made it a priority and learned to do without things occasionally so that we could have what we needed later. Those later things included college money for our children, money to help him when he got sick and eventually died, money for retirement. I retired at 71 and our house and car were paid for. We had enough to cover our bills and a little extra for traveling to visit our children and grandchildren. My pension and social security have given me enough to live comfortably. I'm lucky to live in a small town where my expenses are low. I spend a lot of time gardening now but that takes a lot more sweat than money.*

We asked how she knew when to retire and whether she had any advice on retirement that she would like to share. *I knew it was time to retire because it was time to let the younger teachers take over. If you can't do it* (retirement) *right, don't do it. You want to be sure to leave enough time to do some other fun things.* Pat smiled from ear to ear as she told us this.

Pat Shelley died in April 2007 at the age of 91 and we were very sad to see her go. Her funeral was a joyous celebration of life and she would have approved. We know she was smiling.

Job Performance

Many people expect a negative relationship between age and job performance; that is, they expect older adults to perform at a lower level in the workplace because they are more likely to have reduced strength, reduced sensory abilities, respond slower, and have reduced working memory capacity. Others expect a positive relationship. They expect older adults to perform at a higher level because they have more experience and knowledge. A major meta-analysis performed on the results from 96 different studies with over 38,000 workers, ranging in age from 17 to over 60, and employed in a large variety of jobs, found no overall relationship between age and job performance except for very young workers. Those in their early 20s performed better than those younger than that (McEvoy & Cascio, 1989). Does this mean that age and job performance are unrelated? The answer is that it depends on the skills involved in performing the job and the benefits of job experience.

Table 11-2 present a simplified version of this answer (Warr, 1994). The first column lists cases where the skills involved in a particular job do or do not decline with age. It is important to keep in mind that there may be skills that decline with age but play no role in the performance of a particular job. In cases like that, the decline in skills is irrelevant to job performance and the answer would be no; job skills do not decline (Westerholm & Kilbom, 1997). The second column asks whether performance improves with experience, specifically long-term experience. Nearly everyone performs a job better after doing it for a couple of weeks. Here, however, researchers are interested in whether years, or even

Many professional people continue working into old age.

TABLE 11-2   Effects of Experience and Age on Expected Productivity

Basic job skills decline with age?	Performance improves with experience?	Example of job skills or activities	Expected relation between age and productivity
Yes	Yes	Skilled manual work such as carpentry.	None; age decline is offset by experience.
Yes	No	Rapid processing of new, often unexpected information such as an air traffic controller.	Negative; older workers are less productive.
No	Yes	Making decisions based on knowledge such as a judge.	Positive; older workers are more productive.
No	No	Activities that depend on personality or social skills such as a host.	None; age and experience are not very important.

Source: Modified and reproduced by special permission of the Publisher, Consulting Psychologists Press, Inc., Palo Alto, CA, from *Handbook of Industrial and Organizational Psychology* by H. C. Triandis, M. D. Dunnette, and L. M. Hough, Eds. Copyright 1994 by Consulting Psychologists Press, Inc. All rights reserved. Further reproduction is prohibited without the Publisher's written consent.

decades, of experience still produce gains in performance. One benefit of experience may, of course, be that an experienced worker has found ways to compensate for declines in important skills; think back to discussions of expertise and of selective optimization with compensation in Chapter 8. The responses to these skills and experience questions give four different possibilities. If skills decline and extended experience is beneficial and, thus, offsets the decline, or if skills do not decline but there are no long-term benefits of experience, then we expect to find no relationship between age and job performance. A positive relationship is expected when job skills do not decline but experience is beneficial and a negative relationship is expected when job skills do decline but there are no long-term benefits of experience. If you conducted an analysis combining a large number of jobs, you are likely to find no overall relationship. For most jobs, there is no relationship while for the others, positive (older workers better) and negative (older workers worse) relationships would cancel each other out.

Of course, the relationship between worker age and performance is not quite this simple. The answers to questions regarding the decline of skills and the benefits of experience are not often simply yes or no. There are variations in how much the relevant skills decline and in how much benefit is derived from experience. These variations depend on specific jobs and the people who fill them. Hearing is a skill that plays an important role in many jobs but is far more important for a teacher than for an accountant. Long-term experience is probably of more benefit to a judge than to a dentist. Because of variations such as these, researchers have spent some time looking at very specific jobs. One such study examined the performance of fishers in Okinawa and hunters in Papua, New Guinea. Fishing and hunting are jobs that depend on good sensory skills, speed, muscle strength, and stamina and all of these skills tend to decline with age. At the same time, the experienced fisher and hunter is likely to know far more about the prey, its habits and habitat, and other important factors involved in fishing and hunting. Results showed that, on average, young fishers tended to make more money from their catch than old fishers but the most productive fisher was also the oldest at age 52. For hunters, those who were young and unmarried were the least successful even though they spent the most time at it. The most successful hunters were older and married (Ohtsuka, 1997).

One can think of a number of jobs that appear to be more difficult for older workers because of the physical and mental changes that frequently occur with advanced age. It is unusual to see a professional baseball player, basketball player, figure skater, football (or soccer) player, or gymnast who is over 40. Commercial airline pilots, firefighters, police officers, air traffic controllers, and those in the foreign service still are required to retire by age 65 although some researchers question the legitimacy of such a requirement (Landy, 1994). Close to 7 percent of older workers still are required to retire because of their age (Binstock & George, 1996). These jobs are ones for which the benefits of experience are not thought to offset the decline in skills that can occur with age.

Clearly the relationship between age and job performance is complex, usually nonexistent, at times negative, and at other times positive. Many corporations are aware of this and have devoted considerable effort to attract talented older workers. Table 11-3 is a list of some of these companies named by AARP (2003).

Learning New Procedures

Are older workers able to learn and remember new procedures as well as younger workers? You know the typical changes with age in sensation, perception, reaction time, working memory, and retrieval from episodic memory. We all know that changes in software occur continually and that even grocery stores rearrange where items are to be found. Perhaps older adults have more difficulty than younger adults in adjusting to changes in procedures at work. They may be harder to train. Management generally believes this but the research suggests that training differences depend more on factors other than age.

At the very outset, older workers often are reluctant to participate in training for fear that they will be unable to learn the new procedures or will not perform as well as younger trainees. Some desire separate training groups because of these fears while others do not want to be treated as some special group that needs extra care. Older workers are likely to

---

TABLE 11-3 Some Corporations that Actively Seek Older Workers

Baptist Health South Florida	Adecco Employment Services
Children's Health System	The Aerospace Corporation
Principal Financial Group	SSM Health Care–St. Louis
Bon Secours Richmond Health System	Deere & Company
The Ohio State University Medical Center	Volkswagen of America
Farmers Insurance Group of Companies	Lincoln Financial Group
Whirlpool Corporation	The MITRE Corporation

Source: AARP (2003).

have many of the same false beliefs that others have and so they expect to have difficulties with training (Plett, 1990). Older workers are far more willing to undergo training when they have experienced training previously and when the job continues to be interesting for them (Yeatts et al., 2000). Employers are, however, less likely to recommend or provide training for older workers. Training opportunities for workers 55 and older occur about one-third as often as those for younger workers (Erber & Danker, 1995; Simon, 1996). These negative expectations, on the part of workers as well as management, and the resulting fewer opportunities are important factors in training for older workers.

Once in training, older adults are sometimes slower, need more assistance, and make more mistakes when learning new computer skills than do younger adults (Charness & Bosman, 1992). Other work, however, has not found age differences in training (Garfein et al., 1988) and older workers perform better when certain training procedures are used. In teaching computer skills, such as a new word-processing program or spread sheet, the most effective techniques for younger and especially older learners are those that reduce the demands on working memory by modeling the new procedures and providing menus (Kelly et al., 1994). Older workers also learn to perform computer tasks quicker and perform better when specific goals are set during training. Goal setting is beneficial for a wide range of workers and students too (Hollis-Sawyer & Sterns, 1999). Once trained, older workers perform as well as younger workers when they return to their jobs.

Job Satisfaction

Are older workers less satisfied? Are they burned out and eager for retirement? Most older workers do look forward to retirement (Atchley, 1999) but are, at the same time, generally more satisfied with their jobs than are younger workers (Bernal et al., 1998; White & Spector, 1987). There are a number of possible reasons for this higher level of satisfaction. It may be that young workers have much higher expectations about their jobs than do older workers and when those expectations are not met, they feel dissatisfied. Older workers know from experience not to expect so much and so are more satisfied with much less— or it could be a cohort, rather than age difference. Younger cohort workers have had more experience with computers, cell phones, remote control, and other aspects of modern technology that may not always be present in the workplace. Older cohort workers may be satisfied with much less because they have had much less over the course of their lives. It is possible that it could be due to the fact that older workers have had decades to find the right niche for themselves and tend to have jobs that are comfortable and interesting for them and that they do well. Younger workers, particularly those at an entry level, have not yet found their place. As a result, they are less satisfied. Undoubtedly all of these factors play some role and, if burnout does occur for older workers, these factors seem to be sufficient to offset it so that average satisfaction for older workers is still quite high when compared to younger workers.

Job Discrimination

So why would you not want to hire a worker who is less likely to be injured or involved in an accident on the job, who is likely to be at work every day, who is as productive as any other worker, who can learn new procedures with good training, and who is satisfied with work? If you had workers like this, why would you ever want to get rid of them? The answer, all too frequently, is because they're OLD.

In 1967, the Age Discrimination in Employment Act (ADEA) was passed to protect workers 40 years of age and older from discrimination in hiring, training, dismissal, pay, promotions, retirement (amendment passed in 1986), and benefits (passed in 1990). The law applied to any place of employment with 20 or more employees. Such companies cannot refuse to hire or get rid of workers simply because they're old. In the early 1980s, there was a three-fold increase in the number of cases filed under ADEA and more than 5000 older workers were awarded close to $25 million (Atchley, 1996). In the early 1990s, the number of cases continued to increase but the number of prosecutions declined and many cases were settled out of court (Atchley, 2000). More recently, the number of cases declined and some recent court decisions have made it more difficult for older workers to demonstrate discrimination (Hannson et al., 1997; Ormsbee, 2001). Older workers are less willing to file a case when the odds of winning seem so low (Nicholson, 2000). Companies can afford to spend a lot of time and money to win while older workers have far less of each.

The odds of winning for an older worker have been influenced by decisions made by the courts and those decisions have, until quite recently, seemed to favor companies. For example, Supreme Court rulings suggest that high salaries and eligibility for pension benefits may be nondiscriminatory reasons for dismissing workers and, of course, workers with higher salaries and pension eligibility are typically older workers. The company can argue that such workers were dismissed because of budgetary constraints and not because they were older. In 2000, the court ruled that states were protected from lawsuits filed under the ADEA so older state workers could be fired simply because of age. Since then, state agencies are required to waive their immunity to suit or lose federal funding. In 2005, the Supreme Court ruled that older workers no longer had to prove intention to discriminate. If the impact of a company's actions had more of a negative impact on older than on younger workers, then such actions are not permitted. It is expected that this decision may lead to an increase in cases over the next several years.

Undoubtedly age discrimination occurs in spite of the law but it is difficult to determine its frequency. Older workers are more likely to be dismissed than younger workers, to have more difficulty finding a job once they have lost one, and to begin again at a significantly lower salary than comparable younger workers (Atchley, 2000; Barlett & Steele, 1992; Rix, 2004). Job loss for older workers is particularly high for women and minorities (Flippen & Tienda, 2000). When older workers are dismissed from their jobs, many begin consuming alcohol but typically not in excess (Gallo et al., 2001). One recent study found that older workers who lost their jobs, especially those with limited assets, developed depression and were still depressed 6 years after losing their jobs (Gallo et al., 2006). Companies not wishing to hire older workers can argue, however, that is was not the age of the applicant that made a difference but the outdated job search, resumé, and interview skills that cost the candidate the job. Older workers may take longer to find a job because they are generally less willing than younger workers to relocate and, thus, do not apply for jobs that would require a move. A lower starting salary often is attributed to outdated work skills—which may often be the case especially for older workers not given training opportunities in their prior job.

Companies also may try to influence older workers to leave of their own accord by moving them to another shift, reassigning them to smaller offices, not sending them on business trips as frequently as in the past, showing surprise when they show up for meetings, giving preferable parking spaces to younger employees, replacing requested vacation times with less-desirable ones, and so on. Such actions on the part of an employer cause many older workers to retire early or leave in hopes of finding another job. The chances of finding another job are not, however, high for older workers.

PROJECT **11**
Discrimination Against Older Workers

A major study that looked at discrimination against older workers recruited 142 younger business students (Rosen & Jerdee, 1976b). Students were asked to make decisions about workers in six different situations and in each of the six cases, some were led to believe that the worker was young while others were led to believe that the worker was old. Prior work showed that managers and students held the same typical stereotypes about older workers (see text for some of these stereotypes) in situations like those used in the study (Rosen & Jerdee, 1976a). The following are three of those situations:

- A shipping room employee who was hired only 3 months ago appears to be unresponsive to customer calls for service according to the foreman. How much difficulty is expected in getting the employee to improve and be more responsive?
- A candidate is up for possible promotion to a marketing job that requires "fresh solutions to challenging problems" and "a high degree of creative and innovative behavior." Should the candidate be promoted?
- A position is open that requires a person "who not only knows the field of finance but who is capable of making quick judgments under high risk." Should the applicant be hired?

In addition to receiving one of the three situations just described, participants also were told that the employee, candidate, or applicant was an older or a younger person and in some conditions a picture of an older or younger person accompanied the description.

For the first situation, 65 percent of the students recommended talking to a younger employee but 55 percent recommended replacing an older employee. For the second situation, 54 percent recommended promoting a younger candidate while only 24 percent recommended promoting an older candidate. For the third situation, 25 percent recommended hiring the younger applicant while only 13 percent recommeded hiring the older applicant. As discussed in the text, people tend to have negative views about the abilities of older workers.

For this project, use some of the situations described (or look at the other three from Rosen & Jerdee, 1976b) or write some of your own. In some cases, describe the individual in question as being younger and in other cases as being older. Ask people from different majors or careers and of different ages to make a decision and to explain the basis for their decision.

Did you find age discrimination? If so, were the reasons given for not helping, promoting, or hiring the older person the ones that you expected?

If you did not find age discrimination, could it have to do with the sample you used? Did you use business majors, psychology majors, sociology majors, or a mix of many different majors? Do you expect students in different majors, who have certainly taken many different courses, to have different views about the qualifications and abilities of older workers? What about those in different careers? What about people in different age groups? Why or why not?

In other cases, the encouragement to retire early is done more positively by providing incentives. Incentives are usually in the form of changes in the pension plan offered by the company. For retiring early, an older worker might be given extra years of credit. For example, if 30 years with the company are needed for full pension benefits and the worker only has 25, the five additional years might be purchased if the individual agrees to retire now. Administrators seem to expect, in spite of data to the contrary, that replacing older workers with younger workers will increase productivity. Employers may in some cases save money due to hiring new workers at lower salaries.

Transitions to Retirement.   Two common transitions to retirement from working full time are bridge (to retirement) jobs and retirement planning. Planning may be quite informal or may be through participation in some formal program.

A common belief is that most adults work at a job until age 65 and then retire. In fact, most workers do not fit this pattern. Quite a large number, anywhere between 42 and 78 percent, work at a different job or the same type of job for a different employer before retirement and after leaving their longest held job. These other jobs, **bridge jobs**, serve as a transition to full retirement. They particularly are sought by farm and nonfarm laborers who may need to find a less physically demanding job with the declines in muscle strength and sense organs that can occur in old age. These transition jobs also are sought by those who have been fired but who have not yet given up the search for a new job. The most likely workers to continue in a career job until retirement are professionals, although nearly half of them also find other employment before retiring (Cahill et al., 2006).

Bridge jobs frequently are lower pay and lower status jobs than the individual's longest held job. On average, individuals work at a bridge job for about 5 years before retiring. In many cases, bridge jobs are part-time jobs. Part-time work before retirement is often desired by older workers but can be hard to find. In one survey, 21 percent of older men and 54 percent of older women, still in a full-time job, expressed a strong desire to work part time if such work were available. These workers often expect to stop working before they wish to simply because part-time bridge jobs are fairly difficult to find; so many people want them and so few companies offer them. Over 50 percent of workers who have left their longest held job are employed part time; this trend is especially true for older women workers (Quinn & Kozy, 1996). A majority (57 percent) of professionals who have been employed in a bridge job before full retirement say that they enjoyed that job more than their career job even though the pay was lower (Ruhm, 1991).

It is easy to imagine why a part-time bridge job would be desirable before giving up work entirely. It is difficult to quit work, cold turkey, and plunge into retirement without some transition and a part-time bridge job fills that role nicely for a very large number of older adults. It is unfortunate that more companies do not offer such a transition to their older full-time employees instead of attempting to get rid of them altogether through early retirement incentives. Of course, from the company's point of view, it is expensive to allow older full-time workers to become part-time workers and still continue with full benefits.

Retirement planning, both formal and informal, is another type of transition to full retirement and most older workers do some informal planning as they approach retirement. One large survey of nearly 5000 workers between the ages of 51 and 61 found that 74 percent had a particular retirement date (age or year) in mind while only 12 percent had not yet thought about it; 13 percent believed they would never retire (Ekerdt et al., 2000). People who do less planning for retirement tend to be those who have very positive social relations at work and place high value on their work. One recent survey found that people who responded very positively to items such as "the people I work with are helpful and friendly" and "even if I didn't need the money, I would probably keep on working," were the least likely to be planning for retirement (Kosloski et al., 2001).

Informal retirement planning can, of course, take many different forms and can range from an individual doing some thinking about income after retirement to full family planning of finances, recreation, travel, and where to live after retirement. To assess informal planning among older workers living in a rural community, researchers surveyed 66 adults between the ages of 45 and 64. Participants were asked, among other things, to list retirement issues that were important to them and to list any actions they had taken regarding these important issues. More than half of those responding said that the most important issues were being able to share their experiences with others after they retired, knowing more about Social Security and financial benefits, learning how to adjust to the physical changes that would probably accompany old age, and finding ways to spend time with their children after retirement. In terms of actions taken, more than half had started saving money, determined beneficiaries for insurance, and selected an executor for their estate. Their informal planning had made them aware of the issues that were most important to them but they seemed to take action only on financial matters. Researchers found no gender, age, race, health, or education differences in this pattern of results. One reason for the lack of action on many important issues other than financial matters may be the

Older worker.

paucity of information about these issues (Glass & Flynn, 2000). Participants believe these other issues are very important but do not know how to deal with them or where to find assistance.

While informal planning occurs frequently, only about 5 to 10 percent of older workers participate in formal retirement planning programs. These participants generally have higher income and are more educated older male workers who have already done a fair amount of informal planning (AARP, 1986; Atchley, 2000). Formal programs are far more likely to be offered by larger places of employment and very unlikely in small places or self-employment settings. Even when such programs are offered, however, only about 10 percent of those invited to participate actually do participate (Campione, 1988). It also seems to be the case that the people who most need formal preparation are the least likely to get it. For example, lower income workers are likely to have lower income after retirement and might benefit from some form of financial planning well before retirement. Single people will receive less income from Social Security than married people after retirement. Women may receive less income and/or lose a husband after retirement (see Chapter 14). All of these groups are less likely to have access to formal retirement planning programs (Dennis, 1989; Perkins, 1992).

Formal retirement planning programs always address financial matters such as pension plans but only rarely cover some of the other topics that are important to older workers. To assess the value of formal programs and the importance of various topics that could be covered, 478 adults ranging in age from 50 to 84 and who had already retired were surveyed. The vast majority, 77 percent, thought such programs would be useful while only 5 percent thought they would not be useful (15 percent were not sure and 3 percent did not respond). Retired adults thought that financial information was very important but that information about leisure activities, traveling, creative endeavors, social participation, self-care, and psychological and physical well-being also were very important (Marcellini et al., 1997). The transition to retirement would be easier if more information about these other topics were provided although the information that is provided is helpful (Feldman, 2003). Figure 11-1 illustrates some of the issues that older workers and retirees would like to see included in preretirement planning programs.

People who participate in formal planning programs have done a fair amount of informal planning too. However, the reverse is not true because formal planning programs frequently are not available and when they are available frequently are not used. It could be that the obtained benefits of formal programs are, in fact, due to the informal planning that individuals do on their own. To assess the benefits of formal and informal planning, researchers examined 34 university faculty and staff before and after a formal retirement planning seminar. Results showed that both formal and informal planning were beneficial but in different ways. Both had benefits for participants' expectations about retirement. Informal planning, however, also increased self-efficacy. Self-efficacy, in this case, referred to the individual's confidence in successfully making the transition to retirement. The difference in benefits between the two types of planning is attributed to the belief that it takes longer to change self-efficacy and that informal planning usually goes on for an extended period of time (Taylor-Carter et al., 1997). Both formal and informal planning, particularly when important issues beyond the financial ones are a part of the planning, are beneficial in helping the transition to retirement.

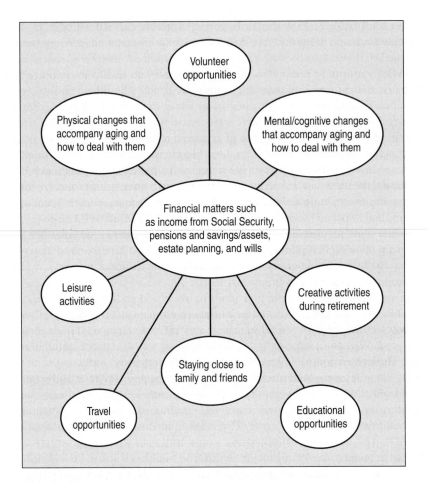

FIGURE 11-1   Some topics that older adults would like to see included in preretirement programs. The inner circle shows programs offered at present while the outer circles indicate kinds of topics that many older adults would like to have included.

Retirement

Retirement refers to a self-determined or voluntary withdrawal from work. Being fired or downsized is not retirement because it is not voluntary. If one is unable to find a new job after being downsized, becomes discouraged, and quits searching, that counts as retirement because quitting is self-determined. Such a retirement would, of course, be an unhappy one while most retirements are more pleasant.

Demographics of Retirement

Chancellor Otto von Bismarck of Germany first established 65 as the retirement age late in the nineteenth century by supplying a pension for people over that age. Of course, not many adults lived to be age 65 in the late nineteenth century so the cost of providing pensions was fairly low. Before the twentieth century in the United States, retirement was rare and short because there were no government financial supports for retired people and people did not live as long. In 1900, the average number of years spent in retirement was 1.2 and retired people were typically supported by their families. People usually retired because they could no longer work. When the U.S. Social Security Act was passed in 1935, it designated 65 as the age of retirement. A prime impetus for Social Security and retirement was to lower the number of people actively looking for a job during the years around the Great Depression in the 1930s (Atchley, 2000). Social Security created jobs for younger workers by vacating positions previously held by older workers. Since then, unemployment has become less of a problem and retirement has come to be an expected event in the lives of most workers and, generally, people look forward to it. It is a chance to share in the nation's wealth that you helped to create.

Who Retires and Why? Most people retire. About 84 percent of men retire by age 65 (Novak, 2006). The reasons for retirement or for remaining employed are many and varied. People who like their work and who are dedicated to their careers are likely to put off retirement. Such people most often are professionals. Social pressure from family and/or friends is another factor. If your spouse retires, he or she may put pressure on you to also retire so that you can spend more time together. Of course, your spouse might also pressure you to continue working. Your retired friends may want you to join them or your work friends may not want you to leave. Attitude is another factor. People who find the idea of retirement to be repugnant and believe retirement means boredom and the end of life also are likely to put it off. Nevertheless, the major reasons for retiring or continuing to work center on finances and health (Adams, 1999; Mutran et al., 1997).

Finances. People who believe they have sufficient funds are more likely to embrace retirement. A reason for continuing to work is that you cannot afford to retire (Parnes & Sommers, 1994). This is the case for many low-income workers who are frequently women and/or minorities. As you already know, such older workers also are more likely to be dismissed from their jobs and to have a difficult time finding another job. They often are forced to retire and research has shown that such forced retirement leads to depression and that, for women, the depression worsens as their husbands become more disabled. Interestingly, for those who retired when they wished, depressive symptoms were actually lower for those who provided care for a spouse (Szinovacz & Davey, 2004).

In one longitudinal examination of retirement, researchers found that those who still had financial responsibility for their children were far less likely to retire. Older men and women who saw their children infrequently went in opposite directions with respect to retirement. Women in this situation tended to remain working while men tended to retire in order to spend more time with their children (Szinovacz & De Viney, 2000). Part of this may be due to the fact that men generally have higher retirement income than do women. This will be discussed when we examine adjustment to retirement.

Health. If you become disabled, you may be forced to retire. This is far more likely for minorities because they are more likely to work as laborers and laborers have the highest rates of disability (Iams, 1986; Taylor & Doverspike, 2003). Studies of coal miners, plumbers, and construction workers have found very high levels of disability for those who work in wet conditions, use vibrating equipment, carry heavy loads, and are exposed to certain chemicals (aspartate transaminase) (Arndt et al., 1998; Calmels et al., 1998). The most common disabilities among other older workers are circulatory disorders, bone diseases like osteoporosis, and mental dysfunction (McCoy & Weems, 1989).

The ill health that leads to retirement is frequently not the ill health of the worker but of a parent or spouse. Becoming a caregiver for a spouse, and retiring as a result, is far more likely for women than men because older men are more likely to need such care (remember, wives are usually younger than husbands) and women of that older cohort are typically less likely to have careers (Savishinsky, 2000). Older men who need to care for a sick wife are also likely to retire (Szinovacz & De Viney, 2000).

Middle-aged adults are, of course, far more likely to be caring for a parent than a spouse and to continue working. A large proportion of women and nearly a quarter of men find themselves in this situation at one time or another and, some work suggests that the stress is greater for women. This situation is far more difficult for low-income workers who are unable to afford a visiting nurse or an adult day care center and who may lose their jobs by spending time caring for an ailing parent (Halpern, 2005). You can easily imagine that the stress for someone working while raising children and caring for a parent would be quite high. There are, however, some qualifications. A stressful job increases the negative effects of stress while caring for a parent, but a rewarding, well-liked job helps alleviate that stress (Lee & Phillips, 2006; Stephens & Townsend, 1997).

Most often, the relationship between stress at home and stress in the workplace leads to conflict and less satisfaction with life and this relationship has been examined a number of times (Ford et al., 2007). One recent study examined this relationship as a function of the type of disability experienced by the parent being cared for. Physical disabilities included sensory problems such as loss or partial loss of hearing and sight, chronic pain, respiratory difficulties, and incontinence; mental disabilities included mental illness and loss of memory. Loss of memory does not refer to the normal changes that occur with age (Chapter 7) but to more severe loss often as a result of dementia (Chapter 12). Results showed that hours spent at work had no overall effect on the stress level of those caring for a physically disabled parent but had a positive influence for those caring for a mentally disabled parent. Time away from the disabled parent and at work helped reduce the stress in this situation (Bainbridge et al., 2006).

When Do Most People Retire?   Although 65 was the established retirement age, people today retire much earlier. This trend toward earlier retirement has been occurring since 1970 in Germany, Japan, and Sweden, as well as the United States (Gendell, 1998). Only 24 percent of women and 44 percent of men still work full time after age 62, which is the lowest age at which one can receive Social Security benefits (Woodbury, 1999). After age 65, these percentages drop to 9 percent of women and 16 percent of men (Parnes & Sommers, 1994). The majority of people over age 62 get Social Security benefits and 75 percent of new recipients every year are retiring before age 65 (U.S. Bureau of the Census, 1992; U.S. Senate Special Committee on Aging, 1992). Because average life expectancy is now over 75, people who retire around age 60 can expect to spend about 15 years in retirement, or 20 percent of their life. A person who lives to be 100 may spend 40 years in retirement, or 40 percent of their life.

Although several factors play a role in the decision of when to retire, health and finances are the two reported most frequently (Fronstin, 1999). Some work suggests that health is a more influential factor in retirement decisions than are finances (Dwyer & Mitchell, 1999; Siddiqui, 1997). For men, cancer, diabetes, and heart attacks are the most frequent and serious health problems leading to early retirement while for women, hypertension is the leading health-related cause for early retirement (Colsher et al., 1988). Health problems account for 60 percent of retirements that occur before the individual is truly ready to retire (Ozawa & Law, 1992).

Married couples report that their spouses are major influences on the decision of when to retire. Men say their wives influenced their retirement mainly by discussing it with them while women say their husbands influenced their retirement by also retiring. Recently, however, many more women are naming financial planning as a major reason for their retirement and are less likely to retire simply because their husband retired. Close to half of 228 couples (43 percent when the man retired and 45 percent when the woman retired) agreed that the retired person's spouse had equal or more influence on the decision (Smith & Moen, 1998). This makes sense because the retirement of one person is certain to influence the life of their marriage partner. Couples almost always discuss retirement as it gets closer and much of the discussion revolves around finances. Both men and women show the highest levels of retirement at ages 62 and 65, which correspond to the ages at which one becomes eligible for Social Security (age 62) and eligible for full benefits (age 65) until recently (see Table 11-4) (Coile, 2003).

TABLE 11-4 Age at Which Retired Persons Receive Full Social Security Benefits

Year of Birth	Age for Full Benefits
1937 or earlier	65
1938	65 plus 2 months
1939	65 plus 4 months
1940	65 plus 6 months
1941	65 plus 8 months
1942	65 plus 10 months
1943–1954	66
1955	66 plus 2 months
1956	66 plus 4 months
1957	66 plus 6 months
1958	66 plus 8 months
1959	66 plus 10 months
1960 and later	67

Source: Information from the Social Security Administration (April 2007).

Where Do People Go when They Retire?   Do people who retire move to Arizona or Florida? A survey of adults age 55 and older found that 84 percent do not want to move (AARP, 1992a). Sometimes, however, people must consider the option of moving. Relocating to a new home, a retirement community, or some form of care facility is likely to be considered at two points, and retirement is the first. When a person retires, they no longer need to live close to work and may consider moving to a location that offers opportunities and housing that are unavailable in their present location. Most, however, do not move when they retire and continue to live in single-family homes in mixed age neighborhoods (Gibler et al., 1997). Those who do move (about 5 percent) often move into a smaller home. About half of these moves are in the same county while one quarter are to a different state (U.S. Bureau of the Census, 1994). The most frequent destinations for those who moved out of their home state were Florida, Arizona, Texas, and North Carolina (Cowper et al., 2000).

As people retire at an earlier age and families live at greater distances from one another than they once did, many believe that postretirement moves will increase. Retired people may move closer to family who were not nearby during their working years. If neither work nor family hold a retired couple to a specific location, then they may look for places that offer skiing, bike trails, or other outdoor activities. They may look for the lower living costs of a small town that is not too far from the part-time employment opportunities and culture of a big city (Howells, 1998). Box 11-1 provides some examples of popular places.

The second point at which movement may be considered is when one loses a spouse or because of serious illness (such as Alzheimer's disease) or disability (such as blindness) that requires family or professional assistance or institutionalization (Bogorad, 1987; Litwak & Longino, 1987). Moving to a retirement community is a likely option for people who experience a decrease in their ability to care for themselves and who live alone with no children living nearby (Silverstein & Zablotsky, 1996). There are many retirement communities and care facilities available for people who find themselves in such circumstances; these are examined in Chapter 13.

In countries less technologically advanced than the United States, Japan, or those in Europe, the pattern of retirement can be quite different than the pattern we have been examining. Box 11-3 describes some aspects of retirement in several of these places.

Phases of Retirement

There is a strong tendency for social science researchers to look for patterns of and regularities in human behavior when major life events occur. The most well-known description of phases of retirement is provided by Robert Atchley (2000; Atchley & Barusch, 2004), who is quick to point out that not all retired people go through these phases. Phases of retirement are only meant "to organize ideas about the issues people face in taking up, playing, and relinquishing the retirement role" (2000, p. 253). Brief case studies of retired people in these phases are presented in Box 11-2.

The first phase is referred to as **preretirement** and has two components, remote and near. People in the **remote** phase are still a long way from retiring but have begun to lay plans for the future. They may, for example, look for a place of employment that has a bet-

BOX **11-1**

Some Top Retirement Locations

We consulted several sources in a search for some of the top retirement locations in the United States. The following are among those thought to be the best.

Bloomington, IN. This is a small friendly community with Indiana University offering cultural events nearly every night. The town is surrounded by gentle hills and many homes are reasonably priced.

Columbia, MO. Four universities are located here and offer ample culture and sports. The city is big enough to offer many of the opportunities of larger cities without a high crime rate.

Holland, MI. This small town is located on an inland lake with beaches. In the winter both sidewalks and streets are heated to melt snow.

Hot Springs, AK. This small town is in the foothills of the Ozark Mountains and numerous recreational opportunities, including a real hot spring, are available.

Prescott, AZ. A small town near the Prescott National Forest with innumerable hiking trails and six golf courses.

Punta Gorda, FL. Sandy beaches and year-long warm climate make this town attractive. More than one-third of the population is 65 and older.

St. Simon Island, GA. This town is filled with local artists and sandy beaches. There is, of course, some risk of hurricanes.

University Triangle, NC. Three major universities are located here and offer many cultural and sporting events and part-time job opportunities.

Walla Walla, WA. This small town attracts a number of retired wine connoisseurs and urban refugees. Three nearby colleges provide educational opportunities in this peaceful community.

Williamsburg, VA. This eighteenth-century colonial town allows one to savor history before heading to one of 15 twenty-first-century golf courses.

Many other places also welcome retirees. Some of the best are Gardnerville Ranchos, NV; Crossville, TN; Del Rio, TX; Georgetown, SC; Ocean Pines, MD; Brookings, OR; Silver City, NM; and Seaford, DE.

Sources: John Howells (1998). *Consumers Digest*; www.bizjournals.com/specials/pages/63.html; and http://money.cnn.com/2000/06/09/senior_living/q_retire_places/. Accessed September 10, 2007.

ter pension plan, invest money for the future, or spend a vacation checking out possible retirement locations (like those in Box 11-1). It is advantageous to begin saving for retirement while you are still young and the remote phase is when that is done, although too many people do not think that far ahead or have any funds to set aside. The **near** phase is shortly before retirement when one begins informing bosses or supervisors, submits a formal letter of retirement, fills out the necessary forms for Social Security, or even trains a new person to take over. Between remote and near phases, workers frequently begin to view their work as far less positive than they did previously and to see it as a source of fatigue or even tension (Ekerdt & DeViney, 1993).

The second phase is the **honeymoon**. Immediately after retirement, many retirees experience an elevated mood. One no longer has to go to work and may feel truly free

Older retirees.

for the first time in a long time. You can set your alarm clock to get up for work and when it goes off, press the button, chuckle, and return to sleep. This is the chance to catch up on that list of chores that need to be done like painting the bathroom, fixing the screen door, and installing that new ceiling fan or to do some things that you've never done before like traveling to the Grand Canyon or starting a garden. The honeymoon phase often is characterized by a flurry of activity while at other times it's more of a rest-and-relaxation phase. It can be a chance to do very little physical activity and spend a lot of time reading. This type of honeymoon phase ordinarily ends when one becomes restless and needs more to do while the more active type of honeymoon ends as people realize they don't have enough money to travel the world and/or they seek a more structured environment (Atchley, 1982). A study of retired women professionals found that, after some time, they needed to reestablish some order in their lives and were most satisfied when they remained active and were able to use the skills they had previously used at work (Price, 2003).

The third phase is the **retirement routine**. The honeymoon is over and the initial flurry of activity calms down or the rest and relaxation becomes more active. It takes some time to find the right routine and initially retired individuals or couples will make several modifications but eventually settle into a regular schedule. They may get up at the same time every morning, have regular daytime activities such as exercise and chores, or activities every few days or a couple of times a week such as shopping, or once a month activities such as an outing or tour. They may do certain chores like cleaning, laundry, or

---

BOX **11-2**

People in Different Phases of Retirement

Ruth is in the **preretirement** phase as she has recently increased her contributions to her savings plan at work. She also is considering switching jobs to get a higher salary for 10 to 15 years before retirement or working an extra weekend shift to boost her salary before retirement. Work hard now to have more to enjoy later.

Pat is a 64-year-old retired dentist who seems to be in the **honeymoon phase**. He and Jeanne, his retired spouse, have enrolled in a literature class at the university. Class begins when they return from a 3-week tour of Europe. Pat and Jeanne take tennis lessons at a local health club. Pat says, "Now I can do all those things that I've waited for years, no decades, to do; we've never felt so alive and haven't been this happy since our first honeymoon, 42 years ago.

Miranda is a 66-year-old retired manager who currently is in the **rest-and-relaxation phase**. She worked over 40 hours a week in a high-stress position and is simply tired. After Miranda retired, she terminated her membership in a health club and spends most of her time at home. Fellow workers bought her a new bicycle as a retirement gift 6 months ago but she has not used it.

Janine is a 59-year-old retired accountant who never made any retirement plans. She left work after becoming dissatisfied with her chances for promotion and the relatively low salary increases she was receiving year after year. Now she cannot find anything to do that she enjoys and all of her friends are still employed. She wishes she had stuck it out, at least for a few more years. Retirement is the biggest mistake she ever made. She is in the **disenchantment phase**.

George and Peggy are both 72 and have been retired for several years. They are in the **retirement routine phase**. Every morning they get up at 8:00, have a relaxed breakfast, and then go for a walk around the nearby park. When they return, George reads the morning paper while Peggy wraps herself in a novel. Lunch is at noon and then they each work on chores for a few hours. Every Monday afternoon they go out to a movie, Tuesdays are for their favorite TV shows, Wednesday is the day for bridge with friends, Thursdays are when each plays poker with their own friends, Fridays are for resting at home, Saturdays are for bingo at the church, and Sundays are for church and catching up with family.

Allen is a 61-year-old retired man who is in the **termination phase**. He is looking for a new job because he needs to make more money before he can retire in the way he hoped he would be able to once he turned 60. After applying for a number of jobs and having two interviews, he finally landed a position last week. He'll make less than he used to and plans on only working for a few more years to build up his savings before retiring again.

---

gardening at a regular time on certain days; get together with family or friends on a regular schedule; attend religious services at the same time every week; watch the same TV shows and go to bed after the evening news. Such a routine can be very comfortable and typically changes little unless or until some other major life change, such as loss of a spouse or serious illness, occurs.

A fourth phase, experienced only by some, is **disenchantment**, which may come before or after a routine has been reached. One may find that their hopes and plans for retirement may have been unrealistic and the reality of their situation and the inability to do all the things they had hoped to do may lead to mild or even major depression. One's plans may be dashed if one becomes disabled or loses a spouse or if available funds are insufficient to finance all the activities dreamed of in the years preceding retirement. A retired person may find that they have nothing to do and that life has become uninteresting without work. However, it is thought that very few retirees actually experience disenchantment. In one longitudinal study, over 300 people were followed from 1975 to 1995 and not one experienced a disenchantment phase following retirement (Atchley, 1999).

A fifth phase is referred to as **termination** and may occur with or without disenchantment. This occurs when the individual returns to work which is, as you know, difficult because jobs for older workers are hard to find. When a retiree returns to work, this is often referred to as **revolving retirement** because most will again retire at a later date. The return to work may have been prompted by disenchantment or by the need for additional funds. It is estimated that about 13 percent of retirees terminate their retirements at least once (Francese, 2004). These five phases of retirement clearly relate to how well one is adjusting to retirement and that adjustment depends on several factors. Adjustment to retirement in other cultures may, however, be quite different than in the United States and Box 11-3 gives a sample of adjustment in other places.

Adjustment to Retirement

Adjustment to retirement is generally very positive for the majority of older adults (Rosenkoetter & Garris, 1998). People tend to look forward to retirement even though they anticipate less income; most people are prepared and have gone through informal, if not formal, planning; and, disenchantment is rare. Worries about retirement and even about broader issues, such as global warming, the numbers of homeless people, and the corruption in government, are generally lower for retired people than for those still working and higher for women than men (Skarborn & Nicki, 2000). The major factors influencing adjustment to retirement and consequent life satisfaction are finances, health, social support, and activity level.

Financial Adjustment. Those who have good income after retirement have better financial adjustment to retirement than those with poor income. Income during retirement is traditionally described as a *three-legged stool*. One leg stands for income from Social Security, one for retirement pensions, and one for personal savings and assets (Gale, 1997).

Economists and financial planners say that an individual's preretirement standard of living can be maintained after retirement as long as the three-legged stool replaces at least 60 percent of preretirement income (Atchley, 1997). After retirement, less income is needed to maintain the same standard that the person had while working. With more leisure time, the retiree can perform tasks that others may have been paid to do in the past; there are fewer people living at home and needing support; expenses are lower (there is no longer a need to maintain a wardrobe for work); often the mortgage is paid off; there are no payroll taxes; and income tax is lower (Gale, 1997). In cases where medical expenses, housing, or transportation costs may be higher than normal, one may need 70 to 80 percent (or more) of preretirement income to maintain the same standard of living.

The first leg of the three-legged stool, **Social Security**, is received by about 95 percent of retired people (AARP, 1994) and replaces, on average, about 44 percent of pre-

B O X **11-3**

Cultural Differences in Retirement

Retirement in fully developed countries such as the United States is the type with which most of us are familiar. In less-developed countries, retirement frequently does not exist as an official time of life and, when it does exist is very different.

One examination of cultural differences involved older adults in Botswana, Ireland, and Hong Kong and compared retirement in these places to that in the United States (Keith et al., 1994). Retirement was viewed and experienced differently in the four countries. In Botswana, the typical physical changes of aging seem to occur earlier and are more obvious. Most work is hard labor which takes a toll on workers sooner than the less-demanding jobs frequently found in other parts of the world. Furthermore, there are fewer opportunities to obtain hearing aids, false teeth, and other assistive devices to maintain functioning or the appearance of youth. Adults retire when they can no longer work but generally remain active in their families. In Zimbabwe, many older adults are very poor and must live in special housing provided by church groups. This housing can be very restrictive or function more like a coop. Coop arrangements are generally preferred (Holmes & Holmes, 1995). In Clifden, Ireland, adults are generally self-employed or work at farming or fishing. Here people never really retire; they simply work less as they grow older and begin to receive a pension to assist them in meeting their needs. In Hong Kong a retired person is an older person who is unable to find or continue steady work and many older adults are unable to find any work at all. Pensions are small and most older retired adults must rely on their children for housing and support. Community homes for older adults in Hong Kong often are crowded and older residents sometimes cease writing to relatives believing it would be better to be thought of as dead than as a resident of one of these old age homes (Holmes & Holmes, 1995). Retirement has more negative connotations in these other cultures. Patterns of retirement in the United States are similar to these places in some ways but different in many others.

Another study examined retirement in Chile, the Dominican Republic, Sri Lanka, and Thailand (Kaiser, 1993). Older adults in all of these countries still were actively involved in domestic activities. The most frequently named domestic activity in Chile and Sri Lanka was household cleaning while in the Dominican Republic it was food preparation and in Thailand it was child care. The most frequently reported source of retirement income was a pension in Chile; retired adults in the other three countries named their children as their primary source of income. In all four countries, retired adults listed finances as their major problem and health was a close second. Their concerns are similar to retired adults in the United States.

retirement income (National Academy on Aging, 1994). You must be 62 years of age to begin receiving partial benefits and, once you have started receiving partial benefits, you can never receive full benefits. The age at which you can retire and receive full benefits depends upon your year of birth and is shown in Table 11-4. If you work beyond your full benefit age without electing to receive Social Security, then your benefits increase from 4.5 percent to 8 percent depending on your year of birth. Social Security benefits are based on average earnings during an individual's working years and are paid at a higher percentage for lower income workers. Although this may seem unfair at first, it makes sense if you think about it. People with higher incomes are able to put more of their income into savings and are more likely to have jobs providing pensions while those with lower incomes have little or no money left for savings. Those with low incomes need more money from Social Security after retirement just to meet the basic costs of living.

It is also important to understand that the Social Security funds received by retired adults come from taxes on current working adults and not from funds contributed over the decades by those now retired. As the number of retired adults increases with the aging of the baby boom generation, many fear that Social Security will have insufficient funds from workers to provide for all the retired adults. In 1970, there were 410 working adults for every 100 retirees; in 1980 the number of working adults per 100 retirees was 320, and in 2025, it is expected that there will be only 200 workers for every 100 retirees. In spite of this, many believe that Social Security will have no problem meeting the needs of these retirees (Rosenblatt, 1999). Three possible solutions often are proposed. One is, of course, to raise Social Security taxes so that each worker is contributing more to the fund for retirees. As you might imagine, this is not a very popular solution. A second suggestion is to privatize some proportion of Social Security and/or to invest a portion in the stock market. Although some prefer this solution, others regard the fluctuations of the market as too risky a place to invest U.S. senior's financial well-being. A third solution is to eliminate the cap on wages taxed for Social Security. Currently people making more than the cap pay no Social Security taxes on money earned over that cap. The cap goes up every year and was $90,000 in 2005, $94,200 in 2006, and $97,500 in 2007. All wages at or under the cap are taxed for Social Security while every dollar over the cap is not. Many argue that eliminating the cap would greatly boost the funds available for Social Security because those making more would pay more. Some believe that this solution has no chance of being implemented because all of our lawmakers make well over the cap and would not like to have their taxes increased. What do you think? Are there any other solutions?

The second leg, **pensions**, replaces about 25 to 30 percent of preretirement income (Gale et al., 1997). About 90 percent of federal, state, or local government workers and 50 percent of private company workers have pension plans available to them. To be eligible for benefits, however, one must work for a required number of years and/or reach a certain age before retiring. Most pension plans do not include any cost-of-living increases after retirement and so the income received remains the same regardless of inflation. Over the last several years, more companies have eliminated pension plans or changed them from defined benefit to defined contribution plans. A defined benefit plan pays a certain amount for workers who have put in the necessary years while the amount received from a contribution plan depends on how much is contributed. To receive the benefits you want, you may have to work a few more years with a contribution than with a benefit plan (Novak, 2006). Some recent work shows that many older adults who have earned pensions have not claimed them. Close to $133 million in pensions benefits are currently waiting for retired adults to apply. For example, estimates suggest that in New York there are $37.49 million in pension benefits owed to 6885 people who have not, for some reason, claimed those benefits. It is thought that many retirees lose track of contributions made to benefit plans early in their careers (Associated Press, 2007).

The third leg is **savings** and **assets**. About two-thirds of retired adults have some savings and assets but income from these assets is less than $500 a year for a quarter of these people and over $5000 for only a third (Radner, 1991). The proportion of preretirement income based on saving and assets is, thus, quite variable.

The biggest asset for most retired people is their home, which may comprise almost half of their net worth (National Academy on Aging, 1994). About 76 percent of older, retired people own their home or are close to paying off their mortgage. Of course, home repairs, utilities, and property taxes are continual expenses for home owners and must be paid from Social Security and pensions. Home equity counts as a major portion of the assets of older adults but is not income that can be used to pay expenses.

If you have Social Security, and the vast majority do, plus a pension and income from assets, perhaps in the form of stocks or long-term investments, then your retirement income is likely to be more than enough to maintain your standard of living. If you do not, but have at least some income from pension or assets, you will probably be fine. If you have no pension or income from your assets but can find a part-time job to supplement your income from social security, then you may also be able to maintain a good standard of living. If you must rely exclusively on Social Security, then your standard of living will decline and you may find it very difficult to pay your bills, particularly if you have one or more medical conditions. This latter situation is more often the case for women and minorities (AARP, 2004a).

Gender and ethnic group financial differences at retirement stem from gender and ethnic group differences at work. Although women have made great advances in the workplace and more women work now than they did 25 years ago, the gender difference still exists. At every age, a greater proportion of men than women are employed (U.S. Bureau of the Census, 1997). Women who are working make less, on average, than working men and tend to be in lower level jobs. Look at the most frequent jobs for men and women shown in Table 11-1. Over 90 percent of the top management positions are held by white men (Riekse & Holstege, 1996). Women are more likely than men to retire involuntarily or to discontinue work at one or more times during their careers as they give birth (perhaps more than once) or leave to care for an aging parent. Workers caring for an older parent are more likely to have difficulties sleeping, frequent headaches, increased anxiety, and be absent from work (Lee, 1997). Both time away from work and changing jobs reduce the opportunity to invest funds in retirement pension plans. Income from pensions following retirement is the largest single gender difference. The pensions of retired women are, on average, only about 60 percent as large as the pensions of retired men and many more men receive pensions than do women (Belgrave, 1988; O'Grady-LeShane, 1996). Furthermore, only about 25 percent of women over the age of 65 receive a pension from a former employer and the median income from a pension is less than $5000 compared to a median of nearly $8000 for men (Richardson, 1999). Largely as a result of these gender differences, many more women than men seek part-time work during retirement. It is estimated that over 60 percent of retired women over the age of 75 work part time (Rix, 2004). It is expected that these gender differences will diminish but not disappear as today's working women reach retirement age. Many more women are employed now than in the past and close to one-third are covered by plans that allow them to designate how their pension funds are invested (compared to about 40 percent of working men) (Sundén & Surette, 1998). Surveys of working women indicate that they are less likely than older cohorts to rely exclusively on their husband's retirement benefits and more likely to evaluate their own earned benefits (Honig, 1998). At the same time, men are more likely than women to plan for retirement in terms of finances and lifestyle factors. It is estimated that over 70 percent of working women have not planned for retirement (Meinecke & Parker, 1997). Fewer women than men, regardless of hours at work, receive retirement information (Onyx, 1998). Married retired couples have higher income than single retired adults. Women are more likely to be single in old age than are men because women live longer than men. About 15 percent of older women but only 8 percent of older men are below the poverty level (AARP, 1994). Women who are also African or Hispanic Americans are doubly disadvantaged. Only 4 percent of white older couples are below the poverty line while 18 percent of African and 22 percent of Hispanic American couples are below that line. For singles, especially women, the rates are much higher. The poverty rates for single white, African, and Hispanic retired men are 14, 48, and 44 percent, respectively. Those rates for single white, African, and Hispanic American women are 26, 61, and 59 percent, respectively (Choi, 1997).

Older African and Hispanic American workers, of either gender, are more likely to be forced into involuntary retirement than are older white American workers (Flippen & Tienda, 2000). This occurs as they are more likely to lose their jobs and then be unable to find new jobs (Choi, 1997). Even for those fortunate enough to keep their job until retirement, African and Hispanic American men earn, on average, only about 60 percent as much as white American men (Hogan et al., 1997). They have had far less money and opportunity to invest in pension programs or savings and assets by the time they reach retirement. The income gap is even larger in retirement than it is in the working years.

Table 11-5 shows average annual income for retired minority and white Americans from Social Security, pensions, and assets. These data were gathered from 3422 married men and show that white Americans earn more in every category but that the biggest gap is in earnings from assets. Social Security earnings by minorities are 72 percent of white American earnings; minority earnings from pensions are 62 percent of white Americans; but minority earnings from assets are only 15 percent of white Americans. Other work shows that for white Americans, 19 percent of total retirement income comes from assets while for African and Hispanic Americans the percentage from assets is only four and seven percent, respectively (Choi, 1997). Although all Americans showed increased income over the last 30 years, the increases were greater for white Americans. Minority Americans have had difficulty acquiring assets to boost their retirement income and to pass on to their children and grandchildren (Hogan, Kim, & Perrucci, 1997).

TABLE 11-5   Average Income for Retired Men from Social Security, Pensions, and Assets

Racial Group	Average Income from		
	Social Security	Pensions	Assets
White Americans	$8767	$3984	$5596
African and Hispanic Americans	$6300	$2491	$ 825

Source: Data from Hogan et al. (1997).

Members of a minority group are said to experience *double jeopardy*. Women and members of minorities have less opportunity to begin or to build up an adequate pension for retirement. This is due to discontinous work, lower pay, and lower status jobs. Older African American women are more likely than any other group to work in cleaning or cooking jobs in private households. Such jobs rarely pay much or offer opportunities to invest a portion of earnings in retirement plans and rarely offer benefits such as health insurance (Rieske & Holstege, 1996). For such disadvantaged workers, retirement may hold no benefits. Such individuals may be forced to work until they can work no longer.

Will the retirement picture get better for minorities and women who work through the twenty-first century and as baby boomers begin to retire? The current differences in retirement finances are expected to diminish as differences in workplace diminish and availability of pensions increase but it will take time before equality is the norm.

Health and Life Satisfaction. Researchers examining health among older adults have generally found lower stress levels among the retired than among those still working (Midanik et al., 1995). In one longitudinal study of satisfaction with retirement, 117 men were followed from preretirement to 7 years after retirement. Researchers measured relief from distress that people felt, energy level, financial and interpersonal satisfaction, feelings of being in control, and overall satisfaction with life. All measures showed an increase after retirement and peaked at about 1 year. After 7 years of retirement, most measures decreased but not as low as they were at preretirement. With retirement, people experienced a gain in perceived control over the events in their lives (Gall et al., 1997). Other work found the same general pattern after retirement although some cross-sectional comparisons have found lower perceived control (Ross & Drentea, 1998).

Of course, the adjustment to retirement is more difficult for those who are forced to retire or who do so for reasons of health or disability (Lehr et al., 1998). Comparisons of measures of distress between those who retire voluntarily and those who retire for health reasons or because they were let go show higher levels of distress, anxiety, and depression among the latter (Sharpley & Layton, 1998; Gallo et al., 2000). Those who retire involuntarily show lower levels of life satisfaction (Schultz et al., 1998).

An old myth that is incorrect is that retirement increases stress and leads to poor health. Retirees were once thought to deteriorate rapidly. Findings like those described show that there is less stress following retirement. Retirement does not lead to poor health but poor health often leads to retirement. Retired people generally do not report a decline in their health but often report increased concern about maintaining the good health that they have (Mein et al., 1998). Good psychological resources before retirement, such as high self-efficacy and good social support, facilitate a successful adjustment to retirement. Improvements in healthy behaviors, such as eating better and exercising more, result from such resources and increase following retirement (Midanik et al., 1995; Wells & Kendig, 1999).

Social Support. It is likely that when you stop going to work every day, your contacts with friends from work will diminish. One might expect to find a lower level of social support for retired people than for people still on the job. Generally, contacts with friends from work do seem to decline with retirement but the quality of friendships and contact with close friends does not (Bossé et al., 1993). Retirement may affect some members of the individual's social network but family and close friends are unaffected. The support of close family members and the worldview of family members are important factors in adjustment to retirement. Families with a strong, positive outlook are better able to deal with potential problems and the social support they provide enables the retiree to succeed in overcoming unforeseen difficulties (Smith, 1997). Some retired people move to retirement communities and lose contact with friends outside of that community. Research shows that those who move to these communities, but maintain close contact with friends outside the retirement community, maintain better mental health and show less depression (Potts, 1997). Losing contact by moving to a retirement community can decrease social support from persons in the inner circles (family members and close friends) and result in a greater number of difficulties. Thus, positive social support, which comes mainly from the closest members of a social support network, is not influenced by retirement but may be influenced by a move away from home following retirement. Perhaps that is one reason why so few people move after retiring.

For a married adult, a prime source of social support is the spouse and this is especially true for men (see Chapter 10). Before retirement, couples frequently worry about the effects that retirement will have on the quality of their marriage and are often more concerned about those effects than about income and health (Hilbourne, 1999). Research, however, indicates that the quality of married life and overall marital satisfaction does not decline when individuals retire and may, in some instances, improve (Vinick & Ekerdt, 1989). Retired couples have fewer complaints than preretirement couples (Kulik, 2001). After retirement, married couples have more time to spend together. Married retirees tend to spend more time doing the household tasks that they did before retirement and to help their partner more with her or his tasks (Kulik, 2001; Szinovacz, 2000). A closeness that may have diminished in the childrearing years may be renewed. Next to the early years of a marriage, the retirement years frequently are reported to be the happiest of all (Rieske & Holstege, 1996).

Activity.   To feel good about yourself and to adjust well to retirement, it may be important to stay busy. The work ethic places a high value on being a productive worker and it has been suggested that we resolve the conflict between retirement and this work ethic by adopting a **busy ethic**. Retired people who stay busy still are regarded as valuable members of society even though they are no longer productive workers (Ekerdt, 1986). Staying busy in retirement refers to a number of different kinds of activities including everyday tasks, travel, education, and volunteer work.

Everyday tasks consume a major share of the busy time of retirees. In a telephone survey of 2592 people, retirees and workers were asked about their typical activities. When retirees were asked what activities they participate in during the day, about 50 percent reported engaging in household chores and family care tasks such as cooking, cleaning, and laundry. Also mentioned was serving as a sitter for grandchildren or as a caregiver for an older relative or spouse. Leisure activities were named by 21 percent and included watching TV, playing golf, walking, playing cards, and visiting friends. These activities are probably closer to what you might expect to find retired people doing. Close to 12 percent reported activities that maintained the house and/or yard and 8 percent did unpaid work for a family business. The activities of retirees involved far less problem solving than the activities of those still working and retirees did not have higher levels of stress (Ross & Drentea, 1998). Other studies found that the most common activities for retirees are reading, watching TV, walking, playing games, arts and crafts, visiting, gardening, traveling, touring, and participating in club events (Roadberg, 1981).

Travel is one form of busy activity and some work shows that the perceived opportunity for travel is one factor that pulls people toward retirement (Shultz et al., 1998). In one survey of still working and retired professors, more than 30 percent listed travel as a planned or as an ongoing activity. Said one retired professor about the difference between his life after retirement and before, "A lot more travel, that's one thing we never had time to do. . . . So, travel with my wife and too, my family, has been the most significant change" (Dorfman & Kolarik, 2005). In another survey, retired men and women were asked what activities they engaged in right after retiring and the most frequent response, given by 21 percent, was travel. When asked what activities they engaged in over the 5 years immediately following their retirement and what activities they would engage in over their next 5 years, travel was the most frequent response to both questions. Travel was associated with more happiness and, as you might guess, with finances; those with higher income traveled more (Staats & Poerfelice, 2003). Nevertheless, some travel is a part of the activities of a great many retirees who may simply take day trips or drive relatively short distances often to visit close members of their social support network.

Some retirees wish they had spent more time in school or completed higher levels of **education**. Retired adults who want to further their education often attend classes at nearby community colleges, 4-year colleges, and universities. Many of these places offer older adults the opportunity to audit classes. Classes that attract the greatest numbers of retired adults are in arts and crafts, literacy training, computers, humanities and social sciences, performing arts, career counseling, and exercise (Atchley, 2000).

There are also educational opportunities outside of the traditional school settings. Shepherd's Centers across the country offer numerous adult education classes on a wide variety of topics. Elder Hostel offers many classes in a variety of settings in the United States and abroad. In the United States and Canada, there are now over 200 separate institutes that cater to retirees and specialize in peer-led learning where students are actively involved in group learning activities (Linnehan & Naturale, 1998).

A fourth way of keeping busy is to serve as a **volunteer** and it has been estimated that close to 40 percent of retired adults are actively involved in volunteer work (Janicki & Ansello, 2000). These volunteers play an important part in the lives of children, adolescents, and adults of all ages as they work in hospitals, schools, and care centers. Surveys of isolated older adults have shown that they benefit greatly from visits and support from retired volunteers (Cheung & Ngan, 2000). The range of volunteer activities is quite large and includes many unusual activities such as writing parking tickets (Zaslow, 2003) and, in Mexico City, wearing sensors to monitor air pollution (Rosenberg & Letrero, 2006). Bank of America, IBM, and General Electric have set up community service programs that are primarily run by retirees from these corporations. Some of the major organizations sponsoring volunteer activities are shown in Table 11-6. A number of cross-sectional studies have found health, longevity, social, and self-esteem benefits for volunteers although it

TABLE 11-6   A Selection of National Volunteer Organizations for Retired Adults

Program	Description
Foster grandparent program	Low-income older adults receive wages for providing support for children who have disabilities.
Retired senior volunteer program	Volunteers over 60 years of age serve as tutors, counselors, and caregivers for children, adolescents, or all age adults.
Senior companion program	Low-income older adults receive wages for helping other older adults who are vulnerable and frail.
Service Corps of Retired Executives (SCORE)	Retired business people offer help to community organizations and small businesses with management problems.
Corporation for National Service	Addresses educational, public safety, and environmental needs.
Volunteers in Service to America (VISTA) and Americorp	Volunteers of any adult age commit at least 1 year to aid the handicapped, homeless, jobless, hungry, or illiterate.

SOCIAL POLICY APPLICATIONS

There has been much discussion about changing retirement and security programs to better meet the needs of older persons. We talked a little about financial support for retired persons and saw that one leg of the three-legged stool, Social Security, is there for the vast majority while the other two legs (pensions and savings/assets) are not. We also saw that Social Security was not meant to be the only support a retired person would have but that, all too often, that is the case. Are there ways to support retired persons without changing Social Security? Many have suggested that policies to enhance working and employment would better meet the needs of today's older adults. Policy changes that have been recommended (by international groups interestingly) include providing financial incentives to keep working and eliminating subsidizing early retirement, employers must have stronger incentives to hire and retain older workers, older workers must be given comprehensive support to retain employability, and, as noted, attitudes toward older workers must improve. On a different track, some suggest that cooperatives might be set up in every community and retired adults could live at such a coop and pay their way by working 20 hours a week caring for less able persons, cleaning, cooking, providing transportation, doing repairs, and so on. Each coop might elect a board of directors that would include representatives from the local city/county government. Coops might be supported by grants from charitable organizations or even AARP in addition to some government funding. Many older adults already choose to live in settings populated exclusively by other older adults and this would be not much different except that those living there would have to work there. One concern is that many frail persons would not be able to take advantage of this option and people who are poor are more likely to be frail. Can you think of a way around this last dilemma so that a coop would be accessible by all? Would there be tasks that even frail persons could provide? Do you think your parents or grandparents would want to live in such a coop? Why or why not?

is not clear whether the volunteering actually led to the benefits or whether healthy and social people are simply more likely to volunteer (Celdrán & Villar, 2007; Young & Glasgow, 1998).

CHAPTER HIGHLIGHTS

- Older workers often are viewed negatively by employers but research shows that such views are mistaken.
- Older workers have fewer injuries and accidents than do younger workers. Time away from work following an accident often is longer for older workers but a large part of this is management's expectation that older adults need longer to heal.
- Older adults in most jobs perform as well as younger adults. Job performance does not always depend on the physical abilities that may decline with age and, in many cases, job experience offsets any declines.
- Older workers are given fewer training opportunities and often avoid such opportunities when given. Older workers can benefit from effective training that reduces demands on working memory and sets specific goals.
- Older workers generally are more satisfied with their jobs than are younger workers, perhaps because they have found the job that is best suited for their abilities and interests.
- In spite of all of these data on older workers, age discrimination in the workplace occurs frequently. The ADEA bars such discrimination and several formal complaints and prosecutions have taken place.
- Suits brought by older workers under the ADEA declined in the 1990s but are expected to rise again since intentional discrimination need no longer be proven.
- Both positive (lowering the age required to receive full pension benefits) and negative (transfer to the night shift) techniques are used to encourage early retirement for older workers.
- Workers preparing to retire frequently seek a bridge job after leaving their longest place of employment. Part-time bridge jobs are attractive but difficult to find.
- Most people do informal planning before retiring but few people do formal planning, which is less available to women and members of minority groups. Many of the topics that people would like to learn about in formal planning sessions are not included although financial matters are always included.
- Most people choose to retire. For others, retirement is a result of poor health or disability. Those who delay retirement are more likely to be professionals or people who expect less retirement income.
- The decision on when to retire is influenced by finances, health, job satisfaction, spouse, and friends. The factors that influence the decision to retire interact with one another differently for different groups.
- Most people do not move after retirement. Movement is more likely after the loss of a spouse or the onset of serious illness.
- Most people look forward to retirement and welcome it as a reward for a lifetime of work.
- There are huge gender, social, and ethnic group differences in retirement. Members of minority groups are more likely to become disabled and forced to leave work. Members of minority groups have less retirement income from Social Security and pensions than do white Americans but the biggest gap is in savings and assets. Women have significantly lower retirement income than men and single people have significantly lower retirement income than married couples. Single women who are members of minority groups have the highest poverty rates in old age.
- A number of retirement phases have been proposed including preretirement (remote and near), honeymoon, routine, disenchantment, and termination.
- Although most retirees expect their income to decline after retirement, most are not bothered by this eventuality and adjust to the finances of retirement with little difficulty.

- The three-legged stool—income from Social Security, pensions, and savings and assets—is sufficient for most married white Americans but less likely to be sufficient for all other groups.
- Health is not affected by retirement nor is quality of social support; most marriages show no change in satisfaction after retirement although some show improvement.
- Retired adults report everyday tasks, travel, education, and volunteer work as important activities for staying busy during retirement.

STUDY QUESTIONS

1. What accounts for the finding of fewer injuries for older workers than for younger workers? What might account for the finding of more time off when an older worker is injured?

2. Older adults often show deficits in physical abilities, sensory abilities, and cognitive abilities, yet, they perform well on the job. Why?

3. Why are younger workers often less satisfied with their jobs than older workers?

4. Describe some of the evidence that suggests that employers discriminate against older adults. What claims do companies make in defense of their actions? Would you recommend that an older worker file suit under the ADEA? Under what conditions? Why or why not?

5. Do you think a presentation of the information in this chapter regarding older workers would be an effective way to reduce age discrimination in business? Why or why not? What other information would you add to employer training?

6. Describe gender and ethnic group differences in formal retirement planning, disability rates, and income after retirement.

7. Describe an older worker who is likely to retire and one who is unlikely to retire. What factors influence the differences between these workers. Describe an interaction of two or more factors.

8. Describe the phases of retirement.

9. How much preretirement income must be earned after retirement to support an individual's standard of living? Why is less income needed? How is this income received (describe the three-legged stool)?

10. How is social support from friends, family, and spouse affected by retirement? How is retirement affected by social support?

11. Retired people often claim to be very busy. What is it that they do?

RECOMMENDED READINGS

The following two short essays will give a glimpse of life as a servant in a private household.
Brooks, G. (2000). At the Burns-Coopers. In E. P. Stoller & R. C. Gibson (Eds.), *Worlds of Difference: Inequality in the Aging Experience* (pp. 187–188), Thousand Oaks, CA: Pine Forge Press.
Childress, A. (2000). Like One of the Family. In E. P. Stoller & R. C. Gibson (Eds.), *Worlds of Difference: Inequality in the Aging Experience* (pp. 189–190), Thousand Oaks, CA: Pine Forge Press.

Bauer-Maglin, N., & Radosh, A. (Eds.). (2003). *Women Confronting Retirement: A Nontraditional Guide.* New Brunswick, NJ: Rutgers U. Press. This book presents views of retirement from many different women who have worked in a wide variety of jobs.

INTERNET RESOURCES

www.eeoc.gov. For information about the ADEA and equal employment opportunities and information concerning Social Security, Medicare, healthcare issues, and age discrimination in employment.

www.ssa.gov, www.pbgc.gov, and *www.dol.gov/dol/pwba.* For information on Social Security, pensions, or welfare benefits for older adults. The National Committee to Preserve Social Security and Medicare also has a website with the latest information on congressional plans to alter these programs and tips on how to talk with your representatives.

www.retirement-living.com. For information about finances, housing options, entertainment, and health care for retired adults living in the mid-Atlantic region.

www.retirementnet.com. For information on different types of retirement communities ranging from those for very active retired adults to those providing care.

www.aarp.org. For general information on older workers and retirees.

www.eeoc.gov. For information about the ADEA and your rights if you or someone you know thinks that they could be a victim of age discrimination in the workplace.

www.sec.gov/investor/pubs/toolkit.htm. A site that can help you answer the question will you have enough income to support your retirement.

www.ssa.gov. For information about Social Security.

www.pbgc.gov/search. Search by last name and the name of the company for which you worked if you think you might be one of those who is owed unclaimed pension benefits.

Aging and Our Survival

PART FOUR

Aging and Our Survival

12 Psychopathology

All interest in disease . . . is only another expression of interest in life.
—*Thomas Mann*

Our fascination with disease is similar in some ways to our fascination with a puzzle. We want to find the solution, however, with diseases, the solution is much more important. In this chapter, we will examine the major disorders of adulthood that affect psychological processes like cognition or emotion. Older adults with one of these serious medical conditions all too frequently are seen as being beyond any help; many of the disorders examined in this chapter are irreversible; there is no cure. Nevertheless, it is our belief that where there is life, there is still hope (Cicero). A cure may not be possible but the time remaining may still be lived and caring always is possible.

In Senior View, Edna Carpenter and Wanda Washburn told about several of the disorders that are examined in this chapter including depression, Parkinson's disease, and Alzheimer's disease. They and everyone interviewed knew someone who had Alzheimer's disease; a large part of the discussion will be centered on this disorder about which Wanda said "a fate worse than death, to me, is Alzheimer's."

Overview

The disorders we will look at in this chapter primarily are cognitive; that is, they disrupt one's ability to think, to remember, and to decide. They are disorders that, like heart disease, cancer, and stroke (Chapters 3, 5, and 14), are primarily disorders of adulthood. Two statistics, prevalence and incidence, are used to determine whether a disorder is more frequent for one age group than another. **Prevalence** is a measure of how many cases there are for a given population for a given period of time while **incidence** is a measure of the number of new cases. For example, if we examine prevalence rates for dementia, or many other disorders, among young, middle-aged, and old adults, we would be likely to find the highest prevalence among older adults. That high rate could be due to young and middle-aged adults getting the disorder but living with it into old age or to old adults being more likely to come down with the disorder or both. To assess this, we would examine incidence over a year and assess how many new cases of dementia have been diagnosed among young, middle-aged, and old adults. We would find the highest incidence rate for dementia among older adults. The crucial comparison, to determine when a disease is likely to strike, is the incidence rate for different age groups. When we find different incidence rates for different age groups, that tells that some age groups are more likely to develop the disorder and that might give clues as to the causes, who to monitor, and how to treat the disorder. As you will learn, incidence rates can vary as a function of gender and ethnic group as well as age. In this chapter we will examine disorders that have high incidence rates in adulthood, particularly in old age. These disorders are alcohol abuse, depression, acute cognitive disorders, and dementias. We will end by looking at those who lovingly care for these people as we examine care giving.

How does one determine whether an individual has a psychopathology? The best procedure involves the administration of several different kinds of tests or measures. A medical doctor may examine blood work to look for nutrient deficiencies or a brain scan to look for evidence of a stroke; a mental health professional may administer a personality inventory and interview the individual, family, and friends; and the individual's behavior might be observed in certain situations. Ordinarily, several measures are made in an attempt to determine whether there is a problem and, what that problem might be. This is an especially important consideration when older persons are undergoing testing because of the existence of multiple medical conditions that can cloud diagnosis.

Older adults are far more likely than younger adults to experience two or even multiple medical conditions (**comorbidity** or **multimorbidity**) (Wolff et al., 2002). In such a case, one disorder might make it more difficult to diagnose the other. A patient with a cognitive impairment and depression may be diagnosed with only one or neither disorder. Think of cooccurring illnesses that you may have had. Is it the flu or a case of food poisoning or an allergy or a head cold or some combination of these? The symptoms and, thus, diagnosis, may not clearly fit any of these single categories because you have more than one problem at the same time. If diagnosis is successful, then it may be that treating one disorder worsens the other. If both are treated, it is possible that the combined treatments create new problems (Yancik et al., 2007). Medical science is in the process of developing a framework to deal with these difficulties but it is always the case that we want multiple assessments, especially with older adults (Karlamangla et al., 2007). Some recent work has examined the quality of care received by patients with multiple conditions and found that quality increased as the number of conditions increased. Some of this effect was due to the fact that people with more conditions generally pay more visits to the doctor and, thus, have a greater chance to receive quality care. Visits are often to specialists, who may provide higher quality care, and the effect was found even with these factors controlled (Higashi et al., 2007). This is good news for older adults who are more likely to have more than one medical condition.

Alcohol Abuse

Although there are a number of substances that adults might abuse, alcohol has received the most attention because it is legal, prevalent, and the most frequent substance use disorder for older adults. Alcohol abuse is characterized by use of alcohol when the individual is aware of the harm it causes and/or uses it in high risk situations, such as driving, and

Senior View

We spoke with Edna Carpenter and Wanda Washburn about some of the disorders discussed in this chapter. Edna was 71 and a widow who used to work as a full-time executive secretary until just 3 years ago. She told us, *my health is pretty good but I have emphysema; probably got it from 40 years of smoking.* Wanda was 73 and was widowed 17 years ago when she was still working as a real estate broker. *I now work part-time at Hertz and I'm going to keep on working as long as I can make it up the office steps.* [She gave us a big smile.] *I've got osteoarthritis and that can be pretty painful.*

We asked about depression. *I don't think older adults are any more depressed than younger adults unless there's something seriously wrong with them,* Wanda told us.

Edna added, *people are more depressed if they let themselves be.*

Wanda said, *I once knew a man who had been depressed for a while and he committed suicide. He had many things wrong with him and couldn't take the pain anymore.*

We also asked about dementia. *I know people who have Parkinson's and some with Alzheimer's too,* said Edna.

I do too, Wanda told us. *My daughter-in-law's mother had Parkinson's but has been able to eliminate some of the tremors with medication. She still has a real hard time swallowing though.*

Edna has a friend with Alzheimer's. *She doesn't know she is in this world; she's not aware of anything. She knew she had Alzheimer's when the doctor diagnosed it and she and her husband had made plans to care for her until she had to be institutionalized about 2 years ago. Of course, I don't think anything makes any difference to her anymore.*

We asked if they would offer any advice to young people. Edna immediately said, *don't smoke, eat right, and get enough exercise.* Wanda said, *I'm really very optimistic. The way they're replacing joints and hearts they'll have everything taken care of by the time you reach old age.*

continues the use for over a month (American Psychiatric Association, 1994). Alcohol abuse can lead to more severe alcohol dependence, also called alcoholism. Dependent individuals show at least three of the following symptoms: tolerance or a need to increase the amount of alcohol to achieve the same effect previously achieved by less alcohol; withdrawal symptoms (such as delirium tremors, hallucinations) when alcohol is discontinued for a period of time; using more alcohol or using it longer than originally intended; not being able to control the use of alcohol; avoiding important work-related, family, or social activities because of alcohol use; and using alcohol even when such use worsens physical or psychological difficulties already present (American Psychiatric Association, 1994). It is estimated that about 7 percent of the U.S. population abuses alcohol or is alcohol dependent (Grant et al., 1994). Alcoholism is far more prevalent among men than women. Close to 20 percent of men will develop alcohol abuse or dependence at some point in their lives; the estimate for women is less than 10 percent (Kessler et al., 1994). Different cultural/ethnic groups also show different levels of alcohol abuse and dependence. Box 12-1 describes some of the differences in greater detail.

The rate of alcoholism among older adults is less than that among younger adults. About 3 percent of adults over 65 abuse alcohol or are dependent. Over all ages of adults, however, the highest rate is for widowers who are 75 and older (Glass et al., 1995; Gurland, 1996). Older alcoholics fall into two general categories. Many are people who began

BOX **12-1**

Alcoholism and Ethnicity

Different ethnic groups in this country show different patterns of alcohol abuse and dependency. The highest rates of alcohol abuse are found for some Native American tribes while other tribes have very low rates (Szlemko et al., 2006). The rate for white Americans is next followed by African Americans who have higher rates than Hispanic and Asian Americans (Aponte et al., 1995). Most researchers suggest that patterns of alcoholism are closely tied to patterns of underemployment, unemployment, poverty, substandard housing, and discrimination. How do you think this relationship works for minorities?

The general pattern of lower levels of alcoholism for older adults than for younger adults is found for white Americans but not for African or Hispanic Americans. African and Hispanic Americans show about the same rate of alcoholism throughout the adult years (Bucholz, 1992). African Americans, perhaps as a result of this continued rate of alcoholism throughout adulthood, show higher rates of death from liver disease than do white Americans. Among different Hispanic American groups, different rates of alcoholism also are found. Cuban Americans show a relatively low rate throughout middle and old age while Mexican American and Puerto Ricans living in the United States show consistently higher rates (Black & Markides, 1994).

Although Prohibition may have had a major influence on the consumption of alcohol of older white Americans it may have had less influence on African Americans who in those days often were excluded from significant participation in American society or Hispanic Americans who are, in large number, more recent immigrants. If this is the case, then we might expect newer cohorts of white Americans to begin to show continued high rates of alcoholism even into old age.

drinking when they were much younger and have continued drinking in their later years. Others are people who began abusing alcohol when they reached old age. These late-onset alcoholics are more often women and are estimated to comprise about one-third of older alcoholics (Dupree & Schonfeld, 1996; Lichtenberg, 1994).

The relatively low rate of alcohol abuse that has been found for older adults is thought to have three important qualifications. The first is an assumed underreporting of alcoholism in older adults. Some older adults are fairly isolated from others who may not detect their alcoholism. Families may hide or ignore a grandparent's excessive drinking believing that it is no one else's business, that the older adult needs alcohol to get by, or that the cost of treatment in terms of money and time would not be worth the effort for someone who may not live much longer anyway. It is thought that doctors often may ignore signs of alcoholism in older patients who they would otherwise attempt to treat in younger patients. They may assume that alcoholism is the least of their patient's worries and can be safely ignored in the face of cancer, stroke, or Alzheimer's disease (Adams & Waskel, 1993; Ankrom et al., 1997).

A second qualification for the low rate of alcoholism found among older adults is that many alcoholics die before reaching old age. Some may perish in auto accidents while others may die of cirrhosis of the liver or Korsakoff's syndrome. Cirrhosis is a degeneration of the liver that most often results from alcohol abuse or dependency (Gallant, 1987). Korsakoff's is a dementia in which the person suffers disorientation, confusion, and irreversible loss of memory. The brain deteriorates and the individual eventually dies. Alcoholics are an unhealthy group of people who typically die earlier than nonalcoholics (Eberling & Jagust, 1995).

The third qualification is that the current low rate of alcoholism among older adults may be a cohort effect. Many of the older adults who are in the low rate of alcoholism group lived through Prohibition (1920–1933). During those years alcohol use was considered a social stigma; it was illegal. Women especially were tainted if they drank. Because most alcoholics begin drinking when they are young (67 percent of older alcoholics began when they were young), the cohorts who were young during Prohibition may have had unusually low rates of alcoholism. Over the next 20 years, the rate of alcoholism for older adults may increase to the level found for younger and middle-age adults (Ganzini & Atkinson, 1996). Some evidence for this prediction comes from longitudinal studies of alcoholism that have found no change in alcohol use for any age adults (Dufour et al., 1988). As today's younger and middle-age adults reach old age, they are likely to bring their current higher rate of alcoholism with them unless deaths from alcohol-related diseases and accidents offset this expected cohort effect.

Depression

Depression is one of three mood disorders. The other two are **mania** which is characterized by exaggerated elation often mixed with intense irritability and **bipolar disorder** which is characterized by severe swings in mood from depression to mania. Both mania and bipolar disorder are less frequent among older adults (Butler et al., 1998).

Depression typically is divided into three different levels. **Depressed mood** is a reaction to an important event such as loss of a pet, a friend moving away, or not geting the job you wanted. Usually the mood lasts no more than a few months, and usually quite less, and seems to be about the same frequency for adults of all ages. **Major clinical depression** is severe and usually comes on as a result of some traumatic event such as loss of a close family member or friend. Symptoms include continual sadness, lack of energy, irritability, difficulty sleeping or oversleeping, weight gain or loss, aches and pains that will not go away, socially isolating oneself, difficulties concentrating and making decisions, feelings of helplessness and hopelessness, and, in many cases, thoughts of death or suicide (Lefton, 1997). To be considered a major depression, a significant number of these symptoms must last at least 2 weeks. A milder form of depression, characterized by low self-esteem, difficulties concentrating and making decisions, low energy, sleep difficulties, and feelings of hopelessness is referred to as **dysthymic disorder**. These three forms of depression are among the more common disorders for adults of all ages.

A common belief among many younger people is that depression increases with old age because older adults have more things to be depressed about. For example, older adults are more likely to become seriously ill with life-threatening diseases such as cancer and cardiovascular disease; to lose major portions of their income with retirement from an active role in the work place; to lose status as a respected member of the working community; to lose friends and relatives to disease and death; to lose their ability to see well, hear well, and move well; and so on.

In spite of this belief, the general finding has been a lower, rather than higher, rate of major depression among older adults (Gatz & Hurwitz, 1990; Hendrie et al., 1995; Lyness et al., 1995). The prevalence of major depression among adults 65 and older is about 1 percent which is the same as or even lower than the prevalence among younger and middle-age adults (Mirowsky & Ross, 1992).

The prevalence of milder depression or dysthymic disorder may be higher in older adults. Table 12-1 shows a depression scale used to assist diagnosis of depression. Using data gathered from scales like this, researchers have found relatively high rates of mild depression among adults 65 and older (Beekman et al., 1995). In one such study, 27 percent of the participating older adults were found to be mildly depressed (Koenig & Blazer, 1992). This is as high as younger adults and together these two groups show much higher rates than adults in their middle years. Across all of these age groups, more women than men are diagnosed with depression. This gender difference, however, seems to vanish after age 80 as the number of depressed men increases from age 60 to 80 until the proportion of depressed men and women is about the same (Barefoot et al., 2001).

Several reasons have been offered for the differences in the prevalence of major and minor depression among older and younger adults. One possibility is that older adults, as members of an older cohort, grew up in times when mental illnesses, such as depression, were a stigma; people tended to keep mental problems to themselves. Thus, members of these older cohorts may be less willing to ask for help when they need it or answer items on a depression scale honestly. If this were, however, the major reason for obtained differences, then it is not at all clear why dysthymic disorder would be high among older adults. A second possibility is that older adults have learned how to deal with depressing events

Depression can occur at any age.

and do not experience depression as deeply. Their high rates of dysthymic disorder may be due to those depressing events and situations that can accompany old age and their better coping strategies learned from experience. They may get depressed as often as young adults but not as deeply. A third possibility is that perhaps there are many older adults suffering with major depression who are simply missed when data are collected using standard methods (Baldwin, 1994). One study found that about half of a group of older adults who showed signs of depression on a standard measure (similar to the one in Table 12-1) were not detected as being depressed by their physicians (Garrard et al., 1998). At present it is not clear which, if any, of these three hypotheses might play a role in the obtained age differences on measures of depression. Most of the factors that produce depression are the same for young and old. When a major and traumatic event occurs, depression is very likely. For example, loss of a pet can produce a depressed mood in adults, adolescents, and children. Continued stress also can produce depression and this is particularly true for those who have daily hassles along with their stress (Kraaij et al., 2002; Nolen-Hoeksema & Ahrens, 2002). It's hard to get any relief from continued stress when you are continually dealing with other, even relatively minor, problems.

There are, however, some age differences in causes of depression. Many older adults, for example, show increased levels of depression after they stop driving (Fonda et

TABLE 12-1   Sample Depression Scale

Answer *yes* or *no* to each of the following questions:

1. Much of the time, do you feel:
   Sad?
   Lethargic?
   Pessimistic?
   Hopeless?
   Worthless?
   Helpless?
2. Much of the time, do you:
   Have difficulty making decisions?
   Have trouble concentrating?
   Have memory problems?
3. Lately, have you:
   Lost interest in things that used to give you pleasure?
   Had problems at work or in school?
   Had problems with your family or friends?
   Isolated yourself from others, or wanted to?
4. Lately, have you:
   Felt low energy?
   Felt restless and irritable?
   Had trouble falling asleep, staying asleep, or getting up in the morning?
   Lost your appetite, or gained weight?
   Been bothered by persistent headaches, stomachaches, backaches, or muscle/joint pains?
5. Lately, have you:
   Been drinking more alcohol than you used to?
   Been taking more mood-altering drugs than you used to?
   Engaged in risky behavior such as not wearing a seat belt or crossing strrets without
   looking?
6. Lately, have you been thinking about:
   Death?
   Hurting yourself?
   Your funeral?
   Killing yourself?

If you answered yes to three or more of these questions, you may be depressed. You should con-
sult your physician or a mental health professional.

Source: From *www.depression.com/health_library/quiz/index/htm* and adapted from material created by the National Institute of Mental Health's Depression Awareness, Recognition, and Treatment Program, Rockville,
Maryland.

al., 2001). In one study, 1700 older adults were followed for 3 years and those who stopped driving during that time showed increased depression and this increase was larger for men than for women (Ragland et al., 2005). It is believed that *cessation of driving* increases depression because of the loss of independence that occurs. In U.S. culture, it is very hard to get around without driving. Why do you think this effect would be greater for men than for women? Cessation of driving is not a frequent cause of depression in younger adults because they rarely cease driving.

Increased disability is another factor influencing depression in older but not younger adults. Research shows that the loss of ability to do activities of daily living (ADLs) and loss of vision are major factors (Choi & Bohman, 2007; Furner et al., 2006). As you might expect, the greater the number of disabilities or other health problems, *comorbidity* and multimorbidity, the more depressive symptoms an individual tends to have (Chapleski et al., 2004). Increased disability is, however, less likely to produce depression when one has good sources of social support (Oxman & Hull, 2001).

Research shows that *loss of social support*, often because of loss of a spouse, increases depression (Choi & Bohman, 2007; Vanderhorst & McLaren, 2005). Loss of a spouse generally results in greater depression for men than for women largely as a result of social network differences between men and women (Chapter 10) (Lee et al., 2001). One might then expect that depression could be lessened by getting out and meeting other people and some work shows that *working as a volunteer* decreases depression (Morrow-Howell, 2003).

Finally, depression is greater for older adults who report that their basic needs are not being met. In a 10-year longitudinal study of over 4000 adults 65 and older, *unmet basic needs* were strong predictors of later depression. Those who did not feel safe in their neighborhood, who did not have enough money to purchase necessities, who had inadequate heat in the winter, and so on were, just as you would expect, more depressed (Blazer et al., 2007).

There are also some gender and ethnic group differences in causes of depression for older adults. Women who suffer from *pain* and who have lost *instrumental support* are more likely to experience depression than men whereas the loss of *emotional support* influences both women and men (Koizumi et al., 2005). In a comparison of African and white Americans, researchers found many of the same causes such as disability and loss of social support, but differences as well. For white Americans, *age* was an important factor and depression increased as age increased. For African Americans, age had no influence but *women* were more depressed than men and those who were *less religious* were more depressed than those who were more religious (Jang et al., 2005).

The relationship between health and depression is fairly strong. Depressed individuals tend to die earlier and, frequently, from heart disease (Schulz et al., 2000). The relationship between health and depression seems to operate in both directions. Individuals who experience a physical illness or impairment often become depressed. Individuals who have depressed personality characteristics tend to become physically ill or impaired (Meeks et al., 2000). Recently researchers compared mortality rates for older adults enrolled at two Montreal hospitals. Some were depressed and some were not and among the former group some had a history of depression and some did not. Age, comorbidity, cognitive impairment, diagnosis, and use of health services over the year before entering the study also were measured. Over more than 4 years, the lowest mortality rates, once all other measured variables were controlled, were for depressed patients with a history of depression (McCusker et al., 2006). It is not clear what the seemingly protective effect of depression is in this case. Perhaps being hospitalized with a major illness is depressing for most and those who are used to dealing with depression, because they have a history, are better able to cope. Further work is needed to clarify these findings and determine under what circumstances depression increases or decreases mortality risk.

Regardless of age or cause of depression, it is treatable. Depressed older adults, like younger adults, often receive prescribed antidepressant medication. Although the rate of use for such medication is reasonably high for institutionalized older adults (36 percent), it is very low (4.2 percent) for depressed older adults living in the community (Newman & Hassan, 1999). Antidepressant medications also have some drawbacks for older adults. One form of antidepressant medication, selective serotonin reuptake inhibitors (SSRIs) has recently been shown to be associated with risk of fracture. Adults, 50 and older, taking this medication were followed for 5 years and were found to have lower bone density, greater risk of falling, and more fractured bones compared to adults not taking SSRIs (Richards et al., 2007). It is not at present clear how this medication influences bone density, falling, and fractures.

Depressed adults frequently engage in talk therapy, in addition to taking medication, to relieve their depression. Research generally supports the benefits of this added therapy and one relatively simple to use—talk therapy is a form of life review where individuals discuss some of the major events of their life. Life review originally was proposed to help older adults deal better with the personal concern of ego integrity versus despair (see Chapter 9). In one examination of the effects of life review, researchers randomly assigned depressed adults 65 and older to a control group that was visited for social assistance or an experimental group that received a form of life review. Both groups were visited for 7 weeks. During life review visits, individuals were asked specific questions about their childhood, adolescence, adulthood, and life in general. For example, they were asked "What is the most pleasant experience you remember from your childhood?"; "Tell me about a day when you were an adolescent and you did something out of the ordinary"; "Tell me a time that you remember experiencing the most pride at work"; and "If everything in your life were to happen exactly the same, what moment would you like to relive." Results showed that this life review greatly reduced depression and increased life satisfaction scores while the control group showed no change at all (Serrano et al., 2004, p. 274).

Of course, not all older adults who are depressed receive this kind of therapy and many are only taking medication. This is fairly common in nursing homes and congregate living facilities. Depression also is fairly common in such institutional settings. Recently, depressed residents of a facility were interviewed regarding their treatment by physicians. Half said they were somewhat or very satisfied and half were dissatisfied. Dissatisfaction was attributed to several different factors. One patient said the physician told her "you are old and must expect these problems" (Mellor et al., 2006, p. 445). Others said the physician never had time to talk and spent very little time trying to help. Some said they saw no reason for the treatment because they were not really depressed. Others said they did not want to talk with anyone about their feelings or problems. These dissatisfied individuals are highly unlikely to get better until researchers can find ways to better treat their depression, and a large part of that seems to be better training of attending physicians and more access to mental health treatment.

Some work has focused on physical activity as a treatment for depression. As you remember from earlier chapters, all systems are integrated and changes in one can influence change in another. Perhaps the increased blood flow and bone and muscle strength that comes from exercise also might make individuals feel better about themselves. To test this, researchers randomly assigned depressed older adults to one of three groups and followed them for 8 weeks. One group received standard care over this period of time while the other two were introduced to progressive resistance training. For these individuals, the maximum load that they could lift was measured and those assigned to high intensity training lifted 80 percent of their maximum load during training while those assigned to low intensity lifted 20 percent. Training took place every week for 3 days. Results showed the greatest benefit for high intensity training and depression was reduced for that group more than for the other two groups (Singh et al., 2005). Some other work shows that aerobic exercise also is beneficial and that even walking can reduce symptoms of depression for older adults but, surprisingly, not for middle-aged adults (Fukukawa et al., 2004). Perhaps that is because middle-aged adults are already walking more than older adults and so, for them, walking is not perceived as something new. In a direct comparison of resistance training and aerobic walking, some work has found a greater reduction of depression for walkers (Penninx et al., 2002).

Different modes of therapy are, of course, more or less successful with different groups of people (Aponte et al., 1995). For example, some recent work suggests that self-reinforcement, which is the ability to control pleasant events, is an effective treatment component for white and Asian American older adults who are depressed. On the other hand perceived control, which is a perception of one's own ability to reduce aversive and increase positive events, is effective for white but not for Asian Americans (Wong et al., 1999). Other work suggests that older African Americans are less likely to report mild depression than are white Americans but far more likely to report thinking about death (Gallo et al., 1998). Unfortunately, many adults, young and old, do not seek treatment and attempt suicide.

Suicide

Major depression is strongly related to suicide; about 15 percent of those who have experienced major depression end their own lives. This is 15 times higher than the suicide rate in the overall population. This is especially true of older adults. People who commit suicide under the age of 40 are more often schizophrenic. Between the ages of 40 and 60, alcoholism is the most frequent diagnosis; for those over 60, depression is the most frequent diagnosis (Conwell, 1995). About 30,000 Americans commit suicide every year.

Suicide rates are quite different for men and women and for adults of different ages. Many more women attempt suicide than men; about 75 percent of suicide attempts are by women. Many more men succeed at suicide than women; about 67 percent of completed suicides are by men (Mynatt & Doherty, 1999). Part of the reason for this difference is the method used. Women tend to use sleeping pills or other drugs and often are found while still alive. Men tend to use more instantly lethal means such as guns or hanging and usually are found after they are dead. Suicide rates for women tend to remain fairly stable and fairly low from young to old adulthood with a slight rise between the ages of 40 and 60. White females have slightly higher suicide rates than African American females. For men, suicide rates vary as a function of both race and age. Such gender and ethnic group differences in suicide are important but it is the relationship between suicide and age that is most striking.

Overall, older adults are more successful at suicide than are younger adults. It has been estimated that about 5 percent of suicide attempts among younger adults are successful while about 25 percent of attempts among older adults are successful (Kastenbaum, 1995). For African American men, the highest suicide rates are at age 20 and at age 80 but are never as high as for white men of any adult age. For white men, the suicide rate starts high in young adulthood and increases dramatically with age. The highest rate of suicide is for older, white men. As you can see from Figure 12-1, no other group comes even close to this high rate which continues to increase until the mid-80s.

Because some suicides are not detected, the rates are probably higher for all of these groups. An older (or younger) adult who simply stops taking important medication may die and be pronounced dead from the disease. A person may do just the opposite and take too much medication and end their life. Then they may be thought of as forgetful rather than suicidal. An older (or younger) adult may intentionally take part in some hazardous activity and be pronounced dead from accidental causes. Regardless of these factors, it is clear that older, white men commit suicide far more often than others.

This finding is not a cohort effect. Older white men have had the highest suicide rate since the turn of the century and, thus, many cohorts have shown this effect (Posner, 1996). One hypothesis frequently mentioned has to do with loss of power and prestige. White males who are still working have more power and prestige than black males and white or black females. With retirement, one may lose that workplace power and prestige and, thus, white males have more to lose than do the other gender and racial groups (McCall, 1991). This loss may result in feelings of worthlessness, depression, and lead to suicide. Another hypothesis suggests that social support is a crucial factor and men generally have fewer people in the inner circle of their social network than do women. Widowers have the highest suicide rate and several studies indicate higher depression and more suicide ideation among those with the lowest levels of social support (Vanderhorst & McLaren, 2005).

Individuals who contemplate and attempt suicide often give warning signs to family, friends, and professionals such as their family doctors. Warning signs include talking about death, giving away valuable possessions, avoiding activities that one ordinarily enjoyed, neglecting personal appearance, and apparent changes in personality or habits. One might, for example, become much more anxious or begin drinking heavily. Such warning signs should be taken seriously.

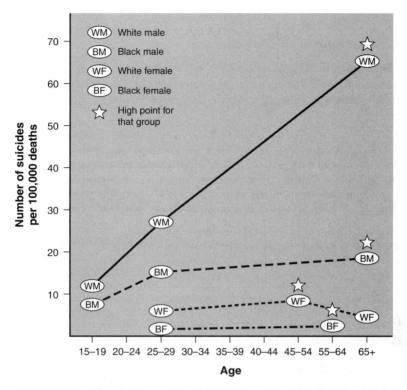

FIGURE 12-1   Graph Comparing Suicide Rates for Old and Young, Male and Female, and White and African Americans.

Source: Adapted from U.S. Census data (1990, 1997).

Acute Cognitive Disorders

The symptoms of cognitive disorders are the same in acute cases and in more severe dementias. The five major symptoms are:

1. *Impaired memory:* Deficits in working memory, such as being unable to remember what just occurred, are usually first followed by deficits in the ability to retrieve information from permanent memory. Usually episodic permanent memory, rather than semantic or procedural, is affected.
2. *Impaired intellect:* Person has difficulty in understanding or comprehending presented information and/or in learning new behaviors. The person may seem to have lost some of their intelligence.
3. *Impaired judgment*: Person cannot make plans or decisions and/or understand the plans and decisions made by others. The individual cannot differentiate between a good and a bad plan or decision.
4. *Impaired orientation*: Person is confused about where they are, what time/date it is, and the identities of others even those who are familiar to them.

5. *Impaired emotionality*: Person displays excessive or very shallow emotions out of proportion to circumstances.

When an older adult shows one or more of these symptoms, one must be careful not to assume that it is an irreversible organic brain syndrome (OBS) or dementia, such as Alzheimer's disease. Although the term **dementia** frequently is used in conversation to refer to many types of cognitive declines, it actually refers to irreversible cognitive declines that result from some organic brain disorder. Too many families, professionals, and older adults are too quick to assume the worst. An older adult who begins to have difficulty keeping track of appointments or forgets things may begin to suspect Alzheimer's disease. Alzheimer's disease is feared among older adults and an individual may begin worrying about having it. Worrying disrupts memory and it may lead to more forgetting and more worrying and so on until the person is convinced that they have Alzheimer's disease. We must try to avoid this downward spiral by first examining other possible causes of changes in cognition before arriving at a diagnosis of Alzheimer's disease or any other dementia (Centofanti, 1998). The first step is to determine whether the cognitive changes are a part of normal aging or whether they are one or more of the five symptoms of a cognitive disorder.

When a problem arises, a number of cognitive tests are used by clinicians to determine whether it is normal aging or a relatively mild cognitive impairment (MCI) or a cognitive disorder. Once confirmed as a disorder, there are a number of other tests (blood tests and brain scans) to determine the type of cognitive disorder. The most widely used cognitive test is the Mini-Mental Status Exam (MMSE; Folstein et al., 1975). This test asks questions that are similar to those shown in Table 12-2. The test has been shown to be quite good at measuring level of cognitive difficulty and equally useful for measuring the degree of impairment regardless of race (Ford et al., 1996). At the same time, it has been criticized for falsely diagnosing individuals with low education or short attention span as having a cognitive disorder and for missing some cases of genuine impairment (Kukull et al., 1994). Because a misdiagnosis could have quite serious consequences, it is typical to use additional tests if a person's MMSE score is low. One of these, the Time and Change Test, takes

TABLE 12-2   Cognitive Test Questions

1. What day is today?
   What is the date?
   What day will it be 2 days from now?
   What date was it 2 days ago?
2. Repeat these words and later I will ask you to remember them:
   TABLE   TREE   HORSE
3. Name as many states as you can.
4. What were the three words that I asked you to remember?
5. Stand up, turn around in a circle, and sit down again.
6. Count backward by fours from 40.
7. Please tell me once again what the three words were that I asked you to remember.

only a couple of minutes to administer but has good reliability. Individuals are asked to look at a clock (with hands) and tell what time it is and to make a dollar in change from quarters, dimes, and nickels placed in front of them (Inouye et al., 1998). Another test, designed to assess visuospatial and construction deficits that are frequently correlated with cognitive and neurological disorders, involves drawing a picture of a clock showing a particular time. People who are able to draw a "normal" clock rarely show any cognitive impairment (Siu, 1991). Difficulties in drawing a clock correlate well with severity of other cognitive disorders (Hill et al., 1995). Some examples of clocks drawn by a normal person and persons with varying cognitive disorders are shown in Figure 12-2. Other work has found that those with beginning dementia are far less able to identify road signs so this too could be used to determine whether or not a problem has progressed beyond a mild impairment (Carr et al., 1998).

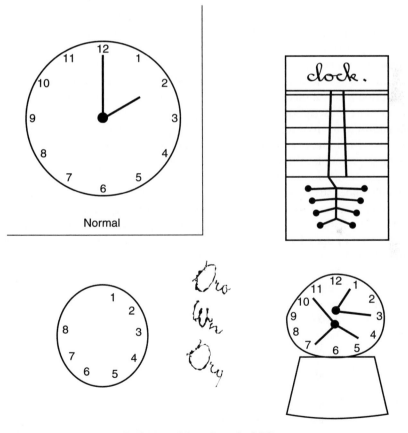

FIGURE 12-2   Sample Clocks as Drawn by a Normal Person and Victims of Cognitive Disorders.

If testing indicates a cognitive disorder, one must still be careful to rule out depression. Depression is very treatable and many cognitive disorders are not. There are several distinctions between a cognitive disorder and depression. Someone with a cognitive disorder will show varying mood over an extended period of observation while a depressed person tends to remain depressed. The answers given on tests like the MMSE tend to be wrong for a person with a cognitive disorder whereas a depressed person is more likely to give no answer at all. Most cognitive disorders have relatively slow onset; things have been getting worse for quite some time. Depression is likely to have a rapid onset following some traumatic event. The presence of such an event suggests depression rather than a problem with cognition. Cognitive loss generally is stable with a cognitive disorder; the person almost always has some difficulty while with depression cognitive loss may appear to be present at one time and not at another (Safford, 1992).

One other important condition to rule out is an **acute cognitive disorder (ACD)** which is reversible and persons frequently show full recovery. About 15 percent of low test scorers have an acute disorder that is typically the result of some disturbance in brain metabolism. There are three common ways in which such a disturbance occurs: polypharmacy, a vitamin deficiency, and/or an electrolyte imbalance.

Polypharmacy refers to interactions among prescription or over-the-counter medications and is one way to disrupt brain metabolism. Some medications produce very different effects when taken with other medications simultaneously. About one-half of all prescription medications are for older adults and more than one-third of older adults take three or more prescription drugs (Park et al., 1992). Some members of older cohorts have been known to hoard drugs and use them at a later date without the advice of a physician. They may think that if it worked before it will work again even though their body chemistry might be quite different from taking other medications. Drug dosage must be carefully monitored for older adults because their liver or kidneys may not function as well, especially under stress. Medications then might be in the body for a longer period of time. All of these factors increase the chances of polypharmacy. Some work suggests that cardiovascular and synthetic drugs are strongly associated with loss of ability to carry out normal activities of daily living (Wolfson et al., 2006). Even some over-the-counter drugs can contribute to ACD and some types of laxatives disrupt memory and cognition. It is always important that each attending physician (endocrinologist, cardiologist, general practitioner, and any others) know of all medications that are being taken. Any potential problem might then be avoided. When polypharmacy does occur, it is typical to discontinue all medications and start again with those necessary for life and add others in one by one. It may take time, but this form of ACD can be fixed.

Brain metabolism can also be disrupted by a **deficiency of vitamin B_6 or B_{12}**. Such deficiencies can cause anxiety, disorientation, memory loss, insomnia, irritability, delusions, hallucinations, and even death. These deficiencies can occur because the individual is not eating the right foods or not taking a multiple vitamin. Good dietary sources of B_6 are chicken, fish, eggs, rice, and soybeans and good sources of B_{12} are red meats. One may, however, be eating the right foods but loss of some stomach lining can cause low absorption. Acid and enzymes produced in the stomach lining help absorb B vitamins and so a deficiency can occur even if one is consuming plenty of B vitamins (Rowe & Kahn, 1998). In this case, the individual may find it necessary to have injections of B vitamins to relieve the symptoms of ACD.

A third disruption of brain metabolism is due to an **imbalance of electrolytes**. The nervous system depends on the presence of positive and negative ions to function correctly and when this balance is disrupted, an ACD can occur. Electrolyte imbalance sometimes occurs after a major surgery and can usually be rectified fairly quickly. If grandmother just had a hip replaced and is now acting confused and disoriented, she may be suffering an ACD from an imbalance of electrolytes. Such an ACD also is frequently referred to as delirium and seems to result from anesthesia. **Delirium** is characterized by the same five cognitive symptoms discussed earlier and can signal the beginning of serious decline, possible dementia, and even death or full recovery. About 20 percent of hospitalized adults, 65 and older, develop delirium for some period of time (Inouye & Ferrucci, 2006). The chances of such development is higher for individuals with lower education levels perhaps because those with higher education have greater cognitive reserves to offset a hopefully temporary disruption of memory and orientation (Jones et al., 2006).

In many cases, the score on a cognitive test is not low enough to indicate ACD or possible dementia but is lower than normal. These are frequently referred to as cases of **mild cognitive impairment (MCI)**. The number of persons with this impairment increases with age; about 5 percent of adults in their 70s, 16 percent in their 80s, and close to a third who are 90 and older show such impairment. The life expectancy of these individuals is greatly reduced compared to the life expectancies of persons who are without such impairment (Suthers et al., 2003). In some cases the MCI continues to worsen and may be the beginning of a slowly developing dementia.

Dementia

Dementia refers to cognitive decline, characterized by the five symptoms, that is usually slow in onset and due to irreversible and increasing damage to the brain. There are many different kinds of dementia and dementia is also found in animals. Box 12-2 describes some animal dementias. The incidence and prevalence rates for dementia are much higher in older adults and increase the older one gets. The prevalence of mild dementia may be as high as 12 percent for all adults 65 and older and the prevalence of moderate to severe cases may be as high as 6 percent (Schulz & O'Brien, 1994). At younger ages, 65 to 75, the prevalence rates are higher for men compared to women (5% to 3.7%) while past the age of 80, the rates are lower for men (13% to 21%). In one study, the rate was examined in 276 adults who were 100 and older in Denmark and 37 percent showed no sign of any cognitive disorder while 51 percent did. Many of those with some disorder had ACD, most often as a result of a vitamin B deficiency (Andersen-Ranberg et al., 2001). The rate of dementia in centenarians has been found to range from almost all tested in some studies to about half in other studies (Calvert et al., 2006). While the incidence of dementia is much higher in older adults, many very old adults remain free from any cognitive disorder at all.

There are quite a large number of different types of dementia and most are easier to diagnose than Alzheimer's. The recommended procedure, when someone shows clear signs of dementia, is to try and rule out as many of these other types as possible before making a diagnosis of probable Alzheimer's. We will follow that procedure here as we go through some of these types on our way to Alzheimer's. To get an idea of where in the

BOX **12-2**

Animal Dementias

Dementia is not a disease of humans alone; probably all animals with brains can experience some form of dementia. Dog dementia or canine cognitive dysfunction syndrome (CDS) frequently occurs in older dogs. Some estimate the prevalence to be as high as 62 percent of older dogs. Such dogs may act confused, not always recognize their owners, bark at night for no reason, turn away when petted, mess in the house, and not wag their tails very frequently. Although the exact cause of CDS is not clear, there are treatments available. The drug Anipryl is often prescribed by veterinarians for CDS. Cinder, shown here, suffered from canine CDS.

Another concern, particularly of hunters and those who eat venison, is mad deer disease or chronic wasting disease (CWD). Like mad cow disease, CWD seems to be caused by a prion that eats away at the brain and results in a form of Creutzfeldt-Jakob disease. A prion is a twisted piece of microscopic protein that is thought to invade nerve cells and convert ordinary proteins into more invading prions. CWD has been documented in both deer and elk in Wyoming and Colorado and is spreading to other states. Human cases have not been confirmed, but are suspected (Miniter, 1999).

brain these dementias are located, refer to Figure 12-3. Let's begin with the less-frequent types.

Less Frequent Forms of Dementia

NeuroAIDS. NeuroAIDS is a result of HIV infection spreading to the brain (Price, 1998). Symptoms include some or all of the five cognitive symptoms plus clumsiness, weakening in the limbs, apathy, and social withdrawal. Eventually the person loses the ability to walk without assistance, loses bowel and bladder control, is confined to bed, and

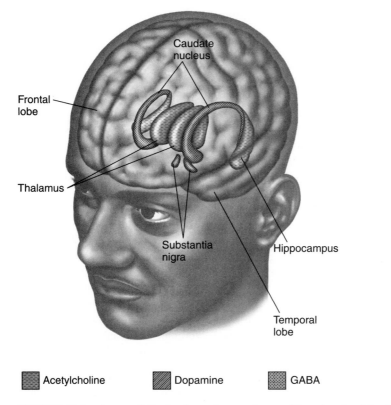

	Acetylcholine		Dopamine		GABA

FIGURE 12-3   Areas of the brain and neurotransmitters involved in chronic OBS.

dies. This deterioration occurs as the HIV infection destroys nerve cells in several areas of the brain and some recent work has shown that dopamine producing areas, the *substantia nigra* in Figure 12-3, are hit hard. Dopamine is one of several chemicals used in the brain to transmit information and control movement and is the key chemical destroyed in Parkinson's disease. The destruction of dopamine areas in neuroAIDS is not as extensive as in Parkinson's. Work has shown that not all AIDS patients develop this dementia, that the dementia occurs at the later stages of AIDS, and that the use of cocaine increases the damage done to dopamine producing cells by the HIV virus (Nath et al., 2000; Sardar et al., 1996).

Korsakoff's Syndrome.   This dementia is primarily due to continual excess alcohol consumption. One version, Wernicke-Korsakoff syndrome, is a result of long-term thiamine (vitamin B_1) deficiency. The most frequent and earliest cognitive symptom is an impairment of working memory. One cannot remember recent events and this suggests that encoding no longer functions well. The individual will not remember the name of someone they just met, where they parked (and that they should not be driving anyway), the score of a game they have been watching, and so on. Afflicted persons resort to confabulation to fill in these blanks in their memories ("oh, it's 3 to 2 or something like that" or "I haven't really been watching very closely") and such confabulations are easily detected by those who know them well or who have been watching the game. Over long periods other cognitive symptoms begin to appear and the damage to the brain is irreversible although the progress of the disease seems to be halted when drinking stops (Butler et al., 1998).

Frontotemporal Dementias.   These types of dementias are centered in the frontal and/or temporal lobes of the brain (see Figure 12-3). They do not occur frequently and usually the first symptoms are social inappropriateness, loss of modesty, and uninhibited sexual behavior. Only later do the typical cognitive symptoms occur and once they do, the individual usually is close to death (Haward, 1977). **Pick's dementia** is one of the better known of these types of dementia and seems to be determined by a single dominant gene. A good example of this dementia occurred when Dr. Allan Zarkin carved his initial (Z) in the abdomen of a mother after successfully delivering her baby by Cesarean section. The doctor was sued and lost his license (Dobnik, 2000; Singleton, 2000). Clearly his cognitive symptoms had not yet begun and his performance of the delivery was flawless but his behavior following that delivery was clearly inappropriate. Recent work has found that the clumps of protein that cause the damage in frontotemporal dementias contain the same damaging protein that is found in the brains of individuals with amyotrophic lateral sclerosis (ALS) (Neumann et al., 2006). This disease killed Lou Gehrig and is often referred to as Lou Gehrig's disease. The disease is well known because of the book *Tuesdays with Morrie* in which Mitch Albom describes the last days of his former professor, Morrie Schwartz, who died of ALS.

Huntington's Disease.   This dementia is caused by a single dominant gene and occurs infrequently. Symptoms typically appear during middle adulthood, 35 to 50 years of age. The disease produces a shortage of the neurotransmitter GABA in the caudate nucleus of the brain (see Figure 12-3). Symptoms include involuntary flicking movements of the arms and legs, an inability to sustain a motor act such as sticking out one's tongue, mood swings, hallucinations, paranoia, and depression. Once the cognitive symptoms appear the individual is usually close to death. Unlike neuroAIDS, dopamine levels seem to be higher than normal in the brains of those with Huntington's (Nemeroff et al., 1983).

Creutzfeldt-Jakob Dementia (CJ).   This is another relatively rare disorder that, unlike most other forms of dementia, has a relatively rapid rate of decline. Death typically occurs within 2 years after diagnosis. CJ is caused by a prion which is a small infectious protein. Because there are many different prions, there are also many different forms of CJ. When prions come into contact with certain types of normal healthy proteins, the healthy proteins change their shape and become prions as well. The infection then spreads rapidly, destroying major areas of the brain. In the later stages of CJ, the brain is so eaten away that it resembles a sponge. Most animal dementias (see Box 12-2) are caused by prions. One form of CJ is **mad cow disease** and it is very likely that consuming beef from infected animals can result in human CJ (DeArmond, 1998). One can also get CJ through blood transfusion from an infected donor because prions are easily passed on in bodily fluids. In one reported case, the donor was not diagnosed with CJ until 18 months after donating blood (Peden et al., 2004). Recently some work with mice suggests a possible future treatment. Mice with scrapie, another prion disease, were given a form of RNA that shuts down the production of a normal protein that is frequently attacked by prions. The cascade of damage might be slowed if the production of such a key protein could be stopped. The treated mice lived, on average, 65 days longer than untreated mice and 65 days is a long time in the life of a mouse (Pfeifer et al., 2006). It will be many years before this treatment can be tested with humans in part because CJ cannot easily be detected in humans in an early enough stage for the treatment to be effective.

All of these less-frequent dementias together account for only about 10 to 15 percent of all dementias. Here are the more frequent forms of dementia.

Vascular Dementia

Vascular dementia is more frequent than the previous dementias discussed. Between 5 and 10 percent; are of this dementia, a form of cardiovascular disease (Corey-Bloom, 2000). Multiple small areas all over the brain are destroyed as small blood vessels become blocked and strokes occur. These strokes produce the cognitive symptoms when they occur in strategic locations or are of a large enough number to reduce cognitive functioning. The early symptoms of vascular dementia include dizziness, headaches, and even passing out. Sometimes the individual will suffer a sudden attack of confusion or even hallucinations. Weakness and fatigue also are quite common but, ordinarily, the cognitive symptoms come much later. Some individuals experience difficulty in swallowing, episodes of laughing or crying, and show kidney failure or scarring of the retina. The symptoms produced depend on which area of the brain has experienced the stroke. Typically, the individual experiences good days and bad days but the good days become less frequent and less good as the disease progresses (Desmond & Tatemichi, 1998). In the early stages, it is difficult to distinguish it from Alzheimer's disease. One promising way of distinguishing the two is to examine the relative ratio of different proteins in the person's spinal fluid but it is too early yet to be certain how effective this technique will be (de Jong et al., 2006). Treatment of vascular dementia involves medications and procedures designed to reduce blood pressure and restore normal blood flow but such treatments, at present, can only slow the progress of the dementia which usually ends with death from a major stroke.

Parkinson's Disease

Parkinson's disease is named for James Parkinson who first described the symptoms in 1817. In the early stages, the individual shows a slowing of movement, called bradykinesia, and then a stooped posture with the head forward and elbows flexed. Walking is done with a shuffling gait and the person shows tremors in their fingers, forearms, eyelids, and tongue. Their face may soon lack emotional expression, speech is often slurred, and the voice becomes a monotone. After some time, the person barely moves at all. The probability of cognitive symptoms is still, however, only 65 percent by age 85 (Chun et al., 1998; Siegert et al., 2006). The average length of life following diagnosis is 8 years.

Although Parkinson's disease usually appears in people over 60, it can appear as early as 30. Actor Michael J. Fox developed Parkinson's before his 30th birthday. Close to 400,000 Americans have Parkinson's disease and the disorder occurs with equal frequency among men and women and people of different races (DiGiovanna, 1994). Without treatment, Parkinson's disease can cause severe disability within 5 years of onset. Increased levels of depression and/or anxiety often accompany Parkinson's (Brod et al., 1998).

Parkinson's disease is one form of **Lewy body dementia (LBD)**. In the early years of the twentieth century, a researcher named Friederich Lewy discovered abnormal proteins disrupting the functioning in the brains of Parkinson's patients and later work showed that these bodies deplete dopamine (and other neurotransmitters such as GABA) in the brain stem, the cerebral cortex, and, in Parkinson's disease, the substantia nigra (see Figure 12-3). These abnormal proteins are called Lewy bodies. LBDs represent about 20 percent of all dementia cases. Susan L. Lindquist found that the abnormal proteins in Lewy bodies and undoubtedly in several other dementias are a result of a misfolding of an ordinarily normal protein. The misfolding is thought to occur during cell division and could be caused by a number of factors. For example, prions may cause misfolding or be misfolded proteins themselves. Some of her work with animals is examining ways to prevent misfoldings and alleviate the symptoms of Parkinson's disease (Cooper et al., 2006).

The factors associated with Parkinson's disease, and presumably with the misfoldings which may underlie the depletion of dopamine, appear to be both genetic and environmental. As you will recall from earlier discussions, we expect both nature and nurture to play some role in nearly every aspect of human development. Eight different genes are associated with Parkinson's and two are directly related to the protein composition of Lewy bodies. Another gene determines the form of an important enzyme that increases or decreases one's susceptibility to certain toxins (Guttman et al., 2003). Some forms of Parkinson's are strongly influenced by a number of environmental agents as well. A good description of the influence of encephalitis can be found in the book and movie *Awakenings* (Sacks, 1999). Some synthetic drugs, such as synthetic heroin, often contain a contaminant that produces Parkinson's (Schneider et al., 1992). Some work suggests that certain pesticides (toxins) are strongly associated with this dementia (Barbeau et al., 1986). Eating the seeds of certain plants, found in Guam, is another risk factor (Spencer et al., 1987). Severe injury to the brain from repeated head trauma is yet another environmental factor and appears to be the reason why champion Muhammed Ali developed Parkinson's. Parkinson's disease is an excellent example of the confluence among genetic and environmental factors.

If the symptoms of Parkinson's disease result from the ever-decreasing availability of dopamine in the brain, then the clearest treatment is to find ways to increase dopamine levels. Dopamine itself cannot be given because it will not cross into the brain from the bloodstream but a precursor of dopamine, L-dopa (also called Levodopa), will and, thus, is one treatment. Unfortunately, maintaining the correct dosage of L-dopa is very difficult because the downward spiral in the brain continues even with such treatment. Too much L-dopa (and dopamine in the brain) produces psychotic, schizophrenic-like symptoms. Because of these difficulties, L-dopa is often a last resort treatment. The mild, antidepressant drug deprenyl inhibits a brain enzyme that breaks down dopamine. Inhibiting this enzyme results in an increase in available dopamine and can slow the progress of Parkinson's disease by as much as 83 percent per year (Pearce, 1992). Some individuals with Parkinson's disease have an electronic device implanted under the skin with a wire attached to the crucial area in the brain. When tremors or rigidity begin, the individual turns on the device by passing a magnet over it. Signals are sent to the brain to stop the tremors and rigidity (Neergaard, 1997). Finally, implants of dopamine-producing tissue from the individual's own adrenal glands or from the brains of human fetuses also have been attempted. This approach has not produced satisfactory results. Implanted fetal tissue takes some time to develop and noticeable changes may take several years. Implants seem to be moderately effective for relatively younger patients but may not benefit adults older than 59. In older patients, the implants frequently produce negative side effects such as uncontolled movement (Freed et al., 2001). Recently, Surmeier and colleagues at Northwestern University began to investigate isradipine, a drug often used to treat hypertension, as a possible way to prevent Parkinson's. In mice, this treatment has had considerable success (Khamsi, 2007).

Alzheimer's Dementia

Alzheimer's dementia or disease, also known as Senile Dementia of the Alzheimer's Type (SDAT), is named for Alois Alzheimer who first described the disease in 1907. Before that time, this and other major declines in cognitive abilities often were not recognized as disease states but were thought to be normal disruptions for old people. It was believed that when you got old, you lost your memory, intelligence, and ability to remain oriented; it was considered to be simply a natural and dreaded part of aging often commonly referred to as senility. Alzheimer was struck by the fact that a woman in her fifties, Auguste D., showed these symptoms long before she should have so he examined her brain after she died and found clear indications of disease. He found massive cell loss in some areas of the brain, tangles of twisted abnormal protein inside nerve cells, and an accumulation of beta amyloid plaque ($A\beta$). These became the markers of Alzheimer's disease and are still the most reliable markers today.

Alzheimer's dementia has been called the cruelest disease. As with some other dementias one can feel oneself slowly vanishing and the effects on family and friends are severe. In the earliest stage of Alzheimer's, no symptoms are observable but undoubtedly tangles and $A\beta$ are beginning to destroy the brain. When the first symptoms appear, it is referred to it as **mild stage Alzheimer's**. These symptoms include difficulty remembering new information such as the name of someone just met or of a book just finished. The person may misplace objects (Where are my keys?; Where did I park?) and have some difficulty driving. Coming up with the right word to complete a thought is more difficult and some fluency is lost. These early symptoms are difficult to distinguish from normal healthy aging. After a period of time, depression frequently occurs. In some cases, delusions (about 22%) and hallucinations (about 10%) also may begin (Mega at al., 1996). In Chapter 7, we talked about one longitudinal study that found many older adults who gave low self-evaluations of their memory sometimes were diagnosed with dementia 2 to 4 years later (Johansson et al., 1997). Perhaps that self-awareness of memory problems is why many at this early stage abandon complex hobbies, some interests, and more difficult chores (Riley, 1999).

As the dementia progresses, one is said to enter the **moderate stage**. Now remote as well as recent memories are difficult to retrieve. Parts of one's past life seem to be gone. The name of the high school and/or college you attended, your own address or phone number, and even the names of friends and relatives become more and more difficult to remember. The ones forgotten last are those who are closest (inner circle of social network) while more distant individuals (outer circle) are lost much sooner. The person may not know what day it is, or where they are, and get lost fairly easily, even when in a familiar environment. As the progression continues, one cannot function alone and requires assistance with meals, cleaning, getting dressed, and most other ADLs. Figure 12-4 shows an assistive device for getting dressed. A person in the moderate stage may be unable to participate in conversation as the difficulty of finding words and of understanding others continue to increase. Agitation may appear and, for some, Sundown syndrome. **Sundown syndrome** is when the disorientation and agitation is greater at night than during the day. These changes do not happen rapidly as one progresses downward through the moderate stage.

Finally, **severe stage** Alzheimer's is reached and the individual is unable to care for themselves at all. Many do not talk at this stage and those who do talk do so in one-word, difficult-to-understand utterances. In the beginnings of this stage, and in the moderate stage, the person may appear to wander aimlessly although it's difficult to know if there might be some purpose known only to the wanderer. Eventually the brain can no longer control walking or most other movements and the person becomes bedridden. In this stage, it is hard to determine whether the individual recognizes anyone, although many families claim that they are still recognized. Eventually the person dies, frequently from pneumonia because of being bedridden for an extended period of time. From the time of first diagnosis, which is usually in the later part of the mild stage or early moderate stage, until death ranges from only 2 up to 18 years with a mean of 7 years (Clark, 2000).

Although this progression is typical, there are some interesting exceptions and big individual differences in the rate at which different mental abilities decline (McCarty et al., 2000). For example, some abilities are preserved even when almost all else is lost. A musician may, for example, still be able to play quite well but only when the musical instrument is placed in her or his hands (Beatty et al., 1997). Extensive longitudinal studies being conducted with nuns in the Catholic order of Notre Dame reveal that some people with Alzheimer's may never show the cognitive symptoms. These nuns are tested and followed throughout their adult lives and one, Sister Mary, showed no signs of cognitive impairment until she died at age 101. At that point, her autopsy showed the cell loss, tangles, and Aβ plaque of Alzheimer's. Perhaps the location of the disease in her brain and her own intelligence allowed her to remain undetected while still alive but at present it is not clear (Snowdon, 1997). It is possible that many, seemingly healthy and mentally intact, older adults have Alzheimer's. Another study looked at brief autobiographies written by these women when they were in their 20s and first joining the order. Researchers found that sentence density in these early writings predicted the occurrence of Alzheimer's 60 or more years later. A low-density sentence is one that expresses a single idea while a high-density sentence expresses several ideas. Low-density sentences predicted Alzheimer's with close to 90 percent accuracy (Riley et al., 2005). This study suggests that Alzheimer's may be in the brain for decades before it can be detected by traditional cognitive tests.

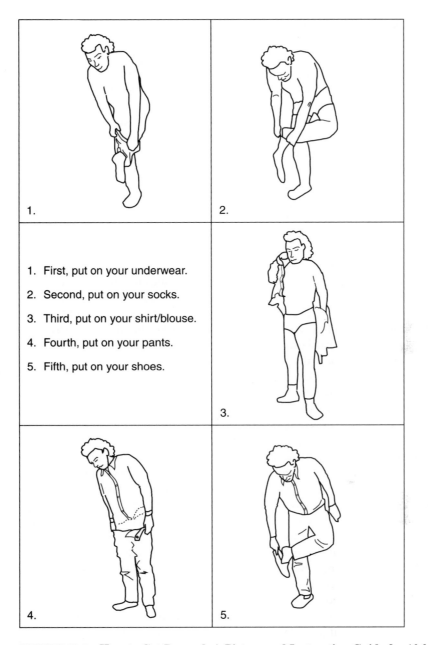

1. First, put on your underwear.

2. Second, put on your socks.

3. Third, put on your shirt/blouse.

4. Fourth, put on your pants.

5. Fifth, put on your shoes.

FIGURE 12-4   How to Get Dressed: A Picture and Instruction Guide for Alzheimer's Patients and Family Caregivers.

Today, Alzheimer's is the most frequent form of dementia accounting for close to 60 percent of all cases. Prevalence and incidence rates increase with age and are slightly higher for women than men (Schulz & Salthouse, 1999). Over the last 5 years, the number of cases has increased by more than 10 percent going from about 4.5 million to over 5 million. As the baby boom generation grows older, the number of Alzheimer's cases will continue to increase and be close to 8 million by 2030 and perhaps more than 16 million by 2050. Some economists suggest that if no changes are made in the ability to treat or prevent Alzheimer's, the cost of providing care for all these people will bankrupt the country. Medicare currently spends, on average, about $4400 for ordinary beneficiaries and over $13,000 for each beneficiary with dementia. Imagine the cost if the number of Alzheimer's cases increases from 5 to 16 million.

Diagnosis.   One important need is to find a reliable way to diagnose the dementia early enough so that early intervention could take place. However, as with many other dementias (Picks, CJ) currently, there is no way to do this and the only certain diagnosis with Alzheimer's occurs at autopsy where tangles and plaques can be measured (Ball & Murdoch, 1997). Cell loss, tangles, and β-amyloid plaque are primarily found in the cortex and hippocampus where acetylcholine is the main neurotransmitter (see Figure 12-3). The cortex is where cognition takes place and the hippocampus is crucial for the formation of new memories. Researchers looking for a way to make the diagnosis earlier have, thus, attempted to use various tests of cognitive abilities. Once one scores low on the MMSE, it is far too late for early diagnosis.

One such study examined those involved in the Baltimore Longitudinal Study of Aging. Over 1400 adults, 60 and older took the WAIS (Chapter 8) and/or the Benton Visual Retention Test (BVRT). The BVRT involves presenting a card with a design on it for 10 seconds and then asking the individual to reproduce that design when the card is removed. There is no time limit and individuals can take as long as they need. The test measures their memory for visual abstract designs and their ability to recreate such designs and a total of 10 cards are presented. In this study, the risk of developing Alzheimer's, up to 15 years after taking the test, was much higher for those who made six or more errors on the test. Performance on the WAIS was not related to risk (Kawas et al., 2003). Another study found impaired classical eyeblink conditioning in one individual 6 years before other standard tests revealed any signs of Alzheimer's (Woodruf-Pak, 2001). A more recent study examined handwriting for individuals with MCI, those diagnosed with early Alzheimer's, and normal controls. Handwriting was assessed using a digitizing tablet that measures time the pen is not in contact with the writing surface, time in contact, and pressure exerted. Participants copied a phone number, a five-item grocery list, a check, the alphabet, and a short paragraph. Those with Alzheimer's showed more time with the pen not in contact and less pressure on the writing pad than did disease-free persons while those with MCI scored between these extremes (Werner et al., 2006). Because those with MCI scored lower than disease-free persons but not as low as those with early Alzheimer's, it will be useful to know how many, if any, of them go on to develop dementia. At present, none of these tests can replace the certain diagnosis that occurs with an autopsy.

Risk Factors.   Other work has focused on identifying the risk factors that are the best predictors of who is likely to get Alzheimer's. These factors may offer clues as to possible diagnostic procedures and to possible causes and treatments. Table 12-3 presents some of the factors that appear to increase or decrease the risk for Alzheimer's. The chances of getting Alzheimer's are greater for individuals with low education, low occupational attainment, or both. A crucial factor in occupation appears to be the complexity of working with people in particular jobs. Although most jobs involve some work with other people, those interactions may be fairly simple as in the case of serving customers or fairly complex as in the case of a negotiator. Research shows that the risk of Alzheimer's is lower for those who have worked in jobs that involved complex interactions with other people. This relationship between cognition and job complexity seems to be independent of education (Andel et al., 2005; 2007). Related work shows that those who are mentally active, and spend time playing games, reading, visiting museums, and solving puzzles have a lower incidence of Alzheimer's (Wilson et al., 2002). It may be that Alzheimer's is simply more difficult to detect in individuals with higher education or more complex occupations or more mental stimulation or that those individuals have greater reserve mental power that delays the onset of some symptoms (Gurland et al., 1995).

The rate of Alzheimer's is higher for women than for men but there are also large differences in incidence and prevalence rates for different racial and ethnic groups. Even when the influence of age, gender, and education variables are removed, African Americans have nearly four times the rate of white Americans and Hispanic Americans have double that rate, up until age 90 (Gurland et al., 1997; Tang et al., 1998). Regardless of gender, race, or ethnic group, individuals with Down's syndrome, who live to old age, are very likely to develop Alzheimer's. Nearly 60 percent of those 65 and older have Alzheimer's dementia with their Down's syndrome (Prasher et al., 2005).

Other factors that increase the risk are the same as those that increase the risk of cardiovascular disease. Hypertension, high cholesterol levels, obesity, smoking, eating a diet high in saturated fats, and not exercising all make Alzheimer's more likely and it is believed that Alzheimer's, like many other disorders, may be due, in part, to inflammation (Grant et al., 2002; Launer, 2005). If this is the case, then use of nonsteroidal anti-inflammatory drugs (NSAIDs) should reduce the risk. In a major study of 2300 persons over a 20-year span, those who used ibuprofen reduced their risk of Alzheimer's by 60 percent; even shorter use reduced the risk by up to 35 percent (Stewart et al., 1997).

TABLE 12-3   Risk Factors for Alzheimer's Dementia

Increased Risk	Decreased Risk
Advanced age	Higher education
Being female	Complex interactions with people at work
African American	Mental activity
Hispanic American	NSAIDs
Down's syndrome	Eating fish
High blood pressure	Physical activity
Obesity	Good nutrition

There are other factors that decrease the risk. The consumption of fish, probably because of inflammation reducing omega-3 fatty acids, reduces the risk of Alzheimer's (Grant et al., 2002). In one comparison of Japanese people living in Japan and in Brazil, the higher rate of Alzheimer's was found for those living in Brazil who no longer eat much fish compared to those living in Japan (Yamada et al., 2002). Physical activity also plays an important role in decreasing the risk of Alzheimer's. A study of over 2000 men, 71 and older, showed that those who walked the most (over 2 miles per day) had the lowest rate of dementia 6 years later (Abbott et al., 2004). In a recent study of women who were 85 and older, those who exercised, more than just walking, 4 or more hours per week were far less likely to develop dementia (Sumic at al., 2007).

Nutrition also seems to play a role in the risk for Alzheimer's. Vitamin B_{12} and antioxidants, vitamins C and E, have also received a fair amount of attention. Some work suggests that individuals with a genetic predisposition toward Alzheimer's are particularly handicapped on some tests of cognition when they also have low levels of B_{12} and it is estimated that close to 10 percent of older adults have such low levels (Bunce et al., 2004). At the same time, other work shows no effect of this B vitamin on cognitive impairment in the general population (Ellinson et al., 2004). Perhaps the tendency for certain genes to result in Alzheimer's is accelerated under conditions in which the individual does not get sufficient B_{12} because of inadequate nutrition or loss of stomach lining (Chapter 3). With respect to other vitamins, two longitudinal studies followed several thousand adults from 4 to 6 years. None had Alzheimer's at the beginning of the study. The first study found a much lower rate of dementia for those who had high intake of vitamins C and E during the course of the study while the second study found a lower rate of Alzheimer's only for those who had a high intake of E from food but not from supplements (Engelhart et al., 2002; Morris et al., 2002). Finally, some work has found a reduced risk of dementia in general for those who consume one to six alcoholic drinks a week (Mukamal et al., 2003). Eating the correct, vitamin-rich foods, with an occasional drink, may help reduce the risk.

Causes. Although all of these risk factors offer clues as to the causes of Alzheimer's, researchers do not yet know exactly how all of the pieces fit together. One distinction of some importance in the search for causes is the distinction between early and late onset Alzheimer's. Early onset cases are those diagnosed before the age of 65 and comprise about 10 percent of all cases. Late onset are those diagnosed at 65 or older and represent the vast majority of cases. Early onset cases progress through the stages and decline much faster than late onset cases (Wilson et al., 2000). In terms of genetics and environment, it appears that early onset cases are more strongly genetic while late onset cases appear to be less so. Over both early and late onset cases, the risk of developing Alzheimer's is six times greater among close relatives of an individual with the disorder than among the general population (Gatz et al., 1997). At the same time, none of the established gene connections can account for more than 2 percent of total Alzheimer's cases (Gatz, 2007).

The genetic factors that are associated with Alzheimer's are not simple and direct. Research suggests that more than a dozen different genes influence susceptibility to Alzheimer's (Bertram et al., 2007) but we will examine only a few. One of these, a gene on chromosome 19, codes for a protein called Apolipoprotein E (ApoE) that functions to transport cholesterol in the body. There are three different forms of this protein, ApoE-2,

ApoE-3, and ApoE-4, and we inherit one from our father and one from our mother (of course we might get the same form from each parent). White Americans and people from China who have two *ApoE-4* genes are more than twice as likely to develop Alzheimer's as those with any other ApoE combination (Blacker et al., 1997; Katzman et al., 1997; Roses & Pericak-Vance, 1995). Having one ApoE-4 gene carries less of a risk than having two (Gatz, 2007). For African and Hispanic Americans, the form of inherited ApoE seems to make no difference; their rates of Alzheimer's are high in all cases. Some work suggests that these groups may average a higher level of cholesterol and that, even with a good form of ApoE, the amount of cholesterol still influences, in some as yet unknown way, the incidence of Alzheimer's perhaps through inflammation. A comparison of African Americans with residents of Yoruba, Africa, found that Americans had much higher levels of Alzheimer's and cholesterol (Hendrie, 2001). Physical activity lowers the risk of Alzheimer's but, while this has been found a number of times, some work has obtained the effect only for those who do not have ApoE-4 (Podewils et al., 2005).

Chromosome 21 carries a gene that codes for an **amyloid precursor protein** (APP). Mutations of this gene may produce a form of APP turned into Aβ (Lewis et al., 2001). An enzyme called β-secretase is implicated in this process because it seems to clip the ends of proteins off at the wrong point, leading to the accumulation of Aβ in the brain (Vassar et al., 1999). Researchers are looking for a chemical inhibitor of this enzyme to reduce the accumulation of Aβ in the brain. Some work suggests that NSAIDs may reduce the risk of Alzheimer's by partially blocking β-secretase (De Strooper & König, 2001; Weggen et al., 2001). Mutations of the *PS1* gene on chromosome 14 and *PS2* on chromosome 1 also seem to be involved in the conversion of APP to Aβ. Figure 12-5 summarizes some of the information on these genetic factors.

There must be environmental factors that play a part in causing Alzheimer's. Comparisons of identical twins who have exactly the same genetic makeup found higher concordance rates for these twins than for fraternal twins (.67 compared to .22) but such estimates suggest that about 25 percent of the variance can be attributed to environmental factors (Gatz et al., 1997). Furthermore, many of the risk factors (see Table 12-3) are clearly environmental.

One environmental factor that has received a lot of attention is aluminum (Grant et al., 2002). Comparisons of Alzheimer's and other brains at autopsy have sometimes found higher levels of aluminum in the former but not always (Xu et al., 1992). Other work has found an increased risk of Alzheimer's in communities with higher concentrations of aluminum in the drinking water (Rondeau et al., 2000). Work with animals shows that such aluminum can travel through the intestines and end up in the brain (Walton et al., 1995) while other work shows that aluminum in the brain can result in degeneration (Yokel, 2000). Much of the aluminum that we come into contact with is through antiperspirant use; almost all antiperspirants contain aluminum. Aluminum has been shown to increase the action of the PS2 gene which may then accelerate the accumulation of Aβ in the brain (Matsuzaki et al., 2004). Aluminum has been found in the tangles in the brains of Alzheimer's victims (Savory et al., 1996) and in the hippocampus of animals (Fattoretti et al., 2003). Aluminum causes Aβ and a protein called tau, to accumulate in the brains of animals (Kawahara, 2005). Tau is a protein that seems to be a major factor in the tangles of Alzheimer's and is coded for by a gene on chromosome 21. Some believe that it is tau,

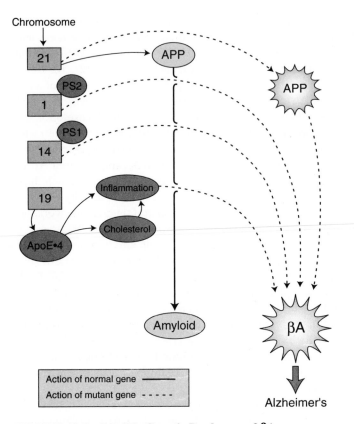

FIGURE 12-5   Possible Genetic Producers of βA.

rather than or in combination with Aβ, that is responsible for the degeneration of the brain. Down's syndrome is a risk factor for Alzheimer's and occurs when chromosome 21 occurs in triplicate rather than as a pair. But is aluminum a cause of Alzheimer's? Researchers cannot say yes although the evidence suggests some connection. Researcher Masahiro Kawahara says that "it should be emphasized that unnecessary exposure to aluminum should be avoided" (2005, p. 178).

Other work on environmental factors has found some evidence for accelerated DNA and free-radical damage in the brains of Alzheimer's victims. It may be that the disease makes the brain more susceptible to such damage (Flirski & Sobow, 2005). Research has found increased consumption of vitamin C in the brains of Alzheimer's victims, suggesting a greater need for this antioxidant protection (Quinn et al., 2003). One longitudinal study found that high levels of antioxidants, particularly beta-carotene, seemed to offer some protection against cognitive decline, especially for those with *ApoE-4* genes (Hu et al., 2006).

Finally, one view suggests that the underlying cause of Alzheimer's may be an accumulation of brain garbage (Chapter 4). Tau, Aβ, metals like aluminum, and other abnormal or dangerous proteins may not be carried away, perhaps due to the actions of genes

PS1 and *PS2*. As a result, the accumulation begins to disrupt the functioning of neurons and eventually the destruction of nerve cells and connections (Sambamurti et al., 2006). Clearly more research is needed to untangle the mystery of what causes Alzheimer's and how best to treat it. At present, the interactions among possible causal factors is quite complex.

Treatments. The best "treatment" for any disease is prevention, or to not get it in the first place. Over the last several years, researchers have been attempting to find a vaccine for Alzheimer's that could prevent the disease from destroying the brain and most of this work has focused on preventing the accumulation of Aβ. The initial work with mice showed that the accumulation of amyloid could be greatly reduced by getting the mouse immune system to regard amyloid as an invader that should be eliminated. To do this, amyloid was combined with substances that provoke an immune response (e.g., cholera toxin). Mice receiving such injections showed very little amyloid accumulation compared to mice not receiving the treatment (Schenk et al., 1999). The work was so promising and Alzheimer's is so devastating that human clinical trials were begun but stopped when some of the patients developed meningoencephalitis. This disease has aspects of both meningitis and encephalitis and is associated with severe disability and mortality. New work is attempting to create a human vaccine that will not produce such an unacceptable side effect (Ghochikyan et al., 2006). It may be 6 or more years before any vaccine is available for human use.

Current pharmacological treatments approved by the Food and Drug Administration include several drugs for mild and moderate stages and one for late-moderate to severe stage Alzheimer's. The mild and moderate stage drugs work to increase the level of acetylcholine by inhibiting the enzyme that sweeps this neurotransmitter in the brain. The first one approved was tacrine (Cognex), which often slowed down the progress of the disease but also frequently caused damage to the liver. Three later drugs—donepezil (Aricept), rivastigmine (Exalon), and galantamine hydrobromide (Reminyl)—were as effective without damaging the liver and so are the preferred treatments today (Gillette-Guyonnet et al., 2006). For later stage Alzheimer's and also for vascular dementia, the drug memantine (Namenda) has been shown to slow progression and works on different receptor cells than do other enzyme inhibitors (Winoblad & Poritis, 1999). That means memantine can be used along with an enzyme inhibitor to produce a broader positive effect (Farlow et al., 2003).

Recently researchers have attempted to find a drug that will break up or inhibit Aβ from causing damage. In animal studies, the antibiotic, clioquinol, has been found to greatly reduce the amount of Aβ in mice brains and clinical trials with humans have begun (Melov, 2002). In one of these studies, 36 moderate to severe stage Alzheimer's patients were randomly assigned to receive clioquinol or a placebo and those receiving the antibiotic showed far less decline over the 9 months of the study and reduced levels of Aβ (Ritchie et al., 2003). Other work has found that resveratrol (see Chapter 5) also clears βA in cells in culture (Marambaud et al., 2005). It is thought that some forms of Aβ are actively involved in creating damage while other forms are not. A dye called congo red seems effective at blocking active Aβ but, unfortunately, will not cross the blood-brain barrier and enter the brain where its potential benefits could be realized (Liu & Schubert, 2006). Work continues to find a chemical that will cross into the brain and deactivate Aβ.

Other work has focused on tau rather than on Aβ. Tau is responsible for the formation of tangles. One study with mice found that a 50 percent tau reduction had no effect on Aβ accumulation but did prevent declines in performance in a water maze. Mice with reduced tau but high levels of Aβ performed as well as control group mice and much better than mice with both tau and Aβ (Roberson et al., 2007).

Some earlier work suggested that *estrogen* might be an effective treatment for Alzheimer's (Giacoboni, 1998). Of course, most women old enough to have dementia are past the age of menopause and so would receive estrogen as a part of hormone replacement therapy (HRT) or as a separate treatment if they are to benefit. Unfortunately, HRT is strongly associated with increased risk of cancer and heart attacks (Rossouw et al., 2002). Furthermore, the Women's Health Initiative, a large longitudinal study found twice the rate of dementia in postmenopausal women receiving estrogen-progesterone therapy (Schumaker et al., 2003). In a more direct examination of the effects of estrogen on Alzheimer's, 97 women with mild to moderate dementia were randomly assigned to receive low or high doses of estrogen or a placebo by wearing a skin patch. Their progress was monitored at 2, 6, 12, and 15 months and, while 74 percent of those in the placebo group worsened, 80 percent of those in the estrogen groups did too (Mulnard et al., 2000). Estrogen does not appear to be an effective treatment for women with Alzheimer's but work on other possible hormone treatments is under way (Casadesus et al., 2006).

Antioxidants, vitamins C and E, are also under investigation as possible treatments for mild stage Alzheimer's. Vitamin E has been shown to slow down the progression of Alzheimer's in some clinical work (Sano et al., 1997). This beneficial effect of vitamin E is increased when vitamin C also is administered (Quinn et al., 2004).

Gingko biloba, which was briefly mentioned in Chapter 6, results in some improvement on cognitive measures for individuals in the early levels of Alzheimer's disease. In a review of the effects of gingko on cognitive performance due to various forms of dementia, gingko was found to be effective in 39 of 40 trials (Kleijnen & Knipschild, 1992). Gingko is frequently recommended although one must be cautious because bleeding under the skin or in the eye has been observed; usage must be monitored (Wincor, 1999).

Some work has focused on the benefits of cognitive stimulation for people with Alzheimer's. As you know, people with higher levels of education and/or more complex jobs and/or who regularly engage in mental activities are less likely to develop Alzheimer's. This suggests that mental stimulation might be an effective way to slow down the progression of the disease once it has begun. Work by Aimee Spector and colleagues found positive results as those receiving stimulating sessions show far less decline and sometimes improvement when compared to those not receiving stimulation (Spector et al., 2003). Stimulation consisted of activities such as using money, playing word games, and discussing current events over a 7-week period. More recently, a comparison of Alzheimer's patients, matched on severity of disease, found improvement for those who engaged in reading aloud and simple arithmetic activities for 6 months (Kawashima et al., 2005).

Person-centered care or validation therapy is yet another treatment that is being used more frequently. The treatment does not generally slow the progression of the disease but does create a warm, friendly environment and greatly reduced agitation (Kitwood, 1993). Such care involves talking about past experiences, and attending to the feelings expressed by the person with dementia. The caregiver may rephrase what the individual said to help

People with confusion due to dementia need a lot of support from caregivers.

communication, maintain good eye contact, gently touch the person, and even use music to bring back memories and relax the person (Toseland et al., 1997). Music therapy, in its simplest form, where older, familiar songs are played, is useful for reducing agitation and can evoke humming, laughing, and even singing (Brotons et al., 1997).

There are a number of treatments that the families of those with Alzheimer's have found to be effective and some of these are presented in Box 12-3. All treatments and even interactions with people who have Alzheimer's, or any other dementia, can be difficult and we need to realize that those difficulties are shared by both caregiver and afflicted. It is never a good idea to argue or become angry with a person who has a dementia because that only increases the difficulty for both persons.

Communication.   Effective communication is one of the most difficult problems for those with Alzheimer's and for those who care for them. Imagine what it might be like if you found yourself only able to understand some of the words that were spoken to you and that you were only able to use some words yourself. People with dementia experience this on a daily basis and the problem only grows worse as the disease progresses. Steven Sabat (2001) spent considerable time examining these difficulties and the cognitive abilities still

BOX **12-3**

Dementia Treatments Used by Families

Families who care for a relative or spouse with Alzheimer's disease or some other form of dementia often devise effective treatments to deal with potential problem behaviors and to calm the confused and/or agitated individual. Here are some examples of a few of those treatments described by the caring family members:

■ At night, mother gets out of bed and wanders. We fear that she may go to the kitchen and turn on the stove or that she may go outside, wander off and be unable to find her way home. Every evening, after she goes to bed, we place a basket of clean laundry beside a chair in the hall near her bedroom. She cannot get to the kitchen or an outside door without going past the laundry and, as a result, she never does. She comes out of her bedroom, sees the laundry, and sits down and folds it all. Once that task is complete, she goes back to bed secure in the feeling that she has accomplished what she set out to do.

■ Several times a week, Grandpa decides it is time that he went home; he has been visiting long enough and has things to do. He is, of course, already at home but no amount of arguing will convince him of that. We deal with this by saying goodbye to him and thanking him for coming over to visit. One of us then offers to walk home with him. We walk down the street a short way, then turn around and head back. When we get back, Grandpa feels comfortable at home. Sometimes he will thank us for coming over to visit him.

■ Nearly every evening my wife and I watch the 11 o'clock news before going to bed. During the news, she will turn to me and say, "You'd better go now; Larry will be home soon and I don't think it's a good idea for you to be here so late." I am Larry but she doesn't recognize me. I learned quickly not to argue with her and play along. I will say that Larry knows I am here and he said it was fine. I will be a perfect gentleman and offer to sleep on the couch because I have no where else to go. Larry should be home any minute and I will clear it with him when he returns. She says, okay and heads off to bed. After a short time, I can go to bed without disturbing her.

■ We have placed a recorder near the TV and it clicks on and delivers messages to Mom at various times throughout the day. At 11:45 AM, it comes on and Dad's voice says, "It's just about lunch time, Honey; I'm feeling hungry, how about you?" Mom will answer and go to the kitchen and fix lunch. It's always the same lunch but it's pretty tasty. Dad always comes home for lunch so when he arrives at noon, lunch is ready and waiting.

■ Here in the nursing home we have a number of Alzheimer's patients who can become quite agitated: We try to avoid drugs and restraints whenever possible and have found that a recorded message from a close family member usually can calm most individuals. When Leo gets agitated, we hand him the phone and tell him it's for him. The recorded message from his brother Tommy always calms him and he'll listen and talk as if he really were on the phone. The same recording can be used again. This is a nice friendly deception that works very well in most cases and is referred to as simulated presence therapy.

held by those with Alzheimer's. He reports cases of caregivers who believe that the people they care for know nothing anymore and of physicians who say that treating a person with Alzheimer's is like practicing veterinary medicine. Those with Alzheimer's are often regarded as no longer being human. Being treated this way can lead to excess disability.

Excess disability refers to problems that are not due to the disease itself but are due to the ways in which the person is treated by others. When others lie to you to get you to do what they wish, do things for you that you can still do yourself, go too fast for you to keep up, or talk about you as if you weren't there, you may develop depression, anxiety, and just give up, not because of your dementia, but because you are treated as an object. Of course, one might say that some of the treatments presented in Box 12-3 involve dishonesty but the key element is whether they lead to excess disability or not. Do they harm or help? The treatments in the box generally are believed to help.

Do people with Alzheimer's know anything? Shouldn't they be treated as children or infants? Sabat says no and gives several examples. In one, a man with Alzheimer's was found going through the pockets of coats as he prepared to leave a support group function. Was he trying to steal something? Was he totally confused? Closer examination showed that he knew exactly what he was doing and had made an intelligent plan. His coat was new and he knew he would not remember it so he placed a familiar object in the pocket so he would know which coat was his. In another example, an institutionalized woman wandered through the halls aimlessly; she seemed to be going nowhere and for no purpose. Closer examination found that she "wandered" when group discussions took place and, because she had great difficulty communicating, she chose to simply take a walk during those times. Individuals with Alzheimer's are aware of their difficulties, try to find strategies for dealing with these problems, and make adaptive changes to their self-identities (Cotrell & Hooker, 2005). Caregivers, whether family members or professionals, need to be patient and do what they can to assist the communication efforts of those with dementia (Smith & Buckwalter, 2005). The burden on these caregivers is, as one might expect, enormous.

Caregiving

Most people who develop Alzheimer's or another dementia are cared for by their family, especially their spouse, rather than in an institution, at least in the early stages (Haley et al., 1987). This places tremendous pressure and strain on the family member(s) who must devote a major part of her or his life to caring for an individual who often has no hope for recovery. These caregivers know that, as time goes by, they may not even be recognized by the person for whom they care (Alspaugh et al., 1999). It is hard, however, to let a loved one go to be cared for in an institution even when they need help with nearly all ADLs. It feels to many family members like abandonment, and have not family members sworn to care for each other through good times and bad? Those who are placed in an institution generally survive for less time than those who are not, although some recent work shows that the timing of the placement is critical. Those who are institutionalized at a later date tend to live as long as those who are not (McClendon et al., 2006). Such work supports those caregivers who believe that the afflicted family member should be kept at home for as long as possible.

Depression levels for these caregivers are well above average and are strongly influenced by the stress they feel and the coping strategies they use to deal with that stress. Those who can maintain a strong sense of mastery, of control over their lives and environments, tend to fare better (Adams et al., 2005). Coping is influenced by stress level and those with high levels of stress tend to adopt more emotion managing strategies while those with lower levels of stress tend to adopt more problem-solving strategies (see

SOCIAL POLICY APPLICATIONS

Considering all of the psychopathologies that you have read about in this chapter, perhaps the one that most people are concerned about is Alzheimer's disease. This is probably because of the increase in prevalence; almost everyone knows someone who has been affected by the disease. On the good side, you have read about the progress being made in treatment as a result of research. On the bad side, researchers have a far way to go. Both more research and better treatment options, including preventive treatment, are needed and there are a few things that you can do to help. As noted before, staying informed about legislation is important. At the time of this writing (July 2007), the Alzheimer's Breakthrough Act of 2007 and the Positive Aging Act were being discussed in Congress. Together, these acts would double the funding for research to attain breakthroughs in diagnosis, prevention, and intervention. The legislation also would create a system for caregiver support which is critical. Finally, another important provision is a tax credit to help families with expenses related to care and a deduction for long-term care insurance. Another provision being discussed is education and awareness that mental illness is not a normal part of aging and is treatable. This could go a long way toward better treatment for depression and other disorders that you read about. Where do you come in? Stay informed and stay active in letting your representatives know that you support these issues. In addition, consider working on your own intervention. As you have read, early results of research indicate that exercise and cognitive activities seem to help tremendously in prevention and treatment of Alzheimer's disease. Consider volunteering, but in a different way than you might have thought. Many groups (scouts, sororities, fraternities, churches, etc.) visit residents in nursing homes or take them things they have made. Next time, plan a cognitive activity to help boost their skills or organize a fun walk for seniors. Not too many like to exercise, but walking with someone interested in hearing your story along the way is a different story. Be creative, give it a try!

Chapter 9; Ross et al., 1997). Some forms of emotion managing strategies, such as not sharing one's feelings, tend to lead to greater alcohol consumption while others, such as reappraising the situation in a positive way, lead to less (Mjelde-Mossey et al., 2004). Traits, as well as coping, are a part of personality and other work shows that caregivers with high levels of neuroticism have less social support and are more likely to experience stress and depression. Those with high levels of extraversion have more social support and less stress and depression (Lee et al., 2006b).

Research has examined African and white American differences in the caregiving experience, stress experienced, and coping. A number of studies have shown that African American caregivers are more likely to report positive aspects of caregiving than their white counterparts and less stress. This positive view and lower stress appear to be due to higher levels of religious belief and African American cultural values. African American caregivers are more like to say "God will reward me" or "it's my duty to take care of my own" (Roff et al., 2004; Williams, 2005). Those African Americans with moderately high involvement in their culture tend to experience fewer health problems as a result of caregiving (Dilworth-Anderson et al., 2004). Recent work has examined coping differences and found that African Americans were more likely to use religion as a coping strategy and to deny problems while white Americans were more likely to use humor and to accept problems (Kosberg et al., 2007).

Caregivers are not the only ones to bear the burden when a family member has Alzheimer's. Grandchildren are especially vulnerable when a grandparent is diagnosed with a severe dementia such as Alzheimer's disease. Even young grandchildren seem able to understand and deal with the decline of a grandparent produced by heart disease, cancer, or severe arthritis. With Alzheimer's disease, however, the grandparent may appear to be quite healthy but in interactions may be unable to remember the grandchild's name, may lose their temper very easily, or may act strange, confused, agitated, and forgetful. This is difficult for young grandchildren who may believe that they are doing something to cause the grandparent to act in this way. Adolescent grandchildren are likely to feel anger, shame, or guilt when around a grandparent with Alzheimer's disease. They may feel very embarrassed by the behavior of a once respected and loved grandparent. Grandchildren need to be told about the disorder, that the grandparent is not intentionally behaving badly, and that the disease is not contagious. The Alzheimer Association has a number of brochures and suggestions that can be helpful for children and adolescents and younger grandchildren. Providing children and grandchildren with tips on how to talk to and deal with the behavior of relatives with dementia can be very beneficial and produce more positive interactions.

One important support for family caregivers is respite care. **Respite care** occurs when the family caregiver(s) is (are) freed from the burden of caring while the older adult in need of care is placed in a care center or a hired home-worker comes to the home to provide the necessary care. Typically this respite lasts for 2 or more weeks. The caregiver receives a well-earned vacation and this time off is very effective in relieving some of the

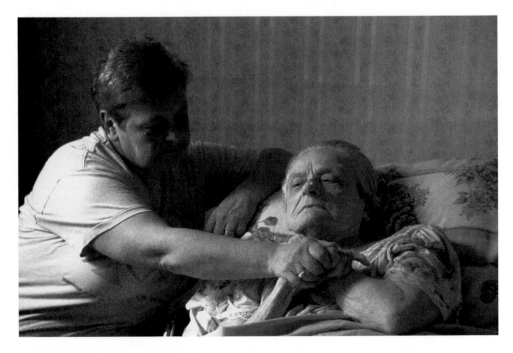

Caregiving can be a very stressful job.

PROJECT **12**

Be a Volunteer

Most of the disorders presented in this chapter will not be witnessed by most readers. We expect, however, that you have had some personal experience with at least one of the disorders. Perhaps you know of an older friend, relative, or neighbor who has abused alcohol. You may have or have had a grandparent with some form of dementia. You may have witnessed depression in a parent or grandparent who has lost a close family member or spouse.

If you have not had any of these experiences, then we recommend that you volunteer in a senior center, for the Alzheimer's Association, or for an adult daycare center to gain some first-hand knowledge of some of these disorders. If you have, then you know the importance of a friendly smile or touch.

Another way to help out is by participating in or helping to organize the raising of funds to support research on these conditions or care for those afflicted. For example, many local Alzheimer's Associations hold an annual Memory Walk to raise funds and would be glad to have your help.

---

stress of caring for another and seems also to improve the functioning of the dependent older adult (Knight, 1993).

In nearly every community, there is a number of support groups for caregivers and frequently for care recipients. Those who participate in these groups report reduced stress and depression as one would expect from perceived social support (Zarit et al., 2004). Support is available online and recent work suggests that these groups may function best when designed to take into account participant's gender, race, and education level (Smyth et al., 2007). Researchers cannot yet heal dementia but daily scientists make great strides in identifying possible causes and effective treatments and caregivers lovingly care for loved ones with dementia. It is our job to learn as much as we can about all of the psychopathologies in order to support those who need our help.

CHAPTER HIGHLIGHTS

- In this chapter we examined several types of psychopathology and the incidence and prevalence of these disorders for different aged persons, males and females, and different ethnic groups.
- Comorbidity and multimorbidity are more frequent for older adults and make diagnosis and treatment more difficult.
- Mood disorders are characterized by moods out of proportion to the existing circumstances and take three forms. Mania, or exaggerated elation, has about the same prevalence among younger and older adults. Major depression, which is less prevalent among older adults while milder depression or dysthymic disorder, is as frequent among older as younger adults. Bipolar disorder is less prevalent among older adults.
- Several hypotheses that attempt to explain these differences in rates of depression include social stigma, better coping strategies, and different symptoms for older adults. All of these mood disorders are treatable.
- Driving cessation, increased disability, and loss of social support are more frequent causes of depression in older than in younger adults.

- Some treatments for depression may have other dangers for older adults (SSRIs) while others are very effective (life review and physical activity).
- Females make more suicide attempts but males are more successful at suicide. The highest rate of suicide is for older white men. This is clearly not a cohort effect and may be due, in part, to the loss of power/money that occurs for older white men.
- Alcoholism is currently higher among younger and middle-age adults than older adults but this difference may be due to a low level of alcoholism among members of the cohort that came of age during Prohibition, the underreporting of alcoholism by family and doctors of older adults, and the unhealthy lifestyle and early death of many alcoholics.
- Cognitive disorders are characterized by symptoms of impaired memory, judgment, intelligence, orientation, and emotionality.
- Diagnosing a cognitive disorder is difficult and requires administration of several tests.
- Mild cognitive impairment increases with age and is considered by some as a first sign of dementia.
- Dementias include neuroAIDS, Korsakoff's syndrome, frontotemporal dementias, Huntington's disease, CJ, vascular dementia, Parkinson's (Lewy body dementias), and Alzheimer's; Alzheimer's is the most frequent dementia.
- Some factors increase the risk of Alzheimer's (e.g., advanced age, high blood pressure) while others decrease the risk (higher education, good nutrition).
- The progression of Alzheimer's is unique to each individual but generally starts with unnoticeable small cognitive decline and ends with severe cognitive impairment. Alzheimer's disease may be present for a long time before any symptoms appear.
- More than a dozen different genes have been implicated in Alzheimer's research and a number of environmental factors (e.g., aluminum) also seem to play an important role.
- Prevention efforts have focused on reducing amyloid plaque. These efforts include injecting chemically treated amyloid to boost the immune system and taking certain nonsteroidal anti-inflammatory drugs that may block the accumulation of proteins that result from the actions of the enzyme β-secretase.
- Treatments for Alzheimer's disease include medications designed to increase the amount of acetylcholine. These work well for mild and moderate levels of the disease.
- There are a number of promising leads toward effective treatments for Alzheimer's.
- People with dementia are still people capable of thinking. Communication is a major problem for them and for their caregivers and can be improved with effort.
- Caregivers of Alzheimer's patients experience a great deal of stress. Respite care has been shown to be one effective way of temporarily relieving the burden of these caregivers.
- A number of therapies have been used with Alzheimer's patients in institutions and in homes. The most popular of these therapies are validation therapy, music therapy, simulated presence therapy, and person-centered care.

STUDY QUESTIONS

1. Which disorders discussed in this chapter are most likely to have a genetic cause and which are most likely to have an environmental cause? Is it ever the case that the cause is entirely genetic or entirely environmental?

2. Why do many people believe that older adults are more likely to be depressed than younger adults? What does the evidence on prevalence rates show?

3. What are some of the signs of a possible suicide attempt?

4. If older adults have lower rates of alcoholism in part because of Prohibition, then what would you expect to happen to other types of drug abuse if drugs were no longer illegal? If it turned out that Prohibition had no effect on alcoholism rates (that is, they don't change as other cohorts enter old age), does that suggest any effect of illegality on rates of use? What do you expect the data to show when it becomes available?

5. If an older relative shows a sudden loss of memory and fears Alzheimer's disease, is there anything that you now know that might help to reassure this person?

6. Describe the types of dementia discussed in this chapter.

7. Describe the steps recommended to reach a diagnosis of Alzheimer's disease. Why are these steps necessary?

8. Describe the three physical changes evident at autopsy in the brain of a person with Alzheimer's disease.

9. What is the cause of Alzheimer's disease? Genetics? ApoE? Aluminum? Other? Does it depend on whether the disease is early or late onset?

10. Why do people with dementia often get treated like objects? What can this lead to?

11. Describe some of the treatments used for Alzheimer's disease including family treatments, drugs, and talk therapies.

12. How do coping strategies used by caregivers vary as a function of stress and race and what strategies are more effective?

RECOMMENDED READINGS

Mace, N. L. & Rabins, P. V. (1999). *The 36-Hour Day* (3rd ed.). Baltimore, MD: Johns Hopkins University Press. This book is a standard for caregivers and provides very valuable information and tips for successful caregiving.

McGowin, D. F. (1993). *Living in the Labyrinth: A Personal Journey Through the Maze of Alzheimer's*. New York: Delta (Dell Publishing). This is a book written by a woman in the earlier stages of Alzheimer's disease. This is an excellent description of some of the cognitive difficulties encountered and the emotional impact of this dreaded disease on the person who has it.

Sabat, S. R. (2001). *The Experience of Alzheimer's Disease: Life Through a Tangled Veil*. Malden, MA: Blackwell. This book presents a number of real-life examples that illustrate the remaining cognitive abilities of persons with Alzheimer's disease and argues strongly for far better treatment.

Shenk, D. (2001). *The Forgetting Alzheimer's: Portrait of an Epidemic*. New York: Doubleday. This book is a very readable and interesting description of Alzheimer's disease from its first description, through past lives, and into the most current research.

INTERNET RESOURCES

www.nami.org. The National Alliance for the Mentally Ill.

www.nimh.nih.gov. National Institute of Mental Health.

www.alz.org. The Alzheimer's Association provides the latest information on Alzheimer's disease, research, and education.

www.alzheimers.org. Alzheimer's Disease Education & Referral Center.

www.parkinsons.org and *www.depression.org.* Good sites for information on Parkinson's and depression.

www.alzgene.org. For information on the genes that increase susceptibility to Alzheimer's.

CHAPTER

13 Healthy/Helpful Environments: Places and People

One's home is like a delicious piece of pie you order in a restaurant on a country road one cozy evening—the best piece of pie you have ever eaten in your life—and can never find again. After you leave home, you may find yourself feeling homesick, even if you have a new home that has nicer wallpaper and a more efficient dishwasher than the home in which you grew up.

—Lemony Snicket

Close your eyes and think about home. What comes to mind? Do you picture one place or several places? What makes up that place? Do you see people as well as buildings, yards, sidewalks, furniture, knick-knacks on shelves? What about the feelings that you have? Is home where your heart is? Is there no place like home? Many of us have warm and fuzzy feelings about the places we call home. Others may have negative feelings about some of the places where they have lived. By the time we reach old age, we have lived in many places and probably have a very complex view of what "home" means.

In this chapter we explore where older people live, what their options are when they need more help, and what makes different environments supportive.

How Spaces Become Places or How We Fit in

The right environment is the one in which we feel comfortable—but what exactly does that mean? We are comfortable when we fit with our surroundings. Powell Lawton and his colleagues at the Philadelphia Geriatric Center proposed an explanation of this fit (Lawton, 1980; Nahemow, 1997). Their theory of **person–environment congruence**, called the ecological theory of aging, explains fit in terms of a how a person operates in any given environment. The theory holds that the ability to complete a task is a result of the congruence between what the environment demands of us (which they call environmental press or demand) and the capabilities of the person attempting the task (which they call competence or person capability). For example, if you have to sit in a hard metal chair for a 3-hour lecture thus requiring you to sit in a certain posture and pay attention, and your back, legs, and brain allow you to do that then you fit this environment, or have person–environment congruence. The important part of Lawton's theory is the "fit" between the person and the

317

environment; neither one alone predicts how comfortable people are or how well they complete daily tasks. If an environment is not all challenging, we give up or get bored. If it is too demanding, we can't perform well. We work best at middle levels of stimulation or demand. What we bring to this fit is important in the middle ranges of demand, but not at the high or low ranges. For example, none of us can see in the pitch dark or glaring bright light; we all function best somewhere in the middle. However, what we bring to the fit, our capabilities, can make a difference in the middle. The better off or more capable we are, the more demands we can handle; the less able we are, the less demands we tolerate to be successful. When you are very tired after spending a long night studying or writing a paper, you have more difficulty concentrating in class. The instructor must be particularly stimulating to keep your attention. If the lights are dimmed for slides and your instructor has a soft soothing voice, you may be headed for a great in-class nap. However, if you had a good night's sleep and a healthy breakfast, you can operate well in even the most boring situations. Powell Lawton and his colleagues proposed the docility hypothesis, which says that individuals with lower capabilities are more vulnerable to environmental demands than people with higher competence. Now, consider some of the changes talked about in old age (Chapters 3 and 6) and the demands of most environments. You can see where some environments would be much more helpful to older adults than others.

Powell Lawton's work has served as the basis for extending the idea of congruence beyond the physical space. It also has spurred much research and work in the design and modification of environments to reduce demand, to improve person capabilities, and to replace tasks for older persons in order to improve person-environment congruence.

Types of Person–Environment Congruence

We operate in environments on a number of levels, so we can fit or not fit on as many levels (Weisman et al., 1997; Rubenstein & Parmelee, 1992). These include fitting in with other people (**social congruence**), being able to move around or work in a given space (**physical congruence**), and feelings about a place and your identity in that space (**psychological congruence**). We go through life choosing environments that fit on all these levels or change environments to adapt to our competencies. As you read the next section, think about how well you fit into the various environments in which you have lived.

Social Congruence.   Social relationships and the importance of social support were discussed in Chapter 10. Social congruence refers to many of the issues discussed there. We are comfortable in environments that allow us the right level of access to people with whom we share good interactions. Many people in old age choose their living arrangements based on where their friends or family are and how easily they will be able to facilitate their social interactions. Some people fit in many social environments; they like all kinds of people. Those who are more social and outgoing might be considered higher in social competence and have a wider range of environmental adaptation. Others who prefer to be alone, who don't make friends easily, are shy, or have hearing or other disabilities may have more trouble adapting to new social environments.

Senior View

We sat down with May Lee who agreed to be interviewed only because her daughter is a colleague and as she said, *I will do anything to help my daughter and her work.* May, who had recently turned 80, was a second-generation Chinese American, born in Savannah, Georgia. *I lived many places in my life, even in Brooklyn, New York, as a child. But I like living in Savannah better than anywhere else because it is familiar, comfortable and feels most like "home."*

May Lee quit school and started working in her mother's grocery store when she was 16. *I didn't mind, my friends were all in the same boat and my family couldn't afford for me to go to school anymore. After I married, we needed more money so we spent our small savings to buy a small grocery store. I kept working there after my husband died. But my store was in a housing project and I didn't feel safe there with all the crime. So I sold my store to the project and have been retired ever since.* We asked her how she handled working and raising a family. *My girls raised themselves,* she laughed. Her daughter, colleague JoAnn, sat in the corner and just shook her head and chuckled.

We asked May Lee to tell us a little about what she thinks about her future home. *I live alone now in a house that I won and is completely paid for. I don't drive but I never did. I never learned to drive; I always took the bus and still do sometimes. I also rely on family and friends to take me grocery shopping, to church, and to the doctor's office.*

A little more than 2 years before our visit, May Lee had an operation to repair a ruptured aneurysm. After the operation, she had a stroke that left her with a little difficulty moving around. This change in mobility prompted her daughters to encourage her to move in with one of them. Jo Ann really wanted her mother to move in with her. *I don't feel that I need help. I do enjoy visiting my daughters. But I would miss my grandchildren in Savannah too much if I moved, and I have a very nice house, all paid for. But I am considering moving in with Jo Ann because I feel sorry for her since she lives alone.* We had to laugh because Jo Ann told us the same thing about her mother!

We asked May Lee to share her perspective on how elders are cared for in the Chinese culture. *Asians treat their elders with a great deal of respect. The oldest son usually takes his mother to live with his family when she gets old. I think Asians respect their elders more than other cultures do. If I could tell young people one thing, it would be, respect your elders, after all they did raise you.*

We ended our interview by asking May Lee if she felt she had a good life. She laughed and said, *Yes, all I do is eat and sleep and the girls come and take me places. I don't worry about old age; I can't think as fast or remember as well but if I can't remember something, I just don't worry about it!*

May Lee passed away recently, not worrying, enjoying life, and living on her own.

Entertaining friends at home is fun at any age.

Psychological Congruence.   Researchers have examined the many ways in which we turn spaces that we occupy into places to which we are attached. Think about the places in your life that hold special meaning for you. Some may be specific buildings, such as the house in which you grew up or your high school. Others may be geographic locations or terrain such as the beach, the mountains, or the vacant lot where you played ball with your friends. When a space that we have lived in becomes a place, part of our identity is defined there. Events occurred there that help define who you are now (Rubenstein & Parmelee, 1992). You have memories of places that make up your personal history and for many of us, the objects in these places have further given us a sense of well-being. Think about your stuffed animal or trophy on a shelf or other reminders of important events in your life. Those items make up your attachment to a place. The longer you live in a place, the more experiences you have there and the more attached you get to that place. For many older people, living in the same house for 30, 40, 50, or more years is not uncommon. Our feelings toward, or psychological congruence to our home, can be very strong as we age. Our attachment to old places remains with us as we add the new spaces we occupy. Attachment to place may be more important in old age than any other time in our life. Attachment to place serves to keep the past alive or provide a sense of continuity. It also strengthens the sense of self and maintains self-image. Finally it represents independence and continued competence (Weiss & Bass, 2002).

Physical Congruence.   The most research and writing on person–environment congruence is in the area of the physical, or what is often called the built, environment. For example, the contribution of light available and your vision ability, predicts completion of reading tasks. Work in aging, and specifically in human factors and aging, has focused on the declining physical strength and stamina in advanced age and how that results in a mismatch with an environment made for younger, stronger people. It is important to know that the physical environment can play a very important role in well-being and remaining independent in old age. If you have difficulty getting around due to arthritis in your knees and hips, everyday tasks are affected. Cooking, cleaning, and shopping can be difficult because they require a good deal of standing and walking. Furthermore, you may have difficulty getting out and interacting with friends and family, which can isolate you and significantly affect your well-being. Depression may result and further jeopardize your ability to remain in your own home. The physical environment impacts us in significant ways. Fitting into an environment that matches our capabilities and allows us to complete our everyday tasks is important at every age.

These different ways that we fit into environments are not separate but rather often overlap. For example, how well we maneuver around the house can affect the way we feel about it and the way we feel about our house can affect whether we invite friends over. Looking to the larger environment, how we feel about our neighborhood, how well we can get around, and how many friends live nearby can all interact to allow us to fit or not fit in that environment. In an interesting study of 8222 persons 70 years and older living in urban neighborhoods across the United States, stability and not social economic status was the most important factor in how well people continued to function in their homes. However, contrary to what you might think, it was not more stable but less-stable neighborhoods that were associated with better health and cognitive and physical function. The authors (Aneshenel et al., 2007) were surprised by the findings and not sure how to interpret the data. Do you have any idea what can explain these surprising results?

Where We Live in Old Age

Older people choose from a variety of housing options, although at any age, finances most often limit those options. The majority of older persons in the community (77%) live in single-family homes. As people need more help, they are most often cared for in their own homes or move in with a relative or friend. Many other options are available such as senior apartments, assisted living facilities, retirement communities, and continuing care retirement communities (CCRC). CCRCs have emerged as extremely popular options for those who can afford them. CCRCs provide a range of housing options from independent living to assisted living to nursing care. An individual can move to another level of care if needed. CCRCs also offer an array of entertainment, recreational, and educational opportunities. They also require long-term contracts and have high monthly rents and substantial entrance fees.

According to the 2000 U.S. census, of the almost 35 million people age 65 and over, approximately 33.5 million (95.7 percent) live in the community and 1.5 million (about 4.3 percent) live in nursing homes (Census Bureau, 2001). As noted in Chapter 1, the number of older persons (particularly those over 85) in the population is growing, those most likely to need some type of long-term care. A concern had been that the population is growing much faster than the supply of nursing home beds. In fact, the number of nursing home beds has dropped over the last 10 to 15 years; however, the need for beds also has dropped.

BOX **13-1**

Cultural Perspectives on Housing for Older Adults

Elderly residents in the United States have a number of housing alternatives and a number of formal care options that they utilize. This is not the case for all elderly citizens, worldwide. The tradition in most societies has been for elderly family members to reside with their children. In fact, lifelong coresidence of extended families has been the norm in most cultures up until the mid-twentieth century. With modernization and industrialization, this pattern is changing. Over the past 50 or so years, most industrialized countries have seen a downward trend in the number of older parents and adult children living together (Aykan & Wolf, 2000). As a result, countries in Europe, Australia, the Mideast, and urban areas in Asia and the Far East have seen a decrease in coresidence and an increase in the number of older adults living alone or with a spouse (Brink, 1998). For example, in Israel in 1985, 27 percent of individuals over 65 lived with children or other family members. However, in 1991 only 2 percent lived with family members (Katan & Werczberger, 1998). Similar changes have been seen in other countries with a concomitant increase in the need for formal care. For example, Japan, with the fastest growing older population in the world, has set housing for the elderly and increasing formal social services as government priorities (Kose, 1998).

Just because families are living separately, this does not mean that families are abandoning their elderly. Adult children all over the world are still very much in contact with their parents and other older relatives and involved with their care. Treas and Chen (2000) observed urban Chinese families and found that very close ties were maintained with parents living separately. They found lots of economic, social, and emotional interdependence. This is a pattern that repeats itself in many countries.

There are a number of countries in which coresidence or extended family living is still the norm. This is most frequently seen in less-modernized or developing countries, such as those in South and Central America, Africa, and in many rural areas of Europe and Asia (Brink, 1998). A combination of traditional cultural family values and economic necessity seem to drive the continuation of this time-old practice. In Korea, 82 percent of older adults live with their adult children, citing the responsibility of younger members to take care of elders as the reason why (Kim, 1998). In India, the extended family is the predominant housing arrangement for elders. Indian sons consider it a duty to take care of their parents and an extreme embarrassment to allow their parents to be sent to nursing homes (Arai, 1998). Aykan and Wolf (2000) suggest that in Turkey, economic well-being is the primary driving force allowing elders to live separately from their adult children.

Keith et al. (1994) conducted a large-scale study of aging in a number of different countries. Some of their most interesting observations were of the !Kung (also called the Bushmen) and Herero peoples of Botswana. In both tribes, elders live either with families or in huts a few feet away from their children. Because of this close proximity, they consider that no elder lives alone. In fact, it is not at all uncommon for elders to share their beds with young children on a regular basis, regardless of where they live. Family members provide the most care for elders in these tribes. The Herero have a very practical tradition in which children from other families are fostered to elders to help provide care. These children and their families consider it a privilege to serve a revered elder. The elders in these situations often include these fostered children in their numbering of extended family members.

Finally, we would like to add a note from a group of indigenous women in rural Guatemala. The group *Heart of Women* is made up of Kakchiqel women whose families were decimated and

BOX 13-1 Continued

the survivors displaced by civil war. They, like many indigenous women in Guatemala, joined together for economic and social support in their recovery efforts. In a discussion of cultural differences in the role of mothers at a recent mother's day celebration, they asked about the practices of family living arrangements in the United States (Personal communication, 2001). On hearing that few extended families live together, they were shocked. They said that they could not imagine living more than two or three houses away from their children, siblings, and parents. Moreover, they felt that their job as mothers extended to their grandchildren and that it would be repaid in their old age when they could be assured of care.

Nursing home occupancy rates have fallen, suggesting that more older persons are opting to stay home and receive services there or in other types of housing like assisted-living facilities. You may already be asking yourself: Where do people who live in assisted living or retirement communities fit in? It is an interesting question with a vague answer. In most surveys, nursing home residents include just that, people living in skilled nursing facilities. All other specialized senior housing usually is grouped into the community dwelling category. However, some housing residences for older persons include a skilled nursing home within a continuum of services. It is unclear whether people in these nursing homes are included only in one category (and which one) or are sometimes doubly counted. Furthermore, people living in assisted living seem to be counted in the noninstitutionalized category, but that is not the case in every study or report. Because of this confusion, the numbers of residents in various housing options is simply an estimate. What is important is that most elderly people are not in institutions but rather are living independently or semi-independently in the community.

Data from the U.S. Census Bureau (2005) indicate the majority (66%) of older noninstitutionalized elders live in a family setting. About 81 percent of older men and 60 percent of older women live with their families. This includes individuals living with a spouse (71% of older men and 41% of older women) and those living with children, siblings, or other relatives (7% of older men, 17% of older women). About 28 percent or 10.5 million people over 65 (three quarters of whom are women; 64% are non-Hispanic white) live alone. Regarding race, non-Hispanic whites and blacks had the highest proportion of people living alone, around 40 percent. The number or people living alone varies significantly by geographic region as well, with Hawaii having the lowest proportion of elders living alone (18%) and Washington, D.C., having the highest rate (36%). The gender differences in those living alone are great, representing 47 percent of older women and 30 percent of older men. An interesting point is the shift over the last 10 to 15 years with more men and fewer women living alone. Can you explain the gender difference based on what you know about longevity and widowhood in old age? What might cohort or societal effects contribute to the explanation? The census bureau reported that about one half of women over 75 years of age in the United States are widows and the majority live alone (2005). The trend is for more people to continue living alone into advanced age. In fact, the fastest growing group of elders living alone are those 85 years and over. What do you think are the implications of this trend for families in particular and for society as a whole? Where do older people live in other countries and other cultures? Box 13-1 presents a cross-cultural glimpse at where people live around the world.

Homeownership.   Another way to look at where older people live is to examine who owns their home and who rents. This is important when you talk about renovations, modifications, or are considering a move. As anyone who has ever lived in a dorm or rented an apartment knows, it is difficult to make even minor changes in a home owned by someone else. On the other hand, anyone who owns a home knows that all maintenance and repairs fall on the owner. Furthermore, when you move out of an apartment or dorm, you have no more money, and usually, less than you did when you moved in. If you own your home, you can build up equity; the money that you paid into your home over the years can provide you with capital to move or to make major modifications. These are important issues to consider as you plan for old age.

In 2003, there were 22.7 million households headed by older persons (U.S. Census, 2005). Of these, 75 percent were owners. It is interesting to note that for these individuals, the median income of homeowners was double the median income of renters. Another interesting fact is that about 50 percent of homes owned by older persons in 1997 were built before 1960 and 6 percent of these homes had significant physical problems. Older homes continue to have repair and maintenance needs compared to younger homes. On a positive note, about 77 percent of older homeowners in 1997 owned their homes free and clear.

Choosing Where to Live.   We have seen the housing choices available to older persons and where people are living now. But are they living where they want to live? Do the places older people choose to live fit them?

We learned that most older people live in single-family homes and that these are long-term residences for most of them. In many surveys, older respondents report the desire to remain in their homes as long as they possibly can, preferably until death. In Chapter 11, we saw that only 5 percent of people choose to move from their homes after retirement. This has been referred to as **aging in place** and reflects attachment to a place and the comfort or fit they have in these homes. Fogel (1992) pointed out that many elderly stay in their homes despite deteriorating neighborhoods, economic hardships, and health-related declines. He suggested that the elderly remain in their homes because of the benefits associated with staying at home, particularly psychological benefits. They like their independence, privacy, and the control they have over the physical environment. Home is familiar, the place where friends are entertained; it is a part of a neighborhood social network. Home is where important family events have taken place. Home is an expression of who you are. Finally, Fogel suggests that many people find meaning or purpose through home maintenance. These all encourage strong emotional attachments, which encourage homeowners to stay.

Does this mean that individuals who move are less attached to their homes? Kahana and Kahana (1996) have been investigating relocation in healthy older persons to determine their reasons for moving. They suggest that for some older people, moving is an adventure that enhances their feelings of personal control and life-satisfaction in late life. For these individuals, the stimulation of new environments is more attractive than the security of a familiar place. Furthermore, for many, the objects in their homes, not the home itself, are the focus of attachment. They can remain attached to their "home" through favorite objects that can be moved and help make a new space feel like an old home (Koenig & Cunningham, 2001).

The Need for Assistance

While we emphasized in Chapter 1 that we are living longer and healthier than ever before, there are still a substantial number of elders who experience difficulty. According to the Department of Health and Human Services (2007), more than half of the older population (52.5 percent) reported having at least one disability in 1997. **Activities of daily living (ADLs)** are very basic physical tasks or motions that we do in the course of everyday life, such as bathing, eating, getting around, getting in and out of chairs or bed, and toileting. **Instrumental activities of daily living (IADLs)** are more complex everyday tasks that require a combination of physical and mental ability. IADLs include tasks such as preparing meals, shopping, cleaning, managing medications, arranging transportation, and using the telephone. Over 4.4 million people (14 percent) had difficulty carrying out ADLs and 6.5 million (21 percent) had problems with IADLs. For the old-old, those numbers dramatically increase with the percentage of those age 80 and over with ADL and IADL problems doubling those of the 65 and over population in total. IADLs tend to be affected first and can be hampered by minor disabilities. For example, if you sprain your ankle, you may have difficulty shopping and cleaning the house. On the other hand, if it is a mild sprain, you simply rearrange your life to complete necessary tasks when you are able. It is usually when daily tasks are interrupted, especially ADLs, that we turn for help.

In an AARP housing survey (2000a), many respondents expressed concern about their ability to stay in their homes due to problems they were experiencing. Eight percent of the survey participants reported that they had difficulty getting around their home with 63 percent of those saying this is a frequent problem. The most common physical functional problem reported was climbing stairs (35 percent). Even so, 82 percent preferred to stay in their homes even if they needed help in caring for themselves (AARP, 2000a). It is not, however, simply physical impairment that determines the need for more support. Stuck and colleagues (Stuck et al., 1999) found that a number of factors can predict functional decline and the need for help. These include cognitive factors, depression, low social contact, low levels of physical activity, number of chronic conditions, low and high BMI, mobility problems, and vision impairment.

Gender and race play a role in decisions to move or remain at home. Older women are more likely than men and African Americans are more likely than whites to remain at home alone (Rubenstein et al., 1992). African Americans receive more informal care than whites as well but this may be due to their higher rates of disability and also cultural expectations (Li & Fries, 2005). Hispanic elderly are much more likely to live with family members than to live alone or be institutionalized. Furthermore, older minority and older single-person households (primarily single women) are more likely than other older households to involve substandard housing and require excessive housing costs. For those with functional difficulties, the burden of home maintenance and repair is even higher because they cannot do many repairs themselves.

Community-Based Long-Term Care

Most care for elders in need comes from family and is unpaid. There are, however, many new programs designed to help elders and their families remain in their homes. Long-term care, the term used to describe all the types of health-related and other supportive services provided to older persons includes a great number of different programs. Some of the more frequently used services are described in Box 13-2.

Community-based home care programs have evolved to meet the need of the many frail elders who wish to remain in their own home or with their family. These programs typically have targeted those with significant problems and at risk for nursing home placement. The goal of many of these programs is to eliminate or delay the need for institutionalization. The most comprehensive of these programs of all inclusive care for the elderly (e.g, PACE) have been studied extensively and found to improve well-being and reduce depression in elders and caregivers participating in adult day care (Gitlin, 2006). For example, Muramatsu et al. (2007) found that living in a state with higher funding for home and community-based services lowered the risk of nursing home admissions for childless seniors.

A major drawback to community-based programs is financing. As you can see in Box 13-3, major health care is covered for elders but other supportive care is not. Many of

---

B O X 13-2

Services for Elders at Home

A number of programs and services are available for elders who need help with daily activities. A wide range of public and private organizations provides these services. The more common programs include:

General Care

Information and referral (I&R)—These are locally operated, often by the local area agency on aging, and provide a central location to obtain information about aging services and programs available in the community. This is almost always a free service.

Companionship services—These can include friendly visitors in the home or over the phone or any combination. Typically these services run about $5 to $15 per hour but may be offered on a sliding scale basis or free through faith-based and volunteer organizations.

Help around the house—This is typically a chore service but may include help with ADLs and IADLS. These services run from $8 to $18 per hour depending on the help needed and the level of skill of the provider. Home care aides charge more than unskilled care providers.

Home modification—This is a range of services aimed at making modifications in the home to improve accessibility for those in need. Services can range from simple tasks like rearranging furniture to enhance mobility to installing ramps and grab bars to major structural changes. Prices range considerably based on the skill of the providers and the degree of modification desired.

BOX 13-2 Continued

Transportation—Special transportation for those with mobility difficulty is usually provided by local public transportation systems or through volunteer organizations. Transportation is often free or low cost but can be very costly depending on the provider and distance traveled.

Nutrition programs—These include a range of services from meals provided in a group setting to meals delivered in the home. Nutrition programs are run by a number of government social service organizations as well as faith-based, volunteer, and private business. Costs range from zero to quite high depending on who is providing the service and qualifications of the person in need.

Geriatric case management—This is a relatively new service in which a geriatric specialist, usually a social worker, provides assessment and ongoing management of the care for an older person in need. Assessment costs range from $200 to $300 and ongoing case management ranges from $60 to $150 per hour depending on the degree of help needed. These are usually paid by the individual and can be provided through social service, health care or community organizations, or by individuals in private practice.

Health Care Programs

In-home health aides—These are minimally trained but licensed individuals who provide personal and low-level health care tasks such as giving medications. Costs run approximately $20 to $50 per hour and may be covered by Medicare, Medicaid, and private insurance. There are typically long waiting lists for in-home aides.

Hospice care—This is a comprehensive program for individuals who have a physician's diagnosis of a terminal illness with 6 months or less to live. The program is designed to provide comprehensive support to individuals to allow them to live out their remaining days in their home. Insurance programs cover hospice care. Read more about hospice care in Chapter 14.

In-home nurses and therapists—These are licensed professionals who deliver specialized care in the home or in an outpatient clinical setting including skilled health care, occupational therapy, physical therapy, mental health therapy, and so on. Prices range from $85 to $150 per hour with insurance covering some of these costs, sometimes.

Adult daycare—These programs typically fall into two categories, adult day social care and adult day health care with the latter including more extensive services. Both are half- or whole-day programs that include supervision, recreation, meals, and some health care and counseling for individuals in a group setting. The typical cost is $150 per day with higher costs for programs with more services. For example, adult daycare for dementia patients can run as much as $200 per day.

Respite programs—These are specialized services for individuals with dementia. Services are designed to give caregivers a break from the daily burden of caring for someone with intense needs. Respite can be provided in the home, in a day program, or in a residential facility for a longer period.

Source: AARP (1996).

BOX 13-3

Financing Long-Term Health Care

Financing long-term health care has become a big concern in this country. Many older people are worried about what might happen if they become debilitated and need extensive care. Many younger and middle-age adults are beginning to consider, not just the needs of their parents in old age, but what types of plans they might make to ensure that their own old age is secure. The concerns focus on how to pay for extensive health care needs, called long-term care, which might arise. These include hospital, doctor, and medication bills as well as the need for rehabilitation, home health care, assisted living, and nursing home services. No one wants or expects to get this sick and as we have seen in this chapter and in Chapter 5, there are many things we can do to stay healthy in old age. The reality, however, is that there are a number of people with chronic and debilitating conditions in old age. Using census data on functional disability and institutionalization rates, the U.S. Department of Health and Human Services estimates that in 2007, 9 million and by 2020, 12 million persons over the age of 65 will need long-term care at some point in their lives (USHHS, 2007). How do people pay for their long-term care? There are several mechanisms for paying for long-term health care, briefly summarized here.

Private Insurance

Most are familiar with this mechanism for paying for health care. It is the most common way that Americans under the age of 65 pay for their health care needs. Comprehensive private insurance usually is tied to employment so, after you retire, this source of health care payment often disappears. You can pay for health insurance on your own but it is very expensive. Moreover, standard health care insurance does not pay for nursing home care and many other long-term care needs. In the last several years, specialized long-term care health insurance policies (LTCI) have been developed to cover expenses not covered by Medicare. A few policies are offered through the federal government and Medicare; these are called Medigap policies and are designed to fill the gaps in Medicare coverage. The cost of LTCI policies range widely, depending on the age of the insured and the benefits chosen. For example, a fairly comprehensive policy purchased at age 55 may cost $3000 per year, but if purchased at age 75 could cost up to $9000 a year. The younger you are when you purchase LTCI, the less expensive it is. Many older people do not plan ahead and end up having to balance the possible costs of care versus the costs of long-term care insurance, with no good solutions. Deductibles and copayments can make private insurance even more costly. Despite the cost, more people are covered by LTCI policies, up from 1.7 million in 1992 to 4.1 million in 1998 (USHHS, 2007).

Medicare

Medicare is a federal health insurance program for people age 65 and over and some younger adults with certain disabilities. Medicare provides near-universal coverage for older Americans. Originally, there were two parts to Medicare, A and B. Part A is called hospital insurance and covers in-patient hospital care, 100 days of skilled nursing home care or rehabilitation following hospitalization, skilled nursing care provided in the home and prescribed by a physician, and fairly comprehensive hospice care for terminally ill persons (6 months or less to live as diagnosed by a physician). Part B, supplemental medical insurance, covers doctor visits paying 80 percent of physician and outpatient service after an annual $100 deductible. Medicare recipients also must pay a monthly premium, which is applied to Part B services. Medicare Part C is called Medicare Advantage and provides services through private HMO or PPO physician groups, similar to many

BOX 13-3 Continued

private insurance plans. You can choose your physician group and most cover the same and sometimes more services than standard Part A and B providers. You still pay a premium to Medicare. Once you have chosen your plan, Medicare pays the HMO or PPO a set amount each month, whether you use the services. There are a number of Medicare Advantage plans to choose from and much research into effectiveness of these plans is ongoing.

Medicare Part D, Prescription Drug Coverage, is the newest component of Medicare Services. Part D provides drug coverage for everyone enrolled in Medicare. This part has options; you must sign up for a specific plan, and there are many, and you pay a monthly premium. The many different plans cover different types of prescriptions and drug-related services. The system has proven quite complex to understand and to manipulate. As the newest service, studies examining effectiveness are just beginning.

You may notice that prescription costs, dental costs, hearing aids and eyeglasses, assistive technologies described in the text, and most long-term care in nursing facilities or at home are not covered. These other costs can be extensive. In 1994, older persons on the average spent $2519 on health care costs not covered by Medicare or other insurance. This does not include nursing home costs of which Medicare covers only 12 percent of the total costs (USHHS, 2007). Unfortunately, many people do not realize that Medicare does not cover long-term nursing home stays. A telephone survey of 1800 persons over the age of 45 revealed that 58 percent thought that Medicare covered all nursing home stays; and, 25 percent planned to rely on Medicare to pay for any nursing home need that might arise (AARP, 2001b).

Medicare is considered an earned benefit and separate trust funds are used to finance both parts. Part A trust fund is financed through current employee and employer contributions (HI on your payroll check is your contribution to the Part A trust fund). Part B is financed by the insurance premiums paid by Medicare recipients (25%) and from general federal revenues (75%). You have to enroll in Medicare once you reach 65 and your premium then is automatically deducted from your Social Security check. If you do not yet receive Social Security, you must pay the premium to Medicare. Parts C and D are funded the same as A and B.

Medicaid

Medicaid is a state and federal cooperative insurance program for people of all ages who are poor. Medicaid is considered a means tested program, referring to the fact that you must meet the requirement of having little or no money (means) in order to receive Medicaid services. The requirement is a fairly complex formula based on size of family, income, assets, and living expenses. Eligibility requirements are set by each state with some overall guidelines established by federal law. Federal law also sets broad limits on type and costs of services but leaves the specifics and management to each individual state. As long as the state complies with the federal regulations, the federal government must match whatever money the state spends on health care services for its citizens. Medicaid eligibility, services, and costs vary greatly from state to state. Those states with higher proportions of poor and older residents spend more of their state budgets on Medicaid health costs. Medicaid pays approximately 46 percent of nursing home costs nationally. Why does it pay so much? The average daily cost of nursing home care is about $194 (with a range of $116 a day in Louisiana to $524 a day in Alaska); very few people can afford to pay for nursing home care on their own, even with substantial savings (AARP, 2001b). Older people often end up spending all of their savings and assets, either before or after they enter a nursing home, and then become eligible for Medicaid. We should note here that eldercare lawyers and financial planners now specialize in helping older people shelter their assets in order to become eligible for

(continued)

B O X **13-3** Continued

Medicaid but yet still be able to pass those assets on to their children. Needless to say, this practice has sparked a lot of controversy. Regardless, most people do not have sufficient private funds for extensive nursing home stays and thus must rely on Medicaid funds. This reliance has put a strain on state budgets as the older population has grown.

Out of-Pocket-Expenses

Without a good long-term care policy, health care costs for frail elderly can be a substantial burden. You may recall our discussion from Chapter 11 about sources of income in old age and see that many people do not have enough money to cover costs if their health is poor. Those people with higher incomes obviously fare better than those with low incomes. Not covered is nonskilled care for frail elderly. Unfortunately, this too can create a financial and psychological burden on older persons and their families. Assisted living is not covered by any except some LTCI plans at this point. Neither is companion care, homemaker services, or daycare programs for frail elders. If your mom is still fairly independent but needs some help cooking or remembering to take her medication, or needs someone to sit with her for a few hours a day, you must pay for this care out of pocket, or do without. Clearly, we have a great number of elderly going without that needed care.

---

the general care services described in the top of Box 13-2, like companionship care, chore service, or medication reminders, are not covered by insurance. Furthermore, when they are covered as part of an all-inclusive plan, funds are regulated by states. There is a significant difference from state to state in what is covered. As a result, many elders go without needed services. The National Association of Area Agencies on Aging reported the results of a survey in 2006 of 1790 towns, counties, and municipalities. They found significant gaps in services in health care, nutrition, exercise programs, and housing modifications. Furthermore, they found that only 46 percent of the places surveyed were looking at strategies to help aging residents (Danhauer & Andrykowski, 2005). Lynch et al. (2005) examined many all-inclusive programs and concluded that elders with chronic care were getting care for health care needs but social and functional needs remained unmet. If you were to decide where money is best spent in caring for frail elders, do you think nursing home or at home with adequate service is better?

Retirement Communities and Assisted Living

For many frail and sick elderly, the ability to remain functional in their home often is compromised and they decide to live with family or in an institution (Worobey & Angel, 1990). Functional ability or how well a person manages daily tasks appears to be a primary factor in an individual's decision to move from home to more supportive care. For some, simply the potential of needing additional help is enough to send them packing to retirement communities or assisted living. In fact, Porter found that subjective perceptions of difficulty in performing ADLs was important to overall function (2007).

How well do people fare in these more supportive settings? A 4-year longitudinal study of 255 residents in a retirement community found that men adjusted better to the move, because they tended to be more active; you may recall from Chapter 10 that men base their friendships on shared activities. Women, however, had more trouble, especially if the new community was far from family and old friends. Interestingly, however, women were very good at keeping up with old friends and family over email and those who did showed little relocation distress (Waldron et al., 2005).

Assisted-living facilities often have eligibility requirements that include the documented need for more support, but not nursing home eligible. In addition, there is usually no or little financial support for these residents (see Box 13-3). For the most part, residents in assisted-living facilities report a high quality of life and low depression (Samus, 2006). Deteriorating cognition, increased age, functional impairment, and severe depression are predictors of nursing home placement from assisted living (Burdick et al., 2005). As we will see with the case in nursing homes, staff and facility characteristics are very important in assisted living resident satisfaction. Staff who are supportive and helpful and residents supportive and helpful to one another (Mitchell & Kemp, 2000), and high-job satisfaction and positive organizational culture all predict resident satisfaction (Sikorska-Simmons, 2006).

Quality of Life in Institutional Environments

People who enter an assisted-living facility or a nursing home are there because they need help with daily tasks. This in itself is difficult for many people to accept. Older adults in residential settings may feel a strong loss of autonomy, choice, and decision making (Kane, 1991). Kane and Caplan (1990) found that the areas of choice most desired by assisted-living residents were choice of roommate, food, visiting rights, and phone privileges. Autonomy in these areas was associated with well-being and better health. In several studies, quality of life also has been shown to be better when residents have good relationships with other residents and staff, participation in social activity, and ability to physically operate in the environment (Mitchell & Kemp, 2000; Ball et al., 2000). Kane and Wilson (1993) conducted a study of residents of assisted living and concluded that despite the higher level of impairment in this group, good adaptation could occur when there was a good fit between the physical and social needs of residents and the resources of the facility. In other words, person-environment congruence predicted well-being.

The goal then is for all facilities to recognize the need, to take into consideration the abilities, needs, and desires of residents in their design and provision of services. Resident rights committees are now ubiquitous in assisted-living facilities and in many nursing homes, resulting in more satisfied and happier residents.

Due to changes in longevity of the very old population coupled with the impact of managed care on the health care system, nursing home residents are older, sicker, and more frail than they have ever been. By definition, a frail elder is one who is experiencing a great deal of limitations due to chronic illness and disability. Studies of quality of life in frail populations have focused on nursing home residents despite the fact that most frail elders still are cared for in their own or their relatives' homes. This is no doubt due to the easy access to institutionalized persons for research studies. Examining quality of life in the community is more difficult. Much of the literature has focused on the negative effects of institutionalization, including increased dependence, isolation, learned helplessness, and not being allowed to make decisions (Cohn & Sugar, 1991).

A closer look at these negative effects reveals that they are reinforced by the environment. Baltes and Wahl (1992) examined dependency behaviors in frail elderly in institutions and living in the community. Dependency behaviors are ones that encourage other people to do things like asking for help or giving up trying to do a task. Researchers found that in both settings dependent behaviors were immediately reinforced; little reinforcement existed for independent behaviors. They also found that staff and family members expected frail elders to be incompetent. Nursing staff and family caregivers felt that they were doing the right thing by providing as much care as they could. The frail elders in this study saw themselves as incompetent and reinforcement from caregivers further encouraged low competence. The cycle is hard to break but changing how staff and family view frail elders is important. Also, it is critical to set up the environment with supports so frail elders can do more things on their own or with minimal help.

Improving the psychological environment is one important way of enhancing competence and independence. Numerous studies have shown that competence and well-being increase by expanding the amount of control institutional residents have in their lives. Giving more control may seem the obvious answer, but it is difficult to run an efficient institution caring for many people and, at the same time, give individuals control over their routines. However, several studies in the 1970s (Langer & Rodin, 1976; Schulz, 1976) showed that having even a little control such as caring for a pet or plant, or determining

Providing the right amount of assistance is key to well-being in nursing home residents.

when visitors would arrive, greatly enhanced well-being in institutionalized frail elders. A study of coping strategies used by nursing home residents found that greater use of meaning-based strategies like positive reappraisal, religious coping, and number of uplifts experienced or perceived, resulted in higher well-being. These are clear avenues for intervention with residents (Danhauer & Andrykowski, 2005).

Harvey and Lawler (2001) demonstrated that when residents and staff work to maintain respect for one another, including improving communication between staff and residents, enhancing the rights of individuals to determine as much of their care as possible, and encouraging control over daily life, nursing home residents have greater feelings of autonomy, lower depression rates, and greater well-being. Although many perceive that nursing homes can be depressing places, and there are some very bad nursing home facilities, they also can be positive places that can be made to feel like home. Little things, such as the terminology used to refer to institutionalized persons (for example, residents not patients) can produce a more positive attitude and make life a little better for those in need of care and support.

An important piece of advice comes from a study of physical environments in nursing homes (Cutler, 2006). He cautions that function is individual and assessing the effects of the environment on function must be done on an individual basis. Global approaches have resulted in significant improvements in public spaces but little change in private spaces. Nursing home residents spend a good deal of time in their rooms and many are very dreary places indeed. The opportunity to provide both function-enhancing and life-enriching features is great if we approach assessment accurately.

Helpful or Enabling Environments

Think back to the discussion of person-environment congruence and you can see that so far we have been discussing the consequence of what happens when older people and their environments do not fit. When we can no longer function well in an environment, we need more support. Traditionally this has meant that we enlist the help of others. We either use our family and friends or pay someone else to help us in our homes or we move to more supportive environments. This type of assistance is most often geared toward replacing task performance rather than providing a person in need with help to complete the task him- or herself. For most older people, a better approach would be to help them perform their tasks so that they can maintain control over their lives and remain independent. Mismatches in physical congruence are the most frequent reason that older people seek more support. There are, however, alternatives to moving.

Human Factors Approach

How can we set up our homes so that we can function better in our old age? The **human factors approach** is uniquely suited to address questions such as these. Human factors engineering is an interdisciplinary field that examines task performance from the perspective of human-environment interaction. The goal is to identify problem areas in tasks as humans perform them and suggest interventions to maximize task performance. Because it is usually easier to change the design of an environment or machine rather than to change the

SOCIAL POLICY APPLICATIONS

Many older adults find it difficult to pay for adequate housing and a number of organizations are working to bring this, and other, issues to the forefront of state and federal lawmakers. The federal government is considering a major overhaul of Medicare and states are studying ways to improve Medicaid coverage for their older citizens. Managed care has impacted federal programs in the same way it has impacted all of the health care world; some say for better, some say for worse. You may be wise to do two things. Consider purchasing long-term care insurance (LTCI) while you are young. The policies are relatively inexpensive. Take an active interest in state and federal discussions of long-term care coverage. Write to your representatives and tell them how you feel. Policy decisions made now can significantly impact your health care options in the future.

characteristics of a person, most human factors research and applications emphasize the design of products and environments to fit the capabilities of people; this is called **ergonomic design**.

Until the 1980s, human factors research focused almost exclusively on the military or civilian work environment. Although a few researchers examined task performance by older workers, no one considered that task performance by older persons in the home was a ripe area for human factors intervention. Martin Faletti was a pioneer in this area. He looked at the work world of most older adults (i.e., the home environment) and proposed using human factors research to identify areas of intervention to bring the home environment more in line with the capabilities of older adults. He and his colleagues (Faletti, 1984; Faletti & Clark, 1984; Czaja et al., 1993) conducted an extensive study of the performance of IADLs by older persons in order to identify the movements necessary to complete a given task (task demands of the home and grocery stores), the capabilities older persons have relevant to their tasks, and areas of possible intervention to improve the everyday task performance of older adults. An example from this research is the finding that 60 percent of IADLs performed by older persons involves lift/lower and push/pull movements while standing. Barr (1994) points out that with these data, specific interventions could be identified to focus on a combination of strength training to improve person capabilities and redesign of the kitchen environment to reduce the stamina demands.

The European ENABLE-AGE project is designed to examine and evaluate the role of housing in promoting healthy aging. Specifically, Susan Iwarsson and her colleagues (Iwarsson et al., 2007; Oswald et al., 2007) conducted a longitudinal test of Lawton's docility hypothesis in 1918 persons aged 75 to 89 from five European countries. Recall that the docility hypothesis states that people with lower capabilities are more vulnerable to demands than those with good capabilities and are less likely to have good congruence or fit in their environment. They defined healthy or successful aging as independence in ADLs and subjective well-being. In support of Lawton's work, the ENABLE project found that it was not capabilities or demand alone but rather the fit between person and environment that predicted ADL performance. They calculated fit, or what they called magnitude of accessibility, using both objective and perceived aspects of housing. Magnitude of accessibility, not disability alone or number of barriers, was related to success in home tasks, particularly for the very old. Housing control beliefs factored strongly in the study outcomes and across all countries. People with external housing control beliefs (recall external control is believing events are due to chance or powerful others) had more intense accessibility problems than those with internal housing control beliefs; both objective and subjective aspects of housing are important to healthy aging.

Home Modification

Most homes have been built using data collected in the military from younger, taller, stronger persons with excellent vision, hearing, and other senses. For example, think about the kitchen cabinets in your home. The top shelf is usually fairly high. This presents no problem for a person who is 6 feet tall, but most older persons (particularly the oldest cohorts) are significantly shorter than that. You may remember from our discussion of functional height changes in Chapter 3 that for the elderly usable or reachable space is greatly reduced. Another example is the thermostat control for heating and cooling the house. It is often located high on the wall and has a small display. There are numerous examples of aspects of home design that do not take into consideration the changing capabilities associated with normal aging, and which further compromise frail elderly. See Project 13 for more information.

A number of modifications have been well-researched that can make a home more livable for those with reduced capabilities. Table 13-1 presents an example of a few typical problem areas and changes that can be made to improve design. Tomita found that the best predictors of assistive device use in frail elders in the community were severity of physical disability, medication intake, and living alone (2004). A study of the effects of incorporating assistive devices and home modifications in community-based care indicated

PROJECT 13
Check Out Your Home

Perhaps your home fits you well, perhaps not. Consider your parents' and grandparents' homes. What aspects of these homes may be poorly designed? In addition to function declining as a result of poor design, accidents also increase. You can improve function and reduce accidents for the elders in your life with simple home alterations. You can start this process by using a simple home checklist. There are several available, and a good, easy-to-use checklist can be found on the AARP website at *www.aarp.org/families/home_designrate_home.*

Use the checklist to go through the homes of your elder relatives and identify areas for improvement. Then sit down with your relative and discuss areas that are problematic and generate ideas for modification. The AARP has a number of suggestions for modification as do several other websites and resources listed at the end of this chapter. Do not be shy about generating your own ideas for improvements. Necessity is the mother of invention and many well-respected home modification ideas have come from older folks and their younger family members making changes to enhance daily living. Once you have generated your to-do list for improvements, you can help make these changes or arrange for professionals (e.g., home repair persons, contractors, engineers, etc.) to make some of the changes. Now you can feel assured that you have made an important difference in the safety and well-being of your loved ones.

TABLE 13-1   Examples of Home Modifications

This table illustrates just a few common problems and modification solutions to enhance performance

Difficulty	Current Design	Better Design	Assistive Device
Problems turning door, stove or cabinet handles (due to arthritis, stroke, general frailty)	Knob handles on doors, stoves, cabinets, etc.	Replace with lever handles	Knob turners
Difficulty seeing controls (due to low vision, cataracts, glaucoma, macular degeneration, etc.)	Controls with small displays (e.g., thermostats—also often mounted high on a wall, telephone dial pads, stove controls)	Replace controls, telephones with models that have larger display faces; mount controls lower on the wall; add additional lighting near controls	Snap-on large control adapters or magnifiers
Trouble getting in and out of the bathtub (due to arthritis, fatigue, other mobility-related problems)	Standard high wall bathtub/shower combinations	Replace standard configuration with a shower separate from the bathtub or a shower only	Bath rails and grab bars installed securely and at appropriate locations and heights
Difficulty reaching (due to shorter stature with age, arthritis or bursitis in shoulders or arms)	Cabinets with top shelves that are quite high	Install movable cabinets	Reacher sticks—be sure to rearrange items on shelves so that lightweight objects (cereal boxes) are on top shelves
Inability to maneuver stairs with a walker or wheelchair	Stairs in entryways and top floor changes; raised thresholds in entryways; deep-pile carpeting, scatter rugs	Live in one-story homes; install ramp entryways; remove thresholds from entryways; replace carpeting with smooth surface flooring; remove scatter rugs	Electric chairlifts in stairways; large-wheel walkers or wheelchairs that maneuver easily on uneven surfaces; environmental control units (ECUs) for remote access of all electric devices
Problems using objects that require a tight grip or precision grip (due to arthritis or hand tremors)	Small-handled utensils, writing instruments, toothbrushes, keys, etc.	Use large-grip designs that replace a small-tight grip with a larger more comfortable hand grip	Build up handles on objects using rubber tubing, tape, or purchased handle enlargers

that use of technology substituted for some help and thus increased independence for the care receivers (Allen et al., 2006).

Home modification includes structural as well as add-on changes. Examples of structural improvements might include widening doorways to accommodate a wheelchair, lowering shelves to improve access, or replacing hard-to-turn knob handles with lever handles. Add-on features can range from low-tech assistive devices like grab-bars or reacher sticks to high-tech use of computers to more easily operate lights, appliances, or any electrical system (Grayson, 1997). Modifications to enhance cognitive performance can be enormously helpful. Medication reminders, alarm systems for appliance controls, and devices to monitor and prevent wandering into unsafe areas are some examples. Examine your own home or your parents' or grandparents' homes with an eye toward enabling design by trying out the project for this chapter.

An important thing to remember is that the design change itself can add demands that are beyond the physical or psychological capabilities of users. For example, a computer-operated thermostat control might be too difficult for someone with cognitive problems. Although older people embrace the use of technology, it can take them longer to learn complex systems (Czaja, 2001) and they are unlikely to consider a change that does not appear useful. Gadgets may be part of baby boomers' lives and will be taken into old age with them but the older generation now is more hesitant to adopt new products (Clark & Gaide, 1986). A relatively new field is providing some guidelines here. **Gerontechnology** (Fozard et al., 2000) is a blend of gerontology and technology with the goal to use technology to prevent, delay, or compensate for declines and to support or enhance opportunities for communication, leisure, learning service, and artistic expression. Gerontechnology promises to bring some interesting changes for future aging.

Many people consider building new homes for retirement or old age. Architects are becoming much more aware of the needs and desires of older homebuilders and are often willing to generate clever designs that incorporate supportive features. A change in the building and product design fields is for universal design of new homes and products. Universal design represents a shift in thinking from adding accessibility features onto standard designs to infusing accessibility into the design of spaces and products so that all people can use the same products and building elements (Connell & Sanford, 2000).

The Eden Alternative (Thomas, 1994) is an interesting new environmental design for nursing home environments. The Eden Alternative is a plan to create a functional and caring nursing home environment by focusing on people living with pets, plants, and younger people. Nursing homes who wish to *Edenize* agree to change their environments so that pets and plants coexist with people and children visit regularly. An evaluation of Edenized homes (Drew & Brooke, 1999) found a number of positive benefits. Residents are more interactive, take less medication for depression, experience fewer bed sores, and fall less frequently. Staff turnover and absenteeism in these facilities also were greatly reduced. Although the research on the beneficial effects of pets on health and well-being for the general population is inconclusive, some evidence points to positive health benefits for institutionalized persons or those experiencing a major stress in their life, such as bereavement (Tucker et al., 1995; Colombo et al., 2006). Based on Rosalie Kane's work on the benefits of autonomy and choice in institutional residents, Rabig has introduced the Green House design (2006). This design for nursing home involves small self-contained homes for 10 or fewer residents. Residents have private rooms and shared common spaces. Nursing assistants are universal workers in that they complete all tasks including cooking, washing, personal care, and health care tasks. Rabig reports early results as positive outcomes for everyone including lower staff turnover and higher job satisfaction and a large number of positive quality-of-life indicators for residents. This is a nursing home design concept to keep watching.

Lever handles are much easier to operate than traditional door knobs.

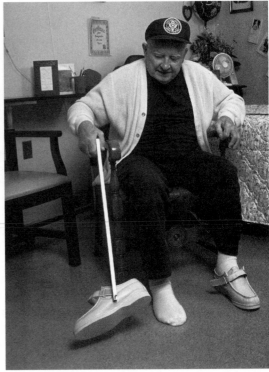

A reacher stick can be invaluable.

An exciting area of research in design is that of environments to enhance function in persons with Alzheimer's disease and other dementias. A number of studies have shown that the environment can play a major role in preventing further problems, and increasing overall function and feelings of independence and well-being in persons with Alzheimer's disease living at home or in institutions (e.g., Lawton, 2001; Charness & Holley, 2001). For example, improving the general ambience, decreasing noise, and increasing lighting in dining areas has been shown to improve the nutritional intake of Alzheimer's patients (McDaniel et al., 2001). Incorporating design features to allow for safe wandering, enhanced sensory experiences, and decreased confusion have led to some very innovative facilities (Charness & Holley, 2001) and designs for home environments (Silverstein & Hyde, 1997). An example of a clever intervention in a dementia unit in a nursing home is described in Box 13-4.

In order to remain in their homes, older people with lower function do what they can do to modify their home or behavior. Most people change their behavior or the way they do tasks before making major changes in the environment (Wylde, 1998), although many make small affordable changes such as using higher wattage light bulbs or installing night lights (AARP, 2000a). Lawton (1982) observed that very frail elders at home make a kind of center of operations, such as an easy chair in front of a TV and surround it with everything that they need, minimizing the need for excessive mobility.

BOX **13-4**

When Is a Door Not a Door?

As part of her master's degree in gerontology at the University of North Carolina at Charlotte, Cynthia Kincaid conducted a study on behavioral management using an environmental intervention with nursing home residents with dementia. She first observed residents in the special care unit for dementia at Courtland Terrace Nursing Home in Gastonia, North Carolina. Residents with dementia exhibit a number of problem behaviors that can make caring for them frustrating and difficult. Ms. Kincaid focused on door testing, or the repeated attempt to open and exit a door.

Door testing can be a problem when residents become anxious, agitated, and even aggressive when the door cannot be opened or worse when they escape through the door to a dangerous location such as outside or a housekeeping or medicine room. She observed residents at the nursing home and recorded a number of door testing and agitation behaviors. She then designed a very clever intervention. She disguised the exit door. She enlisted the help of art students at the local Gaston Community College who painted an underwater fish scene on the wall, covering the problem door (see the following for the before and after photos of the nursing home wall).

In her comparison of premural and postmural behaviors, she observed a significant drop in door testing behaviors after the mural was painted. Additionally, she observed a decrease in agitation and aggressive door testing. Another interesting finding was that premural, one resident repeatedly enlisted the help of other residents resulting in a team effort to open the door. After the mural was painted, she continued to enlist others to walk with her to the door, but the other residents ignored the now-disguised door. It seems clear that using the environment to disguise dangerous or unsafe areas can be an effective and inexpensive intervention with persons with dementia.

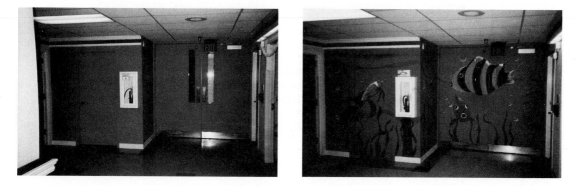

A door in a nursing home before it was disguised with a painting, and the same nursing home door disguised by an underwater scene.

There is a need to encourage service providers and payers (primarily private insurance and Medicare) to incorporate structural modifications, assistive technology, and other environmental interventions to standard care. Currently, there is little to no reimbursement or financial support for environmental changes to accommodate normal changes with age. Programs that include environmental and home management adaptations are more cost effective over the long run than nursing home care (Heumann, 2001).

When we start to see aging as a normal part of life rather than a disease or infirmity to be cured or treated, we can begin to treat ourselves in old age with the same respect we do at other stages of our lives.

CHAPTER HIGHLIGHTS

- How we fit in our environments is called person–environment congruence.
- Lawton's docility hypothesis predicts that those elders with lowered capabilities will be more vulnerable in the face of environmental demands.
- There are three types of congruence: social, psychological, and physical.
- We become attached to places and in old age this leads to a tendency to want to age in place or remain in the home as long as possible.
- Older people live independently in single homes, apartments, and mobile homes.
- Elders in need live in a variety of settings including with their children or other relatives, in places like board and care homes, assisted-living facilities, continuing care retirement communities (CCRCs), in foster care, and in nursing homes.
- The environment can affect quality of life of frail elders, particularly if it restricts autonomy or encourages dependency, a fact common in institutional settings.
- Frail elders living at home receive care from formal (professional) and informal (family and friends) sources.
- Community-based long-term care programs are designed to provide health and supportive services to frail elders in their homes in order to delay or prevent nursing home placement.
- Residents in assisted-living facilties report a fairly high satisfaction with their life and living arrangements.
- Helpful or enabling environments are those designed to augment the capabilities of persons and enhance task performance.
- Human factors look at task performance and generate products and environments that fit human capabilities; for elders, capabilities regarding ADL and IADL tasks are considered.
- Home modification to enhance task performance for elders includes changing architectural features or structural features as well as adding on assistive technology that can range from low-tech gadgets to robotics and sophisticated electronics.
- Gerontechnology is a new field that blends principles of gerontology and technology to generate ergonomic designs for homes and products for older adults.
- The Eden Alternative is a rapidly spreading philosophy of care in which nursing homes are designed to facilitate people living with plants, animals, and having frequent visits from children.
- A holistic approach to achieving person–environment congruence in old age incorporates human services, ergonomic design of products and environments, and public policy and funding solutions.

STUDY QUESTIONS

1. What is person–environment congruence? What are the three different types? Identify the capabilities and demands you are currently bringing to your task of reading and studying. What kind of fit do you have with your environment?

2. What is the difference between younger and older persons in terms of person–environment congruence?

3. What is the docility hypothesis? Give an example of how you might test this hypothesis.

4. What do we mean when we say we have an attachment to a place? Give an example of your own attachments to a place.

5. Identify the various housing options available to older persons.

6. Where and with whom do most older persons live?

7. Describe the difference between continuing care retirement communities, assisted-living facilities, and nursing homes.

8. What are the advantages and disadvantages of homeownership for older adults?

9. What is meant by the term *aging in place*?

10. Describe the findings regarding the effect of environment on quality of life of frail elders.

11. Who is most likely to care for older persons in need?

12. Describe home-based care. Who is most likely to receive this care and what is its effect on care receivers?

13. What predicts satisfaction in retirement communities and assisted-living facilities?

14. What is a helpful or enabling environment?

15. What is the human factors approach and how has it been applied for older adults?

16. What is ergonomic design? Give a few examples.

17. Define ADL and IADL tasks.

18. Provide some examples of problems older people may experience with daily tasks and some environmental solutions for these problems.

19. What is gerontechnology?

20. What do you do when you *Edenize* a nursing home?

21. Describe the Green House Concept design for nursing homes.

RECOMMENDED READING

Pynoos, J., & Cohen, E. (1997). *Home Safety Guide for Older People: Check It Out/Fix It Up*. Washington, DC: Serif Press, Inc. An excellent checklist and guide for improving the safety in your home.

INTERNET RESOURCES

www.carepathways.com. CarePathways provides information on caregiving and facilities.
www.carescout.com. Provides information, ratings, research, and data on eldercare living situations.
www.1sn.com/homehealthcare/. For information on medical supplies.
www.directdme.com/pposcripts/dme_home.asp. Web-retailer for home health care supplies.
www.eldercarelink.com. Offers assistance in finding care for older adults in their homes by finding local home care agencies.

CHAPTER

14 Death and Bereavement

To live in the hearts we leave behind, is not to die.

—Thomas Campbell

Death is a part of the circle of life. It is something we face when those close to us die and, certainly, when we ourselves die. In this chapter, we will examine the most frequent causes of death and the many ways in which people prepare for and face death. We will then examine the survivors, the bereaved, and see, as Thomas Campbell says, that the beloved never die and that the depression of loss can be replaced by the joy of having known such a person.

In Senior View, Tat Kleckley talks about the loss of her parents when she was very young and the loss of other close relatives now that she is older. She says it is very important to have people to talk with after the death of someone close—we will see that the research strongly supports her views. The support of others is crucial at such times.

Death

Before the early 1900s, the most frequent deaths occured in children. Many died during childbirth and those who survived often died from measles, influenza, whooping cough, and other diseases during their early years. Few adults reached old age. Death was much quicker in those days since early detection of a heart problem, cancer, and so on was unlikely given the diagnostic tools and tests available in those years (Lynn, 1991). Treatments were unavailable or fairly ineffective. Because disorders often were not detected until the person was close to death and no effective treatments were available, death was quick. Now, however, disease can be detected much earlier and often treated. People may live with heart disease or cancer for long periods of time after initial diagnosis. A result of advances in medicine is that we live longer and death now occurs more slowly and more frequently in older adults than in children. An older adult is more likely to experience the degeneration that accompanies many diseases and to live for a long time with declining function. Today, the most frequent deaths occur in older adults.

Senior View

Tat Kleckley was 69 years old when we spoke with her about death and bereavement. She lives with her husband.

We're both pretty healthy. When I think about my own life and eventual death, I know I'd like to go on living as long as I'm able to take care of myself; as long as I'm mentally able to think through things. If I get to be a vegetable, then I don't want to live anymore.

I'd rather die at home unless it turns out to be more comfortable for my family and friends for me to be in a hospital. I've already made arrangements for my cremation when I die.

My mother and father both died when I was only 3 and a half. My dad's brother and his wife took my older sister and I to live with them. They raised us as their own children. I also lost some aunts who were very close and my mother-in-law. Losses are never easy and time, more than anything else, takes care of the grief. It took me a year to get over the deep part of grieving because during that first year you think about this time last year when we were doing something together. After that first year you have memories of at least one event, a Christmas or a Fourth of July, that you spent without the deceased. It makes it a little eas-ier but you still grieve within; you still remember the people and you miss them.

We asked what she would recommend to people who are grieving. *They should go out and do things. Don't stay inside by yourself. Most important of all is to talk about it. Part of the healing process is being able to talk about it and to have friends who will listen.*

We will see that Tat is right.

Causes of Death

Table 14-1 shows the leading causes of death in the United States for the year 2002. One hundred years earlier, influenza and pneumonia were the leading causes of death and remain high today at number 7, but many other leading causes of death in those days, such as tuberculosis, diarrhea, diphtheria, and meningitis now are very infrequent (far less than 1%). Even over the last 20 years, there have been some major changes. Deaths from heart disease and cancer, although still very high, have dropped 37 and 6 percent, respectively. Deaths from Alzheimer's disease have increased over 1000 percent (Best, 2007). These changes are attributed to advances in medicine and longer life expectancy. Advances in medicine have successfully treated a number of diseases and those diseases no longer are much of a threat to most people. Increases in life expectancy resulting from a number of factors (see Chapter 5) make many more people susceptible to Alzheimer's and other life-ending dementias. The decline in deaths from heart disease and cancers is, in part, due to the much greater number of deaths because of Alzheimer's.

TABLE 14-1   Major Causes of Death in the United States

Cause of Death	Percentage of Deaths
Heart diseases	28.5
Cancers	22.8
Stroke	6.7
Chronic respiratory diseases	5.1
Accidents	4.4
Diabetes	3.0
Influenza & pneumonia	2.7
Alzheimer's disease	2.4
Kidney diseases	1.7
Septicemia	1.4
Suicide	1.3
Liver diseases	1.1
Hypertension	0.8
Homicide	0.7
All other causes	17.4

Source: National Vital Statistics Report, Volume 53(5), October 2004.

Accidents were ranked seventh in 1900 and are fifth today as a cause of death and, today, the most frequent fatal accidents are those involving a motor vehicle (44% of fatal accidents) followed by falls (18%). Fatal motor vehicle accidents are more frequent for younger adults while fatal falls are more frequent for older adults. The top three causes of death for different age groups in the United States are shown in Table 14-2. Looking at this table, you should notice several things. Cancers are a major cause of death for all groups and this is true for every age group over a year old. Heart diseases, on the other hand, do not become major causes of death until early middle age. Alzheimer's ranks fourth as a

TABLE 14-2   Age Differences in Causes of Death

| Age Group | Leading Causes of Death | | |
	First	Second	Third
15 to 34	Motor vehicle accident	Firearms	Cancers
35 to 54	Cancers	Heart disease	Motor vehicle accidents
55 to 64	Cancers	Heart disease	Respiratory diseases
65 to 74	Heart disease	Cancers	Septicemia
75 to 84	Heart disease	Cancers	Respiratory diseases
85 and older	Heart disease	Cancers	Influenza & pneumonia

Source: National Vital Statistics Report, Volume 50, September 2002.

major cause of death for those 85 and older; it ranks sixth for those between 75 and 84, and eighth for those between 65 and 74. You may be surprised that AIDS is not so high in the United States. Box 14-1 discusses this fact and presents some data on accidental deaths and suicides in a number of other countries.

In addition to these historical and cultural differences in causes of death, there are also some gender differences. For men, suicide and homicide are among the major causes of death; they occur less frequently for women. Men also are more likely than women to have a fatal accident. Women, however, are more likely to die from influenza, pneumonia, and septicemia than are men. Septicemia is a bacterial infection in the blood that rapidly spreads through the body. All infections need to be treated quickly and appropriately to avoid septicemia.

Clearly one way to prolong life is to pay regular visits to the physician. Regular checkups increase the probability of detecting a potentially life-threatening illness, such as hypertension or a cancer, early enough for it to be successfully treated. Some recent work suggests that physician visits account for the largest portion of African and white American differences in longevity (Sherkat et al., 2007). In this study, more than half a million

BOX 14-1
Death Around the World

A major difference in causes of death around the world is in deaths from communicable diseases. **Communicable diseases** are those that can be transmitted from one person to another and include AIDS, influenza, respiratory infections, and measles. These diseases account for 55 percent of the deaths in developing countries but only 14 percent in developed countries. The leading cause of death in developing countries is one of these diseases: AIDS. In 2001, AIDS claimed 2.7 million lives, most of them (1.9 million) in subsaharan Africa. Infectious diseases affect mainly children in these developing countries (*Causes of Death,* 2007).

When one examines deaths from accidents, one finds that they are high in most countries but the top five, in terms of fatal accidents are the Russian Federation, Hungary, Romania, the Czech Republic, and Slovenia. The five lowest death rates from accidents are in the Bahamas, the United Kingdom, the Netherlands, Israel, and Australia. Most fatal accidents in developed countries involve a motor vehicle: the five most dangerous places to drive are Portugal, Greece, Venezuela, Russia, and Slovenia. Of course, one can also examine motor vehicle deaths as a function of miles driven. In that case, the highest rates are for South Korea, Turkey, and Poland (Best, 2007). It is estimated that about 50 percent of motor vehicle fatalities involve alcohol use (Starfield, 2000).

As noted, the suicide rate for older white men in the United States is extraordinarily high (Chapter 12). Generally, the rates for men are higher than for women. In a comparison of several Asian- and English-speaking countries, the highest suicide rate was found for older men and women living in rural China; in this case, women had the higher rate. Rates also were high in Canada, Japan, and the United States while relatively low rates were found in Korea and the United Kingdom. Suicides were higher for older than for younger people in all but three countries: Canada, Ireland, and New Zealand (Pritchard & Baldwin, 2002).

Medicare recipients living in Tennessee were followed for more than 6 years. Over that time period, about 38 percent of African Americans and 32 percent of white Americans died. The strongest explanation of this difference in death rate was that African Americans paid far fewer visits to physicians and researchers suggest that this may be due to past neglect by physicians of this group and their skepticism of medical treatments. Related work shows that for older adults, regardless of race, less-aggressive treatments by physicians became the norm. Those 85 and older may not be expected to live much longer anyway or may not be able to tolerate major surgery or increased pharmaceuticals as well as those between the ages of 65 and 84 (Menec et al., 2007). Finally, some work shows that traditional medical tests used by physicians, such as blood pressure, BMI, and cholesterol levels are good predictors of mortality but some nontraditional measures are even better. Among the nontraditional measures examined were cortisol levels which are good indicators of stress, levels of DHEA, and other markers of immune system functioning and inflammation (Goldman et al., 2006).

Some research indicates a strong role for positive psychology. Those with more negative views and dissatisfaction with their own aging die sooner (Anstey et al., 2001; Maier & Smith, 1999). In a 7-year longitudinal study of several hundred adults 70 and older, those who felt that they were useful to family and friends tended to show no change or slight improvement in their ability to perform ADLs and also were less likely to die over that interval (Gruenewald et al., 2007). Feeling useful to those close to you is a positive way to feel and, as you already know, maintaining good social ties through marriage and friendships increases longevity (Rasulo et al., 2005). A positive attitude, good family and friends, regular checkups, and attention to some nontraditional indicators increase the chances of living longer.

Advance Directives

Because many more people die in old age and death is frequently the end result of some chronic, degenerative disorder, dying can take some time. People now have a more important role in deciding when to continue life and when to die. If you slip into the last stage of Alzheimer's disease and are unable to communicate with others, unable to think, unable to feed or toilet yourself, unable to breathe without a respirator, would you want to continue on life support for as long as possible or would you want someone to pull the plug and let you die? The answer to this question is not as simple as it may first appear because a number of factors are involved and there are several available options.

One factor is the state of mental competence that the individual is in when the question is answered. Persons who are conscious and mentally competent may refuse treatment if they wish. The doctor may say that a cancer might be removed with surgery and that without such surgery you will surely die, but the decision is yours. You can accept surgery, seek a second opinion, or refuse to undergo treatment. However, when a person is not mentally competent, as judged by a court of law or when a person is not conscious to make a decision, then those options are not available to them. Mental competence and/or consciousness may be lost in the advanced stages of dementia or when the individual is in a coma.

The state of being in a coma with severe brain damage and no detectable signs of awareness but a sleep–wake cycle and functioning of the autonomic nervous system, for at least a month is referred to as a **persistent vegetative state** or **PVS**. Such a state can result from a number of different disorders or injuries and may be only temporary, although the probability of recovery is small and grows smaller the longer the state persists. People who remain in a PVS are expected to live close to 7 years with care. If a feeding tube and water are removed, death usually occurs within 2 weeks. Should such a person be kept alive? If they regain consciousness will any of their prior cognitive functioning and memories remain? Such people are kept alive as long as the costs are paid unless there is some prior or advanced directive, such as a living will that specifies actions to be taken or not to be taken in the event of such circumstances. All states recognize the legality of advance directives (High, 1993) and their importance has been underscored by cases such as that of Terri Schiavo described in Box 14-2. There are several different forms of advance directives.

B O X **14-2**

Terri Schiavo

The case of Terri Schiavo received major media attention and drew the president, the Pope, Congress, and eventually the Supreme Court into the debate over care for a person in a persistent vegetative state. Terri was born in Pennsylvania on December 3, 1963. She graduated from high school in 1981 and enrolled at Bucks County Community College where she met her husband in a sociology class. He was her first serious boyfriend. She and Michael were married on November 10, 1984. In 1986, they moved to Florida and 3 months later her parents did too.

Early on the morning of February 25, 1990, Terri collapsed in the hallway of her and Michael's St. Petersburg apartment. She had a heart attack. When paramedics arrived, they found her face down on the floor; she had no pulse and was not breathing. They tried to resuscitate her and rushed her to the hospital. She survived but the long period without oxygen damaged major areas of her brain and she entered a PVS. In 1992, Michael successfully sued the doctor who had been treating Terri before her collapse and was awarded a million dollars, most of which was intended for her care. For many years, Michael and her parents cooperated in her care and prayed for her recovery but in 1998, Michael filed a petition to end her life support. Her feeding tube finally was removed in 2001 but reinserted 2 days later because of a lawsuit filed by her parents to continue all life support. Husband and parents were now locked in a battle over the life of this young woman. Michael said it would be her wish to die while they insisted she must certainly want to live. She had no advance directive.

The battle raged in the courts and media and in 2003 the tube again was removed but reinserted a week later, because Governor Jeb Bush pushed the Florida legislature to pass an emergency act to restore the feeding tube. In 2004, the Florida Supreme Court struck that law down. The U.S. Supreme Court would not hear the case and the U.S. Senate and Congress became involved. In 2005, the Senate passed a bill that would keep the tube in place but passage was delayed in the house. On March 18, the tube again was removed and the parents vowed to appeal to the U.S. Supreme Court. On March 31, 2005, Terri Schiavo died.

(continued)

BOX **14-2** Continued

Would Terri have wanted the tube removed so she could die or would she have wanted all life support continued in the slim hope of recovery? We cannot say for certain as all we know is that her husband and parents disagreed about what she wanted. Her case makes clear the importance of advance directives and at a young, as well as older, age.

A **living will** is a document that specifies the types of treatments that an individual wants and those the person does not want if that individual becomes incompetent or enters a coma or PVS and death is imminent. Living wills are not simple statements saying that no artificial life support is desired; they are frequently far more complex and require the individual to make decisions about treatments wanted or not wanted in a number of different situations. A recent form of living will, called Five Wishes, includes information beyond medical treatments as the person also makes decisions about how comfortable they wish to be, how they want to be treated by others, and what they wish to tell their loved ones (Aging with Dignity, 2007). Table 14-3 provides one example of a part of a traditional living will. Of course, not all possible treatments or situations can be anticipated so it is frequently the case that the directions spelled out in a living will may not directly apply and some interpretation of the individual's wishes must be made by others (Wreen, 2004). Living wills are not usable until death is imminent. A person in a PVS may have wished to have their life ended some time ago but, until death is imminent, their desire to have the "plug pulled," cannot be carried out (Mathes, 2005).

TABLE 14-3   An Example of a Living Will

In this living will, each of the following decisions must be made for each medical procedure in each of four possible situations.

Decisions

I want the treatment.

I want the treatment tried but if there is no clear improvement, then I want it stopped.

I do not want the treatment.

I am undecided.

Medical Procedures

Cardiopulmonary resuscitation

Mechanical/artificial respiration

Artificial nutrition and hydration

Major surgery

Minor surgery

Kidney dialysis

Blood and/or blood products

Invasive diagnostic tests

Simple diagnostic tests

Antibiotics

Pain medication

Situations

I am in a coma or persistent vegetative state with no known hope of regaining awareness or higher mental functions.

I am in a coma or persistent vegetative state with a small probability of full recovery, a slightly higher probability of permanent brain damage, and a much higher probability of dying.

I have brain damage or brain disease that cannot be reversed and I am unable to recognize people or to speak intelligibly. I also have a terminal illness that is very likely to cause my death.

I have brain damage or brain disease that cannot be reversed and I am unable to recognize people or to speak intelligibly. I do not have a terminal illness and may live in this condition for a long period of time.

Try going through each of the four situations and making one of the four decisions for each of the 11 medical procedures. You have 44 decisions to make. Do your decisions depend on the particular situation? Are your decisions different for different medical procedures? In different situations? If so, you have a clearer idea of the complexity involved in preparing a living will.

The **health care durable power of attorney** is a second form of advance directive and specifies another individual as the decision maker for emergency and any other health care decision when the individual is no longer able to make such decisions. In some cases, this other individual may have financial durable power of attorney and makes all financial as well as health care decisions. The health care directive applies to any health decision and is, thus, not restricted to the treatments and situations described in a document or to the imminence of death. Of course, it is extremely important to select a person who will follow your wishes. When a person is in a PVS, there may be much disagreement among family members as to what should or should not be done (see Box 14-2) and that pressure can lead the person with the power to make a decision based on their own needs rather than the wishes of the person they represent (Zweiber & Cassel, 1989). It is important to be certain that the person understands your wishes. In one study, 45 people who made decisions regarding CPR for another person were interviewed. Only one had previously discussed CPR with the person they represented, seven claimed that they knew what the person would have wanted, and 23 had no idea what the individual would have chosen (Sayers et al., 2004). In a similar study, a majority of competent individuals undergoing dialysis believed that their own advance directives could and should be ignored if the doctor decided that it would be best to do so (Sehgal et al., 1992). If one intends to rely on the doctor to make the decision or on a person who has no idea what you would decide if you were able, then there is no need for an advance directive. You simply cast your fate to the wind (Guaraldi, 1962).

Two other types of advance directives are the **do not resuscitate (DNR)** and **do not hospitalize (DNH)** orders. The former specifies that no procedure should be performed to save the person's life in the event of cardiac or respiratory arrest: The DNR can refer only to CPR or to any extraordinary or emergency resuscitation procedures (such as tracheotomy and open heart massage). A DNR is never assumed but must be in writing and in the record. Hospitals will not take verbal DNR instructions. The DNH order specifies that the individual should not be taken to the hospital for treatment in the event of an emergency. The DNH does not rule out lifesaving techniques that might be used where the person resides.

The percentage of older adults with some form of advance directive is fairly small, estimated to be less than 20 percent (High, 1993). This percentage varies for different SES levels and cultural groups. The people who are most likely to have a directive are those who are fairly prosperous, well educated, and not members of minority groups (Sachs, 1994). A number of comparisons show that African Americans are far more likely to desire life support and far less likely to have a DNR directive than are white Americans. Hispanic and Native Americans generally fall between these groups (Eleazer et al., 1996). Chinese, Japanese, Korean, and Mexican older adults are more likely to believe that family members, especially adult children, should be relied on to make the health care decisions when an individual is no longer able to do so (Kwak & Haley, 2005). Attempts that have been made to increase the use of advance directives by providing more information have had only limited success. The Patient Self-Determination Act requires that all health care institutions receiving Medicaid funds must inform patients about advance directives and the patient's right to refuse treatment. Such educational interventions have been found to increase the percentage of people with an advance directive by only a couple of percentage points. Surveys of older adults show that most base their decision to have an advance directive on their own personal experiences of witnessing death and on spiritual (is it morally correct?), emotional (how would my family feel?), and social (would my living in a PVS cause a great burden on my family?) factors and not on public information or information from a health professional (Lambert et al., 2005).

Even when an advance directive has been signed, one cannot be sure that it will be followed. Sometimes the person signing the directive never discusses it with family members or doctors who may not realize that such a directive even exists (Dresser, 1994). Sometimes the existence of an advance directive or its specifics are known by one doctor or department in a hospital but not effectively communicated to professionals in other departments who may care for the individual (Hansot, 1996). Taking time to search a patient's chart for an advance directive in a time of crisis is not generally considered high priority and in some emergencies, charts are not even available. If a patient is in imminent danger of death and transported from an accident at home to a hospital emergency room, heroic efforts to save the individual's life may be undertaken long before the patient's own doctor, lawyer, or family can intervene and make known the contents of the patient's living will, DNR, or DNH orders or the fact that another person with durable power of attorney is supposed to make all decisions in times like these. Even when such orders are known, physicians sometimes ignore them and proceed with every effort to save the individual's life in spite of the individual's wishes (SUPPORT Principal Investigators, 1995). Physicians may fear the possibility of a lawsuit brought by surviving family members or feel that is goes against the Hippocratic oath to let a patient die. Medical personnel have been trained to sustain life and it is often difficult for them to withhold available treatments (Brody et al., 1997).

Euthanasia

Euthanasia, Greek for *good death,* takes two different forms. One form is the refusal to accept life-sustaining technology and efforts by medical personnel or the discontinuing of such technology and efforts already in place. Such refusal is embodied in many of the advance directives just examined and is often referred to as passive euthanasia. Passive euthanasia refers to cases where nothing is done to prolong life. Passive euthanasia is legal and generally accepted by most, but not all, people.

Active euthanasia, on the other hand, refers to cases where specific actions are taken to end life. There are three general forms of active euthanasia.

One form of active euthanasia is when someone kills another person because they believe that other person would be better off dead. It is not the case that the suffering person has asked to die; the killer has decided for them that it would be merciful to hold the pillow over their face, administer poison, or end their life in some relatively painless way. This form is considered murder and is not legal or acceptable, although one occasionally hears of such cases.

A second form of active euthanasia is suicide. We talked briefly about suicide in Chapter 12 when we talked about depression. As you might remember, most people who commit suicide are depressed and the group with the highest suicide rate is older, white men. Although the most frequent diagnosis for older adults who commit suicide has been depression (Conwell, 1995), many also have had a life-threatening and/or terminal illness. Some of these illnesses are more likely to lead to suicide than are others. The incidence of suicide is higher for individuals with cancer, AIDS, epilepsy, and Huntington's chorea than for individuals with blindness, multiple sclerosis, and various forms of dementia (Mishara, 1999).

The third form of euthanasia is **physician-assisted suicide**. In this case, a physician prescribes some drug(s) or assists in some other way to end the life of a person who wished to die. Physician-assisted suicide (PAS) is legal in Oregon and in the Netherlands but is highly regulated. PAS requires at least two doctors to review the case, agree that suicide is a reasonable request based on a determination that the person's circumstances are unbearable and irreversible, that no remedy is foreseeable, that the requester is competent, and that the request has been made more than once over a period of time (Cutter, 1991). Those most likely to seek such assistance are those with high levels of pain and suffering and low quality of life (Mishara, 1999). Several hundred people receive physician-assisted suicide every year in the Netherlands but the rate of requests for this service and the number of completed suicides represents only .2 percent of deaths and has recently dropped to only .1 percent. The number of requests from men and women is about the same and usually a general care practitioner writes the prescription (van der Heide et al., 2007). The first such case in Oregon occurred in March 1998 when a woman in her 80s, suffering from breast cancer, took barbiturates prescribed by her physician. She died in the presence of family members and the physician who assisted her (Murphy, 1998). In the 9 years since the law was passed, a total of 292 patients have died. Most (87%) had cancer, more education than others who died (41% had at least a bachelor's degree), died at home (93%), had hospice care (76%), and had health insurance (97%) (Oregon Department of Human Services, 2006).

There are a number of arguments in favor of and against physician-assisted suicide and discussions can become quite heated. Box 14-3 presents some of these views. At present, 46 states specifically prohibit physician-assisted suicide while only one permits it. Two states, Nevada and Washington, are considering possible legislation. Public opinion

---

B O X 14-3

Physician-Assisted Suicide

Pro

Those in agony should be allowed to die with dignity. Some of these individuals are not capable of ending their own life and/or do not wish to do so because it would create shame for their family. It is truly unmerciful to allow them to experience pain, misery, and suffering without end when they truly wish to die and request assistance. At present, pain medications are given in doses that are too small to relieve the suffering. One may have to wait another 4 hours to get some temporary help and this cycle of brief relief followed by pain and waiting continues until the person dies because physicians fear being accused of malpractice if they give too much medication. Allowing someone to suffer and die a prolonged death is not merciful; physician-assisted suicide is a gentle easy way to end this suffering.

BOX **14-3** Continued

Con

All life is sacred and no one has the right to end their own or anyone else's life. To permit physician-assisted suicide is a dangerous step on a very slippery slope. The old, disabled, and the poor are most vulnerable and may be led to assisted suicide by physicians who have no time for them, know they cannot be cured, and know that they can legally help them die. The right to die could become a duty to die for those without resources in their older years. Legalization of physician-assisted suicide in some cases could lead to assistance whenever suicide is desired rather than just in extreme cases. People with major depression often think about suicide and now could have assistance in ending their life even though depression can be successfully treated. Spending the time to find a way to help alleviate suffering is the compassionate response.

Pro

Everyone has the right to exert as much control as they can over the time, place, and manner of their own death. Those with a terminal illness are, however, denied the right to choose a peaceful and dignified death. People who suffer and wish to die may not know anything about the quickest and least painful means toward that end and should be permitted to receive assistance from a competent professional. Doctors are only permitted to allow a slow painful death from suffocation or starvation as a result of an advance directive to discontinue or not begin treatment. It is the right of any competent, suffering individual to receive assistance in ending their suffering the way they want.

Con

Physician-assisted suicide goes against the entire purpose of medicine. The Hippocratic oath is to do no harm. Medical personnel must always remain hopeful and do the best that can be done for every patient they treat. Physicians cannot become healers for some and executioners for others.

There are, of course, a number of other, related arguments on both sides of this issue. Where do you stand? Why?

---

has been moving in the direction of approval for the procedure when the patient is suffering a painful, terminal illness and requests such assistance (Emanuel et al., 1996). This is not a question that can be settled by conducting more research. In the long run, it will be up to the individual to decide.

Regardless of where you find yourself in the debate over physician-assisted suicide, the major focus should be on providing dignity and relief of pain and suffering for those in need.

Hospice

One program advocating and providing better care for the terminally ill is **hospice**. Hospice has been providing palliative care for over 30 years. Palliative care focuses on helping patients with illnesses be more comfortable by addressing their physical and emo-

Funeral rites vary significantly across cultures.

tional pain and suffering. To qualify for hospice care, a person must have an illness and a life expectancy of 6 months of less. In the last few years, hospice has begun a new separate program for palliative care to those with serious illness regardless of life expectancy. Many hospice programs now offer these as separate palliative care programs. Although the services are the same and the team providing the services are the same, Medicare, Medicaid, and most private insurance companies pay all costs of hospice care but only some costs of palliative care.

Most patients enrolled in hospice programs are older adults (70+ percent) while very few (7 to 8 percent) are under age 45 (National Center for Health Statistics, 1995). Most are dying from cancer (70 to 80 percent) while the remainder typically have AIDS or heart disease (Papalia et al., 1996). A survey of 1700 hospice programs showed that few patients have some form of dementia, such as Alzheimer's disease, as their primary diagnosis (less than 1 percent) although some of those with cancer or heart disease also have a form of dementia as a secondary diagnosis (7 percent). Directors of hospice programs often believe that they do not have the necessary resources to care for late stage dementia patients and it is far more difficult for physicians to be sure that a dementia patient is within 6 months of dying (Hanrahan & Luchins, 1995).

Hospice is not always an easy choice to make and at present it is a choice not made by most although the numbers are growing (Levine, 1995; Sachs, 1994). The individual not only must be close to death but also must be willing to give up several rights in addition to the right to engage in life-sustaining technology and efforts. For example, the patient cannot switch doctors without permission from the team. A hospice team composed of a physician, a nurse, a social worker, and sometimes a lawyer and/or volunteer worker assume responsibility for the person's care under the direction of the physician. Most typically, one or more family members also are involved in caring for the dying person and the family member most likely to be involved is the spouse (Bass et al., 1985–1986). The team makes all decisions regarding care. If an emergency occurs, the team, rather than the individual patient or family, decides whether to call an ambulance or seek hospitalization. In an emergency, one dials the hospice team rather than 911.

Studies have shown that dying persons and their families gain much from hospice. One benefit is that the hospice team makes an effort to lessen any isolation that the person might experience. A few patients dislike this aspect and complain about not having much privacy. Liking or disliking this may be a function of one's level of extraversion (see Chapter 9). The direct involvement of family members in caring for the dying relative is thought to be important for quality care and the well-being of the family following the death (Andershed & Ternestedt, 1998). In this country, most hospice care takes place in the home and home is, for most, a preferred location. Surveys show that close to 90 percent of Americans would prefer to die at home, although almost 75 percent end up dying in a hospital or nursing home (Glasheen & Crowley, 1998). A second benefit is that counseling is continually available for the patient and the family while the person still lives and, for family members, for at least a year after the death. Hospice also helps with all postdeath activities (Kastenbaum, 1993). A third benefit is that pain medication is readily given whenever the dying person feels the need for it and frequently, in their homes, patients or their families are granted control over their own pain medication. Medications that allow the person to continue functioning consciously are preferred by hospice and most patients. Some recent work shows, however, that this free access to pain medication for hospice patients in nursing homes does not always occur. In a comparison of hospice and nonhospice residents living in two nursing homes, researchers found that, although most experienced pain, no more relief was available to hospice than to nonhospice persons (Kayser-Jones et al., 2006). Hospice benefits seem to be more accessible at home than in an institution.

The Dying Experience

The experience of dying depends to a great extent upon the person and the context in which it occurs. Dying alone in pain is a very negative way to die while dying comfortably in the company of loved ones is far more positive. Attempts to describe the experience and to examine the factors involved began with the pioneering work of Elizabeth Kübler-Ross (1969) who observed many dying persons and suggested that they experienced the stages of denial, anger, bargaining, depression, and finally acceptance before meeting death. Later work showed that these experiences were not universal and not really stages at all (Shneidman, 1992) although depression and other emotions are quite common.

Some individuals experience positive emotions, along with the more negative emotions, when confronting death. Dying individuals and their families often find that impending death allows the display of emotions that were previously kept in check and bonds with others may be strengthened. Disagreements that may have festered for years might be resolved in the face of oncoming loss. Some develop insights about others and the world and grow stronger in the face of this hardship (Mead & Willemsen, 1995). Recently 16 hospice patients were interviewed and reported to be experiencing a high quality of life in spite of their terminal diagnosis. They and their primary caregivers were asked about the factors that contributed to their positive outlook. Those factors included a perception of good social support, a stable and comfortable physical environment, effective management of pain, and strong spiritual (not necessarily religious) beliefs (Nakashima & Canda, 2005).

Attitudes toward dying do seem to change with aging. Older adults are thought to be more accepting of death than younger adults (Shneidman, 1992), however, this is not always true. Some older adults are as unaccepting of death as are younger adults and believe that they still have a long life to live even at age 70 or 80 (Howarth, 1998). It may be that the attitudes of older adults toward death are the attitudes of their cohort and that, rather than attitude changing with age, different cohorts have different attitudes (Kastenbaum, 1999). Middle-age and older adults are more likely than younger adults to think about the process of dying rather than death itself (deVries et al., 1993). People of all ages typically express a desire to go quickly, without pain, and while asleep. This type of dying, unfortunately, is not very frequent. Eventually, of course, we all die although we hope, as Thomas Campbell says, to continue to live in the hearts of those we leave behind.

Bereavement

Bereavement refers to survival. The bereaved are those who have survived the death of another. Bereaved individuals are expected to go through the rites of mourning and to experience and show grief.

Mourning

Mourning refers to the socially accepted ways for the bereaved to express grief and to acknowledge that a life has ended. There are enormous cultural differences in mourning and in ways of behaving following the death of another. In some cultures, the dead are immediately removed for burial and not spoken of again. In others, mourning is open and continues for an extended period of time; some people may wear black or black armbands for up to a year after the death. Some religious and cultural differences in mourning are briefly described in Box 14-4.

Some form of funeral and removal of the body as soon as possible are typical for most individuals despite differences in religious beliefs or ethnic origin. In the United States it is typical for a viewing of the body to occur; in 70 to 80 percent of funerals the body is viewed (National Funeral Directors Association, 1997; Riekse & Holstege, 1996). Funerals, body viewing, and burials are expensive. The average cost of a funeral is estimated to be over $6500 in large part due to the average cost of a casket which is $2330. Burial and a burial plot may cost an additional $2500. Tombstones can be quite costly depending on size, type of stone used, and engravings. Table 14-4 shows the range of av-

BOX **14-4**

Selected Religious and Cultural Differences in Mourning

The rituals practiced and regarded as socially acceptable vary as a function of religion and culture (Sweet, 1994). Here are some of these rituals.

Religion

At *Buddhist* funerals, candles and incense are burned near the body until it is taken for burial. One night of viewing is permitted and family wear white while all others wear black. Family members participate in the ceremony and all bow together before the body is taken for burial. Death is viewed as the beginning of one's life and a time of joy as well as sorrow. Japanese Buddhists often give the deceased a new name to mark this beginning and many homes maintain an altar to honor the person on which food and candles are placed on a regular schedule (Morgan, 1986).

Christian funerals involve a service at a church, chapel, funeral home, or burial site and usually occur around 3 to 5 days of the death. Caskets are often open and the body is available for viewing at a funeral home for a couple of days and evenings. Family members wear black. Cremation is acceptable and flowers and gifts are appropriate.

The *Hindu* custom is to dispose of the body before sundown on the day that death occurred. The service is conducted, if possible, by the first-born son. Family members wear white while all others wear dark clothing. Flowers are considered appropriate. All bodies are cremated and formal grieving takes place for at least 13 days following the cremation. In India, cloth-wrapped bodies are often cremated on the banks of the holy river, the Ganges, and slowly moved down the steps as they burn until the ashes can be swept into the river (Jaffrey, 1995).

In *Islam,* the dead are wrapped in cloth by family and friends and buried as soon as possible. At the mosque, all remove their shoes and men and women sit separately. The Iman reads from the Koran and chants. Family members wear black and all file by the body to pay their respects. After the burial, a meal is served; flowers are appropriate.

In *Jewish* culture, burials are very soon after death. Mourners wear black or a piece of black cloth or ribbon attached to their clothing. Caskets are traditionally closed and cremation is frowned upon but not forbidden. At the burial, each person places some dirt on the casket and then a meal is served. For a week of mourning, called shiva, the family receives visitors and all mirrors are covered. For another 30 days, called sheloshim, mourning continues but is diminished and flowers are inappropriate.

Culture

The Athabasken people of Alaska believe that the whole community must support the bereaved; to accomplish this they hold a 3-day ritual called a potlatch. The ritual includes dancing, singing, storytelling, feasting, and giving gifts to the bereaved family members (Simeone, 1991).

In South Africa, the Xhosa culture believes that the dead watch over the living. When a head of household dies, he or she is buried on family land facing the family home to keep an eye on the living. The dead may protect the family or even send some misfortune if he or she becomes angry (Gijana et al., 1989).

The Hmong of southern Asia sacrifice animals, including oxen, to feed the family and the departed. The night before the day of burial, a survivor will sing all night. Burials are in the afternoon and for the next 3 days, food is prepared for the deceased spirit while the deceased becomes

(continued)

> ┃ **B O X** **14-4** Continued
>
> oriented to the afterlife. For 10 additional days, a spot is set at the family table in case the spirit is still present and needs nourishment (Bliatout, 1993).
>
> Among Native Americans, the Hopi view any contact with death to be tainted and dangerous for the living. One must break all ties with the deceased soon after death and get on with life. Grieving is strongly discouraged and the dead are to be forgotten (Mandelbaum, 1959). The Lakota, on the other hand, encourage the open and full expression of grief. Men will sing songs filled with emotion and women will loudly wail and sob (Brokenleg & Middleton, 1993).

TABLE 14-4   Estimated Funeral Costs (in dollars)

Professional services

Minimum (facilities and staff, coordination with cemetery, securing of documents, sheltering remains, and overhead)	1213
Additional services (direction of funeral service, attendants for visitation periods,	347
arrangement of floral and other tributes, attendants for graveside service)	420
Embalming (required by law if body is to be viewed)	175
Other preparation of body for viewing (dressing, cosmetology, hair)	350
Use of facilities for viewing (charge per day)	185
Use of funeral coach to cemetery	33
Acknowledgement cards	53
Memorial folders (100)	

Casket

48-ounce solid bronze	10,778
32-ounce solid bronze	4783
48-ounce solid copper	5340
32-ounce solid copper	4160
16-gauge metal	3604
19-gauge metal	2404
Wooden	1765
20-gauge metal	890

Outer container

Copper	9828
Concrete (with seamless liner, nameplate, and handcrafted design cover)	2875
Concrete (with seamless liner and nameplate)	1127
Wood	196

Cremation

Adult and container provided by purchaser	1200
Disposal of cremated remains	33
Bronze urn	983
Marble urn	315
Vault for urn	315

Prices are based on averages from a number of different funeral homes in February 2001. Many additional caskets, outer containers, and urns are available; those selected include the most and least expensive.

erage prices for professional services, use of facilities, caskets, vaults, and cremation service at a typical funeral home. Vaults are required by some cemeteries in an attempt to keep the ground from subsiding over the casket but are not required by others (Baker & Reyes, 2000).

At the time of death, the family is often far too stressed, troubled, and busy to shop around for the best prices on funeral services. It is thought that many funeral homes take advantage of this situation and charge more than they might if the funeral industry were more competitive or more closely regulated. Funeral directors may try to embarrass or shame families into spending more than they should. "I know you want the very best for your mother," is a phrase heard all too often. Many of these abuses were first brought to light, decades ago, by Jessica Mitford (1963). Funeral home directors argue that abuse does occur but very infrequently. Today Lisa Carlson and the Funeral and Memorial Societies Association work to protect consumers from such abuse (Baker, 1999). In 1994, the Federal Trade Commission adopted standards for funeral practices and ruled that bereaved family members in charge of the funeral must receive written and itemized accounts of all expenses, must not be sold unneeded products or services, and must not be billed for services never rendered (Federal Trade Commission, 1994). In a survey conducted by the AARP, only 8 percent of the general public knew of these rules (Baker & Reyes, 2000). Over the last decade, four large corporations have begun purchasing individual and family-owned funeral homes across the country (Mulder, 1997). At present it is not clear what effect if any this will have on funeral costs.

More families and individuals have begun making funeral arrangements ahead of time (see Project 14). Burial plots frequently are purchased long before death is imminent. Much or all of the expenses can be paid at these prior-to-need times (AARP, 1992a). Although arrangements made ahead of time avoid the rush and stress of making arrangements at the time of death, it appears that they often cost just as much. Carlson says that it is common to tell survivors that the preselected casket is no longer available, then switch to a more expensive substitute (Baker, 1999). Cremation is being used more often than in the not-so-distant past. Cremation, on average, costs about 13 percent as much as a more traditional funeral and burial. Many funeral homes will attempt to convince families who select cremation that embalming should still be done and a casket should be purchased for the journey to the crematory (Baker & Reyes, 2000). There is no need for embalming unless there is a viewing and purchasing a casket for a trip to the crematory is absurd. In Japan, over 90 percent of individuals choose to be cremated (Aiken, 1991). You can purchase caskets, urns, vaults, and other items over the Internet. They are shipped immediately and you can save costs. Funeral expenses are discussed on many money management websites (e.g., www.smartmoney. com). Keeping abreast of current trends and advice could result in substantial savings. Although prepaying funeral costs may be prudent, it is a good idea to think about and plan your funeral to save loved ones this burden and to ensure that your wishes are followed. Project 14 was designed with this in mind.

Mourning rites are the socially accepted and expected ways in which the bereaved behave. For the bereaved, those rites are only the public display of their grief and although mourning is thought to help relieve some of that grief, grief is very powerful.

PROJECT **14**
Plan Your Own Funeral

For this project, we want you to think carefully and seriously about the events that might follow your own death if it were to occur soon. We know that this is not a happy thought but this project can often help people develop important insights into their own desires and preparation for what will one day happen. Try to answer each of the following questions:

- Do you have life insurance to help pay the costs?
- Who would you like notified first of your death? Why did you choose that person?
- Would you rather be buried or cremated or both (in some cases cremation urns are buried)? What type of casket, if any, would you want? If you choose burial, do you have a particular spot or cemetery in mind? If you choose burial, do you want a tombstone? What would you like your tombstone to look like? What, besides your name and dates of birth and death, would you like to have inscribed on the stone? If you wish to be cremated but do not wish to be buried, where and how would you like your ashes to be placed? Why have you chosen as you have?
- Would you like a funeral? If not, why not? If so, who should attend? Will the funeral be in the funeral home, a church, a home, outside, or somewhere else? What clothes do you want to be viewed, buried, or cremated in? Will there be a religious service? What scriptures or religious readings do you want? Why or why not? Will there be music? What songs would you most like to have played at your funeral? Why? Will attendees be expected to do anything special (e.g., say a word or two about you; what do you think they would say)? Should people send flowers or give donations to some organization(s)? Which one(s)? Should attendees accompany you to your burial if that is what you have chosen? Why or why not? Should they bring a flower, toss some dirt into the grave, or perform some other action?
- Do you expect the answers you have given now to be different for you when you have grown old? If so, periodically review your plans and make changes as needed.

You should put this plan away somewhere safe and let someone close to you know where it is. This could save some anguish and concern on the part of your loved ones. They can rest assured that your needs are met and that they have done the right thing for you.

Grief

Grief refers to the emotions experienced and the ways in which one copes with loss. The loss of a close loved one is considered the most stressful event that humans have to face and responses to that loss are extremely variable. Nevertheless, researchers have attempted to discern themes and patterns of grieving that might be common to most bereaved persons.

Bowlby (1980) and others (Parkes, 1998) have proposed four phases and patterns of grieving. *Numbing* is the first. Persons in this phase are unable to fully comprehend that the death has occurred. They do not believe it can be happening. The grieving person might carry on the normal daily activities of eating and sleeping but seem to do so automatically, without conscious awareness. They may appear to be like a robot. This first phase is usually short, lasting only a couple of days and rarely lasting longer than a month.

The second phase is one of *yearning and searching* for the departed loved one and usually is most intense toward the end of the first month following the death. This phase may last as long as a year or even two. Denial is common. Hallucinations may occur or the person may think the deceased is still alive somewhere and can be found if only great effort is made. The bereaved might think that they see or hear the deceased, particulary when alone at home. The desire to find and be with the lost loved one may even lead the bereaved to consider suicide as a way to be together. Any talk of suicide or of joining the deceased should be taken very seriously. Anxiety often appears in this phase as the person strives to be with the lost loved one but is frustrated repeatedly. Anxiety may grow out of the need to perform tasks that were once the domain of the departed loved one. Survivors may have difficulty in learning how to manage household finances or chores.

The third phase is one of *disorganization and despair.* The individual may lose their appetite and their ability to concentrate on any task or conversation. The loss is accepted as being real. Depression is very common in this phase and the individual may withdraw from others and fail to take care of themselves. The survivor may become irritable. Anxiety and guilt are fairly common (Stephenson, 1985; Zisook et al., 1990). The events that led up to the death may be continually thought about as if the person is searching for a clue as to what went wrong and why death had to occur. One may want to relive the last moments, hours, or days in order to do or say the right things. Feelings of anger at the deceased for leaving or guilt for failing to have done more to save the lost loved one frequently occur. The deceased may be seen through rose-colored glasses as having been near perfect, a saint. As time passes, the intensity of these emotions decreases with peaks occurring on important dates such as a birthday or anniversary.

Reorganization is the final phase and also can be very emotional as the bereaved individual attempts to construct a new life. Appetite is usually one of the first things to return to normal (Rosenbloom & Whittington, 1993). The bereaved may begin to care again about appearance and seek social contacts. Social activities become a major part of life. Sometime in the second year of grieving, most individuals notice that they are finally recovering. Some survivors take on some of the mannerisms and habits of the deceased and make them a part of their new self (Stephenson, 1985). This last phase may start toward the end of the first year or as late as 3 to 4 years after the death.

Although these four phases are reasonably good descriptions of the grief process experienced by many survivors, other descriptions also have been proposed. Kübler-Ross proposed the same five stages for grief and for dying (discussed earlier) (Cook & Oltjenbruns, 1998). Worden (1982) proposed four tasks involved in recovering from grief; accepting the reality of the death, feeling the pain, adjusting to the new life, and emotional reinvestment.

It should be kept in mind that none of these models are literally true and that people grieve in different ways. Some may experience all of the emotions and difficulties described while others feel very different emotions and have other difficulties. There is no one correct and healthy way to grieve; there are many. As each person is unique, so is their way of grieving.

The emotions experienced during grief depend to some extent on individual differences but several emotions are common. *Guilt* over not having done enough to save the lost loved one, for not being present when needed, or failing to show enough love seems to occur in about 25 percent of survivors but is usually quite mild (Breckenridge et al., 1986). *Anxiety* also is common although its presence depends to some extent on how it is measured. Feeling tense, nervous, and unable to get things done occurs in about 25 percent (Zisook et al., 1990). When measured as longing, it is present in close to 75 percent (Zisook et al., 1987). Depression is the most common emotion and may actually increase during the first year and be maintained well into the second year of grieving (Kastenbaum, 1999). Some say that the depression never ends although it subsides enough to permit normal functioning (Lund, 1993).

There are instances in which positive emotions and change for the better are associated with grieving. In some individuals, a profound spiritual change takes place and the person develops a new perspective on the meaning of life and their place in the universe (Balk, 1999). Self-confidence may increase as the person witnesses their ability to survive a painful loss. Survivors may feel stronger, more independent, and more capable of facing new crises should they occur (Calhoun & Tedeschi, 1989–1990). Those who grieve the most may, in some instances, experience the most growth in redefining their own goals and understanding their personal existence (Edmonds & Hooker, 1992).

Loss of a Spouse.   Widows are the largest group of bereaved individuals. Several factors contribute to this. As you will remember from Chapter 5, women have a longer life expectancy than men and, on average, live 7 to 8 years longer. Women also tend to marry men who are older than they are. Together, these factors frequently result in situations in which a younger wife loses an older husband. The average age of widowhood for a white woman is 56, for an African American woman it is 49, and for a Hispanic woman 48. After age 65, almost half of women are widowed while only 14 percent of men are. Past age 85, 80 percent of women and 43 percent of men are widowed (U.S. Bureau of the Census, 1990). Widows also are likely to be widowed for much longer periods of time than are widowers because they live longer and are much less likely to remarry. Because this is such a large group of individuals, both widows and widowers have received considerable research attention.

With the loss of a spouse, particularly a spouse of a long time, many unwelcome changes occur. The survivor has lost *a,* perhaps *the,* major role in their life. They are no longer a husband or a wife. Couples who were close friends with the couple before the death may attempt to continue including the bereaved spouse in activities but the spouse may feel out of place with intact couples and may tend to stay away after the funeral. In any marriage, there are shared tasks and tasks that are primarily handled by one or the other spouse. After the loss of a marriage partner, the survivor is faced with no one to share tasks with and many tasks to take on that were the other person's domain. One may have to learn to pay the bills and organize finances, to cook, do the laundry and keep the house clean, tend to the automobile, and so on. For some, these tasks are overwhelming.

As you might expect, widowhood significantly reduces the income for the surviving spouse. If both were working at the time of loss, as much as 70 percent of total income might be lost. If only one worked and that one died, all income might be lost and Social

Those in grief need support.

Security benefits could be all that remains. The death of a husband generally results in a greater loss of income than death of a wife because men have higher average incomes. The drop in total income for a white American widow is about 40 percent, for a Hispanic American widow about 27 percent, and for an African American widow about 55 percent. This drop in income is, of course, a difficulty for all widows but because Hispanic and African American widows have lower income to begin with, the loss can lead to poverty (Angel et al., 2007).

Sidney Zisook and his colleagues conducted a longitudinal investigation of grieving in 350 men and women living in San Diego who lost a spouse. They examined anxiety, depression, changes in immune function, and increased use of medications, alcohol, and cigarettes. Anxiety was more frequent among younger than older survivors, more frequent among women than men, and more frequent when a loss of income accompanied the loss of spouse. Among widows, 85 percent lost major income following the death of a husband. Younger women who lost a spouse and, thus, a major source of income were the most likely to experience severe anxiety. Anxiety did not decline significantly during the first 7 months of grief (Zisook et al., 1990; Zisook et al., 1990).

In terms of depression, Zisook and colleagues found 24 percent showed significant depression 2 months after the loss of a spouse. That incidence barely changed at 7 months (23 percent) but dropped to 16 percent at 13 months. Even over 2 years after the death, 14 percent of bereaved widows and widowers still showed some symptoms of depression. Those most likely to experience depression were younger survivors, and those who had a

SOCIAL POLICY APPLICATIONS

The economic consequences of widowhood are far more severe for minority women than for any other group. The loss of a working husband produces a loss of income that frequently brings poverty even if the woman continues to work. Income from Social Security is nowhere near enough to offset this drop so many older minority women must continue to work for very low wages until they can do so no longer. Social Security, of course, was never intended to be full retirement income in the first place. When originated, the assumption was that of a traditional marriage with a male breadwinner. His benefits, not just from Social Security, would take care of the couple in their final years (Herd, 2006). Things have changed dramatically since then and divorce is more frequent, life expectancy has increased, the proportion of older adults is increasing, and many believe Social Security cannot continue in its present form. As we ponder ways to assure the availability of Social Security for future generations (see Chapter 11), we must consider the plight of older minority widows. Ways must be found to help assure their security without stigmatizing them as a welfare group (Angel et al., 2007). This will not be an easy task but any changes in Social Security must recognize the needs of these very vulnerable individuals.

---

past history of depression (Zisook & Shuchter, 1991, 1993; Zisook et al., 1997). A 10 year, longitudinal study of 2104 Swedish twins, ages 26 to 87, looked at depression, loneliness, and life satisfaction. Cross-sectional comparisons were made between twins where one was widowed and the other was still married, and longitudinal comparisons were made between an individual's depression, loneliness, and life satisfaction before and after the death of a spouse. Both comparisons showed increased depression and loneliness and lower life satisfaction for up to 3 years following the death. These effects were diminished in the oldest-old, those over age 80 (Lichtenstein et al., 1996). What do you think this says about genetic contributions?

Of course the grief shown by the bereaved varies as a function of a number of factors (e.g., how close they were, age, gender). George Bonanno and colleagues described five different categories of bereaved individuals. Some individuals were depressed before the loss and remain depressed (about 8%), some showed increased depression following the loss and remained depressed for quite some time (about 16%), some became depressed with the loss but the depression abated over time (about 11%), some are depressed before the loss but their depression lessened with time (about 10%), and some were resilient and showed much lower rates of depression and were able to handle their loss well (about 46%). Those who were resilient and those who suffered depression after the loss but improved did not have as much difficulty as the other three groups in coping, adjusting, and remaining healthy (Bonanno et al., 2002; 2004).

Other work compared the grief experienced by men and women and both tend to show depression (Quigley & Schatz, 1999). Following the loss of a spouse, men spend more time alone, experience more boredom, and experience less affection from others than women during the early years of bereavement but eventually these differences disappear (Nieboer et al., 1998–1999). In one comparison of married men and women and bereaved men and women, all over 65, it was found that bereaved women were adjusting quite well, although more depressed than married women while bereaved men were far more depressed than married men. Married men were the least depressed of all four groups. Bereaved men lost a major part of their relatively happy lives when they lost the inner circle of their social network, their wife (Lee et al., 2001). Some work indicates that when a person has served as a caregiver for their now-deceased spouse, women take longer to recover from their depression than do men (Tweedy & Guarnaccia, 2006). Finally, some work shows that bereaved women are more dependent on their children, especially for financial and legal advice, than are bereaved men (Ha et al., 2006). Do you think this difference is due to cohort? The work also shows that widows with higher levels of education are less dependent.

Physical health also might decline after loss of a spouse. Bereaved individuals use more medication, call in sick more often, and have more doctor visits than comparable married persons. You already know that bereaved individuals lose their appetite and fail to eat very well for some time after the loss (Rosenbloom & Whittington, 1993). To see if widowhood or depression influenced functioning of the immune system, researchers compared 21 middle-age widows to 21 married women matched on age, length of marriage, physical and mental health, and no current or recent alcohol or drug abuse. All women were evaluated for 13 months. Impaired immune system functioning was found but only for the six widows who had major depression (Zisook et al., 1994). Depression, resulting from widowhood, can lower the efficiency of the survivor's immune system possibly producing increased risk for serious illness. Finally, research has shown that alcohol and medication use and cigarette smoking are likely to increase for 6 to 13 months after the loss of a spouse before returning to prior levels of use (Zisook et al., 1990). Increased medication, alcohol, and cigarette use are very unhealthy. Changes in physical health are most likely to occur in middle age bereaved adults (Wolinsky & Johnson, 1992).

Because health decreases for some period of time after the loss of a spouse, one might expect to find higher levels of **mortality** among the bereaved than among those still married and that is exactly what a number of studies have found. Bereaved individuals are more likely to die than comparable married persons of the same age. This greater likelihood of death lasts for close to 12 months and is greater for men than for women (Bowling, 1987; Stroebe, 1998). Several explanations have been offered for this finding.

One explanation has been that unhealthy people tend to marry other unhealthy people so, when one dies, the other unhealthy person also is likely to die. A related explanation argues that the death of both husband and wife, within a year of each other, is the result of both living in an unhealthy environment. Neither of these explanations are supported by evidence (Schafer et al., 1995). A third explanation claims that people who marry are genetically similar to one another and that it is the influence of those genetic factors that leads to death for both. This explanation also is unsupported (Lichtenstein et al., 1996).

Recent work suggests that the elevated mortality rate for the surviving spouse may be due to two factors: stress and diminished social support. Researchers know that the loss of a spouse is, for most survivors, an emotional and physical stressful event and they have seen that anxiety is one of the more common emotions during grief. Researchers also know that one's spouse is nearly always a major source of social support, especially for men. With stress and without the support of a spouse, one may neglect or be more likely to forget to take medication, keep doctor's appointments, dress warmly in winter, wear a hat in summer, and so on. It is assumed that men are more likely to neglect such tasks without a wife to remind them. After losing a spouse, the use of alcohol and tobacco increases for some time. Death from accidents and cirrhosis of the liver are especially high for bereaved men (Rogers, 1995) and the suicide rate is highest for older men who have recently lost their wife (Li, 1995).

One recent study examined mortality for married men and women whose spouse died or was hospitalized. Hospitalization as well as death resulted in increased mortality rates. During the first 30 days of hospitalization of a spouse, the death rate for the other spouse was nearly as great as for spouses who lost a husband or wife. Again, the death rate was higher for men than for women and for both, the rate depended on the reason for hospitalization of the spouse. The mortality rate was highest when the reason for hospitalization was some illness that left the hospitalized spouse unable to physically or mentally function well. So, hip fractures, psychiatric disorders, and dementia more often led to death of the healthy spouse than did other illnesses. Over the course of the year, mortality rates were highest during the first 3 and last 6 months and researchers believe that the early deaths may be largely due to stress while the later ones may be largely due to the loss of social support (Christakis & Allison, 2007).

One final factor influencing recovery from grief for a lost spouse is remarriage. Bereaved individuals who remarry or cohabitate show an increase in life satisfaction and reductions in stress and depression. Men are more likely than women to remarry in part because there are more women than men and men rely more than women on social support from a spouse (Belle, 1987). Some work has found that the best predictors of who will remarry are different for men and women. In a longitudinal study of widows and widowers 25 months after the loss, over 60 percent of the men but only 19 percent of the women were remarried or seriously involved in a relationship. For women, age was a predictor while for men income and education were predictors. Women who were younger than 65 were more likely to remarry and men with higher income and more education were more likely to remarry (Schneider et al., 1996). Why do you think this might be?

Although the mortality rate is higher for bereaved spouses during that first year and the likelihood of remarriage is not so high for women, most adjust and reorganize their lives. Within 2 years of the death, nearly 80 percent are getting along successfully though, of course, the sense of loss always remains (Lund et al., 1993).

Loss of Another. Although loss of a spouse has received the most attention from gerontology researchers, there are, of course, a number of other losses that occur all too frequently. About 40 percent of adults over 60 have lost a sibling and about 10 percent have lost an adult child (Moss & Moss, 1989; Moss et al., 1986–1987). In one study, several hundred adults, 65 and older, were followed for 2½ years to see how often different types of loss occurred. Bereaved individuals reported loss of a spouse 8 percent of the time while loss of a friend occurred for 37 percent and loss of a family member, other than a spouse, occurred for half of the participants. African Americans reported more frequent loss of a nonspousal family member than did white Americans and a part of this difference is assumed to be the closer ties with extended family for African Americans who may be more aware of losing more distant relatives. Loss of a friend was reported more frequently by women than men and it is thought that this may be due in part to the greater likelihood of women having friends in the inner circles of their social networks and, thus, being more aware of their demise (Williams et al., 2007).

The grief experienced with the loss of a sibling depends to some extent upon how close the siblings were. Recall the types of sibling relationships discussed in Chapter 10. Those with the closest relationships report the greatest sense of loss and deeper depression than those who were less close. At the same time, some of these same individuals report their loss as having made them stronger (Moss & Moss, 1989). Because children and surviving spouse generally are closer to the deceased, it is believed that the surviving sibling typically receives less emotional support when in fact they might need quite a lot (Cicirelli, 1995).

Loss of a close friend leads to a sense of loss and many bereaved individuals report becoming closer to their other friends (about 45%) while nearly a quarter report making new friends. About 45 percent report becoming more aware of their own aging and mortality and having a greater appreciation of life following such loss (Roberto & Stanis, 1994).

Loss of a Child or Grandchild.   The loss of a child, particularly a young child, can be devastating for parents and some never recover (Rando, 1991). The loss of an adult child also is very intense (DeSpelder & Strickland, 1992) and some evidence suggests it may be more intense than the loss of a spouse (Moss & Moss, 1995). The likelihood of guilt and self-blame occurs most often when the death is accidental, and accidents are the leading cause of death in children and young adolescents (ages 1 to 14). In a comparison of 44 bereaved spouses, 40 adult children who lost a parent, and 36 parents who lost a child younger than 18, several measures of images/thoughts, acute separation, and grief were taken at 1 month, 10 weeks, 7 months, and 13 months after the death. The most severe reactions were for parents who lost a child. Those who lost a spouse showed more grief than adult children who lost a parent (Middleton et al., 1998). A part of this difference may be due to the fact that the death of a child, especially one under 18, is usually unexpected.

Some researchers have examined the reactions of grandparents when their grandchild dies. The strongest reactions seem to be a blunting of emotion and feelings of guilt. Grandparents feel numb, confused, restless, and struggle with the belief that it was their time, not their grandchild's time, to die. Grandparents report a strong need to remain in contact with their own child, the parent of the lost grandchild (Fry, 1997).

The most likely persons to lose a child are the oldest-old because their children also are old. In such cases, one can easily envision the heartbreak that comes when one's child, particularly in the absence of any grandchildren, dies. One may feel truly alone with no link to the future. There may be nothing left to live for particularly if the spouse also is gone. Unfortunately, this group has not yet received much research attention.

Loss of a Parent.   Most people lose their parents before they themselves retire. Half have lost both parents by the time they are in their 50s and 75 percent have lost both parents before age 65 (Winsborough et al., 1991). Although the loss of a parent is not usually as severe as the loss of a child or spouse, it still presents many difficulties that are unique. *First,* loss of a parent is usually the loss of the oldest relationship in an individual's life.

Your parents have been a part of your life since your birth. *Second,* loss of a parent may be seen as a signal that your turn is next. Parents may represent the cohort just before yours and their loss means that death is on its way. *Third,* loss of parents means loss of a household and perhaps the very house where you grew up and were raised (Dainoff, 1989). Such losses may be felt for quite some time.

Surveys of adult children who have lost a parent show that 25 percent report continuing social and/or emotional problems 1 to 5 years after the death. Physical disorders, such as frequent fatigue, aches and pains, and illness, are common in half of the survivors (Scharlach & Fredriksen, 1993). Loss of a parent when the bereaved is still a child is thought to influence that person well into their own old age (Krause, 1993a).

The loss of a child is more intense in some cultures and less intense in others. In many parts of the world, the death of an older person is viewed as a greater loss. A mature person has goals that finally may be within reach and has entered into many relationships with other people. All of that will be lost with the death of a mature person (Jecker & Schneiderman, 1994; Kilner, 1990).

> In Africa, people are sadder about the death of an old man than about that of a newborn baby. The old man represented a wealth of experience that might have benefitted the tribe, whereas the newborn baby had not lived and could not even be aware of dying. In Europe, people are sad about the newborn baby because they think he might well have done wonderful things if he had lived. On the other hand, they pay little attention to the death of the old man, who had already lived his life anyway. (Werber, 1998, p. 227)

In U.S. culture, the death of the young is seen as more severe and unfair than the death of an older person. The young are viewed as having great potential and being the future whereas older people already have lived a full life (Jecker & Schneiderman, 1994). They may have no more potential. Parents may see their own children as a way of attaining immortality. After the parents are gone, their children and children's children will live on. Loss of an older parent is sad but is only the loss of a part of the past (Yalom, 1989).

Unexpected Death.   One might think that a sudden, unexpected death would result in more severe grief reactions than a slower, expected death. In the case of an expected death, one has time to prepare for the loss and to say goodbye to the dying person. One might understand the cause of death. In the case of an unexpected death there is no time to prepare or say goodbye. The death may not make sense to the survivors (Epstein, 1993). Generally, these predictions are supported. In one major study, 224 survivors who had not expected a relative or close friend to die were compared to 173 who expected the death of a relative or close friend. Unexpected deaths were defined as death from murder, suicide, car accident, stroke, heart attack, drowning, fire, aneurysm, or plane crash. Expected deaths were defined as death from cancer, AIDS, diabetes, or other chronic disorders. Individuals in the unexpected death group had more bereavement difficulties than those in the expected death group. This was especially true for individuals who lost a person to murder, suicide, or accident. Age played a role in the findings because more younger survivors lost a loved one unexpectedly while more older survivors had expected to lose a loved one. Age did not, however, interact with the effects of type of death. Unexpected death was more severe for both older and younger survivors (Hayslip et al., 1998–1999).

One aspect of unexpected death that might, in part, account for increased feelings of anger or guilt is that such deaths often are viewed as having been preventable. One might think "If only I had not let Sarah drive after knowing she had been drinking"; or "If only I had paid more attention to the signals that Jeff sent about his intended suicide"; or "If only I had warned Tameka and Simon not to take the short cut through that part of town." When bereaved individuals rate the preventability of a loss, those who rate the death as preventable show much higher levels of irritability, sleep problems, crying, missing the person, and anger and guilt (Guarnaccia et al., 1999).

When the death is from suicide, feelings of guilt and anger and the belief that the death was preventable typically are very strong. Survivors may become obsessed with thoughts about how they could or should have prevented the tragedy. In such a situation, where help often is needed the most, help is frequently absent. The comforting support of others often is diminished when a suicide has occurred because families may restrict funeral services and withdraw from all but the very closest friends. Suicide carries a social stigma and neither survivors nor friends may want to talk about it. Friends and family members themselves may avoid contact with the immediate survivors of a suicide because such contact is unpleasant and people may not know what is appropriate to say and do. Friends may even blame the immediate family for failing to prevent the death. As a result, survivors may be abandoned (Stillion, 1996). Survivors also may doubt their own self-worth, feeling that they were not important enough for the deceased to go on living to spend more time with them. In one study, persons who lost a spouse to suicide were compared with those who lost a spouse to a more natural death and to those who were still married. Although survivors of the natural death showed great grief, they also showed some recovery at 6 and 18 months. Survivors of a suicide still showed intense grief at 12 months with no sign of any recovery until 18 months after the death (Farberow et al., 1992). Survivors of a suicide experience greater levels of depression, anger, anxiety, guilt, and the other emotions of grief for a longer period of time and with less social support. As one father said of his daughter who committed suicide: "Suicide is not a solitary act. A beloved person thinks that she is killing herself, but she also kills a part of us" (Bolton, 1986, p. 202).

One aspect of expected death that might, in part, account for lower levels of grief when compared to unexpected death is **anticipatory grief**. When one begins grieving while the person is still alive, and if the amount of grief is finite, then some of it may already be gone when the person finally dies (Lindemann, 1944; Lundin, 1984). The research findings are not, however, supportive of this hypothesis. Some work has found that widows benefit from the opportunity to prepare funeral arrangements and to deal with insurance and pensions with their spouse before they die but, after the death, they are as filled with grief as those without such opportunity to prepare (O'Bryant, 1990–1991). It has been suggested that anticipatory grief is an entirely different kind of grieving from that which follows death and, therefore, cannot lessen the grief that follows death (Duke, 1998).

It is often the case that when death is expected that the spouse has been the caregiver for the deceased. Caring for a spouse with dementia or a terminal illness can be a great strain and caregivers are likely to experience far more depression than noncaregivers while the spouse is still alive (see Chapter 12). In comparisons of bereaved caregivers and noncaregivers, however, research has often found that surviving caregivers, particularly those who were very strained by the tasks involved in providing care, did not show as much of an increase in depression following the loss as did noncaregivers or caregivers with less strain. They also did not increase their own health risk behaviors such as smoking more, failing to take medication, not getting enough rest, or missing appointments with physicians as did the other two groups. The loss of their spouse may have lessened their burden (Schulz et al., 2001). It may not be anticipatory grief that lessens grieving but grieving may be lessened when the physical, mental, and emotional strain that was borne before the death was very great on the caregiver. Such caregivers may feel released from their burden knowing that they have done everything they could for their lost spouse.

Support for the Bereaved

What can be done to support the bereaved? What kinds of support are most welcome and what kinds are not? Clearly the answers to these questions depend to some extent upon the bereaved person, type of loss, and type of death. What helps one individual may not help another. It is estimated that close to 25 percent of the bereaved could, however, benefit from professional intervention. In a study of 350 newly bereaved widows and widowers, researchers found that 10 percent were experiencing the symptoms of posttraumatic stress disorder (PTSD) 2 months after the death and that 7 percent were still experiencing PTSD 25 months after the death. A diagnosis of PTSD is reflected in the individual spending a lot of time thinking about the loss, feeling that the lost person is with them at times, being numb, feeling lonely even when others are around, having no interest in anything, finding visits to the cemetery or looking at pictures to be too painful, having trouble falling asleep, having trouble concentrating, and feeling tense. The incidence of PTSD is highest (36 percent) in those who lose a loved one to an accident or suicide (Zisook et al., 1998).

Besides a diagnosis of PTSD, other behaviors on the part of the bereaved may predict a future need for counseling. Individuals who show the most conspicuous reactions are thought to be at very high risk for mental breakdown (Zisook & Shuchter, 1990). In addition to early and very strong emotional reactions, some individuals experience excessive confusion and lowered self-esteem. Those who avoid help and activity, who avoid keeping busy, and who show excessive crying may need counseling (Lund et al., 1985). It is important to keep in mind, however, that grief is an individual experience and that even when these behaviors are present, it may or may not signal a need for professional intervention. Most bereaved individuals do not need professional help and are able to cope quite well with their loss (O'Bryant & Hansson, 1995).

Intervention, professional or not, may, of course, take many forms including support from friends and family, to conventional therapeutic techniques, to drug therapy. Some work, however, suggests that antidepressant medications that reduce the symptoms of depression do not seem to reduce the intensity of grief (Prigerson et al., 1995). In addition to the more conventional techniques, some interventions are thought to be particularly useful for bereaved individuals. They are bibliotherapy, writing, self-help groups, and continued support from family and friends.

Bibliotherapy, which refers to the use of literature in therapy, has frequently been used with children and is beginning to be used with older adults (Brett, 1992; Cook & Olt-jenbruns, 1998). It is thought that reading about others who have had similar experiences may help the bereaved develop insight into their own situation and develop effective coping strategies. For family and friends, reading may help them understand and emphathize with some of the grief being experienced by the bereaved (Klingman, 1985).

For some, **writing** may serve as an effective way to cope with the grief of losing a loved one. The expression of grief by writing about it, even if only for oneself, can help the individual develop insights into their own reactions. By rereading writings done closer to the actual death and comparing them to current writings, one may see the signs of recovery. Writings shared with others may help to open the lines of communication to aid the healing process (Lattanzi & Hale, 1984).

Self-help groups typically are composed of people who share some common experience, such as the loss of a spouse, and generally meet regularly to assist each other in

Bibliotherapy.

coping with that experience (Lieberman, 1993). Many churches and communities offer such groups and the American Association of Retired Persons (AARP) has a program of peer support called the Widowed Persons Service (WPS). This program pairs widows or widowers with another person or persons of the same gender who also lost a spouse but not as recently. The person who has already survived the same loss is usually very empathetic and able to offer helpful tips on coping with the loss. This program grew out of Silverman's (1986) Widow-to-Widow program. Comparisons of survivors who participate in self-help groups with those who do not has shown that the bereaved in a self-help group seem to go through the same process of grieving but in a shorter period of time. Their return to normal functioning is quicker (Vachon et al., 1980). Other work indicates that self-help groups are most helpful for those who have lower self-esteem, poorer mental health, and less life satisfaction. Those with higher self-esteem, better mental health, and more life satisfaction often become more depressed when in a self-help group (Caserta & Lund, 1993). Support groups on the Internet have more recently been used by many bereaved individuals. They are, of course, very convenient and one can use these chat support groups as frequently as one desires.

Finally, the continued **support of family and friends** can be most helpful for grieving survivors. Persons without such support are thought to suffer grief more intensely and for a longer period of time. In interviews conducted with 115 widows, 6 months after the loss of a spouse, the 20 percent who reported a need for help were those who also reported few friends and not being close with their children (Goldberg et al., 1988). When bereaved individuals have been asked about the support of family members, the behaviors that were named as most helpful were others being available when needed; others expressing their concern by asking how the bereaved was doing, staying in touch by visiting, phoning, or writing; offering invitations to social gatherings; providing physical work, transportation, financial, or legal assistance; and giving care packages containing food and other needed items (Rigdon et al., 1987). Unfortunately, for many of the bereaved, these helping behaviors are discontinued soon after the funeral. It is important for families and friends to realize that grieving is not over so soon and social support is most helpful when it continues.

Bereavement, and grief are not often the topics of everyday conversation in spite of the widespread presence of loss. As you know, it is not just older adults who lose close loved ones. For college students, it is estimated that more than 25 percent are in the first year of grief following the loss of a family member and 30 percent following the loss of a friend, no matter when the measure is taken (Balk & Vesta, 1998). If you are among these bereaved or among friends or family of bereaved individuals we hope that the information we have provided in this chapter will be of some help to you in coping with your loss or helping others cope with theirs.

CHAPTER HIGHLIGHTS

■ This chapter examined death and bereavement. Today death is far more likely to occur for older adults whereas in the past children were the more likely to die. This is a result of our extended life expectancy; the major causes of death today are different than they were 100 years ago and different for different aged adults. Younger adults are more likely to die of AIDS, older adults of Alzheimer's disease, and both young and old of heart disease and cancer.

- Advance directives, such as living wills, durable power of attorney, DNR, and DNH orders are legal in all states but are not yet used very frequently. Family members and physicians often resist such orders even when they are aware of them.
- Euthanasia takes several different forms and physician-assisted suicide is the most controversial.
- Hospice and palliative care programs for the terminally ill serve family as well as patient and seem to be beneficial although the research that has been conducted has certain problems. People who choose hospice may be different in important ways (more accepting of death?) from those who they are compared with when hospice programs are evaluated.
- There is much variety and many cultural differences in funeral/mourning rituals. Funeral, burial, and cremation costs are quite high. Federal law and consumer advocates urge caution when purchases are made in such a time of stress.
- The process of grieving is individual but some theorists have proposed stages. The emotions of anxiety and depression are very common and, in many cases, anger and guilt also occur. The effects on grief when the lost person is a spouse have been frequently studied. Such grief can last a very long time and be associated with decreased health and increased mortality for the surviving spouse during the first year. Several hypotheses for this finding have been offered but most were found wanting. Remarriage is one coping mechanism for the widowed. Loss of a child, loss of a grandchild, and loss of a parent are all difficult. The former, however, is often regarded as the worst loss possible in this country but not in other cultures. The influence of an unexpected death on the grief of survivors is far worse and accompanied by more anger and guilt than in cases of expected death. The perceived preventability of the death seems to be a factor in this finding but the anticipatory grief of the expected death is not. Those who have experienced much physical, mental, and emotional strain as caregivers for a now-deceased spouse seem to experience less grief.
- At the end of the chapter we looked at the probability that a bereaved individual might experience PTSD and require professional intervention. Bibliotherapy, writing, and self-help groups have been proposed as special means of dealing with grief. The continued support of family and friends is the most frequent support available for the bereaved.

STUDY QUESTIONS

1. Describe some of the differences in leading causes of death for different aged adults and the changes in leading causes over the last 100 years. What factors are responsible for the differences and changes?

2. Describe the types of advance directives and the difficulties that can occur when life-and-death decisions must be made.

3. Describe the arguments for and against the legalization of physician-assisted suicide. Where do you stand on this issue?

4. What is hospice? What is palliative care? What benefits does one gain and what rights does one lose when enrolling in hospice?

5. Describe the funeral rites practiced in different cultures.

6. What are the stages of grief proposed by Bowlby?

7. Describe the negative and positive emotions that are often a part of grieving.

8. What hypotheses have been proposed to account for the higher mortality rate for widowed men and women? Are any of these hypotheses supported by research findings?

9. What factors influence the likelihood of remarriage after the loss of a spouse?

10. What factors make an unexpected death more difficult for survivors? What factor, expected to play a role, does not and why?

11. Discuss the likelihood of a bereaved individual requiring professional help to cope with their loss and the types of help, professional and otherwise, that might be available.

RECOMMENDED READINGS

Albom, M. (1997). *Tuesdays with Morrie: An Old Man, a Young Man, and Life's Greatest Lesson.* New York: Doubleday. A young man meets on Tuesdays with his old college professor, Morrie, who is dying of amylotrophic lateral sclerosis (Lou Gehrig's disease). Morrie teaches many worthwhile lessons before dying.

Mannino, J. D. (1997). *Grieving Days, Healing Days.* Boston: Allyn & Bacon. This workbook provides an abundance of exercises, activities, and insights for those who have lost or wish to help someone else who has lost a close loved one.

Phillips, K. (1996). *White Rabbit.* Boston: Houghton Mifflin. An amusing last day on earth for Ruth Hubble is described.

INTERNET RESOURCES

www.funerals.org/famsa. Information about consumer's rights and affordable and meaningful funerals, from the Funeral and Memorial Societies Association.

www.ftc.gov. A brochure published by the federal government that is intended to protect consumers who are shopping for funerals. From the homepage, click on Consumer Protection, then on Seniors' Issues, and you will find the brochure under Funerals: A Consumer Guide.

www.nho.org/. The National Hospice Organization.

www.Oregon.gov/DHS/ph/pas/faqs.shtml. For information on physician-assisted suicide in Oregon.

www.startribune.com/a2834. Several websites display the last words spoken by some famous (and also infamous) people.

PART FIVE

Aging and You

CHAPTER
15 Looking to the Future

Light tomorrow with today.

—*Elizabeth Barrett Browning*

As we come to the end of this text, the words of Elizabeth Barrett Browning seem clearer than ever. You now know what aging is like for most people; you know quite a lot about older people; you know how cultural, environmental, and genetic factors influence aging; and you know what choices you can make to improve your own chances of aging successfully.

In this last chapter, we review the principles and issues raised in Chapter 2, examine the well-being of today's older adults, and describe some of the factors that play an important role in their life satisfaction. Living for a long time is not the most important factor. Almost everyone, young and old, responds to the question "do you want to live to be very old?" with the qualifier "yes, if my mind is good" or "yes, if I am in good shape." We will use the four divisions of this book, aging and our bodies, minds, selves, and survival, to foresee how things might be for you when you reach old age. You undoubtedly know by now that we are fairly optimistic about most things having to do with human aging and tend to see the future as being better than the present and we will strive to end on that positive note.

This chapter's Senior View is with a not-yet-older adult—you. Take a moment and think about your answers to the questions and, if you wish, send your self-interview and we'll post it on the website accompanying this text.

Principles and Issues

In Chapter 2, we talked about some of the guiding principles and major issues in gerontology research. Here we would like to refresh your memory and review some of the examples with which you are now familiar.

As a first principle, we said that *development is a lifelong process* and that should now be very clear to you. From birth to death, development is taking place. We take with us all that has occurred before. *Development is multidisciplinary* and that also must be very clear. We have looked at research and theory on adult development and aging from the

Senior View

Because this chapter focuses on future aging, we thought it might be appropriate to have you be the subject of this last senior view. We would like you to sit back and relax and complete the following interview. Thank you, and please feel free to share your answers with us; we would love to hear from you!

Before you read the following questions, think forward about 60 or 70 years into the future. Think about what life will be like, how society will look, where you will be, and finally what aging will be like for you.

Interview About Your Future

How will you look?

How healthy will you and your friends be?

What physical activities will you undertake?

What will be your overall physical condition?

What will be your best and worst aspects of memory?

Will you be wise in old age?

Who will be in your immediate and extended family? How often will you see them?

Who will you live with and where will you live?

How many friends will you have and what will you do together?

How often will you get together with friends?

What will your religious or spiritual life be like?

What roles will you hold?

When will you retire?

What will you do in retirement?

How will you get around?

What will driving be like for you and others?

What recreational activities will you enjoy? How will this change?

What will TV and movies be like?

How, when, and where will you die?

Do you think society will treat older persons differently? If so, how?

Go ask these same questions to a few of your friends and see how their answers may differ from yours; you should see a big difference in your response compared to others who are not "aging smart" as you are now.

---

disciplines of biology, economics, medicine, psychology, and sociology. The findings from these varied disciplines are not isolated from one another but combine and interact to give a more complete view of human aging. Think, for example, of how information from these disciplines guides in our understanding of adjustment to retirement.

Development is composed of gains and losses and you can easily find many examples of both in earlier chapters. As we grow older, we gain perspective, skills, and knowledge, while we may lose quickness, physical ability, and some of those closest to us. *Development shows plasticity.* Factors operating in our environment and the choices we make can alter the gains and losses experienced. Regardless of how old we grow, we are never set in stone. *Development is embedded in history* and you have seen many examples where the influence of cohort is greater than the influence of age. This is particularly true for measures of intelligence and personality traits. *Development occurs within a context* and societal, cultural, and familial, as well as economic contexts exert considerable influence on the choices made in life.

Four major developmental issues guide much of the research in gerontology; the first of these is **nature–nurture**. Determining the relative contributions of genetics and environment to a particular aspect of human aging is a central issue in much research. We have seen that this research generally suggests that genetics plays a bigger role in some physical changes such as balding, in the stability of personality traits, and in some disorders such as Alzheimer's and other dementias. On the other hand, environment seems to play a bigger role in longevity, the development of wisdom, and management of caregiving. All aspects of aging are influenced by both.

A second issue is whether aging is **mechanistic** or **organismic**. Passive mechanistic changes seem to occur in the slowing that occurs with age, and many physical changes such as the accumulation of lipofuscin, the yellowing of the lens of the eyes, and the increased wrinkling with age. Other changes seem more organismic and depend on our own activities. To remain cognitively healthy, we must actively exercise our minds and stay engaged in intellectual pursuits. As with nature–nurture, most of development involves mechanistic and organismic factors but it is almost always the case that our own activities, our own choices, play a bigger role in our own successful aging.

A third issue is **stability–change**. Our personality traits, our sensory and procedural memories, and our social networks remain relatively stable as we grow older while our coping strategies, our working memory, and our immune systems show significant change. By now you know that everything shows some change and this issue is better thought of as being a continuum from very little to quite a lot of change for different aspects of aging.

Finally, when change occurs, we are interested in whether it is relatively **continuous** or **discontinuous**. The changes that occur in most physical components, in our sense organs and perception, and in the progression of dementia are relatively slow and continuous while changes in hormone levels for women, engaging in generative acts, or the environment in which we live are more abrupt. The issue of continuity–discontinuity, like all other issues, is better thought of as a continuum.

You have learned a lot in this course and from this text and should take a moment now to think of other examples that fit these four issues.

Age and Well-Being

We have already discussed a number of factors that influence well-being and life satisfaction. For example, people generally are more satisfied when they can perceive that they have good social support from others; when they have some personality traits but not others (e.g., neuroticism); when they are relatively healthy; when they have sufficient funds; when they can avoid or cope effectively with stress; and when they have a generally positive outlook on life. At the same time, people generally have a lower sense of well-being when they develop a disability, become ill, lose family members and friends, lose their job, and are lonely (Lyubomirsky, 2001). Because many of these negative events are more likely for older than for younger adults, many expect that older adults will have lower levels of well-being and life satisfaction. They will be less happy than younger adults.

In fact, any finding of greater happiness, well-being, or life satisfaction among older adults has been regarded as surprising and has been referred to as the **paradox of**

well-being. A paradox is a statement that seems to contain a contradiction; it runs counter to expectations. To say that older adults are happy seems paradoxical; they are expected to be far less happy because of all those negative events. Investigations of well-being and age often have measured life satisfaction and/or the prevalence of positive and negative emotions. Table 15-1 provides an example of how positive and negative emotions might be measured in such research.

In a major review of the literature and an examination of data collected in a number of different cultures, researchers looked at the relationship between a number of important factors and life satisfaction, pleasant emotions, and unpleasant emotions (Diener & Suh, 1998; Diener et al., 1999). These studies showed that one internal factor, personality, is one of the strongest correlates of well-being. Traits such as extraversion and optimism are related to the presence of pleasant emotions while neuroticism is related to unpleasant emotions. One external factor, income, is not strongly related to any of the measures of

---

TABLE 15-1   **Measuring Positive and Negative Emotions**

Use this scale* to answer the following questions:

    1 = none of the time
    2 = a little of the time
    3 = some of the time
    4 = most of the time
    5 = all of the time

During the past 30 days, how much of the time did you feel

    a. worthless   _____
    b. that everything was an effort   _____
    c. full of life   _____
    d. joyful   _____
    e. hopeless   _____
    f. loved   _____
    g. in good spirits   _____
    h. anxious   _____
    i. commitment to another   _____
    j. guilty   _____
    k. sad   _____
    l. calm and peaceful   _____

Add up your scores for the positive emotion items (c, d, f, g, i, and l) and then for the negative emotion items (a, b, e, h, j, and k). Which score is higher, the positive or negative emotions? A higher score means more of that type of emotion over the last 30 days. Remember that this is not a valid or reliable measure but rather an example of the types of questions used to measure emotions. As with all of our examples, it is designed to give an idea about your emotions, not a true score. Measures similar to this one are the way in which researchers often assess positive and negative emotional aspects of well-being.

---

* Components of this sample scale were adapted from the work of Mroczek & Kolarz (1998).

well-being within a culture. People with low incomes are nearly as happy as those with much higher incomes. People living in wealthy countries, however, are generally happier than those living in poorer countries. Religion and spirituality are positively related to overall well-being. Very religious or spiritual people generally are happier. Men are typically happier than women and show more pleasant emotions. In all these studies, life satisfaction did not decline with age and in many studies was found to increase.

Another cross-sectional study focused on emotions in nearly 3000 men and women between the ages of 25 and 74. Age, gender, and marital status were strongly related to reported emotions. Both older men and women showed higher levels of positive emotions than did younger adults. The lowest level of negative emotions was for older, married men. Unmarried men, and women, married or not, showed very little change in amount of negative emotion as a function of age. It is not that they were negative but that their level of negative emotions did not vary. These researchers tell us that "older people are happier than other adults" (Mroczek & Kolarz, 1998, p. 1346).

Of course, because these are all cross-sectional studies, it may simply be that older cohorts are more positive than younger cohorts. You know that levels of neuroticism are generally higher in younger cohorts (see Chapter 9) and neuroticism is associated with a number of negative emotions and less satisfaction with life. One longitudinal study examined life satisfaction over a 22-year period for nearly 2000 men. The life satisfaction of these men was measured every 3 years beginning in 1978. Results showed that life satisfaction was highest at age 65 and showed some decline thereafter. The decline appears to be due, in part, to lower levels of satisfaction for those who were within a year of their own death and, of course, the probability of death increases with age (Mroczek & Spiro, 2005).

Generally cross-sectional and longitudinal research show that older adults have levels of life satisfaction and positive emotions as high as or higher than younger adults. You are, of course, familiar with the benefits of positive emotions from our earlier discussions of positive psychology. Perhaps older adults are happier because unhappy people are less likely to reach old age. Try Project 15 before reading further.

You might remember in our discussion of Alzheimer's disease that we told you about the nun study being conducted by Snowdon (1997). Remember that he examined autobiographies that nuns wrote when they first joined their convents in their early 20s and 30s and then he related their writing styles to rates of Alzheimer's disease in their 80s and 90s. Along with colleagues (Danner et al., 2001), he used those same autobiographies to look more generally at longevity patterns in late life related to emotional content in early life. They found that women whose autobiographies contained more positive emotions lived significantly longer than women who used few positive emotions in their life stories. By itself, this finding could mean that people with positive experiences while they are young live longer or that people with positive feelings about their experiences live longer. Some closely related work suggests that it is our attitude toward our experiences rather than the experiences themselves that is most important. Researchers looking at another aspect of positive emotions developed an optimism–pessimism scale to be used with the MMPI (Maruta et al., 2000). In a longitudinal examination of survival rates, they found that there was a lower risk of death, over a 30-year period, for those scoring higher in optimism. One reason then for a generally positive outlook on life for older adults is that those with a less-positive view are less likely to live to old age.

PROJECT 15
AUTOBIOGRAPHY PROJECT

For this project, think and write a short sketch of your life. This account should not contain more than 200 to 300 words. You might include:

- Your place of birth
- Information about your parents and grandparents
- Interesting and edifying events of your childhood
- The schools you attended
- Influences that led you to pursue a college degree
- Influences on your choice of major/career field
- Any outstanding events in your life.

Do not read any further until you write your autobiography!

Now analyze the content of your autobiography for the presence of emotions. Carefully go through your autobiography and identify each word that reflects an emotional experience. Underline or highlight these words to make the next step easier to do. Be sure to include only those words that reflect an emotion you experienced, not what elicited the emotion or what you did in response to the emotion. For example, let's say you wrote, "When I was 10 years old, my grandmother passed away. I was so sad that I cried for several hours." The only word that you would underline or highlight here is the word *sad*.

Now classify each underlined word as having a positive, negative, or neutral connotation. For example, happiness, amusement, hope, love, and accomplishment are all positive words. Anger, contempt, fear, sadness, and shame are examples of negative words. Surprise is an example of a neutral emotion word. If you have trouble identifying or classifying words, ask a friend to help. Now add up the number of positive and negative words separately that you have written in your autobiography.

What you have done is very similar to what the nuns were instructed to do in the study discussed in the text. Researchers classified emotional words in essentially the same way you did (Danner et al., 2001). Did your autobiography contain more positive or more negative emotion words? Do you think this reflects your general attitude toward life or were you feeling particularly positive or negative today? Will you live longer or should you consider finding ways to be more positive in your reflections and your interpretations of daily life to increase your chance of living longer? How do you think this relates to the discussion of life stories in Chapter 9?

Good health and longer life are associated with a positive outlook and several studies have been conducted to examine the factors involved in producing these benefits. For example, it's easy to see that people with a more positive outlook are more fun to be around than are those with a more negative view. Those with a positive outlook are, thus, more likely to have larger, more stable, and socially supportive networks. We discussed the benefits of social support earlier (Chapters 10 and 12). You know that social support is most effective when it is perceived as such and a person with a positive outlook may not only have more supporters but also be more likely to say "they're helping me because they love me" rather than "they're helping me because they have to." A positive outlook may be an effective way of handling stress. One may try to see a bright side of bad situations and handle stress with some humor. Stress is damaging to health, in part, because it depletes our resources over time and suppresses the functioning of our immune system (Chapter 5). Some work found a strong association between positive mood and immune system functioning when older adults have been faced with a stressful move to another residence (Lutgendorf et al., 1999). One measure of immune function, the population of natural killer cells (Chapter 3), is higher for those who are more satisfied with their lives (Tsuboi et al., 2005). Although these studies could indicate that higher levels of killer cells produce more satisfaction, many think it's the other way around. Life satisfaction lowers stress and lowered stress does not damage the immune system; those with more negative attitudes experience more stress and, as a result of that, have lower levels of immune functioning.

Other work indicates that the ability to manage one's emotions, particularly anger, results in a higher level of well-being (Carstensen et al., 2003). In one study, several hundred adults between the ages of 18 and 88 were measured for life satisfaction, positive and negative emotions, anger frequency and management, anxiety, and depression. Results showed that older adults did not experience anger as often or as intensely as younger adults and when they did experience anger, they were better able to manage it. They did not lose their temper but instead were able to calm themselves. This ability to manage anger was largely responsible for their lower levels of negative affect and anxiety and their higher levels of life satisfaction. Older adults also had higher levels of positive emotions but this result was not related to anger management (Phillips et al., 2006).

To maintain a positive attitude, particularly in the face of some negative event, one must be able to put that event into a broader context and believe that overall, things are pretty good. Our evaluation of our present satisfaction with life depends, to some extent, upon cognitive processes that we use in comparing our life with the lives of others and of other times (Albert, 1977). Researchers have examined the cognitive processes used by older adults when they evaluate their satisfaction with life and found that many say the best time in life was in their 30s but that present life is very good. Those who report positive periods in their lives tend to base their evaluation on general positive feelings and an overall positive sense while negative evaluations are more frequently based on specific negative events. Satisfaction with old age was most often based on temporal comparisons between the general situations for older adults today with the general situation for older adults in the past. Those with relatively high levels of life satisfaction believe that things are much better today than in the past (Mehlsen et al., 2005). Are they right?

Still other work has found that group activities help to produce and maintain higher levels of well-being. For example, some work has shown that a group exercise program not only increases health and well-being for previously sedentary older adults but also increases their happiness. The social aspect of the program seemed to be the main reason for the obtained increases in happiness (McAuley et al., 2001). Providing support for others and volunteering also seem to have positive effects on well-being. When helping others it is important to not provide more assistance than is actually needed because, as seen, in Chapter 13, that can result in lower well-being and more dependence for the person(s) being helped. One should focus on minimizing any negative interactions and reinforcing the fact that support is always available when and if needed. This benefits both the person helping and the person being helped (Liang et al., 2001).

In short, older adults generally are quite satisfied with their lives and report high levels of well-being; these positive feelings appear to be due to a number of factors. Old age is certainly a time well worth living.

The Future

As you know from Chapters 1 and 5, life expectancy has increased dramatically over the past 100 years. Some gerontologists caution that as people live longer, they may become less happy because they will have seen, heard, and done everything that there is to do. Older adults will be able to say in every situation "been there, done that." They also will be less unhappy because they will have had numerous sad experiences. They will become somewhat bland and may even hope for death when everything around them appears to be

Be happy, live longer.

SOCIAL POLICY APPLICATIONS

Social policies usually are based on the objective needs of the members of the society and/or the desires of those members. Most often the basic needs that policies are meant to ensure are food, shelter, health, safety, and education. Policies frequently are based on increasing income to achieve satisfaction. Perhaps policy makers should consider subjective well-being when considering changes in current or the introduction of new policy. We know that those with higher levels of well-being are less likely to be absent from work, are more productive workers, are more likely to serve as volunteers, are more engaged in healthy behaviors such as exercise, and are more supportive of others who may need assistance. Policy makers interested in promoting prosocial behaviors and executives interested in increasing profits should measure well-being and use it, along with needs and desires, when determining the best social policy (Dolan & White, 2007). Such measures were used to assess different types of compensation for people living near noisy Schiphol airport in Amsterdam and well-being measures showed that the most cost-effective and efficient policy was an expansion of a home insulation program (van Praag & Baarsma, 2005). Planning in this way may be much more beneficial than simply considering capital expansion.

a repeat. We think this is an absurd belief. It could possibly occur if all progress ceased and one could have been everywhere and done everything. We expect that there will be plenty to do for everyone wishing to participate and participants are very unlikely to get bored. In this section, we look at the changes expected for future cohorts of older adults; for you when you grow old. New discoveries, opportunities, and knowledge, however, become available continually.

Our Future Bodies

Many researchers believe that the first person to live to be 150 years old is alive right now. Why do you think they believe this? Our discussion of increases in longevity in Chapter 5 may help answer this question. Perhaps that first person to reach 150 is you. Jean Calment's record of 122 (see Chapter 1) will be broken a number of times over the next few decades, and before the year 2050, someone will live to be 150. Because women, on average, live longer than men, it is most likely to be a woman who first reaches 150. Will 150 be the life span for humans, the maximum number of years that a human can live? A number of gerontologists say there is no reason to assume an upper limit and we will be better off if we plan for the possibility of more people living to very advanced ages.

Life expectancy will certainly continue to increase although there are disagreements about how high it will go and how soon it will get there. The Social Security Administration projects a life expectancy of 77.5 for men and 82.9 for women born in 2050. Other estimates run as high as 81.6 for men and 87 for women (Wilmoth, 1998). Remember that life expectancy is based on an estimate of when half of the birth cohort still is living. These projections are quite impressive when you think about it. A very large proportion of the population will be older adults for the foreseeable future.

Why will life expectancy be longer in the future? A number of factors play a role in this projection. We expect longer lives because people will be in better health. We expect better health for several reasons. First more people are expected to exercise on a regular basis and eat more nutritionally than in the past or present. As you know, the proportion of people engaging in regular aerobic and resistance exercise is woefully small at present. Most people know that exercise is beneficial. The difficult part has been convincing people that they have time for such activities (Leventhal et al., 2001). Not everyone will be exercising by the time you are an older adult, just a higher proportion than today. As you know, there's even a newer computer game that enables players to stand and move as they play. Do you currently exercise?

We also expect more people to eat more nutritional foods. We see more of a demand for organic produce and locally grown food as people learn of more widespread problems with foods that travel great distances. A smaller proportion of people smoke cigarettes now than 10 years ago and we expect that proportion to continue to drop. Of course there will always be people who won't wear seat belts or helmets and who will smoke or who will continue to eat high-calorie fast foods, but most informed people will choose healthy over unhealthy behaviors. The research on health and longevity is progressing rapidly and the Internet has made more of the latest information available to greater numbers of people. It has become easier to be an informed person. Today older adults are being taught to use the Internet to gain access to information about health. Even older adults with no prior experience learn rapidly and find information in which they have interest. Said one participant, "I found that the computer is a powerful tool. . . . Now I can go to the NIH site to learn about any health problem or treatment. You can find anything you need to on the Net" (Bertera et al., 2007, p. 493). Undoubtedly you already use the Internet to obtain information about a number of topics important to you. In fact, the Internet probably will become even easier to access and use and contain even more valid and reliable information.

Life expectancy is expected to be strongly influenced by medical science. There will be more effective diagnostic procedures and treatments for heart disease, cancers, AIDS, and Alzheimer's disease over the next 5 to 10 years. More physicians will be trained to understand older adults and their situation and increases in such training are already beginning (Laditka et al., 2007). Treatments and options will be better tailored to meet the needs of older adults (or is it older cohorts). When you reach age 70, you will have lived through different times than those who are only in their 20s.

With the rapid gains in knowledge of the human genome, researchers may soon be far more successful at replacing vital organs and tissues with body parts grown from our own cells. Some geneticists predict that researchers will use an individual's DNA to grow human organs in animals and harvest them when needed. The supply will be virtually unlimited. Others believe researchers will be able to stimulate regeneration of heart and other tissue within the patient's body and that even fingers (arms, legs, entire bodies) will be regenerated within the next 50 years (Randerson & Sample, 2006). We expect new medicines to increase life expectancy and work now is investigating drugs designed to activate a class of genes called sirtuins. Sirtuins may prevent certain diseases, such as amyotrophic lateral sclerosis (see Chapter 12) from ever developing (Treen, 2006) and, as said earlier, the best treatment for a disease is to not get it in the first place. Of course, we will need to find ways to make these medical advances available to many more people than the wealthiest of the population if they are truly to increase life expectancy.

Of course, having a long life expectancy is nothing to look forward to if you spend your last 20 or more years disabled and sick. The term used to refer to declining health and increasing disability is **morbidity**. Many gerontologists believer that, instead of long life, with long years of morbidity, there will be a compression of morbidity. Figure 15-1 illustrates the current situation for many adults as health declines over time as one grows older and one may still live for many years in very poor health. The figure also illustrates the compression of morbidity hypothesis as a future trajectory where people spend most of their lives in relatively good health and die soon after a late life decline begins. The number of years spent in illness will be far less than they are now (Fries, 1980). This is not an easy hypothesis to test but some work does show that people who exercise and take care of themselves postpone disability for a decade or more compared to those who do not exercise regularly (Fries, 1999). Should we count on an increased aging population that is healthy or one in need of services? Without some compression of morbidity, we may find we do not have sufficient funds to provide care for an ever-increasing and morbid older population. Researchers believe, however, that you will eat right, exercise, and make the right choices to stay healthy well into your own old age.

Our Future Minds

As you know from discussion in Chapters 6, 7, and 8, a number of changes in cognition and thinking occur as we grow older. Some of these changes can be linked to the mental slowing that takes place in older brains that were discussed in Chapter 6. Some of these changes are gains, such as higher levels of knowledge and, in many cases, wisdom (Chapter 8). By 2060, we expect older adults to perform at much higher levels on most measures of cognition than older adults do today. We believe, however, that this difference

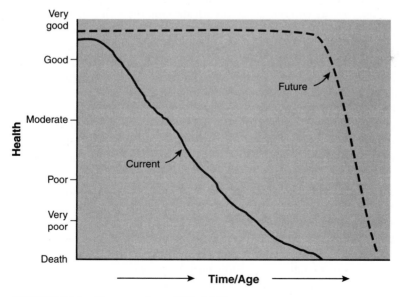

FIGURE 15-1   Compression of Morbidity

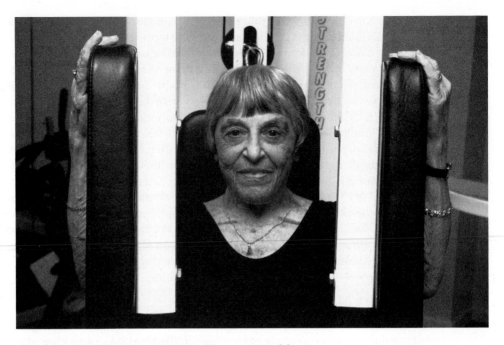

Exercising will always be an important key to successful aging.

will be a result of cohort rather than age. Members of younger cohorts will know much more in their older years than members of older cohorts, today's older adults, ever knew. We are in the Information Age. Television, radio, cell phones, computers, and the Internet have delivered an enormous amount of knowledge that is easy to access. The technology only will improve as will our ability to sift through the *junk* and quickly concentrate on real fact. At the same time, we expect cross-sectional comparisons to continue to find age differences. When you are in the older cohort in 2060, the younger cohort of that time (those born in 2040) will probably perform better than you will on any timed test and on many measures of episodic memory. You, however, will know more and be an expert at some tasks and, perhaps, at life itself. You may be wise.

We believe that more effective measures of adult intelligence than those discussed in Chapter 8 will be created and in use by 2060. Standard IQ tests will probably still be used to measure some aspects of intelligence for young and old but measures of specific adult abilities also will be available. Those abilities include getting along well with diverse groups of people, avoiding conflict, planning real-world activities/events, being able to argue a position effectively, being persuasive, being able to take another's point of view, and having a broad perspective. We are confident that psychologists will create standardized tests to measure many of these adult abilities.

You will benefit from the results of the many studies looking at improving intelligence into old age. New games and other recreation outlets will capitalize on the desire we all have to remain mentally sharp. **Elderhostel**, a very popular program for adults over the age of 60 offers educational classes combined with social opportunities in settings around the world. This and Shepard Centers, discussed in Chapter 11, are two examples of successful programs aimed at enhancing intellectual abilities in older adults. Current work that has examined perceptions of successful aging among older adults found that they regard the opportunity to continue learning as one very important factor (Duay & Bryan, 2006). Learning provides an enjoyable social experience and older students are far more likely than younger students to see that both teacher and student benefit and learn from each other. For those of you in classes that contain both "traditional age" and "nontraditional age" students, do you see any evidence of this mutual learning? Lifelong learning institutes provide much more than intellectual stimulation. Learners experience enhanced self-esteem, a supportive and nurturing community, and a chance to expand social networks (Lamb & Brady, 2005).

Some prognosticators expect that as distance learning becomes more widespread in the twenty-first century, we will see a change in the average age of on-campus students. Younger students who work will take many more classes online while retired older adults will take many more classes on campus and, perhaps, even reside in dorms (Kressley & Huebschmann, 2002). Campuses may become, to some extent, senior centers. How would you prefer to take your classes? Why? It is just as easy to see older adults being online as often as younger adults with very little change in average age of on-campus students. Studies that have compared training of old and young adults to use new technology found that both young and old benefit from the same types of training and learn equally well (see Chapter 11). In a recent comparison of young and old computer users, guided action and guided attention training techniques were directly compared. Guided action training presents very specific steps to be taken to complete a task while guided attention directs the learner to focus attention on certain aspects of the task. Table 15-2 gives an example of each technique as it might be used to teach a novice to change the font when using the Microsoft Word software. Results showed that guided action training was effective for instances where the action guide would always be available but guided attention was far more effective for young and old who could then go on to new tasks in the absence of very specific instructions (Hickman et al., 2007). Such effective use of the computer and the Internet might be of most benefit for older adults who have some difficulty in getting around because of disability or loss of driver's license or living in a rural area. Several studies have

TABLE 15-2   Guided Action and Guided Attention Instructions for Changing Font in MS WORD

Guided Action	Guided Attention
Click on "Format"	Find appropriate pull-down menu
Click on "Font"	Select font menu
Scroll through choices in upper left box	Look at available choices
Click on desired font	Make selection
Click "OK" box at bottom	Approve selection

Source: Based on Hickman et al. (2007).

found that older Internet users experience a number of benefits including higher levels of psychological well-being and lower perceived stress than older nonusers (Chen & Persson, 2002; Wright, 2000). Perhaps such difficulties in getting around will be far-less frequent when you grow older. Either way, we expect continued benefits from all learning environments including Internet use.

Will your memory function well when you are older? Will you be able to solve problems, make decisions, and respond quickly? Will you perform better than those who are older now? Some recent work suggests that the answers to these questions are yes. Recently researchers examined normal cognitive functioning in several hundred older adults. High school IQ, physical and social activities, and education level data were available for these older adults who had graduated from high school 60 or more years earlier. Their current cognitive functioning was measured using the Telephone Interview for Cognitive Status (a measure similar to the MMSE; Welsh et al., 1993), a test of episodic memory (recalling a story), verbal fluency (name as many animals as possible within 1 minute), and central processing speed (say the months of the year backward as quickly as possible). Results showed that current cognitive functioning was strongly predicted by early IQ and education but not by physical and social activities. Those who were smarter in high school and who continued their education had higher levels of cognitive functioning when they were in their 70s (Fritsch et al., 2007). To increase your chances of functioning well in the future, stay in school.

Our minds are expected to function in the future as they do now but we will have access to much more information and far more quickly than today. Medical science will have found many more effective techniques to preserve the functioning of the sense organs and we may all carry computers with us wherever we go. Will all this knowledge be beneficial or will we end up staring at monitors rather than exercising? We must believe that greater knowledge will be beneficial and that we will act on it. We will know the benefits of exercise and do it regularly.

Our Future Selves

With advances in methodology and an understanding of the role of genetics, we expect to have a much firmer grasp on the concept of personality that were discussed in Chapter 9. Furthermore, we will be better able to identify the role of personality in everyday life and behavior. With this understanding, we can better see what is under our control and what we need to learn to live with. For example, if we find that temperament is a lifelong, genetically linked propensity to behave in certain ways *and* we develop definitive ways to measure it, we can make a lot of progress in adjusting to life. We can help children from a young age to understand their propensities and to identify environments that complement these temperaments rather than work against them. Learning how to do this early in life can make doing it in adulthood and old age a habit.

We do not expect any major changes in the quality of social relationships over the next few decades. As noted in Chapter 10, people will still be close to and value their relationships with family members as they have for all of recorded history. People still will make and value friends. We do, however, expect a greater proportion of individuals to participate in Internet communities. You may not lose touch with your college roommates or classmates as so many other cohorts have done in the past. It will be easy to keep up via email. Older and younger adults in 2060 will have friends all over the world connected by the Internet and social networking communities. It will become a small world (after all). Recently, a technology consulting company, Accenture, has begun to develop "the Virtual Family Dinner" so that families separated by great distances can still enjoy each other's company over the dinner table. Microphones and cameras in each home send the information to speakers and monitors in the other home. Grandparents in New York can eat and converse with children and/or grandchildren in several different locations—although it may be a bit early for those kids in California to eat dinner. Such technology may influence older adults to eat better and more than they would without such social contact (Babwin, 2006). By the time you're a grandparent, such virtual visits might be commonplace.

We expect that by 2060, most societies and most individuals will have far greater respect for diversity. Part of this will result from worldwide friendships via the Internet and part of it will result from efforts in this country. This is an important goal to strive for and we believe that your generations may be our best hope in achieving tolerance and peaceful coexistence.

We expect to see great changes in the work world. We saw in Chapter 11 that already the nature of work has changed and it is expected to continue to evolve. Particularly interesting to the study of aging is the move to more individuals working for themselves and out of their own homes. If this trend continues, it will be ideal for older adults because they can work part-time and still travel and enjoy different versions of retirement. We also expect to see much better personal planning for retirement as changes in government and employer provided financial support in old age evolve. Politics will play a strong role here and older voters are a strong voting block. As their numbers increase, their influence on political outcomes probably will increase. There may be some very interesting things happening in legislation benefiting older adults in the next 20 to 40 years. It would be wise to pay attention and continue to vote.

Our Future Survival

We are optimistic that an effective way of halting or even preventing Alzheimer's disease will soon be found. As you know from discussions in Chapter 12, there are many promising leads for a vaccination and for medications that will break down Aß in the brain. Of course, it is possible that the breakdown of or immunization against Aß will not have the desired effect if the tangles resulting from an aberrant form of tau are the real culprit as some research suggests (Roberson et al., 2007). Nevertheless effective treatments may be available soon. Combined with a reliable way of diagnosing the dementia in its early stage, researchers can prevent the deterioration that is so widespread today.

Of course, it is not just Alzheimer's disease that will be more effectively diagnosed and treated over the next several decades. All forms of dementia as well as cardiovascular diseases, cancers, and AIDS will become less of a threat. Already many physicians view heart disease and many cancers as chronic, not terminal, disorders. By 2060, there will be major changes in the top causes of death just as there were major changes between the early years of the twenty and of the twenty-first centuries. In the less-developed nations, deaths from communicable diseases are expected to decline and be more like death rates in the more fully developed countries. In the more developed countries, deaths from communicable diseases may, however, increase for a (hopefully brief) period of time as drug-resistant bacterial infections, such as staph and *E. coli,* infect greater numbers of people and as more people travel worldwide and increase exposure. The overuse of antibiotics and of bacteria-killing soaps, cleaning liquids, hair gels, and even breath mints will result in very strong enemies and science will have to work hard to thwart them.

As noted in earlier chapters, older adults typically take more medications than younger adults and these medications are not metabolized as quickly (see kidney function in Chapter 3). Slower metabolism, especially if combined with dehydration, can result in dangerously high levels of medications in the bloodstream. Some believe that as the understanding of the human genome progresses, this problem will lessen because researchers will discover unexpected links among various disorders and then be able to use only one medication to treat those that are linked. Older adults may still be taking more medications than younger adults but far fewer than they take now (Johnson, 2004).

Death and disease will not, of course, disappear. As life expectancy increases, we will witness new forms of genetic disorders that we have not yet seen (or recognized) and that only appear in very old age. People still will die but life will be longer and healthier than it is today.

We hope to see a better understanding and treatment of death and dying. As stated in Chapter 14, these processes are a part of life and need to be discussed openly. Euthanasia and physician-assisted suicide continue to make news as society struggles with these important ethical decisions. One important step in that direction is the growing knowledge of advanced directives or living wills. As more people understand these documents, life-and-death decisions can be made long before they become too difficult emotionally to make. We expect the percentage of people having advanced directives will rise from 18 percent, currently, to a majority of the population. The lost life of young Terri Schiavo will have a positive influence on the lives of many others as they take steps to prepare their own advanced directives.

We also expect to see some change in funeral and burial customs although changes in such rituals and procedures are bound to occur at a very slow rate and depend heavily on acceptance by many cultures. More people are choosing cremation now than in the past but recent examinations of cremation suggest that it is not the most environmentally friendly procedure. Although ashes may be placed almost anywhere and land saved from cemetery use, the pollutants released and energy used by cremation are most unwelcome consequences. Because of these problems, it is expected that there will be more use of green cemeteries. Green cemeteries place a body, without casket or embalming fluids, in the ground, most often in a wooded location. The body deteriorates naturally. In 2007, there were green cemeteries in California, Florida, New York, South Carolina, Texas, and Washington and they are under consideration in Colorado, Illinois, Iowa, Michigan, Minnesota, New Mexico, Wisconsin, and parts of Canada. Muslim cultures have used green burials for centuries.

Based on the research and progress seen and discussed in Chapter 13, the environment that we build will undergo significant changes and become more ergonomic in our old age. Universal design of buildings and products will provide us with more livable environments at all ages. We suspect that technology will play an important role in the home environments over the next few decades. The **Smarthouse** is already in production. You may have seen prototypes of this house if you have ever gone to Disneyland or Disney World and visited their future exhibits. The Smarthouse is a joint public and private venture that has resulted in a home design that incorporates a central wiring system hooked to an electronic gateway system. All devices that are currently electronic, and many that can be converted to electronic operation are run from the central gateway system. Terminals in every room and remote access will allow you to operate virtually everything in your home from one place. You can use your computer at work or your handheld remote device to lock a door, turn on the oven, or see who is at the door and talk to them via a video cell phone, for example. Even more important for frail elderly is the ability to monitor several aspects of health using the electronic health checker. You and your doctor can be automatically alerted to any potential problems. In Japan, there is now a teapot, referred to as the "i-pot"

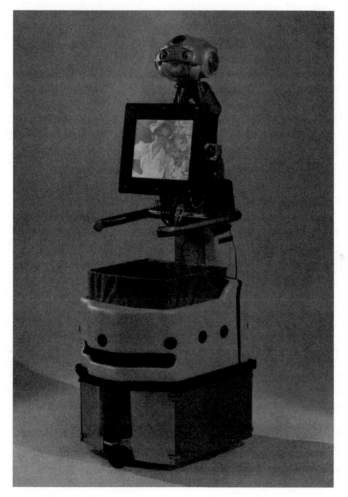

Robot Pearl, one of Carnegie Melon University's Nursebots.

("i" for information), that is used regularly to boil water for tea and sends an email message, to a person of your choice, whenever it is used. Your family can know you're all right because your tea pot has told them that you made tea today; if no such message is received, they can contact you or call for help (Doi, 2005). Green tea is beneficial and now even the pot in which it is made can watch over older adults. What electronic device(s) used daily in the homes of American older adults could be designed to serve this need?

In the future, housing for older adults (e.g., nursing homes) will become homes for older adults. Incorporation of human and environmental supports to enhance independence will be routine. Residents will have the opportunity to take on responsibility for pets and/or plants if they wish. They will be able to make their own choices as to interior design. They will have more freedom to come and go as they please, get up and go to bed as they wish, eat when they're hungry, and have sexual relations in private. As individuals become ill or experience disability, they will not lose these freedoms but instead gain additional support. Technology will play an important role in facilities for frail older adults and in private homes as well. Smarthouse and i-pot–type monitoring can make it possible for older adults to remain in their homes if they choose to do so. In residential facilities, technology will enhance health care delivery and help alleviate an anticipated shortage in nursing and care staff. Nursebot, developed by Carnegie Mellon University, is already being used in the Pittsburgh area to efficiently monitor patients and deliver medications. Older adults will be far more respected than they currently are. We will treat older adults as we would wish to be treated when we are older.

Aging is not something to fear or run away from; it is to be embraced for all its gains and losses. The knowledge you now have will help light your way as you age. You may say with Robert Browning, "grow old along with me, the best is yet to be."

CHAPTER HIGHLIGHTS

- There are many examples in aging of the six developmental principles: development is a lifelong process, is multidisciplinary, is composed of gains and losses, shows plasticity, is embedded in history, and occurs within a context.
- The central issues at the core of developmental research, nature–nurture, mechanistic–organismic, stability–change, and continuous–discontinuous, are clearly in evidence in the aging research discussed.
- The paradox of well-being is a seeming contradiction that well-being or happiness is quite high for older adults when older adults should be experiencing events that would seem likely to lower their well-being.
- Three components of well-being—life satisfaction, positive emotions, and negative emotions—have been examined in their relationship to internal and external factors.
- Both internal and external factors affect well-being at all ages; internal factors related to well-being include religion/spirituality, gender, and most strongly, personality, but not age; external factors related only slightly to well-being include education and marital status but not income.
- Older adults are as satisfied with life or more satisfied than younger adults. A part of this finding appears to be that less-satisfied people do not live as long as those who are optimistic.
- Those with a more positive outlook may live longer because of higher levels of perceived social support, better functioning immune systems, more effective management of negative emotions such as anger, and the cognitive processes involved in making social and temporal comparisons.

- Life-long happiness appears to be good for you. The nun study found that nuns who used more positive emotions in autobiographies written in their younger years lived longer than nuns who used fewer positive emotions.
- Life expectancy will continue to increase in the future.
- There is a great controversy about whether there is an upper limit on lifespan or how long we could possibly live; some believe it has and will continue to hold steady at 120 to 125 years of age while others predict the first person to live to 150 years of age is alive right now and that we may live even beyond that age.
- Another controversy is whether we can continue to live healthier into old age and show compression of morbidity or shorten the length of time we are unhealthy in old age; some believe we can and will live very healthy right until we die in very old age; others believe we will not and that we may just postpone morbidity into very advanced age and still live even longer.
- We expect an increase in knowledge and better understanding and use of memory processes in old age in the future.
- Tomorrow's older adults, like many older adults today, will embrace the Internet and be quite skilled at finding desired information. Information about health will influence the way we choose to live.
- Both your level of education and IQ when you're young predict cognitive functioning when you're old.
- Social relationships may strengthen as access to friends and family improves through the use of the Internet, email, videophones, and other technology.
- The work world will undergo significant changes that bear close watching.
- Advances in science and health care research and treatment will increase our knowledge about, prevention of, and treatment of Alzheimer's disease and other pathologies and psychopathologies that are seen in late life.
- The most frequent causes of death in old age will probably change as once terminal diseases like cancer and heart disease transform into curable or chronic conditions.
- The building environment will undergo changes as designs better suited to our abilities are incorporated in homes and institutions, including the use of advanced technology.

STUDY QUESTIONS

1. Give an example of human aging illustrating each of the six principles of development.
2. For each of the four central developmental issues, provide an example from aging research that was not used in this chapter.
3. What is the paradox of well-being and what does research say about this contradiction?
4. Describe the relationship between well-being and internal and external factors.
5. What are some of the reasons for the general finding of high levels of well-being, life satisfaction, and happiness among older adults?
6. What are some predictions regarding life expectancy, life span, and health in old age in the future?
7. What are some predictions about the future regarding memory and intelligence in old age?
8. What are some predictions regarding personality, social relationships, and the work world for future elderly?
9. What are some predictions regarding psychopathology, death and dying, and the building environment for future older persons?
10. What additional predictions about aging have you thought about?

RECOMMENDED READINGS

Rowe, J. W. & Kahn, R. L. (1998). *Successful Aging.* New York: Pantheon Books. This book presents a very readable, optimistic view of how individuals can control their own health and experience successful aging. There is an emphasis on the lifestyle choices that we all can make right now. The information presented comes from a major study conducted and supported by the MacArthur Foundation.

Qualls, S. H. & Abeles, N. (2000). *Psychology and the Aging Revolution: How We Adapt to Longer Life.* Washington, DC: American Psychological Association. This is an edited book with a number of different authors who write about the expanding number of years spent in retirement, changes in needs and abilities with advanced age, and the likelihood of successful aging in U.S. changing culture.

Vaillant, G. E. (2002). *Aging Well: Surprising Guideposts to a Happier Life from the Landmark Harvard Study of Adult Development.* New York: Little, Brown. This book presents information about aging well and some surprising suggestions for remaining happy.

INTERNET RESOURCES

www.aoa.gov. For information on aging in the twenty-first century.

www-2.cs.cmu.edu/~nursebot. The Nursebot Project site at Carnegie Mellon University.

www.smarthouse.com. For the latest on the smart house.

www.allwellbeing.com/ag/aging or *www.healthinaging.org.* For information about well-being, aging, and longevity.

www.NIHseniorhealth.gov. A good source for very specific information on caring for an older adult with Alzheimer's, good exercises for older adults, and many more of the topics discussed in this book.

www.forestofmemories.com. For information about green cemeteries.

REFERENCES

AARP (1999). The AARP grandparenting survey. Washington, DC: Author.

Abbott, R. D., White, L. R., Russ, W., Masuki, K. H., Crub, J. D., and Petrovich, J. (2004). Walking and dementia in physically capable elderly men. *Journal of the American Medical Association, 292,* 1447–1453.

Abraham, J. D. & Hansson, R. O. (1995). Successful aging at work: An applied study of selection, organization, optimization, and compensation through impression management. *Journals of Gerontology: Psychological Sciences, 50B,* P94–P103.

Ackerman, P. L. & Rolfhus, E. L. (1999). The locus of adult intelligence: Knowledge, abilities, and nonability traits. *Psychology & Aging, 14,* 314–330.

Adams, A. J., Wang, L. S., Wong, L. & Gould, B. (1988). Visual acuity changes with age: Some new perspectives. *American Journal of Optometry & Physiological Optics, 65,* 403–406.

Adams, G. A. (1999). Career-related variables and planned retirement age: An extension of Beehr's model. *Journal of Vocational Behavior, 55,* 221–235.

Adams, K. B., Smyth, K. A., & McClendon, M. J. (2005). Psychosocial resources as moderators of the impact of spousal dementia caregiving on depression. *Journal of Applied Gerontology, 24,* 475–489.

Adams, K. F., Schatzkin, A., Harris, T. B., Kipnis, V., Mouw, T., Ballard-Barbash, R., Hollenbeck, A., & Leitzmann, M. F. (2006). Overweight, obesity, and mortality in a large prospective cohort of persons 50 to 71 years old. *The New England Journal of Medicine, 355,* 763–778.

Adams, S. L. & Waskel, S. A. (1993). Late onset alcoholism: Stress or structure. *Journal of Psychology, 127,* 329–334.

Aday, R. H., Evans, E. & Sims, C. R. (1991). Youth's attitudes toward the elderly: The impact of intergenerational partners. *Journal of Applied Gerontology, 10,* 372–384.

Adelman, M. (1990). Stigma, gay lifestyles, and adjustment to aging: A study of later-life gay men and lesbians. *Journal of Homosexuality, 20,* 1–7.

Ade-Ridder, L. (1990). Sexuality and marital quality among older married couples. In T. H. Brubaker (Ed.), *Family relationships in later life* (2nd ed., pp. 48–67). Newbury Park, CA: Sage.

Aging with Dignity (2007). Five wishes. www.agingwithdignity.org/5wishes.html. Accessed May 21, 2007.

Aiken, L. (1991). *Dying, death, and bereavement.* Boston: Allyn & Bacon.

Aiken, L. R. (1995). *Aging: An introduction to gerontology.* London: Sage.

Ajrouch, K. J., Blandon, A. Y., & Antonucci, T. C. (2005). Social networks among men and women: The effects of age and socioeconomic status. *Journal of Gerontology: Social Sciences, 60B,* S311–S317.

Albert, S. (1977). Temporal comparison theory. *Psychological Review, 84,* 485–503.

Albom, M. (1997). *Tuesdays with Morrie.* New York: Doubleday.

Aldwin, C. M. & Revenson, T. A. (1987). Does coping help? A reexamination of the relationship between coping and mental health. *Journal of Personality & Social Psychology, 53,* 337–348.

Aldwin, C. M., Sutton, K. J., Chiara, G., & Spiro, A. (1996). Age differences in stress, coping, and appraisal: Findings from the Normative Aging Study. *Journal of Gerontology: Psychological Science, 51B,* P179–P188.

Alfaro-Acho, A., Snih, S. A., Raji, M. A., Kuo, Y-F., Markides, K. S., & Ottenbacher, K. J. (2006). Handgrip strength and cognitive decline in older Mexican Americans. *Journal of Gerontology: Medical Sciences, 61A,* 859–865.

Allaire, J. C., & Marsiske, M. (1999). Everyday cognition: Age and intellectual ability correlates. *Psychology & Aging, 14*, 627–644.

Allen, S., Resnik, L., & Roy, J. (2006). Promoting independence for wheelchair users: The role of home accommodations. *The Gerontologist, 46*, 115–123.

Alley, D., Suthers, K., & Crimmins, E. (2007). Education and cognitive decline in older Americans. *Research on Aging, 29*, 73–94.

Allport, G. W. (1937). *Personality: A psychological interpretation*. New York: Holt, Rinehart, & Winston.

Alspaugh, M. E. L., Zarit, S. H., & Greene, R. (1999). Longitudinal patterns of risk for depression in dementia caregivers: Objective and subjective primary stress as predictors. *Psychology & Aging, 14*, 34–43.

Amato, P. R. & Rogers, S. J. (1997). A longitudinal study of marital problems and subsequent divorce. *Journal of Marriage & the Family, 59*, 612–624.

American Association of Retired Person Bulletin. (September, 2003), 10–11.

American Association of Retired Person Magazine. (November/December, 2003), 45–51.

American Association of Retired Person Magazine. (September/October, 2006). 30.

American Association of Retired Persons (2004a). *Baby boomers envision retirement II: A survey of baby boomers expectations for retirement*. Washington, DC: Author.

American Association of Retired Persons. (1986). *Work and retirement: Employees over 40 and their views*. Washington, DC: Author.

American Association of Retired Persons. (1993). *A portrait of older minorities*. Washington, DC: Author.

American Association of Retired Persons. (1994). *A profile of older Americans*. Washington, DC: Author.

American Association of Retired Persons. (1995). *Images of aging in America*. Washington, DC: AARP.

American Association of Retired Persons. (2000). *Fixing to stay: A national survey on housing and home modification issues*. Washington, DC: Author.

American Association of Retired Persons. (2001). *The costs of long-term care: Public perceptions versus reality*. Washington, DC: Author.

American Cancer Society. (1991). *Cancer facts and figures for minority Americans–1991*. Atlanta, GA: Author.

American Cancer Society. (1994). *Cancer facts and figures–1994*. Atlanta, GA: Author.

American Geriatrics Society, British Geriatrics Society, & American Academy of Orthopaedic Surgeons Panel on Falls Prevention. (2001). Guidelines for the prevention of falls in older persons. *Journal of the American Geriatric Society, 49*, 664–672.

American Psychiatric Association. (1994). *Diagnostic and statistical manual of mental disorders* (4th ed.). Washington, DC: Author.

American Psychological Association. (2003). *Ethical principles of psychologists and code of conduct*. Washington, DC: Author.

Andel, R., Crowe, M., Pedersen, N. L., Mortimer, J., Crimmins, E., Johansson, B., & Gatz, M. (2005). Complexity of work and risk of Alzheimer's disease: A population-based study of Swedish twins. *Journal of Gerontology: Psychological Sciences, 60B*, P251–P258.

Andel, R., Kåreholt, I., Parker, M. G., Thorslund, M., & Gatz, M. (2007). Complexity of lifetime occupation and cognition in advanced old age. *Journal of Aging and Health, 19*, 397–415.

Andersen-Ranberg, K., Vasegaard, L., & Jeune, B. (2001). Dementia is not inevitable: A population-based study of Danish centenarians. *Journal of Gerontology: Psychological Sciences, 56B*, P152–P159.

Andershed, B. & Ternestedt, B-M. (1998). Involvement of relatives in the care of the dying in different care cultures: Involvement in the dark or in the light. *Cancer Nursing, 21*, 106–116.

Anderson, S. A., Russell, C. S., & Schumm, W. R. (1983). Perceived marital quality and family life-cycle categories. *Journal of Marriage & the Family, 45,* 127–139.

Aneshensal, C. S., Wight, R. G., Miller-Martinez, D., Botticello, A. L., Karlamangla, A. S., & Seeman, T. (2007). Urban neighborhoods and depressive symptoms in older adults. *Journal of Gerontology: Social Sciences, 62B,* S52–S59.

Angel, J. L., Jiménez, M. A., & Angel, R. J. (2007). The economic consequences of widowhood for older minority women. *The Gerontologist, 47,* 224–234.

Ankrom, M., Thompson, J., Finucane, T., & Fingerhood, M. (1997). *Gender differences in alcohol use and abuse in the homebound elderly and their caregivers.* Paper presented at the 50th annual meeting of the Gerontological Society of America.

Anstey, K. J., Luszcz, M. A., Giles, L. C., & Andrews, G. R. (2001). Demographic, health, cognitive, and sensory variables as predictors of mortality in very old adults. *Psychology & Aging, 16,* 3–11.

Antonucci, T. C. & Akiyama, H. (1991). Social relationships and aging well. *Generations, 15* (1), 39–44.

Antonucci, T. C. & Akiyama, H. (1997). Concerns with others at midlife: Care, comfort, or compromise? In M. E. Lachman & J. B. James (Eds.), *Multiple paths of midlife development* (pp. 147–169). Chicago: University of Chicago Press.

Antonucci, T. C. (1990). Social supports and social relationships. In R. H. Binstock & L. K. George (Eds.), *The handbook of aging and the social sciences* (3rd ed., pp. 205–227). New York: Academic Press.

Antonucci, T. C. (2001). In J. E. Birren & K. W. Schaie (Eds.). *The handbook of the psychology of aging.* (5th ed., pp. 427–453). New York: Academic Press.

Antonucci, T. C., Fuhrer, R., & Dartigues, J. F. (1997). Social relations and depressive symptomatology in a sample of community-dwelling French older adults. *Psychology & Aging, 12,* 189–195.

Aponte, J. F., Rivers, R. Y., & Wohl, J. (1995). *Psychological interventions and cultural diversity.* Boston: Allyn & Bacon.

Aquilino, W. S. (1997). From adolescent to young adulthood: A prospective study of parent-child relations during the transition to adulthood. *Journal of Marriage & the Family, 59,* 670–686.

Arai, S. (1998). Housing facilities for the elderly in India. In S. Brink (Ed.). *Housing older people: An international perspective* (pp. 87–94). New Brunswick, NJ: Transaction Publishers.

Araujo, A. B., Mohr, B. A., & McKinlay, J. B. (2004). Changes in sexual function in middle-aged and older men: Longitudinal data form the Massachusetts Male Aging Study. *Journal of the American Geriatrics Society, 52,* 1502–1509.

Arber, S., & Ginn, J. (1991). *Gender and later life: A sociological analysis of resources and constraints.* London: Sage.

Ardelt, M. (1997). Wisdom and life satisfaction in old age. *Journal of Gerontology: Psychological Sciences, 52B,* P15–P27.

Aria, M. (2006). Elder abuse in Japan. *Educational Gerontology, 32,* 13–23.

Arndt, V., Brenner, H., Rothenbacher, D., Zschenderlein, B., Fraisse, E., & Fliedner, T. M. (1998). Elevated liver enzyme activity in construction workers: Prevalence and impact on early retirement and all-cause mortality. *International Archives of Occupational & Environmental Health, 71,* 405–412.

Associated Press. (April 3, 2007). Agency finds 32,000 unclaimed benefits. Available from www.msnbc.com/id/17929857/. Accessed April 3, 2007.

Atchley, P. & Andersen, G. J. (1998). The effect of age, retinal eccentricity, and speed on the detection of optic flow components. *Psychology & Aging, 13,* 297–308.

Atchley, R. C. (1982). The process of retirement: Comparing women and men. In M. Szinovacz (Ed.), *Women's retirement* (pp. 153–168). Beverly Hills, CA: Sage.

Atchley, R. C. (1996). Retirement. In J. E. Birren (Ed.), *Encyclopedia of gerontology*, Vol. 2 (pp. 437–449). New York: Academic Press.

Atchley, R. C. (1997). Retirement income security: Past, present, and future. *Generations*, 9–12.

Atchley, R. C. (1999). *Continuity and adaptation in aging: Creating positive experiences*. Baltimore, MD: Johns Hopkins University Press.

Atchley, R. C. (2000). *Social forces and aging: An introduction to social gerontology*. Stamford, CT: Wadsworth.

Atchley, R. C., & Barusch, A. S. (2004). *Social forces and aging* (10th ed.). Belmont, CA: Wadsworth/Thompson.

Austad, S. N. (1997). *Why we age*. Nye York: John Wiley & Sons.

Aviv, A. (2006). Telomeres and human somatic fitness. *Journal of Gerontology: Medical Sciences, 61A*, 871–873.

Aykan, H. & Wolf, D. A. (2000). Traditionality, modernity, and household composition: Parental-child coresidence in contemporary Turkey. *Research on Aging, 22*, 395–421.

Babwin, D. (Dec. 24, 2006). Dine together virtually. *The Charlotte Observer*, 7A.

Baddeley, A.D., & Logie, R.H. (1999). Working memory: The multiple-component model. In A. Miyake & P. Shah (Eds.). *Models of working memory* (pp. 28–61). Cambridge: Cambridge University Press.

Bafefoot, J. C., Mortensen, E. L., Helms, M. J., Avlund, K., & Schroll, M. (2001). A longitudinal study of gender differenes in depressive symptoms from age 50 to 80. *Psychology & Aging, 16*, 342–345.

Bagby, R. M., Joffe, R. T., Parker, J. D. A., Kalemba, V., & Harkness, K. L. (1995). Major depression and the five-factor model of personality. *Journal of Personality Disorders, 9*, 224–234.

Bainbridge, H. T. J., Cregan, C., Kulik, C. T. (2006). The effect of multiple roles on caregiver stress outcomes. *Journal of Applied Psychology, 91*, 490–497.

Baker, B. & Reyes, K. (2000, March-April). Now that death has become big business, who can you trust? *Modern Maturity*, 60–67, 73.

Baker, B. (1999, November). *AARP Bulletin, 40*, 18–20.

Baldwin, R. C. (1994). Is there a distinct type of major depression in the elderly? *Journal of Psychopharmocology, 8*, 177–184.

Balin, A. K. (1982). Testing the free radical theory of aging. In Adelman & Roth (Eds.), *Testing the theories of aging*. Boca Raton, FL: CRC Press.

Balk, D. E. & Vesta, L. C. (1998). Psychological development during four years of bereavement: A longitudinal case study. *Death Studies, 22*, 23–41.

Balk, D. E. (1999). Bereavement and spiritual change. *Death Studies, 23*, 485–493.

Ball, K. Berch, D. B., Helmers, K. F., Jobe, J. B., Leveck, M. D., Marsiske, M., et al. (2002). Effects of cognitive training interventions with older adults: A randomized controlled trial. *JAMA, 288*, 2271–2281.

Ball, M. J. & Murdoch, G. H. (1997). Consensus recommendations for the postmortem diagnosis of Alzheimer's disease. *Neurobiology of Aging, 18*, S1.

Ball, M. M., Whittington, F. J., Perkins, M. M., Patterson, V. L., Hollingsworth, C., King, S., & Combs, B. (2000). Quality of life in assisted living: Viewpoints of residents. *Journal of Applied Gerontology, 19*, 304–325.

Ball. K., Berch, D. B., Helmers, K. F., Jobe, J. B., Leveck, M. D., Marsiske, M., Morris, J. N., Rebok, G. W., Smith, D. M., Tennstedt, S. L., Unverzagt, F. W., & Willis, S. L.; for the ACTIVE Study Group. Effects of cognitive training interventions with older adults. *Journal of the American Medical Association, 288*, 2271–2281.

Baltes, M. M., & Wahl, H. W. (1992). The dependency support script in institutions: Generalization to community settings. *Psychology & Aging, 7*, 409–418.

Baltes, P. B. (1987). Theoretical propositions of life-span developmental psychology: On the dynamics between growth and decline. *Developmental Psychology, 23*, 611–626.

Baltes, P. B. (1993). The aging mind: Potential and limits. *The Gerontologist, 33*, 580–594.

Baltes, P. B. & Graf, P. (1996). Psychological aspects of aging: Facts and frontiers. In D. Magnussen (Ed.), *The life span development of individuals: Behavioral, neurobiological, and psychosocial perspectives*. (pp. 427–459). Cambridge, England: Cambridge University Press.

Baltes, P. B. & Labouvie, G. V. (1973). Adult development of intellectual performance: Description, explanation, and modification. In C. Eisdorfer & M. P. Lawton (Eds.), *The psychology of adult development and aging*. Washington, DC: American Psychological Association.

Baltes, P. B. & Smith, J. (1990). Toward a psychology of wisdom and its ontogenesis. In R. J. Sternberg (Ed.), *Wisdom: Its nature, origins, and development*. (pp. 87–120). Cambridge, England: Cambridge University Press.

Baltes, P. B. & Staudinger, U. M. (1993). The search for a psychology of wisdom. *Current Directions, 2*, 75–80.

Baltes, P. B. & Staudinger, U. M. (2000). Wisdom: A metaheuristic (pragmatic) to orchestrate mind and virtue toward excellence. *American Psychologist, 55*, 122–136.

Baltes, P. B., & Graf, P. (1996). Psychological aspects of aging: Facts and frontiers. In D. Magnussen (Ed.) *The life span development of individuals: Behavioral, neurobiological, and psychosocial perspectives* (pp. 427–459). Cambridge, England: Cambridge University Press.

Baltes, P. B., & Labouvie, G. V. (1973). Adult development of intellectual performance: Description, explanation, and modification. In C. Eisdorfer & M. P. Lawton (Eds.), *The psychology of adult development and aging*. Washington, DC: American Psychological Association.

Baltes, P. B., & Smith, J., (1990). Toward a psychology of wisdom and its ontogenesis. In R. J. Sternberg (Ed.), *Wisdom: Its nature, origins, and development* (pp. 87–120). Cambridge, England: Cambridge University Press.

Baltes, P. B., & Staudinger, U. M. (1993). The search for a psychology of wisdom. *Current Directions, 2*, 75–80.

Baltes, P. B., & Staudinger, U. M. (2000). Wisdom: A metaheuristic (pragmatic) to orchestrate mind and virtue toward excellence. *American Psychologist, 55*, 122–136.

Baltes, P. B., Staudinger, U. M., Maercker, A., & Smith, J. (1995). People nominated as wise: A comparative study of wisdom-related knowledge. *Psychology & Aging, 10*, 155–166.

Barbeau, A., Roy, M., Cloutier, T., Plasse, L., & Paris, S. (1986). Environmental and genetic factors in the etiology of Parkinson's disease. In M. D. Yar & K. J. Bergman (Eds.), *Advances in neurology* (pp. 299–306). New York: Raven Press.

Barbee, E. L. (1989). Worries, aging, and desires to be younger in a sample of American middle-aged women. *Medical Anthropology, 12*, 117–129.

Barclay, L. L., Zemcov, A., Blass, J. P., & Sansone, J. (1985). Survival in Alzheimer's disease and vascular dementia. *Neurology, 35*, 834–840.

Barefoot, J. C., Maynard, K. E., Beckham, J. C., Brummett, B. H., Hooker, K., & Siegler, I. C. (1998). Trust, health, and longevity. *Journal of Behavioral Medicine, 21*, 517–526.

Barefoot, J. C., Mortensen, E. L., Helms, M. J., Avlund, K., & Schroll, M. (2001). A longitudinal study of gender differences in depressive symptoms from age 50 to 80. *Psychology & Aging, 16*, 342–345.

Barer, B. M. (2001). The "grands and greats" of very old black grandmothers. *Journal of Aging Studies, 15*, 1–11.

Barker, J. C. (1997). Between humans and ghosts: The decrepit elderly in a Polynesian society. In J. Sokolovsky (Ed.). *The cultural context of aging*, (pp. 295–314). New York: Bergin & Garvey Publishers.

Barlett, D. L., & Steele, J. B. (1992). *America: What went wrong?* Kansas City: Andrews & McMeel.

Barlow, J. H., Cullen, L. A., Foster, N. E., Harrison, K., & Wade, M. (1999). Does arthritis influence perceived ability to fulfill a parenting role? Perceptions of mothers, fathers, and grandparents. *Patient Education & Counseling, 37*, 141–151.

Barnhill, W. (1998). On the road: Older drivers under closer scrutiny. *AARP Bulletin, 39*, 1, 14, 18.

Barr, R. A. (1994). Human factors and aging: The operator-task dynamic. In R. P. Abeles, H. C. Gift, & M. G. Ory (Eds.), *Aging and quality of life* (pp. 202–215). New York: Springer.

Barrouillet, P., Bernardin, S., & Camos, V. (2004). Time constraints and resource sharing in adults' working memory spans. *Journal of Experimental Psychology: General, 133*, 83–100.

Barrouillet, P., Bernardin, S., & Camos, V. (2004). Time constraints and resource sharing in adults' working memory spans. *Journal of Experimental Psychology General, 133*, 83–100.

Bartali, B., Frongillo, E. A., Bandinelli, S., Lauretani, F., Semba, R. D., Fried, L. P., & Ferrucci, L. (2006). Low nutrient intake is an essential component of frailty in older persons. *Journal of Gerontology: Medical Sciences, 61A*, 589–593.

Bartoshuk, L. M., Rifkin, B., Marks, L. E., & Bars, P. (1986). Taste and aging. *Journal of Gerontology, 41*, 51–57.

Bass, D. M., Garland, T. N., & Otto, M. E. (1985-1986). Characteristics of hospice patients and their caregivers. *Omega, 16*, 51-68.

Bauer-Maglin, N., & Radosh, A. (Eds.). (2003). *Women confronting retirement: A nontraditional guide*. New Brunswick, NJ: Rutgers U. Press.

Baur, J. A., Pearson, K. J., Price, N. L., Jaimeson, H. A., Lerin, C., Kalra, A., et al. (2006). Resveratrol improves health and survival of mice on a high–calorie diet. *Nature, 1–6*.

Bayley, N. & Oden, M. (1955). The maintenence of intellectual ability in gifted adults. *Journal of Gerontology, 10*, 91–107.

Beatty, W. W., Brumback, R. A., & Vonsattel, J-P. G. (1997). Autopsy-proven Alzheimer diseases in a patient with dementia who retained music skill in life. *Archives of Neurology, 54*, 1448.

Becker, D., Faraday, N., Yanek, L., Moy, T., & Becker, L. (November, 2006). *Casual chocolate consumption and platelet activity*. Paper presented at the meetings of the American Heart Association, Chicago, Illinois.

Becker, J. T. & Milke, R. M. (1998). Cognition and aging in a complex work environment: Relationships with performance among air traffic control specialists. *Aviation, Space, & Environmental Medicine, 69*, 944–951.

Bedford, V. H. (1996). Sibling relationships in middle and old age. In R. Blieszner & V. H. Bedford (Eds.), *Aging and the family: Theory and research* (pp. 201–222). Westport, CT: Praeger.

Beekman, A. T. F., Deeg, D. J. H., van Tillburg, T., & Smit, J. H. (1995). Major and minor depression in later life: A study of the prevalence and risk factors. *Journal of Affective Disorders, 36*, 65–75.

Béland, F., Zunzunegui, M-V., Alvarado, B., Otero, A., & del Ser, T. (2005). Trajectories of cognitive decline and social relations. *Journal of Gerontology: Psychological Sciences, 60B*, P320–P330.

Belgrave, L. L. (1988). The effects of race differences in work history, work attitudes, economic resources, and health in women's retirement. *Research on Aging, 10*, 383–398.

Belle, D. (1987). Gender differences in the social moderators of stress. In R. Barrett, L. Biener, & G. Baruch (Eds.), *Gender and stress*, New York: Free Press.

Belsky, J. (1999). *The psychology of aging*. Pacific Grove, CA: Brooks/Cole.

Bem, S. L. (1974). The measurement of psychological androgyny. *Journal of Consulting & Clinical Psychology, 42*, 155–162.

Benson, H., Dusek, J. A., Sherwood, J. B., Lam. P., Bethea, C. F., Carpenter, W., et al. (2006). Study of the therapeutic effects of intercessory prayer (STEP) in cardiac bypass patients: A multicenter randomized trial of uncertainty and certainty of receiving intercessory prayer. *American Heart Journal, 151*, 934–942.

Berger, R. M. (1990). Men together: Understanding the gay couple. *Journal of Homosexuality, 19*, 31–49.

Berger, R., Rothman, I., & Rigaud, G. (1994). Nonvascular causes of impotence. In A. H. Bennett (Ed.), *Impotence: Diagnosis and management of erectile dysfunction* (pp. 106–123). Philadelphia: W. B. Saunders.

Bergman, M., Blumenfeld, V. G., Casardo, D., Dash, B., Levitt, H., & Margulios, M. K. (1976). Age-related decrement in hearing for speech: Sampling and longitudinal studies. *Journal of Gerontology, 31*, 533–538.

Berkman, L. (1986). Social networks, support, and health: Taking the next step forward. *American Journal of Epidemiology, 123*, 559–562.

Berkman, L. F. (1995). The role of social relations in health promotion. *Psychosomatic Medicine, 57*, 245–254.

Berkman, L. & Breslow, L. (1983). *Health and ways of living: The Alameda County study*. New York: Oxford University Press.

Bernal, D., Snyder, D., & McDaniel, M. (1998). The age and job satisfaction relationship: Do its shape and strength still evade us? *Journal of Gerontology: Psychological Sciences, 53B*, P287–P293.

Berry, J. M., West, R. L., & Dennehey, D. M. (1989). Reliability and validity of the Memory Self-Efficacy Questionnaire (MSEQ). *Development Psychology, 25*, 701–713.

Bertera, E. M., Bertera, R. L., Morgan, R., Wuertz, E., & Attey, A. M. O. (2007). Training older adults to access health information. *Educational Gerontology, 33*, 483–500.

Bertram, L., McQueen, M. B., Mullin, K., Blacker, D., & Tanzi, R. E. (2007). Systematic meta-analyses of Alzheimer disease genetic association studies: The AlsGene database. *Nature Genetics, 39*, 17–23.

Best, B. (2007). Causes of death. Available from www.benbest.com/lifeext/causes.html. Accessed May 16, 2007.

Best, D. L., Hamlett, K. W., & Davis, S. W. (1992). Memory complaint and memory performance in the elderly: The effects of memory skill training and expectancy change. *Applied Cognitive Psychology, 6*, 405–416.

Bezerra-Flanders, W., & Clark, J. C. (2006). Perspectives of elder abuse and neglect in Brazil. *Educational Gerontology, 32*, 63–72.

Bieman-Copland, S., & Ryan, E. B. (1998). Age-biased interpretation of memory successes and failures in adulthood. *Journal of Gerontology: Psychological Sciences, 53B*, P105–P111.

Binet, H. (1903). The experimental study of intelligence. Paris, France: Schleicher.

Binstock, R. H. & George, L. K. (Eds.) (1996). *Handbook of aging and the social sciences* (4th ed.) New York: Academic Press.

Birren, J. E. (1985). Age, competence, creativity, and wisdom. In R. N. Butler & H. P. Gleason (Eds.), *Productive aging: Enhancing vitality in later life.* (pp. 25–41). New York: Springer.

Bishop, J. M. & Krause, D. R. (1984). Depictions of aging and old age on Saturday morning television. *The Gerontologist, 24*, 91–94.

Black, S. A., & Markides, K. (1994). Americans, Cuban Americans, and Mainland Puerto Ricans. *International Journal of Aging & Human Development, 39*, 97–103.

Blacker, D., Haines, J. L., Rodes, L., Terwedow, H., Harrell, L. E., Perry, R. T., Bassett, S. S., Chase, G., Meyers, D., Albert, M. S., & Tanzi, R. (1997). ApoE-4 and age of onset of Alzheimer's disease. *Neurology, 48*, 139–147.

Blackwell, T., Yaffe, K., Ancoli-Israel, S., Schneider, J. L., Cauley, J. A., Hillier, T. A., Fink, H. A., & Stone, K. L. (2006). Poor sleep is associated with impaired cognitive function in older women: The study of osteoporotic fractures. *Journal of Gerontology: Medical Sciences, 61A*, 405–410.

Bladbjerg, E. M., Andersen-Ranberg, K., de Maat, M. P. M., Kristensen, S. R., Jeune, B., Gram, J., & Jespersen, J. (1999). Longevity is independent of common variations in genes associated with cardiovascular risk. *Thrombosis & Haemostasis, 82*, 1100–1105.

Blanchard-Fields, F. (1986). Reasoning on social dilemmas varying in emotional saliency: An adult developmental perspective. *Psychology & Aging, 1*, 325–333.

Blanchard-Fields, F. & Camp, C. (1990). Affect, individual differences, and real world problem solving across the adult life span. In T. Hess (Ed.), *Aging and cognition: Knowledge organization and utilization* (pp. 461–497). Amsterdam: North Holland.

Blanchard-Fields, F., Jahnke, H. C., & Camp, C. (1995). Age differences in problem-solving style: The role of emotional saliency. *Psychology & Aging, 10*, 173–180.

Blanchard-Fields, F., Stein, R., & Watson, T. L. (2004). Age differences in emotion-regulation strategies in handling everyday problems. *Journal of Gerontology: Psychological Sciences, 59B*, P261–P269.

Blatt-Eisengart, I., & Lachman, M. E. (2004). Attributions for memory performance in adulthood: Age differences and mediation effects. *Aging, Neuropsychology, & Cognition, 11*, 68–79.

Blaum, C. S., Ofstedal, M. B., Langa, K. M., & Wray, L. A. (2003). Functional status and health outcomes in older Americans with diabetes mellitus. *Journal of the American Geriatric Society, 51*, 745–753.

Blazer, D. G., Sachs-Ericsson, N., & Hybels, C. (2007). Perception of unmet basic needs as a predictor of depressive symptoms among community-dwelling older adults. *Journal of Gerontology: Medical Sciences, 62A*, 191–195.

Bliatout, B. T. (1993). Hmong death customs: Traditional and acculturated. In D. P. Irish, K. F. Lundquist, & V. J. Nelsen (Eds.), *Ethnic variations in dying, death, and grief: Diversity in universality* (pp. 79–100). Washington, DC: Taylor & Francis.

Blick, K. A. & Howe, J. B. (1984). A comparison of the emotional content of dreams recalled by young and elderly women. *Journal of Psychology, 116*, 143–146.

Bogorad, L. (1987). Emerging trends in rental retirement housing. *Journal of Real Estate Development* (Winter), 7–17.

Bolton, I. (1986). Death of a child by suicide. In T. Rando (Ed.), *Parental loss of a child* (pp. 201–212). Champaign, IL: Research Press.

Bonanno, G. A., Wortman, C. B., & Nesse, R. M. (2004). Prospective pattern of resilience and maladjustment during widowhood. *Psychology & Aging, 19*, 260–271.

Bonanno, G. A., Wortman, C. B., Lehman, D. R., Tweed, R. G., Haring, M., Sonnega, J., et al. (2002). Resilience to loss and chronic grief: A prospective study from pre-loss to 18 months post-loss. *Journal of Personality & Social Psychology, 83*, 1150–1164.

Bonomi, A. E., Anderson, M. L., Reid, R. J., Carrell, D., Fishman, P. A., Rivara, F. P., & Thompson, R. S. (2007). Intimate partner violence in older women. *The Gerontologist, 47*, 34–41.

Boon, S. D. & Brussoni, M. J. (1996). Young adults' relationships with their "closest" grandparents: Examining emotional closeness. *Journal of Social Behavior & Personality, 11*, 439–458.

Booth-Kewley, S. & Vickers, R. R. (1994). Associations between major domains of personality and health behavior. *Journal of Personality, 62*, 281–298.

Boring, E. G. (1950). *A history of experimental psychology*. New York: Appleton-Century-Crofts.

Bossé, R., Aldwin, C. M., Levenson, M., Spiro, A. III, Mroczek, D. K. (1993). Changes in social support after retirement: Longitudinal findings from the normative aging study. *Journal of Gerontology: Psychological Sciences, 48*, P210–217.

Botwinick, J. (1984). *Aging and behavior: A comprehensive integration of research findings*. New York: Springer.

Boucher, N., Dufeu-Duchesne, T., Vicaut, E., Farge, D., Effros, R. B., & Schächter, F. (1998). CD28 expression in T cell aging and human longevity. *Experimental Gerontology, 33*, 267–282.

Boutet, I., & Faubert, J. (2006). Recognition of faces and complex objects in younger and older adults. *Memory & Cognition, 34*, 854–864.

Bowlby, J. (1980). *Attachment and loss: Loss, sadness, and depression, 3*. New York: Basic Books.

Bowling, A. (1987). Mortality after bereavement: A review of the literature on survival periods and factors affecting survival. *Social Science & Medicine, 24*, 117–124.

Brackbill, Y., & Kitch, D. (1991). Intergenerational relationships: A social exchange perspective on joint living arrangements among the elderly and their relatives. *Journal of Aging Studies, 5*, 77–97.

Brand, F. N., Kiely, D. K., Kannel, W. B., & Myers, R. H. (1992). Family patterns of coronary heart disease mortality: The Framingham longevity study. *Journal of Clinical Epidemiology, 45*, 169–174.

Brandtstädter, J. (1992). Personal control over development: Some developmental implications of self-efficacy. In R. Schwarzer (Ed.), *Self-efficacy: Thought control of action* (pp. 127–145). Washington, DC: Hemisphere.

Brandtstädter, J. & Greve, W. (1994). The aging self: Stabilizing and protective processes. *Developmental Review, 14*, 52–80.

Brant, L. J. & Fozard, J. L. (1990). Age changes in pure tone thresholds in a longitudinal study of normal aging. *Journal of the Acoustic Society of America, 88*, 813–820.

Brébion, G. (2003). Working memory, language comprehension, and aging: Four experiments to understand the deficit. *Experimental Aging Research, 29*, 269–301.

Brecher, E. M. (1984). *Love, sex, and aging*. Boston: Little, Brown.

Breckenridge, J. N., Gallagher, D., Thompson, L. W., & Peterson, J. (1986). Characteristic depressive symptoms of bereaved elders. *Journal of Gerontology, 41*, 163–168.

Bretschneider, J. G. & McCoy, N. L. (1988). Sexual interest and behavior in healthy 80- to 102-year olds. *Archives of Sexual Behavior, 17*, 109–129.

Brett, D. (1992). *More Annie stories: Therapeutic storytelling techniques*. New York: Magination Press-Brunner/Mazel.

Brod, M., Mendelsohn, G. A., & Roberts, B. (1998). Patients' experiences of Parkinson's disease. *Journal of Gerontology: Psychological Sciences, 53B*, P213–P222.

Brody, H., Campbell, M. L., Faber-Langendoen, K., & Ogle, K. (1997). Withdrawing intensive life sustaining treatment: Recommendations for compassionate clinical management. *New England Journal of Medicine, 336*, 652–657.

Brokenleg, M. & Middleton, D. (1993). Native Americans: Adapting, yet retaining. In D. P. Irish, K. F. Lundquist, & V. J. Nelsen (Eds.), *Ethnic variations in dying, death, and grief: Diversity in university* (pp. 101–113). Washington, DC: Taylor & Francis.

Brotons, M., Koger, S., & Pickett-Cooper, P. (1997). Music and dementias: A review of literature. *Journal of Music Therapy, 34*, 204–245.

Brown, A. S. (1989). *How to increase your memory power*. Glenview, IL: Scott Foresman.

Brown, S. C., & Park, D. C. (2003). Theoretical models of cognitive aging and implications for translational research in medicine. *The Gerontologist, 43*, 57–67.

Brown, S. L., Lee, G. R., & Bulanda, J. R. (2006). Cohabitation among older adults: A national portrait. *Journal of Gerontology: Social Sciences, 61B*, S71–S79.

Bucholz, K. K. (1992). Alcohol abuse and dependence from a psychiatric epidemiologic perspective. *Alcohol Health & Research World, 16*, 197–208.

Buehlman, K. T., Gottman, J. M., & Katz, L. F. (1992). How a couple views their past predicts their future: Predicting divorce from an oral history interview. *Journal of Family Psychology, 5*, 295–318.

Bumpass, L. L., & Lu, H–H. (2000). Trends in cohabitation and implications for children's family contexts in the United States. *Population Studies, 54*, 29–41.

Bunce, D., Kivipelto, M., & Wahlin, Å. (2004). Utilization of cognitive support in episodic free recall as a function of Apolipoprotein and vitamin B12 or folate among adults aged 75 years and older. *Neuropsychology, 18*, 362–370.

Buono, M. D., Urciuoli, O., & de Leo, D. (1998). Quality of life and longevity: A study of centenarians. *Age & Ageing, 27*, 207–216.

Burdick, D. J., Rosenblatt, A., Samus, Q. M., Steele, C., Baker, A., Harper, M., Mayer, L., Brandt, J., Rabins, P. V., & Lyketsos, C. G. (2005). Predictors of functional impairment in residents of assisted-living facilities: The Maryland Assisted Living Study. *Journal of Gerontology: Medical Sciences, 60A*, 258–264.

Burleson, M. H., Gregory, W. L., & Trevarthen, W. R. (1995). Heterosexual activity:

Busjahn, A., Freier, K., Faulhaber, H. D., Li, G. H., Rosenthal, M., Jordan, J., Hoehe, M. R., Timmermann, B., & Luft, F. C. (2002). Beta-2 adrenergic receptor gene variations and coping styles in twins. *Biological Psychology, 61* (1–2), 97–109.

Butler, R. N. (1969). Ageism: Another form of bigotry. *Gerontologist, 9*, 243–246.

Butler, R. N., Lewis, M. I., & Sunderland, T. (1998). *Aging and mental health: Positive psychosocial and biomedical approaches.* Boston: Allyn & Bacon.

Cabelof, D. C., Raffoul, J. J., Ge, Y., Van Remmen, H., Matherly, L. H., & Heydari, A. R. (2006). Age-related loss of the DNA repair response following exposure to oxidative stress. *Journal of Gerontology: Biological Sciences, 61A*, 427–434.

Cahill, K. E., Giandrea, M. D., & Quinn, J. F. (2006). Retirement patterns from career employment. *The Gerontologist, 46*, 514–523.

Cahill, S., South, K., & Spade, J. (2000). *Public policy issues affecting gay, lesbian, bisexual, and transgender elders.* New York: The Policy Institute of the National Gay and Lesbian Task Force.

Calfas, K. J., Long, B. J., Sallis, J. F., Wooten, W. J., Pratt, M., & Patrick, K. (1996). A controlled trial of physician counseling to promote the adoption of physical activity. *Preventive Medicine, 25*, 225–233.

Calhoun, L. G. & Tedeschi, R. G. (1989–1990). Positive aspects of critical life problems: Recollections of grief. *Omega, 20*, 265–272.

Calmels, P., Ecochard, R., Blanchon, M. A., Charbonnier, C., Cassou, B., & Gonthier, R. (1998). Relation between locomotion impairment, functional independence in retirement, and occupational strain resulting from work carried out during working life. Study of a sample population of 350 miners in the Loire valley in France. *Journal of Epidemiology & Community Health, 52*, 283–288.

Calvert, J. F., Jr., Hollander-Rodriguez, J., Kaye, J., & Leahy, M. (2006). Dementia-free survival among centenarians: An evidence–based review. *Journal of Gerontology: Medical Sciences, 61A*, 951–956.

Campbell, A. J., Reinken, J., Allan, B. C., & Martinez, G. S. (1981). Falls in old age: A study of frequency and related clinical factors. *Age & Ageing, 10*, 264–270.

Campione, W. A. (1988). Predicting participation in retirement preparation programs. *Journal of Gerontology: Social Sciences, 43*, S91–S95.

Cappola, A. R., Xue, Q-L., Walston, J. D., Leng, S. X., Ferrucci, L., Guralnik, J., & Fried, L. P. (2006). DHEAS levels and mortality in disabled older women: The women's health and aging study I. *Journal of Gerontology: Medical Sciences, 61A*, 957–962.

Cardelli, M., Marchegiani, F., Cavallone, L., Olivieri, F., Giovagnetti, S., Mugianesi, E., Moresi, R., Lisa, R. & Franceschi, C. (2006). A polymorphism of the YTHDF2 gene (1p35) located in an Alu-rich genomic domain is associated with human longevity. *Journal of Gerontology Biological Sciences, 61A*, 547–556.

Carnes, B. A., Olshansky, S. J., & Grahn, D. (1996). Continuing the search for a law of mortality. *Population & Development Review, 19*, 231–264.

Carnes, B. A., Olshansky, S. J., Gavrilov, L., Gavrilova, N., & Grahn, D. (1999). Human longevity:

Nature vs. nurture-fact or fiction. *Perspectives in Biology & Medicine, 42*, 422–441.

Carr, D. B., LaBarge, E., Dunnigan, K., & Storandt, M. (1998). Differentiating drivers with dementia of the Alzheimer's type from healthy older persons with a traffic sign naming test. *Journal of Gerontology: Medical Sciences, 53A*, M135–M139.

Carskadon, M. A. (1982). Sleep fragmentation, sleep loss, and sleep needs in the elderly. *Gerontologist, 22*, 187.

Carstensen, L. L. (1992). Social and emotional patterns in adulthood: Support for socioemotional selectivity theory. *Psychology and Aging, 7*, 331–338.

Carstensen, L. L. (1995). Evidence for a lifespan theory of socioemotional selectivity. *Current Directions in Psychological Science, 4*, 151–156.

Carstensen, L. L. & Charles, S. T. (1998). Emotion in the second half of life. *Current Directions in Psychological Science, 7*, 144–149.

Carstensen, L. L. & Freund, A. M. (1994). The resilience of the aging self. *Developmental Review, 14*, 81–92.

Carstensen, L. L., Fung, H. H., & Charles, S. T. (2003). Socio-emotional selectivity theory and the regulation of emotion in the second half of life. *Motivation & Emotion, 27*, 103–123.

Carstensen, L. L., Gottman, J. M., & Levenson, R. W. (1995). Emotional behavior in long-term marriage. *Psychology & Aging, 10*, 140–149.

Casadesus, G., Garrett, M. R., Webber, K. M., Hartzler, A. W., Atwood, C. S., Perry, G., Bowen, R. L., & Smith, M. A. (2006). The estrogen myth: Potential use of Gonadotropin-releasing hormone agonists for the treatment of Alzheimer's disease. *Drugs in R & D, 7*, 187–193.

Caserta, M. S., & Gillett, P. A. (1998). Older womens' feelings about exercise and their adherence to an aerobic regimen over time. *The Gerontologist, 38*, 602–609.

Caserta, M. S., & Lund, D. A. (1993). Intrapersonal resources and the effectiveness of self-help groups for bereaved older adults. *The Gerontologist, 33*, 619–629.

Caspari, R., & Lee, S–H. (2006). Is human longevity a consequence of cultural change or modern biology? *American Journal of Physical Anthropology, 129*, 512–517.

Causes of Death. (2007). Available from http://ucatlas.ucsc.edu/health/causeprint.html. Accessed May 16, 2007.

Cavanaugh, J. C. (1996). Memory self-efficacy as a key to understanding memory change. In F. Blanchard-Fields & T. M. Hess (Eds.), *Perspectives on cognitive changes in adulthood and aging.* (pp. 488–507). New York: McGraw-Hill.

Cavanaugh, J. C. (1998). Friendships and social networks among older people. In I. H. Nordhus, G. R. Vanden Bos, S. Berg, & P. Fromholt (Eds.), *Clinical geropsychology* (pp. 137–140). Washington, DC: APA.

Cebelof, D. C., Raffoul, J. J., Ge, Y., Van Remmen, H., Matherly, L. H., & Heydari, A. R. (2006). Age-related loss of the DNA repair response following exposure to oxidative stress. *Journal of Gerontology: Biological Sciences, 61A*, 427–434.

Ceci, S. J. & Liker, J. K. (1986). A day at the races: A study of IQ, expertise, and cognitive complexity. *Journal of Experimental Psychology: General, 115*, 255–266.

Celdrán, M., & Villar, F. (2007). Volunteering among older Spanish adults: Does the type of organization matter? *Educational Gerontology, 33*, 237–251.

Centers for Disease Control and Prevention (2002). Cohabitation, marriage, divorce, and remarriage in the United States. Data from the National Survey of Family Growth, Dept. of Health & Human Services.

Centofanti, M. (1998). Fear of Alzheimer's undermines health of elderly patients. *APA Monitor, 29*, 1 & 33.

Cerella, J., Rybash, J., Hoyer, W., & Commons, M. L. (1993). *Adult information processing: Limits on loss.* San Diego, CA: Academic Press.

Chapleski, E. E., Kaczynski, R., Gerbi, S. A., & Lichtenberg, P. A. (2004). American Indian elders and depression: Long-term effects of life events. *Journal of Applied Gerontology, 23*, 40–57.

Chapman, B. P., Duberstein, P. R., Sörensen, S., & Lyness, J. M. (2006). Personality and perceived health in older adults: The five factor model in primary care. *Journal of Gerontology: Psychological Sciences, 61B*, P362–P365.

Charlotte Observer. (January 7, 1995). 6A.

Charness, N. (1981). Search in chess: Age and skill differences. *Journal of Experimental Psychology: Human Perception & Performance, 7*, 467–476.

Charness, N. & Bosman, E. A. (1992). Human factors and aging. In F. I. M. Craik & T. A. Salthouse (Eds.), *The handbook of aging & cognition* (pp. 495–551). Hillsdale, NJ: Erlbaum.

Charness, N. & Holley, P. (2001). Human factors and environmental support for Alzheimer's disease. *Aging and Mental Health, 5*, 65–3.

Chasteen, A. L., Schwarz, N., & Park, D. C. (2002). The activation of aging stereotypes in younger and older adults. *Journal of Gerontology: Psychological Sciences, 57B*, P540–P547.

Cheesman, M. F. (1997). Speech perception by elderly listeners: Basic knowledge and implications for audiology. *Journal of Speech-Language Pathology and Audiology, 21*, 104–110.

Chen, Y., & Persson, A. (2002). Internet use among young and older adults: Relation to psychological well-being. *Educational Gerontology, 28*, 731–744.

Chen, Y., & Sun, Y. (2003). Age differences in financial decision making: Using simple heuristics. *Educational Gerontology, 29*, 627–635.

Cherlin, A. & Furstenberg, F. (1985). Styles and strategies of grandparenting. In V. L. Bengston & J. Robertson (Eds.), *Grandparenthood*. Beverly Hills, CA: Sage.

Cherry, K. E., & Smith, A. D. (1998). Normal memory aging. In M. Hersen & V. B. Van Hasselt (Eds.), *Handbook of clinical geropsychology* (pp. 87–110). New York: Plenum Press.

Cheung, C. & Ngan, M. (2000). Contributions of volunteer networking to isolated seniors in Hong Kong. *Journal of Gerontological Social Work, 33*, 79–100.

Chipperfield, J. G., & Havens, B. (2001). Gender differences in the relationship between marital status transitions and life satisfaction in later life. *Journal of Gerontology: Psychological Sciences, 56B*, P176–186.

Chiriboga, D. A. (1989). Mental health at the midpoint: Crisis, challenge, or relief? In S. Hunter & M. Sundel (Eds.), *Midlife myths: Issues, findings, and practical implications* (pp. 116–144). Newbury Park, CA: Sage.

Choi, N. G. (1997). Racial differences in retirement income: The roles of public and private income sources. *Journal of Aging & Social Policy, 9*, 21–42.

Choi, N. G., & Bohman, T. M. (2007). Predicting the changes in depressive symptomatology in later life. *Journal of Aging & Health, 19*, 152–177.

Christakis, N. A., & Allison, P. D. (2007). Mortality after the hospitalization of a spouse. *New England Journal of Medicine, 354*, 719–730.

Christensen, A. J., Ehlers, S. L., Wiebe, J. S., Moran, P. J., Raichle, K., Femeyhough, K., & Lawton, W. J., (2002). Patient personality and mortality: A 4-year prospective examination of chronic renal insufficiency. *Health Psychology, 21*, 315–320.

Christensen, P. R., & Guilford, J. P. (1957a). *Associational Fluency I, Form A*. Redwood City, CA: MindGarden.

Christensen, P. R., & Guilford, J. P. (1957b). *Ideational Fluency I, Form A*. Redwood City, CA: MindGarden.

Christensen, P. R., & Guilford, J. P. (1958a). *Expressional Fluency, Form A*. Redwood City, CA: MindGarden.

Christensen, P. R., & Guilford, J. P. (1958b). *Word Fluency, Form A*. Redwood City, CA: MindGarden.

Christensen, P. R., Merrifield, P. R., & Guilford, J. P. (1958). *Consequences*. Redwood City, CA:

MindGarden.

Chu, L-W., Chiu, A. Y. Y., & Chi, I. (2006). Impact of falls on the balance, gait, and activities of daily living functioning in community-dwelling Chinese older adults. *Journal of Gerontology: Medical Sciences, 61A*, 399–404.

Chun, M. R., Schofield, P., Stern, Y., Tatemechi, T. K., & Mayeux, R. (1998). The epidemiology of dementia among the elderly: Experience in a community-based registry. In M. F. Folstein (Ed.), *Neurobiology of primary dementia* (pp. 1–26). Washington, DC: American Psychiatric Press.

Cicirelli, V. G. (1985). The role of siblings as family caregivers. In W. J. Sauer & R. T. Coward (Eds.), *Social support networks and the care of the elderly* (pp. 93–107). New York: Springer.

Cicirelli, V. G. (1995). Siblings. In G. L. Maddox et al., *The encyclopedia of aging* (2nd ed., pp. 951–954). New York: Springer.

Clancy, S. M. & Hoyer, W. J. (1988). Effects of age and skill on domain specific search. In V. L. Pateri & G. J. Groen (Eds.), *Proceedings of the tenth conference of the Cognitive Science Society.* (pp. 398–404). Hillsdale, NJ: Erlbaum.

Clark, C. M. (2000). Clinical manifestations and diagnostic evaluation of patients with Alzheimer's disease. In C. M. Clark & J. Q. Trojanowski (Eds.), *Neurodegenerative dementias* (pp. 95–114). New York: McGraw–Hill.

Clark, M. C., Foos, P. W., Briand, J., Briand, R., & Ripplinger, J. (2006, Nov.). *Perchance to dream: Gender and age differences in dream content of African Americans.* Paper presented at the meetings of the Gerontological Society of America, Dallas, Texas.

Clark, R. F. & Goate, A. M. (1993). Molecular genetics of Alzheimer's disease. *Archives of Neurology, 50*, 1164–1167.

Clarke, S. (1995). *Advance report of final divorce statistics, 1989 and 1990, 43*(9). Hyattsville, MD: National Center for Health Statistics.

Clayton, V. P. & Birren, J. E. (1980). The development of wisdom across the lifespan: A reexamination of an ancient topic. *Life-Span Development & Behavior, 3*, 103–135.

Cleek, M. G. & Pearson, T. A. (1985). Perceived causes of divorce: An analysisn of interrelationships. *Journal of Marriage & the Family, 47*, 179–183.

Cleveland, J. N. & Shore, L. M. (1996). Work and employment. In J. E. Birren (Ed.), *Encyclopedia of Gerontology, 2*, (pp. 627–639). New York: Academic Press.

Cohen, C., Teresi, J., & Holmes, D. (1985). Social networks, stress, and physical health: A longitudinal study of an inner-city elderly population. *Journal of Gerontology, 40*, 478–486.

Cohen, G. (1993). Memory and aging. In G. M. Davies & R. H. Logic (Eds.), *Memory in everyday life* (pp. 419–459). Amsterdam: North Holland.

Cohen, G. D. (2000). *The creative age: Awakening human potential in the second half of life.* New York: Quill, Harper-Collins.

Cohen, G. D. (2006). Research on creativity and aging: The positive impact of the arts on health and illness. *Generations*, 7–15.

Cohen, S. (1988). Psychosocial models of the role of social support in the etiology of physical disease. *Health Psychology, 7*, 269–297.

Cohen, S. & Herbert, T. B. (1996). Health psychology: Psychological factors and physical disease from the perspective of human psychoneuroimmunology. *Annual Review of Psychology, 47*, 113–142.

Cohen, S., & Pressman, S. D. (2006). Positive affect and health. *Current Directions in Psychological Science, 15*, 122–125.

Cohen-Mansfield, J., Parpura-Gill, A., & Golander, H. (2006). Utilization of self-identity roles for designing interventions for persons with dementia. *Journal of Gerontology: Psychological Sciences, 61B*, P202–P212.

Cohler, B. J. (1982). Personal narrative and life course. In P. Baltes & O. G. Brim (Eds.), *Life span development and behavior* (Vol. 4, pp. 205–241). New York: Academic Press.

Cohn, J. & Sugar, J. A. (1991). Determinants of quality of life in institutions: Perceptions of frail older residents, staff, and families. In J. E. Birren & J.E Lubben (Eds). *The concept and measurement of quality of life in the frail elderly* (pp. 28–49). San Diego: Academic Press.

Cohn, L., Feller, A. G., Draper, M. W., Rudman, J. W., & Rudman, D. (1993). Carpal tunnel syndrome and gynecomastia during growth hormone treatment of elderly men with low circulating IGF-I concentrations. *Clinical Endocrinology, 39,* 417–425.

Coile, C. (2003). *Retirement incentives and couples' retirement decisions.* Chestnut Hill, MA: Center for Retirement Research at Boston College.

Colcombe, S., & Kramer, A. F. (2003). Fitness effects on the cognitive function of older adults: A meta-analysis. *Psychological Science, 14,* 125–130.

Cole, E. R. & Stewart, A. J. (1996). Meanings of political participation among Black and White women: Political identity and social responsibility. *Journal of Personality & Social Psychology, 71,* 130–140.

Coleman, P. G. (1999). Creating a life story: The task of reconciliation. *Gerontologist, 39,* 133–139.

Coleman, P. G., Ivani-Chalian, C., & Robinson, M. (1998). The story continues: Persistence of life themes in old age. *Ageing & Society, 18,* 389–419.

Coleman, P. G., Ivani-Chalian, C., & Robinson, M. (1999). Self and identity in advanced old age: Validation of theory through longitudinal case analysis. *Journal of Personality, 67,* 819–849.

Colonia-Willner, R. (1998). Practical intelligence at work: Relationship between aging and cognitive efficiency among managers in a bank environment. *Psychology & Aging, 13,* 45–57.

Colsher, P. L., Dorfman, L. T., & Wallace, R. B. (1988). Specific health conditions and work-retirement status among the elderly. *Journal of Applied Gerontology, 7,* 485–503.

Columbo, G., Buono, M. D., Smania, K., Raviola, R. &DeLeo, D. (2006). Pet therapy and institutionalized elderly: A study on 144 cognitively unimpaired subjects. *Archives of Gerontology and Geriatrics, 42,* 207–216.

Comfort, A. (1964). *Ageing: The biology of senescence.* New York: Holt, Rinehart, & Winston.

Conger, R. D., Cui, M., Bryant, C. M., & Elder, G. H., Jr. (2000). Competence in early adult romantic relationships: A developmental perspective on family influences. *Journal of Personality & Social Psychology, 79,* 224–237.

Connell, B. R. & Sanford, J. A. (1999). Research implications of universal design. In E. Steinfeld & G.S. Danford (Eds.). *Enabling environments: Measuring the impact of environment on disability and rehabilitation* (pp. 35–57). New York: Plenum Press.

Connides, I. A. (1992). Life transitions and the sibling tie: A qualitative study. *Journal of Marriage & the Family, 54,* 972–982.

Connides, I. A. (1994). Sibling support in older age. *Journal of Gerontology: Social Sciences, 49,* S309–S317.

Conwell, Y. (1995). Suicide among elderly persons. *Psychiatric Services, 46,* 563–564.

Cook, A. S., & Oltjenbruns, K. A. (1998). *Dying and grieving: Life span and family perspectives.* New York: Harcourt Brace College Publishers.

Cooney, T. M., Schaie, K. W., & Willis, S. L. (1988). The relationship between prior functioning on cognitive and personality variables and subject attrition in longitudinal research. *Journal of Gerontology: Psychological Sciences, 43,* P12–P17.

Cooper, A. A., Gitler, A. D., Cashikar, A., Haynes, C. M., Hill, K. J., Bhullar, B, et al. (2006). _-Synuclein blocks ER-Golgi traffic and Rab1 rescues neuron loss in Parkinson's models. *Science, 313,* 324–328.

Corey-Bloom, J. (2000). Dementia. In S. K. Whitboure (Ed.), *Psychopathology in later adulthood* (pp. 217–243). New York: John Wiley & Sons.

Cornelius, S. W. & Caspi, A. (1987). Everyday problem solving in adulthood and old age. *Psychol-*

ogy & Aging, 2, 144–153.

Cornelius, S. W., & Capsi, A. (1987). Everyday problem solving in adulthood and old age. *Psychology & Aging, 2*, 144–153.

Costa, P. T., Jr. & McCrae, R. R. (1988). Personality in adulthood: A six year longitudinal study of self-reports and spouse ratings on the NEO Personality Inventory. *Journal of Personality & Social Psychology, 54*, 853–863.

Costa, P. T., Jr. & McCrae, R. R. (1994). Set like plaster? Evidence for the stability of adult personality. In T. E. Heatherton & J. L. Weinberger (Eds.), *Can personality change?* (pp. 21–41). Washington, DC: American Psychological Association.

Costa, P. T., Jr., McCrae, R. R., Zonderman, A. B., Barbano, H. E., Lebowitz, B., & Larson, D. M. (1986). Cross-sectional studies of personality in a national sample: 2. Stability in neuroticism, extraversion, and openness. *Psychology & Aging, 1*, 144–149.

Costa, P. T., Jr., Yang, J., & McCrae, R. R. (1998). Aging and personality traits: Generalizations and clinical implications. In I. H. Nordhus, G. R. VandenBos, S. Berg, & P. Fromholt (Eds.), *Clinical geropsychology* (pp. 33–48). Washington, DC: American Psychological Association.

Cotrell, V., & Hooker, K. (2005). Possible selves of individuals with Alzheimer's disease. *Psychology & Aging, 20*, 285–294.

Coward, R. T., Horne, C., & Dwyer, J. W. (1992). Demographic perspectives on gender and family caregiving. In J. W. Dwyer & R. T. Coward (Eds.), *Gender, families, and elder care* (pp. 18–33). Newbury Park, CA: Sage.

Cowper, D. C., Longino, C. F., Jr., Kubal, J. D., Manheim, L. M., Dienstfrey, S. J., & Palmer, J. M. (2000). The retirement migration of U. S. veterans, 1960, 1970, 1980, and 1990. *Journal of Applied Gerontology, 19*, 123–137.

Craik, F. I. M. & Jennings, J. M. (1992). Human memory. In F. I. M. Craik & T. A. Salthouse (Eds.), *The handbook of aging and cognition* (pp. 51–110). Hillsdale, NJ: Erlbaum.

Crawford, S., & Channon, S. (2002). Dissociation between performance on abstract tests of executive function and problem solving in real-life type situations in normal aging. *Aging & Mental Health, 6*, 12–21.

Creasey, G. L. & Kaliher, G. (1994). Age differences in grandchildren's perceptions of relations with grandparents. *Journal of Adolescence, 17*, 411–426.

Cress, M. E., Buchner, D. M., Questad, K. A., Esselman, P. C., deLateur, B. J., & Schwartz, R. S. (1999). Exercise: Effects on physical functional performance in independent older adults. *Journal of Gerontology: Medical Sciences, 54A*, M242–M248.

Crichton, M. (1990). *Jurassic park*. New York: Ballantine.

Crimmins, E. M., Hayward, M. D., & Seeman, T. (2004). Race/ethnicity, socioeconomic status and health. In N. B. Anderson, R. A. Bulatao, & B. Cohen (Eds.), *Critical perspectives on racial and ethnic differences in health in late life* (pp. 310–352). Washington, DC: National Research Council.

Crimmins, E. M., Reynolds, S. L., & Saito, Y. (1999). Trends in health and ability to work among the older working-age population. *Journal of Gerontology: Social Sciences, 54B*, S31–S40.

Crystal, S. & Shea, D. (1990). Cumulative advantage, cumulative disadvantage, and inequality among elderly people. *Gerontologist, 30*, 437–443.

Csikszentmihalyi, M. (1996). *Creativity: Flow and the psychology of discovery and invention*. New York: HarperCollins.

Cumming, R. G., Salkeld, G., Thomas, M., & Szonyi, G. (2000). Prospective study of the impact of fear of falling on activities of daily living, SF-35 scores, and nursing home admission. *Journal of Gerontology: Medical Sciences, 55A*, M299–M305.

Cummings, S. M., Kropf, N. P., & DeWeaver, K. L. (2000). Knowledge of and attitudes toward aging among non-elders: Gender and race differences. *Journal of Women & Aging, 12*, 77–91.

Cunningham, W. R. & Brookbank, J. W. (1988). *Gerontology: The Psychology, Biology, and Sociology of Aging*. New York: Harper & Row.

Cutler, L. J., Kane, R. A., Degenholtz, H. B., Miller, M. J. & Grant, L. (2006). Assessing and comparing physical environments for nursing home residents: Using new tools for greater research specificity. *The Gerontologist, 46*, 42–51.

Cutter, M. A. G. (1991). Euthanasia: Reassessing the boundaries. *Journal of National Institute of Health Research, 3*, 59–61.

Czaja, S. J. (2001). Technological change and the older worker. In J. E. Birren & K. W. Schaie (Eds.), *Handbook of the psychology of aging* (5th ed., pp. 547–568). San Diego, CA: Academic Press.

Czaja, S. J., Weber, R. A., Nair, S. N., & Clark, M. C. (1993). A human factors analysis of ADL activities: A capability-demand approach (Special Issue). *Journal of Gerontology, 47*, 44–48.

Dail, P. W. (1988). Prime-time television portrayals of older adults in the context of family life. *The Gerontologist, 28*, 700–706.

Dainoff, M. (1989). Death and other losses. *Humanistic Judaism, 17*, 63–67.

Danhauer, S. C., & Andrykowski, M. A. (2005). Positive psychosocial functioning in later life: Use of meaning-based coping strategies by nursing home residents. *Journal of Applied Gerontology, 24*, 299–318.

Danner, D. D., Snowdon, D. A., & Friesen, W. V. (2001). Positive emotions in early life and longevity: Findings from the Nun study. *Journal of Personality and Social Psychology, 80*, 804–813.

Davey, A., & Szinovacz, M. E. (2004). Dimensions of marital quality and retirement. *Journal of Family Issues, 25*, 431–464.

Davies, R., Lacks, P., Storandt, M., Bertelson, A. D. (1986). Countercontrol treatment of sleep-maintenance insomnia in relation to age. *Psychology & Aging, 1*, 233–238.

de Benedictis, G., Rose, G., Carrieri, G., de Luca, M., Falcone, E., Passarino, G., Bonafé, M., Monti, D., Baggio, G., Bertolini, S., Mari, D., Mattace, R., & Franceschi, C. (1999). Mitochondrial DNA inherited variants are associated with successful aging and longevity in humans. *FASEB Journal, 13*, 1532–1536.

de Jong, D., Jansen, R. W. M. M., Kremer, B. P. H., & Verbeek, M. M. (2006). Cerebrospinal fluid amyloid β_{42}/phosphorylated tau ratio discriminates between Alzheimer's disease and vascular dementia. *Journal of Gerontology: Medical Sciences, 61A*, 755–758.

De Strooper, B. & König, G. (2001). An inflammatory drug prospect. *Nature, 414*, 159–169.

de Zwart, B. C., Broersen, J. P., Frings-Dresen, M. H., & van Dijk, F. J. (1997). Repeated survey on changes musculoskeletal complaints relative to age and work demands. *Occupational & Environmental Medicine, 54*, 793–799.

DeArmond, S. J. (1998). Prion diseases: The spectrum of etiologic and pathogenic mechanisms. In M. F. Folstein (Ed.), *Neurobiology of primary dementia* (pp. 83–118). Washington, DC: American Psychiatric Press.

Deary, I. J., & Der, G. (2005). Reaction time explains IQ's association with death. *Psychological Science, 16*, 64–69.

Deberdt, W. (1994). Interaction between psychological and pharmocological treatment in cognitive impairment. *Life Sciences, 55*, 2057–2066.

Dement, W., Richardson, G., Prinz, P., Carskadon, M., Kripke, D., & Czeisler, C. (1985). Changes of sleep and wakefulness with age. In C. E. Finch & E. L. Schneider (Eds.), *Handbook of the biology of aging* (2nd edition). New York: Van Nostrand Reinhold, 692–717.

Demos, V. & Jache, A. (1981, September 22). Return to sender please. *Women's Day*, 20.

Dennerstein, L., Randolph, J., Taffe, J., Dudley, E., & Burger, H., (2002). Hormones, mood, sexuality, and the menopausal transition. *Fertility & Sterility, 77*, S42–S48.

Denney, N. W., & Palmer, A. N. (1981). Adult age differences on traditional and practical problem-solving, *Journal of Gerontology, 36*, 323–328.

Denney, N. W., & Pearce, K. A. (1989). A developmental study of practical problem solving in adults. *Psychology & Aging, 4*, 438–442.

Dennis, H. & Migliaccio, J. (1997, Summer). Redefining retirement: The baby boomer challenge. *Generations*, 45–50.

Dennis, H. (1989). The current state of preretirement planning. *Generations, 13*, 38–41.

Dennis, W. (1966). Creative productivity between the ages of twenty and eighty years. *Journal of Gerontology, 21*, 1–18.

Dennis, W. (1968). Creative productivity between the ages of twenty and eighty years. In B. L. Neugarten (Ed.), *Middle age and aging*. Chicago: University of Chicago Press.

DePaola, S. J., Griffin, M., Young, J. R., & Neimeyer, R. A. (2003). Death anxiety and attitudes toward the elderly among older adults: The role of gender and ethnicity. *Death Studies, 27*, 335–354.

Dergance, J. M., Calmbach, W. L., Dhanda, R., Miles, T. P., Hazuda, H. P., & Mouton, C. P. (2003). Barriers to and benefits of leisure time physical activity in the elderly: Differences across cultures. *Journal of the American Geriatrics Society, 51*, 863–868.

Desmond, D. W. & Tatemichi, T. K. (1998). Vascular dementia. In M. F. Folstein (Ed.), *Neurobiology of primary dementia* (pp. 167–190). Washington, DC: American Psychiatric Press.

DeSpelder, L. A., & Strickland, A. L. (1992). *The last dance: Encountering death and dying*. Mountain View, CA: Mayfield Press.

deVries, B., Bluck, S., & Birren, J. E. (1993). The understanding of death and dying in a lifespan perspective. *The Gerontologist, 33*, 366–372.

Dickey, M. (1996). Melatonin: Does it work? *The Washingtonian, 31*, 33.

Diehl, M., Willis, S. L., & Schaie, K. W. (1995). Everyday problem solving in older adults: Observational assessment and cognitive correlates. *Psychology & Aging, 10*, 478–491.

Diener, E. & Suh, M. E. (1998). Subjective well-being and age: An international analysis. In K. W. Schaie & M. P. Lawton (Eds.), *Annual review of gerontolgy and geriatrics: Vol. 17. Focus on emotion and adult development* (pp. 304–324). New York: Springer.

Diener, E., Suh, E. M., Lucas, R. E., & Smith, H. L. (1999). Subjective well-being: Three decades of progress. *Psychological Bulletin, 125*, 276–302.

DiGiovanna, A. G. (1994). *Human aging: Biological perspectives*. New York: McGraw-Hill.

Dilworth-Anderson, P., Goodwin, P. Y., & Williams, S. W. (2004). Can culture help explain the physical health effects of caregiving over time among African American caregivers? *Journal of Gerontology: Social Sciences, 59B*, S138–S145.

Dinsmoor, R. (1996). Elixers of youth: Which work, which don't, which might? *Diabetes Self-Management, 13*, 51–58.

Dittman-Kohl, F. & Baltes, P. B. (1990). Toward a neofunctionalist conception of adult intellectual development: Wisdom as a prototypical case of intellectual growth. In C. Alexander & E. Langer (Eds.), *Higher stages of human development: Perspectives on adult growth*. (pp. 54–78). New York: Oxford University Press.

Dittman-Kohli, F., Lachman, M. E., Kliegl, R., & Baltes, P. B. (1991). Effects of cognitive training and testing on intellectual efficacy beliefs in elderly adults. *Journal of Gerontology: Psychological Sciences, 46*, P162–P164.

Dixon, R. A. & Hultsch, D. F. (1983). Structure and development of metamemory in adulthood. *Journal of Gerontology, 38*, 682–688.

Dixon, R. A. & Hultsch, D. F. (1999). Intelligence and cognitive potential in late life. In J. C. Cavanaugh & S. K. Whitbourne (Eds.), *Gerontology: Interdisciplinary perspectives* (pp. 213–237). New York: Oxford University Press.

Dobnik, V. (Jan. 22, 2000). Doctor carved his intials on patient. *Charlotte Observer*.

Doi, E. (April 9, 2005). Special tea kettles keep eye on elderly, isolated in Japan. *The Charlotte Observer*, 24A.

Dolan, P., & White, M. P. (2007). How can measures of subjective well-being be used to inform public policy? *Perspectives on Psychological Science, 2*, 71–85.

Doll, R. (1997). One for the heart. *British Medical Journal, 315*, 1664–1668.

Doll, R., & Peto, R. (1994). Mortality in relation to consumption of alcohol: 13 years' observations on male British doctors. *British Medical Journal, 309*, 911–918.

Dorfman, L. T., & Kolarik, D. C. (2005). Leisure and the retired professor: Occupation matters. *Educational Gerontology, 31*, 343–361.

Doty, R. L., Shaman, P., Appelbaum, S. L., Bigerson, R., Sikorski, L., & Rosenberg, L. (1984). Smell identification ability: Changes with age. *Science, 226*, 1441–1443.

Dresser, R. (1994). Advance directives: Implications for policy. *Hastings Center Report, 24*, 52–55.

Drew, J. C. & Brooke, V. (1999). Changing a legacy: The Eden Alternative nursing home. *The Annals of Long-Term Care, 7*, 115–121.

Duay, D. L., & Bryan, V. C. (2006). Senior adults' perceptions of successful aging. *Educational Gerontology, 32*, 423–445.

Dufour, M., Colliver, J., Stinson, F., & Grigson, B. (1988). *Changes in alcohol consumption with age: NHANES I epidemiologic followup*. Paper presented at the annual meeting of the American Public Health Association, Boston.

Duke, S. (1998). An exploration of anticipatory grief: The lived experience of people during their spouses' terminal illness and in bereavement. *Journal of Advanced Nursing, 28*, 829–839.

Dunlosky, J., Kubat-Silman, A. K., & Hertzog, C. (2003). Training monitoring skills improves older adults' self-paced associative learning. *Psychology & Aging, 18*, 340–345.

Dupree, L. W. & Schonfeld, L. (1996). Substance abuse. In M. Hersen & V. B. Van Hasselt (Eds.), *Psychological treatment of older adults: An introductory text* (pp. 281–297). New York: Plenum Press.

Dustman, R. E., Ruhling, R. O., Russell, E. M., Shearer, D. E., Bonekat, W., Shigeoka, J. W., Woods, J. S., & Bradford, D. C. (1984). Aerobic exercise training and improved neuropsychological function of older adults. *Neurobiology of Aging, 5*, 35–42.

Dwyer, D. S. & Mitchell, O. S. (1999). Health problems as determinants of retirement: Are self-rated measures endogenous? *Journal of Health Economics, 18*, 173–193.

Eberling, J. L., & Jagust, W. J. (1995). Imaging studies of aging, neurodegenerative disease, and alcoholism. *Alcohol World Health & Research, 19*, 279–286.

Eckert, J. K. & Rubinstein, R. L. (1999). Older men's health: Sociocultural and ecological perspectives. *Medical Clinics of North America, 83*, 1151–1172.

Edmonds, S. & Hooker, K. (1992). Perceived changes in life meaning following bereavement. *Omega, 25*, 307–318.

Effects on depressive symptoms. *Journal of Gerontology: Social Sciences, 59B*, S333–S342.

Einstein, G. O., McDaniel, M. A., Manzi, M., Cochran, B., & Baker, M. (2000). Prospective memory and aging: Forgetting intentions over short delays. *Psychology & Aging, 15*, 671–683.

Ekerdt, D. J. (1986). The busy ethic: Moral continuity between work and retirement. *Gerontologist, 26*, 239–244.

Ekerdt, D. J., & DeViney, S. (1993). Evidence for a preretirement process among older male workers. *Journals of Gerontology, 48*, S35–S43.

Ekerdt, D. J., Kosloski, K., & DeViney, S. (2000). The normative anticipation of retirement by older workers. *Research on Aging, 22,* 3–22.

Eleazer, G. P., Hornung, C. A., Egbert, C. B., Egbert, J. R., Eng, C., Hedgepeth, J. et al. (1996). The relationship between ethnicity and advance directives in a frail older population. *Journal of the American Geriatrics Society, 44,* 938–943.

Ellinson, M., Thomas, J., & Patterson, A. (2004). A critical evaluation of the relationship between serum vitamin B12, folate, and total homocysteine with cognitive impairment in the elderly. *Journal of Human Nutrition and Dietetics, 17,* 371–383.

Emanuel, E. J., Fairclough, D. L., Daniels, E. R., & Clarridge, B. R. (1996). Euthanasia and physician assisted suicide: Attitudes and experiences of oncology patients, oncologists, and the public. *Lancet, 347,* 1805–1810.

Endeshaw, Y. W., Ouslander, J. G., Schnelle, J. F., & Bliwise, D. L. (2007). Polysomnographic and clinical correlates of behaviorally observed daytime sleep in nursing home residents. *Journal of Gerontology: Medical Sciences, 62A,* 55–61.

Engelhart, M. J., Geerlings, M. I., Ruitenberg, A., van Swieten, J. C., Hofman, A., Witteman, J. C. M. & Breteler, M. M. B. (2002). Dietary intake of antioxidants and risk of Alzheimer's disease. *Journal of the American Medical Association, 287,* 3223–3229.

Epel, E., Lapidus, R., McEwen, B., & Brownell, K. (2000). Stress may add bite to appetite: A laboratory study of stress-induced cortisol and eating behavior in women. *Psychoneuroendocrinology, 26,* 37–49.

Epel, E., Lin, J., Wilhelm, F. H., Wolkowitz, O. M., Cawthon, R., Adler, N. E., Dolbier, C., Mendes, W. B., & Blackburn, E. H. (2006). Cell aging in relation to stress arousal and cardiovascular disease risk factors. *Psychoneuroendocrinology, 26,* 277–287.

Epstein, S. (1993). Bereavement from the perspective of cognitive-experiential self-theory. In M. S. Stroebe, W. Stroebe, & R. O. Hansson (Eds.), *Handbook of bereavement: Theory, research, and intervention* (pp. 112–128). New York: Cambridge University Press.

Erber, J. T. & Danker, D. C. (1995). Forgetting in the workplace: Attributions and recommendations for young and older-employees. *Psychology & Aging, 10,* 565–569.

Ericsson, K. A. & Charness, N. (1994). Expert performance: Its structure and acquisition. *American Psychologist, 49,* 725–747.

Erikson, E. H. (1963). *Childhood and society* (2nd ed.). New York: Norton.

Erikson, E. H. (1968). *Identity, youth, and crisis.* New York: Norton.

Erikson, E. H. (1982). *The life cycle completed: A review.* New York: Norton.

Erikson, E. H., Erikson, J. M., & Kivnick, H. Q. (1986). *Vital involvement in old age.* New York: W. W. Norton.

Eriksson, B. G., Hessler, R. M., Sundh, V., & Steen, B. (1999). Cross-cultural analysis of longevity among Swedish and American elders: The role of social networks in the Gothenburg and Missouri longitudinal studies compared. *Archives of Gerontology & Geriatrics, 28,* 131–148.

Escobedo, L. G. & Peddicord, J. P. (1996). Smoking prevalence in US birth cohorts: The influence of gender and education. *American Journal of Public Health,* 231–236.

Evert, J., Lawler, E., Bogan, H., & Peris, T. (2003). Morbidity profiles of centenarians: Survivors, delayers, and escapers. *Journal of Gerontology: Medical Sciences, 58A,* 232–237.

Faletti, M. V. (1984). Human factors research and functional environments for the aged. In I. Altman, J. Wohlwill, & M.P. Lawton (Eds.). *Human behavior and the environment: Vol. 7. The elderly and the environment.* New York: Plenum Press.

Faletti, M. V. & Clark, M. C. (1984). A capability-demand approach to the aged in technological environments: A case for improved task analysis. In P. K. Robinson, J. Livingston, & J.E. Birren (Eds.). *Aging and technological advances.* New York: Plenum Press.

Farberow, N. L., Gallagher-Thompson, D., Gilewski, M., & Thompson, L. (1992). Changes in grief and mental health. *Journal of Gerontology: Psychological Sciences, 47*, P357–P366.

Farlow, M. R., Tariot, P., Grossberg, G. T., Gergel, I., Grahm, S., & Jin, J. (2003). Memantine/donepezil dual therapy is superior to placebo/donepezil therapy for treatment of moderate to severe Alzheimer's disease. *Neurology, 60*, A412.

Fattoretti, P., Bertoni–Freddari, C., Balietti, M., Mocchegiani, E., Scancar, J., Zambenedetti, P., & Zatta, P. (2003). The effect of chronic aluminum (III) administration on the nervous system of aged rats: Clues to understand its suggested role in Alzheimer's disease. *Journal of Alzheimer's Disease, 5*, 437–444.

Faulkner, K. A., Cauley, J. A., Zmuda, J. M., Griffin, J. M., & Nevitt, M. C. (2003). Is social integration associated with the risk of falling in older community-dwelling women? *Journal of Gerontology: Medical Sciences, 58A*, 954–959.

Faulks, S. C., Turner, N., Else, P. L., & Hulbert, A. J. (2006). Calorie restriction in mice: Effects on body composition, daily activity, metabolic rate, mitochondrial reactive oxygen species production, and membrane fatty acid composition. *Journal of Gerontology: Biological Sciences, 61A*, 781–794.

Federal Trade Commission, Division of Consumer Protection. (1994). *Funeral industry practices.* Washington, DC: U. S. Superintendent of Documents.

Feifel, H. & Strack, S. (1989). Coping with conflict situations: Middle-aged and elderly men. *Psychology & Aging, 4*, 26–33.

Feig, B. (1998). Fortifying body and soul. *Food & Beverage Marketing, 17*(6), 30–31.

Fein, G., Feinberg, I., Insel, T. R., Antorbus, J. S., Price, L. J., Floyd, T. C., & Nelson, M. A. (1985). Sleep mentation in the elderly. *Psychophysiology, 22*, 218–225.

Feldman, D. C. (2003). Endgame: The design and implementation of early retirement incentive programs. In G. A. Adams & T. A. Beehr (Eds.), *Retirement: Reasons, processes, and results* (pp. 83–114). New York: Springer.

Feng, D., Silverstein, M., Giarrusso, R., McArdle, J. J., & Bengston, V. L. (2006). Attrition of older adults in longitudinal surveys: Detection and correction of sample selection bias using multigenerational data. *Journal of Gerontology: Social Sciences, 61B*, S323–S328.

Ferenac, M., Polan_ec, D., Huzak, M., Pereira-Smith, O. M., & Rubelj, I. (2005). Early-senescing human skin fibroblasts do not demonstrate accelerated telomere shortening. *Journal of Gerontology: Biological Sciences, 60A*, 820–829.

Ferrara, C. M., Goldberg, A. P., Ortmeyer, H. K., & Ryan, A. S. (2006). Effects of aerobic and resistive exercise training on glucose disposal and skeletal muscle metabolism in older men. *Journal of Gerontology: Medical Sciences, 61A*, 480–487.

Ferraro, K. F. (1992). Cohort changes in images of older adults. *Gerontologist, 32*, 296–304.

Ferraro, K. F., Thorpe, R. J., Jr., McCabe, G. P., Kelley-Moore, J. A., Jiang, Z. (2006). The color of hospitalization over the adult life course: Cumulative disadvantage in Black and White? *Journal of Gerontology: Social Sciences, 61B*, S299–D306.

Fetveit, A., Skjerve, A., & Bjorvatn, B. (2003). Bright light treatment improves sleep in institutionalized elderly: An open trial. *International Journal of Geriatric Psychiatry, 18*, 520–526.

Fichten, C. S., Libman, E., Creti, L., Bailes, S., & Sabourin, S. (2004). Long sleepers sleep more and short sleepers sleep less: A comparison of older adults who sleep well. *Behavioral Sleep Medicine, 2*, 2–23.

Finch, C. E. (1998). Variations in senescence and longevity include the possibility of negligible senescence. *Journal of Gerontology: Biological Sciences, 53A*, B235–B239.

Finch, C. E. & Tanzi, R. E. (1997). Genetics of aging. *Science, 278*, 407–411.

Fisk, J. E. & Warr, P. (1996). Age and working memory: The role of perceptual speed, the central executive, and the phonological loop. *Psychology & Aging, 11*, 316–323.

Fitzgerald, J. M. & Lawrence, R. (1984). Autobiographical memory across the life span. *Journal of*

Gerontology, 39, 692–699.

Flaherty, M. G. & Meer, M. D. (1994). How time flies: Age, memory, and temporal compression. *Sociological Quarterly, 35*, 705–721.

Flavell, J. H. (1985). *Cognitive development*. Upper Saddle River, NJ: Prentice Hall.

Fleeson, W. & Heckhausen, J. (1997). More or less "me" in past, present, and future: Perceived lifetime personality during adulthood. *Psychology & Aging, 12*, 125–136.

Flippen, C. & Tienda, M. (2000). Pathways to retirement: Patterns of labor force participation and labor market exit among the pre-retirement population by race, Hispanic origin, and sex. *Journal of Gerontology: Social Sciences, 55B*, S14–S27.

Flirski, M., & Sobow, T. (2005). Biochemical markers and risk factors of Alzheimer's disease. *Current Alzheimer Research, 2*, 47–64.

Fogel, B. S. (1992). Psychological aspects of staying at home. *Generations, 16*, 15–19.

Fogler, J. & Stern, L. (1994). *Teaching memory improvement to adults*. Baltimore, MD: Johns Hopkins University Press.

Foley, D. J., Monjan, A. A., Brown, S. L. et al. (1995). Sleep complaints among elderly persons: An epidemiologic study of three communities. *Sleep, 18*, 425–432.

Folkman, S., Lazarus, R. S., Pimley, S., & Novacek, J. (1987). Age differences in stress and coping processes. *Psychology & Aging, 2*, 171–184.

Folstein, M. F., Folstein, S. E., & McHugh, P. R. (1975). "Mini-Mental State," a practical method for grading the cognitive state of patients for the clinician. *Journal of Psychiatric Research, 12*, 189–198.

Fonda, S. J., Wallace, R. B., & Herzog, A. R. (2001). Changes in driving patterns and worsen-ing depressive symptoms among older adults. *Journal of Gerontology: Social Sciences, 56B*, S343–S351.

Foos, P. W. (1995). Working memory resource allocation by young, middle-aged, and old adults. *Experimental Aging Research, 21*, 239–250.

Foos, P. W. (1997). Effects of memory training on anxiety and performance in older adults. *Educational Gerontology, 23*, 243–252.

Foos, P. W. (2001). A self-reference exercise for teaching life expectancy. *Teaching*

Foos, P. W. & Clark, M. C. (April, 1994). *Cross-cultural similarities and differences in images of aging*. Paper presented at the annual meeting of the Southern Gerontological Society, Charlotte, NC.

Foos, P. W., & Sarno, A. J. (1998). Adult age differences in semantic and episodic memory. *Journal of Genetic Psychology, 159*, 297–312.

Foos, P. W., Boone, D., & Clark, M. C. (2003, Nov.). *The absence of adult age differences in divergent thinking: Implications for creativity*. Paper presented at the annual meetings of the Gerontological Society of America, San Diego, California.

Foos, P. W., Clark, M. C., & Terrell, D. (2006). Adult age, gender, and race group differences in images of aging. *Journal of Genetic Psychology, 167*, 309–325.

Ford, G. R., Haley, W. E., Thrower, S. L., West, C. A. C., & Harrell, L. E. (1996). Utility of Mini-Mental State Exam scores in predicting functional impairment among white and African American dementia patients. *Journal of Gerontology: Medical Sciences, 51A*, M185–M188.

Ford, M. T., Heinen, B. A., & Langkamer, K. L. (2007). Work and family satisfaction and conflict: A meta-analysis of cross-domain relations. *Journal of Applied Psychology, 92*, 57–80.

Fozard, J. L. (1990). Vision and hearing in aging. In J. E. Birren & K. W. Schaie (Eds.), *Handbook of the psychology of aging* (3rd ed., pp. 150–170). San Diego, CA: Academic Press.

Fozard, J. L., Rietsema, J., Bouma, H., & Graafmans, J. A. M. (2000). Gerontechnology: Creating enabling environments for the challenges and opportunities of aging. *Educational Gerontology, 26*, 331–344.

Fozard, J. L., Vercruyssen, M., Reynolds, S. L., & Hancock, P. A. (1994). Age differences and changes in reaction time: The Baltimore Longitudinal Study of Aging. *Journal of Gerontology: Psychological Sciences, 49*, P179–P189.

Fraas, M., Lockwood, J., Neils-Strunjas, J., Shidler, M., Krikorian, R., & Weiler, E. (2002). "What's his name?" A comparison of elderly participants' and undergraduate students' misnamings. *Archives of Gerontology & Geriatrics, 34*, 155–165.

Fraisse, P. (1984). Perception and estimation of time. *Annual Review of Psychology, 35*, 1–36.

Francese, P. (2004). Labor of love. *American Demographics, 26*, 40–41.

Frassetto, L. A., Todd, K. M., Morris, C., Jr., & Sebastian, A. (2000). Worldwide incidence of hip fracture in elderly women: Relation to consumption of animal and vegetable foods. *Journal of Gerontology: Medical Sciences, 55A*, M585–M592.

Frazier, L. D., & Waid, L. D. (1999). Influences on anxiety in later life: The role of health status, health perceptions, and health locus of control. *Aging & Mental Health, 3*, 213–220.

Fredrickson, B. L. & Carstensen, L. L. (1990). Choosing social partners: How old age and anticipated endings make people more selective. *Psychology & Aging, 5*, 335–347.

Freed, C. R., Greene, P. E., Breeze, R. E., Tsai, W-Y., DuMouchel, W., Kao, R., Dillon, S., Winfield, H., Culver, S., Trojanowski, J. Q., Eidelberg, D., & Fahn, S. (2001). Transplantation of embryonic dopamine neurons for severe Parkinson's disease. *The New England Journal of Medicine, 344*, 710–719.

Fried, L. F., Shlipak, M. G., Stehman-Breen, C., Mittalhenkle, A., Seliger, S., Sarnak, M., Robbins, J., Siscovick, D., Harris, T. B., Newman, A. B., & Cauley, J. A. (2006). Kidney function predicts the rate of bone loss in older individuals: The cardiovascular health study. *Journal of Gerontology: Medical Sciences, 61A*, 743–748.

Friedman, H. S., Tucker, J. S., Schwartz, J. E., Martin, L. R., Tomlinson-Keasey, C., Wingard, D. L., & Criqui, M. H. (1995). Childhood conscientiousness and longevity: Health behaviors and cause of death. *Journal of Personality & Social Psychology, 68*, 696–703.

Friedman, H. S., Tucker, J. S., Schwartz, J. E., Tomlinson-Keasey, C., Martin, L. R., Wingard, D. L., & Criqui, M. H. (1995). Psychosocial and behavioral predictors of longevity. *American Psychologist, 50*, 69–78.

Fries, J. F. (1980). Aging, natural death, and the compression of morbidity. *New England Journal of Medicine, 303*, 130–136.

Fries, J. F. (1999). *Preparing for a long life: Functional capacity.* Presented at the U.S. Administration on Aging Symposium, "Longevity in the new American century" Baltimore, MD, March 29–30. Available from *www.aoa.gov/Baltimore99/J.F. Fries-bio.html.*

Friis, R. H., Nomura, W. L., Ma, C. X., & Swan, J. H. (2003). Socioepidemiologic and health-related correlates of walking for exercise among the elderly: Results from the longitudinal study of aging. *Journal of Aging & Physical Activity, 11*, 54–66.

Fritsch, T., McClendon, M. J., Smyth, K. A., Lerner, A. J., Friedland, R. P., & Larsen, J. D. (2007). Cognitive functioning in healthy aging: The role of reserve and lifestyle factors early in life. *The Gerontologist, 47*, 307–322.

Fronstin, P. (1999). Retirement patterns and employee benefits: Do benefits matter? *Gerontologist, 39*, 37–47.

Fry, P. S. (1997). Grandparents' reactions to the death of a grandchild: An exploratory factor analytic study. *Omega, 35*, 119–140.

Fukukawa, Y., Nakashima, C., Tsuboi, S., Kozakai, R., Doyo, W., Niino, N., Ando, F., & Shimokata, H. (2004). Age differences in the effect of physical activity on depressive symptoms. *Psychology & Aging, 19*, 346–351.

Funderbunk, B., Damron-Rodriguez, J., Storms, L. L., & Solomon, D. H. (2006). Endurance of undergraduate attitudes toward older adults. *Educational Gerontology, 32*, 447–462.

Funkhouser, A. T., Hirsbrunner, H. P., Cornu, C., & Bahro, M. (1999). Dreams and dreaming among the elderly: An overview. *Aging & Mental Health, 3*, 10–20.

Furner, S. E., Wallace, K., Arguelles, L., Miles, T., & Goldberg, J. (2006). Twin studies of depressive symptoms among older African American women. *Journal of Gerontology: Psychological Sciences, 61B*, P355–P361.

Fuzhong, L., Harmer, P., Fisher, K. J., McAuley, E., Chaumeton, N., Eckstrom, E., & Wilson, N. L. (2005). Tai chi and fall reductions in older adults: A randomized controlled trial. *Journal of Gerontology: Medical Sciences, 60A*, 187–194.

Gale, W. G. (1997, Oct.). When baby boomers retire: The coming challenge. *Current* (396), 8–12.

Gall, T. L., Evans, D. R., & Howard, J. (1997). The retirement adjustment process: Changes in the well-being of male retirees across time. *Journal of Gerontology: Psychological Sciences, 52B*, P110–P117.

Gallagher, W. (1993). Midlife myths. *Atlantic Monthly, 271*, 51–68.

Gallant, M. (1987). *Alcoholism: A guide to diagnosis, intervention, and treatment.* New York: Norton.

Gallo, J. J., Cooper-Patrick, L., & Lesikar, S. (1998). Depressive symptoms of Whites and African Americans aged 60 years and older. *Journal of Gerontology: Psychological Sciences, 53B*, P277–P286.

Gallo, W. T., Bradley, E. H., Dubin, J. A., Jones, R. N., Falba, T. A., Teng, H-M., & Kasl, S. V. (2006). The persistence of depressive symptoms in older workers who experience involuntary job loss: Results from the Health and Retirement Survey. *Journal of Gerontology: Social Sciences, 61B*, S221–S228.

Gallo, W. T., Bradley, E. H., Siegel, M., & Kasl, S. V. (2000). Health effects of involuntary job loss among older workers: Findings from the Health and Retirement Survey. *Journal of Gerontology: Social Sciences, 55B*, S131–S140.

Gallo, W. T., Bradley, E. H., Siegel, M., & Kasl, S. V. (2001). The impact of involuntary job loss on subsequent alcohol consumption by older workers: Findings from the health and retirement survey. *Journal of Gerontology: Social Sciences, 56B*, S3–S9.

Gambrell, R. D. (1987). Estrogen replacement therapy for the elderly woman. *Medical Aspects of Human Sexuality, 21*(5), 81–93.

Ganzini, L. & Atkinson, R. M. (1996). Substance abuse. In J. Sadavoy, L. W. Lazarus, L. F. Jarvik, & G. T. Grossberg (Eds.), *Comprehensive review of geriatric psychiatry II* (2nd ed., pp. 659–692). Washington, DC: American Psychiatric Press.

Gardner, A. W. & Poehlman, E. T. (1995). Predictors of the age-related increase in blood pressure in men and women. *Journal of Gerontology: Medical Sciences, 50A*, M1–6.

Gardner, H. (1993). *Multiple intelligences: The theory in practice.* New York: Basic Books.

Garfein, A. J., Schaie, K. W., & Willis, S. L. (1988). Microcomputer proficiency in later-middle-aged and older adults: Teaching old dogs new tricks. *Social Behaviour, 3*, 131–148.

Garfinkel, D. & Zisapel, N. (1998). The use of melatonin for sleep. *Nutrition, 14*, 53.

Garrard, J., Rolnick, S. J., Nitz, N. M., Luepke, L., Jackson, J., Fischer, L. R., Leibson, C., Bland, P. C., Heinrich, R., & Waller, L. A. (1998). Clinical detection of depression among community-based elderly people with self-reported symptoms of depression. *Journal of Gerontology: Medical Sciences, 53A*, M92–M101.

Garstka, T. A., Schmitt, M. T., Branscombe, N. R., & Hummert, M. L. (2004). How young and old adults differ in their responses to perceived age discrimination. *Psychology & Aging, 19*, 326–335.

Gatz, M. (2007). Genetics, dementia, and the elderly. *Current Directions in Psychological Science, 16*, 123–127.

Gatz, M., & Hurwitz, M. (1990). Are old people more depressed? Cross-sectional data on Center for Epidemiological Studies depression scale factors. *Psychology & Aging, 5*, 284–290.

Gatz, M., Pedersen, N. L., Berg, S., Johansson, K., Mortimer, J., Posner, S. F., Viitane, M., Winblad,

B., & Anlbom, P. (1997). Heritability for Alzheimer's disease: The study of dementia in Swedish twins. *Journal of Gerontology: Medical Sciences, 52A*, M117–M125.

Gavrilov, L. A., Gavrilova, N. S., Semenova, V. G., Evdokushkina, G. N., Krut'ko, V. N., Gavrilova, A. L., Evdokushkina, N. N., & Kushnareva, Y. E. (1998). Life-span inheritance in humans: Effects of paternal and maternal longevity on offspring life-span. *Doklady Biological Sciences, 360*, 281–283.

Gavrilova, N. S., Gavrilov, L. A., Evdokushkina, G. N., Semyonova, V. G., Gavrilova, A. L., Evdokushkina, N. N. et al. (1998). Evolution, mutations, and human longevity: European royal and noble families. *Human Biology, 70,* 799–804.

Gazmararian,J. A., Baker, D. W., Williams, M.V., Parker, R. M., Scott, T. L., Green, D. C., et al. (1999). Health literacy among Medicare enrollees in a managed care organization. *Journal of the American Medical Association, 281*, 545–551.

Gellis, Z. D., Sherman, S., & Lawrance, F. (2003). First year graduate social work students' knowledge of and attitude toward older adults. *Educational Gerontology, 29*, 1–16.

Gendell, M. (1998). Trends in retirement age in four countries, 1965–95. *Monthly Labor Review, 121* (8), 20–30.

Gerbner, G., Gross, L., Signorielli, N., & Morgan, M. (1980). Aging with television: Images on television dramas and conceptions of social reality. *Journal of Communication, 30*, 37–47.

Gerstorf, D., Herlitz, A., & Smith, J. (2006). Stability of sex differences in cognition in advanced old age: The role of education and attrition. *Journal of Gerontology: Psychological Sciences, 61B*, P245–P249.

Ghochikyan, A., Petrushina, I., Lees, A., Vasilevko, V., Movsesyan, N., Karapetyan, A., Agadjanyan, M. G., & Cribbs, D. H. (2006). A_-immunotherapy for Alzheimer's disease using mannan-amyloid-beta peptide immunoconjugates. *DNA & Cell Biology, 25*, 571–580.

Giacobini, E. (1998). Aging, Alzheimer's disease, and estrogen therapy. *Experimental Gerontology, 33*, 865–869.

Gibler, K. M., Lumpkin, J. R., & Moschis, G. P. (1998). Making the decision to move to retirement housing. *Journal of Consumer Marketing, 15*, 44–54.

Gijana, E. W. M., Louw, J., & Manganyi, N. C. (1989). Thoughts about death and dying in an African sample. *Omega, 20*, 245–258.

Gilewski, M. J., Zelinski, E. M., & Schaie, K. W. (1990). The Memory Functioning Questionnaire for assessment of memory complaints in adulthood and old age. *Psychology & Aging, 5*, 482–490.

Gillette-Guyonnet, S., Andrieu, S., Cortes, F., Nourhashemi, F., Cantet, C., Ousset, P-J. et al., (2006). Outcome of Alzheimer's disease: Potential impact of cholinesterase inhibitors. *Journal of Gerontology: Medical Sciences, 61A*, 516–520.

Giltay, E. J., Kamphuis, M. H., Kalmijin, S., Zitman, F. G., & Kromhout, D. (2006). Dispositional optimism and the risk of cardiovascular death: The Zutphen Elderly Study. *Archives of Internal Medicine, 166*, 431–436.

Giovino, G. A., Henningfield, J. E., Tomar, S. L., Escobedo, L. G., & Slade, J. (1995). Epidemiology of tobacco use and dependence. *Epidemiological Review, 17*, 48–65.

Gitlin, L. N., Reever, K., Dennis, M. P., Mathieu, E. & Hauck, W. W. (2006). Enhancing quality of life of families who use adult day services: Short- and long-term effects of the Adult Day Services Plus program. *The Gerontologist, 46*, 630–639.

Glaser, R. (1986). Intelligence as acquired proficiency. In R. J. Sternberg & D. K. Detterman (Eds.), *What is intelligence? Contemporary viewpoints on its nature and definition.* (pp. 77–83). Norwood, NJ: Ablex.

Glasheen, L. K. & Crowley, S. L. (1998, May). A family affair: Hospice eases the way at life's end. *AARP Bulletin, 39*(5), 2, 10–11, 13.

Glass, A. L. & Holyoak, K. J. (1986). *Cognition.* New York: Random House.

Glass, J. C., Jr. & Flynn, D. K. (2000). Retirement needs and preparation of rural middle-aged persons. *Educational Gerontology, 26*, 109–134.

Glass, J. C., Jr., Mustian, R. D., & Carter, L. R. (1986). Knowledge and attitudes of health-care providers toward sexuality in the institutionalized elderly. *Educational Gerontology, 12*, 465–475.

Glass, T. A., Prigerson, H., Kasl, S. V., & Mendes de Leon, C. F. (1995). The effects of negative life events on alcohol consumption among older men and women. *Journal of Gerontology, 50B*, 5205–5216.

Gold, D. T. (1989). Sibling relationships in old age: A typology. *International Journal of Aging & Human Development, 28*, 37–51.

Gold, D. T. (1990). Late-life sibling relationships: Does race affect typological distribution? *Gerontologist, 30*, 741–748.

Gold, D. T., Woodbury, M. A., & George, L. K. (1990). Relationship classification using grade of membership analysis: A typology of sibling relationships in late life. *Journal of Gerontology: Social Sciences, 45*, S43–S51.

Goldberg, E. L., Comstock, G. W., & Harlow, S. D. (1988). Emotional problems and widowhood: Problems and possibilities. *Journal of Gerontology: Social Sciences, 43*, S206–S208.

Goldman, N., Turra, C. M., Glei, D. A., Seplaki, C. L., Lin, Y-H., & Weinstein, M. (2006). Predicting mortality from clinical and nonclinical biomarkers. *Journal of Gerontology: Medical Sciences, 61A*, 1070–1074.

Goldstein, I. & Hatzichristou, D. G. (1994). Epidemiology of impotence. In A. H. Bennett (Ed.), *Impotence: Diagnosis and manangement of erectile dysfunction* (pp. 1–17). Philadelphia: W. B. Saunders.

Goodman, C. C. (2003). Multigenerational triads in grandparent-headed families. *Journal of Gerontology: Social Sciences, 58B*, S281–S289.

Goodpaster, B. H., Park, S. W., Harris, T. B., Kritchevsky, S. B., Nevitt, M., Schwartz, A. V. et al. (2007). The loss of skeletal muscle strength, mass, and quality in older adults: The health, aging, and body composition study. *Journal of Gerontology: Medical Sciences, 61A*, 1059–1064.

Grant, B. S., Harford, T. C., Dawson, D. A., Chou, P., Dufour, M., & Pickering, R. (1994). Prevalence of *DSM-IV* alcohol abuse and dependency: United States, 1992. *Alcohol, Health, & Research World, 18*, 243–248.

Grant, W. B., Campbell, A., Itzhaki, R. F., & Savory, J. (2002). The significance of environmental factors in the etiology of Alzheimer's disease. *Journal of Alzheimer's Disease, 4*, 179–189.

Grayson, P. J. (1997). Technology and home adaptation. In S. Lanspery & J. Hyde (Eds.). *Staying put: Adapting places instead of people* (pp. 55–74). Amityville, New York: Baywood Publishing.

Grossman, A. H., D'Augelli, A. R., & Hershberger, S. L. (2000). Social support networks of lesbian, gay, and bisexual adults 60 years of age and older. *Journal of Gerontology: Psychological Sciences, 55B*, P171–P179.

Gruenewald, T. L., Karlamangla, A. S., Greendale, G. A., Singer, B. H., & Seeman, T. E. (2007). Feelings of usefulness to others, disability, and mortality in older adults: The MacArthur Study of Successful Aging. *Journal of Gerontology: Psychological Sciences, 62B*, P28–P37.

Guaraldi, V. (1962). *Cast your fate to the wind*. On *The Best of Vince Guaraldi* (record album). New York: downloaded from www.EncoreMusic.com/piano September 20, 2007.

Guarnaccia, C. A., Hayslip, B., Jr., & Landry, L. P. (1999). Influence of perceived preventability of the death and emotional closeness to the deceased: A test of Bugen's model. *Omega, 39*, 261–276.

Guilford, J. P. (1956). The stucture of intellect. *Psychological Bulletin, 53*, 267–293.

Guilford, J. P. (1967). *The nature of human intelligence*. New York: McGraw-Hill.

Guralnik, J. M., Butterworth, S., Wadsworth, M. E. J., & Kuh, D. (2006). Childhood socioeconomic status predicts physical functioning a half century later. *Journal of Gerontology Medical Sciences, 61A,* 694–701.

Gurland, B. (1996). Epidemiology of psychiatric disorders. In J. Sadavoy, L. W. Lazarus, L. F. Jarvik, & G. T. Grossberg (Eds.), *Comprehensive review of geriatric psychiatry II* (2nd ed., pp. 3–41). Washington, DC: American Psychiatric Press.

Gurland, B., Wilder, D., Cross, P., Phil, M., Lantigua, R., Teresi, J., Barrett, V., Stern, Y., & Mayeux, R. (1995). Relative rates of dementia by multiple case definitions, over two prevalence periods, in three sociocultural groups. *American Journal of Geriatric Psychiatry, 3,* 6–20.

Gurland, B., Wilder, D., Lantigua, R., Mayeux, R., Stern, Y., Chen, J., Cross, P., & Killeffer, E. (1997). Differences in rates of dementia between ethno-racial groups. In L. G. Martin & B. J. Soldo (Eds.), *Racial and ethnic differences in the health of older Americans* (pp. 233–269). Washington, DC: National Academy Press.

Guttman, D. L. (1987). *Reclaimed powers: Men and women in later life.* Evanston, IL: Northwestern University Press.

Guttman, M., Kish, S. J., & Furukawa, Y. (2003). Current concepts in the diagnosis and management of Parkinson's disease. *Canadian Medical Association, 168,* 293–301.

Ha, J-H., Carr, D., Utz, R. L., & Nesse, R. (2006). Older adults' perceptions of intergenerational support after widowhood. *Journal of Family Issues, 27,* 3–30.

Habermas, T. & Bluck, S. (2000). Getting a life: The emergence of the life story in adolescence. *Psychological Bulletin, 126,* 748–769.

Hagstadius, S. & Risberg, J. (1989). Regional cerebral blood flow characteristics and variations with age in resting normal subjects. *Brain & Cognition, 10,* 28–43.

Haley, W. E., Brown, S. L., & Levine, E. G. (1987). Family caregiver appraisals of patient behavioral disturbance in senile dementia. *Clinical Gerontologist, 6,* 25–34.

Hall, G. S. (1922). *Senescence: The last half of life.* New York: Appleton.

Halpern. D. F. (2005). Psychology at the intersection of work and family. *American Psychologist, 60,* 397–409.

Hamilton, J. B. (1948). The role of testicular secretions as indicated by the effects of castration in man and by studies of pathological conditions and short lifespan associated with maleness. *Recent Progress in Hormone Research, 3,* 257–324.

Hamner, T. J. & Turner, P. H. (1996). *Parenting in comtemporary society.* Boston: Allyn & Bacon.

Hannson, R. O., DeKoekkoek, P. D., Neece, W. M., & Patterson, D. W. (1997). Successful aging at work: Annual review, 1992–1996: The older worker and transitions to retirement. *Journal of Vocational Behavior, 51,* 202–233.

Hanrahan, P. & Luchins, D. J. (1995). Access to hospice programs in end-stage dementia: A national survey of hospice programs. *Journal of the American Geriatric Society, 43,* 56–59.

Hansot, E. (1996). A letter from a patient's daughter. *Analysis of Internal Medicine, 125,* 149–151.

Harris, L. A., & Dollinger, S. M. C. (2002). Individual differences in personality traits and anxiety about aging. *Personality & Individual Differences, 34,* 187–194.

Harris, M. B. (1994). Growing old gracefully: Age concealment and gender. *Journal of Gerontology: Psychological Sciences, 49,* P149–P159.

Harris, S. B. (1996). For better or worse: Spouse abuse grown old. *Journal of Elder Abuse & Neglect, 8,* 1–33.

Hart, R. W., & Setlow, R. B. (1982). DNA repair and life span of mammals. In P. C. Hanawalt & R. B. Setlow (Eds.), *Molecular mechanisms for repair of DNA,* Part B. New York: Plenum.

Harter, S. (1990). Identity and self development. In S. Feldman & G. E Elliott (Eds.), *At the threshold: The developing adolescent.* Cambridge, MA: Harvard University Press.

Harvey, G. & Lawler, J. The rights of elderly people in a nursing home: A little creativity, a lot of respect, a taste for adventure, and an allergy for bureaucracy. In L. F. Heumann, M. E. McCall, & Boldy, D. P. (Eds.). *Empowering frail elderly people: Opportunities and impediments in hous-*

ing, health, and support service delivery (pp. 155–173). Westport, CT: Praeger Publishers.

Harwood, J., & Lin, M-C. (2000). Affiliation, pride, exchange, and distance in grandparents' accounts of relationships with their college-aged grandchildren. *Journal of Communication, 50*(3), 31–47.

Haught, P. A., Walls, R. T., Laney, J. D. Leavell, A., & Stuzen, S. (1999). Child and adolescent knowledge and attitudes about older adults across time and states. *Educational Gerontology, 25,* 501–517.

Havighurst, R. J. (1972). *Developmental tasks and education.* New York: McKay.

Haward, L. R. C. (1977). Cognition in dementia presenilis. In W. L. Smith & M. Kinsbourne (Eds.), *Aging and dementia* (pp. 189–202). New York: Spectrum Publications.

Hawkes, W. G., Wehren, L., Orwig, D., Hebel, R., & Magaziner, J. (2006). Gender differences in functioning after hip fracture. *Journal of Gerontology: Medical Sciences, 61A,* 495–499.

Hayashi, T., Ito, I., Kano, H., Endo, H., & Iguchi, A. (2000). Estriol (E3) replacement improves endothelial function and bone mineral density in very elderly women. *Journal of Gerontology: Biological Sciences, 55A,* B183–B190.

Hayflick, L. (1965). The limited in vitro lifetime of human diploid cell strains. *Experimental Cell Research, 37,* 614–636.

Hayflick, L. (1996). *How and why we age.* New York: Ballantine Books.

Hayslip, B., Jr., Ragow-O'Brien, D., & Guarnaccia, C. A. (1998–1999). The relationship of cause of death to attitudes toward funerals and bereavement adjustment. *Omega, 38,* 297–312.

Hayslip, B., Shore, J., Henderson, C. E., & Lambert, P. L. (1998). Custodial grandparenting and the impact of grandchildren with problems on role satisfaction and role meaning. *Journal of Gerontology: Social Sciences, 53B,* S164–S173.

Hazan, H. (1996). *From first principles: An experiment in aging.* Westport, CT: Bergin & Garvey.

Health Care Finance Administration. (2007). National Health Expenditures, 2001. Available from *www.hcfa.gov.*

Healy, B. P. (1997). A sage brain, a sturdy skeleton, and a funny bone: A longevity lesson from Madame Calment. *Journal of Women's Health, 6,* 503–504.

Heckhausen, J. (1997). Developmental regulation across adulthood: Primary and secondary control of age-related challenges. *Developmental Psychology, 33,* 176–187.

Heidrich, S. M., & Denney, N. W. (1994). Does social problem solving differ from other types of problem solving during the adult years? *Experimental Aging Research, 20,* 105–126.

Heller, K. S. & Wilber, L. A. (1990). Hearing loss, aging, and speech perception in reverberation and noise. *Journal of Speech and Hearing Research, 33,* 149–155.

Helson, R. & Wink, P. (1992). Personality change in women from the early 40s to the early 50s. *Psychology & Aging, 7,* 46–55.

Helson, R. (1993). The Mills classes of 1958 and 1960: College in the fifties, young adulthood in the sixties. In K. D. Hulbert & D. T. Schuster (Eds.), *Women's lives through time* (pp. 190–210). San Francisco, CA: Jossey-Bass.

Hendrie, H. C. (2001). Exploration of environmental and genetic risk factors for Alzheimer's disease: The value of cross-cultural studies. *Current Directions in Psychological Science, 10,* 98–101.

Hendrie, H. C., Callahan, C. M., Levitt, E. E., Hui, S. L., Musick, B., Austrom, M. G., Nurnberger, J. I. Jr., & Tierney, W. M. (1995). Prevalence rates of major depressive disorders: The effect of varying the diagnostic criteria in an older primary care population. *American Journal of Geriatric Psychiatry, 3,* 119–131.

Henry, J. D., MacLeod, M. S., Phillips, L. H., & Crawford, J. R. (2004). A meta-analytic review of prospective memory and aging. *Psychology & Aging, 19,* 27–39.

Hermann, M. (1998, March-April). A call for calcium. *Modern Maturity,* 66–67.

Hertzog, C., Dixon, R. A., & Hultsch, D. F. (1990). Relationships between metamemory, memory predictions, and memory task performance in adults. *Psychology & Aging, 5*, 215–227.

Heslop, P., Smith, G. D., Carroll, D., Macleod, J., Hyland, F., & Hart, C. (2001). Perceived stress and coronary heart disease risk factors: The contribution of socioeconomic position. *British Journal of Health Psychology, 6*, 167–178.

Heumann, J. F. (2001). The role of the built environment in holistic delivery of home and community based care services to frail elderly. In L. F. Heumann, M. E. McCall, & Boldy, D. P. (Eds.). *Empowering frail elderly people: Opportunities and impediments in housing, health, and support service delivery* (pp. 119–136). Westport, CT: Praeger Publishers.

Hickman, J. M., Rogers, W. A., & Fisk, A. D. (2007). Training older adults to use new technology. *Journals of Gerontology: Series B, 62B* (Special Issue I), 77–84.

Higashi, T., Wenger, N. S., Adams, J. L., Fung, C., Roland, M., McGlynn, E. A. et al., (2007). Relationship between number of medical conditions and quality of care. *New England Journal of Medicine, 356*, 2496–2504.

High, D. M. (1993). Advance directives and the elderly: A study of intervention strategies to increase use. *The Gerontologist, 33*, 342–349.

Hilbourne, M. (1999). Living together full time? Middle-class couples approaching retirement. *Aging & Society, 19*, 161–183.

Hill, R., Bäckman, L., Wahlin, A., & Winblad, B. (1995). Visuospatial performance in very old demented persons. *Dementia, 6*, 49–54.

Hoch, C. C., Reynolds III, C. F., Buysse, D. J., Monk, T. H., Nowell, P., Begley, A. E., Hall, F., & Dew, M. A. (2001). Protecting sleep quality in later life: A pilot study of bed restriction and sleep hygiene. *Journal of Gerontology: Psychological Sciences, 56B*, P52–P59.

Hofferberth, B. (1994). The efficacy of Egb 761 in patients with senile dementia of the Alzheimer's type, a double-blind, placebo-controlled study on different levels of investigation. *Human Psychopharmacology Clinical & Experimental, 9*, 215–222.

Hogan, R., Kim, M., & Perrucci, C. C. (1997). Racial inequality in men's employment and retirement earnings. *Sociological Quarterly, 38*, 431–438.

Holland C. A., & Rabbitt, P. M. A. (1992). People's awareness of their age-related sensory and cognitive deficits and the implications for road safety. *Applied Cognitive Psychology, 6*, 217–231.

Hollis-Sawyer, L. A. & Sterns, H. L. (1999). A novel goal-oriented approach for training older adult computer novices: Beyond the effects of individual difference factors. *Educational Gerontology, 25*, 661–684.

Holloszy, J. O. (1998). Longevity of exercising rats: Effect of an antioxidant supplemented diet. *Mechanisms of Ageing & Development, 100*, 211–219.

Holmes E. R. & Holmes L. D. (1995). *Other cultures, elder years* (2nd ed.). Thousand Oaks, CA: Sage.

Holmes, D. S. (1987). The influence of meditation versus rest on physiological arousal: A second examination. In M. A. West (Ed.), *The psychology of meditation*. New York: Oxford University Press.

Holtzman, R. E., Rebok, G. W., Saczynski, J. S., Kouzis, A. C., Doyle, K. W., & Eaton, W. W. (2004). Social network characteristics and cognition in middle-aged and older adults. *Journal of Gerontology: Psychological Sciences, 59B*, P278–P284.

Honig, M. (1998). Married women's retirement expectations: Do pensions and Social Security matter? *American Economic Review, 88*, 202–206.

Horn, J. L. (1982). The theory of fluid and crystallized intelligence in relation to concepts of cognitive psychology and aging in adulthood. In F. I. M. Craik & S. Trehub (Eds.), *Aging and cognitive processes*. New York: Plenum.

Horner, K. L., Rushton, J. P., & Vernon, P. A. (1986). Relation between aging and research productivity. *Psychology & Aging, 1*, 319–324.

Hornyak, M., & Trenkwalder, C. (2004). Restless leg syndromes and periodic limb movement disorder in the elderly. *Journal of Psychosomatic Research, 56*, 543–548.

Horowitz, A., Brennan, M., Reinhardt, J. P., & MacMillan, T. (2006). The impact of assistive device use on disability and depression among older adults with age-related vision impairments. *Journal of Gerontology: Social Sciences, 61B*, S274–S280.

Hortobágyi, T., Zheng, D., Weidner, M., Lambert, N. J., Westbrook, S., & Houmard, J. A. (1995). The influence of aging on muscle strength and muscle fiber characteristics with special reference to eccentric strength. *Journal of Gerontology: Biological Sciences, 50B*, B399–406.

Howarth, G. (1998). "Just live for today", living, caring, ageing, and dying. *Aging & Society, 18*, 673–689.

Howells, J. (1998). The best places to retire in America. *Consumers Digest, 37*(5), 67–70.

Hu, P., Bretsky, P., Crimmins, E. M., Guralnik, J. M., Reuben, D. B., & Seeman, T. E. (2006). Association between serum beta-carotene levels and decline of cognitive function in high-functioning older persons with or without Apolipoprotein E 4 alleles: MacArthur studies of successful aging. *Journal of Gerontology: Medical Sciences, 61A*, 616–620.

Huang, T-T., Carlson, E. J., Gillespie, A. M., Shi, Y., & Epstein, C. J. (2000). Ubiquitous overexpression of CuZn superoxide dismutase does not extend life span for mice. *Journal of Gerontology: Biological Sciences, 55A*, B5–B9.

Hulicka, I. M. (1982). Memory functioning in late adulthood. In F. I. M. Craik & S. Trehub (Eds.), *Aging and cognitive processes* (pp. 331–351): New York: Plenum.

Hull, R. H. (1980). Talking to the hearing-impaired older adult. *Asha, 22* (Journal of the American Speech, Language, Hearing Association), 427.

Hultsch, D. F., Hertzog, C., Small, B. J., & Dixon, R. A. (1999). Use it or lose it: Engaged lifestyle as a buffer of cognitive decline in aging? *Psychology & Aging, 14*, 245–263.

Hurd, L. C. (1999). 'We're not old': Older women's negotiation of aging and oldness. *Journal of Aging Studies, 13*, 419–439.

Huyck, M. H. (1990). Gender differences in aging. In J. E. Birren & K. W. Schaie (Eds.), *Handbook of the psychology of aging* (pp. 124–132). San Diego, CA: Academic Press.

Iams, H. M. (1986). Characteristics of the longest job for newly disabled workers: Findings from the New Beneficiary Survey. *Social Security Bulletin, 49*(12), 13–18.

Ice, G. H., King, S. V., Owino, E., & Anastasia, Sister P. (November, 2006). *KeNew Yorkan grandparents raising grandchildren: Perspectives of discipline and misbehavior.* Paper presented at the annual meetings of the Gerontological Society of America, Dallas, TX.

Idler, E. L. & Kasl, S. V. (1997a). Religion among disabled and nondisabled persons I: Cross-sectional patterns in health practices, social activities, and well-being. *Journal of Gerontology: Social Sciences, 52B*, S294–S305.

Idler, E. L. & Kasl, S. V. (1997b). Religion among disabled and nondisabled persons II: Attendance at religious services as a predictor of the course of disability. *Journal of Gerontology: Social Sciences, 52B*, S306–S316.

Ingram, D. K., Weindruch, R., Spangler, E. L., Freeman, J. R., & Wolford, R. L. (1987). Dietary restriction benefits learning and motor performance of aged mice. *Journal of Gerontology, 42*, 78–81.

Inouye, S. K., & Ferrucci, L. (2006). Elucidating the pathophysiology of delirium and the interrelationship of delirium and dementia. *Journal of Gerontology: Medical Sciences, 61A*, 1277–1280.

Inouye, S. K., Robison, J. T., Froehlich, T. E., & Richardson, E. D. (1998). The Time and Change Test: A simple screening test for dementia. *Journal of Gerontology: Medical Sciences, 53A*, M281–M286.

Irwin, M. R., Pike, J. L., & Cole, J. C. (2003). The effects of a behavioral intervention, Tai Chi Chih, on Varicella-Zoster virus specific immunity and health functioning in older adults. *Psychosomatic Medicine, 65,* 824–830.

Isingrini, M., Fontane, R., Taconnat, L., & Duportal, A. (1995). Aging and encoding in memory: False alarms and decision criteria in a word-pair recognition task. *International Journal of Aging & Human Development, 41,* 79–88.

Iwarsson, S. Wahl, H-W., New Yorkgren, C., Oswald, F., Sixsmith, A., Sixsmith, J., Széman, Z., & Tomsone, S. (2007). Importance of the home-environment for healthy aging: Conceptual and methodological background of the European ENABLE-AGE Project. *The Gerontologist, 47,* 78–84.

Jacobs, E. & Worcester, R. (1990). *We British: Britain under the MORI-scope.* London: Weidenfeld & Nicholson.

Jacoby, L. L., & Rhodes, M. G. (2006). False remembering in the aged. *Current Directions in Psychological Science, 15,* 49–53.

Jaffrey, M. (1995). Cremation along the Ganges. In J. O. Reilly & L. Habegger (Eds.), *Traveler's tales: India.* San Francisco, CA: Traveler's Tales Inc.

James, L. E., & Burke, D. M. (2000). Phonological priming effects on word retrieval and tip-of-the-tongue experiences in young and older adults. *Journal of Experimental Psychology: Learning, Memory, & Cognition, 26,* 1378–1391.

Jang, Y., Borenstein, A. R., Chiriboga, D. A., & Mortimer, J. A. (2005). Depressive symptoms among African American and white older adults. *Journal of Gerontology: Psychological Sciences, 60B,* P313–P319.

Janicki, M. P., & Ansello, E. F. (Eds.). (2000). Community supports for aging adults with lifelong disabilities. Baltimore, MD: Brookes.

Jansari, A. & Parkin, A. J. (1996). Things that go bump in your life: Explaining the reminiscence bump in autobiographical memory. *Psychology & Aging, 11,* 85–91.

Jarvik, L. F. & Cohen, D. A. (1973). A biobehavioral approach to intellectual changes with aging. In C. Eisdorfer & M. P. Lawton (Eds.), *The psychology of adult development and aging.* Washington, DC: American Psychological Association.

Jecker, N. S. & Schneiderman, L. J. (1994). Is dying young worse than dying old? *The Gerontologist, 34,* 66–72.

Jee, S. H., Sull, J. W., Park, J., Lee, S-Y., Ohrr, H., Guallar, E., & Samet, J. M. (2006). Body-mass index and mortality in Korean men and women. *The New England Journal of Medicine, 355,* 779–787.

Johansson, B. & Zarit, S. H. (1997). Early cognitive markers of the incidence of dementia and mortality: A longitudinal population-based study of the oldest old. *International Journal of Geriatric Psychiatry, 12,* 53–59.

Johansson, B., Allen-Burge, R., & Zarit, S. H. (1997). Self-reports on memory functioning in a longitudinal study of the oldest old: Relation to current, prospective, and retrospective performance. *Journal of Gerontology: Psychological Sciences, 52B,* P139–P146.

Johansson, B., Zarit, S. H., & Berg, S. (1992). Changes in cognitive functioning of the oldest old. *Journal of Gerontology: Psychological Sciences, 47,* P75–P80.

Johnson, C. (2004). Promised land or purgatory? *Scientific American Special Edition, 14* (3), 92–97.

Johnson, C. & Troll, L. E. (1994). Constraints and facilitators to friendships in late late life. *Gerontologist, 34,* 79–87.

Johnson, D. R. & Johnson, J. T. (1982). Managing the older worker. *Journal of Applied Gerontology, 1,* 58–66.

Johnson, S. M., Karvonen, C. A., Phelps, C. L., Nader, S., & Sanborn, B. M. (2003). Assessment of analysis by gender in the Cochrane reviews as related to treatment of cardiovascular disease. *Journal of Womens Health, 12,* 449–457.

Johnson, T. R. (1995). The significance of religion for aging well. *American Behavioral Scientist,*

39, 186–208.

Jones, D. C. & Vaughn, K. (1990). Close friendships among senior adults. *Psychology & Aging, 5*, 451–457.

Jones, H. E. (1959). Intelligence and problem-solving. In J. E. Birren (Ed.), *Handbook of aging and the individual: Psychological and biological aspects.* Chicago, IL: University of Chicago Press.

Jones, R. N., Yang, F. M., Zhang, Y., Kiely, D. K., Marcantonio, E. R., & Inouye, S. K. (2006). Does educational attainment contribute to the risk for delirium? A potential role for cognitive reserve. *Journal of Gerontology: Medical Sciences, 61A*, 1307–1311.

Joubert, C. E. (1990). Subjective expectations of the acceleration of time with aging. *Perceptual & Motor Skills, 70*, 334.

Juan-Espinosa, M., Cuevas, L., Escorial, S., & Garcia, L. F. (2006). Testing the indifferentiation hypothesis during childhood, adolescence, and adulthood. *The Journal of Genetic Psychology, 167*, 5–15.

Kahana, E. & Kahana, B. (1996). Conceptual and empirical advances in understanding aging well through proactive adaptation. In V. L. Bengston (Ed.). *Adulthood and aging: Research on continuities and discontinuities* (pp. 18–40). New York: Springer.

Kahn, J. R., & Fazio, E. M. (2005). Economic status over the life course and racial disparities in health. *Journal of Gerontology: Series B, 60B*, (Special Issue II), 76–84.

Kahn, R. L. & Antonucci, T. C. (1980). Convoys over the life course: Attachment, roles, and social support. In P. B. Baltes & O. G. Brim (Eds.), *Life-span development and behavior* (Vol. 3, pp. 254–286). New York: Academic Press.

Kaiser, M. A. (1993, Winter). The productive roles of older people in developing countries. *Generations, 17*, 65–69.

Kalavar, J. M. (2001). Examining ageism: Do male and female college students differ? *Educational Gerontology, 27*, 507–513.

Kane, R. & Wilson, K. B. (1993). *Assisted living in the United States: A new paradigm for residential care for frail older persons?* Washington, DC: American Association of Retired Persons.

Kane, R. A. (1991). Personal autonomy for residents in long-term care: Concepts and issues of measurement. In J. E. Birren, & J. E. Lubben (Eds.). *The concept and measurement of quality of life in the frail elderly* (pp. 315–334). San Diego: Academic Press.

Kane, R. A. & Caplan, A. L. (Eds.) (1990). *Everyday ethics: Resolving dilemmas in nursing home life.* New York: Springer.

Kannel, W. B. (1996). Cardioprotection and antihypertensive therapy: The key importance of addressing the associated coronary risk factors (The Framingham Experience). *American Journal of Cardiology, 77*, 6B–11B.

Kaplan, G., Barell, V., & Lusky, A. (1998). Subjective state of health and survival among elderly adults. *Journal of Gerontology: Social Sciences, 43*, S114–S120.

Kaplan, R. M., Patterson, T. L., & Groessl, E. J. (2004). Outcome assessment for resource allocation in primary care. In R. G. Frank, S. H. McDaniel, J. H. Bray, & M. Heldring (Eds.), *Primary care psychology* (pp. 293–315). Washington, DC: American Psychological Association.

Karlamangla, A. S., Singer, B. H., McEwen, B. S., Rowe, J. W., & Seeman, T. E. (2002). Allostatic load as a predictor of functional decline: MacArthur studies of successful aging. *Journal of Clinical Epidemiology, 55*, 696–710.

Karlamangla, A., Tinetti, M., Guralnik, J., Studenski, S., Wetle, T., & Reuben, D. (2007). Comorbidity in older adults: Nosology of impairment, diseases, and conditions. *Journal of Gerontology: Medical Sciences, 62A*, 296–300.

Karlin, W. A., Brondolo, E., & Schwartz, J. (2003). Workplace social support and ambulatory cardiovascular activity in New York City traffic agents. *Psychosomatic Medicine, 65*, 167–176.

Kastenbaum, R. (1993). Re-constructing death in postmodern society. *Omega, 27*, 75–89.

Kastenbaum, R. (1995). To which self be true? *Contemporary Gerontology, 2*, 34–37.

Kastenbaum, R. (1999). Dying and bereavement. In J. C. Cavanaugh & S. K. Whitbourne (Eds.), *Gerontology: An interdisciplinary perspective* (pp. 155–185), New York: Oxford University Press.

Kaszniak, A. W. (1990). Psychological assessment of the aging individual. In J. E. Birren & K. W. Schaie (Eds.), *Handbook of the psychology of aging* (3rd ed., pp. 427–445). San Diego, CA: Academic Press.

Katan, Y. & Werczberger, E. (1998). Housing for elderly people in Israel. In S. Brink (Ed.). *Housing older people: An international perspective* (pp. 35–48). New Brunswick, NJ: Transaction Publishers.

Katchadourian, H. (1987). *Fifty: Midlife in perspective*. New York: Freeman.

Kato, K., & Pedersen, N. L. (2005). Personality and coping: A study of twins reared apart and twins reared together. *Behavior Genetics, 35*, 147–158.

Katzko, M. W., Steverink, N., Dittmann-Kohli, F., & Herrera, R. R. (1998). The self-concept of the elderly: A cross-cultural comparison. *International Journal of Aging & Human Behavior, 46*, 171–187.

Katzman, R., Zhang, M. Y., Chen, P. J., Gu, N., Jiang, S., Saitoh, T., et al. (1997). Effects of apolipoprotein E on dementia and aging in the Shanghai Survey of Dementia. *Neurology, 49*, 779–785.

Kaufman, G. & Uhlenberg, P. (1998). Effects of life course transitions on the quality of relationships between adult children and their parents. *Journal of Marriage & the Family, 60*, 924–938.

Kawahara, M. (2005). Effects of aluminum on the nervous system and its possible link with neurodegenerative diseases. *Journal of Alzheimer's Disease, 8*, 171–182.

Kawas, C. H., Corrada, M. M., Brookmeyer, R., Morrison, A., Resnick, S. M., Zonderman, A. B., & Arenberg, D. (2003). Visual memory predicts Alzheimer's disease more than a decade before diagnosis. *Neurology, 60*, 1089–1093.

Kawashima, R., Okita, K., Yamazaki, R., Tajima, N., Yoshida, H., Taira, M., et al. (2005). Reading aloud and arithmetic calculation improve frontal function of people with dementia. *Journal of Gerontology: Medical Sciences, 60A*, 380–384.

Kayser-Jones, J., Kris, A. E., Miaskowski, C. A., Lyons, W. L., & Paul, S. M. (2006). Hospice care in nursing homes: Does it contribute to higher quality pain management? *The Gerontologist, 46*, 325–333.

Keith, J., Fry, C. L., Glascock, A. P., Ikels, C., Dickerson-Putman, J., Harpending, H. C., & Draper, P. (1994). *The aging experience: Diversity and commonality across cultures*. Thousand Oaks, CA: Sage.

Kelly, C. L., Charness, N., Mottram, M., & Bosman, E. (1994). *The effect of cognitive aging and prior computer experience on learning to use a word processor*. Paper presented at the Cognitive Aging Conference, Atlanta, GA.

Kelman, H. R., Thomas, C., Kennedy, G. J., & Cheng, J. (1994). Cognitive impairment and mortality in older community residents. *American Journal of Public Health, 84*, 1255–1260.

Kennedy, G. E. (1992). Shared activities of grandparents and grandchildren. *Psychological Reports, 70*, 211–227.

Kessler, R. C., McGonagle, K. A., Zhao, S., Nelson, C. B., Hughes, R., Eshleman, S., Wittchen, H., & Kendler, K. S. (1994). Lifetime and 12-month prevalence of *DSM-III R* psychiatric disorders in the United States. *Archives of General Psychiatry, 51*, 8–19.

Khamsi, R. (2007). Hypertension drug protects against Parkinson's. *New Scientist*. Available from www.newscientist.com. Accessed June 11, 2007.

Kim, M. (1998). Housing policies for the elderly in Korea. In S. Brink (Ed.). *Housing older people: An international perspective* (pp. 61–72). New Brunswick, NJ: Transaction Publishers.

Kimmel, D. C. (1990). *Adulthood and aging: An interdisciplinary, developmental view*. New York:

Wiley & Sons.

King, V., & Scott, M. E. (2005). A comparison of cohabiting relationships among older and younger adults. *Journal of Marriage & the Family, 67,* 271–285.

Kirschbaum, J. (1988). Effect on human longevity of added dietary chocolate. *Nutrition, 14,* 869.

Kitayama, S., Markus, H., Matsumoto, H., & Norasakkunkit, V. (1997). Individual and collective processes in the construction of the self: Self-enhancement in the United States and self-criticisms in Japan. *Journal of Personality & Social Psychology, 72,* 1245–1267.

Kitwood, T. (1993). Towards a theory of dementia care: The interpersonal process. *Ageing & Society, 13,* 51–67.

Kivnick, H. Q. & Sinclair, H. M. (1996). Grandparenthood. In J. E. Birren (Ed.), *Encyclopedia of gerontology* (Vol. 1, pp. 611–623). New York: Academic Press.

Kivnick, H. Q. (1982). Grandparenthood: An overview of meaning and mental health. *Gerontologist, 22,* 59–66.

Kleemeier, R. W. (1962). Intellectual change in the senium. *Proceeding of the Social Statistics Section of the American Statistical Association,* 290–295.

Kleijnen, J. & Knipschild, P. (1992). Gingko biloba for cerebral insufficiency. *British Journal of Pharmacology, 34,* 352–358.

Kligman, A. M., Grove, G. L., & Balin, A. K. (1985). Aging of human skin. In C. E. Finch & E. L. Schneider (Eds.), *Handbook of the biology of aging.* (2nd ed.), New York: Van Nostrand Reinhold, 820–841.

Kline, D. W. & Schieber, F. (1985). Vision and aging. In J. E. Birren & K. W. Schaie (Eds.), *Handbook of the psychology of aging* (2nd ed.). New York: Van Nostrand Reinhold.

Klingman, A. (1985). Responding to a bereaved classmate: Comparison of two strategies for death education in the classroom. *Death Studies, 9,* 449–454.

Knight, B. (1993). A meta-analytic review of interventions for caregiver distress. *The Gerontologist, 32,* 249–257.

Koenig, C. S., & Cunningham, W. R., (2001). Adulthood relocation: Implications for personal-ity, future orientation, and social partner choices. *Experimental Aging Research, 27,* 197–213.

Koenig, H. G. & Blazer, D. G. (1992). Mood disorders and suicide. In J. E. Birren, R. B. Sloane, & G. D. Cohen (Eds.), *Handbook of mental health and aging* (2nd ed., pp. 379–407). San Diego: Academic Press.

Koenig, H. G. (1995). Religion as a cognitive schema. *International Journal for the Psychology of Religion, 5,* 31–37.

Koenig, H. G., Hays, J. C., Larson, D. B., George, L. K., Cohen, H. S., McCullogh, M. E., Meador, K. G., & Blazer, D. G. (1999). Does religious attendance prolong survival? *Journal of Gerontology: Medical Sciences, 53A,* M426–M434.

Koivumaa-Honkanen, H., Honkanen, R., Viinamaki, H., Heikkila, K., Kaprio, J., & Koskenvuo, M. (2000). Self-reported life-satisfaction and 20-year mortality in healthy Finnish adults. *American Journal of Epidemiology, 152,* 983–991.

Koizumi, Y., Awata, S., Kuriyama, S., Ohmori, K., Hozawa, A., Seki, T., Matsuoka, H., & Tsuji, I. (2005). Association between social support and depression status in the elderly: Results of a 1-year community-based prospective cohort study in Japan. *Psychiatry & Clinical Neurosciences, 59,* 563–569.

König, J., & Leembruggen–Kallberg, E. (2006). Perspectives on elder abuse in Germany. *Educational Gerontology, 32,* 25–35.

Kosberg, J. I., Kaufman, A. V., Burgio, L. D., Leeper, J. D., & Sun, F. (2007). Family caregiving to those with dementia in rural Alabama. *Journal of Aging & Health, 19,* 3–21.

Kose, S. (1998). Housing elderly people in Japan. In S. Brink (Ed.). *Housing older people: An in-*

ternational perspective (pp. 125–140). New Brunswick, NJ: Transaction Publishers.

Kosloski, K., Ekerdt, D., & DeViney, S. (2001). The role of job-related rewards in retirement planning. *Journal of Gerontology: Psychological Sciences, 56B*, P160–P169.

Kozma, A., Stones, M. J., & Hannah, T. E. (1991). Age, activity, and physical performance: An evaluation of performance models. *Psychology & Aging, 6*, 43–49.

Kraaij, V., Arensman, E., & Spinhoven, P. (2002). Negative life events and depression in elderly persons: A meta-analysis. *Journal of Gerontology: Psychological Sciences, 57B*, P87–P94.

Kramer, D. A. & Woodruff, D. S. (1986). Relativistic and dialectical thought in three adult age groups. *Human Development, 29*, 280–290.

Kranczer, S. (1998). Changes in longevity by State. *Statistical Bulletin, 79*(3), 29–36.

Krause, N. (1993). Early parental loss and personal control in later life. *Journal of Gerontology: Psychological Sciences, 48*, P100–P108.

Krause, N. (1995a). Religiosity and self-esteem among older adults. *Journal of Gerontology: Psychological Sciences, 50B*, P236–P246.

Krause, N. (1997). Religion, aging, and health: Current status and future prospects. *Journal of Gerontology: Social Sciences, 52B*, S291–S293.

Krause, N. (2001). Social suppot. In *Handbook of aging and the social sciences*, (5th ed., pp. 273–294). New York: Academic Press.

Kressin, N. R., Spiro, A., III, Bosse, R., & Garcia, R. I. (1999). Personality traits and oral self-care behaviors: Longitudinal findings form the normative aging study. *Psychology & Health, 14*, 71–85.

Kressley, K. M., & Huebschmann, M. (2002). The 21st century campus: Gerontological perspectives. *Educational Gerontology, 28*, 835–851.

Krucoff, M. W., Crater, S. W., Gallup, D., Blankenship, J. C., Cuffe, M., Guarneri, M., et al., (2005). Music, imagery, touch, and prayer as adjuncts to interventional cardiac care: The Monitoring and Actualisation of Noetic Trainings (MANTRA) II randomised study. *The Lancet, 366*, 211–217.

Kübler-Ross, E. (1969). *On death and dying*. New York: Macmillan.

Kukull, W., Larson, E., Teri, L., Bowen, J., McCormick, W., & Pfanschmidt, M. (1994). The Mini-Mental State Examination score and the clinical diagnosis of dementia. *Clinical Epidemiology, 47*, 1061–1067.

Kulik, L. (2001). Marital relationships in late adulthood: Synchronous versus asynchronous couples. *International Journal of Aging & Human Development, 52*, 323–339.

Kurdek, L. A. (1995a). Developmental changes in relationship quality in gay male and lesbian cohabiting couples. *Developmental Psychology, 31*, 86–94.

Kurdek, L. A. (1995b). Lesbian and gay couples. In A. R. D'Augelli & C. J. Patterson (Eds.), *Lesbian, gay, and bisexual identities over the lifespan* (pp. 243–261). New York: Oxford University Press.

Kuriyama, S., Shimazu, T., Ohmori, K., Kikuchi, N., Nakaya, N., Nishino, Y., Tsubuno, Y., & Tsuji, I. (2006). Green tea consumption and mortality due to cardiovascular disease, cancer, and all causes in Japan: The Ohsaki study. *Journal of the American Medical Association, 296*, 1255–1265.

Kwak, J., & Haley, W. E. (2005). Current research findings on end-of-life decision making among racially or ethnically diverse groups. *The Gerontologist, 45*, 634–641.

Laboratory Medicine. (1996). No. 9, 567.

Labouvie-Vief, G. (1992). A neo-Piagetian perspective on adult cognitive development. In R. J. Sternberg & C. A. Berg (Eds.), *Intellectual development* (pp. 197–228). New York: Cambridge University Press.

Labouvie-Vief, G., Diehl, M., Tarnowski, A., & Shen, J. (2000). Age differences in adult personality: Findings from the United States and China. *Journal of Gerontology: Psychological Sciences, 55B*, P4–P17.

Lacey, H. P., Smith, D. M., & Ubel, P. A. (2006). Hope I die before I get old: Mispredicting happiness across the lifespan. *Journal of Happiness Studies, 7*, 167–182.

Lachman, M. E. (1983). Perceptions of intellectual aging: Antecedent or consequnce of intellectual functioning? *Developmental Psychology, 19*, 482–498.

Lachman, M. E. (1985). Personal efficacy in middle and old age: Differential and normative patterns of change. In G. H. Elder, Jr. (Ed.), *Life course dynamics: Trajectories and transitions, 1968–1980*. Ithaca, NY: Cornell University Press.

Lachman, M. E. (1986). Loss of control in aging research: A case for multidimensional and domain-specific assessment. *Psychology & Aging, 1*, 34–40.

Lachman, M. E. (2006). Perceived control over age-related declines. *Current Directions in Psychological Science, 15*, 282–286.

Lachman, M. E., Andreolletti, C., & Pearman, A. (2006). Memory control beliefs: How are they related to age, strategy use and memory improvement? *Social Cognition, 24*, 359–385.

Lachs, M. S. & Pillemer, K. (1995). Abuse and neglect of elderly persons. *New England Journal of Medicine, 332*(7), 437–443.

Laditka, S. B., Jenkins, C. L., Eleazer, G. P., & Kelsey, S. G. (2007). Geriatric expertise among medical school faculty: Preparing for the challenges of an aging population. *Educational Gerontology, 33*, 469–482.

Laflamme, L. & Menckel, E. (1995). Aging and occupational accidents: A review of the literature of the last three decades. *Safety Science, 21*, 145–161.

Lakatta, E. G. (1990a). Changes in cardiovascular function with aging. *European Heart Journal, 11c*, 22–29.

Lakatta, E. G. (1990b). Heart and circulation. In E. L. Schneider & J. W. Rowe (Eds.), *Handbook of the biology of aging* (3rd edition). San Diego, CA: Academic Press, 181–217.

Lamb, R., & Brady, E. M. (2005). Participation in lifelong learning institutes: What turns members on? *Educational Gerontology, 31*, 207–224.

Lambert, H. C., McColl, M. A., Gilbert, J., Wong, J., Murray, G., & Shortt, S. E. D. (2005). Factors affecting long-term-care residents' decision-making processes as they formulate advance directives. *The Gerontologist, 45*, 626–633.

Landi, F., Cesari, M., Onder, G., Lattanzio, F., Gravina, E. M., & Bernabei, R. (2004). Physical activity and mortlity in frail, community-living elderly patients. *Journal of Gerontology: Medical Sciences, 59A*, 833–837.

Landman, J., Kotkin, A. M., Shu, W., Droller, M. J., & Liu, B. C-S. (1997). Vitamin D inhibits telomerase activity and tumor cell invasion in human prostrate cancer LNCap cells. *Surgical Forum, 48*, 758.

Landy, F. J. (1994, July–August). Mandatory retirement age: Serving the public welfare? *Psychological Science Agenda: American Psychological Association*, 10–11, 20.

Lane, C. J., & Zelinski, E. M. (2003). Longitudinal hierarchical linear models of the Memory Functioning Questionnaire. *Psychology & Aging, 18*, 38–53.

Langer, E. J. & Rodin, J. (1976). The effects of choice and enhanced personal responsibility for the aged: A field experiment in an institutional setting. *Journal of Personality and Social Psychology, 34*, 191–198.

Langer, R., Criqui, M., & Reed, D. (1992). Lipoprotein and blood pressure as biological pathways for effects of moderate alcohol consumption on coronary heart disease. *Circulation, 85*, 910–915.

Lapp, D. C. (1992). *Maximizing your memory power*. New York: Barron's Educational Series.

Lasher, K., & Faulkender, P. J. (1993). Measurement of aging anxiety: Development of the Anxiety about Aging Scale. *International Journal of Aging & Human Development, 37*, 247–259.

Laslett, P. (1985). Societal development and aging. In R. A. Binstock & E. Shanas (Eds.), *Handbook of aging and the social sciences.* (2nd ed.), New York: Van Nostrand Reinhold.

Lattanzi, M., & Hale, M. E. (1984). Giving grief words: Writing during bereavement. *Omega, 15*, 45–52.

Lauer, J. & Lauer, R. (1985). Marriages made to last. *Psychology Today, 19*, 22–26.

Lauer, R. H., Lauer, J. C., & Kerr, S. T. (1990). The long-term marriage: Perceptions of stability and satisfaction. *International Journal of Aging & Human Development, 31*, 189–195.

Launer, L. J. (2005). The epidemiologic study of dementia: A life-long quest? *Neurobiology of Aging, 26*, 335–340.

Laver, G. D., & Burke, D. M. (1993). Why do semantic priming effects increase in old age? *Psychology & Aging, 8*, 34–43.

Lawton, M. P. (1980). *Environment and aging.* Belmont, CA: Brooks-Cole.

Lawton, M. P. (1982). Competence, environmental press, and adaptation. In P. Lawton, P. G. Windley, & T. O. Byerts (Eds.). *Aging and the environment: Theoretical approaches* (pp. 33–59). New York: Springer.

Lawton, M. P. (2001). The physical environment of the person with Alzheimer's disease. *Aging and Mental Health, 5*, 56–64.

Lawton, M. P., Kleban, M. H., Rajagopal, D., & Dean, J. (1992). Dimensions of affective experience in three age groups. *Psychology & Aging, 7*, 171–184.

Lazowski, D-A., Eccleston, N. A., Myers, A. M., Paterson, D. H., Tudor-Locke, C., Fitzgerald, C., Jones, G., Shima, N., & Cunningham, D. A. (1999). A Randomized outcome evaluation of group exercise programs in long-term care institutions. *Journal of Gerontology: Medical Sciences, 54A*, M621–M628.

Lee, G. R., DeMaris, A., Bavin, S., & Sullivan, R. (2001). Gender differences in the depressive effect of widowhood in later life. *Journal of Gerontology: Social Sciences, 56B*, S56–S61.

Lee, I. M. & Paffenbarger, R. S. (1998). Life is sweet: Candy consumption and longevity. *British Medical Journal, 317*, 1683–1684.

Lee, I-M., Cook, N. R., Gaziano, J. M., Gordon, D., Ridker, P. M., Manson, J. E., Hennekens, C. H., & Buring, J. E. (2005). Vitamin E in the primary prevention of cardiovascular disease and cancer. *Journal of the American Medical Association, 294*, 56–65.

Lee, J. A. (1997). Balancing elder care responsibilities and work: Two empirical studies. *Journal of Occupational Health Psychology, 2*, 220–228.

Lee, J. A., & Phillips, S. J. (2006). Work and family: Can you have it all? *The Psychologist-Manager Journal, 9*, 41–57.

Lee, S., Hooker, K., Monahan, D., Frazier, L. D., & Shifren, K. (2006, Nov.). Personality traits predict mental health of spouse caregivers. Paper presented at the annual meeting of the Gerontological Society of America, Dallas, Texas.

Lee, S-Y. D., Gazmararian, J. A., & Arozullah, A. M. (2006). Health literacy and social support among elderly Medicare enrollees in a managed care plan. *Journal of Applied Gerontology, 25*, 324–337.

Lee, T. R. (1985). Kinship and social support of the elderly: The case of the United States. *Aging & Society, 5*, 19–38.

Lee, T. R., Mancini, J. A., & Maxwell, J. W. (1990). Sibling relationships in adulthood: Contact patterns and motivations. *Journal of Marriage & the Family, 52*, 431–440.

Lee, W., & Hotopf, M. (2005). Personality variation and age: Trait instability or measurement unreliability? *Personality & Individual Differences, 38*, 883–890.

Lefton, L. A. (1997). *Psychology.* Boston: Allyn & Bacon.

Lehman, H. C. (1953). *Age and achievement.* Princeton, NJ: Princeton University Press.

Lehr, U., Jüchtern, J. C., Schmitt, M., Sperling, U., Fischer, A., Grünendahl, M., & Minnemann, E. (1998). Anticipation and adjustment to retirement. *Aging Clinical & Experimental Research, 10*, 358–367.

Lerner, R. M. (1986). *Concepts and theories of human development* (2nd ed.). New York: Random House.

Levenson, H. (1974). Activism and powerful others: Distinctions within the concept of internal-external control. *Journal of Personality Assessment, 38*, 377–383.

Levenson, R. W., Carstensen, L. L., & Gottman, J. M. (1993). Long-term marriage: Age, gender, and satisfaction. *Psychology & Aging, 8*, 301–313.

Leventhal, H., Rabin, C., Leventhal, E. A., & Burns, E. (2001). Health risk behavior and aging. In J. E. Birren & K. W. Schaie (Eds.), *Handbook of the psychology of aging* (5th ed., pp. 186–214). San Diego, CA: Academic Press.

Levin, J. S. (1994). Investigating the epidemiological effects of religious experience: Findings, explanations, and barriers. In J. S. Levin (Ed.), *Religion in aging and health* (pp. 3–17). Thousand Oaks, CA: Sage.

Levin, J. S. (1998). Religion, health, and psychological well-being in older adults: Findings from three national surveys. *Journal of Aging & Health, 10*, 504–532.

Levine, D. (1995, June). Choosing a nursing home. *American Health*, 82–84.

Levine, J. A., Lanningham-Foster, L. M., McCrady, S. K., Krizan, A. C., Olson, L. R., Kane, P. H., Jensen, M. D., & Clark, M. M. (2005). Interindividual variation in posture allocation: Possible role in human obesity. *Science, 307*, 584–586.

Levinson, D. J. (1996). *Seasons of a woman's life*. New York: Alfred Knopf.

Levitt, M. J. (2000). Social relations across the life span: In search of unified models. *International Journal of Aging and Human Development, 51*, 71–84.

Levy, B. & Langer, E. (1994). Aging free from negative stereotypes: Successful memory in China and among the American deaf. *Journal of Personality & Social Psychology, 66*, 989–997.

Levy, B. R. (1999). The inner self of the Japanese elderly: A defense against negative stereotypes of aging. *International Journal of Aging & Human Development, 48*, 131–144.

Levy, B. R., Slade, M. D., & Gill, T. M. (2006). Hearing decline predicted by elders' stereotypes. *Journal of Gerontology, Psychological Sciences, 61B*, P82–P87.

Levy, B. R., Slade, M. D., & Kasl, S. V. (2002). Longitudinal benefits of positive self-perceptions of aging on functional health. *Journal of Gerontology: Psychological Sciences, 57B*, P409–P417.

Lewis, C. A., & Cruise, S. M. (2006). Religion and happiness: Consensus, contradictions, comments and concerns. *Mental Health, Religion, & Culture, 9*, 213–225.

Lewis, J., Dickson, D. W., Lin, W. L., Chisholm, L., Corral, A., Jones, G. et al. (2001). Enhanced neurofibrillary degeneration in transgenic mice expressing mutant tau and APP. *Science, 293*, 1487–1491.

Li, G. (1995). The interaction effect of bereavement and sex on the risk of suicide in the elderly: An historical cohort study. *Social Science & Medicine, 40*, 825–828.

Li, L. W. & Fries, B. R. (2005). Elder disability as an explanation for racial differences in informal health care. *The Gerontologist, 45*, 206–215.

Liang, J., Krause, N. M., & Bennet, J. M. (2001). Social exchange and well-being: Is giving better than receiving? *Psychology & Aging, 16*, 511–523.

Lichtenberg, P. A. (1994). *A guide to psychological practice in geriatric long term care*. Binghamton, New York: Haworth.

Lichtenstein, M. J., Pruski, L. A., Marshall, C. E., Blalock, C. L., Lee, S., & Plaetke, R. (2003). Sentence completion to assess children's views about aging. *The Gerontologist, 43*, 839–848.

Lichtenstein, P., Gatz, M., Pedersen, N. L., Berg, S., & McClearn, G. E. (1996). A co-twin-control study of response to widowhood. *Journal of Gerontology: Psychological Sciences, 51B,* P279–P289.

Lieberman, M. A. (1993). Bereavement self-help groups: A review of conceptual and methodological issues. In M. S. Stroebe, W. Stroebe, & R. O. Hansson (Eds.), *Handbook of bereavement: Theory, research, & intervention* (pp. 411–426). New York: Cambridge University Press.

Lifshitz, H. (2002). Attitudes toward aging in adult and elderly people with intellectual disability. *Educational Gerontology, 28,* 745–759.

Lindauer, M. S. (1998). Artists, art, and art activities: What do they tell us about aging? In C. Adams-Price (Ed.), *Creativity and successful aging: Theoretical and empirical approaches* (pp. 237–250). New York: Springer.

Lindemann, E. (1944). Symptomatology and management of acute grief. *American Journal of Psychiatry, 101,* 141–148.

Lindenberger, U., Scherer, H., & Baltes, P. B. (2001). The strong connection between sensory and cognitive performance in old age: Not due to sensory acuity reductions operating during cognitive assessment. *Psychology & Aging, 10,* 196–205.

Linnehan, M. & Naturale, C. (1998). The joy of learning in retirement. *Journal of Physical Education, Recreation, & Dance, 69,* 32–33.

Litwak, E. & Longino, C. F., Jr. (1987). Migration patterns among the elderly. *Gerontologist, 27,* 266–272.

Liu, J. H., Zingmond, D. S., McGory, M. L., SooHoo, N. F., Ettner, S. L., Brook, R. H., Ko, C. Y. (2006). Disparities in the utilization of high-volume hospitals for complex surgery. *Journal of the American Medical Association, 296,* 1973–1980.

Liu, Y., & Schubert, D. (2006). Treating Alzheimer's disease by inactivating bioactive amyloid _ peptide. *Current Alzheimer Research, 3,* 129–135.

Ljungquist, B., Berg, S., Lanke, J., McClearn, G. E., & Pedersen, N. L. (1998). The effect of genetic factors for longevity: A comparison of identical and fraternal twins in the Swedish Twin Registry. *Journal of Gerontology: Medical Sciences, 53A,* M441–M446.

Lombardi, W. J. & Weingartner, H. (1995). Pharmacological treatment of impaired memory function. In A. D. Baddeley, B. A. Wilson, & F. N. Watts (Eds.), *Handbook of memory disorders* (pp. 577–601). Chichester, England: Wiley.

Long, G. M. & Crambert, R. F. (1990). The nature and basis of age-related changes in dynamic visual acuity. *Psychology & Aging, 5,* 138–143.

Lorber, D. L., & Lagana, D. (1997). Mirror on your health: A guided tour of yourself. *Diabetes Self-Management, 14,* 66–72.

Lu, T., Pan, Y., Kao, S-Y., Li, C., Kohane, I., Chan, J., & Yankner, B. A. (2004). Gene regulation and DNA damage in the ageing human brain. *Nature, 429,* 883–891.

Lund, D. A. (1993). Widowhood: The coping response. In R. Kastenbaum (Ed.), *Encyclopedia of adult development* (pp. 537–541), Phoenix, AZ: Onyx Press.

Lund, D. A., Caserta, M. S., & Dimond, M. F. (1993). The course of spousal bereavement in later life. In M. S. Stroebe, W. Stroebe, & R. Hansson (Eds.), *Handbook of bereavement: Theory, research, and intervention* (pp. 240–254). New York: Cambridge University Press.

Lund, D. A., Caserta, M. S., Connelly, J. R., Dimond, M. F., Johnson, R. J., & Poulton, J. L. (1985). Identifying elderly with coping problems after two years of bereavement. *Omega, 16,* 212–223.

Lundin, T. (1984). Morbidity following sudden and unexpected bereavement. *British Journal of Psychiatry, 144,* 84–88.

Luria, A. R. (1968). *The mind of a mnemonist.* New York: Basic Books.

Lutgendorf, S. K., Vitaliano, P. P., Tripp-Reimer, T., Harvey, J. H., & Lubaroff, D. M. (1999). Sense of coherence moderates the relationship between life stress and natural killer cell activity in healthy older adults. *Psychology & Aging, 14,* 552–563.

Lynch, M., Estes, C. L., & Hernandez, M. (2005). Chronic care initiatives for the elderly: Can they bridge the gerontology-medicine gap? *Journal of Applied Gerontology, 24,* 108–124.

Lyness, J. M., Cox, C., Curry, J., Conwell, Y., King, D. A., & Caine, E. D. (1995). Older age and the underreporting of depressive symptoms. *Journal of the American Geriatrics Society, 43,* 216–221.

Lynn, J. (1991). Dying well. *Generations, 15*(1), 69–72.

Lyubomirsky, S. (2001). Why are some people happier than others? The role of cognitive and motivational processes in well-being. *American Psychologist, 56,* 239–249.

Lyyra, T-M., & Heikkinen, R-L. (2006). Perceived social support and mortality in older people. *Journal of Gerontology: Social Sciences, 61B,* S147–S152.

Lyyra, T-M., Törmäkangas, T. M., Read, S., Rantanen, T., & Berg, S. (2006). Satisfaction with present life predicts survival in octogenarians. *Journal of Gerontology: Psychological Sciences, 61B,* P319–P326.

Mack, R. B. (1997). "Grow dumb along with me": Misuse of DHEA (dehydroepiandrosterone). *North Carolina Medical Journal, 58,* 144–146.

Mahoney, D. & Restak, R. (1998). *The longevity strategy: How to live to 100 using the brain-body connection.* New York: John Wiley & Sons.

Maier, H., & Smith, J. (1999). Psychological predictors of mortality in old age. *Journal of Gerontology: Psychological Sciences, 54B,* P44–P54.

Maitland, S. B., Herlitz, A., Nyberg, L., Bäckman, L., & Nilsson, L-G. (2004). Selective sex differences in declarative memory. *Memory & Cognition, 32,* 1160–1169.

Malacrida, R., Genoni, M., Maggioni, A. P., Spataro, V., Parish, S., Phil, D., Palmer, A., Collins, R., & Moccetti, T. (1998). A comparison of the early outcome of acute myocardial infarction in women and men. *New England Journal of Medicine, 338,* 8–14.

Malatesta, C. Z. & Kalnok, M. (1984). Emotional experience in younger and older adults. *Journal of Gerontology, 39,* 301–308.

Mancil, G. L. & Owsley, C. (1988). 'Vision through my aging eyes' revisited. *Journal of the American Optometric Association, 59,* 288–294.

Mandelbaum, D. G. (1959). Social uses of funeral rites. In H. Feifel (Ed.), *The meaning of death.* New York: McGraw-Hill.

Manson, J. E., Willett, W. C., Stampfer, M. J., Colditz, G. A., Hunter, D. J., Hankinson, S. E., Hennekens, C. D., & Speizer, F. E. (1995). Body weight and mortality among women. *New England Journal of Medicine, 333,* 677–685.

Marambaud, P., Zhao, H., & Davies, P. (2005). Resveratrol promotes clearance of Alzheimer's disease Amyloid-β peptides. *Journal of Biological Chemistry, 280,* 37377–37382.

Marcellini, F., Sensoli, C., Barbini, N., & Fioravanti, P. (1997). Preparation for retirement: Problems and suggestions of retirees. *Educational Gerontology, 23,* 377–388.

Markides, K. S., & Eschbach, K. (2005). Aging, migration, and mortality: Current status of research on the Hispanic paradox. *Journal of Gerontology: Series B, 60B,* (Special Issue II), 68–75.

Marsiglio, W. & Donnelly, D. (1991). Sexual relations in later life: A national study of married persons. *Journal of Gerontology: Social Sciences, 46,* S338–S344.

Marsiske, M., & Willis, S. L. (1998). Practical creativity in older adults' everyday problem solving: Life-span perspectives. In C. E. Adams-Price (Ed.), *Creativity and aging: Theoretical and empirical approaches* (pp. 73–113). New York: Springer.

Marsiske, M., Lang, F. B., Baltes, P. B., & Baltes, M. M. (1995). Selective optimization with compensation: Life-span perspectives on successful human development. In R. A. Dixon & L. Bäckman (Eds.), *Compensating for psychological deficits and declines: Managing loss and promoting gains.* (pp. 35–79). Mahwah, NJ: Erlbaum.

Martin, A., Prior, R., Shukitt-Hale, B., Cao, G., & Joseph, J. A. (2000). Effect of fruits, vegetables, or Vitamin E-rich diet on Vitamins E and C distribution in peripheral and brain tissues: Implication for brain function. *Journal of Gerontology: Biological Sciences, 55A,* B144–B151.

Martin, P., Bishop, A., Poon, L., & Johnson, M. A. (2006). Influence of personality and health behaviors on fatigue in late and very late life. *Journal of Gerontology: Psychological Sciences, 61B,* P161–P166.

Martin, P., Bishop, A., Poon, L., & Johnson, M. A. (2006). Influence of personality and health behaviors on fatigue in late and very late life. *Journal of Gerontology: Psychological Sciences, 61B,* P161–P166.

Martin, T. C. & Bumpass, L. L. (1989). Recent trends in marital disruption. *Demography, 26,* 37–51.

Maruta, T., Colligan, R. C., Malinchoc, M., & Offord, K. P. (2000). Optimists vs. pessimists: Survival rate among medical patients over a 30-year period. *Mayo Clinic Proceedings, 75,* 140–143.

Masoro, E. J. (2002). *Caloric restriction: A key to understanding and modulating aging.* Amsterdam: Elsevier.

Masunaga, H. & Horn, J. (2001). Expertise and age-related changes in components of intelligence. *Psychology & Aging, 16,* 293–311.

Mathes, M. (2005). Terri Schiavo and end–of–life decisions: Can law help us out? *MEDSBURG Nursing, 14,* 200–202.

Matsuzaki, S., Manabe, T., Katayama, T., Nishikawa, A., Yanagita, T., Okuda, H., et al. (2004). Metals accelerate production of the aberrant splicing isoform of the presenilin-2. *Journal of Neurochemistry, 88,* 1345–1351.

Matthias, R. E., Lubben, J. E., Atchison, K. A., & Schweitzer, S. O. (1997). Sexual activity and satisfaction among very old adults: Results from a community-dwelling Medicare population survey. *Gerontologist, 37,* 6–14.

Mayr, U. & Kliegl, R. (2000). Complex semantic processing in old age: Does it stay or does it go? *Psychology & Aging, 15,* 29–43.

McAdams, D. P. (1994a). *The person: An introduction to personality psychology* (2nd ed.). Fort Worth, TX: Harcourt Brace.

McAdams, D. P. (1994b). A psychology of the stranger. *Psychological Inquiry, 5,* 145–148.

McAdams, D. P. (1994c). Can personality change? Levels of stability and growth in personality across the life span. In T. F. Heatherton & J. L. Weinberger (Eds.), *Can personality change?* (pp. 299–314). Washington, DC: American Psychological Association.

McAdams, D. P. (1995). What do we know when we know a person? *Journal of Personality, 63,* 365–396.

McAdams, D. P. (1998). The role of defense in the life story. *Journal of Personality, 66,* 1125–1146.

McAdams, D. P. & de St. Aubin, E. (1992). A theory of generativity and its assessment through self-report, behavioral acts, and narrative themes in autobiography. *Journal of Personality & Social Psychology, 62,* 1003–1015.

McAdams, D. P., de St. Aubin, E., & Logan, R. L. (1993). Generativity among young, midlife, and older adults. *Psychology & Aging, 8,* 221–230.

McAdams, D. P., Diamond, A., de St. Aubin, E., & Mansfield, E. (1997). Stories of committment: The psychosocial construction of generative lives. *Journal of Personality & Social Psychology, 72,* 678–694.

McArdle, P. F., Pollin, T. I., O'Connell, J. R., Sorkin, J. D., Agarwala, R., Schäffer, A. A., Streeten, E. A., King, T. M., Shuldiner, A. R., & Mitchell, B. D. (2006). Does having children extend life span? A genealogical study of parity and longevity in the Amish. *Journal of Gerontology: Med-*

ical Sciences, 61A, 190–195.

McArdle, W. D., Katch, F. I., & Katch, V. L. (1991). *Exercise physiology: Energy, nutrition, and human performance* (3rd ed.). Philadelphia, PA: Lea & Egbert.

McAuley, E., Blissmer, B., Marquez, D. X., Jerome, G. J., Kramer, A. F., & Katula, J. (2001). Social relations, physical activity, and well-being in older adults. *Preventive Medicine: An International Journal Devoted to Practice and Theory, 31*, 608–617.

McCabe, J., & Hartman, M. (2003). Examining the locus of age effects on complex span tasks. *Psychology & Aging, 18*, 562–572.

McCall, P. L. (1991). Adolescent and elderly white male suicide trends: Evidence of changing well-being? *Journal of Gerontology: Social Sciences, 46*, S43–S51.

McCarty, H. J., Roth, D. L., Goode, K. T., Owen, J. E., Harrell, L., Donovan, K., & Haley, W. E. (2000). Longitudinal course of behavior problems during Alzheimer's disease: Linear versus curvilinear patterns of decline. *Journal of Gerontology: Medical Sciences, 55A*, M200–M206.

McClendon, M. J., Smyth, K. A., & Neundorfer, M. M. (2006). Long-term care placement and survival of persons with Alzheimer's disease. *Journal of Gerontology: Psychological Sciences, 61B*, P220–P227.

McConatha, J. T., Hayta, V., Riesser-Danner, L., & McConatha, D. (2004). Turkish and U.S. attitudes toward aging. *Educational Gerontology, 30*, 169–183.

McConatha, J. T., Schnell, F., Volkwein, K., Riley, L., & Leach, E. (2003). Attitudes toward aging: A comparative analysis of young adults from the United States and Germany. *International Journal of Aging & Human Development, 57*, 203–215.

McCoy, J. L. & Weems, K. (1989). Disabled worker beneficiaries and disabled SSI recipients. *Social Security Bulletin, 52*(5), 15–28.

McCrae, R. R. & Costa, P. T., Jr. (1990). *Personality in adulthood.* New York: Guilford Press.

McCrae, R. R., Arenberg, D., & Costa, P. T. (1987). Declines in divergent thinking with age: Cross-sectional, longitudinal, and cross-sequential analyses. *Psychology & Aging, 2*, 130–137.

McCrae, R. R., Costa, P. T. Jr., de Lima, M. P., Simões, A., Ostendorf, F., Angleitner, A., Marušič, I., Bratko, D., Caprara, G. V., Barbaranelli, C., Chae, J-H., & Piedmont, R. L. (1999). Age differences in personality across the adult life span: Parallels in five cultures. *Developmental Psychology, 35*, 466–477.

McCusker, J., Cole, M., Ciampi, A., Latimer, E., Windholz, S., & Belzile, E. (2006). Does depression in older medical patients predict mortality? *Journal of Gerontology: Medical Sciences, 61A*, 975–981.

McDaniel, J. H., Hunt, A., Hackes, B., & Pope, J. F. (2001). Impact of dining room environment on nutritional intake of Alzheimer's residents: A case study. *American Journal of Alzheimer's Disease, 15*, 29–302.

McDonald-Miszczak, L., Hertzog, C., & Hultsch, D. F. (1995). Stability and accuracy of metamemory in adulthood and aging: A longitudinal analysis. *Psychology & Aging, 10*, 553–564.

McElreath, D. D. (1996). What is a grandmother. Ddmac@juno.com.

McEvoy, G. M. & Cascio, W. F. (1989). Cumulative evidence of the relationship between employee age and job performance. *Journal of Applied Psychology, 74*, 11–17.

McFadden, S. H. (1999). Religion, personality, and aging: A life span perspective. *Journal of Personality, 67*, 1081–1104.

McGaugh, J. L. (2000). Memory-A century of consolidation. *Science, 287*, 248–251.

McGue, M., & Christensen, K. (2002). The heritability of level and rate-of-change in cognitive functioning in Danish twins age 70 years and older. *Experimental Aging Research, 28*, 435–451.

Mead, S. C., & Willemsen, H. W. A. (1995). Crisis of the psyche: Psychotherapeutic considerations on AIDS, loss and hope. In L. Sherr (Ed.), *Grief and AIDS* (pp. 115–127). Chichester, England: John Wiley & Sons.

Meeks, S., Murrell, S. A., & Mehl, R. C. (2000). Longitudinal relationships between depressive symptoms and health in normal older and middle-aged adults. *Psychology & Aging, 15,* 100–109.

Mega, M. S., Cummings, J. L., Fiorello, T., & Gornbein, J. (1996). The spectrum of behavioral changes in Alzheimer's disease. *Neurology, 46,* 130–135.

Mehlsen, M., Thomsen, D. K., Viidik, A., Olesen, F., & Zachariae, R. (2005). Cognitive processes involved in the evaluation of life satisfaction: Implications for well-being. *Aging & Mental Health, 9,* 281–290.

Mein, G., Higgs, P., Ferrie, J., & Stansfield, S. A. (1998). Paradigms of retirement: The importance of health and ageing in the Whitehall II study. *Social Science & Medicine, 47,* 535–545.

Meinecke, A. & Parker, T. (1997). Women and retirement. *National Educational Secretary, 62*(3), 18.

Mellor, D., Davison, T., McCabe, M., George, K., Moore, K., & Ski, C. (2006). Satisfaction with general practitioner treatment of depression among residents of aged care facilities. *Journal of Aging & Health, 18,* 435–457.

Melov, S. (2002). '...and C is for Clioquinol'-The AβCs of Alzheimer's disease. *Trends in Neuroscience, 25,* 121–123.

Menec, V. H., Lix, L., Nowicki, S., & Ekuma, O. (2007). Health care use at the end of life among older adults: Does it vary by age? *Journal of Gerontology: Medical Sciences, 62A,* 400–407.

Menotti, A., Giampaoli, S., & Seccareccia, F. (1998). The relationship of cardiovascular risk factors measured at different ages to prediction of all-cause mortality and longevity. *Archives of Gerontology & Geriatrics, 26,* 99–111.

Meshel, D. S., & McGlynn, R. P. (2004). Intergenerational contact, attitudes, and stereotypes of adolescents and older people. *Educational Gerontology, 30,* 457–479.

Metter, E. J., Schrager, M., Ferrucci, L., & Talbot, L. A. (2005). Evaluation of movement speed and reaction time as predictors of all-cause mortality in men. *Journal of Gerontology: Biological Sciences, 60A,* 840–846.

Midanik, L., Sokhikian, K., Ransom, L. J., & Tekawa, I. S. (1995). The effect of retirement on mental health and health behaviors: The Kaiser Permanente Retirement Study. *Journal of Gerontology, 50B,* S59–S61.

Middleton, R. A., & Byrd, E. K. (1996). Psychosocial factors and hospital readmission status of older persons with cardiovascular disease. *Journal of Applied Rehabilitation Counseling, 27,* 3–10.

Middleton, W., Raphael, B., Burnett, P., & Martinek, N. (1998). A longitudinal study comparing bereavement phenomena in recently bereaved spouses, adult children, and parents. *Australian & New Zealand Journal of Psychiatry, 32,* 235–241.

Miller, G. E., & Blackwell, E. (2006). Turning up the heat: Inflammation as a mechanism linking chronic stress, depression, and heart disease. *Current Directions in Psychological Science, 15,* 269–272.

Miller, P. N., Miller, D. W., McKibbin, E. M., & Pettys, G. L. (1999). *New York Times,* July 3, 1997.

Miller, R. A. (1999). Kleemeier Award Lecture: Are there genes for aging? *Journal of Gerontology: Biological Sciences, 54A,* B297–B307.

Miller, R. B., Henesath, K., & Nelson, B. (1997). Marriage in middle and later life. In T. D. Hargrave & S. M. Hanna (Eds.), The aging family: *New visions in theory, practice, and reality* (pp. 178–198). New York: Bruner/Mazel.

Mills, R. B., Vermette, V., & Malley-Morrison, K. (1998). Judgments about elder abuse and college students' relationship with grandparents. *Gerontology & Geriatrics Education, 19*(2), 17–30.

Minaker, K. L., & Rowe, J. W. (1982). Gastrointestinal system. In J. W. Rowe & R. W. Besdine (Eds.), *Health and disease in old age.* Boston: Little, Brown.

Miner-Rubino, K., Winter, D. G., & Steward, A. J. (2004). Gender, social class, and the subjective experience of aging: Self-perceived personality change from early adulthood to late midlife. *Personality & Social Psychology Bulletin, 30,* 1599–1610.

Miniter, F. (1999). Mad deer disease: Can venison kill you? *Outdoor Life, 204,* 44–46.

Minkler, M. & Fuller-Thomson, E. (2000). Second time around parenting: Factors predictive of grandparents becoming caregivers for their grandchildren. *International Journal of Aging & Human Development, 50,* 185–200.

Minkler, M., Fuller-Thomson, E., Miller, D., & Driver, D. (1997). Depression in grandparents raising grandchildren: Results of a national longitudinal study. *Archives of Family Medicine, 6,* 445–452.

Mirowsky, J. & Ross, C. E. (1992). Age and depression. *Journal of Health & Social Behavior, 33,* 187–205.

Mishara, B. L. (1999). Synthesis of research and evidence on factors affecting the desire of terminally ill or seriously chronically ill persons to hasten death. *Omega, 39,* 1–70.

Mitchell, J. M. & Kemp, B. J. (2000). Quality of life in assisted living homes: A multidimensional analysis. *Journal of Gerontology: Psychological Sciences, 55B,* P117–P127.

Mitford, J. A. (1963). *The American way of death.* New York: Simon & Schuster.

Mjelde-Mossey, L. A., Barak, M. E. M., & Knight, B. G. (2004). Coping behaviors as predictors of drinking practices among primary in-home dementia caregivers. *Journal of Applied Gerontology, 23,* 295–308.

Modak, S. P., Deobagkar, D. D., Leubagfeller, G., Connet, C., & Basu-Modak, S. (1986). Genetic information in aging cells. In A. H. Bittles & K. J. Collins (Eds.), *The biology of human aging* (pp. 17–32). London: Cambridge University Press.

Modern Maturity. (July–August, 1997). R.

Moore, R. D., & Pearson, T. A. (1986). Moderate alcohol consumption and coronary heart disease. *Medicine, 65,* 242–267.

Morgan, J. D. (1986). Death, dying, and bereavement in China and Japan: A brief glimpse. *Death Studies, 10,* 265–272.

Morgan, M. W. (1988). Vision through my aging eyes. *Journal of the American Optometric Association, 59,* 278–280.

Morris, M. C., Evans, D. A., Bienias, J. L., Tangney, C. C., Bennett, D. A., Aggarwal, N., Wilson, R. S., & Scherr, P. A. (2002). Dietary intake of antioxidant nutrients and the risk of incident Alzheimer disease in a biracial community study. *Journal of the American Medical Association, 287,* 3230–3237.

Morris, M. C., Evans, D. A., Tangney, C. C., Bienias, J. L., & Wilson, R. S. (2006). Associations of vegetable and fruit consumption with age-related cognitive change. *Neurology, 67,* 1370–1376.

Morrow, D., Clark, D., Tu, W., Wu, J., Weiner, M., Steinley, D., & Murray, M. D. (2006). Correlates of health literacy in patients with chronic heart failure. *The Gerontologist, 46,* 669–676.

Morrow, D., Leirer, V., Altieri, P., & Fitzsimmons, C. (1994). When expertise reduces age differences in performance. *Psychology & Aging, 9,* 134–148.

Morrow-Howell, N., Hinterlong, J., Rozario, P. A., & Tang, F. (2003). Effects of volunteering on the well-being of older adults. *Journal of Gerontology: Social Sciences, 58B,* S137–S145.

Morse, J. M., Prowse, M. D., & Morrow, N. A. (1985). A retrospective analysis of patient falls. *Canadian Journal of Public Health, 76,* 116–118.

Moss, M. S. & Moss, S. Z. (1995). Death and bereavement. In R. Blieszner & V. H. Bedford (Eds.), *Handbook of aging and the family* (pp. 422–439). Westport, CT: Greenwood Press.

Moss, S., & Moss, M. (1989). The impact of the death of an elderly sibling. *American Behavioral Scientist, 33,* 94–106.

Moss, M., Lesher, L., & Moss, S, (1986–1987). Impact of the death of an adult child on elderly parents: Some observations. *Omega, 17*, 209–218.

Mozaffarian, D., & Rimm, E. B. (2006). Fish intake, contaminants, and human health: Evaluating the risks and benefits. *Journal of the American Medical Association, 296*, 1885–1899.

Mroczek, D. K. & Kolarz, C. M. (1998). The effect of age on positive and negative affect: A developmental perspective on happiness. *Journal of Personality & Social Psychology, 75*, 1333–1349.

Mroczek, D. K., & Spiro, A., III. (2005). Change in life satisfaction during adulthood: Findings from the Veterans Affairs Normative Study of Aging. *Journal of Personality & Social Psychology, 88*, 189–202.

Mroczek, D. K., & Spiro, A., III. (2007). Personality change influences mortality in older men. *Psychological Science, 18*, 371–376.

Mukamal, K. J., Kuller, L. H., Fitzpatrick, A. L., Longstreth, W. T. J., Mittleman, M. A., & Siscovick, D. S. (2003). Prospective study of alcohol consumption and risk of dementia in older adults. *Journal of the American Medical Association, 289*, 1405–1413.

Mukamal, K. J., Mittleman, M. A., Longstreth, W. T., Jr., Newman, A. B., Fried, L. R., & Siscovick, D. S. (2004). Self–reported alcohol consumption and falls in older adults: Cross-sectional and longitudinal analyses of the Cardiovascular Health Study. *Journal of the American Geriatrics Society, 52*, 1174–1179.

Mulder, J. T. (1997, June 29). Death care giant tightens grip on central New York. *Syracuse Herald American*, D4–D9.

Mulnard, R. A., Cotman, C. W., Kawas, van Dyck, C. H., C., Sano, M., Doody, R., Koss, E., Pfeiffer, E., Jin, S., Gamst, A., Grundman, M., Thomas, R., & Thal, L. J. (2000). Estrogen replacement therapy for treatment of mild to moderate Alzheimer disease. *Journal of the American Medical Association, 283*, 1007–1015.

Muramatsu, N., Yin, H., Campbell, R. T., Hoyem, R. L., Jacob, M. A., & Ross, C. O. (2007). Risk of nursing home admission among older Americans: Do states' pending on home- and community-based services matter? *Journal of Gerontology: Social Sciences, 62B*, S169–S178

Murphy, K. (1998, March 26). Doctor assists Oregon suicide. *The Charlotte Observer*, A10.

Murphy, S. L., Dubin, J. A., & Gill, T. M. (2003). The development of fear of falling among community-living older women: Predisposing factors and subsequent fall events. *Journal of Gerontology: Medical Sciences, 58A*, 943–947.

Musick, M. A., Herzog, A. R., & House, J. S. (1999). Volunteering and mortality among older adults: Findings from a national sample. *Journal of Gerontology: Social Sciences, 54B*, S173–S180.

Musil, C. M., & Ahmad, M. (2002). Health of grandmothers: A comparison by caregiver status. *Journal of Aging & Health, 14*, 96–121.

Musil, C. M., Warner, C. B., Zauszniewski, J. A., Jeanblanc, A. B., & Kercher, K. (2006). Grandmothers, caregiving, and family functioning. *Journal of Gerontology: Social Sciences, 61B*, S89–S98.

Mutran, E. J., Reitzes, D. C., & Fernandez, M. E. (1997). Factors that influence attitudes toward retirement. *Research on Aging, 19*, 251–273.

Mynatt, C. R. & Doherty, M. E. (1999). *Understanding human behavior*. Boston: Allyn & Bacon.

Nahemow, L. (1997). The ecological theory of aging: Powell Lawton's legacy. In R. L. Rubenstein, M. Moss, & M. H. Kleban, (Eds.). *The many dimensions of aging* (pp. 22–40). New York: Springer.

Nakashima, M., & Canda, E. R. (2005). Positive dying and resiliency in later life: A qualitative study. *Journal of Aging Studies, 19*, 109–125.

Nath, A., Anderson, C., Jones, M., Maragos, W., Booze, R., Mactutus, C., Bell, J., Hauser, K., & Mattson, M. (2000). Neurotoxicity and dysfunction of dopaminergic systems associated with AIDS dementia. *Journal of Psychopharmacology, 14*, 222–227.

National Academy on Aging. (1994). *Old age in the 21st century*. Syracuse, New York: Syracuse

University, the Maxwell School.

National Alliance for Caregiving & American Association of Retired Persons. (1997). *Family caregiving in the U.S.: Findings from a national survey.* Washington, DC: Authors.

National Association of Area Agencies on Aging (Na4). (2006). *Shaping communities for a maturing America.* Washington, DC: Author.

National Center for Health Statistics. (1995). *Health: United States, 1994*, Hyattsville, MD: Public Health Service.

National Center for Health Statistics. (2003). *National Vital Statistics Reports, 51, 5.*

National Funeral Directors Association. (1997). *Funeral services and expenses.* Northbrook, IL: Office of Public Affairs.

National Institute on Aging. (1993). *Bound for good health: A collection of Age Pages.* Washington, DC: U. S. Government Printing Office.

National Vital Statistics Report (October, 2004). Volume 53(5). Washington, DC: U. S. Government. Available at www.benbest.com/lifeext/causes.html. Accessed on May 16, 2007.

Nawrot, T. S., Staessen, J. A., Gardner, J. P., & Aviv, A. (2004). Telomere length and possible link to X chromosome. *Lancet, 363*, 507–510.

Neely, A. S. & Backman, L. (1995). Effects of multifactorial memory training in old age: Generalizability across tasks and individuals. *Journal of Gerontology: Psychological Sciences, 50B*, P134–P140.

Neergaard, L. (March, 1997). Relief from shaking of Parkinson's. *Charlotte Observer.*

Neisser, U. (1967). *Cognitive psychology.* New York: Meredith.

Neisser, U., Boodoo, G., Bouchard, T., Boykin, A., Brody, N., Ceci, S., Halpern, D. F., Loehlin, J. C., Perloff, R., Sternberg, R. J., & Urbina, S. (1996). Intelligences: Knowns and unknowns. *American Psychologist, 51*, 77–101.

Nemeroff, C. B., Youngblood, W. W., Manberg, P. J., Prange, A. J., & Kizer, J. S. (1983). Regional brain concentrations of neuropeptides in Huntington's chorea and schizophrenia. *Science, 221*, 972–975.

Netz, Y., Wu, M-J., Becker, B. J., & Tenenbaum, G. (2005). Physical activity and psychological well-being in advanced age: A meta-analysis of intervention studies. *Psychology & Aging, 20*, 272–284.

Neugarten, B. L., & Neugarten, D. A. (1987, May). The changing meanings of age. *Psychology Today*, 29–33.

Neumann, M., Sampathu, D. M., Kwong, L. K., Truax, A. C., MicseNew Yorki, M. C., Chou, T. T., et al. (2006). Ubiquitinated TDP-43 in frontotemporal lobar degeneration and amyotrophic lateral sclerosis. *Science, 314*, 130–133.

Newman, S. C. & Hassan, A. I. (1999). Antidepressant use in the elderly population in Canada: Results from a national survey. *Journal of Gerontology: Medical Sciences, 54A*, M527–M530.

Newman-Hornblum, J., Attig, M., & Kramer, D. A. (1980, August). *The use of sex-relevant Piagetian tasks in assessing cognitive competence among the elderly.* Paper presented at the annual meeting of the American Psychological Association, Toronto.

Newsom, J. T. & Schulz, R. (1996). Social support as a mediator in the relation between functional status and quality of life in older adults. *Psychology & Aging, 11*, 34–44.

Ng, D. M., & Jeffrey, R. W. (2003). Relationships between perceived stress and health behaviors in a sample of working adults. *Health Psychology, 22*, 638–642.

Nicholson, T. (2000, May). EEOC sees new trends: Age bias "alive and well". *AARP Bulletin, 41(5)* 3, 6–7.

Nieboer, A. P., Lindenberg, S. M., & Ormel, J. (1998–1999). Conjugal bereavement and well-being of elderly men and women: A preliminary study. *Omega, 38*, 113–141.

Nilsson, I., Löfgren, B., Fisher, A. G., & Bernspång, B. (2006). Focus on leisure repertoire in the oldest old; The Umeå 85+ study. *Journal of Applied Gerontology, 25*, 391–405.

Nobre, P. J., & Pinto-Gouveia, J. (2006). Dysfunctional sexual beliefs as vulnerability factors for sexual dysfunction. *The Journal of Sex Research, 43*, 68–75.

Nock, S. L. (1995). A comparison of marriages and cohabiting relationships. *Journal of Family Issues, 16*, 53–76.

Nolen-Hoeksema, S. & Ahrens, C. (2002). Age differences and similarities in the correlates of depressive symptoms. *Psychology & Aging, 17*, 116–124.

Norton, M. (2002). Fighting the effects of aging. *Vegetarian Times, 302*, 81.

Novak, M. (2006). *Issues in aging.* Boston: Allyn & Bacon.

Nyberg, L., Bäckman, L., Erngrund, K., Olofsson, U., & Nilsson, L. G. (1996). Age differences in episodic memory, semantic memory, and priming: Relationships to demographic, intellectual, and biological factors. *Journal of Gerontology; Psychological Sciences, 51B*, P234–P240.

Nyberg, L., Maitland, S. B., Rönnlund, M., Bäckman, L., Dixon, R. A., Wahlin, Å., & Nilsson, L-G. (2003). Selective adult age differences in an age-invariant multifactor model of declarative memory. *Psychology & Aging, 18*, 149–160.

O'Brian, C. A., & Goldberg, A. (1999). Lesbians and gay men inside and outside families. In N. Mandell & A. Duffy (Eds.), *Canadian families: Diversity, conflict, and change.* Toronto: Harcourt Brace.

O'Bryant, S. L. & Hansson, R. O. (1995). Widowhood. In R. Blieszner & V. H. Bedford (Eds.), *Handbook of aging and the family* (pp. 440–458). Westport, CT: Greenwood Press.

O'Bryant, S. L. (1990–1991). Forewarning of a husband's death: Does it make a difference for older widows? *Omega, 22*, 227–239.

O'Connell, J. F., Hawkes, K., & Jones, N. G. B. (1999). Grandmothering and the evolution of *Homo erectus. Journal of Human Evolution, 36*, 461–485.

O'Grady-LeShane, R. (1996). Older women workers. In W. H. Crown (Ed.), *Handbook on employment and the elderly* (pp. 103–109). Westport, CT: Greenwood Press.

O'Hanlon, A. M., & Brookover, B. C. (2002). Assessing changes in attitudes about aging: Personal reflections and a standardized measure. *Educational Gerontology, 28*, 711–725.

Öberg, P. & Tornstam, L. (1999). Body images among men and women of different ages. *Ageing & Society, 19*, 629–644.

Ogin, T., Hard, G. C., Schwartz, A. G., & Magee, P. N. (1990). Investigation into the effect of DHEA on renal carcinogenesis induced in the rat by a single dose of DMN. *Nutrition & Cancer, 14*, 57–68.

Ohtsuka, R. (1997). Aging and efficacy of work: A methodological discussion. *Journal of Human Ergology, 26*, 159–164.

Okoye, U. O., & Obikeze, D. S. (2005). Stereotypes and perceptions of the elderly by the youth in Nigeria: Implications for social policy. *Journal of Applied Gerontology, 24*, 439–452.

Olshansky, S. J., Carnes, B., & Cassel, C. (1993). The aging of the human species. *Scientific American, 268*, 46–52.

Oman, D. & Reed, D. (1998). Religion and mortality among the community-dwelling elderly. *American Journal of Public Health, 88*, 1469–1475.

Oregon Department of Human Services (2006). 2006 Annual Report on the Death with Dignity Act. Available from www.Oregon.gov/DHS/ph/pes. Accessed June 15, 2007.

Ormsbee, T. J. (2001). An age-old story-Forget about layoffs-the problem for IT workers over the age of 40 is just getting an interview. *Infoworld, 23*, 40–42.

Ostir, G. V., Markides, K. S., Peek, M. K., & Goodwin, J. S. (2001). The association between emotional well-being and the incidence of stroke in older adults. *Psychosomatic Medicine, 63*, 210–215.

Oswald, F., Wahl, H-W., Schilling, O., New Yorkgren, C., Fänge, A., Sixsmith, A., Sixsmith, J., Széman, Z., & Tomsone, S. & Iwarsson, S. (2007). Relationships between housing and healthy aging in very old age. *The Gerontologist, 47*, 96–107.

Otten, M. W., Teutsch, S. M., Williamson, D. F., & Marks, J. S. (1990). The effect of known risk factors on the excess mortality of black adults in the United States. *Journal of the American Medical Association, 263*, 845–850.

Oxman, T. E. & Hull, J. G. (2001). Social support and treatment response in older depressed primary care patients. *Journal of Gerontology: Psychological Sciences, 56B*, P35–P45.

Oxman, T. E., Freeman, D. H., & Manheimer, E. D. (1995). Lack of social participation or religious strength and comfort as risk factors for death after cardiac surgery in the elderly. *Psychosomatic Medicine, 57*, 5–16.

Ozawa, M. N. & Law, S. W-O. (1992). Reported reasons for retirement: A study of recently retired workers. *Journal of Aging & Social Policy, 4*(3/4), 35–51.

Pak, S. K., Olsen, L. K., & Mahoney, B. S. (2000). The relationships of health behaviors to perceived stress, job satisfaction, and role modeling among health professionals in South Korea. *International Journal of Community Health Education, 19*, 65–76.

Palmore, E. B. (1971). Attitudes toward aging as shown by humor. *Gerontologist, 11*, 181–186.

Palmore, E. B. (1986). Attitudes toward aging shown by humor: A review. In L. Nahemow, K. A. McCluskey-Fawcett, & P. E. McGhee (Eds.), *Humor and aging* (pp. 101–118). San Diego, CA: Academic Press.

Panzer, A., Lottering, M-L., Bianchi, P., Glencross, D. K., Stark, J. H., & Seegers, J. C. (1998). Melatonin has no effect on the growth, morphology, or cell cycle of human breast cancer (MCF-7), cervical cancer (HeLa), osteosarcoma (MG-63), or lymphoblastoid (TKG). *Cancer Letters, 122*, 17.

Papalia, D. E., Camp, C. J., & Feldman, R. D. (1996). *Adult development and aging*. New York: McGraw-Hill.

Park, D. C., Morrell, R. W., Frieske, D., & Kincaid, D. (1992). Medication adherence behaviors in older adults: Effects of external cognitive supports. *Psychology & Aging, 7*, 252–256.

Park, D. C., Smith, A. D., & Cavanaugh, J. C. (1990). Metamemories of memory researchers. *Memory & Cognition, 18*, 321–327.

Parker, R. M., Ratzan, S. C., & Lurie, N. (2003). Health literacy: A policy challenge for advancing high-quality health care. *Health Affairs, 22*, 147–153.

Parkes, C. M. (1998). Bereavement in adult life. *British Medical Journal, 316*, 856–859.

Parnes, H. S. & Sommers, D. G. (1994). Shunning retirement: Work experience of men in their seventies and early eighties. *Journal of Gerontology: Social Sciences, 49*, S117–S124.

Patterson, C. J. (2000). Family relationships of lesbians and gay men. *Journal of Marriage and the Family, 62*, 1052–1069.

Pearce, J. M. S. (1992). *Parkinson's disease and its management*. New York: Oxford University Press.

Pearls, R. (1931). Studies on human longevity: IV: The inheritance of longevity. *Annals of Human Biology, 3*, 245–269.

Peck, R. C. (1968). Psychological developments in the second half of life. In B. L. Neugarten (Ed.), *Middle age and aging*. Chicago, IL: University of Chicago Press.

Peden, A. H., Head, M. W., Ritchie, D. I., Bell, J. E., & Ironside, J. W. (2004). Preclinical vCJD after blood transfusion in a PRNP codon 129 heterozygous patient. *The Lancet, 364*, 527–531.

Pedri, S., & Hesketh, B. (1993). Time perception: Effects of task speed and delay. *Perceptual & Motor Skills, 76*, 599–608.

Peeke, P. (2005). *Body for life for women*. New York: Rodale.

Penninx, B. W. J. H., Rejeski, W. J., Pandya, J., Miller, M. E., Di Bari, M., Applegate, W. B., & Pahor, M. (2002). Exercise and depressive symptoms: A comparison of aerobic and resistance exercise effects and physical function in older persons with high and low depressive symptomatology. *Journal of Gerontology: Psychological Sciences, 57B,* P124–P132.

Penninx, B. W. J. H., van Tilburg, T., Kriegsman, D. M. W., Deeg, D. J. H., & van Eijk, J. T. M. (1997). Effects of social support and personal coping resources on mortality in older age: The longitudinal study in Amsterdam. *American Journal of Epidemiology, 146,* 510–519.

Peplau, L. A. (1991). Lesbian and gay relationships. In J. C. Gonsiorek & J. D. Weinruch (Eds.), *Homosexuality: Research implications for public policy.* Newbury Park, CA: Sage.

Perkins, K. (1992). Psychosocial implications of woman and retirement. *Social Work, 37,* 526–527.

Perls, T., Silver, M. H., & Lauerman, J. F. (1999). *Living to 100: Lessons in living to your maximum potential at any age.* New York: Basic.

Perreira, K. M. (2002). Excess alcohol consumption and health outcomes: A 6-year follow-up of men over 50 form the health and retirement study. *Addiction, 97,* 301–310.

Peters, A. & Liefbroer, A. C. (1997). Beyond marital status: Partner history and well-being in old age. *Journal of Marriage & the Family, 59,* 687–699.

Peterson, J. & Rosenblatt, R. (1986, March 23). Life past 85: Often sweet but painful. *Los Angeles Times,* I-1,26.

Pfeifer, A., Eigenbrod, S., Al-Khadra, S., Hofmann, A., Mitteregger, G., Moser, M., Bertsch, U., & Kretzschmar, H. (2006). Lentivector-mediated RNAi efficiently suppresses prion protein and prolongs survival of scrapie-infected mice. *Journal of Clinical Investigation, 116,* 3204–3210.

Phillips, L. H., Henry, J. D., Hosie, J. A., & Milne, A. B. (2006). Age, anger, and well-being. *Aging & Mental Health, 10,* 250–256.

Piaget, J. (1972). Intellectual evolution from adolescence to adulthood. *Human Development, 15,* 1–12.

Pillemer, K. & Suitor, J. J. (1991). "Will I ever escape my child's problems?" Effects of adult children's problems on elderly parents. *Journal of Marriage & the Family, 53,* 585–594.

Pletcher, S. D., Khazael, A. A., & Curtsinger, J. W. (2000). Why do life spans differ? Partitioning mean longevity differences in terms of age-specific mortality parameters. *Journal of Gerontology: Biological Sciences, 55A,* B381–B389.

Plett, P. (1990). Training opportunities for older workers. In H. L. Sheppard (Ed.), *The future of older workers* (pp. 87–103). Tampa, FL: International Exchange Center on Gerontology.

Plomin, R., DeFries, J. C., McClearn, G. E., & Rutter, M. (1997). *Behavioral genetics,* New York: Freeman.

Podewils, L. J., Guallar, E., Kuller, L. H., Fried, L. P., Lopez, O. L., Carlson, M., & Lyketsos, C. G. (2005). Physical activity, *APOE* genotype, and dementia risk: Findings from the Cardiovascular Health Cognition Study. *American Journal of Epidemiology, 161,* 639–651.

Poon, L. W. (1985). Differences in human memory with aging: Nature, causes, and clinical implications. In J. Birren & K. W. Schaie (Eds.), *Handbook of the psychology of aging* (2nd ed., pp. 427–462). New York: Van Nostrand Reinhold.

Pope, M. (1997). Sexual issues for older lesbians and gays. *Topics in Geriatric Rehabilitation, 12,* 53–60.

Porter, E. (2007). Scales and Tales: Older women's difficulty with daily tasks. *Journal of Gerontology: Social Sciences, 62B,* S153–S159.

Porter, J. R. & Svec, F. (1996). DHEA diminishes fat food intake in lean and obese Zucker rats. *Annals of the New York Academy of Sciences, 774,* 329–331.

Posner, R. A. (1996). *Aging and old age.* Chicago: University of Chicago Press.

Potts, M. K. (1997). Social support and depression among older adults living alone: The importance of friends within and outside of a retirement community. *Social Work, 42,* 348–362.

Power, A. E. (2004). Slow-wave sleep, acetylcholine, and memory consolidation. *Proceedings of the National Academy of Science, 101,* 1795–1796.

Prasher, V. P., Fung, N., & Adams, C. (2005). Rivastigmine in the treatment of dementia in

Alzheimer's disease in adults with Down's syndrome. *International Journal of General Psychiatry, 20*, 496–498.

Price, C. A. (2003). Professional women's retirement adjustment: The experience of reestablishing order. *Journal of Aging Studies, 17*, 341–355.

Price, R. W. (1998). Implications of the AIDS dementia complex viewed as an acquired genetic neurodegenarative disease. In M. F. Folstein (Ed.), *Neurobiology of primary dementia* (pp. 213–234). Washington, DC: American Psychiatric Press.

Prigerson, H. G., Frank, E., Kasl, S., & Reynolds, C. F., III. (1995). Complicated grief and bereavement-related depression as distinct disorders: Preliminary empirical validation in elderly bereaved spouses. *The American Journal of Psychiatry, 152*, 22–36.

Priplata, A. A., Niemi, J. B., Harry, J. D., Lipsitz, L. A., & Collins, J. J. (2004). Vibrating insoles and balance control in elderly people. *The Lancet, 362*, 1123–1124.

Pritchard, C., & Baldwin, D. S. (2002). Elderly suicide rates in Asian and English-speaking countries. *Acta Psychiatrica Scandinavica, 105*, 271–275.

Pudrovska, T., Schieman, S., & Carr, D. (2006). Strains of singlehood in later life: Do race and gender matter? *Journal of Gerontology: Social Sciences, 61B*, S315–S322.

Quam, J. K. & Whitford, G. (1992). Adaptation and age-related expectations of older gay and lesbian adults. *The Gerontologist, 32*, 367–374.

Quandt, S. A., Stafford, J. M., Bell, R. A., Smith, S. L., Snively, B. M., & Arcury, T. A. (2006). Predictors of falls in a multiethnic population of older rural adults with diabetes. *Journal of Gerontology: Medical Sciences, 61A*, 394–398.

Quigley, D. G. & Schatz, M. S. (1999). Men and women and their responses in spousal bereavement. *The Hospice Journal, 14*, 65–78.

Quinn, J. F., & Kozy, M. (1996). Role of bridge jobs in the retirement transition: Gender, race, and ethnicity. *The Gerontologist, 36*, 363–372.

Quinn, J. F., Montine, K. S., Moore, M., Morrow, J. D., Kaye, J. A., & Montine, T. J. (2004). Suppression of longitudinal increase in CSF F2-isoprostanes in Alzheimer's disease. *Journal of Alzheimer's Disease, 6*, 93–97.

Quinn, J., Suh, J., Moore, M. M., Kaye, J., & Frei, B. (2003). Antioxidants in Alzheimer's disease-vitamin C delivery to a demanding brain. *Journal of Alzheimer's Disease, 5*, 309–313.

Rabi, K. (2006). Israeli perspectives on elder abuse. *Educational Gerontology, 32*, 49–62.

Rabig, J., Thomas, W., Kane, R., Cutler, L.J., & McAlilly, S. (2006). Radical redesign of nursing homes: Applying the Green House concept in Tupelo, Mississippi. *The Gerontologist, 46*,533–539.

Radner, D. B. (1991). Changes in the incomes of age groups: 1984 to 1989. *Social Security Bulletin*, 54.

Ragland, D. R., Satariano, W. A., & MacLeod, K. E. (2005). Driving cessation and increased depressive symptoms. *Journal of Gerontology: Medical Sciences, 60A*, 399–403.

Rahhal, T. A., Hasher, L., & Colcombe, S. J. (2001). Instructional manipulations and age differences in memory: Now you see them, now you don't. *Psychology & Aging, 16*, 697–706.

Randerson, J., & Sample, I. (Nov. 16, 2006). Life in 2056: Longer, healthier, and not alone. Guardian Unlimited. Available from www.guardian.co.uk/science/story. Accessed November 16, 2006.

Rando, T. A. (1991). Parental reaction to the loss of a child. In D. Papadatos & C. Papadatos (Eds.), *Children and death*. New York: Hemisphere Publishers.

Rantanan, T., Harris, T., Leveille, S. G., Visser, M., Foley, D., Masaki, K., & Guralnik, J. M. (2000). Muscle strength and body mass index as long term predictors of mortality in initially healthy men. *Journal of Gerontology: Medical Sciences, 55A*, M168–M173.

Rapuri, P. B., Gallagher, J. C., & Smith, L. M. (2007). Smoking is a risk factor for decreased physical performance in elderly women. *Journal of Gerontology: Medical Sciences, 62A,* 93–100.

Rasulo, D., Christensen, K., & Tomassini, C. (2005). The influence of social relations on mortality in later life: A study of elderly Danish twins. *The Gerontologist, 45,* 601–608.

Ratcliff, R., Spieler, D., & McKoon, G. (2000). Explicitly modeling the effects of aging on response time. *Psychonomic Bulletin & Review, 7,* 1–25.

Ratcliff, R., Thapar, A., & McKoon, G. (2001). The effects of aging on reaction time in a signal detection task. *Psychology & Aging, 16,* 323–341.

Ravussin, E. (2005). A NEAT way to control weight? *Science, 307,* 530–531.

Rebok, G. W. (1987). *Life-span cognitive development.* New York: Holt, Rinehart, & Winston.

Reese, C. M., & Cherry, K. E. (2006). Effects of age and ability on self–reported memory functioning and knowledge of memory aging. *The Journal of Genetic Psychology, 167,* 221–240.

Rein D., Paglieroni, T. G., Pearson, D. A., Wun, T., Schmitz, H. H., Gosselin, R., & Keen, C. L. (2000). Cocoa and wine polyphenols modulate platelet activation and function. *The Journal of Nutrition, 130,* 2120S–2126S.

Reinhardt, J. P., Boerner, K., & Benn, D. (2003). Predicting individual change in support over time among chronically impaired older adults. *Psychology & Aging, 18,* 770–779.

Reitzes, D. C., & Mutran, E. J. (2004). Grandparent identity, intergenerational family identity, and well-being. *Journal of Gerontology: Social Sciences, 59B,* S213–S219.

Rexbye, H., Petersen, I., Iachina, M., Mortensen, K., McGue, M., Vaupel, J. W., & Christensen, K. (2005). Hair loss among elderly men: Etiology and impact on perceived age. *Journal of Gerontology: Medical Sciences, 60A,* 1077–1082.

Reynolds, C. A., Finkel, D., Gatz, M., & Pedersen, N. L. (2002). Sources of influence on rate of cognitive change over time in Swedish twins: An application of latent growth models. *Experimental Aging Research, 28,* 407–433.

Richards, J. B., Papaioannou, A., Adachi, J. D., Joseph, L., Whitson, H. E., Prior, J. C., & Goltzman, D. (2007). Effects of selective serotonin reuptake inhibitors on the risk of fracture. *Archives of Internal Medicine, 167,* 188–194.

Richardson, V. E. (1999). Women and retirement. *Journal of Women & Aging, 11,* 49–66.

Rideout, C. A., Linden, W., & Barr, S. I. (2006). High cognitive dietary restraint is associated with increased cortisol excretion in postmenopausal women. *Journal of Gerontology: Medical Sciences, 61A,* 628–633.

Riekse, R. J. & Holstege, H. (1996). *Growing older in America.* New York: McGraw-Hill.

Rigdon, I. S., Clayton, B. C., & Dimond, M. (1987). Toward a theory of helpfulness for the elderly bereaved: An invitation to a new life. *Advances in Nursing Science, 9*(2), 32–43.

Riggs, K. M., Lachman, M. E., & Wingfield, A. (1997). Taking charge of remembering: Locus of control and older adults' memory for speech. *Experimental Aging Research, 23,* 237–256.

Riley, K. P. (1999). Assessment of dementia in the older adult. In P. A. Lichtenberg (Ed.), *Handbook of assessment in clinical gerontology* (pp. 134–166). New York: John Wiley & Sons.

Riley, K. P., Snowden, D. A., Desrosiers, M. F., & Markesbery, W. R. (2005). Early life linguistic ability, late life cognition function, and neuropathology: Findings from the Nun Study. *Neurobiology of Aging, 26,* 341–347.

Ritchie, C. W., Bush, A. I., Mackinnon, A., Macfarlane, S., Mastwyk, M., MacGregor, L. et al. (2003). Metal-protein attenuation with idodchorhydroxquin (Clioquniol) targeting A_ amyloid deposition and toxicity in Alzheimer's disease. *Archives of Neurology, 60,* 1685–1691.

Rix, S. E. (2004). *Aging and work: A view from the United States.* Washington, DC: AARP Public Policy Institute.

Roadberg, A. (1981). Perceptions of work and leisure among the elderly. *Gerontologist, 21,* 142–145.

Roberson, E. D., Scearce-Levie, K., Palop, J. J., Yan, F., Cheng, I. H., Wu, T., Gerstein, H., Yu, G-Q., & Mucke, L. (2007). Reducing endogenous tau ameliorates amloid _-induced deficits in an

Alzheimer's disease mouse model. *Science, 316*, 750–754.

Roberto, K. A. (1997). Qualities of older women's friendships: Stable or volatile? *International Journal of Aging & Human Development, 44*, 1–14.

Roberto, K. A., & Stanis, P. (1994). Reactions of older women to the death of their close friends. *Omega, 29*, 17–27.

Roberto, K. A. & Stroes, J. (1992). Grandchildren and grandparents: Roles, influences, and relationships. *International Journal of Aging & Human Development, 34*, 227–239.

Roberto, K. A., Gold, D. T., & Yorgason, J. B. (2004). The influence of osteoporosis on the marital relationships of older couples. *Journal of Applied Gerontology, 23*, 443–456.

Roberts, B. W., Walton, K. E., & Viechtbauer, W. (2006). Patterns of mean-level change in personality traits across the life course: A meta-analysis of longitudinal studies. *Psychological Bulletin, 132*, 1–25.

Roberts, S. D. & Zhou, N. (1997). The 50 and older characters in the advertisements of *Modern Maturity*: Growing older, getting better? *Journal of Applied Gerontology, 16*, 208–220.

Robine, J. M. & Allard, M. (1998). The oldest human. *Science, 279*, 1834.

Robinson, J. A. (1976). Sampling autobiographical memory. *Cognitive Psychology, 8*, 578–595.

Robinson, J. D. & Skill, T. (1995). The invisible generation: Portrayals of the elderly on prime-time television. *Communication Reports, 8*, 111–119.

Robles, T. F., & Kiecolt-Glaser, J. K. (2003). The physiology of marriage: Pathways to health. *Physiology & Behavior, 79*, 409–416.

Rodewald, H-R. (1998). The thymus in the age of retirement. *Nature, 396*, 630–631.

Roff, L. L., Burgio, L. D., Gitlin, L., Nichols, L., Chaplin, W., & Hardin, J. M. (2004). Positive aspects of Alzheimer's caregiving: The role of race. *Journal of Gerontology: Psychological Sciences, 59B*, P185–P190.

Rogers, R. G. (1995). Marriage, sex, and mortality. *Journal of Marriage & the Family, 57*, 515–526.

Rondeau, V., Commenges, D., Jacqmin-Gadda, H., & Dartigues, J. F. (2000). Relation between aluminum concentrations in drinking water and Alzheimer's disease: An 8-year follow-up study. *American Journal of Epidemiology, 152*, 59–66.

Rosen, B. & Jerdee, T. H. (1976a). The nature of job-related age stereotypes. *Journal of Applied Psychology, 61*, 180–183.

Rosen, B. & Jerdee, T. H. (1976b). The influence of age stereotypes on managerial decisions. *Journal of Applied Psychology, 61*, 428–432

Rosenberg, E., & Letrero, I. L. (2006). Using age, cohort, and period to study elderly volunteerism. *Educational Gerontology, 32*, 313–334.

Rosenblatt, R. A. (1999, Jan. 14). U.S. can afford boomers' retirement, study says. *Charlotte Observer*, 11A.

Rosenbloom, C. A., & Whittington, F. J. (1993). The effects of bereavement on eating behaviors and nutrient intakes in elderly widowed persons. *Journal of Gerontology: Social Sciences, 51B*, S223–S229.

Rosenkoetter, M. M. & Garris, J. M. (1998). Psychosocial changes following retirement. *Journal of Advanced Nursing, 27*, 966–976.

Roses, A. D. & Pericak-Vance, M. (1995). Alzheimer's disease and other dementias. In E. H. Emery & D. L. Rimoin (Eds.), *Principles and practice of medical genetics* (3rd ed.), Edinburgh: Churchill Livingstone.

Rosnick, C. B., Small, B. J., Graves, A. B., & Mortimer, J. A. (2004). The association between health and cognitive performance in a population-based study of older adults: The Charlotte county health aging study (CCHAS). *Aging Neuropsychology & Cognition, 11*, 89–99.

Ross, C. E. & Drentea, P. (1998). Consequences of retirement activities for distress and the sense of personal control. *Journal of Health & Social Behavior, 39,* 317–334.

Ross, I. K. (1995). *Aging of cells, humans, and societies.* Dubuque, IA: Wm. C. Brown.

Ross, S. (1991). Subjective acceleration of time with aging. *Perceptual & Motor Skills, 72,* 289–290.

Rossouw, J. E., Anderson, G. L., Prentice, R. L., LaCroix, A. Z., Kooperberg, C., Stefanick, M. L. et al. (2002). Risks and benefits of estrogen plus progestin in healthy postmenopausal women: Principal results from the women's health initiative randomized controlled trial. *Journal of the American Medical Association, 288,* 321–333.

Rothermund, K., & Brandstädter, J. (2003). Coping with deficits and losses in later life: From compensatory action to accommodation. *Psychology & Aging, 18,* 896–905.

Rotter, J. B. (1966). Generalized expectancies for internal versus external control of reinforcement. *Psychological Monographs, 80* (1, Whole No. 609).

Roughan, P. A., Kaiser, F. E., & Morley, J. E. (1993). Sexuality and the older woman. *Clinics in Geriatric Medicine, 9,* 87–106.

Rowe, J. W. & Kahn, R. L. (1998). *Successful aging.* New York: Pantheon Books.

Rubenstein, R. L. & Parmelee, P. A. (1992). Attachment to place and the representation of the life course by the elderly. *Human Behavior and Environment: Advances in Theory and Research, 12,* 139–163.

Rubenstein, R. L., Kilbride, J. C., & Nagy, S. (1992). *Elders living alone: Frailty and the perception of choice.* Hawthorne, NY: Aldine de Gruyter.

Rudman, D., Feller, A. G., Nagraj, H. S., Gergans, G. A., Lalitha, P. Y., Goldberg, A. F., Schlenker, R. A., Cohn, L., Rudman, I. W., & Mattson, D. E. (1990). Effects of human growth hormone in men over 60 years old. *New England Journal of Medicine, 323,* 1–6.

Ruhm, C. (1991). *Bridge employment and job stopping in the 1980s* (Americans Over 55 at Work Program, Background Paper Series, No. 3). New York: Commonwealth Fund.

Runyan, W. M. (1980). The life satisfaction chart: Perceptions of the course of subjective experience. *Iternational Journal of Aging & Human Development, 11,* 45–64.

Ruth, J. E. & Birren, J. E. (1985). Creativity in adulthood and old age: Relations to intelligence, sex, and mode of testing. *International Journal of Behavioral Development, 8,* 99–109.

Ryan, E. B., & See, S. K. (1993). Age-based beliefs about memory changes for self and others across adulthood. *Journal of Gerontology: Psychological Sciences, 48,* P199–P201.

Ryckman, R. M. & Malikioski, M. (1975). Relationship between locus of control and chronological age. *Psychological Reports, 36,* 655–658.

Sabat, S. R. (2001). *The experience of Alzheimer's disease: Life through a tangled veil.* Malden, MA: Blackwell.

Sachs, G. A. (1994). Improving care of the dying. *Generations, 18,* 19–22.

Sack, R. L., Hughes, R. J., Edgar, D. M., & Lewy, A. J. (1997). Sleep-promoting effects of melatonin: At what dose, in whom, under what conditions, and by what mechanisms? *Sleep, 20,* 908.

Sacks, O. (1999). *Awakenings.* New York: Vintage Publishing.

Safford, F. (1992). Differential assessment of dementia and depression in elderly people. *Gerontology for Health Professionals.* Washington, DC: National Association of Social Workers Press.

Salthouse, T. A. & Babcock, R. L. (1991). Decomposing adult age differences in working memory. *Developmental Psychology, 27,* 763–776.

Salthouse, T. A. (1984). Effects of age and skill in typing. *Journal of Experimental Psychology: General, 113,* 345–371.

Salthouse, T. A. (1985). Speed of behavior and its implications for cognition. In J. E. Birren & K. W. Schaie (Eds.), *Handbook of the psychology of aging* (2nd ed., pp. 400–426). New York: Van Nostrand Reinhold.

Salthouse, T. A. (1990). Working memory as a processing resource in cognitive aging. *Developmental Review, 10,* 101–124.

Salvio, M. A., Wood, J. M., Schwartz, J., & Eichling, P. S. (1992). Nightmare prevalence in the healthy elderly. *Psychology & Aging, 7*, 324–325.

Samani, N. J., Boultby, R., Butler, R., Thompson, J. R., & Goodall, A. H. (2001). Telomere shortening in atherosclerosis. *Lancet, 358*, 472–473.

Sambamurti, K., Suram, A., Venugopal, C., Prakasam, A., Zhou, Y., Lahiri, D. K., & Greig, N. H. (2006). A partial failure of membrane protein turnover may cause Alzheimer's disease: A new hypothesis. *Current Alzheimer Research, 3*, 81–90.

Samus, Q. M., Rosenblatt, A., ONew Yorkike, C., Steele, C., Baker, A., Harper, M., et al. (2006). Correlates of caregiver-rated quality of life in assisted living: The Maryland Assisted Living Study. *Journal of Gerontology: Psychological Sciences, 61B*, P311–P314.

Sands, R. G. & Goldberg-Glen, R. S. (2000). Factors associated with stress among grandparents raising their grandchildren. *Family Relations, 49*, 97–105.

Sano, M., Ernesto, C., Thomas, R. G., Klauber, M. R., Schafer, K., Grundman, M., Woodbury, P., Growdon, J., Cotman, C. W., Pfeiffer, E., Schneider, L. S., & Thal, L. J. (1997). A controlled trial of selegiline, alpha-tocopherol or both as treatments for Alzheimer's disease: The Alzheimer's disease cooperative study. *New England Journal of Medicine, 336*, 1216–1222.

Sardar, A. M., Czudek, C., & Reynolds, G. P. (1996). Dopamine deficits in the brain: The neurochemical basis of parkinsonian symptoms in AIDS. *Neuroreport, 7*, 910–912.

Sasser-Coen, J. R. (1993). Qualitative changes in creativity in the second half of life: A life-span developmental perspective. *Journal of Creative Behavior, 27*, 18–26.

Satariano, W. A., DeLorenze, G. N., Reed, D., & Schneider, E. L. (1996). Imbalance in an older population. *Journal of Aging & Health, 8*, 334–358.

Savishinsky, J. S. (2000). *Breaking the watch: The meaning of retirement in America.* Ithaca: Cornell U. Press.

Savory, J., Exley, C., Forbes, W. T., Huang, Y., Joshi, J. G., Kruck, T., et al. (1996). Can the controversy of the role of aluminum in Alzheimer's disease be resolved? What are the suggested approaches to this controversy and methodological issues to be considered? *Journal of Toxicology and Environmental Health, 48*, 615–635.

Sayers, G. M., Beckett, N., Waters, H., & Turner, C. (2004). Surrogates' decisions regarding CPR, and the fallacy of substituted judgment. *The Journal of Clinical Ethics, 15*, 340–345.

Schacter, D. L. (1992). Understanding implicit memory: A cognitive neuroscience approach. *American Psychologist, 47*, 559–569.

Schächter, F. (1998). Causes, effects, and constraints in the genetics of human longevity. *American Journal of Human Genetics, 62*, 1008–1014.

Schafer, C., Quesenberry, C. P., Jr., & Wi, S. (1995). Mortality following a conjugal bereavement and the effects of a shared environment. *American Journal of Epidemiology, 141*, 1142–1152.

Schaie, K. W. & Hertzog, C. (1983). Fourteen-year cohort sequential studies of adult intelligence. *Developmental Psychology, 19*, 531–543.

Schaie, K. W. (1965). A general model for the study of developmental change. *Psychological Bulletin, 64*, 92–107.

Schaie, K. W. (1977). Quasi-experimental research designs in the psychology of aging. In J. E. Birren & K. W. Schaie (Eds.), *Handbook of the psychology of aging.* New York: Van Nostrand Reinhold.

Schaie, K. W. (1979). The primary mental abilities in adulthood: An exploration in the development of psychometric intelligence. In P. B. Baltes & O. G. Brim (Eds.), *Life-span development and behavior* (Vol. 2, pp. 67–115). New York: Academic Press.

Schaie, K. W. (1983). The Seattle Longitudinal Study: A twenty-one year investigation of psychometric intelligence. In K. W. Schaie (Ed.), *Longitudinal studies of adult personality development* (pp. 64–155). New York: Guilford Press.

Schaie, K. W. (1989). Individual differences in rate of cognitive change in adulthood. In V. L.

Bengston & K. W. Schaie (Eds.), *The course of later life: Research and reflections* (pp. 68–83). New York: Springer Publishing.

Schaie, K. W. (1990a). Developmental designs revisited. In H. W. Reese & S. H. Cohen (Eds.), *Lifespan developmental psychology: Methodological issues*. Hillsdale, NJ: Erlbaum.

Schaie, K. W. (1990b). Intellectual development in adulthood. In J. E. Birren & K. W. Schaie (Eds.), *Handbook of the psychology of aging*. (pp. 291–309). San Diego, CA: Academic Press.

Schaie, K. W. (1994). The course of adult intellectual development. *American Psychologist, 49*, 304–313.

Schaie, K. W. (2005). *Developmental influences on adult intelligence: The Seattle Longitudinal Study*. New York: Oxford University Press.

Schaie, K. W., & Willis, S. L. (1991). *Adult development and aging* (3rd ed.). New York: Harper Collins.

Scharlach, A. E., & Fredriksen, K. I. (1993). Reactions to the death of a parent during midlife. *Omega, 27*, 307–319.

Schenk, D., Barbour, R., Dunn, W., Gordon, G., Grajeda, H., Guido, T., Hu, K., Huang, J., Johnson-Wood, K., Khan, K., Kholodenko, D., Lee, M., Liao, Z., Lieberberg, I., Motter, R., Mutter, L., Soriano, F., Shopp, G., Vasquez, N., Vandevert, C., Walker, S., Wogulis, M., Yednock, T., Games, D., & Seubert, P. (1999). Immunization with amyloid-b attentuates Alzheimer-disease-like pathology in the PDAPP mouse. *Nature, 400*, 173.

Schiavi, R. C. (1999). *Aging and male sexuality*. Cambridge, UK: Cambridge University Press.

Schmidt, S. R. (1991). Can we have a distinctive theory of memory? *Memory & Cognition, 19*, 523–542.

Schmucker, D. L. (1998). Aging and the liver: An update. *Journal of Gerontology: Biological Sciences, 53A*, B315–B320.

Schneider, B. (1997). Psychoacoustics and aging: Implications for everyday listening. *Journal of Speech-Language Pathology and Audiology, 21*, 111–124.

Schneider, D. S., Sledge, P. A., Shuchter, S. R., & Zisook, S. (1996). Dating and remarriage over the first two years of widowhood. *Annals of Clinical Psychiatry, 8*, 51–57.

Schneider, J. S., Pope, A., Simpson, K., Taggart, J., Smith, M. G., & DiStefano, L. (1992). Recovery from experimental Parkinsonism in primates with Gml ganglioside treatment. *Science, 256*, 843–846.

Schulman, G. L. (1999). Siblings revisited: Old conflicts and new opportunities in later life. *Journal of Marital & Family Therapy, 25*, 517–524.

Schultz, K. S., Morton, K. R., & Weckerle, J. R. (1998). The influence of push and pull factors on voluntary and involuntary early retirees' retirement decision and adjustment. *Journal of Vocational Behavior, 53*, 45–57.

Schulz, R. (1976). Effects of control and predictability on the physical and psychological well-being of the institutionalized aged. *Journal of Personality and Social Psychology, 33*, 563–573.

Schulz, R. & Heckhausen, J. (1996). A life span model of successful aging. *American Psychologist, 51*, 702–714.

Schulz, R. & O'Brien, A. T. (1994). Alzheimer's disease caregiving: An overview. *Seminars in Speech and Language, 15*, 185–194.

Schulz, R. & Salthouse, T. (1999). *Adult development & aging*. Upper Saddle River, NJ: Prentice Hall.

Schulz, R., Beach, S. R., Lind, B., Martire, L. M., Zdaniuk, B., Hirsch, C., Jackson, S., & Burton, L. (2001). Involvement in caregiving and adjustment to death of a spouse: Findings form the Caregiver Health Effects Study. *Journal of the American Medical Association (JAMA), 285*, 3123–3129.

Schulz, R., Martire, L. M., Beach, S. R., & Scheier, M. F. (2000). Depression and mortality in the elderly. *Current Directions in Psychological Science, 9*, 204–208.

Schumaker, S. A., Legault, C., Rapp, S. R. et al. (2003). Estrogen plus progestin and the incidence of dementia and mild cognitive impairment in postmenopausal women: The Women's Health Initiative Memory Study: A randomized controlled trial. *Journal of the American Medical Association, 289*, 2651–2662.

Schwartz, C. K. & Simmons, J. P. (2001). Contact quality and attitudes toward the elderly. *Educational Gerontology, 27*, 127–137.

Scogin, F. R., Storandt, M., & Lott, L. (1985). Memory skills training, memory complaints, and depression in older adults. *Journal of Gerontology, 40*, 562–568.

Seeman, T. E., Singer, B. H., Rowe, J. W., Horwitz, R. I., & McEwen, B. S. (1997). Price of adaptation-allostatic load and its health consequences. *Archives of Internal Medicine, 157*, 2259–2268.

Segraves, R. T. & Segraves, K. B. (1995). Human sexuality and aging. *Journal of Sex Education & Therapy, 21*, 88–102.

Sehgal, A., Galbraith, A., Chesney, M., Schonfeld, P., Charles, G., & Lo, B. (1992). How strictly do dialysis patients want their advance directives followed? *Journal of the American Medical Association, 267*, 59–63.

Seidman, S. N. & Rieder, R. O. (1994). A review of sexual behavior in the United States. *American Journal of Psychiatry, 151*, 330–341.

Sekuler, R. & Blake, R. (1994). *Perception* (3rd ed.). New York: McGraw-Hill.

Sell, D. R., Lane, M. A., Johnson, W. A., Masoro, E. J., Mock, O. B., Reiser, K. M., Fogarty, J. F., Cutler, R. G., Ingram, D. K., Roth, G. S., & Monnier, V. M. (1996). Longevity and the genetic determination of collagen glycoxidation kinetics in mammalian senescence. *Proceeding of the National Academy of Science, 93*, 485–490.

Seltzer, J. A. (2000). Families formed outside of marriage. *Journal of Marriage & the Family, 62*, 1247–1268.

Seltzer, M. M., & Karnes, J. (1988). An early retirement incentive program: A case study of Dracula and Pinocchio complexes. *Research on Aging, 10*, 342–357.

Serdula, M. K., Williamson, D. F., Anda, R. F., Levy, A., Heaton, A., & Byers, T. (1994). Weight control practices in adults: Results of a multistate telephone interview. *American Journal of Public Health, 84*, 1821–1824.

Seripa, D., Franceschi, M., Matera, M. G., Panza, F., Kehoe, P. G., Gravina, C. et al. (2006). Sex differences in the association of Apolipoprotein E and Angiotensin-converting enzyme gene polymorphisms with healthy aging and longevity: A population-based study from southern Italy. *Journal of Gerontology: Biological Sciences, 61A*, 918–923.

Serrano, J. P., Latorre, J. M., Gatz, M., & Montanes, J. (2004). Life review therapy using autobiographical retrieval practice for older adults with depressive symptomatology. *Psychology & Aging, 19*, 272–277.

Seynnes, O., Singh, M. A. F., Hue, O., Pras, P., Legros, P., & Bernard, P. L. (2004). Physiological and functional responses to low-moderate versus high-intensity progressive resistance training in frail elders. *Journal of Gerontology: Medical Sciences, 59A*, 503–509.

Sharpley, C. F. & Layton, R. (1998). Effects of age of retirement, reason for retirement, and pre-retirement training on psychological and physical health during retirement. *Australian Psychologist, 33*, 119–124.

Shea, M. T., Leon, A. C., Mueller, T. I., Solomon, D. A., Warshaw, M. G., & Keller, M. B. (1996). Does major depression result in lasting personality change? *American Journal of Psychiatry, 153*, 1404–1410.

Sheehy, G. (1992). *The silent passage: Menopause*. New York: Random House.

Sherkat, D. E., Kilbourne, B. S., Cain, V. A., Hull, P. C., Levine, R. S., & Husaini, B. A. (2007). The impact of health service use on racial differences in mortality among the elderly. *Research on Aging, 29*, 207–224.

Shniedman, E. (1992). *Death: Current perspectives* (3rd ed.). Mountain View, CA: Mayfield.

Shultz, K. S., Morton, K., & Weckerle, J. (1998). The influence of push and pull factors on voluntary and involuntary retirees retirement decision and adjustment. *Journal of Vocational Behavior, 53*, 45–57.

Siddiqui, S. (1997). The impact of health on retirement behaviour: Empirical evidence from West Germany. *Health Economics, 6*, 425–438.

Siebert, D. C., Mutran, E. J., & Reitzes, D. C. (1999). Friendship and social support: The importance of role identity to aging adults. *Social Work, 44*, 522–533.

Siedlecki, K. L., Salthouse, T. A., & Berish, D. E. (2005). Is there anything special about the aging of source memory? *Psychology & Aging, 20*, 19–32.

Siegert, R. J., Taylor, K. D., Weatherall, M., & Abernethy, D. A. (2006). Is implicit sequence learning impaired in Parkinson's disease? A meta-analysis. *Neuropsychology, 20*, 490–495.

Siegler, I. C. (1983). Psychological aspects of the Duke longitudinal studies. In K. W. Schaie (Ed.), *Longitudinal studies of adult psychological development*. New York: Guilford Press.

Siegler, I. C. & Costa, P. T. (1994). Personality and breat cancer screening behaviors. *Annals of Behavioral Medicine, 16*, 347–351.

Siegler, I. C. & Gatz, M. (1985). Age patterns in locus of control. In E. Palmore, E. Busse, G. Maddox, J. Nowlin, & I. Siegler (Eds.), *Normal aging III*. Durham, NC: Duke University Press.

Sikorska-Simmons, E. (2006). Linking resident satisfaction to staff perceptions of the work environment in assisted living: A multilevel analysis. *The Gerontologist, 46*, 590–598

Silverman, P. R. (1986). *Widow-to-widow*. New York: Springer.

Silverstein, M. & Zablotsky, D. L. (1996). Health and social precursors of later life retirement-community migration. *Journal of Gerontology: Social Sciences, 51B*, S150–S156.

Silverstein, N. M. & Hyde, J. (1997). The importance of consumer perspective in home adaptation of Alzheimer's households. In S. Lanspery & J. Hyder (Eds.). *Staying put: Adapting the places instead of the people* (pp. 91–112). Amityville, New York: Baywood.

Simeone, W. E. (1991). The northern Athabaskan potlatch: The objectification of grief. In D. R. Counts & D. A. Counts (Eds.), *Coping with the final tragedy: Cultural variations in dying and grieving* (pp. 157–167). Amityville, NY: Baywood.

Simmons, T., & Dye, J. L. (2003). *Grandparents living with grandchildren, 2000*. Washington, DC: U. S. Census Bureau.

Simoes, E. J., Byers, T., Coates, R. J., Serdula, M. K., Mokdad, A. H., & Heath, G. W. (1995). The association between leisure time physical activity and dietary fat in American adults. *American Journal of Public Health, 85*, 240–244.

Simon, R. (1996). Too damn old. *Money, 25*(7), 88–126.

Simonton, D. K. (1989). The swan song phenomenon: Last works effects for 172 classical composers. *Psychology & Aging, 4*, 42–47.

Simonton, D. K. (1990). Creativity and wisdom in aging. In J. E. Birren & K. W. Schaie (Eds.), *Handbook of the psychology of aging* (3rd ed., pp. 320–329). San Diego, CA: Academic Press.

Simonton, D. K. (1991). Creative productivity through the adult years. *Generations, 15*, 13–16.

Simonton, D. K. (1998). Career paths and creative lives: A theoretical perspective on late-life potential. In C. Adams-Price (Ed.), *Creativity and successful aging: Theoretical and empirical approaches* (pp. 3–18). New York: Springer.

Sims, R. V., McGwin, G., Jr., Allman, R. M., Ball, K., & Owsley, C. (2000). Exploratory study of incident vehicle crashes among older drivers. *Journal of Gerontology: Medical Sciences, 55A*, M22–M27.

Singh, N. A., Stavrinos, T. M., Scarbek, Y., Galambos, G., Liber, C., & Singh, M. A. F. (2005). A randomized controlled trial of high versus low intensity weight training versus general practitioner care for clinical depression in older adults. *Journal of Gerontology: Medical Sciences, 60A*, 768–776.

Singleton, D. (2000, February 13). Obstetrician, carved-up patient settle lawsuit. *Charlotte Observer*, A12.

Sininger, Y. S., & Cone-Wesson, B. (2006). Asymmetric cochlear processing mimics hemisphere specialization. *Science, 305*, 1581.

Sinnott, J. D. (1991). What do we do to help John? A case study of postformal problem solving in a family making decisions about an acutely psychotic member. In J. D. Sinnott & J. C. Cavanaugh (Eds.). *Bridging paradigms: Positive development in adulthood and cognitive aging.* (pp. 203–219). New York: Praeger.

Siu, A. (1991). Screening for dementia and investigating its causes. *Internal Medicine, 115*, 122–132.

Skarborn, M. & Nicki, R. (2000). Worry in pre- and post-retirement persons. *International Journal of Aging & Human Development, 50*, 61–71.

Sliwinski, M. (1997). Aging and counting speed: Evidence for process specific slowing. *Psychology & Aging, 12*, 38–49.

Small, B. J. & Bäckman, L. (1997). Cognitive correlates of mortality: Evidence from a population-based sample of very old adults. *Psychology & Aging, 12*, 309–313.

Smith, D. B. & Moen, P. (1998). Spousal influence on retirement: His, her, and their perceptions. *Journal of Marriage & the Family, 60*, 734–744.

Smith, D. W. E. (1993). *Human longevity.* New York: Oxford University Press.

Smith, G. E., Petersen, R. C., Ivnik, R. J., Malec, J. F., & Tangalos, E. G. (1996). Subjective memory complaints, psychological distress, and longitudinal change in objective memory performance. *Psychology & Aging, 11*, 272–279.

Smith, J. & Baltes, P. B. (1990). Wisdom-related knowledge: Age/cohort differences in response to life-planning problems. *Developmental Psychology, 26*, 494–505.

Smith, J., Staudinger, U. M., & Baltes, P. B. (1994). Occupational settings facilitating wisdom-related knowledge: The sample case of clinical psychologists. *Journal of Consulting & Clinical Psychology, 66*, 989–999.

Smith, M. (1979). The portrayal of elders in magazine cartoons. *The Gerontologist, 19*, 408.

Smith, M. E. (1935). Delayed recall of previously memorized material after twenty years. *Journal of Genetic Psychology, 47*, 477–481.

Smith, M. E. (1951). Delayed recall of previously memorized material after forty years. *Journal of Genetic Psychology, 79*, 337–338.

Smith, M. E. (1963). Delayed recall of previously memorized material after fifty years. *Journal of Genetic Psychology, 102*, 3–4.

Smith, M., & Buckwalter, K. (2005). Behaviors associated with dementia. *American Journal of Nursing, 105*, 40–52.

Smith, S. D. (1997). The retirement transition and the later life family unit. *Public Health Nursing, 14*, 207–216.

Smith, T. W. (2006). Personality as risk and resilience in physical health. *Current Directions in Psychological Science, 15*, 227–231.

Smoke, S. (1996). *The bill of rights and responsibilities: A book of common sense.* Los Angeles: General Publishing Group.

Smyth, K. A., Rose, J. H., McClendon, M. J., & Lambrix, M. A. (2007). Relationships among caregivers' demographic characteristics, social support ratings, and expectations of computer-mediated support groups. *Journal of Applied Gerontology, 26*, 58–77.

Snow, C. M., Shaw, J. M., Winters, K. M., & Witzke, K. A. (2000). Long-term exercise using weighted vests prevents hip bone loss in postmenopausal women. *Journal of Gerontology: Medical Sciences, 55A*, M489–M491.

Snowdon, D. A. (1997). Aging and Alzheimer's disease: Lessons from the Nun Study. *Gerontologist, 37*, 150–156.

Snowdon, D. A., Gross, M. D., & Butler, S. M. (1996). Antioxidants and reduced functional capacity in the elderly: Findings from the nun study. *Journal of Gerontology: Medical Sciences, 51A*, M10–M16.

Social Security Administration (2007). Available at www.ssa.gov. Accessed on April 14, 2007.

Sofikitis, N., Miyagawa, I., Dimitriadis, D., Zavos, P., Sikka, S., & Hellstrom, W. (1995). Effects of smoking on testicular function: Semen quality and sperm fertilizing capacity. *Journal of Urology, 154*, 1030–1034.

Sohal, R. S. & Allen, R. G. (1985). Relationship between metabolic rate, free radicals, differentiation, and aging: A united theory. In A. D. Woodhead, A. D. Blackett, & A. Hollaender (Eds.), *Molecular Biology of aging*, New York: Plenum Press, 75–104.

Sokolovsky, J. (1997). *The cultural context of aging*. (2nd ed.). New York: Bergin & Garvey Publishers.

Solomon, J. C. & Marx, J. (1995). "To grandmother's house we go:" Health and school adjustment of children raised solely by grandparents. *Gerontologist, 35*, 386–394.

Soper, B., Rosenthal, G., Milford, G. E., & Akers, J. B. (1992). A comparison of self-reported dream themes for traditional and older college students. *College Student Journal, 26*, 20–24.

South, S. J. & Lloyd, K. M. (1995). Spousal alternatives and marital dissolution. *American Sociological Review, 60*, 21–36.

Spector, A., Thorgrimsen, L., Woods, B., Royan, L., Davies, S., Butterworth, M., & Orrell, M. (2003). Efficacy of an evidence-based cognitive stimulation therapy programme for people with dementia. *British Journal of Psychiatry, 183*, 248–254.

Spencer, P. S., Nunn, P. B., Hugon, J., Ludolph, A. C., Ross, S. M., Roy, D. N., & Robertson, R. C. (1987). Guam amyotrophic lateral scelorosis-Parkinsonism- dementia linked to a plant excitant neurotoxin. *Science, 237*, 517–522.

Spencer, W. D. & Raz, N. (1995). Differential effects of aging on memory for content and context: A meta-analysis. *Psychology & Aging, 10*, 527–539.

Spillman, D. (1990). Survey of food and vitamin intake responses reported by university students experiencing stress. *Psychological Reports, 66*, 499–502.

Spirduso, W. W., & Clifford, P. (1978). Replication of age and physical activity effects on reaction and movement time. *Journal of Gerontology, 33*, 26–30.

Spirduso, W. W., & McRae, G. P. (1990). Motor performance and aging. In J. E. Birren and K. W. Schaie (Eds.), *Handbook of the psychology of aging* (3rd ed., pp. 184–200). New York: Academic Press.

Staats, S., & Pierfelice, L. (2003). Travel: A long-range goal of retired women. *The Journal of Psychology, 137*, 483–494.

Stampfer, M. J., Kang, J. H., Chen, J., Cherry, R., & Grodstein, F. (2005). Effects of moderate alcohol consumption on cognitive function in women. *New England Journal of Medicine, 352*, 245–253.

Starfield, B. (2000). Is US health really the best in the world? *Journal of the American Medical Association, 284*, 483–485.

Starr, B. D. & Weiner, M. B. (1981). *Sex and sexuality in the mature years*. New York: McGraw-Hill.

Staudinger, U. M., Maciel, A. G., Smith, J., & Baltes, P. B. (1998). What predicts wisdom-related performance? A first look at personality, intelligence, and facilitative experiential contexts. *European Journal of Personality, 12*, 1–17.

Stephens, M. A. P., & Townsend, A. L. (1997). Stress of parent care: Positive and negative effects of women's other roles. *Psychology & Aging, 12*, 376–386.

Stephenson, J. S. (1985). *Death, grief, and mourning: Individual and social realities*. New York: Free

Press.

Steptoe, A., Lipsey, Z., & Wardle, J. (1998). Stress, hassles, and variations in alcohol consumption, food choice, and physical exercise. *British Journal of Health Psychology, 3*, 51–63.

Sternberg, R. J. (1985). *Beyond IQ: A triarchic theory of human intelligence*. New York: Cambridge University Press.

Sternberg, R. J. (2004). What is wisdom and how can we develop it? *Annals of the American Academy of Political and Social Science, 591*, 164–174.

Sterns, H. L., Barrett, G. V., & Alexander, R. A. (1985). Accidents and the aging individual. In J. E. Birren & K. W. Schaie (Eds.), *Handbook of the psychology of aging* (2nd ed., pp. 703–724). New York: Van Nostrand Reinhold.

Steunenberg, B., Beekman, A. T. F., Deeg, D. J. H., & Kerkhof, J. F. M. (2006). Personality and the onset of depression in late life. *Journal of Affective Disorders, 92*, 243–251.

Stevens, N. L., Martina, C. M. S., & Westerhof, G. J. (2006). Meeting the need to belong: Predicting effects of a friendship enrichment program for older women. *The Gerontologist, 46*, 495–502.

Stevens-Long, J. (1990). Adult development: Theories past and future. In R. Nemiroff & C. Colarusso (Eds.), *New dimensions in adult development* (pp. 125–169). New York: Basic Books.

Stewart, A. J. & Ostrove, J. M. (1998). Women's personality in middle age. *American Psychologist, 53*, 1185–1194.

Stewart, A. J. & Vandewater, E. A. (1993). The Radcliffe Class of 1964: Career and family social clock projects in a transitional cohort. In K. D. Hulbert & D. T. Schuster (Eds.), *Women's lives through time* (pp. 235–258). San Francisco, CA: Jossey-Bass.

Stewart, A. J. & Vandewater, E. A. (1998). The course of generativity. In D. P. McAdams & E. De St. Aubin (Eds.), *Generativity and adult development: Psychosocial perspectives on caring for and contributing to the next generation* (pp. 75–100). Washington, DC: American Psychological Association Press.

Stewart, A. J., Ostrove, J. M., & Helson, R. (2001). Middle aging in women: Patterns of personality change from the 30's to the 50's. *Journal of Adult Development, 8*, 23–37.

Stewart, W. F., Kawas, C., Corrada, S. M., & Mettter, E. J. (1997). Risk of Alzheimer's disease and duration of NSAID use. *Neurology, 48,* 626–632.

Stillion, J. M. (1996). Survivors of suicide. In K. J. Doka (Ed.), *Living with grief after sudden loss* (pp. 41–71). Bristol, PA: Taylor & Francis.

Stoller, E. P. & Gibson, R.C. (2000). *Worlds of difference: Inequality in the aging experience*. Newbury Park: CA: Sage.

Stone, A. (1993). Sleep and aging. *Dialogue: The Emory clinic magazine, 63*, 5–8.

Stoner, S. B. & Panek, P. E. (1985). Age and sex differences with the Comfrey Personality Scales. *Journal of Psychology, 119*, 137–142.

Stoner, S. B. & Spencer, W. B. (1986). Age and sex differences on the State-Trait Personality Inventory. *Psychological Reports, 59*, 1315–1319.

Stowe, R., Rosenblatt, R., & Foster, R. D. (1997, Sept.–Oct.). MM reports: Friends. *Modern Maturity, 40W*, 38–45.

Strawbridge, W. S., Cohen, R. D., Shema, S. J., & Kaplan, G. A. (1997). Frequent attendance at religious services and mortality over 28 years. *American Journal of Public Health, 87*, 957–961.

Stroebe, M. S. (1998). New directions in bereavement research: Exploration of gender differences. *Palliative Medicine, 12*, 5–12.

Strom, R. D., Heeder, S. D., & Strom, P. S. (2005). Performance of black grandmothers: Perceptions of three generations of females. *Educational Gerontology, 31*, 187–205.

Strom, R., Strom, S., Collinsworth, P., Strom, P., & Griswold, D. (1996). Black grandparents: Curriculum development. *International Journal of Aging & Human Development, 43*, 119–134.

Stuck, A. E., Walthert, J. M. Nikolaus, T., Bula, C., Hohmann, C., & Beck, J. C. (1999). Risk factors for functional status decline in community-living elderly people: A systematic literature review. *Social Science and Medicine, 48*, 445–469.

Sumic, A., Michael, Y. L., Carlson, N. E., Howieson, D. B., & Kaye, J. A. (2007). Physical activity and the risk of dementia in oldest old. *Journal of Aging & Health, 19*, 242–259.

Sundén, A. E. & Surette, B. J. (1998). Gender differences in the allocation of assets in retirement savings plans. *American Economic Review, 88*, 207–211.

SUPPORT Principal Investigators. (1995). A controlled study to improve care for seriously ill hospitalized patients: The study to understand prognosis and preferences for outcomes and risks of treatments. *Journal of the American Medical Association, 274*, 1591–1598.

Suthers, K., Kim, J. K., & Crimmins, E. (2003). Life expectancy with cognitive impairment in the older population of the United States. *Journal of Gerontology: Social Sciences, 58B*, S179–S186.

Swayne, L. E. & Greco, A. J. (1986). The portrayal of older Americans in television commercials. *Journal of Advertising, 16*, 47–54.

Sweet, L. (1994, August 27). In memorium: A user's guide on how to behave at funerals of different faiths. *Edmonton Journal, 47*, A10.

Szinovacz, M. E. (1998). Grandparents today: A demographic profile. *Gerontologist, 38*, 37–52.

Szinovacz, M. E. (2000). Changes in housework after retirement: A panel analysis. *Journal of Marriage & the Family, 62*, 78–92.

Szinovacz, M. E., & Davey, A. (2004). Retirement transitions and spouse disability:

Szinovacz, M. E. & De Viney, S. (2000). Marital characteristics and retirement decisions. *Research on Aging, 22*, 470–498.

Szinovacz, M. E., DeViney, S., & Atkinson, M. P. (1999). Effects of surrogate parenting on grandparents' well-being. *Journal of Gerontology: Social Sciences, 54B*, S376–S388.

Szlemko, W. J., Wood, J. W., & Thurman, P. J. (2006). Native Americans and alcohol: Past, present, and future. *Journal of General Psychology, 133*, 435–451.

Tang, M., Stern, Y., Marder, K., Bell, K., Gurland, B., Lantigua, R., Andrews, H., Feng, L., Tycko, B., & Mayeux, R. (1998). The APOE-a4 allele and the risk of Alzheimer disease among African Americans, Whites, and Hispanics. *Journal of the American Medical Association, 279*, 751–755.

Tangri, S. & Jenkins, S. (1993). The University of Michigan Class of 1967: The women's life paths study. In K. D. Hulbert & D. T. Schuster (Eds.), *Women's lives through time* (pp. 259–281). San Francisco, CA: Jossey-Bass.

Taylor, M. A., & Doverspike, D. (2003). Retirement planning and preparation. In G. A. Adams & T. A. Beehr (Eds.), *Retirement: Reasons, processes, and results* (pp. 53–82). New York: Springer.

Taylor, M. G., & Lynch, S. M. (2004). Trajectories of impairment, social support, and depressive symptoms in later life. *Journal of Gerontology: Social Sciences, 59B*, S238–S246.

Taylor, R. J. & Chatters, L. M. (1986). Patterns of informal support to elderly black adults: Family, friends, and church members. *Social Work, 31*, 432–438.

Taylor-Carter, M. A., Cook, K., & Weinberg, C. (1997). Planning and expectations of the retirement experience. *Educational Gerontology, 23*, 273–288.

Teitelman, J. (1990). Sexuality and aging. In I. Parham, L. Poon, & I. Siegler (Eds.), *Aging curriculum content for education in the social-behavioral sciences*. New York: Springer.

Tennant, C. (2000). Work stress and coronary heart disease. *Journal of Cardiovascular Risk, 7*, 273–276.

Terracciano, A., McCrae, R. R., Brant, L. J., & Costa, P. T., Jr. (2005). Hierarchical linear modeling analyses of the NEO-PI-R scales in the Baltimore Longitudinal Study of Aging. *Psychology & Aging, 20*, 493–506.

Thomas, J. L., Sperry, L., & Yarbrough, M. S. (2000). Grandparents as parents: Research findings and policy recommendations. *Child Psychology & Human Development, 31*, 3–22.

Thomas, W. H. (1994). *The Eden Alternative: Nature, hope, and nursing homes.* Sherburne, NY: Eden Alternative Foundation.

Tinetti, M. E. (1989). Instability and falling in elderly patients. *Seminars in Neurology, 9*, 39–45.

Tinetti, M. E., Gordon, C., Sogolow, E., Lapin, P., & Bradley, E. H. (2006). Fall-risk evaluation and management: Challenges in adopting geriatric care practices. *The Gerontologist, 46*, 717–725.

Tomita, M. R., Mann, W. C., Fraas, L. F., & Stanton, K. M. (2004). Predictions of the use of assistive devices that address physical impairments among community based frail elders. *Journal of Applied Gerontology, 23*, 141–155.

Torre, F. La, Silipigni, A. M., Orlando, A., Torre, C, La, & Aragonia, M. (1997). Free radicals, telometers, and telomerase role in aging and cancerogenesis. *Minerva Medica, 88*, 205–214.

Toseland, R. W., Diehl, M., Freeman, K., Manzanares, T., Naleppa, M., & McCallion, P. (1997). The impact of validation group therapy on nursing home residents with dementia. *Journal of Applied Gerontology, 16*, 31–50.

Treas, J. & Chen, J. (2000). Living arrangements, income pooling, and life course in urban Chinese families. *Research on Aging, 22*, 238–261.

Treen, J. (2006, Sept.–Oct.). Living longer: The future. AARP the Magazine. Available from www.aarpmagazine.org/health/living. Accessed October 6, 2006.

Triveldi, D. P., & Khaw, K. T. (2001). Dehydroepiandrosterone sulfate and mortality in elderly men and women. *Journal of Clinical Endocronoligical Metabolism, 86*, 4171–4177.

Troll, L. E. & Skaff, M. M. (1997). Perceived continuity of self in very old age. *Psychology & Aging, 12*, 162–169.

Tsuboi, H., Kawamura, N., Hori, R., Kobayashi, F., Iwasaki, Y., Takeuchi, H., & Fukino, O. (2005). Depressive symptoms and life satisfaction in elderly women are associated with natural killer cell number and cytotoxicity. *International Journal of Behavioral Medicine, 12*, 236–243.

Tucker, J. S., Friedman, H. S., Tsai, C. M., & Martin, L. R. (1995). Playing with pets and longevity among older people. *Psychology and Aging, 10*, 3–7.

Tulving, E. (1985). How many memory systems are there? *American Psychologist, 40*, 385–398.

Tuomi, K., Ilmarinen, J., Seitsamo, J., Huuhtanen, P., Martikainen, R., Nygård, C-H., & Klockars, M. (1997). Summary of the Finnish research project (1981–1992) to promote the health and work ability of aging workers. *Scandanavian Journal of Work & Environmental Health, 23*, 66–71.

Tweedy, M. P., & Guarnaccia, C. A. (November, 2006). *Changes in depression of caregiver wives and husbands following death of a spouse with dementia.* Paper presented at the annual meetings of the Gerontological Society of America, Dallas, Texas.

U.S. Census Bureau. (1990), *Statistics,* 111th edition, Washington, DC: U.S. Government Printing Office.

U.S. Census Bureau. (1992). *Sixty-five plus in America, Current Population Reports Special Studies,* Washington, DC: U.S. Government Printing Office.

U.S. Census Bureau. (1993). Population projections of the U.S. by age, sex, race, and Hispanic origin data: 1993 to 2050. *Current Population Reports.* P-25, No. 1104, U.S. Department of Commerce.

U.S. Census Bureau. (1994). *Geographic mobility: March 1992 to March 1993, Current Population Reports,* Washington, DC: U.S. Government Printing Office.

U.S. Census Bureau. (1997). *Statistical abstracts of the United States: 1997.* Washington, DC: U.S. Government Printing Office.

U.S. Census Bureau. (1998). Marital status and living arrangements: March 1997 (Update). Washington, DC: United States Department of Commerce News. Available from *www.census.gov/population/www/socdemo/ms-la.html.*

U.S. Census Bureau. (2000). Population projections of the U.S. by age, sex, race, and Hispanic origin data: 1995 to 2050. *Current Population Reports*. P-25, No. 11304, U.S. Department of Commerce.

U.S. Census Bureau. (2001). Current population survey, March 2000. Washington, DC: Author. Available from *www.census.gov/population/www/socdemo/age/pp1-147/tab05.txt*. Accessed September 11, 2001.

U.S. Census Bureau. (2005). Current Housing Reports, Series H150/97, *American housing survey for the United States: 2005*. Washington DC: U.S. Government Printing Office.

U.S. Department of Health & Human Services. (1992). *Health, United States, 1991, & prevention profile* (DHHS/PHS Publication No. 92-1232). Washington, DC: U.S. Government Printing Office.

U.S. Department of Health & Human Services. (2003). *Smoking and health: A national status report* (DHHS/PHS/Child Development Publication No. 87-8396). Washington, DC: U.S. Government Printing Office.

U. S. Department of Health & Human Services (2007). *Center for Medicare and Medicaid Services: Health Insurance & Assistance Programs*. Washington, DC: U. S. Government Printing Office.

U.S. Senate Special Committee on Aging. (1992). *Aging America: Trends and projections*. Washington, DC: U.S. Government Printing Office.

Uchino, B. N., Cacioppo, J. T., & Kiecolt-Glaser, J. K. (1996). The relationship between social support and physiological processes: A review with emphasis on underlying mechanisms and implications for health. *Psychological Bulletin, 119*, 488–531.

Uhlenberg, P. L. & Cooney, T. M. (1990). Family size and mother-child relations in later life. *Gerontologist, 30*, 618–625.

Umberson, D., & Williams, K. (2005). Marital quality, health, and aging: Gender equity? *Journal of Gerontology: Series B, 60B*, 109–112.

Umberson, D., Williams, K., Powers, D. A., Liu, H., & Needham, B. (2006). You make me sick: Marital quality and health over the life course. *Journal of Health & Social Behavior, 47*, 1–16.

Vachon, M. L. S., Sheldon, A. R., Lancee, W. J., Lyall, W. A. L., Rogers, J., & Freeman, S. J. J. (1980). A controlled study of self-help intervention for widows. *American Journal of Psychiatry, 137*, 1380–1384.

Vaillant, G. & McArthur, C. (1972). Natural history of male psychologic health. I: The adult life cycle from 18 to 50. *Seminars in Psychiatry, 4*, 415–427.

Valdes, A. M., Andrew, T., Gardner, J. P., Kimura, M., Oelsner, E., Cherkas, L. F., Aviv, A., & Spector, T. D. (2005). Obesity, cigarette smoking, and telomere length in women. *The Lancet, 366*, 662–664.

Valenzano, D. R., Terzibasi, E., Genade, T., Catteneo, A., Domenici, L., & Cellerino, A. (2006). Reserveratrol prolongs lifespan and retards the onset of age-related markers in short–ived vertebrate. *Current Biology, 16*, 296–300.

van der Heide, A., Onwuteaka-Philipsen, B. D., Rurup, M. L., Buiting, H. M., van Delden, J. J. M., Hanssen-de Wolf, J. E. et al. (2007). End-of-life practices in the Netherlands under the Euthanasia Act. *New England Journal of Medicine, 356*, 1957–1965.

van Langingham, J., Johnson, D. R., & Amato, P. (2001). Marital happiness, marital duration, and the U-shaped curve: Evidence from a five-wave panel study. *Social Forces, 79*, 1313–1341.

van Meurs, J. B. J., Dhonukshe–Rutten, R. A. M., Pluijm, S. M. F., van der Klift, M., de Jonge, R., Lindemans, J., de Groot, L. C. P. G. M., Hofman, A., Witteman, J. C. M., van Leeuwen, J. P. T. M., Breteler, M. M. B., Lips, P., Pols, H. A. P., & Uitterlinden, A. G. (2004). Homocysteine levels and the risk of osteoporotic fracture. *New England Journal of Medicine, 350*, 2033– 2041.

Vandenbroucke, J. P. (1998, April 4). Maternal inheritance of longevity. *The Lancet, 351*, 1064.

Vanderhorst, R. K., & McLaren, S. (2005). Social relationships as predictors of depression and suicidal ideation in older adults. *Aging & Mental Health, 9*, 517–525.

Van-de-Ven, P. Rodden, P., Crawford, J., & Kippax, S. (1997). Comparative demographic and sexual profile of older homosexually active men. *Journal of Sex Research, 34*, 349–360.

Vasil, L. & Wass, H. (1993). Portrayal of the elderly in the media: A literature review and implications for educational gerontologists. *Educational Gerontology, 19*, 71–85.

Vassar, R., Bennett, B. D., Babu–Khan, S., Kahn, S., Mendiaz, E. A., Denis, P., et al. (1999). Beta-secretase cleavage of Alzheimer's amyloid precursor protein by the transmembrane aspartic protease BACE. *Science, 288*, 735–740.

Vaupel, J. W., Carey, J. R., Christensen, K., Johnson, T. E., Yashin, A. I., Holm, N. V., Iachine, I. A., Kannisto, V., Khazaeli, A. A., Liedo, P., Longo, V. D., Zeng, Y., Manton, K. G., & Curtsinger, J. W. (1998). Biodemographic trajectories of longevity. *Science, 280*, 855–860.

Verdonck-de Leeuw, I. M., & Mahieu, H. F. (2004). Vocal aging and the impact on daily life: A longitudinal study. *Journal of Voice, 18*, 193–202.

Verhaeghen, P., & Cerella, J. (2002). Aging, executive control, and attention: A review of meta-analyses. *Neuroscience & Biobehavioral Reviews, 26*, 849–857.

Viljanen, A., Era, P., Kaprio, J., Pyykkö, I., Koskenvuo, M., & Rantanen, T. (2007). Genetic and environmental influences on hearing in older women. *Journal of Gerontology: Medical Sciences, 62A*, 447–452.

Vinick, B. H. & Ekerdt, D. J. (1989). Retirement and the family. *Generations, 13*, 53–56.

Von Sydow, K. (1992). An investigation of female sexuality in middle and higher age. *Journal of Gerontology, 25*, 105–112.

Wakayama, T., Shinkai, Y., Tamashiro, K., Niida, H., Blanchard, D. C., Blanchard, R. J., Ogura, A., Tanemura, K., Tachibana, M., Perry, A. C. F., Colgan, D. F., Mombaerts, P., & Yanagimachi, R. (2000). Cloning of mice to six generations. *Nature, 407*, 318–319.

Waldron, V. R., Gitelson, R., & Kelley, D. L. (2005). Gender differences in social adaptation to a retirement community: Longitudinal changes and the role of mediated communication. *Journal of Applied Gerontology, 24*, 283–298.

Walford, R. L. (1969). *The immunologic theory of aging.* Baltimore, MD: Williams & Wilkins.

Walker, B. L., Osgood, N. J., Richardson, J. P., & Ephross, P. H. (1998). Staff and elderly knowledge and attitudes toward elderly sexuality. *Educational Gerontology, 24*, 471–489.

Wallen, K., & Lovejoy, J. (1993). Sexual behavior: Endocrine function and therapy. In J. Shulkin (Ed.), *Hormonal pathways to mind and brain.* New York: Academic Press.

Walton, J., Tuniz, C., Fink, D., Jacobsen, G., & Wilcox, D. (1995). Uptake of trace amounts of aluminum into the brain from drinking water. *NeuroToxicology, 16*, 187190.

Warr, P. (1994). Age and employment. In H. C. Triandis, M. D. Dunnette, & L. M Hough (Eds.), *Handbook of industrial & organizational psychology, 4,* (pp. 485–550). Palo Alto, CA: Consulting Psychologists Press, Inc.

Warren, C. A. B. (1998). Aging and identity in premodern times. *Research on Aging, 20*, 11–35.

Weekes, N. Y., MacLean, J., & Berger, D. E. (2005). Sex, stress, and health: Does stress predict health symptoms differently for the two sexes? *Stress & Health: Journal of the International Society for the Investigation of Stress, 21*, 147–156.

Weggen, S., Eriksen, J. L., Das, P., Sagi, S. A., Wang, R., Pietrzik, C. U., Findlay, K. A., Smith, T. E., Murphy, M. P., Butler, T., Kang, D. E., Marquez-Sterling, N., Golde, T. E., & Koo, E. H. (2001). A subset of NSAIDs lower amyloidogenic Ab42 independently of cyclooxygenase activity. *Nature, 414*, 212–216.

Wegman, D. H. (1999). Older workers. *Occupational Medicine: State of the Art Reviews, 14*, 537–557.

Weindruch, R. (1996, January). Caloric restriction and aging. *Scientific American*, 46–52.

Weisberg, R. W. (1986). *Creativity.* New York: W. H. Freeman.

Weisburger, J. H. (1991). Carconigenesis in our food and cancer prevention. *Advances in Experimental Medicine & Biology, 289*, 137–151.

Weisman, G. D., Chaudhury, H., & Moore, K. D. (1997). Theory and practice of place: Toward an integrative model. In R. L. Rubenstein, M. Moss, & M. H. Kleban, (Eds.). *The many dimensions of aging* (pp. 3–21). New York: Springer.

Weiss, R. & Kasmauski, K. (1997). Aging: New answers to old questions. *National Geographic, 192*, 2–31.

Weiss, R. S. & Bass, S. A. (2002). *Challenges of the third age: Meaning and purpose in later life.* London, England: Oxford University Press.

Welch, D. C. & West, R. L. (1995). Self-efficacy and mastery: Its application to issues of environmental control, cognition, and aging. *Developmental Review, 15*, 150–171.

Welford, A. (1984). Psychomotor performance. *Annual Review of Gerontology & Geriatrics, 4*, 237–274.

Wells, Y. D. & Kendig, H. L. (1999). Psychological resources and successful retirement. *Australian Psychologist, 34*, 111–115.

Welsh, K. A., Breitner, J. C. S., & Magruder–Habib, K. M. (1993). Detection of dementia in the elderly using telephone screening of cognitive status. *Neuropsychiatry, Neuropsychology, & Behavioral Neurology, 6*, 103–110.

Wenger, G. C. & Jingming, L. (2000). Family support in Beijing (China) and Liverpool (UK): Differences and similarities. *Hallym International Journal of Aging, 2*, 85–91.

Wenger, G. C., Davies, R., Shahtahmasebi, S., & Scott, A. (1996). Social isolation and loneliness in old age: Review and model refinement. *Aging & Society, 16*, 333–358.

Werber, B. (1998). *Empire of the ants.* New York: Bantam Books.

Werner, P., Rosenblum, S., Bar–On, G., Heinik, J., & Korczyn, A. (2006). Handwriting process variables discriminating mild Alzheimer's disease and mild cognitive impairment. *Journal of Gerontology: Psychological Sciences, 61B*, P228–P236.

Westerholm, P. & Kilbom, Å. (1997). Aging and work: The occupational health services' perspective. *Occupational & Environmental Medicine, 54*, 777–780.

Whitbourne, S. K. (1985). The life-span construct as a model of adaptation in adulthood. In J. E. Birren & K. W. Schaie (Eds.), *Handbook of the psychology of aging* (2nd ed., pp. 594–618). New York: Van Nostrant Reinhold.

Whitbourne, S. K. (1989). Comments on Lachman's "Personality and aging at the crossroads." In K. W. Schaie & C. Schooler (Eds.), *Social structure and aging: Psychological processes* (pp. 191–198). Hillsdale, NJ: Erlbaum.

Whitbourne, S. K. (1996). *The aging individual: Physical and psychological perspectives.* New York: Springer Publishing Co.

Whitbourne, S. K. (2001). *Adult development and aging: Biopsychosocial perspectives.* New York: John Wiley & Sons.

Whitbourne, S. K. & Sherry, M. S. (1991). Subjective perceptions of the life span in chronic mental patients. *International Journal of Aging & Human Development, 33*, 65–73.

Whitbourne, S. K. & Waterman, A. S. (1979). Psychological development during the adult years: Age and cohort comparisons. *Developmental Psychology, 15*, 373–378.

Whitbourne, S. K., Zuschlag, M. K., Elliot, L. B., & Waterman, A. S. (1992). Psychosocial development in adulthood: A 22-year sequential study. *Journal of Personality & Social Psychology, 63*, 260–271.

White, A. T. & Spector, P. E. (1987). An investigation of age-related factors in the age-job satisfaction relationship. *Psychology & Aging, 2*, 261–265.

White, N. & Cunningham, W. R. (1988). Is terminal drop pervasive or specific? *Journal of Gerontology: Psychological Sciences, 44*, P141–P144.

Wilk, C. A. & Kirk, M. A. (1995). Menopause: A developmental stage, not a deficiency disease. *Psychotherapy, 32*, 233–241.

Willander, J., & Larsson, M. (2006). Smell your way back to childhood: Autobiographical odor memory. *Psychonomic Bulletin & Review, 13*, 240–244.

Willcox, B. J., Willcox, D. C., He, Q., Curb, J. D., Suzuki, M. (2006). Siblings of Okinawan residents share lifelong mortality advantages. *Journal of Gerontology: Biological Sciences, 61A*, 345–354.

Willcox, B. J., Yano, K., Chen, R., Willcox, D. C., Rodriguez, B. L., Masaki, K. H., Donlon, T., Tanaka, B., & Curb, J. D. (2004). How much should we eat? The association between energy intake and mortality in a 36-year follow-up study of Japanese-American men. *Journal of Gerontology: Biological Sciences, 59A*, 789–795.

Williams, B. R., Baker, P. S., Allman, R. M., & Roseman, J. M. (2007). Bereavement among African American and white older adults. *Journal of Aging & Health, 19*, 313–333.

Williams, D. R. (2005). The health of U. S. racial and ethnic populations. *Journal of Gerontology: Series B, 60B*, (Special Issue II), 53–62.

Williams, E. (1988). Health promotion and aging: Alcohol. In Surgeons General's Workshop, *Health promotion and aging*. Washington, DC: U.S. Government Printing Office.

Williams, G. C. (1997). *The PoNew York fish's glow*. New York: Basic Books, Harper & Collins.

Williams, I. C. (2005). Emotional health of black and white dementia caregivers: A contextual examination. *Journal of Gerontology: Psychological Sciences, 60B*, P287–P295.

Willis, S. L. (1990). Current issues in cognitive training research. In E. A. Lovelace (Ed.), *Aging and cognition: Mental processes, self-awareness, and interventions* (pp. 263–280). Amsterdam: North Holland.

Wilmoth, J. R. (1998). The future of human longevity: A demographer's perspective. *Science, 280*, 395–397.

Wilson, R. S., Gilley, D. W., Bennett, D. A., Beckett, L. A., & Evans, D. A. (2000). Person-specific paths of cognitive decline in Alzheimer's disease and their relation to age. *Psychology & Aging, 15*, 18–28.

Wilson, R. S., Mendes de Leon, C. F., Barnes, L. L., Schneider, J. A., Bienias, J. L., Evans, D. A., et al. (2002). Participation in cognitively stimulating activities and risk of incident Alzheimer's disease, *Journal of the American Medical Association, 287*, 742–748.

Wilson, R. S., Mendes de Leon, C. F., Bienias, J. L., Evans, D. E., & Bennett, D. A. 2004). Personality and mortality in old age. *Journal of Gerontology: Pychological Sciences, 59B*, P110–P116.

Wincor, M. Z. (1999). Gingko biloba for dementia: A reasonable alternative? *Journal of the American Pharmaceutical Association, 39*, 415–416.

Wink, P., & Dillon, M. (2003). Religiousness, spirituality, and psychosocial functioning in late adulthood: Findings from a longitudinal study. *Psychology & Aging, 18*, 916–924.

Winoblad, B., & Poritis, N. (1999). Memantine in severe dementia: Results of the M-BEST study (Benefit and Efficacy in severely demented patients during treatment with memantine). *International Journal of Geriatric Psychiatry, 14*, 135–146.

Winsborough, H. H., Bumpass, L. L., & Aquilino, W. S. (1991). *The death of parents and the transition to old age*. Paper presented at the annual meetings of the Population Association of America, Washington, DC.

Wojciechowski, W. C. (1998). Issues in caring for older lesbians. *Journal of Gerontological Nursing, 24*, 28–33.

Wolf, R. S. (1998). Domestic elder abuse and neglect. In I. H. Nordhus, G. R. VandenBos, S. Berg, & P. Fromholt (Eds.), *Clinical geropsychology* (pp. 161–165). Washington, DC: American Psychological Association.

Wolf, S. & Kurtz, J. (1975). Positive adjustment and involvement during aging and expectancy for internal control. *Journal of Consulting & Clinical Psychology, 43*, 173–178.

Wolf, S. L., Barnhart, H. X., Kutner, N. G., McNeely, E., Coogler, C., Xu, T., & the Atlanta FICSIT

Group. (1996). Reducing frailty and falls in older persons: An investigation of Tai Chi and computerized balance training. *Journal of the American Geriatrics Society, 44*, 489–497.

Wolff, J. L., Starfield, B., & Anderson, G. (2002). Prevalence, expenditures, and complications of multiple chronic conditions in the elderly. *Archives of Internal Medicine, 162*, 2269–2276.

Wolfson, L., Whipple, R., Derby, C., Judge, J., King, M., Amerman, P., Schmidt, J., & Smyers, D. (1996). Balance and strength training in older adults: Intervention gains and Tai Chi maintenance. *Journal of the American Geriatrics Society, 44*, 498–506.

Wolfson, T., Ayotte, B. J., Margrett, J. A., & Willis, S. L. (2006, Nov.). *Relation between medication type and functional ability in older adults.* Paper presented at the annual meetings of the Gerontological Society of America, Dallas, Texas.

Wolinsky, F. D. & Johnson, R. J. (1992). Widowhood, health status, and the use of health services by older adults: A cross-sectional and prospective approach. *Journal of Gerontology, Social Sciences, 47*, S8–S16.

Wong, S. S., Heiby, E. M., Kameoka, V. A., & Dubanoski, J. P. (1999). Perceived control, self-reinforcement, and depression among Asian American and Caucasian American elders. *Journal of Applied Gerontology, 18*, 46–62.

Woo, E., & Sharps, M. J. (2003). Cognitive aging and physical exercise. *Educational Gerontology, 29*, 327–337.

Woodbury, R. G. (1999). Early retirement in the United States. *Statistical Bulletin, 80*(3), 2–7.

Woodruff-Pak, D. S. (2001). Eyeblink classical conditioning differentiates normal aging from Alzheimer's disease. *Integrative Physiological & Behavioral Science, 36*, 87–108.

Worden, J. W. (1982). *Grief counseling and grief therapy: A handbook for the mental health practitioner.* New York: Springer.

Worldwatch Institute. (1994). *Vital signs.* New York: Norton.

Worobey, J. L. & Angel, R. J. (1990). Functional capacity and living arrangements of unmarried elderly persons. *Journal of Gerontology: Social Sciences, 45*, S95–S101.

Wray, L. A., Alwin, D. F., McCammon, R. J. (2005). Social status and risky health behaviors: Results from the health and retirement study. *Journal of Gerontology: Series B, 60B,* (Special Issue II), 85–92.

Wreen, M. J. (2004). Hypothetical autonomy and actual autonomy: Some problem cases involving advance directives. *The Journal of Clinical Ethics, 15*, 319–333.

Wright, D. (2000). Computer-mediated social support, older adults, and coping. *Journal of Communication, 50*(3), 100–118.

Wrosch, C. & Heckhausen, J. (1999). Control processes before and after passing a developmental deadline: Activation and deactivation of intimate relationship goals. *Journal of Personality & Social Psychology, 77*, 415–427.

Wrosch, C., Heckhausen, J., & Lachman, M. E. (2000). Primary and secondary control strategies for managing health and financial stress across adulthood. *Psychology & Aging, 15*, 387–399.

Wylde, M. A. (1998). Consumer knowledge of home modifications. *Technology and Disability, 8*, 51–68.

Xu, N., Majidi, V., Markesbery, W. R., & Ehmann, W. D. (1992). Brain aluminum in Alzheimer's disease using an improved GFAAS method. *Neurotoxicity, 13*, 735–743.

Yalom, I. D. (1989). *Love's executioner and other tales of psychotherapy.* New York: Harper Collins.

Yamada, TR., Kadekaru, H., Matsumoto, S., Inada, H., Tanahe, M., Moriguchi, E. H., et al. (2002). Prevalance of dementia in the older Japanese-Brazilian population. *Psychiatry & Clinical Neurosciences, 56*, 71–75.

Yancik, R., Ershler, W., Satariano, W., Hazzard, W., Cohen, H. J., & Ferrucci, L. (2007). Report of the National Institute on Aging Task Force on comorbidity. *Journal of Gerontology: Medical Sciences, 62A*, 275–280.

Yeatts, D. E., Folts, W. E., & Knapp, J. (2000). Older workers' adaption to a changing workplace:

Employment issues for the 21st century. *Educational Gerontology, 26*, 565–582.

Yee, B. W. K. & Weaver, G. D. (1994). Ethnic minorities and health promotion: Developing a "culturally competent" agenda. *Generations, 18*, 39–44.

Yen, S. S. C., Morales, A. J., & Khorram, O. (1996). Replacement of DHEA in aging men and women. *Annals of the New York Academy of Sciences, 774*, 128–142.

Yerkes, R. M. (Ed.). (1921). Psychological examining in the United States Army. *Memoirs of the National Academy of Sciences, 15*, 1–890.

Yoakam, J. R. (1999). Beyond the wrinkle room: Challenging ageism in gay male culture. *Dimensions*, San Francisco, ASA, Mental Health & Aging Network, 3, 7.

Yokel, R. A. (2000). The toxicology of aluminum in the brain: A review. *NeuroToxicology, 21*, 813–828.

Yong-Xing, M., Zan-Sun, W., Yue, Z., Shu-Ying, C., Zheng-Yan, Y., Long, Q., Jian-Ying, Y., Shu-Qi, C., Jian-Gang, Z., & Lin, H. (1998). Behavior pattern, arterial partial pressure of oxygen, superoxide dismutase, micro-blood flow state and longevity or aging. *Mechanisms of Aging and Development, 100*, 187–196.

Yoon, C., Hasher, L., Feinberg, F., Rahhal, T. A., & Winocur, G. (2000). Cross-cultural differences in memory: The role of culture-based stereotypes about aging. *Psychology & Aging, 15*, 694–704.

Young, F. W., & Glasgow, N. (1998). Voluntary social participation and health. *Research on Aging, 20*, 339–362.

Youngstedt, S. D., Kripke, D. F., Klauber, M. R., Sepulveda, R. S., & Mason, W. J. (1998). Periodic leg movements during sleep and sleep disturbances in elders. *Journal of Gerontology: Medical Sciences, 53A*, M391–M394.

Yu, B. P. (1995). Putative interventions. In E. J. Masoro (Ed.). *Handbook of psyiology, Section II: Aging*. New York: Oxford University Press.

Yusef, S., Hawken, S., O[MWT1]umpauu, T., et al. (2004). Effects of potentially modifiable risk factors associated with myocardial infarction in 52 countries (the INTERHEART study): Case-control study. *Lancet, 364*, 937–952.

Zacks, R. T., Hasher, L., Doren, B., Hamm, V., & Attig, M. S. (1987). Encoding and memory of explicit and implicit information. *Journal of Gerontology, 42*, 418–422.

Zanasi, M., De Persis, S., Caporali, M., & Siracusano, A. (2005). Dreams and age. *Perceptual & Motor Skills, 100*, 925–938.

Zarit, S. H., Femia, E. E., Watson, J., Rice-Oeschger, L., & Kakos, B. (2004). Memory club: A group intervention for people with early-stage dementia and their care partners. *The Gerontologist, 44*, 262–269.

Zaslow, J. (2003, February 3). The granny patrol: Florida recruits elderly volunteers. *The Wall Street Journal, Global Action on Aging* online. Available at www.globalaging.com/elderrights /us/recru.html. Accessed October 4, 2003.

Zavos, P. M., Correa, J. R., Antypas, S., Zarmakoupis-Zavos, P. N., & Zarmakoupis, C. N. (1998). Effects of seminal plasma from cigarette smokers on sperm viability and longevity. *Fertility & Sterility, 69*, 425–429.

Zimprich, D., & Martin, M. (2002). Can longitudinal changes in processing speed explain longitudinal changes in fluid intelligence? *Psychology & Aging, 17*, 690–695.

Zisook, S. & Shuchter, S. R. (1990). Hovering over the bereaved. *Psychiatric Annal, 20*, 327–333.

Zisook, S. & Shuchter, S. R. (1991). Depression through the first year after the death of a spouse. *American Journal of Psychiatry, 148*, 1346–1352.

Zisook, S. & Shuchter, S. R. (1993). Major depression associated with widowhood. *The American Journal of Geriatric Psychiatry, 1*, 316–326.

Zisook, S., Chentsova-Dutton, Y., & Shuchter, S. R. (1998). PTSD following berreavement. *Annals of Clinical Psychiatry, 10*, 157–163.

Zisook, S., Mulvihill, M., & Shuchter, S. R. (1990). Widowhood and anxiety. *Psychiatric Medicine, 8*, 99–116.

Zisook, S., Paulus, M., Shuchter, S. R., & Judd, L. L. (1997). The many faces of depression following spousal bereavement. *Journal of Affective Disorders, 45*, 85–95.

Zisook, S., Schneider, D., & Shuchter, S. R. (1990). Anxiety and bereavement. *Psychiatric Medicine, 8*, 83–96.

Zisook, S., Shuchter, S. R., & Lyons, L. (1987). Predictors of psychological reactions during the early course of bereavement. *Psychiatric Clinics North America, 10*, 355.

Zisook, S., Shuchter, S. R., & Mulvihill, M. (1990). Alcohol, cigarette, and medication use during the first year of widowhood. *Psychiatric Annals, 20*, 318–326.

Zisook, S., Shuchter, S. R., Irwin, M., Darko, D. F., Sledge, P., & Resovsky, K. (1994). Bereavement, depression, and immune function. *Psychiatry Research, 52*, 1–10.

Zonderman, A. B., Siegler, I. C., Barefoot, J. C., Williams, R. B., & Costa, P. T., Jr. (1993). Age and gender differences in the content scales of the Minnesota Multiphasic Personality Inventory. *Experimental Aging Research, 19*, 241–257.

Zopf, P. E., Jr. (1992). *Mortality patterns and trends in the United States*. Westport, CT: Greenwood Press.

Zucker, A. N., Ostrove, J. M., & Stewart, A. J. (2002). College-educated women's personality development in adulthood: Perceptions and age differences. *Psychology & Aging, 17*, 236–244.

Zweibel, N. R., & Cassel, C. K. (1989). Treatment choices at the end of life: A comparison of decisions by older patients and their physician selected proxies. *The Gerontologist, 29*, 615–621.

NAME INDEX

Abbot, R. D., 304
Abeles, N., 396
Abraham, J. D., 160
Ackerman, P. L., 153
Adams, A. J., 114
Adams, G. A., 255
Adams, K. B., 311
Adams, K. F., 86
Adams, S. L., 281
Aday, R. H. 16
Adelman, M., 222
Ade-Ridder, L., 222
Ahmad, M., 229
Ahrens, C., 283
Aiken, L., 359
Aiken, L. R., 115, 119, 124
Ajrouch, K. J., 211
Akiyama, H., 210
Albert, S., 383
Albom, M., 296, 374
Aldwin, C. M., 194, 202
Allard, M., 83, 108
Allen, R. G., 74, 336
Alley, D., 136
Allison, P. D., 336
Allport, G., 179
Alspaugh, M. E. L., 311
Alzheimer, A., 299
Amato, P. R., 220
Andel, R., 303
Andersen-Ranberg, K., 293
Anderson, G. J., 114
Anderson, S. A., 215
Andrykowski, M. A., 330, 333
Aneshenel, C. S., 321
Angel, J. L., 363
Angel, R. J., 330
Ankrom, M., 281
Ansello, E. F., 269
Anstey, K. J., 346
Antonucci, T. C., 103, 208, 209, 210, 211, 212, 231
Aponte, J. F., 287
Aquilino, W. S., 219
Arai, M., 217
Arai, S., 322
Araujo, A. B., 222

Arber, S., 223
Ardelt, M., 164
Arndt, V., 25
Atchley, P., 114
Atchley, R. C., 215, 225, 228, 231, 237, 248, 249, 253, 255, 260, 262, 269
Atkinson, R. M., 281
Austad, S. N., 70
Aviv, A., 69
Aykan, H., 322

Baarsma, B. E., 385
Babcock, R. L., 135
Babwin, D., 391
Bäckman, L., 144, 155
Bagby, R. M., 200
Bainbridge, H. T. J., 256
Baker, B., 359
Baldwin, D. S., 345
Baldwin, R. C., 283
Balin, A. K., 74
Balk, D. E., 362, 372
Ball, K., 161
Ball, M. J., 302
Ball, M. M., 331
Baltes, M. M., 332
Baltes, P. B., 21, 23, 155, 160, 162, 163, 164, 170
Barbee, E. L., 16
Barefoot, J. C., 103, 282
Barer, B. M., 228
Barlett, D. L., 229
Barlow, J. H., 229
Barnhill, W., 115
Barr, R. A., 334
Barrouillet, P., 135
Bartali, B., 87
Bartoshuk, L. M., 119
Barusch, A. S., 258
Bauer-Maglin, N., 273
Bass, D. M., 355
Bass, S. A., 320
Bauer, J. A., 94
Bayley, N., 152
Bear, L. W., 238
Beatty, W. W., 300
Becker, D., 91

Bedford, V. H., 225
Beekman, A. T. F., 282
Béland, F., 212
Belgrave, L. L., 265
Belle, D., 366
Belsky, J., 158
Bem, S. L., 63
Benson, H., 237
Berger, R. M., 218, 223
Bergman, M., 117
Berkman, L., 102, 231
Bernal, D., 248
Berry, J. M., 140
Bertera, E. M., 386
Bertram, L., 304
Best, B., 345
Best, D. L., 145
Bezerra-Flanders, W., 217
Bieman-Copland, S., 143
Binet, A., 151
Binstock, R. H., 247
Birren, J. E., 122, 162, 163, 165
Bishop, J. M., 13
Black, S. A., 280
Blacker, D., 305
Blackwell, T., 62, 97
Bladjerg, E. M., 84
Blair, S. N., 89
Blake, R., 114
Blanchard-Fields, F.,, 159, 189, 190, 191
Blatt-Eisengart, I., 141
Blaum, C. S., 124
Blazer, D. G., 282, 285
Blick, K. A., 63
Bluck, S., 196
Bogorad, L., 258
Bohman, T. M., 285
Bolton, I., 369
Bonanno, G. A., 364
Bonomi, A. E., 217
Boon, S. D., 228
Booth-Kewley, S., 200
Boring, E. G., 121
Bosman, E. A., 248
Bossé, R., 268
Botwinick, J., 165
Boucher, N., 56

465

SUBJECT INDEX

Page/Photo Credits

279:    Left- Ali Metcalf, UNC Charlotte
        Right- Foos & Clark
283:    David Young-Wolff/PhotoEdit
294:    Ruth E. Stephenson, Queens University of Charlotte
309:    Tom Raymond/Stone Allstock/Getty Images
313:    Jeff Greenberg/PhotoEdit